THE NEW INTERNATIONAL COMMENTARY
ON THE
OLD TESTAMENT

General Editors

R. K. HARRISON
(1968–1993)

ROBERT L. HUBBARD, JR.
(1994–   )

The Book of
HOSEA

J. ANDREW DEARMAN

WILLIAM B. EERDMANS PUBLISHING COMPANY
GRAND RAPIDS, MICHIGAN / CAMBRIDGE, U.K.

Published 2010 by
Wm. B. Eerdmans Publishing Co.
2140 Oak Industrial Drive N.E., Grand Rapids, Michigan 49505 /
P.O. Box 163, Cambridge CB3 9PU U.K.

Printed in the United States of America

16 15 14 13 12 11 10   7 6 5 4 3 2 1

Library of Congress Cataloging-in-Publication Data

Dearman, J. Andrew, 1951-
The book of Hosea / J. Andrew Dearman.
p.   cm. — (The new international commentary on the Old Testament)
Includes bibliographical references and indexes.
ISBN 978-0-8028-2539-1 (cloth: alk. paper)
1. Bible. O.T. Hosea — Commentaries.   I. Title.

BS1565.53.D43   2010
224′.6077 — dc22

2010005261

www.eerdmans.com

CONTENTS

v

GENERAL EDITOR'S PREFACE

Long ago St. Paul wrote: "I planted, Apollos watered, but God gave the growth" (1 Cor. 3:6, NRSV). He was right: ministry indeed requires a team effort — the collective labors of many skilled hands and minds. Someone digs up the dirt and drops in seed, while others water the ground to nourish seedlings to growth. The same team effort over time has brought this commentary series to its position of prominence today. Professor E. J. Young "planted" it forty years ago, enlisting its first contributors and himself writing its first published volume. Professor R. K. Harrison "watered" it, signing on other scholars and wisely editing everyone's finished products. As General Editor, I now tend their planting, and, true to Paul's words, through four decades God has indeed graciously "[given] the growth."

Today the New International Commentary on the Old Testament enjoys a wide readership of scholars, priests, pastors, rabbis, and other serious Bible students. Thousands of readers across the religious spectrum and in countless countries consult its volumes in their ongoing preaching, teaching, and research. They warmly welcome the publication of each new volume and eagerly await its eventual transformation from an emerging "series" into a complete commentary "set." But as humanity experiences a new century of history, an era commonly called "postmodern," what kind of commentary series is NICOT? What distinguishes it from other similarly well-established series?

Its volumes aim to publish biblical scholarship of the highest quality. Each contributor writes as an expert, both in the biblical text itself and in the relevant scholarly literature, and each commentary conveys the results of wide reading and careful, mature reflection. Ultimately, its spirit is eclectic, each contributor gleaning interpretive insights from any useful source, whatever its religious or philosophical viewpoint, and integrating them into his or her interpretation of a biblical book. The series draws on recent methodological innovations in biblical scholarship, for example, canon criticism, the so-called "new literary criticism," reader-response theories, and sensitivity to gender-based and ethnic readings. NICOT volumes also aim to be irenic in tone, summarizing and critiquing influential views with fairness while defending their own. Its list of contributors includes male and female scholars from a number of Christian faith-groups. The diversity of contributors and their freedom to draw on all relevant methodologies give the entire series an exciting and enriching variety.

What truly distinguishes this series, however, is that it speaks from within that interpretive tradition known as evangelicalism. Evangelicalism is an informal movement within Protestantism that cuts across traditional denominational lines. Its heart and soul is the conviction that the Bible is God's inspired Word, written by gifted human writers, through which God calls humanity to enjoy a loving personal relationship with its Creator and Savior. True to that tradition, NICOT volumes do not treat the Old Testament as just an ancient literary artifact on a par with the *Iliad* or *Gilgamesh*. They are not literary autopsies of ancient parchment cadavers but rigorous, reverent wrestlings with wonderfully human writings through which the living God speaks his powerful Word. NICOT delicately balances "criticism" (i.e., the use of standard critical methodologies) with humble respect, admiration, and even affection for the biblical text. As an evangelical commentary, it pays particular attention to the text's literary features, theological themes, and implications for the life of faith today.

Ultimately, NICOT aims to serve women and men of faith who desire to hear God's voice afresh through the Old Testament. With gratitude to God for two marvelous gifts — the Scriptures themselves and keen-minded scholars to explain their message — I welcome readers of all kinds to savor the good fruit of this series.

ROBERT L. HUBBARD JR.

AUTHOR'S PREFACE

I am grateful for the opportunity to contribute a volume on Hosea for the NICOT series. The material has made the effort a difficult task. Just ask anyone else who has translated and commented on this complicated text, and if they are honest, they too will acknowledge the difficulties! I am also grateful for the feedback of classes and study groups with whom I have had the privilege of sharing my observations on this exquisite prophetic book. Their comments and questions have reminded me repeatedly of the book's significant role in the unfolding drama of redemption set forth in the canonical Scriptures.

The series editor, Professor Robert Hubbard, is a friend and mentor. His comments on an earlier version of the commentary have saved me from a number of errors of both omission and commission. Of course, the problems that remain are of my own making. Translations of Scripture are my own unless otherwise noted.

When it comes to gratitude, my wife and family are always on my mind. In particular, this volume is dedicated to my sister Lizabeth Dearman Sanderford, someone who has kept the faith and been a helper of many (Rom. 16:2).

J. Andrew Dearman
Austin, TX

ABBREVIATIONS

AAT	Ägypten und Altes Testament
AB	Anchor Bible
ABD	D. N. Freedman, ed., *The Anchor Bible Dictionary.* 6 vols. New York: Doubleday, 1992.
ABRL	Anchor Bible Reference Library
AJSL	*Americal Journal of Semitic Languages and Literatures*
ANET	J. B. Pritchard, ed., *The Ancient Near Eastern Texts Relating to the Old Testament.* 3rd ed. Princeton: Princeton University Press, 1969.
AOAT	Alter Orient und Altes Testament
ATD	Das Alte Testament Deutsch
BASOR	*Bulletin of the American Schools of Oriental Research*
BBB	Bonner biblische Beitrag
BETL	Bibliotheca ephemeridum theologicarum lovaniensium
BHS	*Biblia Hebraica Stuttgartensia.* Ed. K. Elliger and W. Rudolph. Stuttgart: Deutsche Bibelstiftung, 1977.
Bib	*Biblica*
BibOr	Biblica et orientalia
BIS	Biblical Interpretation Series
BJRL	*Bulletin of the John Rylands Library*
BR	*Biblical Research*
BTB	*Biblical Theology Bulletin*
BZ	*Biblische Zeitschrift*
BZAW	Beihefte zur Zeitschrift für die alttestamentliche Wissenschaft
CAT	Commentaire de l'Ancien Testament

CBET	Contributions to Biblical Exegesis and Theology
CBQ	*Catholic Biblical Quarterly*
ConBOT	Coniectanea biblica, Old Testament
COS	*The Context of Scripture.* Ed. W. W. Hallo. 3 vols. Leiden: Brill, 1997-2002.
CT	Cuneiform Texts
CTM	Calwer theologische Monographien
DJD	Discoveries in the Judaean Desert
ESV	English Standard Version
EvT	*Evangelische Theologie*
FAT	Forschungen zum Alten Testament
FCB	Feminist Companion to the Bible
FOTL	Forms of the Old Testament Literature
FRLANT	Forschungen zur Religion und Literatur des Alten und Neuen Testaments
GKC	W. Gesenius, *Hebrew Grammar.* Ed. E. Kautzsch. Trans. A. E. Cowley. 2nd ed. Oxford: Clarendon, 1910.
HALOT	L. Koehler et al., *The Hebrew and Aramaic Lexicon of the Old Testament.* Trans. M. E. J. Richardson et al. Repr. in 2 vols. Leiden: Brill, 2001.
HAT	Handbuch zum Alten Testament
HBS	Herders Biblische Studien
HBT	*Horizons in Biblical Theology*
HSM	Harvard Semitic Monographs
HTR	*Harvard Theological Review*
IBHS	Bruce K. Waltke and M. O'Connor, *An Introduction to Biblical Hebrew Syntax.* Winona Lake, IN: Eisenbrauns, 1990.
ICC	International Critical Commentary
IEJ	*Israel Exploration Journal*
Int	*Interpretation*
JBL	*Journal of Biblical Literature*
JCS	*Journal of Cuneiform Studies*
JETS	*Journal of the Evangelical Theological Society*
JNES	*Journal of Near Eastern Studies*
JNSL	*Journal of Northwest Semitic Languages*
JPS	Jewish Publication Society version
JSJ	*Journal for the Study of Judaism*
JSJSup	JSJ Supplement
JSOT	*Journal for the Study of the Old Testament*
JSOTSup	JSOT Supplement

KAT	Kommentar zum Alten Testament
LHBOTS	Library of Hebrew Bible/Old Testament Studies
LXX	Septuagint
MT	Masoretic Text
NAC	New American Commentary
NASB	New American Standard Bible
NEB	New English Bible
NIV	New International Version
NRSV	New Revised Standard Version
OBO	Orbis biblicus et orientalis
OTE	*Old Testament Essays*
OTL	Old Testament Library
OTS	*Oudtestamentische Studiën*
PEQ	*Palestine Exploration Quarterly*
PL	Patrologia latina. Ed. J.-P. Migne. 221 vols. Paris: Migne, 1844-64.
PTSDSSP	Princeton Theological Seminary Dead Sea Scrolls Project
RB	*Revue biblique*
RevQ	*Revue de Qumran*
RHPR	*Revue d'histoire et de philosophie religieuses*
SBL	Society of Biblical Literature
SBLAB	SBL Academia Biblica
SBLDS	SBL Dissertation Series
SBLMS	SBL Monograph Series
SBLSymS	SBL Symposium Series
SHANE	Studies in the History of the Ancient Near East
SJOT	*Scandinavian Journal of the Old Testament*
SSN	Studia semitica neerlandica
SWBA	Social World of Biblical Antiquity
TA	*Tel Aviv*
TDOT	G. J. Botterweck et al., eds., *Theological Dictionary of the Old Testament*. Trans. J. T. Willis et al. Vol. 1-. Grand Rapids: Eerdmans, 1974–.
TLZ	*Theologische Literaturzeitung*
VT	*Vetus Testament*
WBC	Word Biblical Commentary
WMANT	Wissenschaftliche Monographien zum Alten und Neuen Testament
WTJ	*Westminster Theological Journal*
ZAW	*Zeitschrift für die alttestamentliche Wissenschaft*
ZDPV	*Zeitschrift des Deutschen Palästina-Vereins*

INTRODUCTION

I. ORIGINS AND TRANSMISSION

The book of Hosea owes its origins to one Hosea, the son of Beeri, and his anonymous supporters/disciples. Hence the common title of the work as "Hosea." Apart from inferences in the book itself, nothing else is known about him or his family. Internal clues mark him as an Israelite, an inhabitant of the kingdom of Israel, to whom the vast majority of his prophetic compositions are directed. They indicate also a context for his prophetic activity, the mid- and later part of the 8th century B.C., when Israel struggled to maintain its identity in a treacherous international environment and was rent from within by competing religious and political factions.[1] No call narrative is preserved in the book to mark him specifically as a prophetic figure or to provide a clear indication of his profession. Some elements of his dramatic family circumstances, however, are provided in chs. 1–3.

Hosea was an accomplished poet as well as a prophetic figure, a wordsmith whose oral presentations were likely perceived as artful but eccentric. That they were also deemed inspired by God is the primary reason that they were preserved in written form. They interpret the calamities that struck Israel as self-inflicted and the consequences of rebellion against YHWH. Moreover, the projections of a reunion with Judah and transformation for both provide grounds for hope in the future.

In literary terms his book is among the most poetic of the prophetic collections in the OT,[2] particularly in the allusive character of individual units of speech and a propensity for metaphor and simile. It is, therefore, one of the most difficult to interpret. He himself may well have had a hand

---

1. See below, III, "Historical Background to Hosea's Prophecy."
2. Gerald Morris, *Prophecy, Poetry and Hosea* (JSOTSup 219; Sheffield: Sheffield Academic Press, 1996).

3

in initial collections of his prophecies, so that they might be disseminated more widely in his own day and preserved for later generations, but unfortunately we know nothing about his role in such a process. His prophetic efforts were spread out over three decades or so, coming to an end at some point at or near the siege of Samaria (2 Kgs. 17:1-6). Only a small portion of the book preserves first-person speech (e.g., 3:1-3) that may be attributed to Hosea; the rest of the book represents him or someone else in speaking roles. It is likely that anonymous disciples had a role in collecting and editing what became the book of Hosea, but one reason for the uniqueness of the book may be that he was a literary figure as well as a prophetic one. Perhaps his prophetic tasks included literary composition as well as speaking and interpreting visions. For decades scholarship has been dedicated to the proposition that prophets were speakers, not authors; however, in the case of Hosea this presupposition is being reassessed.[3] In any case, once a work was deemed worthy of preservation through writing down, scribes carried out the tasks of copying and editing.[4]

"There is little or nothing in the present text that requires its completion later than the end of the eighth century."[5] This is a statement worthy of some reflection. On the one hand, it suggests a relatively short time between the prophetic activity of Hosea himself and a penultimate form of the book by his name. It is a point of view adopted undogmatically in the present work. On the other hand, one must acknowledge that too many variables are at work in interpreting the book to make this a firm conclusion. While nothing in the book clearly reflects an exilic or postexilic date, some interpreters continue to posit significant additions to the Hosea materials after the fall of Jerusalem in 587/586 B.C. (see below). By the end of the 8th century, for example, the kingdom of Israel had been incorporated into the Assyrian Empire and Judah faced its own crises in relating to the Assyrians. Israel's fall was predicted by Hosea, but the aftermath offered a changed situation in which to reflect upon his prophecies. It is not clear from the book's contents whether Hosea himself lived to see the fall of Samaria (ca. 722). We should reckon, therefore, with the possibility that the book (as opposed to the earlier [oral?] presentations by the prophet) originated in the aftermath of Samaria's fall and was produced in Judah by refugees from the Assyrian onslaught. Public

3. See the comments in A. A. Macintosh, *A Critical and Exegetical Commentary on Hosea* (ICC; Edinburgh: T & T Clark, 1997), p. lv. The analysis of the book by F. I. Andersen and D. N. Freedman, *Hosea: A New Translation with Introduction and Commentary* (AB; Garden City, NY: Doubleday, 1980), also works on the assumption that Hosea himself may have been a literary figure.

4. Karel van der Toorn, *Scribal Culture and the Making of the Hebrew Bible* (Cambridge: Harvard University Press, 2007).

5. Andersen and Freedman, *Hosea*, p. 317.

dissemination of Hosea's prophecies would provide confirmation that Israel's political demise was an act of YHWH's judgment. It is certainly to Judah that we should look for an early written collection of Hosea's prophecies, even if not the first one, and in Judah also for the subsequent preserving of them.[6] Hezekiah's resurgent and reforming policies in Judah offer a plausible context for the collecting of prophetic oracles and national traditions.[7] In the superscription to the book, Hezekiah is the fourth and last Judean king named. And he may be the model for the reference to "David" in 3:5, the king who would be head over both Israel and Judah (1:11 [MT 2:2]).[8]

In spite of the summary offered above, a wide disparity exists among scholars with regard to the early editorial history of the book and its dating. Much of this has to do with broader conclusions about the development of religious traditions in Israel and Judah and how those in the book of Hosea fit the developmental models. For example, it has been proposed that the book is composed of two parts, one going back to a 9th-century prophet (chs. 1–3), when the struggle against baalism was at its height, and the second going back to an 8th-century prophet (chs. 4–14).[9] This has failed to persuade, given the stronger evidence for connections between the two parts of the book as a reflection of a common author/speaker. Two recent studies further illustrate the continuing disparity regarding origins. One concludes that the book was essentially put together in the 720s, while another finds very little in the book that can be attributed to Hosea himself, and little more that can be

6. So Grace I. Emmerson, *Hosea: An Israelite Prophet in Judean Perspective* (JSOTSup 28; Sheffield: JSOT Press, 1984). The references to Judah in the book of Hosea are an issue for both the transmission of the book and its interpretation. Some of them are widely believed to be editorial additions from one or more Judean perspectives as a way to update the prophecies for a Judean readership. See the comments below under II.B, Literary Features and Composition: Written Composition and Outline.

7. See Jonathan Rosenbaum, "Hezekiah's Reform and the Deuteronomic Tradition," *HTR* 72 (1979) 23-43; Andersen and Freedman, *Hosea*, p. 53, who speak of a "reform party" in Judah in the first half of the 7th century; W. Schniedewind, *How the Bible Became a Book* (Cambridge: Cambridge University Press, 2004), pp. 64-90, who has an extensive discussion of the writing traditions that either originated or emerged publicly in the time of Hezekiah, including Hosea; and Israel Finkelstein and Neil Asher Silberman, "Temple and Dynasty: Hezekiah, the Remaking of Judah and the Rise of the Pan-Israelite Ideology," *JSOT* 30 (2006) 259-85.

8. The long tradition associated with the book has resulted in some chapter and verse differences between the Hebrew text (MT) and the vast majority of modern English translations. The system followed in the commentary is the common one of citing the numbering in English versions first, followed by the MT. For example, 1:10 in English is 2:1 in Hebrew, and it will be cited as 1:10 (MT 2:1).

9. H. L. Ginsberg, "Hosea, Book of," *Encyclopedia Judaica* (2nd ed.; New York: Macmillan, 2007), 9:547-58.

attributed even to the preexilic period.[10] There are, of course, mediating positions, but in one sense these serve to illustrate the lack of consensus over the origins and early transmission of the book.[11]

With respect to my viewpoint, two matters are decisive. The first is the persuasiveness of the conclusion that little or nothing in the book itself requires a date later than the end of the 8th century B.C. As noted, elements of the book may have originated at a later, or even considerably later, date, but nothing in the vocabulary itself or allusion to historical events demands such a conclusion. For example, the terminology of "return" *(šûb)* is frequent in the book. It has to do primarily with Israel's repentance and return to YHWH, however, not with Israel's return to the land (a favorite exilic and postexilic theme). In the one place that a return of Israelites from dispersion is explicitly described, they come from Egypt and Assyria, two entities with extensive interaction with Israel in the second half of the 8th century B.C. And the verb used is *yāšab,* "to settle," rather than *šûb.* With the employment of the lexeme *šûb* in Hosea, one would expect it to be associated with a return to the land if exilic or postexilic additions to the text were made.

The second matter is acceptance of the final form of the text as the proper focus of attention. This is not a rejection of historical analysis or denial of literary growth in the Hosea tradition, but an attempt to see these matters as interpreting events in the second half of the 8th century. That is what they purport to do. In the commentary I accept some examples of editorial updating and consider others as an option, without losing sight of the task at hand, which is to interpret a received text.

With respect to Judah and the production of the Hosea book, there are

10. For the early date see W. Gisin, *Hosea: Ein literarisches Netzwerk beweist seine Authentizität* (BBB 139; Berlin: Philo, 2002). An earlier work that attributes the vast amount of the book to Hosea and early disciples is the detailed commentary by Andersen and Freedman, *Hosea.* For the later date see Susanne Rudnig-Zelt, *Hoseastudien: Redaktionskritische Untersuchungen zur Genese des Hoseabuches* (FRLANT 213; Göttingen: Vandenhoeck & Ruprecht, 2006). A study that also concludes the book is essentially the work of later editors is that of Gale A. Yee, *Composition and Tradition in the Book of Hosea: A Redaction Critical Investigation* (SBLDS 102; Atlanta: Scholars Press, 1987).

11. Two examples of a mediating position would be the commentary of H. W. Wolff, *Hosea,* trans. G. Stansell (Hermeneia; Philadelphia: Fortress, 1974), who sees a development in stages from Hosea himself through a final touch up in the postexilic period; and Macintosh, *Hosea,* who attributes a major portion of the book to Hosea and sees the editorial work on it as primarily preexilic. The study of Marti Nissinen, *Prophetie Redaktion und Fortschreibung im Hoseabuch: Studien zum Werdegang eines Prophetenbuches im Lichte von Hos. 4 und 11* (AOAT 231; Neukirchen-Vluyn: Neukirchener Verlag, 1991), offers a careful reading of two chapters and concludes that a layered development of the book took place, beginning with the prophet and developing over time.

clear links between Hosea and the book of Jeremiah, the latter a Judean literary production from the late 7th/early 6th century.[12] The two books correspond in numerous matters of vocabulary and theme, whatever form of Hosea's prophecies the author(s) of Jeremiah drew upon. This is consistent with the view that a penultimate Hosea book was a product of prophetic circles during the reign of Hezekiah (or Manasseh) and was kept in circulation in subsequent decades to influence reformist movements.[13] Indeed, Jeremiah's reception of essential elements from Hosea is solid evidence that a collection of Hosea's prophecies was extant in Judah before the fall of Jerusalem in 587/586. For good reason Jeremiah has been called Hosea's "spiritual son" and "most devoted imitator."[14]

At some point in the postexilic period, Hosea's prophecies were collected with other "minor" prophets to form the Book of the Twelve. There may have been earlier stages in the process of collecting the prophetic oracles of the Minor Prophets, but a scroll for the Twelve was likely completed by the 2nd century B.C.[15] The Wisdom of Jesus Ben Sirach (49:10), dating ca. 130 B.C., refers to the "twelve prophets," indicating that they are a recognized collection. Hosea is placed first among the Twelve, which may reflect a conviction that he is the earliest of them[16] or that the collection is the largest from the 8th-century contributors. In recent years interpreters have looked at

12. Martin Schulz-Rauch, *Hosea und Jeremia: Zur Wirkungsgeschichte des Hoseabuches* (CTM A16; Stuttgart: Calwer, 1996); H. Lalleman-de Winkel, *Jeremiah in Prophetic Tradition: An Examination of the Book of Jeremiah in the Light of Israel's Prophetic Traditions* (CBET 26; Leuven: Peeters, 2000).

13. It was suggested as far back as the patristic period that Hosea himself went to Judah in the immediate aftermath of Samaria's fall. See Eugen J. Pentiuc, *Long-Suffering Love: A Commentary on Hosea with Patristic Annotations* (Brookline, MA: Holy Cross Orthodox Press, 2002), p. 6.

14. For the former see Edmond Jacob, "Osée," in Jacob et al., *Les petits prophètes*, vol. 1: *Osée, Joël, Abdias, Jonas, Amos* (CAT 11a; Neuchâtel: Delachaux & Niestlé, 1965), p. 10; for the latter, Morris, *Prophecy, Poetry and Hosea*, p. 70.

15. Martin Beck, "Das Dodekapropheton als Anthologie," *ZAW* 118 (2006) 558-81.

16. It is widely held among modern scholars that Amos was earlier than Hosea, but the evidence for this is not decisive. They are more likely contemporaries, at least overlapping one another during the reign of Jeroboam II, with Hosea's public role in Israel lasting longer than that for Amos. The superscription of each book has them prophesying in the reigns of Uzziah of Judah and Jeroboam II of Israel, while Hosea's presence is extended until the reign of Hezekiah in Judah. Some have seen Amos's task in Israel coming to an end with the expulsion from Bethel (7:10-17), which occurred in the reign of Jeroboam II. That is possible, but a text like 6:1-7, if from Amos, suggests that his prophetic work continued into the 730s. See J. J. M. Roberts, "Amos 6:1-7," in *Understanding the Word: Essays in Honour of Bernhard W. Anderson,* ed. J. T. Butler et al. (JSOTSup 52; Sheffield: JSOT Press, 1985), pp. 155-66.

the collection of the Twelve as a whole and asked about editorial arrangements and intertextual relations.[17] It has been suggested that the collection bears marks of editorial work to facilitate an intracollection reading. If so, there is little evidence that Hosea has undergone an updated arrangement. It is more likely that as the initial "book" Hosea sets a tone for what follows.[18]

There is manuscript evidence for the Book of the Twelve from the region of the Dead Sea dating to the last century B.C. and the 1st century A.D. The evidence exists in both Hebrew and Greek. Fragments in Hebrew from the majority of chapters in Hosea have been found, along with small portions of a *pesher*-style analysis of the book.[19] The latter demonstrate that Hosea was studied and his words applied to the time of the readers in Palestinian Judaism. Portions of Hosea in Greek translation were discovered in a cave in Nahal Hever (Wadi Murabba'at).[20] They were part of a leather copy of the Book of the Twelve. Citations and allusions to Hosea in the NT are further evidence for the book's importance in Judaism and early Christianity. Thus with regard to the origins of the book and the transmission of the Hosea traditions, we have more evidence with which to work than with many other preexilic books. Ironically, the identifiable stages in the book's transmission and influence are not matched by a textual tradition free of difficulties.

17. James D. Nogalski and Marvin Sweeney, eds., *Reading and Hearing the Book of the Twelve* (SBLSymS 15; Atlanta: SBL, 2000); Paul L. Redditt and Aaron Schart, eds., *Thematic Threads in the Book of the Twelve* (BZAW 325; Berlin: de Gruyter, 2003); James D. Nogalski, "Recurring Themes in the Book of the Twelve: Creating Points of Contact for Theological Reading," *Int* 61 (2007) 125-36.

18. See the comments in Rainer Albertz, "Exile as Purification: Reconstructing the 'Book of the Four,'" in *Thematic Threads,* ed. Redditt and Schart, pp. 245-50; and A. Schart, "The First Section of the Book of Twelve Prophets: Hosea-Joel-Amos," *Int* 61 (2007) 138-52.

19. These are 4Q166 and 4Q167. See James Charlesworth, ed., *The Dead Sea Scrolls: Hebrew, Aramaic, and Greek Texts with English Translations,* vol. 6B: *Pesharim, Other Commentaries, and Related Documents* (PTSDSSP; Louisville: Westminster John Knox, 2002), pp. 113-31. 4Q166 contains 2:6-11 (MT 8-14) with commentary *(pesher)*. 4Q167 is 38 fragments, showing portions of chs. 5, 6, 8. For additional fragments see Eugene Ulrich et al., *Qumran Cave 4,* vol. X: *The Prophets* (DJD 15; Oxford; Clarendon, 1997), 4QXII^c, 4QXII^d, 4QXII^g.

20. Emanuel Tov, *The Greek Minor Prophets Scroll from Nahal Hever (8HevXIIgr)* (DJD 8; Oxford: Clarendon, 1990).

II. LITERARY FEATURES AND COMPOSITION

A. LITERARY FEATURES

The received texts of Hosea (Hebrew or MT; Greek versions) are among the most difficult in the OT. "With the possible exception of Job, the book of Hosea has the dubious distinction of having the most obscure passages of the entire Hebrew Bible. . . . The text is traditionally regarded as the most corrupt and poorly preserved of the Hebrew Bible."[21]

There are several reasons for this. One may be the vagaries of handling the text over time, with the inevitable errors associated with sight and hearing in the repetitive task of copying. The MT of Hosea appears to have suffered more in the centuries of transmission than that of most other books. The other reasons are likely due to Hosea himself, and they made the preservation of the text more difficult for the tradents who handed it on. His poetic elliptical style, frequent shift of subject, penchant for wordplay and assonance, formidable vocabulary, and even elements of a northern dialect,[22] all contribute to the difficulty of handling and interpreting the text. Interpreters vary considerably whether to describe a feature in the text as a corruption or an anomaly. On the one hand, there are corruptions in the Hebrew text and examples of befuddled rendering in the early versions. On the other hand, there are also examples where "standard" Hebrew syntax is violated, but it is likely that some of these are either the product of Hosea's individualistic poetry or reflect aspects of speech in his day that simply deviate from the norm. Difficulties with the text of Hosea are noted as far back as Jerome, the greatest Christian biblical scholar of his day, who began his commentary with the following:

> If in the interpretation of all the prophets we stand in need of the intervention of the Holy Spirit . . . how much more should the Lord be invoked in interpreting Hosea and in St. Peter's words should it be said, "Expound for us this parable" (Mt 15.15); more especially is this the case since the author himself wrote at its end, "Whoso is wise, let him understand these things" . . . thereby giving a precise indication of the obscurity of the book.[23]

---

21. C. L. Seow, "Hosea, Book of," *ABD* 3:292. Andersen and Freedman, *Hosea,* p. 66: "The text of Hosea competes with Job for the distinction of containing more unintelligible passages than any other book of the Hebrew Bible."

22. Macintosh, *Hosea,* pp. liv-lvii, has the best discussion of Hosea's dialectical peculiarities.

23. Quoted from Macintosh, *Hosea,* liii.

It is not that the text is hopelessly corrupt — far from it — but that every translation of Hosea has degrees of certainty and uncertainty, depending on the passage in question. Modern translations navigate between the MT, various early versions, and comparative Semitics, as well as the proposals of earlier interpreters for emendation, in search of coherence for readers. That is the case with the rendering offered in this volume, and no one will be happier than I will be to find new and more firm options for old difficulties I was unable to unravel.

Three prominent features of the book are reasons for its uniqueness: the use of metaphors (including similes), paronomasia or wordplays, and allusions to prior national history. In terms of frequency of use, the book exceeds all other prophetic books in these three areas. Hosea has the distinction of being the prophetic book most poetic in the employment of metaphor and wordplay, and most historical with respect to allusions to prior national traditions.

Recent decades have seen a marked increase of interest in metaphors in the OT, with several studies dedicated to Hosea.[24] It is not necessary here to review various theories of metaphor in any detail, but only to offer some brief definitions of terms for when they appear elsewhere. Suffice it to say that a metaphor is "a figure of speech whereby we speak about one thing in terms of which are seen to be suggestive of another."[25] A simile is a type of metaphor in which the preposition "like" or "as" functions to compare one thing in terms of another. In the analyses of metaphor the "one thing" can be referred to as a *tenor* or a *target domain,* while the "terms of the suggested other" are the *vehicle* or *source domain.* Thus YHWH's statement in 14:5 (MT 6), "I will be like the dew to Israel," has the "tenor" of divine care and refreshment of Israel which is compared to or explicated by the "vehicle" of dew, an important phenomenon for agricultural produce in Syria-Palestine during the dry summer season.[26] It is important to stress that metaphors and similes are not simply literary devices, but also evidence of cognition:

---

24. A good survey of the matter can be found in Pierre van Hecke, ed., *Metaphor in the Hebrew Bible* (BETL 187; Leuven: Leuven University Press, 2005). See also Paul A. Kruger, "Prophetic Imagery: On Metaphors and Similes in the Book of Hosea," *JNSL* 14 (1988) 143-51; Gören Eidevall, *Grapes in the Desert: Metaphors, Models, and Themes in Hosea 4–14* (ConBOT 43; Stockholm: Almqvist & Wiksell, 1996); Brigitte Seifert, *Metaphorisches Reden von Gott im Hoseabuch* (FRLANT 166; Göttingen: Vandenhoeck & Ruprecht, 1996); Emmanuel O. Nwaoru, *Imagery in the Prophecy of Hosea* (AAT 41; Wiesbaden: Harrassowitz, 1999).

25. This is the widely recognized definition of Janet Soskice, *Metaphors and Religious Language* (Oxford: Clarendon, 1985), p. 15.

26. See further appendix 3, "Flora and Fauna Metaphors in Hosea," and the excursus below on "Similes and Metaphors for Political Actions in Hosea 4–14."

Metaphor is considered not so much as a way in which people speak, but rather as a way in which people think. We use metaphors in our language because, to a large extent, we think metaphorically. The essence of metaphor, according to cognitive linguistics, is that we make use of our knowledge of one conceptual domain (the source) in order to gain new understanding of a second, non-related domain (the target).[27]

Hosea, for certain, does not simply employ metaphors as clever literary devices, but thinks metaphorically, making connections between phenomena in order to instruct an audience. Some of his conceptual comparisons he may have inherited; others undoubtedly were the product of his fertile mind and more particularly his search for coherence in his historical context. For him both nature and history were not impersonal autonomous spheres but revelatory of God. In one sense divine activity was the great tenor (target domain) to which Hosea employed a variety of vehicles (source domain) for explication. Elsewhere I propose that a root metaphor (a model that holds together a variety of images) for the prophet Hosea is that of God as head of his household.[28] While the household metaphor certainly does not undergird the significance of every other metaphor used for YHWH or Israel in the book, it assists us, the readers, to see coherence in such different metaphors for YHWH as husband, father, shepherd, farmer, and king. Rather than thinking of these as disparate means of portrayal, they are rooted in the source domains of family and property. Various ways of portraying Israel as YHWH's spouse, child, land, inheritance, and animals are similarly rooted in this encompassing metaphor.

Excursus: Similes and Metaphors for Political Actions in Hosea 4–14

In Hosea's poetic descriptions of Israel, Ephraim, and Judah's failures, one often cannot easily distinguish between indications of political actions (e.g., a coronation, a coup, international diplomacy) and those related to the cult (e.g., sacrifice, polytheism, veneration of images). Charges of rejecting or rebelling against YHWH fit either sphere of activity. This difficulty is true particularly of Hos. 1–3, the first major subsection of the book, where the root metaphor is that of YHWH's household, symbolized in Gomer and the children, and the primary imagery is that of harlotry and future reconciliation. Most interpreters (rightly) have seen the imagery primarily in covenantal terms, where Israel's polytheism is rejected, but there may be political overtones as well to Gomer's lovers.

27. Pierre van Hecke, "Conceptual Blending: A Recent Approach to Metaphor. Illustrated with the Pastoral Metaphor in Hos 4,16," in *Metaphor in the Hebrew Bible*, pp. 218-19. The "source domain" is essentially the vehicle and the "target domain" is the tenor.
28. See below, IV.B, "Hosea's Theology: Israel Is YHWH's Household."

In chs. 4–14, the second major section of the book, the root metaphor of Israel as YHWH's household is still at work, but the actions of Israel are variously depicted with sharp and cutting comparisons. Some of these continue the concern of covenantal faithlessness defined primarily as polytheism, syncretism, and idolatry.[29] Nevertheless, as the following list demonstrates, there are a number of poetic analogies for Israel and Ephraim in the realm of politics and international relations. For the most part they are allusive and elusive. They do not, for example, come with the names of any foreign rulers.[30] Both Assyria and Egypt are mentioned repeatedly in the book, and Israel's entanglements with them are lampooned in multiple ways. The tenor (target domain) is the folly of Israel in its political search for security. The vehicles (source domains) are drawn from a variety of fields.

Political imagery appears more frequent in chs. 7–8 than elsewhere in the book. The two chapters, whatever the prehistory of individual units within them, now employ satire and scorn repetitively to portray Israel's dangerous engagement in political intrigue and international affairs. It is unlikely, therefore, that we should read Hos. 4–14 as a sequential presentation of Israel's history, but more as a thematic collection of prophecies and poetic portrayals drawn from Hosea's efforts.

4:3	"mourning land"
5:1	"snare and net"
5:3-4; 6:10; 9:1 (?)	"harlotry"
5:7	"giving birth to strange children"[31]
5:13	"sickness and wound"
6:4	"dissipating morning dew"
6:9	"marauding bandits"
7:1	"bandits and thieves"
7:4-6	"adulterers, like a heated oven"
7:8	"mixed among the nations, yet a half-baked cake"
7:11	"silly dove, without sense"
7:16	"deceitful bow"[32]
8:7	"sowing wind and reaping a storm"
8:8a	"swallowed up" (cf. 8:7b)
8:8b	"[a broken] vessel no one wants"
8:9	"solitary wild donkey"
8:10b	"burden"[33]
9:1	"hiring lovers"

29. This section also has the language of lovers, harlotry, and adultery used in chs. 1–3, and on occasion this terminology is applied to political moves undertaken by Israel or within the state's leadership (cf. 8:9).

30. One probable exception is the reference to Shalman in 10:14.

31. The strange children may stand for the results of ill-conceived state actions in the political realm or for the failures of the priesthood.

32. This could refer either to a slack bow incapable of drawing an arrow or to a bent bow that might snap and injure the archer.

33. The term applies to the press or the subservience of vassalage.

10:4	"justice sprouts like poisonous plants in a field"
10:7	"a stick floating on water"
12:1	"shepherding the wind and pursuing the east wind"
12:7	"an oppressive merchant"
13:13	"an ill-timed birth"

Wordplays are similar to, and can be a part of, metaphorical expression. And as with metaphors, we should not think of wordplay as merely a literary or rhetorical device, but as a conceptual mnemonic device. Just as a metaphor speaks of one thing in terms suggestive of another, Hosea's wordplays speak of one thing in terms of a suggested other that to his mind has a linguistic point of contact.[34] Thus the unflattering depiction of Ephraim (*'eprayim*) as a "wild ass" *(pĕre')* in 8:9 has the mnemonic value of connecting similarly spelled terms from different semantic fields. A number of his wordplays evoke popular etymologies and even etiologies, some of which are employed elsewhere in the OT. For example, he indicates in 12:3 (MT 4) that Jacob supplanted *('āqab)* his brother in the womb and in his maturity he strove *(śārâ)* with God. The first verb is a pun on the name Jacob *(ya'ăqōb)*, and the second verb is a pun on the name Israel *(yiśrā'ēl)*. Both wordplays are known from the book of Genesis (25:26; 27:35; 32:28 [MT 29]). Not only do these wordplays evoke elements about ancestral lore, they are intended also as comparisons to the Jacob/Israel of Hosea's day.

I treat the allusions to historical tradition, including stories of prenational ancestors, more fully below.[35] There are clear references to the ancestors Jacob and Esau, and to the people Israel in Egypt and the wilderness. There are also references to prior national history in the land of promise, some of which likely go back to the period of the judges and the rise of the monarchy. These are more difficult to pin down, however, given their allusiveness. We might think of some of these things as analogous to later haggadah and in service to a narrative-based typology.[36] By "typology" I mean a perceived correspondence between events and persons in different eras. The past is employed to understand the significance of the present and the future. So, for example, the rehearsal of the ancestor Jacob's life in ch. 12 exposes current Israel's precarious position before YHWH unless repentance and transformation take place. Regarding the future, the new mar-

34. Morris, *Prophecy, Poetry, and Hosea,* pp. 147-51, offers a substantial list of perceived wordplays in Hosea.

35. See below, IV.A, "Hosea's Theology: Narrative and Community Identity."

36. Michael Fishbane, *Biblical Interpretation in Ancient Israel* (Oxford: Clarendon, 1985), pp. 298-300, 311-12, 361, 377-78, 398-99. He uses both haggadah and typology to describe Hosea's interpretation of historical tradition.

13

riage between YHWH and Israel in Hos. 2:14-20 (MT 16-22) is predicated on the prior election of Israel in the wilderness (2:14 [MT 16]; 9:10a; 12:9 [MT 10]; 13:4-5). Most of Hosea's allusions to the past, when used to identify or reveal something about the present, are rooted in historical tradition and have a narrative context.[37] As a poet, Hosea has points in common with other poetic renderings of historical tradition, notably Ps. 106 and Deut. 32.[38]

The issue at hand is the significance of this phenomenon in introducing the book. We might phrase the issue differently by asking what the appeal to the past has in common with metaphor and wordplay, since these three phenomena are major characteristics of the unique text that makes up the book. The suggested answer is twofold. All three items have a point of comparison as a focal point.[39] Elements from historical tradition are brought forth as means to interpret the present and project a future. And in complementary fashion, all three have explanatory potential, in that the focal point potentially brings to light new or different ways to grasp the matter under scrutiny. A wild ass (8:9) or grapes in a wilderness (9:10) offer new foci for thinking about Israel, as does the predator lion (5:14) or evergreen tree (14:8 [MT 9]) for YHWH.

In the case of Hosea, the book offers to readers various ways to identify and to explain why Israel fell to the Assyrians. One can say that Israel sinned and YHWH judged, which is true as far as it goes, but the instructive power comes from the imaginative portrayal of the major figures, YHWH and Israel. Hence the potential power of metaphor, wordplay, and historical typology as means of rendering Hosea's perceptions. Furthermore, the future is not determined simply by the past national failure. It lies open to be a recreation of another past, that of covenant and intimate communion, indeed the surpassing of that former era as only a new creation can offer. Such matters can be perceived in faith and only glimpsed from afar, and a prosaic recounting of them is seldom persuasive.

The poetry in Hosea has a number of characteristic poetic line forms.

---

37. Dwight R. Daniels, *Hosea and Salvation History* (BZAW 191; Berlin: de Gruyter, 1990), notes that "historical tradition is the lens through which Hosea perceives God and Israel" (p. 130), but hesitates to use the term "typology." I do not mind the general nature of the term, for it is not intended to define a particular method of citing and applying traditional materials as much as a way of perceiving connections that are rooted in historical tradition and are narrative-based. Indeed, it is a way of thinking theologically.

38. See appendix 5, "Psalm 106 and Hosea"; and appendix 2, "Song of Moses and Hosea."

39. Nwaoru, *Imagery*, p. 1: "Hosea perceives a common quality in different events and creates relation between them."

Both bicola and tricola are found. An example of the former is 13:12, a classic synonymous parallelism:

> Clause/colon A: The *iniquity* of Ephraim is <u>bound up</u>;
> Clause/colon B: his *sin* is <u>stored up</u>.

The parallelism employs a *noun* word pair and a <u>verb</u> word pair in which each term of the pair reinforces the other as a synonym.

Verses may comprise two bicola or more. An example is 5:14,[40] with two of them:

> (A) For I am like a lion to Ephraim,   (B) and like a young lion to the house of Judah.
> (A′) Indeed, I myself will tear and depart,   (B′) bear away and there will be no deliverer.

The colon in each line reinforces the other. Verse 14 also contains the simile of YHWH as a lion. The tenor is divine judgment that neither Ephraim nor Judah can escape. The vehicle is the lion that overwhelms its prey and kills it.

Among the tricola poetic forms, 8:8 is typical (see also 8:9; 9:3):

> (A) Israel is swallowed up; (B) now they are among the nations, (C) like a vessel no one desires.

One also encounters the pattern of two bicola + one. An example is 2:19-20 (MT 21-22), spread over two verses and keyed to the repetition of the verb *'āraś,* "to take in marriage":

> (A) I will take you in marriage for myself forever; (B) I will take you in marriage for myself by means of righteousness and justice, (C) and by means of devoted loyalty and compassion;
> (A′) And I will take you in marriage by giving faithfulness, (B′) and you will know YHWH.

An uncommon form is a verse with two tricola, as in 9:6:

> (A) For behold, they will go from destruction; (B) Egypt will gather them, (C) Memphis will bury them.

> (A′) Their precious silver? (B′) Thistles will possess them, (C′) briars will be in their tents.

---

40. Some other examples are in 4:16; 5:3, 8; 9:10.

Of course, much of the prophetic speech in Hosea is composed of mixed poetic forms and includes elements of prose. Hosea thus gives classic form analysis a headache on this account and also because of the relative lack of introductory and concluding formulas.[41] In this regard Hosea is markedly different from the book of Amos, a prophetic contemporary. When one adds frequent shifts of subject, then both the identification of literary units and potential connections between them are made more difficult. These matters, particularly the compressed style and frequent shifts of subject, prompted Jerome's understated comment centuries ago: "Hosea is concise and speaks as it were in detached sayings."[42]

It is possible that the emphasis on prophecy as oral speech is generally correct, but somewhat misleading with regard to Hosea. Instead of a collection of brief, originally oral presentations, Hosea may contain somewhat longer literary pieces. Units the size of modern chapters (or more) are possible. In one sense this would be the opposite of Jerome's surmise. In any case, the frequent shift of person in Hosea's text may be difficult to follow for modern or ancient readers, but it is not a sign of incoherence or the haphazard splicing together of small units of speech.[43]

B. WRITTEN COMPOSITION AND OUTLINE

Hosea's 197 verses in 14 chapters are a medieval arrangement of a text handed down for centuries. But its formation as a literary work shows signs of editing from earlier times. It has a superscription (1:1) introducing Hosea and his context, and an epilogue or conclusion (14:9 [MT 10]) urging discernment in the reading of the book. Between these two points it has two major sections, chs. 1–3 and 4–14, with the latter section in two collections or large panels (4:1–11:11; 11:12–14:8 [MT 12:1–14:9]). The first three chapters are primarily concerned with Hosea's marriage and family as the metaphorical means to understand the relationship between YHWH and Israel. Chapters 4–14 are made up of prophetic speeches addressed to Israel and Ju-

---

41. See the complicated survey of options from a form-critical perspective in Ehud Ben Zvi, *Hosea* (FOTL XXIA/1; Grand Rapids: Eerdmans, 2005). A basic study of speech units and their editorial linking is that of Martin J. Buss, *The Prophetic Word of Hosea: A Morphological Study* (BZAW 111; Berlin: Töpelmann, 1969). The study by Gisin, *Hosea,* concentrates on catchwords and linking phrases.

42. PL 28:1015.

43. L. J. de Regt, "A Genre Feature in Biblical Prophecy and the Translator: Person Shift in Hosea," in *Past, Present, Future: The Deuteronomistic History and the Prophets,* ed. J. C. de Moor and H. F. van Rooy (OTS 44; Leiden: Brill, 2000), pp. 230-50.

dah. In the proposed outline of the book, these chapters will be subdivided into the two panels noted above.

Hosea 1–3 is not an original literary unity, but it is now composed in such a way as to invite its reading as a whole. There is a long history of interpretation concentrating on these three chapters, which is the subject of an extended introduction in the commentary section. There is third-person reporting in 1:2-9, 10-11, paralleled with first-person speaking in 2:1-23 (MT 3-25); 3:1-5. The speaker in chs. 2–3 alternates between Hosea and YHWH. Hosea 1–3 can be outlined briefly as follows:

I. Superscription	1:1
II. Hosea's Family	1:2–3:5
A. Marriage, Children, and Judgment on Israel	1:2-9
B. Reversal of the Judgment and Restoration of Israel and Judah	1:10–2:1 (MT 2:1-3)
C. Charge against the Mother as a Sign of the Case against Israel	2:2-13 (MT 4-15)
D. Reversal of the Judgment against Israel and Its Transformation	2:14-23 (MT 16-25)
E. Love Her Again as a Sign that YHWH Loves Israel and Judah	3:1-5

The outline of the first section above shows that a linear presentation of events in Hosea's marriage and family (the vehicle or source domain) is not provided. It is the same case in presenting the relationship between YHWH and Israel (the tenor or target domain). Instead, the presentation alternates between judgment and renewal. This sets a pattern that is discernible also in chs. 4–14, where the two panels proposed have both judgment and renewal themes.

The remaining parts of the book may be outlined as follows:

III. God and His People	4:1–11:11
A. YHWH's Case against the People	4:1-3
B. "Spirit of Harlotry"	4:4–5:7
1. Priesthood and People	4:4-19
2. Government and People	5:1-7
C. Alarm over Israel and Judah	5:8–7:7
1. A Lion against Ephraim and Judah	5:8-15
2. Failed Repentance and Failed Relationships	6:1-11a
3. Their Deeds Encompass Them	6:11b–7:2
4. All Adulterers and the Kings Have Fallen	7:3-7
D. Israel Is Mixed and Swallowed Up among the Nations	7:8–9:9

A theme for chs. 4–14 comes in the "case" *(rîb)* announced by YHWH against Israel in 4:1-3. Most of what then follows in 4:4–11:11 is but a variation on the theme of Israel and Judah's culpability and coming judgment. Again, the theme is not developed in chronological or linear fashion, but the poetry circles around the fundamental point and presents it from various angles. In 11:8-9, however, YHWH declares himself moved by compassion and committed to the continuing existence of Israel, his beloved son (11:1). A depiction of scattered Israelites coming back to the promised land follows (11:10-11). Thus a major section of prophecies devoted to uncovering transgressions concludes with restoration and forgiveness.

Culpability and judgment, however, return again in 11:12 (MT 12:1)–13:16. The comparison with Jacob in ch. 12 has elements of judgment and possible change for Israel, with the harshest language against the people reserved for ch. 13. In ch. 14, by contrast, it is the possibility of Israel's repentance and the declaration of YHWH's healing restorative power that take center stage. Thus chs. 4–14 provide a recapitulation of the theme of sin-judgment-renewal presented in chs. 1–3. One can see this recapitulation in the ways that the three major sections (II-IV) begin and end.

1:2 Go, take for yourself a wife of harlotry, and (have) children of harlotry, for the land commits great harlotry against YHWH.

3:5 Afterward the Israelites shall return and seek YHWH their God and David their king, and they will be in awe before YHWH and his goodness in the latter days.

III. God and His People   4:1–11:11

  4:1 YHWH has a case against the inhabitants of the land. There is no faithfulness, no loving-kindness, and no knowledge of God in the land.

  11:11 They will come trembling like a sparrow from Egypt and like a dove from Assyria, and I will settle them in their homes, says YHWH.

IV. God and His People   11:12–14:8 (MT 12:1–14:9)

  11:12 (MT 12:1) Ephraim surrounds me with deception; the house of Israel (surrounds me) with deceit.

  14:8b (MT 9b) I am like a luxuriant cypress. From me comes your fruit.

Even with the widespread recognition that the book has two (or three) major sections of material, interpreters still vary widely in their sense of the relationship of the various literary units in chs. 4–14. As noted above, the book has a low percentage of introductory and concluding formulas (e.g., "Hear this word" or "says YHWH") by which to gauge the beginning and end of literary units. Change of subject and speaker, which occurs frequently in the book, is an inconsistent marker for determining the extent of a literary unit. Such changes may or may not indicate the beginning of new units or topics.

The references to Judah in the book are largely obscured in this outline, but as noted earlier, they play an important role in the question of the book's editorial history in reaching its final form. The references are as follows: ten references to "Judah" (1:1; 4:15; 5:5, 13; 6:4, 11; 8:14; 10:11; 11:12 [MT 12:1]; 12:2 [MT 3]), three to the "house of Judah" (1:7; 5:12, 14), and one to the "descendants of *(běnê)* [or people of] Judah" (1:11 [MT 2:2]). We may set aside the reference in the superscription, for the whole verse is an editorial introduction. Of the remaining references, the following are possibly or likely editorial: 1:7; 4:15; 5:5; 6:11; 8:14; 10:11; 11:12 (MT 12:1). "Editorial" can mean several things. Hosea himself may have updated his own material in the task of preparing it for written preservation or in light of changing contexts. Second, when the Hosea materials were taken to Judah in the aftermath of the fall of Samaria, then additional editorial work likely resulted in an early form of the book. What, however, if an early collection made its way to Judah before the fall of Samaria? There is nothing implausible about Hosean materials being transmitted to Judah in the aftermath of Tiglath-pileser III's campaign in the region in 733-732, which resulted in both destruction and dislocation of people in Israel. Third, it is also possible that such updating of the Hosean materials is the work of reformist circles during the time of Josiah and Jeremiah. Just as Jeremiah himself was decisively influenced by the Hosean materials, so their updating for presentation in Judah may have continued into the exilic period.

Three of the references to Judah are positive (1:7; 1:11 [MT 2:2]; 11:12 [MT 12:1]). That they are positive is no reason in and of itself to see them as editorial, although each has been defined as such by some interpreters. If 1:7 and 11:12 are additions to Hosea's material, as is possible, then that should be determined primarily on the basis of literary and semantic criteria rather than geography and political affiliation.

The same approach should be taken with respect to the "positive" elements in the book of Hosea. There is a long tradition in the historical analysis of Israelite prophecy that some or all of the restoration passages in the preexilic prophets are to be dated as exilic or later.[44] Fortunately, current interpreters are less likely to make such sweeping judgments for some or all of three reasons. One is that more emphasis is put on literary analysis, recognizing that poetic qualities make precise historical analysis difficult and that the book is first a literary document and secondarily a historical artifact. A second is a related concern to deal with texts in their final form and to spend less time reconstructing their earlier hypothetical forms.[45] A third, also related, is reticence to make sweeping historical judgments. This matter can be the loss of confidence in historical judgments due to excesses in the past or to the (increasingly postmodern) conviction that historical analysis is a form of ideological control.

There is no reason to deny to Hosea the view that God can both judge and transform his people. Such is, after all, the witness of the book. If editors can produce a scroll with texts of judgment and a projected future transformation, then why should Hosea be denied that same outlook? It may be, for example, that as a northerner Hosea would not refer positively to a future Davidic ruler (3:5),[46] but we must be aware of controlling presuppositions about what he could or could not have envisioned in a future that only

---

44. A classic example of this with respect to the book of Hosea is the detailed commentary by W. R. Harper, *A Critical and Exegetical Commentary on Amos and Hosea* (ICC; New York: Scribner's, 1905), who denies to Hosea the prophet all the texts in the book that indicate Israel's future restoration. For a more recent version of the same conclusion, see William F. Stinespring, "The Problem of Theological Ethics in Hosea," in *Essays in Old Testament Ethics (J. Philip Hyatt, In Memoriam)*, ed. James L. Crenshaw and John T. Willis (New York: Ktav, 1974), pp. 131-44.

45. The commentary by F. Landy, *Hosea* (Readings; Sheffield: Sheffield Academic Press, 1995), is an example of a "sequential" reading of the Hebrew text, without extended speculation on the history behind it.

46. See the excursus on "David Their King" at 3:5.

YHWH can bring to pass. Certainly, there is no compelling reason to deny him the hope for a reunion of Israel and Judah under one head, as expressed in 1:11 (MT 2:2).

Nevertheless, we should not draw lines in the sand with respect to affirming the work of the prophet Hosea and then dismissing or denigrating the work of editors in the collecting and composing of the book. The text is a gift. If one can affirm that God worked through Hosea, son of Beeri, then one can give that same affirmation to editors of his work, whatever their role.

III. HISTORICAL BACKGROUND
TO HOSEA'S PROPHECY

The superscription to the book of Hosea names four kings of Judah and one of Israel in whose days the prophet carried out his work. The total years of reign for the kings of Judah span most of the 8th century B.C. Jeroboam II, the one king of Israel named in the superscription, reigned through much of the first half of the 8th century. Internal clues to the book put the vast majority of the prophecies in the mid-8th century, ca. 760-720 B.C., with Israel, not Judah, as the primary audience addressed by Hosea.

During the first half of the 8th century Israel enjoyed something of a respite after decades of off-and-on struggles with Assyria and the Arameans of Damascus.[47] Both the Assyrians and the Arameans were primarily involved in their own internal matters, so that under Jeroboam II Israel managed to expand its own holdings for a brief period of time (2 Kgs. 14:25-28), although the details remain obscure. Efforts to expand from both Assyria and Damascus, however, soon resurfaced during Hosea's day.

Long-reigning monarchs in both Israel and Judah provided stability during the time of respite. Jeroboam II ruled 41 years (2 Kgs. 14:23) in Israel, and Uzziah (Azariah) reigned 52 years (2 Kgs. 15:2).[48] In Uzziah's case

47. The subject in question is discussed in standard histories of Israel and Judah, which should be consulted for more extensive treatments of the period in question. For further documentation and English translations of the Neo-Assyrian inscriptions, see H. Tadmor, *The Inscriptions of Tiglath-Pileser III King of Assyria: Critical Edition, with Introductions, Translations and Commentary* (Jerusalem: Israel Academy of Sciences and Humanities, 1994); W. W. Hallo, ed., *The Context of Scripture,* vol. 2: *Monumental Inscriptions from the Biblical World* (Leiden: Brill, 2000), pp. 161-200 (various texts translated by many different scholars); Anson F. Rainey and R. Steven Notley, *The Sacred Bridge: Carta's Atlas of the Biblical World* (Jerusalem: Carta, 2006), pp. 225-35.

48. Chronological reconstructions of the divided monarchy in the second half of the 8th century inevitably vary among scholars. The dates included in what follows are

his years of reign likely included a period when he was coregent with his father Amaziah (ca. 787-776), and certainly included a time when he was ill and his son Jotham ruled in his stead as coregent (2 Kgs. 15:5; ca. 750-735). Jeroboam II reigned in Israel from ca. 793/791 to 752/750. He was the third ruler in succession after Jehu, who founded a dynasty in 842/841 through assassination of the last Omride ruler, and who soon after paid tribute to the Assyrian ruler Shalmaneser III. The situation in Israel changed radically, however, with the death of Jeroboam II. He was succeeded by his son Zechariah (2 Kgs. 15:8-10; cf. 10:30), who six months later was assassinated by one Shallum son of Jabesh, who then took over the government in Samaria.[49] The prophecy against the "house of Jehu" and the "kingdom of the house of Israel" in Hos. 1:4 reflects these events. One month later, Shallum himself was dispatched by Menahem son of Gadi (2 Kgs. 15:14-17), who ruled for ten years. Are these changes in rulers the context for the statement, "they made kings, but not through me" (Hos. 8:4)?[50]

In 745 Tiglath-pileser III ascended the throne in Assyria and rapidly began the process of restoring authority to the central government and engaging in territorial expansion. He turned his attention to north Syria in the first years of his reign, finally reducing the heavily fortified city of Arpad. This was a wake-up call to states in the eastern Mediterranean littoral and Egypt. A second came with the taking of Kullani, biblical Calno/Calneh, in 738.[51] At some point between 743 and his death, Menahem paid tribute to

---

largely those of Kenneth Kitchen, *On the Reliability of the Old Testament* (Grand Rapids: Eerdmans, 2003), pp. 26-32, but it should be emphasized that they are approximate and that no reconstruction is certain due to the difficulties inherent in the data.

Apart from the superscription, the prophecy of Hosea preserves only one named reference to an Israelite king (Jehu in 1:4) and no dates at all. For the purposes of interpreting the prophecy, therefore, precise chronological reconstruction is not usually required. In the summary that follows there are some indications of different options regarding the dating of political events or reigns of monarchs where they may play into the interpretation of Hosea, but not full discussions of chronological options.

49. Jabesh is possibly a personal name, but it may also refer to the city Jabesh, as in Jabesh-gilead. If the latter, it is another example of the role of Gilead in the affairs of Israel. An army officer named Pekah assassinated Pekahiah in Samaria with the assistance of fifty men from Gilead (2 Kgs. 15:25).

50. Cf. Hos. 7:3-7; 13:9-11. These texts may also reflect one of the later times of dynastic difficulties in Israel such as the murders of Pekahiah and Pekah.

51. Cf. Amos 6:2. An enigmatic figure from this period, Azriyau of Yaudi, who was a ringleader in the opposition to Tiglath-pileser III in Syria, has been identified by some with Azariah/Uzziah of Judah. See the discussion in Tadmor, *Inscriptions,* pp. 273-74, who is cautiously inclined to identify the two. If the figure is the king of Judah, which is not certain (as Tadmor acknowledges), then this would be the first recorded tribute extracted from Judah. Otherwise, the first recorded is that of Ahaz in 734/733.

Tiglath-pileser III at least once and likely more than that. His tribute paying has multiple attestations. During a campaign against the Medes in 737 Tiglath-pileser III had a stele erected describing his imposition of tribute on a list of rulers. Menahem is on that list.[52] For various reasons interpreters have concluded that the list of tribute bearers contains parts of an older list and is not the result solely of the campaign against the Medes. Menahem is named also in a tribute list contained in the Assyrian king's annals (738?).[53] In 2 Kgs. 15:19-20 Pul (i.e., Tiglath-pileser III) receives a thousand talents of silver from Menahem in order to "strengthen Menahem's hold" on the kingdom of Israel. One way to read this last text is that Tiglath-pileser III actually moved against Israel with an army, but no record survives of that effort, and the text may mean nothing more than a threatening gesture or ominous signal from the Assyrian side. It is not clear either whether this biblical account reflects another payment from Menahem in addition to that noted in Assyrian sources.

Menahem intended to found a dynasty, and at his death he was succeeded by his son Pekahiah (2 Kgs. 15:22-26). Since Menahem was bound by oath and tribute to Tiglath-pileser III, this transition no doubt came with Assyrian approval. Pekahiah reigned two years only and was assassinated by an army officer of a similar name, Pekah, who was accompanied by fifty men from Gilead. There may have been additional factors at work in this act beside ambition and aggression on Pekah's part. He may have been anti-Assyrian in his outlook. The compiler(s) of the narrative gives Pekah twenty years of reign (15:27), an impossibly long time given the years assigned to other Israelite rulers and the synchronisms of their rule with those known in Egypt and Assyria. A common suggestion is that Pekah had a base of support in Gilead and that the length of his reign includes time when he "ruled" in Gilead as well. If so, Pekah may have been the leader of a regional faction not fully integrated with or loyal to the ruling house in Samaria. Moreover, the proximity of Gilead to Aramean influence is one way to account for Pekah's later alliance with Rezin of Damascus (see below). Did Pekah think of himself as ruling Israel from Gilead, while Menahem and Pekahiah ruled

---

52. L. D. Levine, *Two Neo-Assyrian Stelae from Iran* (Toronto: Royal Ontario Museum, 1972); Tadmor, *Inscriptions,* Stele III A5. Rezin of Damascus and Itobaal of Tyre are also on the list. See the discussion below on the possibility of collusion on the part of Damascus, Israel, and Tyre.

53. Tadmor, *Inscriptions,* Annals 13*:10 with parallel in Annals 27:2. The date is that preferred by Tadmor. On some chronological reconstructions Menahem's death is earlier than 738, ca. 743/742. See further M. Coogan, "Tyre and Tiglath Pileser III: Chronological Notes," *JCS* 25 (1973) 96-99; M. Weippert, "Menahem von Israel und seine Zeitgenossen in einer Steleinschrift des assyrischen Königs Tiglath Pileser III. aus dem Iran," *ZDPV* 89 (1973) 26-53; Rainey and Notley, *Sacred Bridge,* pp. 225-27.

over Ephraim?[54] The curious bifurcation between Israel and Ephraim in Hos. 5:5 could reflect such a state of affairs.

At some point after consolidating his power Pekah emerges in the biblical text in an alliance with Rezin, the ruler of Damascus. Several motives may have been at work in the alliance, but as noted above, opposition to Assyrian control was likely one of them. Pekah may have been a ringleader for anti-Assyrian factions in Israel even before his seizure of the throne in Samaria. Various clues, however, suggest that Rezin was the instigator and leading partner in the alliance between the ruling houses of Damascus and Israel.[55] Meanwhile, the sickly Uzziah finally died in Judah and his son and long-time coregent Jotham became king. His sole rule was short-lived. The sixteen years accorded him in 2 Kgs. 15:33 almost certainly includes his time as coregent (from ca. 751/750 B.C.). During his reign, perhaps in 736, Rezin and Pekah began encroaching against Judah (15:37). At Jotham's death he was succeeded by his son Ahaz.

A variety of texts (2 Kgs. 16:5-9; Isa. 7:1-9; 2 Chr. 28:1-21) narrate a move by Rezin and Pekah against Ahaz and Jerusalem, likely soon after Ahaz's accession to the throne (735/734). This move is known as the Syro-Ephraimite or Israelite-Aramean War.[56] It is almost certainly reflected in various Hosean prophecies, but their allusiveness makes identifying specific references to the struggle mostly guesswork. Isaiah records the consternation evoked in Jerusalem and among the house of David by the aggressive alliance. The Chronicler reports quite a battle and the seizure of prisoners from Judah (2 Chr. 28:5-16). One goal of the two aggressors was to replace Ahaz

---

54. Assyrian references to Menahem describe him as from either the "city" (URU; Annals 13*:10 and 27:2) or the "land" (KUR; Stele III A 5) of Samaria, whereas other Israelite rulers are described as "Israelite" or "from the house [or land] of Omri." This may be nothing more than variation in terminology. It could reflect, however, recognition that Menahem and his son ruled over a more limited area and that Pekah in Gilead and Rezin from Damascus controlled territory that had been previously part of Israel. See further Andersen and Freedman, *Hosea*, pp. 34-35; Stuart A. Irvine, "The Southern Border of Syria Reconstructed," *CBQ* 56 (1994) 21-41; Nadav Na'aman, "Rezin of Damascus and the Land of Gilead," *ZDPV* 111 (1995) 107-8.

55. See Stuart A. Irvine, *Isaiah, Ahaz, and the Syro-Ephraimitic Crisis* (SBLDS 123; Atlanta: Scholars Press, 1990), who proposes that Rezin attempted to build an anti-Assyrian coalition to help create a greater Syria like that of his predecessor Hazael. Hiram of Tyre (successor to Itobaal) played a role in the coalition.

56. The bibliography is extensive. For further references and discussions, see R. Tomes, "The Reason for the Syro-Ephraimitic War," *JSOT* 59 (1993) 55-71; Brad E. Kelle, *Hosea 2: Metaphor and Rhetoric in Historical Perspective* (SBLAB 20; Atlanta: SBL, 2005), pp. 182-99. For concentration on the Assyrian sources and a more detailed reconstruction of the Assyrian campaigns than provided here, see Peter Dubovský, "Tiglath-pileser III's Campaigns in 734-732 B.C.: Historical Background of Isa 7; 2 Kgs 15–16 and 2 Chr 27–28," *Bib* 87 (2006) 153-70.

with a certain son of Tabeel (Isa. 7:6). Perhaps the mysterious figure is a Tyrian prince and son of the Itobaal who paid tribute along with Menahem and Rezin to Tiglath-pileser III a few years earlier.[57] The narrative in 2 Kgs. 16 has Ahaz appealing to Tiglath-pileser III with tribute, whereupon Tiglath-pileser III moves on Damascus and kills Rezin. The Assyrian texts do not provide any clarity in the timing of the campaigns vis-à-vis Ahaz's bribe.

The texts do preserve a series of campaigns in the years 734-732 that bring the Assyrian army into Phoenicia, Philistia (Gaza), and against Damascus.[58] When these events are joined with the report in 2 Kgs. 15:29 that Tiglath-pileser III captured several Israelite cities during Pekah's reign[59] and took captives back to Assyria, a broader context for the Syro-Ephraimite War emerges. Rezin and Pekah (and their Tyrian supporters) sought to expand their influence in the region and to maintain control of international trade and the route to Egyptian markets. Perhaps the ruler of Gaza or certain other Philistine rulers were involved, or even Egypt itself. Some have speculated that Rezin and Pekah wanted to force Ahaz and Judah into an anti-Assyrian coalition. In any case, the consequences for Israel and for Damascus were devastating. Destruction levels at major Israelite cities such as Dan, Hazor, and Megiddo are mute but effective testimony to the Assyrian ravages and rebuilding programs.[60] While Samaria itself was spared, Damascus apparently received more severe treatment.

By 732/731 Samaria was left as a rump state with much reduced territory and severe tribute owed to Assyria. Nothing is said in the Assyrian Annals, however, about either a capture or submission of Pekah. He apparently maintained his anti-Assyrian posture until the bitter end. Given the success of the Assyrian regional campaigns, Pekah fell victim to a conspiracy and was assassinated by Hoshea the son of Elah (2 Kgs. 15:30). A plausible date for this is 732/731. According to Tiglath-pileser III, he confirmed Hoshea on the throne, thereby making Israel a vassal.[61] Jerusalem and the house of Da-

---

57. See further J. Andrew Dearman, "The Son of Tabeel (Isaiah 7:6)," in *Prophets and Paradigms: Essays in Honor of Gene M. Tucker,* ed. S. B. Reid (JSOTSup 229; Sheffield: Sheffield Academic Press, 1996), pp. 33-47. Another possibility is that the son of Tabeel is from Transjordan and perhaps even related to Tobiah the Ammonite (in Ezra–Nehemiah) and the later Tobiads.

58. One reference notes that Hiram of Tyre and Rezin of Damascus are involved together in some form of collusion (Tadmor, *Inscriptions,* Summary 9:r.5). It is possible that the Philistines were also involved; see C. S. Ehrlich, "Coalition Politics in Eighth Century B.C.E. Palestine: The Philistines and the Syro-Ephraimite War," *ZDPV* 107 (1991) 48-58.

59. The territories listed in Isa. 9:1 (MT 8:23) probably reflect the onslaught of the Assyrians at this time.

60. Ephraim Stern, *Archaeology of the Land of the Bible,* vol. 2: *The Assyrian, Babylonian, and Persian Periods, 732-332 BCE* (ABRL; New York: Doubleday, 2001), 3-57.

61. Tadmor, *Inscriptions,* Summary 4:17-18 and 9:r.10.

vid were spared as a result of Ahaz's submission to the Neo-Assyrian overlord. Thus, as a result of the Assyrian western campaigns, both Israel and Judah were subjugated.

Tiglath-pileser III died in 727 and was succeeded by Shalmaneser V.
Very little survives about the latter ruler, who died in 722. Challenges to
Shalmaneser's rule were inevitable in the aftermath of Tiglath-pileser III's
death. At some point (726-724) Hoshea declined to send tribute to
Shalmaneser and sent an appeal for aid to "So, king of Egypt" (2 Kgs. 17:4).
The syntax of the text and the name So have caused no little discussion. "So"
is either an abbreviation for Osorkon IV or a garbled reference to the western
Egyptian city of Sais, where for a time the Egyptian government had its seat.
At least the appeal to Egypt is clear. According to the brief account in 2 Kgs.
17:4-6, Shalmaneser responded by moving against Samaria. Hoshea was ar-
rested or captured, Samaria was besieged for three years, and the city fell in
the ninth year of his reign (722). There is no confirmation of the three-year
siege in surviving Assyrian records,[62] but arguments from silence are no reason to doubt a siege of the city and its subsequent fall. Since Sargon II,
Shalmaneser's successor, claims to have subdued Samaria, discussion remains over the details of Samaria's final collapse.[63]

From the terse biblical account, it is possible to work out a plausible
sequence of events in the nine years attributed to Hoshea, but a number of
matters are left open by the nature of the sources. This is particularly true regarding the relationship between Samaria and Assyria during the end of
Tiglath-pileser III's reign and the early part of Shalmaneser's. For example,
J. H. Hayes and J. K. Kuan have proposed that Samaria was part of a regional
revolt during Tiglath-pileser III's seventeenth year (728), and this was when
Hoshea first withheld tribute to Assyria.[64] A campaign to restore control was

62. The nonbiblical texts for Shalmaneser's reign are sparse. See the discussion of
the Babylonian Chronicle (1.i.28), which briefly comments on Shalmaneser's reign and
an attack on a city, in H. Tadmor, "The Campaigns of Sargon II of Assur: A
Chronological-Historical Study," *JCS* 12 (1958) 39-40. It is now generally agreed that the
city attacked by Shalmaneser was Samaria. Josephus records that the Assyrian king
Shalmaneser invaded Phoenicia and forced compliance from a number of cities (*Ant.*
9.283-87). For detailed discussions of the circumstances of Samaria's siege and fall, see
Bob Becking, *The Fall of Samaria: An Historical and Archaeological Study* (SHANE 2;
Leiden: Brill, 1992); and two studies by K. Lawson Younger, "The Deportations of the Is-
raelites," *JBL* 117 (1998) 201-27; "The Fall of Samaria in Light of Recent Research,"
CBQ 61 (1999) 461-82.

63. For Sargon's inscriptions and his claims regarding Samaria, see the translations of K. Lawson Younger Jr., *COS* 2:293-98.

64. J. H. Hayes and J. K. Kuan, "The Final Years of Samaria (730-720)," *Bib* 72
(1991) 153-81. The campaign depends on a fragmentary reference in the Assyrian Eponym
Chronicle. Not all historians concur that the campaign in question is against Damascus.

underway when Tiglath-pileser III died and was succeeded by Shalmaneser. The report in 2 Kgs. 17:3 that Hoshea paid tribute to Shalmaneser is then placed in Shalmaneser's accession year (726). Hoshea's embassy to Egypt (17:4) came in the next year. Shalmaneser's response was to come up against Samaria again, remove Hoshea, and begin the process of making the rump state a province of Assyria. Samaria, however, refused to acquiesce and instead appointed an Israelite government.[65] Shalmaneser was then forced to return and lay siege to Samaria. This would be a third military move against Samaria by Shalmaneser. While it is possible that Shalmaneser attacked Samaria as early as 726, or that an unnamed Israelite king followed Hoshea, both depend upon an uncertain reconstruction of the Assyrian Eponym Chronicle and obscure references in Hosea.

As noted above, there is also difficulty in sorting out the chain of events surrounding the death of Shalmaneser and the fall of Samaria. One can argue on the basis of the biblical text that Samaria fell to Shalmaneser, and on the basis of his annals that the city fell to Sargon II. Indeed, one can argue that both claims are rooted in fact. The most straightforward interpretation of the biblical text is that Samaria surrendered to Shalmaneser. The report in 2 Kgs. 17:6 says that "the king of Assyria" took the city, but the only king mentioned in the context is Shalmaneser (17:3; Sargon is not named in 2 Kings). Nothing precludes the siege having lasted two years or more and, from the Assyrian viewpoint, having come to a satisfactory conclusion before Shalmaneser died in 722. In his annals Sargon claims that he engaged Samaria militarily and sent 27,000 people into exile. The question is when. Was it directly on the heels of his predecessor, so that in essence Sargon claims what was really the work of Shalmaneser, or was there a gap in time and another submission of Samaria, this time to Sargon? One can make a reasonable case that Sargon took action against Samaria in 720/719, his second regnal year, when Hamath fomented rebellion in the area and Egypt abetted it.[66] Sargon claims to have defeated them all. Thus ended the political state of Israel over two hundred years after its birth in reaction against oppressive policies of Solomon and

65. Hayes and Kuan, "Final Years," 167-68, suggest that the charge in Hos. 8:4, "they made a king, but not through me," is the prophet's assessment of the appointment of an Israelite king (unnamed in any surviving source) after the removal of Hoshea.

66. M. Christine Tetley, "The Date of Samaria's Fall as a Reason for Rejecting the Hypothesis of Two Conquests," *CBQ* 64 (2002) 59-77, proposes that there was indeed a three-year conquest of Samaria, but that it was accomplished by Sargon II from 720 to 718. She accepts the claim that Samaria fell in the 9th year of Hoshea (2 Kgs. 17:6), but believes that Hoshea was not appointed king by Tiglath-pileser III until 728/727. Her conclusions have (rightly) been questioned by B. Kelle, "Hoshea, Sargon, and the Final Destruction of Samaria: A Response to M. Christine Tetley with a View Toward Method," *SJOT* 17 (2003) 226-43.

Rehoboam. Its separatist beginnings were affirmed by prophetic word (1 Kgs. 11:29-39) and its demise was accounted for by prophetic word.

As a result of the Assyrian attacks on Israel and Samaria, the population in and around Jerusalem increased markedly as people fled the conflicts.[67] The area between Shechem and Bethel was apparently the most affected by population shifts.[68] With the displaced people moving south came also those who brought the traditions of Hosea's prophetic ministry, perhaps including some from Hosea's own circle of support. The book in its penultimate and then final form was created and preserved in Judah. Although there is no reason to doubt that the prophet included words about Judah in his prophetic work, it is also likely that the edited version of the book in Judah received some updates. A clear example is the superscription to the work, with its four kings of Judah that includes Hezekiah, the ruler whose reign lasted at least until the turn of the century.[69] Hezekiah was a reforming monarch and one who made overtures to the northern population (2 Kgs. 18:3-8; 2 Chr. 29–31). As noted in the discussion of the book's composition, the reign of Hezekiah would be a plausible setting for putting the book in essentially its present form.

In outline form, a sketch of the events is as follows:

750-749	Death of Jeroboam II
749	Assassination of Zechariah, son of Jeroboam II, six months later by Shallum
749/748	Assassination of Shallum by Menahem one month later
748-738	Reign of Menahem in Israel
745	Accession to the throne in Assyria by Tiglath-pileser III (also called Pul[u])
743-738	Tribute(s) paid by Menahem to Tiglath-pileser III
738-736	Reign of Pekahiah
736-735	Rezin of Damascus and Pekah of Israel put pressure on Judah under Jotham

67. M. Broshi, "The Expansion of Jerusalem in the Reigns of Hezekiah and Manasseh," *IEJ* 24 (1974) 21-26; Ronny Reich and Eli Shukron, "The Urban Development of Jerusalem in the Late Eighth Century B.C.E.," in *Jerusalem in Bible and Archaeology: The First Temple Period,* ed. Andrew Vaughn and Anne Killebrew (SBLSymS 18; Atlanta: SBL, 2003), pp. 209-18; Nadav Na'aman, "When and How did Jerusalem Become a Great City? The Rise of Jerusalem as Judah's Premier City in the Eighth-Seventh Centuries B.C.E.," *BASOR* 347 (2007) 21-56.

68. Finkelstein and Silberman, "Temple and Dynasty," 265-69.

69. The chronology of Hezekiah's reign is very complicated. See the discussion in the commentary on Hos. 1:1. It is possible that Hezekiah was appointed vice-regent under Ahaz in 728/727. If so, then his political and religious influence briefly overlapped the prophetic work of Hosea.

735-734	Syro-Ephraimite War; Rezin and Pekah move against Jerusalem and Ahaz, new king in Jerusalem
734-732/731	Tiglath-pileser III campaigns against Phoenicia, Philistia, Israel, and Damascus
732/731	Hoshea assassinates Pekah and is confirmed on throne by Tiglath-pileser III
728/727	Hezekiah coregent in Judah?
727	Tiglath-pileser III dies and is succeeded by Shalmaneser V; Hoshea pays tribute
726-724	Hoshea withholds tribute, appeals to Egypt for aid, and is captured by Shalmaneser
724-722	Shalmaneser lays siege to Samaria; refugees flee south to Jerusalem and Judah
722	Samaria falls; Shalmaneser dies and is succeeded by Sargon II
720	Rebel elements in Samaria are involved with Hamath in rebellion against Sargon
720/719	Sargon subdues Samaria and sends a wave of inhabitants into exile

IV. HOSEA'S THEOLOGY

A. NARRATIVE AND COMMUNITY IDENTITY

A prophetic book like that of Hosea can be understood as an occasional document. It is occasioned by the circumstances of Israel in the second half of the 8th century and presents a portion of one side of a give-and-take between prophet and receiving community. It does not, therefore, present theological views in systematic form, but addresses the particulars that occasioned prophetic responses. The NT epistles, particularly those of Paul, are sometimes described as occasional writings, pastoral responses to particular matters in early Christian communities rather than, say, essays on theological subjects for young churches. The epistles also preserve a portion of one side of a give-and-take between apostle and congregation. A book like Hosea distills prophetic responses over more than twenty years and is edited for public presentation, while a letter like 1 Corinthians comes a few months after Paul has been in Corinth; nevertheless, the two documents still share the characteristics of occasioned response.

Hosea, like an epistle writer, does not present his theology abstractly, but responds from his theological convictions to the issues of his day. He does have a matrix that formed him and from which he developed a worldview and a corresponding set of convictions about theological integrity in common life. In literary and conceptual terms, we might describe Hosea's matrix and resulting worldview as a narrative, a story-shaped ethos that he absorbed and that subsequently shaped his approach to his prophetic task. Working backward from his occasioned responses, we can reconstruct at least some of the narrative substructure of his theology.[70] In doing so, it is helpful to recognize that "narrative frameworks are created by communities, not by autonomous individuals."[71] Hosea was at once a member of a national community and of a smaller, particular community, both with traditions to define identity. The latter community was almost certainly some form of what we might call an opposition party. If anything is clear, it is that Hosea opposed the leading social-religious institutions in the Israel of his day. His particular community, whatever its origins, would have held similar convictions. The two communities, national and particular, had traditions that overlapped and diverged, and correspondingly, religious practices that overlapped and diverged. Where they diverged, Hosea offered his criticisms.

The reconstruction of Hosea's narrative theology is related to, but somewhat different from, the question of earlier biblical traditions known to him. It is related in that the evidence for both depends on what is preserved in the book of Hosea as references for his hearers/readers. It is different in that a concern for identifying a particular tradition history (e.g., Israel's wilderness tradition) may show that Hosea draws on traditions somewhat different from those now contained elsewhere in the OT. Furthermore, these individual traditions still require integration with others before one can define a narrative-based matrix that shaped the theological convictions of the prophet and his particular community. It is the case that we cannot always sort out the relative importance of the various traditions that Hosea drew upon, but some elements seem primary or fundamental to him. Following a proposal of Ray Van Leeuwen, those deemed most influential will be described as "base texts (tra-

70. Readers will recognize here the influence of Richard Hays's work on Pauline thought, including the subtitle of his work, *The Faith of Jesus Christ: An Investigation of the Narrative Substructure of Galatians 3:1–4:11* (2nd ed.; Grand Rapids: Eerdmans, 2002). The occasional letter draws on a recognized narrative. Similarly, Michael Fishbane, *Biblical Interpretation in Ancient Israel* (Oxford: Clarendon, 1985), proposes that a dynamic is at work with Hosea (and other biblical writers) whereby historical tradition *(traditio)* is passed along *(traditum)*, interpreted, and actualized for application in the community. Hosea draws on narratives and prescriptive materials in haggadic and typological fashion to apply his message at a point of crisis in Israelite history.

71. Joel Kaminsky, *Corporate Responsibility in the Hebrew Bible* (JSOTSup 196; Sheffield: Sheffield Academic Press, 1995), p. 181. We should not think of Hosea as a lone ranger, even if we are unable to locate his supportive community. They were certainly involved in the preservation of his (their?) materials.

ditions)."[72] These would be the hallmarks of the *traditum* (received tradition) adapted and applied by Hosea.

It is possible by way of beginning to characterize Hosea's narrative about the *past and present* as having three periods to it. We should be wary, however, of defining the periods too linearly or in a one-dimensional way. Hosea's overlapping metaphors, the circularity of the book's presentation of his thought, and the typological manner in which he applies inherited traditions to define Israel past and present all complicate any simple historical periodization. On the other hand, a three-period schema is a helpful heuristic device. The first relates to the period of Israel's ancestors. Hosea knows traditions about Jacob and Bethel (12:2-6 [MT 3-7]) and cites a promise for the future that is now part of the ancestral accounts in Genesis (1:10 [MT 2:1]; Gen. 22:17; 32:12 [MT 13]). Yet, as far as the book of Hosea is concerned, the ancestral period plays a subsidiary role to the two massively influential periods that follow, namely, the exodus and wilderness wandering, followed by the settlement and life in the promised land. The second period, which interpreters sometimes shorten by referring to the "wilderness period," is a time that the prophet appropriates through a variety of metaphors and with a number of allusions. The root metaphor is that of Israel as YHWH's household (with roles for marriage and children). The third period is the time of Israel's life in the promised land reaching to Hosea's own day. It is difficult to say precisely how the prophet saw the transition between the latter two periods, as he says virtually nothing about the traditions of settlement in the land.[73] His reference to the apostasy at Baal-peor (9:10) may be a transition point between them.[74]

The categories of exposition that follow are not organized around the three periods, although they are presupposed in them. The categories them-

---

72. Ray Van Leeuwen, "Scribal Wisdom and Theodicy in the Book of the Twelve," in *In Search of Wisdom: Essays in Memory of John G. Gammie,* ed. Leo G. Perdue et al. (Louisville: Westminster John Knox, 1993), pp. 31-51, shows the formative influence of Exod. 34:6-7, what he describes as a "base text (or its tradition)," in several of the Minor Prophets. His discussion of Hosea is on pp. 34-39. While his proposal seems correct for Hosea and his editors, I will propose a few other base texts as well.

73. His prophetic contemporary Amos notes YHWH's acts in granting Israel a life in the promised land and in raising up prophets and nazirites for Israel's edification (2:9-12).

74. For further discussion and bibliography regarding Hosea and the importance placed on Israel's prior history, see Dwight R. Daniels, *Hosea and Salvation History* (BZAW 191; Berlin: de Gruyter, 1990); Else Kragelund Holt, *Prophesying the Past: The Use of Israel's History in the Book of Hosea* (JSOTSup 195; Sheffield: Sheffield Academic Press, 1995). Hosea also understands that Israel has a future in which God's saving promises will be realized. That future is linked by typology to God's prior redemptive acts on Israel's behalf.

selves are more thematic, in keeping with the primary mode of the book's own presentation. They are followed by more extended reflections on two lenses through which Hosea appropriates his base texts and frames them. The first is the metaphor of Israel as YHWH's household, and the second is the metaphor of national covenant as marriage.

1. "I am YHWH your God from/since the land of Egypt" (12:9 [MT 10]; 13:4); "Out of Egypt I called my son" (11:1). These related affirmations are a primary clue to the defining narrative that nurtured Hosea, providing him his theological identity, and from which he drew prophetic insight. In kernel form it is certainly drawn from a base text. The canonical form of the narrative of YHWH redeeming Israel from Egypt (and its aftermath in nation forming) is the Pentateuch and portions of the Former Prophets.[75] The Psalter also contains poetic renditions of Israel's earlier history (e.g., Pss. 78, 105, 106), noting the primacy of the exodus event. These poetic recitals do not draw woodenly from the canonical narrative formulation of the Pentateuch any more than Hosea does. At times the particulars of their angles of visions differ from the narrative presentation in the Pentateuch, just as Hosea's does. Examples of Hosea's independence of terminology and allusion regarding Israel's prior history will be cited in the relevant commentary sections. Given the difficulties of dating individual traditions in multilayered works like the Pentateuch and Psalter, one can note similarities and draw comparisons between them and the prophet, but one cannot determine that Hosea knew Exodus or Deuteronomy or Ps. 106 in essentially the forms in which they now exist. That he shares some materials in common with them will have to suffice for comparison.[76] It is clear that accounts existed in Hosea's day of YHWH's acquisition of Israel in Egypt and his guidance of them to the land of promise. Hosea drew upon them as authoritative resources. Whether he knew them in written or oral form likely varied among accounts. If Hosea's prophetic charges against Israel are to be believed, then many of his contemporaries did not draw the same conclusions from those accounts that the prophet did.[77]

75. For a narrative-based approach to these portions of the OT, see the work by John Goldingay and its felicitous title, *Old Testament Theology,* vol. 1: *Israel's Gospel* (Downers Grove, IL: InterVarsity Press, 2003).

76. On the commonalities between Hosea and the poetic texts of Deut. 32 and Ps. 106, see appendixes 2 and 5, respectively. With respect to a book like Exodus, note the comment of F. C. Fensham, "The Marriage Metaphor in Hosea for the Covenant Relationship between the Lord and His People," *JNSL* 12 (1984) 76: "It is clear that Hosea was familiar with the greatest part of Exodus." Perhaps this should be qualified slightly to say that he seems familiar with much of the narrative traditions in Exodus.

77. Amos 3:1-2 also uses the election tradition as a base text with which to engage the prophet's audience.

The significance of the base text of YHWH's acquisition is developed metaphorically with Israel as his household (see B below). Here is an intersection between a base text and narrative matrix with the root metaphor of Israel as YHWH's household. Thus for Hosea Israel can be spouse and/or child or even delectable grapes discovered in the wilderness (9:10a). In the marriage metaphor, Israel is the spouse who owes fidelity to her husband YHWH. One cannot tell if the household metaphor is part of Hosea's base text or if he drew the analogy with marriage and family based on the covenantal exclusivism that he inherited (see discussion in B below). Israel's sonship is explicit in Exod. 4:22, where Israel is YHWH's "firstborn son."[78] In the role of son, Israel has a "calling" to represent the head of the household.

In acquiring Israel, YHWH saved them. Hosea applies the term "savior/deliverer" (môšîa', 13:4) to YHWH, since he brought up ('ālâ) Israel from Egypt to the land of promise (12:13 [MT 14]). In keeping with Hosea's narrative logic, this event can be seen in familial terms: YHWH loved his son and called him from Egypt (11:1). We might think of this datum in Hosea's narrative the way the Decalogue begins a summary of Israel's covenant ethos with a prologue affirming that YHWH is "your God, who brought you out from the land of Egypt" (Exod. 20:2).[79] This is a base text from which other matters about Israel derive their significance.

Hosea knows that the unique name of Israel's Deity is associated with the choosing and rescue of Israel (Hos. 1:9). In the canonical account, Moses is addressed from a burning bush and told that the God of the ancestors is named YHWH (often pronounced "Yahweh"; Exod. 3:1-15). The setting is Mt. Sinai in the wilderness, the place where Moses will later return with the people. That account has a pun on God's name that links its etymology to the verb hāyâ, "to be." Thus God declares that he "will be" with Moses, that "I will be whom I will be," and that Moses is to tell the people in Egypt that "I am" has sent him to them (3:12-15). One may debate how much of the tradi-

---

78. Deuteronomy also has Israel collectively as YHWH's "children" (14:1; cf. 32:5-6).

79. Hosea uses the verb "bring up" (Hiphil of 'ālâ) to describe the event of the exodus in 12:13 (MT 14) and plays on the same verb in 1:11 (MT 2:2). The prologue to the Decalogue uses the verb "bring out" (Hiphil of yāṣā') in Exod. 20:2 and Deut. 5:6. Thomas B. Dozeman, "Hosea and the Wandering Wilderness Tradition," in *Rethinking the Foundations: Historiography in the Ancient World and in the Bible: Essays in Honour of John Van Seters*, ed. S. McKenzie and T. Römer (BZAW 294; New York: de Gruyter, 2000), pp. 59-62, suggests that the formula with "brought up" is tied to the view that the goal is the land of promise, while the formula with "brought out" emphasizes the saving aspect of the tradition. He also suggests that the latter formula is the one adopted by the Deuteronomistic movement and that it may be later in date than the former expression.

tion now embedded in Exod. 3:1-15 Hosea knew, but he knows the pun on the divine name and its significance as explicated there.[80] The Deity who identifies himself as YHWH declared himself to be with and for Israel in the wilderness.

2. "You shall know no other deity except for me, for there is no savior except for me. I knew you in the wilderness" (Hos. 13:4-5); "I found Israel like grapes in the wilderness" (9:10a). A household has only one "head." Hosea understands YHWH to be not only the savior of Israel but also the exclusive Lord of his people. The "knowing" that the prophet attributes to both YHWH and Israel is a relational term that excludes other intimates from the covenantal bond. The verb can be used in the context of marriage to signify the intimate act leading to conception (cf. Gen. 4:1). YHWH "knew" Israel in the sense of calling them and choosing them as his own. From Israel's side, therefore, "to know" YHWH means to reciprocate his committed choice and to obey his instruction. There are both relational and cognitive aspects to the "knowledge of God" expected of Israel.[81]

For Israel there is no other savior. Hosea held to a robust monolatry, and as noted, developed its implications for Israel by analogy with the household members of wife and children. He is the earliest writing prophet to make the metaphorical connection between covenant and marriage. That robust monolatry is also present in the first commandment of the Decalogue ("no other gods before me," Exod. 20:3; Deut. 5:7), whose preface states that YHWH brought Israel out of Egyptian slavery (Exod. 20:2; Deut. 5:6).[82] Indeed, the second commandment is a polemic against the making of images and venerating them, because YHWH is a jealous God (Exod. 20:4-6; Deut. 5:8-10; cf. Exod. 34:6-7, 14). Divine images were also a subject of Hosea's polemic (see 7 below). It is only a short step from divine jealousy and covenantal exclusivism to the marriage metaphor.

One can argue, of course, that texts like the Decalogue, Exod. 32–34, and the poetic Song of Moses in Deut. 32 are later in written formulation than Hosea. Yet even if that is correct, the substance of their compositions

---

80. Cf. Exod. 3:15 with Hos. 12:5 (MT 6).

81. Joy Philip Kakkanattu, *God's Enduring Love in the Book of Hosea: A Synchronic and Diachronic Analysis of Hosea 11,1-11* (FAT 2/14; Tübingen: Mohr Siebeck, 2006), pp. 120-26.

82. Exod. 34:14: "You shall not worship any other deity, for YHWH — whose name is Jealous — is a jealous God"; Deut. 32:12: "YHWH alone guided him [= Israel] and there was no foreign deity with him"; 32:39: "I am he and there is no deity except for me." Deut. 6:4-5 is essentially a positive formulation of the first commandment of the Decalogue. The comprehensive "oneness" of YHWH has as its corollary a command for Israel to love him comprehensively (and thus to exclude the love of other deities).

likely is not later.[83] One can succinctly describe the thrust of Hosea's prophecy by saying that it is a sustained application of the prologue and first two commandments of the Decalogue to the crises he perceives for Israel in his day. These, in particular, are a base text/tradition that casts its influence across the book of Hosea.[84]

Hosea seems to use the "wilderness" in geographic and metaphorical senses. In a geographic sense it is the place between Egypt and the promised land, where YHWH "found" and "married" Israel (cf. Jer. 2:2-3). From the perspective of existence in the land of promise, evoking the wilderness is metaphorical. It stands for an arid, foreboding place in which human life is at risk unless sustained by divine care (Hos. 2:3 [MT 5]).

In Hos. 2:14 (MT 16) YHWH intends to allure Israel back to the wilderness/desert.[85] This is part of the typology of marriage for covenant, with the "wilderness," the former place of covenant making, serving as the future place of marriage renewal. Hosea's eschatology, if that is the right term to use for his concept of Israel's future restoration, is patterned on the past.[86] His appropriation of the wilderness period in Israel's prior history, therefore, is positive in this form of the typology, unlike the canonical narrative, where numerous examples of Israel's faithlessness are also portrayed (e.g., Exod. 32–34; Num. 16:1-50). In this regard Hosea's angle of presentation is like that in Ps. 105, which celebrates what YHWH accomplished from Egypt through the wilderness to the promised land. This does not mean that Hosea knew no traditions of Israelite disobedience in the wilderness, only that the wilderness is the positive setting for his marriage and covenant typology. He

83. For example, Hosea almost certainly knows the substance of the narratives in Exod. 32–34, as his vocabulary demonstrates, but in what form he knew it remains an open question. See the comments by Ruth Scoralick, *Gottes Güte und Gottes Zorn: Die Gottesprädikationen in Exodus 34.6f und ihre intertextuellen Beziehungen zum Zwölfprophetenbuch* (HBS 33; Freiburg: Herder, 2002), pp. 73-130, 145-60, particularly the comments on 145, 152.

84. Much of the substance of Exod. 34:6-7 is contained in Exod. 20:2-6; Deut. 5:6-10; see appendix 10, "YHWH's Self-Definition (Exod. 34:6-7) and Hosea." Helmut Utzschneider, *Hosea, Prophet vor dem Ende: Zum Verhältnis von Geschichte und Institution in der alttestamentlichen Prophetie* (OBO 31; Göttingen: Vandenhoeck & Ruprecht, 1980), pp. 102-3, proposes that Hosea drew upon the prologue to the Decalogue plus the first two commandments in their "Deuteronomistic edited version."

85. See further Dozeman, "Hosea and Wandering Wilderness Tradition." The observations that follow differ from Dozeman's conclusion that in the explicit references to the exodus and wilderness the prophet is "not dependent on, but is laying the foundation for salvation history" (p. 69).

86. This is the same typology for Jeremiah (2:2-8; 31:31-34): marriage in the wilderness, guidance to the promised land, Israel and Judah's defections, YHWH's declared intent to make a new covenant.

employs vocabulary and themes in common with Ps. 106, which has a number of references to Israelite failure in the wilderness wandering. Comparing Pss. 105 and 106 and the bits of tradition employed by Hosea demonstrates the multiformed way that any one composer draws upon memory of the past. The prophet appears to know something of the "golden calf" tradition[87] and certainly knows a form of the apostasy at Baal-peor (cf. 9:10b with Num. 25). The incident at Baal-peor may or may not be considered part of the "wilderness period" in Hosea's viewpoint. In the canonical version, it is part of the sojourn in the plains of Moab (Num. 22:1; 25:1). For Hosea it is a negative illustration from Israel's past, whether or not he included it in the wilderness traditions known to him. Israel did not have an idyllic past or a perfect marriage with YHWH before the crises of Hosea's day.[88]

3. "I will love them freely" (Hos. 14:4 [MT 5]). The language of love flows naturally from the concept of Israel as YHWH's household, yet it is rooted in the great mystery of divine choice, not natural descent. Hosea shares with Deuteronomy the vocabulary of "love" (*'āhab*) as a motivation for YHWH's choice of Israel. Surprisingly, that vocabulary does not occur in Amos, Isaiah of Jerusalem, or Micah, Hosea's prophetic contemporaries, though each of them presupposes that God had graciously drawn Israel and Judah to himself. Not only do Hosea and Deuteronomy share this vocabulary, they draw similarly on the traditions that employ it. In Deuteronomy one cannot move behind the mystery of divine election of and love for Israel (4:37; 7:6-8; 10:15; 23:5), even when the narrative itself moves back from slavery in Egypt to earlier promises to ancestors. The presenting issue is divine initiative. YHWH's gracious initiating election is simply the primary affirmation about

87. Daniels, *Hosea and Salvation History,* pp. 59-61, concludes that Hosea's positive rendition of the wilderness tradition means that he could not have known of the tradition of the apostasy with the golden calf at Sinai. The severe criticism in Hosea about bovine imagery in Israel (see 7 below) would have to be rooted in something else. This plausible conclusion seems based on a view that Hosea had a linear and exclusively idealized view of the wilderness period. Given Hosea's multiple metaphors and employment of different traditions, the balance of probability seems to be with a multiformed appropriation of the past. A transgression at the mountain of God did not result in the end of Israel according to Exod. 32–34, and so it may not have been fatal to the metaphors of marriage and adoption in interpreting God's claim upon Israel and his guidance of them in the wilderness to the promised land.

88. There is no evidence that Hosea romanticized the experience of the desert and a return to it, as has sometimes been claimed in the past; see P. Humbert, "Osée, le prophète bedouin," *RHPR* 1 (1921) 97-118. The wilderness is the place where YHWH claimed Israel; there is no reason to think that the prophet saw the values of monotheism or communal rigor more rooted in a "desert ideal" as opposed to the debaucheries of sedentary existence.

God from which other matters, such as rescue from Egypt, preservation in the wilderness, and guidance to the promised land, take their source. In Hosea's case, the narrative of divine calling is the fount from which the significance of Israel's origins and identity is drawn, although he too has knowledge of traditions that precede the exodus from Egypt (11:8; 12:2-6, 12 [MT 3-7, 13]). So when the prophet is commanded to "go again, love a woman,"[89] Hosea is personally re-presenting an authoritative narrative in which God has "loved the Israelites" (3:1).

4. "By a prophet YHWH brought Israel from Egypt, and by a prophet he was kept" (12:13 [MT 14]). The prophet in question is almost certainly Moses, although he is not named explicitly in the book of Hosea.[90] In the Pentateuch Moses is described through his manifold tasks: he judges the people, officiates at sacrifice, and mediates instruction between YHWH and people. In Deuteronomy, however, Moses is the prophet par excellence (18:15-19; 34:10-12).[91] It is not clear whether Deut. 18:18 intends a prophetic office patterned on the portrait of Moses or is simply indicating that the institution of prophecy is one of God's continuing provisions for Israel. These two are not mutually exclusive. And since Hosea does not name any other prophets, we do not know for certain that he made any connections between the paradigm of Moses and subsequent prophets (Samuel, Elijah?). It is likely, however, that he did (cf. Hos. 6:5; 12:10 [MT 11]). YHWH spoke to prophets and provided comparisons by their hand (12:10 [MT 11]). Such an affirmation almost certainly influenced Hosea's sense of prophecy as one of YHWH's institutional gifts to Israel and the particulars of his own task.[92]

89. Cf. the instruction to love God in Deut. 6:5; 10:12; 11:1, 13, 22.

90. W. F. Albright, "Samuel and the Beginnings of the Prophetic Movement," in *Interpreting the Prophetic Tradition,* ed. H. Orlinsky (Cincinnati: Hebrew Union College Press, 1969), p. 157, has proposed that two prophets are represented by the Hebrew parallelism in 12:13 (MT 14). The first is Moses, who brought Israel out from Egypt; and the second is Samuel, who helped preserve Israel in difficult circumstances. In this context he calls attention to the pairing of Moses and Samuel in Jer. 15:1.

91. Moses' prophetic tasks are also described in Num. 11:24-30; 12:1-15. In 12:7-8 Moses is affirmed by God as "faithful in all my household *(bayit);* with him I speak mouth to mouth." The first clause would be a model of prophecy consonant with Hosea's understanding of Moses as someone who led and preserved Israel, YHWH's household. It is an apt description also of a prophetic office or role to which Hosea may have aspired.

92. Hos. 6:5 probably indicates that other prophets before Hosea had charged Israel with defection from YHWH and announced judgment to the people. He likely saw himself in line with these figures going back to Moses. A dissenting opinion regarding 6:5 is offered by Margaret Odell, "Who Were the Prophets in Hosea?" *HBT* 18 (1996) 79-82. She proposes that the prophets described in 6:5 incited the people to follow a fatal course of action.

The difficult text of 9:8a probably defines a prophet as a "watchman/sentinel"

A prophet in Hosea's understanding is one who represents YHWH's "words" in the public realm, since all of Israel's institutional life is answerable to YHWH for continuing legitimacy.[93] Perhaps we might say that what Hosea inherited about Israel's origins and identity is rooted in Moses' prophetic acts and applied in Israel's history by prophets who were before Hosea. Moses was "called" (Exod. 3:4) to lead Israel, who in turn was "called" from Egypt (Hos. 11:1). The identity of God's household, therefore, is a result of its calling. In some ways Israel collectively is a prophetic community (may "all YHWH's people be prophets," Num. 11:29). It definitely has priestly roles (Hos. 4:4-19) to play as well, but both prophetic and priestly roles are consistent with being led by Moses. They are two sides of a coin (so Exod. 19:6). Hosea's concern for Israel's identity is thus properly a prophetic task in two senses. First, it is a way to think of Israel as YHWH's elect household. Second, it is a way for Hosea to think of his own role in calling Israel to task.[94]

5. "They have broken my covenant and transgressed my instruction" (8:1). Covenant and instruction, what we might call in summary fashion the "covenantal ethos," is another of the linguistic and thematic connections between Deuteronomy and Hosea. They both use the term *bĕrît* ("covenant") to describe YHWH's acquisition of Israel and his binding of himself to them. In requiring a loyal response, YHWH also provided instruction for it. "Torah" is his gracious gift by which they might obediently respond to him. It is the case that Hosea, unlike Deuteronomy, never mentions Horeb (or Sinai) as the place of covenant making. His references to Moses and to the wilderness, however, serve a similar function. It was through Moses and in the wilderness that God became Israel's exclusive Lord. The covenantal ethos that YHWH graciously grants Israel is the heart and soul of Deuteronomy, a re-

---

(*ṣōpeh*) over Israel. On Hosea's understanding of prophets and prophecy, see further E. Zenger, "'Durch Menschen zog ich sie . . . (Hos 11,4)': Beobachtungen zum Verständnis des prophetischen Amtes im Hoseabuch," in *Künder des Wortes, Beiträge zur Theologie der Propheten: Josef Schreiner zum 60. Geburtstag,* ed. L. Ruppert et al. (Würzburg: Echter Verlag, 1982), pp. 183-202.

93. Note the parallelism between "prophets" and "words from YHWH's mouth" in 6:5. This is also the functional definition of one who follows Moses (Deut. 18:18). Hosea understands prophecy itself to be an Israelite social/religious institution, even as he offers severe criticism of Israel's institutional life from within it. See further Utzschneider, *Hosea.*

94. Ernst Sellin, "Hosea und das Martyrium des Mose," *ZAW* 46 (1928) 26-34, proposed that Hosea knew a tradition of Moses' death on behalf of Israel's guilt, based on his interpretation of 6:4-6; 12:14 (MT 15)–13:1. It is an unlikely interpretation in spite of the vigor with which Sellin defended it.

newal document set in the plains of Moab, where in his last will and testament Moses recalls and adapts instructional matter from Sinai for life in the promised land. In his own way, Hosea remembers and adapts, while calling Israel back to a confession that preceded their own day.

The connection with the concerns of Deuteronomy is so close that interpreters essentially have two choices by way of response. Either Hosea shares some central affirmations with Deuteronomy and the reform-minded circles behind it (even if Deuteronomy had not yet reached a stable or final written form), or a later Deuteronomy inherits some elements from Hosea and elaborates on them. One version of the latter option has an editor expanding some of Hosea's own traditions by adding the specifically "Deuteronomistic" material in 8:1b. The former option is more likely, as is the Hosean origin of 8:1.

The prologue to the great Sinai pericope (Exod. 19:1–Num. 10:10) also contains vocabulary and thematic material consistent with Hosea. YHWH is said to have borne Israel to the mountain in the wilderness "on eagle's wings" and to seek obedience from the people to "his covenant" (Exod. 19:4-5). The prologue is a conditional articulation: If the people adhere to the covenantal ethos, YHWH would make them collectively a "kingdom of priests and a holy nation" (19:6).[95] Hosea likely draws on these same themes. The eagle imagery is reversed (Hos. 8:1; see 6 below) in the historical moment of judgment, and the language of holiness (qādaš) is employed in the critique of people and priesthood (4:14).[96]

6. "An eagle is upon the house of YHWH" (8:1). The prophet constructs the image of the bird of prey swooping down on its target. It is a familiar image, culturally speaking, but it has a literary counterpart in the tradition of curses for violation of YHWH's covenant. The Pentateuch contains extensive lists of blessings and curses associated with the covenant YHWH instituted with Israel (Lev. 26:1-45; Deut. 27:11–28:68), and Hosea's announced judgments on Israel draw on similar traditions.[97] In the Deuteronomic formulation of the

95. John A. Davies, *A Royal Priesthood: Literary and Intertextual Perspectives on an Image of Israel in Exodus 19:6* (JSOTSup 395; London: T & T Clark International, 2004), particularly pp. 199-203, where the author discusses possible ways in which Hosea draws on Exod. 19:6. The substance of the prologue (Exod. 19:4-6) is likely another base text that has shaped the perspective of both Hosea and his editors.

96. Some scholars attribute the passage in Exod. 19:4-6 to the same hand(s) responsible for Deuteronomy. The literature on this matter is large. In addition to the various commentaries, see Jean Louis Ska, "Ex 19,3-8 et les parénèses deutéronomiques," in *Biblische Theologie und gesellschaftlicher Wandel: Für Norbert Lohfink*, ed. G. Braulik, W. A. Gross, and S. McEvenue (Freiburg: Herder, 1993), pp. 307-14.

97. Douglas K. Stuart, *Hosea–Jonah* (WBC 31; Waco: Word, 1987), pp. xxxi-

covenant ethos, there is a curse for disobedience, where YHWH will bring a nation from afar upon the people, like a swooping eagle upon its prey (Deut. 28:49). Such a formulation is a likely source of influence for the prophet. The maledictions in Deuteronomy are listed not only as warnings; they serve almost as predictions of what is inevitable (cf. 30:1), given Israel's sinful propensities. They serve also as public witnesses of self-incurred judgment, if/when Israel does not respond obediently. Thus some are to be proclaimed, spoken out loud, as reminders to Israel (Deut. 27:11-26).

Hosea's repeated charges that Israel has rejected or rebelled against YHWH are linked time and again to the negative consequences of those actions. In drawing the connection between disobedience and disaster, Hosea is both performing a prophetic function and representing the covenantal ethos in public. He is also drawing on deeply held convictions from the ancient world about act and consequence.[98] A formulation of that conviction is embedded in one of Hosea's base texts in the description of YHWH as one who "visits" *(pāqad 'al)*, that is, "brings upon" people, the transgressions they themselves have committed (Exod. 20:5; 34:6-7). It is a formulation that explicitly connects a perpetrator's negative act to negative consequences contained in it.

7. "Your calf is wretched, O Samaria!" (8:5).[99] Such heated language represents Hosea's fundamental critique of idolatry. Is he an innovator in such criticism or is this too part of his inheritance?[100] It is likely that Hosea criticizes his contemporaries for something that had been part of Yahwistic worship for some time, namely depicting YHWH in bovine form, but that does not make his criticism innovative. Various textual witnesses place a calf image in Is-

---

xliii, provides an extensive list of curses from the Pentateuch that he believes are related to Hosea's announcements of judgment upon Israel. He states, furthermore, that "although Hosea's style was in many ways original, his message was not at all innovative. Hosea's task was simply to warn that Yahweh intended to enforce the terms of his covenant" (p. 7). See also Delbert Hillers, *Treaty-Curses and the Old Testament Prophets* (BibOr 16; Rome: Pontifical Biblical Institute, 1964).

98. Patrick D. Miller, *Sin and Judgment in the Prophets: A Stylistic and Theological Analysis* (SBLMS 27; Chico, CA: Scholars Press, 1982).

99. For this translation of 8:5a, see the comments in the body of the commentary. One plausible alternative is the rendering of NRSV: "Your calf is rejected, O Samaria."

100. That Hosea is a "religious innovator" in the critique of the calf is proposed by Niels Peter Lemche, "The God of Hosea," in *Priests, Prophets and Scribes: Essays on the Formation of Second Temple Judaism in Honour of Joseph Blenkinsopp,* ed. Eugene C. Ulrich (JSOTSup 149; Sheffield: JSOT Press, 1992), pp. 241-57. It is better to think of Hosea as "conservative" in the classical sense of conserving and applying tradition from the past (which included criticism of the calf), and as a radical reformer in his application of his convictions.

rael's past (Exod. 32; Deut. 9:16-21; 1 Kgs. 12:26-28; Ps. 106:19-20) and relate the image to Yahwism. None, however, accepts the image as legitimate,
and we are at the mercy of our sources. The book of Exodus devotes a chapter to the making of the calf at Mt. Sinai and two chapters to the responses of
Moses and YHWH to the people's folly (Exod. 32–34). These three chapters
contain a critique of calf iconography and veneration, a presentation of Moses' intercession on the people's behalf, and a proclamation of YHWH as
gracious and compassionate yet jealous for his people. These themes, and
even some of the same vocabulary, are part of the book of Hosea. They proceed from the basic claims of the covenant ethos as defined in the Decalogue,
including an aniconic requirement (Exod. 20:3-6). Hosea's calf criticism
may also draw upon the cultic traditions of Bethel (and Dan?) that go back to
Jeroboam I. According to 1 Kgs. 12:26-33, the first king of the breakaway
kingdom installed a golden calf at Bethel and Dan. The writers see these actions as a sin (v. 30). In some complicated ways, the narratives of Exod. 32
and 1 Kgs. 12:28-29 are related, although it is very difficult to sort out the
lines of dependence. Jeroboam also constituted non-Levitical priests to serve
at various shrines in the land. In any case, it is likely that Hosea is simply one
of several, even if he was in the minority, to draw upon these traditions in his
role as a prophetic judge of Israel. We might think also of his prophetic role
as a religious reformer who desires removal of certain practices and a return
to those that have been ignored or repressed.[101]

8. "She does not know that I gave her the grain, new wine, and oil" (2:8 [MT
10]). This affirmation comes in the extended metaphorical portrayal of the
wounded husband, whose wife has sought these things from others. Thus not
only is YHWH Israel's Lord since Egypt, he is the Lord of his "land" (9:3)
where such commodities are produced. Unlike his contemporary Amos (5:8;
9:6), Hosea does not describe YHWH as a creator deity. Nevertheless, nothing could be farther from Hosea's truth than that YHWH is the God of covenant and history, as opposed to fertility and blessing. In the broad Canaanite
world, creation was the work of the high god El, the head of the typical
Canaanite pantheon. Fertility and its related blessings came from him and the
gods and goddesses, including several Baal deities, who constituted the various pantheons. Hosea's monolatry assumes not only the exclusivity of

---

101. Lemche, "God of Hosea," pp. 243-44, acknowledges that "religious reform-
ers" would be a plausible description of a prophet like Hosea, if it is historically correct
that a form of Yahwistic monotheism was present early in Israel's history. For the possibility that Hosea was a Levitical priest from the circles disenfranchised by Jeroboam I, see
Wolff, *Hosea,* pp. xxii-xxiii; idem, "Hoseas geistige Heimat," *TLZ* 81 (1956) 83-94; S. L.
Cook, "The Lineage Roots of Hosea's Yahwism," *Semeia* 87 (1999) 145-61.

YHWH in his covenantal claim on Israel, but also his supremacy regarding other deities and their presumed roles in history and nature. Indeed, Hosea likely conceived of YHWH as the name of the creator El, but this cannot be known for certain. Hosea explicitly rejects *ba'al* as a legitimate title for YHWH, while proclaiming that the tasks of fertility and sustenance are his (2:16-23 [MT 18-25]). In his household, which includes his land, YHWH is the Deity of blessing, fertility, and sustenance, fulfilling the roles assigned to other deities in the various pantheons. In Hosea's portrayal of future restoration, YHWH initiates covenantal blessings with the animals of the field, and from the heavens themselves, to produce grain, new wine, and oil in his land.

In Hosea's narrative logic, YHWH is the Lord of covenant and land, providing his corporate household with what it needs. Is this behind the description of YHWH as Israel's "maker" (8:14)? It seems that in polemical response to polytheism and perceived syncretism, Hosea does not reject the broad Canaanite worldview in toto. At one level, it would be virtually impossible for him to do so. As a land and as a people, Israel was Canaanite, even as it had unique elements in its history that differentiated it from its neighbors. Essential elements of that worldview are adapted in Hosea's thinking and enfolded within the covenantal ethos of a monolatrous Yahwism.[102]

9. "The Israelites and the Judeans shall gather as one. They shall appoint for themselves a single head" (1:11 [MT 2:2]). This is a prophecy of a transformed future that YHWH will bring in after judgment. The question with respect to Hosea's theological matrix is whether this depiction of a new community is drawn from it or comes from his later editors. Since the marriage metaphor is based on covenant broken and covenant renewed, it is certainly plausible that Hosea's new community is similarly patterned: tribal kingdom divided and tribal kingdom reunited. It is altogether likely that in Israel as well as Judah there were hopes for a future union of the larger tribal kingdom. Hosea's depiction assumes that the division between Israel and Judah, which had lasted nearly two hundred years by his day, was tragic and would be healed. What about the form of government? "Single head" is a general term for leadership. It could refer to the leadership of a judge *(šōpēṭ)* or more specifically a monarch *(melek),* both of which are part of Israel's institutional history.

One way to read Hosea's uncompromising judgment on Israel is that its political separation from Judah was viewed by him as tragic and flawed

102. W. S. Boshoff, "Yahweh as God of Nature: Elements of the Concept of God in the Book of Hosea," *JNSL* 18 (1992) 13-24. Note the comment of Andersen and Freedman, *Hosea,* p. 242, that with Hosea's description in 2:8, "we are close to the claim of Yahweh to be *the* fertility god."

from the beginning. If this is correct (and it may not be), then it is more likely that he inherited this judgment and that it contributes to the comprehensiveness of his institutional critique. The story line of 1–2 Kings, while acknowledging Judah's failures and YHWH's instigation in Israel's separation from Judah, represents essentially this assessment. The division of the tribal kingdom was tragic, even if Solomon and Rehoboam had exercised bad judgment on certain matters. The approach taken in 2 Chronicles is more uncompromising, for it rarely even mentions the northern kingdom, apart from the efforts of Judean kings like Hezekiah and Josiah to bring northern elements back into the fold. Of course, both Kings and Chronicles are Judean documents, and one wonders to what degree a northern prophet like Hosea would have shared this approach to monarchical history. One can say, however, that the book of Hosea is consistent with it, since the depiction of the "latter days" in 3:5 has the Israelites coming back to "David their king." A number of scholars have plausibly concluded that this reference to David is part of the Judean editing of Hosea's words, an update on the prophet's own prediction of a "single head" for the reunited kingdom.[103]

Hosea refers a number of times to violence and faithlessness in Israel, some of which may reach back to events at the beginning of the monarchy or even to the premonarchical period and not to events of the prophet's own day (e.g., 5:1; 6:8-9; 9:9, 15; 10:9, 14-15; 12:11 [MT 12]). If we could gain more clarity on some of these, then we might be clearer on the question of Hosea's assessment of Israel's monarchical history. We are on relatively safe ground with one proposal. Hosea's negative assessment of Israel, beginning with announced judgment on the Jehu dynasty, was thoroughgoing. We cannot get behind this to know for certain whether Hosea was antimonarchical in principle, preferring a more loosely organized tribal confederation; a monarchist who saw grave problems with the royal administration of his day; or more particularly a northern prophet who preferred the Davidic dynasty as the one head of the united tribal confederation over the corruption of his day. The book's portrayal follows this last option, with an expressed hope that Israel will return to YHWH and David their king in the latter days. Only in dramatic transformation and change would Israel be saved and bring to fulfillment the conclusion of the grand narrative Hosea represented and applied.[104]

10. Hosea's narrative theology is presented uniquely through his metaphors, wordplays, and historical typology, exceeding all other prophets in the rela-

---

103. See the excursus on "David Their King" at 3:5.

104. In postmodern terminology Hosea had a metanarrative; so Ben Zvi, *Hosea*, pp. 8-9. It defined not only the past and present in the three periods noted previously, but also the future in a transformation to come, with one or more periods included in it.

tive frequency of their employment. These means of presentation character-ize him as a poet and theological critic of his contemporaries, but they are more than literary devices and theological broadsides. They are the ways that the prophet appropriated his tradition, connecting it with Israel's crises of identity and his convictions about divine activity in the world.[105] In the next two sections I discuss two metaphors further: the root metaphor of Israel as YHWH's household, and the metaphor of covenant as marriage.

Not only does Hosea interpret Israel's history, past, present, and fu-ture; in doing so, he opens new windows on YHWH's ways in the world for hearers/readers. The book opens with the metaphor of Israel as the harlotrous land in defection from YHWH. It ends with a projection of YHWH as a luxu-riant tree nurturing a penitent Israel. Such imagery reveals history interpreted with poetic license and flair, but to those with discernment (14:9 [MT 10]), the connections drawn by Hosea reveal far more than that.

B. ISRAEL IS YHWH'S HOUSEHOLD

Many commentators have remarked on the centrality of the marriage meta-phor in Hosea and how it is used side by side with that for parent and child. In anthropological terms, what holds these two together is the "household," a social institution whose importance can be seen in the prevalence of kinship terminology in defining relationships in the ancient world.[106] Hebrew does not have an exact counterpart to the English term "family," but the common noun *bayit* ("house") is used similarly to refer to a "household" of related members. The noun represents a family, typically in its extended form of three or four generations, and its possessions. So, for example, the tenth com-mandment as formulated in Exod. 20:17 forbids the coveting of the neigh-bor's "house" *(bayit),* which is then elaborated upon by reference to the wife, servants, animals, or anything else that belongs to the neighbor. A related term is *bêt 'āb,* literally "house of the father," since the broader cultural world of which Israel was a part had various laws and customs that defined a house-hold by the adult male at its head.

105. Kakkanattu, *God's Enduring Love,* p. 110: "Hosea does not make any re-markable distinction between the past and the present. For him, the history of the Yahweh-Israel relationship is a continuum marked by Yahweh's constancy and perseverance in his election of Israel and Israel's disloyalty to him."

106. L. E. Stager, "The Archaeology of the Family in Ancient Israel," *BASOR* 260 (1985) 1-35. A basic taxonomy is the extended family *(bêt 'āb),* followed by the clan *(mišpāḥâ),* followed by the tribe *(šēbeṭ).* In the premonarchical period Israel was a tribal-based association or confederation. With the advent of monarchy, Israel became a tribal-based kingdom.

With respect to the interpretation of Hosea, the institution of marriage has received far more attention than that of the household, perhaps because of the striking presentation of the prophet's marriage to Gomer in Hos. 1–3.[107] In terms of social structure, however, the household is the primary institution, with marriage as a constituent part, just as children are given identity as members of the household, whether by birth or by adoption. This primary institution appears to be the vehicle (source domain) of a root metaphor employed by Hosea to portray Israel and Judah as YHWH's household. It is a lens through which Hosea interprets the grand narrative of YHWH's acquisition of Israel in Egypt and preservation of them in the wilderness. Through it one sees that even in Hos. 1–3, where the marriage of Gomer and Hosea is presented in detail as a prophetic sign-act, the children and the land also have their roles to play in representing Israel because they too are part of the household.[108] Moreover, the conceptual influence of the household extends beyond Hos. 1–3, as can be seen in various aspects of Hosea's terminology (see below).

In the ancient Semitic world, kinship, whether real or contrived, was a primary symbolic key to the profile of nation-states and tribal confederations.[109] With respect to Israel and Judah, both took their names from an ancestor. Both entities, furthermore, could and did take the prefix "house of" with the name of their ancestor as a political designation. Similarly, a king's family (his "house" or dynasty) could give its name to the people or territory governed, incorporating them symbolically into his larger patrimonial domain. Thus the administrative identity of Judah is encapsulated in the term "house of David" (Isa. 7:2, 13; 22:22) or that of Israel in "house of Omri" or "house of Jehu," depending on the ruling dynasty.[110]

---

107. It has been proposed that the marriage metaphor is the "theory-constitutive metaphor" (the term is P. Ricoeur's) that informs the book of Hosea as a whole. See the discussion in Morris, *Prophecy, Poetry and Hosea*, p. 135.

108. Laurie J. Braaten, "Hosea's Land Theme in the Book of the Twelve," in *Thematic Threads*, ed. Redditt and Schart, pp. 104-32, recognizes that the family rather than the marriage metaphor is the root metaphor for Hosea. He notes also the metaphorical roles and importance of the land in the book. I prefer the term "household," however, precisely because the property of the family is integral to it and because it adheres more closely to the Hebrew terminology. See also Nwaoru, *Imagery*, pp. 96-109, who treats the metaphors of YHWH as husband and father under the rubric of "family."

109. See Frank M. Cross, "Kinship and Covenant in Ancient Israel," in *From Epic to Canon: History and Literature in Ancient Israel* (Baltimore: Johns Hopkins University Press, 1998), pp. 3-21; J. David Schloen, *The House of the Father as Fact and Symbol: Patrimonialism in Ugarit and the Ancient Near East* (Leiden: Brill, 2001).

110. A 9th-century Aramaic inscription from Tell Dan refers to the "house of David" (so Alan Millard, *COS* 2:162). The 9th-century inscription of Mesha, king of Moab, mentions triumphing over Omri and his "house" (lines 6-7) and possibly also the "house

There is ample evidence that the household metaphor reflects Hosea's own orientation and is not for him residual vocabulary from a bygone period of his grand narrative.[111] The primary evidence begins with the marked portrayal of the prophet's own household in chs. 1–3 as a symbol of the relationship between YHWH and Israel. Gomer, the individual children, and even the land (1:2) all represent Israel in its relationship with YHWH. Israel itself can be designated elsewhere as YHWH's "son" (11:1; cf. Exod. 4:22). Five times the state is referred to as the "house of Israel" (Hos. 1:4, 6; 5:1; 6:10; 11:12 [MT 12:1]). Similarly, its southern sibling is the "house of Judah" (1:7; 5:12, 14). There are also references to the "house of Jehu" (1:4) and an anonymous "house of the king" (5:1). The significance of kinship is evident, whether as part of the extended household metaphor in Hos. 1–3, or in scattered references elsewhere. For example, in the projection of a future restoration, there is reference to the gathering of the "sons of Judah" and the "sons of Israel" (1:11 [MT 2:2]) and "children" coming trembling to YHWH (11:10). They can speak to one another as "brothers" and "sisters" (2:1 [MT 3]) and are collectively called "children of the living God" (1:10 [MT 2:1]). The Lord's house is a multitribal kinship network (šēbeṭ, lit. "tribe," 5:9), and the youth of a tribe are its "children" (9:16).

YHWH is represented as speaking directly of "my house" in 9:15, and Israel is designated as "YHWH's land" in 9:3. Since in the OT the term "house of YHWH" most frequently refers to the temple in Jerusalem, it may seem initially that a temple in Israel (Samaria, Bethel) is the intended referent in 9:15. Hosea, however, is not likely to refer to a threat on Jerusalem's temple as an explanation of the failures of the northern kingdom.[112] And there are good reasons in chs. 8–9 to see "house" and "land" as essential equivalents, both indicating Israel as YHWH's household. For example, the eagle over "YHWH's house" in 8:1 is more likely a reference to Israel as YHWH's patrimony under corporate threat rather than an oblique reference to an otherwise unnamed Yahwistic temple. In 9:4 the reference to the "house of YHWH" occurs in a context of cultic practices during a time of punishment and expulsion from the land. For reasons given in the commentary section, it is best also to see "house" in 9:4 as a synonym for his "land" in 9:3. The "house of 'his' [= a

---

of David" (line 31, tentative reconstruction). Neo-Assyrian texts contain references to Israel as the "house" or "land" of Omri (e.g., *ANET,* pp. 284, 285).

111. How widespread the application of the patrimonial or household model to Israel's structure and self-understanding is debatable. It appears fundamental to Hosea, however. For further discussion with regard to Iron Age Israel and other evidence, see Daniel Master, "State Formation Theory and the Kingdom of Israel," *JNES* 60 (2001) 117-31.

112. Those scholars who think that "YHWH's house" in 8:1 (or in 9:4, 15) refers to the Jerusalem temple typically regard the reference as a Judean gloss.

prophet's] god" in 9:8 is likely a reference to a temple. An unknown prophet is addressed by Hosea, and the temple cannot be further identified. In 9:15 YHWH declares "hatred" for evildoers, whom he will "drive" out of his house and no longer "love." His terminology is replete with allusions to divorcing a wife for cause and expelling her from "his house" (cf. Deut. 24:1-4). It is much more likely, therefore, that YHWH's house in Hos. 9:15 refers to his household than to an otherwise unidentified temple. This is in keeping with the marriage and divorce typology of Hos. 1–3.

The problem for any ambiguous reference in Hosea to a "temple" of YHWH is the prophet's thorough and polemical rejection of a flawed Israelite worship, wherever it is offered in the realm and to whomever it is offered, even YHWH. On the one hand, there can be no doubt of Yahwistic shrines in Israel during Hosea's day[113] (cf. Amos 5:21-25; 7:13; 9:1); on the other hand, one is hard-pressed to identify a temple *(bayit, hêkāl)* in Israel on the basis of Hosea's book alone.[114] The polemical references to Bethel (e.g., 10:5, 15), which likely do presuppose a temple, depend on other texts for confirmation (1 Kgs. 12:26-33; Amos 7:13). Hosea's terminology for cultic worship elsewhere points to hilltop shrines with trees (4:13), to "high places *(bāmôt)* of iniquity" (10:8), and above all to altars for sacrifice (8:11; 10:1-2, 8; 12:11 [MT 12]). All of Israel's current cultic practices are polemically judged as worthless and defiling.

The equation of YHWH's "land" and "house" in Hosea has resonance in various places in the OT. He is not the only prophet to equate the two. It is clear, for example, in Jeremiah, heir to several of Hosea's theological convictions.[115] In Jer. 2:7 and 16:18 occur the synonymous pair YHWH's "land" and "inheritance" *(naḥălâ).* In 12:7-10 several items are linked that collectively present Judah as YHWH's household/patrimony: "house" *(bayit),* "inheritance" *(naḥălâ;* 3 times), "beloved" *(yĕdidût),*[116] "vineyard" *(kerem),* and "pleasant portion" *(ḥelqat ḥemdâ).*

---

113. One thinks in this context of Elijah's complaint that the "altars" for YHWH had been torn down in his day (1 Kgs. 19:10). This presupposes more than one Yahwistic shrine, whatever it reflects about temples.

114. In Hosea the one occurrence of *hêkāl,* which can mean "palace" or "temple," is in a context that refers to public buildings (8:14), but not specifically to a temple.

115. See the discussion in the commentary section on 9:4. For further examples and helpful discussion, see also Utzschneider, *Hosea,* pp. 182-85. Utzschneider regards the concept of Israel as "YHWH's land" to be primary for Hosea and regards the references to YHWH or God's house in 8:1; 9:4, 15, as representatives of it. For reasons cited above, I would reverse this conceptual link and make household primary. It is the case that the land personified can represent Israel (1:2), even as it remains YHWH's patrimony (9:3).

116. The term is likely one of familial endearment.

In his treatment of Hos. 8:1, H. W. Wolff has suggested that the term "'house of Yahweh' might be a prophetic parallel to the political expression 'house of Omri.'"[117] This is a helpful proposal and deserves expansion. In Hosea's day it might well have been a prophetic and polemical alternative to current internal political designations such as "house of Jehu" or even "house of the kingdom of Israel" (1:4). Hosea drew political consequences from his prophetic interpretation of a national story line in which YHWH had rescued Israel from Egypt, "married" the people in the wilderness, and brought them home. Once established there, YHWH's household can have only one head, just as the land belonging to the household has one Lord.[118] What Wolff calls a "prophetic parallel" might be rooted more particularly in what Hosea received about the work of Moses as prophetic agent in leading Israel. Alone of the 8th-century prophets, Hosea records that YHWH brought Israel out from Egypt by a prophet and that Israel was preserved by a prophet (12:13 [MT 14]). This could mean that Hosea allows only a subsidiary role for human kingship under the aegis of YHWH, indeed, something similar to the polity set out in Deuteronomy, which has a single section on the duties of a king, and they include being instructed by the contents of YHWH's torah (Deut. 17:14-20).

As a root metaphor, the patrimonial household is more important than a way to explain certain literary expressions of Hosea. It is a conceptual symbol, a way of thinking, not just a way of oral or literary expression, though these are certainly included. It is versatile in the sense that it allowed him to integrate a number of elements from his narrative traditions about Israel's past into his perception of Israel's historical crisis. The metaphor functions like a map to explain origins, journey, and destination. Through it the prophet drew connections from his theological matrix of exodus-wilderness-fruitful land and shaped his critique of religious practice, social structure, and political relations. The exclusive service, the covenantal ethos that YHWH demands from "his" people, is like that of the household ethos, in which the wife and children are expected to honor and to obey the patrimonial head. The family property is an integral part of the household, representing familial identity and inheritance, while giving of its fruitfulness to support them. Thus Israel's breaking of the covenant is a threat to the life of the Lord's house (8:1) and a pollution of his land (9:3-4). Its faithlessness is harlotry and adultery, whether represented by the land (1:2), Gomer (2:2 [MT 4]), or the children (2:4 [MT 6]). The treachery of Israel and Ephraim against YHWH is like the bearing of illegitimate children (5:7) or the acts of an in-

117. Wolff, *Hosea,* p. 137. Andersen and Freedman, *Hosea,* p. 203, note also in passing the identity of the land as the "house of Yahweh."

118. See above, IV.A, "Hosea's Theology: Narrative and Community Identity."

corrigible son (11:1-2).[119] Correspondingly, in the period of restoration, Israel will be called "children of the living God" (1:10 [MT 2:1]; 2:23 [MT 25]). YHWH will betroth himself to "Gomer," overcoming her harlotries (2:19-20 [MT 21-22]), and speak to the land, so that it will be fruitful once again (2:21-22 [MT 23-24]). It is a household restored.

Hosea offers withering critiques of Israel's entangling alliances with other deities and with other states. The household metaphor helps us understand why. Such exclusivism fits the profile expected of a household in both cultic activities and political relationships. Family members owe allegiance to the head of the household.

The following lists show the political designations of Israel and Judah in the book of Hosea and related household terminology.

Political Designations

    I. Israel: 25 times
       House of Israel *(bêt yiśrā'ēl):* 1:6; 5:1; 6:10; 11:12 (MT 12:1)
       Rule of *(mamlĕkût)* the house of Israel: 1:4
       Descendants of Israel *(bĕnê-yiśrā'ēl):* 1:10, 11 (MT 2:1-2); 3:1, 4,
         5; 4:1
       Tribes of Israel *(šibṭê yiśrā'ēl):* 5:9
   II. Ephraim: 34 times
  III. Jacob: 10:11; 12:2 (MT 3)
  IV. My (= YHWH) people *('ammî):* 1:9-10; 2:1 (MT 3); 2:23 (MT 25;
      2 times); 4:6, 8, 9, 12; 6:11; 11:7
   V. Samaria: 7:1; 8:5, 6; 10:7; 13:16 (MT 14:1)
       Inhabitants of Samaria *(šĕkan šōmĕrôn):* 10:5
  VI. Judah: 1:1; 4:15; 5:5, 13; 6:4, 11; 8:14; 10:11; 11:12 (MT 12:1);
      12:2 (MT 3)
       House of Judah *(bêt yĕhûdâ):* 1:7; 5:12, 14
       Descendants of Judah *(bĕnê-yĕhûdâ):* 1:11 (MT 2:2)

119. Hosea's understanding of the covenant or bond between Israel and YHWH is not that of an indigenous relationship, based on a form of henotheism in which people and land were naturally YHWH's possession. See the discussion of marriage and covenant that follows. Land and people are his through historical acts. Hosea knows and employs the claims that YHWH had redeemed his people from Egypt, led them in the wilderness, and gifted them with "his" land (13:4-5). The covenant ethos is founded on that redemption and it presupposes fidelity in worship and service (cf. 13:4 with Exod. 20:2-3; Deut. 5:6-7). Historical acquisition, covenant ethos, and future redemption can be incorporated into the household metaphor.

VII. House of Jehu: 1:4
    House of the king: 5:1
VIII. House of YHWH: 8:1; 9:4
    My (= YHWH) house: 9:15
  IX. Land of YHWH: 9:3

Household Terminology for the People in Hosea

    I. Children of harlotry: 1:2-9; 2:4 (MT 6)
      Wife of harlotry: Hos. 1–3
   II. Descendants of Israel: 1:10, 11 (MT 2:1-2); 3:1, 4, 5; 4:1
      Descendants of Judah: 1:11 (MT 2:2)
  III. Children of the living God: 1:10 (MT 2:1)
  IV. Brothers and sisters: 2:1 (MT 3)
   V. YHWH's son: 11:1
      YHWH's children: 11:10
  VI. Ephraim is an unwise son: 13:13

Household terminology for YHWH

    I. Husband: 2:16 (MT 18): That YHWH is metaphorically the hus-
      band of Israel is implied in the family typology of Hos. 1–3
   II. Father/parent: 1:10; 11:1, 3-4, 10
  III. Groom: 2:19-20 (MT 21-22): YHWH is also the head of the fam-
      ily, as he is providing the "bride-price"
  IV. Shepherd: 4:16: A task shared by members of a household
   V. Animal husbandry: 10:11; 11:4

C. COVENANT AND MARRIAGE

1. Basic Terminology in Hosea and the OT

The institutions of covenant and marriage are variously related in the OT. Hosea's metaphorical "joining" of the two institutions in symbolic act and poetic presentation is one of the most widely recognized aspects of the book bearing his name. Marriage is the metaphorical vehicle (source domain) that renders God's covenant with Israel, the tenor (target domain).

In theological terms the word "covenant" *(bĕrît)* refers to God's relationship with another entity that is initiated by God and established by his solemn word (promise or oath).[120] A covenant instituted by God is not a parity relationship. In making a covenant with an entity God may or may not require a response. In the OT God establishes a covenant with Noah and all living beings, with Abraham and his descendants, with Israel through Moses, with Levi and the Levites, with David and his descendants; and through the prophets God promises a new and everlasting covenant in the future for his people.[121] The social and religious understandings of marriage in the OT included, at least for some (such as Hosea and other prophets), the view that marriage was a covenant between husband and wife,[122] and a suitable way to conceive of the covenant YHWH established with Israel, the people of his household.

In Hosea the term "covenant" *(bĕrît)* is used five times. Two of those refer to the covenant YHWH extended to Israel to be his people after his rescue of them from Egypt (6:7; 8:1; cf. 11:1 and 13:4-5). Another refers to a future in which YHWH makes a covenant with aspects of the created order for the purpose of bringing to fruition a cosmic community of security and blessing (2:18 [MT 20]). Hosea's conception of a national covenant with Israel is likely influenced by the claim that the people collectively are called to be YHWH's "royal priesthood and a holy nation" (Exod. 19:4-6) in the land YHWH granted them and by the first two commandments of the Decalogue.[123] His primary criticism of his contemporaries is based on their

120. On covenant see R. Smend, *Die Bundesformel* (Zurich: EVZ, 1963); Lothar Perlitt, *Bundestheologie im Alten Testament* (Neukirchen-Vluyn: Neukirchener Verlag, 1969); D. J. McCarthy, *Old Testament Covenant: A Survey of Current Opinions* (London: Blackwell, 1972); Ernst Kutsch, *Verheissung und Gesetz: Untersuchungen zum sogennanten "Bund" im Alten Testament* (BZAW 131; Berlin: de Gruyter, 1973); E. W. Nicholson, *God and His People: Covenant and Theology in the Old Testament* (New York: Oxford University Press, 1986); J. H. Walton, *Covenant: God's Purpose and God's Plan* (Grand Rapids: Zondervan, 1994); Rolf Rendtorff, *The Covenant Formulary: An Exegetical and Theological Investigation,* trans. Margaret Kohl (Edinburgh: T & T Clark, 1998); Steven L. McKenzie, *Covenant* (St. Louis: Chalice, 2000); R. B. Salters and A. D. H. Mayes, eds., *Covenant as Context: Essays in Honour of E. W. Nicholson* (New York: Oxford University Press, 2003); Paul R. Williamson, *Sealed with an Oath: Covenant in God's Unfolding Purpose* (Downers Grove, IL: InterVarsity Press, 2007).

121. Gen. 9:8-17; 15:1-21; 17:1-22; Exod. 6:4-5; 19:4-6; 24:3-8; Jer. 31:31-34; 33:21; Ezek. 16:60-62; 37:26; Mal. 2:4-5.

122. Ezek. 16:8, 59-62; Jer. 2:2-3; Mal. 2:14. See G. P. Hugenberger, *Marriage as a Covenant: A Study of Biblical Law and Ethics Governing Marriage Developed from the Perspective of Malachi* (VTSup 52; Leiden: Brill, 1994); Elaine J. Adler, "The Background for the Metaphor of Covenant as Marriage in the Hebrew Bible" (Ph.D. diss.; University of California at Berkeley, 1990).

123. See John A. Davies, *A Royal Priesthood: Literary and Intertextual Perspec-*

failure to be faithful to their covenantal calling. This conviction about Israel's identity is joined in the book with the marital metaphor, so that Israel's failures are compared to prostitution and adultery. Hosea 12:1 (MT 2) refers to making a covenant with Assyria and carrying oil to Egypt, which puts the term in the sphere of international relations, indicating more specifically treaty relations or diplomatic agreements. A political context seems probable also for the more obscure reference in 10:4. Thus Hosea employs the term *běrît* in two senses: one relates to political agreements between peoples, and the other represents YHWH's initiation of a relationship with Israel or another aspect of creation.

Some scholars think that the covenantal references in 6:7 and 8:1 are not derived from Hosea or the 8th century B.C., but are the work of later redactors, who were influenced by the innovative covenantal theology of Deuteronomy, a book in their view to be dated no earlier than the reign of Josiah (d. 609 B.C.) and essentially reaching its final form no earlier than the Babylonian exile.[124] This conclusion is sometimes also extended to 2:18 (MT 20) and its reference to a covenant, on the assumption that a prophet of judgment like Hosea would not himself have prophesied a future transformation. That would have fallen to his editors, so that what remains are the political references in 10:4 and 12:1 (MT 2). In response, one should say that quite apart from the term *běrît* in 6:7 and 8:1b, the assumptions of a national relationship with YHWH are deeply embedded in the claims of the book, as are the expectations that YHWH would eventually heal Israel's defection. It would take quite radical surgery to remove all of them completely from the time of the prophet to the book's compilers.[125]

---

tives on an Image of Israel in Exodus 19:6 (JSOTSup 395; London: T &T Clark International, 2004).

124. A vigorous statement of this position is that of Perlitt, *Bundestheologie im Alten Testament.* For his treatment of the texts in Hosea, see pp. 139-52. Regarding 8:1, see his summary comments on p. 150: "Hosea knows nothing of a (perhaps two-sided obligating) treaty of YHWH with Israel . . . therefore in Hosea YHWH is neither the God of Sinai nor is the administration of justice grounded in the Sinai covenant." In this he follows essentially the view of J. Wellhausen, *Prolegomena to the History of Israel,* trans. J. S. Black and A. Menzies (Edinburgh: A. & C. Black, 1885), who believed that the preaching of the great prophets like Hosea, Amos, and First Isaiah broke the national assumption of a natural bond between YHWH and people, which was subsequently replaced by a more contractual understanding in Deuteronomy and the Priestly sources. Nicholson, *God and His People,* pp. 186-88, also agrees essentially with the innovative accomplishments of the preexilic prophets, but thinks that *běrît* in Hos. 6:7 and 8:1 is original to the prophet and that it is possible that Hosea himself "first coined such a notion" of a *běrît* between YHWH and Israel. In any case, he thinks that the notion originated in the 8th century B.C.

125. Such surgery is attempted in the recent dissertation of Susanne Rudnig-Zelt,

With respect to the term *bĕrît,* the question is not whether Hosea knew the term, but whether he ever used it for the bond that YHWH instituted with Israel. Is the concept of YHWH's covenant in Deuteronomy so innovative, so specifically defined and context-bound, that one must differentiate it from that presupposed in the marital and sonship metaphors that are clearly integral to Hosea? As one expression among several for the YHWH-Israel relationship in Hosea, the term *bĕrît* in 6:7 and 8:1 may well entail specific nuances such as an analogy with treaties and related political relationships (cf. 12:1 [MT 2]) or association with oaths and self-maledictions (cf. 10:4).[126] In the final analysis the term fits contextually and theologically in 6:7 and 8:1 as a complement to the household metaphors of marriage and children. The household metaphor, which Hosea so assiduously developed, and the term *bĕrît* go hand-in-hand in the book. If one were to ask Hosea about the origins of the covenant relationship YHWH instituted with Israel, the book at least points to an answer: it was brought into being at the time when YHWH redeemed Israel from slavery and guided them by a prophet (12:13 [MT 14] = Moses; 13:4-5) to the land of promise. Most likely these convictions were part of the authoritative tradition that Hosea inherited, even if he developed them in unique ways.

When one steps away from the books of Hosea and Deuteronomy, it is important to note that the two social institutions of covenant and marriage have similar formulas and shared vocabulary (see below).[127] This similarity of shared vocabulary extends also to the political institution of international relations among states (i.e., treaties) and to texts for adopting family members.[128]

Hoseastudien: Redaktionskritische Untersuchungen zur Genese des Hoseabuches (FRLANT 213; Göttingen: Vandenhoeck & Ruprecht, 2006). According to her improbable thesis, the vast majority of the book of Hosea is the work of later redactors, not that of the 8th-century prophet.

126. See James Barr, "Some Semantic Notes on the Covenant," in *Beiträge zur alttestamentlichen Theologie: Festschrift für Walther Zimmerli zum 70. Geburtstag,* ed. Herbert Donner et al. (Göttingen: Vandenhoeck & Ruprecht, 1977), p. 37: "The possibility that the theological use of the covenant is Deuteronomic, and that the silence of the earlier prophets was simply because they knew nothing of such a covenant, is something that has to be faced realistically. Yet with all the will in the world it is a little hard to believe that the covenant of Yahweh with Israel became significant only so late." In his study Barr points out that the term *bĕrît* is opaque, with essentially no synonyms, but capable of association with a range of theological convictions. See also the commentary on Hos. 10:4.

127. S. T. Sohn, *The Divine Election of Israel* (Grand Rapids: Eerdmans, 1991), pp. 10-44; Hugenberger, *Marriage as Covenant,* pp. 216-79.

128. The literature on the relationship between suzerainty treaties and Israelite conceptions of a national covenant instituted by YHWH is enormous. For bibliography and discussion, see Kitchen, *Reliability of the Old Testament,* pp. 283-306. On the metaphor of adoption and its formulas see Janet L. R. Melnyk, "When Israel Was a Child: An-

Marriage and adoption contracts in particular use terse reciprocal formulations that function as "performative language," to use a term from modern linguistics. As a common element in all of these spheres, kinship appears to be the matrix from which influential portions of their terminology were drawn.[129]

Interpreters should be cautious, however, in trying to define too explicitly how covenant and marriage are linked, even granting their roots in kinship practices, or more particularly which formula for relationship preceded the other. For example, was the common terminology first attached to marriage and adoption and then subsequently adapted for use in the religious sphere of the covenant God made with Israel? Intuitively one would answer yes, since marriage and adoption were societal institutions that existed long before YHWH's acquisition of Israel.

Nevertheless, it is interesting to ask a similar question from a different angle: Was the theological language for covenant, which is related to the political spheres of international treaties, loyalty oaths, and royal grants, adapted for the institution of marriage by prophets like Hosea? This also makes sense. As noted above, there is no evidence that the institution of marriage in Israel was widely understood theologically as a covenant before certain prophets joined the two. Instead of trying to unravel the mysteries of first influences or to reconstruct a linear development, it is better simply to acknowledge a conceptual analogy between covenant and marriage made theologically fruitful in the OT. In the case of Hosea, his particular formulations of covenant, adoption, and marriage seem rooted in his conception of Israel as YHWH's household, a primary social institution and the bedrock of kinship. This is the root metaphor, the conceptual symbol, that he employs to interpret the theological traditions he inherited and applied to the life of Israel.

It is possible that Hosea was the "first to employ the metaphor of husband for the deity, casting Israel in negative female imagery as God's adulterous wife."[130] The claim is certainly more plausible than the one that denies

---

cient Near Eastern Adoption Formulas and the Relationship between God and Israel," in *History and Interpretation: Essays in Honour of John H. Hayes,* ed. M. Patrick Graham et al. (JSOTSup 173; Sheffield: JSOT Press, 1993), pp. 245-59. The marriage metaphor is not employed in the international treaty tradition, but the language of father and son is. See F. C. Fensham, "Father and Son Terminology for Treaty and Covenant," in *Near Eastern Studies in Honor of W. F. Albright,* ed. H. Goedicke (Baltimore: Johns Hopkins University Press, 1971), pp. 121-35.

129. Cross, "Kinship and Covenant," in *From Epic to Canon,* pp. 3-21, proposes that the terminology and thought forms associated with covenant theology in the OT emerge from the matrix of kinship.

130. The quotation is from G. Yee, "Hosea," in *Women's Bible Commentary,* ed. C. Newsom and S. Ringe (Louisville: Westminster John Knox, 1998), p. 207. M. Weinfeld, *Deuteronomy and the Deuteronomic School* (1972; repr. Winona Lake, IN: Eisen-

Hosea the employment of *bĕrît* as a theological term to define Israel's call-ing. Of the prophetic texts that make explicit the analogy of marriage with covenant, Hosea is indeed the earliest.[131] Possibly, however, there are ante-cedents to his use of the marital metaphor in the language of God's jealousy *(qānā')* with respect to Israel's forbidden veneration of other deities in the Si-nai covenant. Such language in the Decalogue (e.g., Exod. 20:5) and else-where in the Sinai pericope (Exod. 34:14) could be rooted in the understand-ing that the covenant God established with Israel is like the exclusive intimacy established in marriage.[132] The question is related, at least in part, to the place of Hosea in the YHWH-alone movement in Israel, which urged the exclusive worship of YHWH upon the people.[133] Possibly Hosea was the first "writing" prophet in Israel to champion the monolatrous service of YHWH; but if true, this would not necessarily make him a theological innovator, only the first in a surviving, literary chain of evidence.

Whatever the historical development of these institutions in Israel, it is surprising that, according to present knowledge, neither marriage nor cov-enant was used elsewhere in the ancient Near East to define an exclusive rela-tionship between deity and people. The marital metaphor for covenant is thus unique to the OT, whether or not Hosea is the first to employ it, as is the re-lated emphasis on God's jealousy or zealousness for his people.[134] It is not likely, therefore, that Hosea drew his marriage metaphor from the various Canaanite fertility cults. From them the prophet received sexual imagery of the divine world relating to sky and land and perhaps sexually related cultic acts employed as sympathetic magic, but not the metaphorical marriage of deity and people. It is almost certainly an inner-Israelite development

---

brauns, 1992), pp. 81-82, says that the marital metaphor is at best latent in the covenant traditions of the Pentateuch, so that "we must conclude that the prophets were responsible for the development of the idea of marital love between God and Israel."

131. See R. Abma, *Bonds of Love: Methodic Studies of Prophetic Texts with Mar-riage Imagery (Isaiah 50:1-3 and 54:1-10, Hosea 1-3, Jeremiah 2-3)* (SSN 40; Assen: Van Gorcum, 1999).

132. Cf. Num. 5:14, 30, with reference to the jealousy of a husband for his wife. In Num. 25:1-13 is the account of Israel "playing the harlot" with the daughters of Moab. The reaction of YHWH is one of extreme jealousy (25:10-12). The root *qn'* does not occur in Hosea, however.

133. See the discussion in Bernhard Lang, *Monotheism and the Prophetic Minor-ity* (SWBA 1; Sheffield: Almond, 1983), pp. 13-56. Cf. p. 30: "The book of Hosea must be regarded as the oldest classical document of the movement [that Israel should worship YHWH alone]."

134. On God's jealousy see Num. 25:10-12; Deut. 6:15; 32:16; Ps. 78:58; Joel 2:18; Zech. 1:14; 8:2. Bernhard Oestreich, *Metaphors and Similes for Yahweh in Hosea 14:2-9(1-8): A Study of Hoseanic Pictorial Language* (Frankfurt: Peter Lang, 1998), pp. 118-21, proposes that the motif of divine jealousy is behind the marital metaphor in Hosea.

through which the prophet both engages and critiques the broader Canaanite world of which he and Israel were constituent parts.

2. Covenant and Marriage Formulas and Their Institutional Settings

What is commonly known as the covenant formula in the OT comes in several variations. Three examples are:

> Jer. 7:23: "I will be your God and you shall be my people."[135]
> Exod. 6:7: "I will take you for my people and I will be your God."
> Ezek. 14:11: "They will be my people and I will be their God."

In each instance the reciprocal element is clear: YHWH is Israel's God and Israel is YHWH's people. The verb "to be" *(hāyâ)* is used twice in Jer. 7:23. In Exod. 6:7 *hāyâ* is the second verb, but in the first clause God "takes" *(lāqaḥ)* Israel, a term commonly used in marriage. In both texts God speaks in the first person and Israel is addressed in second person plural. In Ezek. 14:11 the verb *hāyâ* is used twice; the first is Qal perfect (with *waw* conversive) third person plural, and the second is Qal imperfect first person singular. One can see the similarities with Hos. 1:2-3, where Hosea is commanded to go and take *(lāqaḥ)* for himself a woman (see Gen. 4:19; Exod. 6:20), and the descriptive rehearsal in Ezek. 16:8 that YHWH married Jerusalem: "I entered into a covenant *(bĕrît)* with you . . . and you became mine *(wattihĕyî lî)*" (see also Ruth 4:13).

In Jewish Aramaic texts from Elephantine are four apparently identical declarations of marriage.[136] The declaration is:

> She is my wife and I am her husband from this day and henceforth.

In a mythological Akkadian text Ereshkigal says to Nergal:

> You are my husband, I will be your wife. . . .
> You be master, I will be mistress.[137]

---

135. Note the close similarity with a formula for or declaration of adoption in 2 Sam. 7:14: "I will be a father for him [= his father] and he will be a son for me [= my son]," which has numerous parallels in ancient Near Eastern adoption contracts. This particular declaration comes in the context of God's promise to build a *house* for David (7:11). Elsewhere, God's binding promise to David and his house is called a "covenant" (2 Sam. 23:5).

136. The marital documents are B2.6, B3.3, B3.8, and B6.1 in Bezalel Porten and Ada Yardeni, *Textbook of Aramaic Documents from Ancient Egypt,* vol. 2: *Contracts* (Jerusalem: Hebrew University, 1989).

137. My translation. Cf. *ANET,* p. 104.

The reciprocal binding through declarative style is clear, even though there are differences of genre, language, and grammar. In the Aramaic declarations the verb "to be" is not written but understood, as is common in declaratory statements. The declaration is made by the husband and the possessive pronouns are suffixes on the nouns "wife" and "husband" rather than affixed to the preposition *lĕ,* as in the covenant formulas cited above. The Akkadian text is a plea from a goddess to a god, and the language of "husband" and "wife" is parallel to the terms for "master" *(bēl)* and "mistress" *(bēltu).* (The corresponding terms in Hebrew for the latter two would be *ba'al* and *ba'ălâ.)* Declarations include first-, second-, and third-person speech.

One may compare briefly in this context the language for adoption. In Hammurabi's Law Code (§170) the performative element is the spoken word: "(You are) my children." A contract from the time of King Nebuchadnezzar states: "Give me your seventeen-day-old-son . . . and he will be my son."[138]

Divorce formulas in Near Eastern literature are similarly terse in what they declare about marital status. In essence they represent the legal dissolving of the status "X is husband and Y is wife." A marriage document in Old Babylonian preserves the double declaration: "You are not my wife. . . . You are not my husband."[139]

The Aramaic marital documents from Elephantine contain statements of actions that could lead to divorce. For example, in the marriage of Ananiah and Jehoishma it is recorded: "If Ananiah stands in an assembly and says, 'I hate my wife Jehoishma, she shall not be my wife.' If Jehoishma hates her husband Ananiah and says to him, 'I hate you, I will not be your wife,' then. . . ."[140]

There are parallels to the declarative prophecies in Hos. 1:9b, where the naming of the third child is because "you all are not my people," and in 2:2 (MT 4), where the children are commanded by their father to tell their mother: "She is not my wife and I am not her husband." We probably should not think of 1:9b or 2:2 (MT 4) as an official divorce declaration, but they do function to reverse a marriage declaration (de facto). The difference is slight, yet significant, since it is not clear that Hosea and Gomer were officially divorced. Perhaps we should think of these declarations in 1:9 and 2:2 (MT 4) as employing

138. See, respectively, *ANET,* pp. 173, 547; see discussion in Melnyk, "When Israel Was a Child," p. 251, who in n. 20 cites also an Aramaic contract from Egypt in which a child named Yeheniah is adopted with the declaration: "He will be my son."

139. CT 48:50. From a later period one can find the same statements in the third person: "She is not my wife," "He is not my husband." For these and further references see Hugenburger, *Marriage as Covenant,* p. 219.

140. Porten and Yardeni, *Contracts,* B3.8.21-22, 24-25.

the recognized rhetoric of the day,[141] but not as legal performative speech. In modern American society, persons who say by way of a conversational commitment, "as God is my witness" or "till death do us part," are not participating in either a formal trial scene or an official marriage ceremony, but adapting what are recognized as fundamental declarations to make a point with solemnity. Such language has *Sitze im Leben* in trials or weddings, but it is the analogy they evoke with solemn declarations of truth and fidelity that give them cogency in public parlance. Similarly, Hosea's deployment of the marriage/covenant metaphor was public parlance intended to provoke Israel, not to provide precise details on the legal status of his marriage.[142]

Marriage and divorce presuppose obligations and standards with respect to property. Thus in Israelite marriage there are matters of bride-price and dowry and obligations on the part of the husband to provide materially for his wife. In divorce a wife is sent from the house of the husband with a writ of divorce (Deut. 24:1). When divorce is for cause (her infidelity or infertility), the property settlement for her will be different than otherwise, since the assets she brought to the marriage such as a dowry may be kept by the husband. The question has been raised, based on texts like Hos. 2:3, 9-10 (MT 5, 11-12), whether punitive measures such as stripping naked were also part of the sending away of the divorced woman.[143] On the one hand, a woman divorced for cause may have had to leave her clothes with her husband, if they were property he provided for her. On the other hand, we lack evidence that such acts as exposing genitals were a form of punishment for a wife's indiscretion.

International treaties employ the terminology of "love" to describe the relationship established between suzerain and vassal.[144] Such a cultural con-

---

141. See M. J. Geller, "The Elephantine Papyri and Hos. 2,3: Evidence for the Form of the Early Jewish Divorce Writ," *JSJ* 8 (1977) 139-48.

142. Cf. Hos. 9:15, where YHWH "hates" evildoers in Gilgal and will drive them from "his house." Perhaps this reflects rejection of political activity in Gilgal using divorce-like terminology.

143. For a comparative approach, see R. Westbrook, "Adultery in Ancient Near Eastern Law," *RB* 97 (1990) 542-80. Westbrook proposes that in Israel the husband of a woman found guilty of adultery had several options. Execution of the adulteress is one, but monetary fines and physical punishment, such as stripping and physical exposure, were also possible. Others have argued that the imagery of stripping and shameful exposure elsewhere in the OT connect it with the imagery of the vanquished and destroyed city, which is personified as a female (Isa. 47:1-4; 52:1-2; Jer. 13:22-27; Ezek. 16; 23; Nah. 3:1-7). See further Kelle, *Hosea 2*, 90-93, and bibliography cited there.

144. See W. Moran, "The Ancient Near Eastern Background of the Love of God in Deuteronomy," *CBQ* 25 (1963) 77-87; S. Ackerman, "The Personal Is Political: Covenantal and Affectionate Love (*'āhēb, 'ahăbâ*) in the Hebrew Bible," *VT* 52 (2002) 437-58; Kelle, *Hosea 2*.

text may have influenced the Deuteronomic language of YHWH loving his people or the people being commanded to love him, since Deuteronomy is an explicitly covenantal book with some formal similarities to treaty documents. Lists of curses for infractions are part of treaty texts, for loyalty is understood as a sacred obligation to maintain because it is undergirded by an oath. Deuteronomy includes not only pointed injunctions against the Canaanite cults but also extensive lists of curses for disobedience. These dynamics may translate to the marriage and covenant metaphor in Hosea as well, particularly in the terminology of "lovers" and in the extensive judgmental language on Israel for disobedience. The "lovers" polemicized against in Hos. 2 include various Canaanite deities and their cults, and possibly national deities of neighboring states and even their human leadership, since the latter sought to entangle Israel in alliances that might require among other things the recognition of their deities.

3. Marriage and Covenant after Hosea

The prophetic model of marriage and covenant in Hosea grows from the root metaphor of Israel as YHWH's household/family. That kinship matrix gives particular shape to the ways in which the book of Hosea develops the model. The marriage model itself, however, is found also in the subsequent prophets Jeremiah, Ezekiel, and Second Isaiah, who express different aspects of the model. The cities of Jerusalem and Samaria are sisters married to YHWH. The fruitfulness of the land and the population of the cities are put in familial terms, referring to Jerusalem as a widow or divorced mother, the land as barren and unhusbanded, all of whom will nevertheless have children in YHWH's good time.

The NT carries over the metaphor of covenant and marriage, placing it first in the service of Christology. The church is the bride of Christ, joined to him by the Spirit as a result of his resurrection from the dead (1 Cor. 6:14-17; 2 Cor. 11:2; Eph. 5:22-33). The Holy City as mother and bride is also adapted, whereby "Jerusalem who is above, our mother" (Gal. 4:26), is the eternal abode. This is a form of ecclesiology. When seen by John, she is the heavenly city adorned as a bride, whose spouse is the Lamb (Rev. 21:2, 9).

Hosea is thus an early and primary witness to themes of central importance in biblical theology. The book represents Israel's history as an unfolding drama with an eschatological future more glorious than its past. The people reside under a self-incurred judgment, which will strike them grievously during the prophet's day. The cosmic community will be transformed, however, and one from David's line will rule the redeemed people. That community is YHWH's beloved household, united to him through a covenant graciously extended to people and cosmos.

V. BIBLIOGRAPHY

Abma, Richtsje. *Bonds of Love: Methodic Studies of Prophetic Texts with Marriage Imagery (Isaiah 50:1-3 and 54:1-10, Hosea 1–3, Jeremiah 2–3).* SSN 40. Assen: Van Gorcum, 1999.

Ackerman, Susan. "The Personal Is Political: Covenantal and Affectionate Love (*'āhēb, 'ahăbâ*) in the Hebrew Bible." *VT* 52 (2002) 437-58.

————. *Under Every Green Tree: Popular Religion in Sixth-Century Judah.* HSM 46. Atlanta: Scholars Press, 1992.

Ackroyd, Peter. "Hosea and Jacob." *VT* 13 (1963) 245-59.

Adler, Elaine J. "The Background for the Metaphor of Covenant as Marriage in the Hebrew Bible." Ph.D. diss. University of California at Berkeley, 1990.

Albright, William F. "Samuel and the Beginnings of the Prophetic Movement." Pages 151-76 in *Interpreting the Prophetic Tradition.* Ed. H. Orlinsky. Cincinnati: Hebrew Union College Press, 1969.

Amsler, Samuel. "Les prophètes et la communication par les actes." Pages 194-201 in *Werden und Wirken des Altes Testament: Festschrift für Claus Westermann zum 70. Geburtstag.* Ed. R. Albertz et al. Göttingen: Vandenhoeck & Ruprecht, 1980.

Andersen, Francis I., and David Noel Freedman. *Hosea: A New Translation with Introduction and Commentary.* AB. Garden City, NY: Doubleday, 1980.

Arnold, Patrick. "Hosea and the Sin of Gibeah." *CBQ* 51 (1989) 447-60.

Balz-Cochois, H. "Gomer oder die Macht der Astarte: Versuch einer feministischen Interpretation von Hos. 1–4." *EvT* 42 (1982) 37-65.

Barr, James. "Some Semantic Notes on the Covenant." Pages 23-38 in *Beiträge zur alttestamentlichen Theologie: Festschrift für Walther Zimmerli zum 70. Geburtstag.* Ed. Herbert Donner et al. Göttingen: Vandenhoeck & Ruprecht, 1977.

Barré, Michael. "New Light on Hos. VI 2." *VT* 28 (1978) 129-41.

Barrick, W. Boyd. "On the Meaning of *bêt-ha/bāmôt* and *bātê-habbāmôt* and the Composition of the Kings History." *JBL* 115 (1996) 621-42.

Baumann, Gerlinde. *Love and Violence: Marriage as Metaphor for the Relationship between YHWH and Israel in the Prophetic Books.* Trans. Linda M. Maloney. Collegeville, MN: Liturgical Press, 2003.

Beale, G. K., and D. A. Carson, eds. *Commentary on the New Testament Use of the Old Testament.* Grand Rapids: Baker Academic, 2007.

Beck, Martin. "Das Dodekapropheton als Anthologie." *ZAW* 118 (2006) 558-81.

Becker, Joachim. *Messianic Expectation in the Old Testament.* Trans. David E. Green. Philadelphia: Fortress, 1980.

Becking, Bob. *The Fall of Samaria: An Historical and Archaeological Study.* SHANE 2. Leiden: Brill, 1992.

————. "West Semites at Tell Šēh Hamad: Evidence for the Israelite Exile?" Pages 153-66 in *Kein Land für sich allein: Studien zum Kulturkontakt in Kanaan, Israel/Palästina und Ebirnâri für Manfred Weippert zum 65. Geburtstag*. Ed. U. Hübner and E. A. Knauf. OBO 186. Göttingen: Vandenhoeck & Ruprecht, 2002.

Ben Zvi, Ehud. *Hosea*. FOTL XXIA/1. Grand Rapids: Eerdmans, 2005.

————. "Observations on the Marital Metaphor of YHWH and Israel in Its Ancient Israelite Context: General Consideration and Particular Images in Hosea 1.2." *JSOT* 28 (2004) 363-84.

Bons, Eberhard, ed. *"Car c'est l'amour qui me plaît, non le sacrifice . . .": Recherches sur Osée 6:6 et son interprétation juive et chrétienne*. JSJSup 88. Leiden: Brill, 2004.

Boshoff, W. S. "Yahweh as God of Nature: Elements of the Concept of God in the Book of Hosea." *JNSL* 18 (1992) 13-24.

Boudreau, George R. "Hosea and the Pentateuchal Traditions: The Case of the Baal of Peor." Pages 121-31 in *History and Interpretation: Essays in Honour of John H. Hayes*. Ed. M. Patrick Graham et al. JSOTSup 173. Sheffield: JSOT Press, 1993.

Braaten, Laurie J. "Hosea's Land Theme in the Book of the Twelve." Pages 104-32 in *Thematic Threads in the Book of the Twelve*. Ed. Paul R. Redditt and Aaron Schart. BZAW 325. Berlin: de Gruyter, 2003.

Brenner, Athalya, and Fokkelien van Dijk Hemmes. *On Gendering Texts: Female and Male Voices in the Hebrew Bible*. BIS 1. 1993. Repr. Leiden: Brill, 1996.

Broshi, Magen. "The Expansion of Jerusalem in the Reigns of Hezekiah and Manasseh." *IEJ* 24 (1974) 21-26.

Brueggemann, Walter. *Tradition and Crisis: A Study in Hosea*. Richmond: John Knox, 1968.

Burke, Trevor J. *Adopted into God's Family: Exploring a Pauline Metaphor*. Downers Grove, IL: InterVarsity Press, 2006.

Buss, Martin J. *The Prophetic Word of Hosea: A Morphological Study*. BZAW 111. Berlin: Töpelmann, 1969.

Caquot, André. "Osée et la Royauté." *RHPR* 41 (1961) 123-46.

Cassuto, Umberto. *Biblical and Oriental Studies*. Vol. 1: *Bible*. Trans. I. Abrahams. Jerusalem: Magnes, 1973.

Chambers, R. Scott. "Who Is the Real El? A Reconstruction of the Prophet's Polemic in Hosea 12:5a." *CBQ* 68 (2006) 611-30.

Charlesworth, James, et al., eds. *The Dead Sea Scrolls: Hebrew, Aramaic, and Greek Texts with English Translations*. Vol. 6B: *Pesharim, Other Commentaries, and Related Documents*. PTSDSSP. Louisville: Westminster John Knox, 2002.

Conzelmann, Hans. *1 Corinthians*. Trans. J. W. Leitch. Hermeneia. Philadelphia: Fortress, 1975.

Coogan, M. "Tyre and Tiglath Pileser III: Chronological Notes." *JCS* 25 (1973) 96-99.

Cook, S. L. "The Lineage Roots of Hosea's Yahwism." *Semeia* 87 (1999) 145-61.

Coote, Robert B. "Hosea XII." *VT* 21 (1971) 389-402.

Cornelius, Izak. *The Many Faces of the Goddess: The Iconography of the Syro-Palestinian Goddesses Anat, Astarte, Qedeshet, and Asherah c. 1500-1000* BCE. OBO 204. Göttingen: Vandenhoeck & Ruprecht, 2004.

Crenshaw, James L. *Education in Ancient Israel: Across the Deadening Silence*. ABRL. New York: Doubleday, 1998.

Cross, Frank M. *From Epic to Canon: History and Literature in Ancient Israel*. Baltimore: Johns Hopkins University Press, 1998.

Daniels, Dwight R. *Hosea and Salvation History: The Early Traditions of Israel in the Prophecy of Hosea*. BZAW 191. Berlin: de Gruyter, 1990.

Davies, Graham I. *Hosea*. Sheffield: JSOT Press, 1993.

Davies, John A. *A Royal Priesthood: Literary and Intertextual Perspectives on an Image of Israel in Exodus 19.6*. JSOTSup 395. London: T & T Clark International, 2004.

Day, John. "Pre-Deuteronomic Allusions to the Covenant in Hosea and Psalm lxxviii." *VT* 36 (1986) 1-12.

Day, Peggy. "A Prostitute Unlike Women: Whoring as Metaphoric Vehicle for Foreign Alliances." Pages 167-73 in *Israel's Prophets and Israel's Past: Essays on the Relationship of Prophetic Texts and Israelite History in Honor of John H. Hayes*. Ed. Brad E. Kelle and Megan Bishop Moore. LHBOTS 446. London: T & T Clark, 2006.

Dearman, J. Andrew. "Baal in Ancient Israel: The Contribution of Some Place Names and Personal Names to the Understanding of Early Israelite Religion." Pages 173-91 in *History and Interpretation: Essays in Honour of John H. Hayes*. Ed. M. Patrick Graham et al. JSOTSup 173. Sheffield: JSOT Press, 1993.

———. "Marriage in the Old Testament." Pages 53-67 in *Biblical Ethics & Homosexuality: Listening to Scripture*. Ed. R. L. Brawley. Louisville: Westminster John Knox, 1996.

———. "The Son of Tabeel (Isaiah 7:6)." Pages 33-47 in *Prophets and Paradigms: Essays in Honor of Gene M. Tucker*. Ed. Stephen Breck Reid. JSOTSup 229. Sheffield: Sheffield Academic Press, 1996.

———. "YHWH's House: Gender Roles and Metaphors for Israel in Hosea." *JNSL* 25 (1999) 97-108.

DeRoche, Michael. "Structure, Rhetoric and Meaning in Hos. iv 4-10." *VT* 33 (1983) 185-98.

Dever, William G. *Did God Have a Wife? Archaeology and Folk Religion in Ancient Israel.* Grand Rapids: Eerdmans, 2005.

Dobbie, R. "The Text of Hosea 9:8." *VT* 5 (1955) 199-203.

Dozeman, Thomas B. "Hosea and the Wandering Wilderness Tradition." Pages 55-70 in *Rethinking the Foundations: Historiography in the Ancient World and in the Bible: Essays in Honour of John Van Seters.* Ed. S. McKenzie and T. Römer. BZAW 294. New York: de Gruyter, 2000.

Driver, S. R. *A Critical and Exegetical Commentary on Deuteronomy.* ICC. Edinburgh: T & T Clark, 1902.

Dubovsky, Peter. "Tiglath-pileser III's Campaigns in 734-732 B.C.: Historical Background of Isa. 7; 2 Kgs 15–16 and 2 Chr. 27–28." *Bib* 87 (2006) 153-70.

Ehrlich, C. S. "Coalition Politics in Eighth Century B.C.E. Palestine: The Philistines and the Syro-Ephraimite War." *ZDPV* 107 (1991) 48-58.

Eidevall, Göran. *Grapes in the Desert: Metaphors, Models, and Themes in Hosea 4–14.* ConBOT 43. Stockholm: Almqvist & Wiksell, 1996.

Emerton, John. "The Biblical High Place in Light of Recent Study." *PEQ* 129 (1997) 116-32.

Emmerson, Grace I. *Hosea: An Israelite Prophet in Judean Perspective.* JSOTSup 28. Sheffield: JSOT Press, 1984.

Fensham, F. C. "Father and Son Terminology for Treaty and Covenant." Pages 121-35 in *Near Eastern Studies in Honor of W. F. Albright.* Ed. H. Goedicke. Baltimore: Johns Hopkins University Press, 1971.

———. "The Marriage Metaphor in Hosea for the Covenant Relationship between the Lord and His People." *JNSL* 12 (1984) 71-78.

Feuillet, A. "'S'asseoir à l'ombre' de l'époux." *RB* 78 (1971) 391-405:

Finkelstein, Israel, and Neil Asher Silberman. "Temple and Dynasty: Hezekiah, the Remaking of Judah and the Rise of the Pan-Israelite Ideology." *JSOT* 30 (2006) 259-85.

Fishbane, Michael. *Biblical Interpretation in Ancient Israel.* Oxford: Clarendon, 1985.

Fuller, Russell. "A Critical Note on Hosea 12:10 and 13:4." *RB* 98 (1991) 343-57.

Fuss, Barbara. *"Dies ist die Zeit, von der geschrieben ist . . .": Die expliziten Zitate aus dem Buch Hosea in den Handschriften von Qumran und im Neuen Testament.* Münster: Aschendorff, 2000.

Galambush, Julie. *Jerusalem in the Book of Ezekiel: The City as Yahweh's Wife.* SBLDS 130. Atlanta: Scholars Press, 1992.

Garrett, D. A. *Hosea, Joel.* NAC. Nashville: Broadman and Holman, 1997.

Geller, M. J. "The Elephantine Papyri and Hos. 2, 3: Evidence for the Form of the Early Jewish Divorce Writ." *JSJ* 8 (1977) 139-48.

Gelston, Anthony. "Kingship in the Book of Hosea." *OTS* 19 (1974) 71-85.

Ginsberg, Harold Louis. "Hosea, Book of." *Encyclopedia Judaica.* Ed. Fred Skolnik. 2nd ed. 22 vols. New York: Macmillan, 2007. 9:547-58.

Gisin, W. *Hosea: Ein literarisches Netzwerk beweist seine Authentizität.* BBB 139. Berlin: Philo, 2002.

Gleis, Matthias. *Die Bamah.* BZAW 251. Berlin: de Gruyter, 1997.

Goldingay, John. *Old Testament Theology.* Vol. 1: *Israel's Gospel.* Downers Grove, IL: InterVarsity Press, 2003.

Gomes, Jules F. *The Sanctuary of Bethel and the Configuration of Israelite Identity.* BZAW 368. New York: de Gruyter, 2006.

Good, E. M. "Hosea 5:8–6:6: An Alternative to Alt." *JBL* 85 (1966) 273-86.

Graetz, Naomi. "God Is to Israel as Husband Is to Wife: The Metaphoric Battering of Hosea's Wife." Pages 126-45 in *A Feminist Companion to the Latter Prophets.* Ed. A. Brenner. FCB 8. Sheffield: Sheffield Academic Press, 1995.

Harper, William R. *A Critical and Exegetical Commentary on Amos and Hosea.* ICC. New York: Scribner's, 1905.

Hayes, J. H. *Amos, the Eighth-Century Prophet: His Times and His Preaching.* Nashville: Abingdon, 1988.

Hayes, J. H., and J. K. Kuan. "The Final Years of Samaria (730-720)." *Bib* 72 (1991) 153-81.

Hayes, Katherine M. *"The Earth Mourns": Prophetic Metaphor and Oral Aesthetic.* SBLAB 8. Atlanta: SBL, 2002.

Hess, Richard. *Israelite Religions: An Archaeological and Biblical Survey.* Grand Rapids: Baker Academic, 2007.

Hillers, Delbert. *Treaty-Curses and the Old Testament Prophets.* BibOr 16. Rome: Pontifical Biblical Institute, 1964.

Holladay, William L. "Chiasmus, the Key to Hosea XII 3-6." *VT* 16 (1966) 53-64.

Holt, Else Kragelund. *Prophesying the Past: The Use of Israel's History in the Book of Hosea.* JSOTSup 195. Sheffield: Sheffield Academic Press, 1995.

Hong, Seong-Hyuk. *The Metaphor of Illness and Healing in Hosea and Its Significance in the Socio-Economic Context of Eighth-Century Israel and Judah.* Studies in Biblical Literature 95. New York: Peter Lang, 2006.

Hornsby, T. J. "'Israel Has Become a Worthless Thing': Re-reading Gomer in Hosea 1–3." *JSOT* 82 (1999) 115-28.

Hugenberger, Gordon P. *Marriage as a Covenant: A Study of Biblical Law and Ethics Governing Marriage Developed from the Perspective of Malachi.* VTSup 52. Leiden: Brill, 1994.

Humbert, Paul. "Osée, le prophète bedouin." *RHPR* 1 (1921) 97-118.

Irvine, Stuart A. "Enmity in the House of God (Hosea 9:7-9)." *JBL* 117 (1998) 645-53.

————. *Isaiah, Ahaz, and the Syro-Ephraimitic Crisis.* SBLDS 123. Atlanta: Scholars Press, 1990.

————. "Politics and Prophetic Commentary in Hosea 8:8-10." *JBL* 114 (1995) 292-94.

————. "Relating Prophets and History: An Example from Hosea 13." Pages 158-66 in *Israel's Prophets and Israel's Past: Essays on the Relationship of Prophetic Texts and Israelite History in Honor of John H. Hayes.* Ed. Brad E. Kelle and Megan Bishop Moore. LHBOTS 446. London: T & T Clark, 2006.

————. "The Southern Border of Syria Reconstructed." *CBQ* 56 (1994) 21-41.

Jacob, Edmond. "Osée." Pages 9-98 in Jacob, C.-A. Keller, and S. Amsler, *Les petits prophètes.* Vol. 1: *Osée, Joël, Abdias, Jonas, Amos.* CAT 11a. Neuchâtel: Delachaux & Niestlé, 1965.

Jeremias, Jörg. "Der Begriff 'Baal' im Hoseabuch und seine Wirkungsgeschichte." Pages 86-103 in *Hosea und Amos: Studien zu den Anfängen des Dodekapropheton.* Tübingen: Mohr, 1986.

————. *Der Prophet Hosea.* ATD 24/1. Göttingen: Vandenhoeck & Ruprecht, 1983.

Johnston, Philip S. *Shades of Sheol: Death and Afterlife in the Old Testament.* Downers Grove, IL: InterVarsity Press, 2002.

Kakkanattu, Joy Philip. *God's Enduring Love in the Book of Hosea: A Synchronic and Diachronic Analysis of Hosea 11,1-11.* FAT 2/14. Tübingen: Mohr Siebeck, 2006.

Kaminsky, Joel. *Corporate Responsibility in the Hebrew Bible.* JSOTSup 196. Sheffield: Sheffield Academic Press, 1995.

Keefe, Alice A. *Woman's Body and the Social Body in Hosea.* JSOTSup 338. Sheffield: Sheffield Academic Press, 2001.

Keel, Othmar. *Goddesses and Trees, New Moon and Yahweh: Ancient Near Eastern Art and the Hebrew Bible.* JSOTSup 261. Sheffield: Sheffield Academic Press, 1998.

Keel, Othmar, and Christoph Uehlinger. *Gods, Goddesses, and Images of God in Ancient Israel.* Trans. Thomas H. Trapp. Minneapolis: Fortress, 1998.

Kelle, Brad E. *Hosea 2: Metaphor and Rhetoric in Historical Perspective.* SBLAB 20. Atlanta: Society of Biblical Literature, 2005.

————. "Hoshea, Sargon, and the Final Destruction of Samaria: A Response to M. Christine Tetley with a View Toward Method." *SJOT* 17 (2003) 226-43.

Kitchen, K. A. *On the Reliability of the Old Testament.* Grand Rapids: Eerdmans, 2003.

Kletter, Raz. *The Judean Pillar-Figurines and the Archaeology of Asherah.* Oxford: Tempus Reparatum, 1996.

Koenen, Klaus. *Bethel: Geschichte, Kult und Theologie.* OBO 192. Göttingen: Vandenhoeck & Ruprecht, 2003.

Krause, Deborah. "A Blessing Cursed: The Prophet's Prayer for Barren Womb and Dry Breasts in Hosea 9." Pages 191-202 in *Reading Between the Texts: Intertextuality and the Hebrew Bible.* Ed. D. N. Fewell. Louisville: Westminster John Knox, 1992.

Kruger, Paul A. "'I will hedge her way with thornbushes' (Hosea 2,8): Another Example of Literary Multiplicity?" *BZ* 43 (1999) 92-99.

———. "Israel, the Harlot." *JNSL* 11 (1987) 107-16.

———. "Prophetic Imagery: On Metaphors and Similes in the Book of Hosea." *JNSL* 14 (1988) 143-51.

———. "Yahweh's Generous Love: Eschatological Expectations in Hosea 14:2-9." *OTE* 1 (1988) 27-48.

Kuhnigk, Willibald. *Nordwestsemitische Studien zum Hoseabuch.* BibOr 27. Rome: Biblical Institute Press, 1974.

Kutsch, Ernst. *Verheissung und Gesetz: Untersuchungen zum sogennanten 'Bund' im Alten Testament.* BZAW 131. Berlin: de Gruyter, 1973.

Lalleman-de Winkel, H. *Jeremiah in Prophetic Tradition: An Examination of the Book of Jeremiah in the Light of Israel's Prophetic Traditions.* CBET 26. Leuven: Peeters, 2000.

Landy, Francis. *Hosea.* Readings. Sheffield: Sheffield Academic Press, 1995.

Lang, Bernhard. *Monotheism and the Prophetic Minority: An Essay in Biblical History and Sociology.* SWBA 1. Sheffield: Almond, 1983.

Lapsley, Jacqueline. "Feeling Our Way: Love for God in Deuteronomy." *CBQ* 65 (2003) 350-69.

Lemaire, André. "Essai d'interprétation historique d'une nouvelle inscription monumentale moabite." *CRAIBL* 1 (2005) 95-108.

Lemche, Niels Peter. "The God of Hosea." Pages 241-57 in *Priests, Prophets and Scribes: Essays on the Formation of Second Temple Judaism in Honour of Joseph Blenkinsopp.* Ed. Eugene C. Ulrich. JSOTSup 149. Sheffield: JSOT Press, 1992.

Levine, L. D. *Two Neo-Assyrian Stelae from Iran.* Toronto: Royal Ontario Museum, 1972.

Machinist, Peter. "Hosea and the Ambiguity of Kingship in Ancient Israel." Pages 153-81 in *Constituting the Community: Studies on the Polity of Ancient Israel in Honor of S. Dean McBride Jr.* Ed. John T. Strong and Steven S. Tuell. Winona Lake, IN: Eisenbrauns, 2005.

Macintosh, A. A. *A Critical and Exegetical Commentary on Hosea.* ICC. Edinburgh: T & T Clark, 1997.

———. "Hosea and the Wisdom Tradition." Pages 124-32 in *Wisdom in Ancient Israel: Essays in Honour of J. A. Emerton.* Ed. J. Day, R. P. Gordon, and H. G. M. Williamson. Cambridge: Cambridge University Press, 1995.

Master, Daniel. "State Formation Theory and the Kingdom of Israel." *JNES* 60 (2001) 117-31.

Mays, James Luther. *Hosea: A Commentary.* London: SCM Press, 1969.

McCarthy, D. J. "Hosea XII 2: Covenant by Oil." *VT* 14 (1964) 215-21.

McCartney, Dan, and Peter Enns. "Matthew and Hosea: A Response to John Sailhamer." *WTJ* 63 (2001) 97-105.

McComiskey, Thomas Edward. "Hosea." Pages 1-237 in *The Minor Prophets: An Exegetical and Expository Commentary.* Vol. 1. *Hosea, Joel, and Amos.* Ed. McComiskey. Grand Rapids: Baker, 1992.

————. "Prophetic Irony in Hosea 1.4: A Study of the Collocation פקד על and Its Implications for the Fall of Jehu's Dynasty." *JSOT* 58 (1993) 93-101.

McKenzie, Steven L. *Covenant.* St. Louis: Chalice, 2000.

Melnyk, Janet L. R. "When Israel Was a Child: Ancient Near Eastern Adoption Formulas and the Relationship between God and Israel." Pages 245-59 in *History and Interpretation: Essays in Honour of John H. Hayes.* Ed. M. Patrick Graham et al. JSOTSup 173. Sheffield: JSOT Press, 1993.

Mettinger, T. N. D. *No Graven Image? Israelite Aniconism in Its Ancient Near Eastern Context.* ConBOT 42. Stockholm: Almqvist & Wiksell, 1995.

————. *The Riddle of Resurrection: "Dying and Rising Gods" in the Ancient Near East.* ConBOT 50. Stockholm: Almqvist & Wiksell, 2001.

Miller, Patrick D. *Sin and Judgment in the Prophets: A Stylistic and Theological Analysis.* SBLMS 27. Chico, CA: Scholars Press, 1982.

Moberly, R. W. L. "'God Is Not a Human That He Should Repent' (Numbers 23:19 and 1 Samuel 15:29)." Pages 112-23 in *God in the Fray: A Tribute to Walter Brueggemann.* Ed. T. Linafelt and T. Beal. Minneapolis: Fortress, 1998.

Morris, Gerald. *Prophecy, Poetry and Hosea.* JSOTSup 219. Sheffield: Sheffield Academic Press, 1996.

Na'aman, Nadav. "Rezin of Damascus and the Land of Gilead." *ZDPV* 111 (1995) 107-8.

————. "When and How Did Jerusalem Become a Great City? The Rise of Jerusalem as Judah's Premier City in the Eighth-Seventh Centuries B.C.E." *BASOR* 347 (2007) 21-56.

Na'aman, Nadav, and Ran Zadok. "Assyrian Deportations to the Province of Samerina in the Light of Two Cuneiform Tablets from Tel Hadid." *TA* 27 (2000) 159-88.

Neef, H. D. *Die Heilstraditionen Israels in der Verkündigung des Propheten Hosea.* BZAW 169. New York: de Gruyter, 1987.

Nelson, Richard D. "Priestly Purity and Prophetic Lunacy: Hosea 1.2-3 and 9.7." Pages 115-33 in *The Priests in the Prophets: The Portrayal of Priests, Prophets and Other Religious Specialists in the Latter Prophets.* Ed. L. L. Grabbe and A. Ogden Bellis. JSOTSup 408. New York: T & T Clark, 2004.

Nicholson, Ernest W. *God and His People: Covenant and Theology in the Old Testament.* Oxford: Clarendon, 1986.

Nielsen, Kirsten. *Yahweh as Prosecutor and Judge: An Investigation of the Prophetic Lawsuit (Rîb Pattern)*. Trans. Frederick Cryer. JSOTSup 9. Sheffield: JSOT Press, 1978.

Nissinen, Marti. *Prophetie Redaktion und Fortschreibung im Hoseabuch. Studien zum Werdegang eines Prophetenbuches im Lichte von Hos. 4 und 11.* AOAT 231. Neukirchen-Vluyn: Neukirchener Verlag, 1991.

Nogalski, James D. "Recurring Themes in the Book of the Twelve: Creating Points of Contact for a Theological Reading." *Int* 61 (2007) 125-36.

Nogalski, James D., and Marvin Sweeney, eds. *Reading and Hearing the Book of the Twelve.* SBLSymS 15. Atlanta: SBL, 2000.

Nwaoru, Emmanuel O. *Imagery in the Prophecy of Hosea.* AAT 41. Wiesbaden: Harrassowitz, 1999.

Odell, Margaret. "Who Were the Prophets in Hosea?" *HBT* 18 (1996) 78-95.

Oestreich, Bernhard. *Metaphors and Similes for Yahweh in Hosea 14:2-9(1-8): A Study of Hoseanic Pictorial Language.* Frankfurt: Peter Lang, 1998.

O'Kennedy, D. F. "Healing as/or Forgiveness? The Use of the Term רפא in the Book of Hosea." *OTE* 14 (2001) 458-74.

Olyan, Saul. "'In the Sight of Her Lovers': On the Interpretation of *nablūt* in Hos. 2,12." *BZ* 36 (1992) 255-61.

Patterson, Richard D. "Parental Love as a Metaphor for Divine-Human Love." *JETS* 46 (2003) 205-16.

Paul, Shalom. *Amos.* Hermeneia. Minneapolis: Fortress, 1991.

Pentiuc, Eugen J. *Long-Suffering Love: A Commentary on Hosea with Patristic Annotations.* Brookline, MA: Holy Cross Orthodox Press, 2002.

Perlitt, Lothar. *Bundestheologie im Alten Testament.* WMANT 36. Neukirchen-Vluyn: Neukirchener Verlag, 1969.

Polley, Max E. *Amos and the Davidic Empire: A Socio-Historical Approach.* New York: Oxford University Press, 1989.

Porten, B., and A. Yardeni. *Textbook of Aramaic Documents from Ancient Egypt.* Vol. 2: *Contracts.* Jerusalem: Hebrew University, 1989.

Porteous, Norman W. "The Prophets and the Problem of Continuity." Pages 11-25 in *Israel's Prophetic Heritage: Essays in Honor of James Muilenburg.* Ed. B. W. Anderson and W. Harrelson. New York: Harper & Brothers, 1962.

Porter, Stanley E. *The Messiah in the Old and New Testaments.* Grand Rapids: Eerdmans, 2007.

Rainey, Anson F. "Looking for Bethel: An Exercise in Historical Geography." Pages 269-73 in *Confronting the Past: Archaeological and Historical Essays on Ancient Israel in Honor of William G. Dever.* Ed. Seymour Gitin et al. Winona Lake, IN: Eisenbrauns, 2006.

Rainey, Anson F., and R. Steven Notley. *The Sacred Bridge: Carta's Atlas of the Biblical World.* Jerusalem: Carta, 2006.

Redditt, Paul L., and Aaron Schart, eds. *Thematic Threads in the Book of the Twelve*. BZAW 325. Berlin: de Gruyter, 2003.

Regt, Lénart de. "A Genre Feature in Biblical Prophecy and the Translator: Person Shift in Hosea." Pages 230-50 in *Past, Present, Future: The Deuteronomistic History and the Prophets*. Ed. J. C. de Moor and H. F. van Rooy. OTS 44. Leiden: Brill, 2000.

Reich, Ronny, and Eli Shukron. "The Urban Development of Jerusalem in the Late Eighth Century B.C.E." Pages 209-18 in *Jerusalem in Bible and Archaeology: The First Temple Period*. Ed. Andrew Vaughn and Ann E. Killebrew. SBLSymS 18. Atlanta: SBL, 2003.

Rendtorff, Rolf. *The Covenant Formula: An Exegetical and Theological Investigation*. Trans. Margaret Kohl. Edinburgh: T & T Clark, 1998.

Ritschl, Dietrich. "God's Conversion: An Exposition of Hosea 11." *Int* 15 (1961) 286-303.

Roberts, J. J. M. "Amos 6:1-7." Pages 155-66 in *Understanding the Word: Essays in Honour of Bernhard W. Anderson*. Ed. J. T. Butler et al. JSOTSup 52. Sheffield: JSOT Press, 1985.

Robinson, T. H. "Hosea." Pages 1-54 in Robinson and Friedrich Horst, *Die zwölf kleinen Propheten*. 2nd ed. HAT 14. Tübingen: Mohr, 1954.

Rosenbaum, Jonathan. "Hezekiah's Reform and the Deuteronomic Tradition." *HTR* 72 (1979) 23-43.

Rowley, H. H. "The Marriage of Hosea." *BJRL* 39 (1956-57) 200-233.

Rudnig-Zelt, Susanne. "Die Genese des Hoseabuches: Ein Forschungsbericht." Pages 351-86 in *Textarbeit: Studien zu Texten und ihrer Rezeption aus dem Alten Testament und der Welt Israels. Festschrift für Peter Weimar zum Vollendung seines 60. Lebensjahres*. Ed. K. Kiesow and T. Meurer. AOAT 294. Münster: Ugarit, 2003.

————. *Hoseastudien: Redaktionskritische Untersuchungen zur Genese des Hoseabuches*. FRLANT 213. Göttingen: Vandenhoeck & Ruprecht, 2006.

Rudolph, Wilhelm. *Hosea*. KAT 13/1. Gütershloh: Gerd Mohn, 1966.

Sailhamer, John H. "Hosea 11:1 and Matthew 2:15." *WTJ* 63 (2001) 87-96.

Sanders, Paul. *The Provenance of Deuteronomy 32*. OTS 37. Leiden: Brill, 1996.

Schart, Aaron. "The First Section of the Book of Twelve Prophets: Hosea-Joel-Amos." *Int* 61 (2007) 138-52.

Schloen, J. David. *The House of the Father as Fact and Symbol: Patrimonialism in Ugarit and the Ancient Near East*. Studies in the Archaeology and History of the Levant 2. Winona Lake: Eisenbrauns, 2001.

Schmitt, J. J. "Gender Correctness and Biblical Metaphors: The Case of God's Relation to Israel." *BTB* 26 (1996) 96-106.

————. "The Gender of Ancient Israel." *JSOT* 26 (1983) 115-25.

————. "The Wife of God in Hosea 2." *BR* 24 (1989) 5-18.

————. "Yahweh's Divorce in Hosea 2 — Who Is That Woman?" *SJOT* 9 (1995) 119-32.

Schniedewind, William M. *How the Bible Became a Book.* Cambridge: Cambridge University Press, 2004.

————. "The Search for Gibeah: Notes on the Historical Geography of Central Benjamin." Pages 711-22 in vol. 2 of *"I Will Speak the Riddle of Ancient Times": Archaeological and Historical Studies in Honor of Amihai Mazar on the Occasion of His Sixtieth Birthday.* Ed. A. M. Maeir and P. de Miroschedji. Winona Lake, IN: Eisenbrauns, 2006.

Schulz-Rauch, Martin. *Hosea und Jeremia: Zur Wirkungsgeschichte des Hoseabuches.* CTM A16. Stuttgart: Calwer, 1996.

Schüngel-Straumann, H. "God as Mother in Hosea 11." Pages 194-218 in *A Feminist Companion to the Latter Prophets.* Ed. A. Brenner. FCB 8. Sheffield: Sheffield Academic Press, 1995.

Scoralick, Ruth. *Gottes Güte und Gottes Zorn: Die Gottesprädikationen in Exodus 34.6f und ihre intertextuellen Beziehungen zum Zwölfprophetenbuch.* HBS 33. Freiburg: Herder, 2002.

Seifert, Brigitte. *Metaphorisches Reden von Gott im Hoseabuch.* FRLANT 166. Göttingen: Vandenhoeck & Ruprecht, 1996.

Sellers, O. R. "Hosea's Motives." *AJSL* 41 (1924-25) 243-47.

Sellin, Ernst. "Hosea und das Martyrium des Mose." *ZAW* 46 (1928) 26-34.

Seow, C. L. "Hosea 14:10 and the Foolish People Motif." *CBQ* 44 (1982) 212-24.

Setel, T. D. "Prophets and Pornography: Female Sexual Imagery in Hosea." Pages 86-95 in *Feminist Interpretations of the Bible.* Ed. L. Russell. Oxford: Blackwell, 1985.

Sherwood, Yvonne. *The Prostitute and the Prophet: Hosea's Marriage in Literary-Theoretical Perspective.* JSOTSup 212. Sheffield: Sheffield Academic Press, 1996.

Smend, Rudolph. *Die Bundesformel.* Zurich: EVZ, 1963.

Smith, Mark S. "The Death of 'Dying and Rising Gods' in the Biblical World: An Update, with Special Reference to Baal in the Baal Cycle." *SJOT* 12 (1998) 257-313.

Sohn, S. T. *The Divine Election of Israel.* Grand Rapids: Eerdmans, 1991.

Soskice, Janet. *Metaphors and Religious Language.* Oxford: Clarendon, 1985.

Spieckermann, Hermann. "Barmherzig and gnädig ist der Herr . . . ." *ZAW* 102 (1990) 1-18.

————. "God's Steadfast Love: Towards a New Conception of Old Testament Theology." *Bib* 81 (2000) 305-27.

Stacy, W. D. *Prophetic Drama in the Old Testament.* London: Epworth, 1990.

Stager, L. E. "The Archaeology of the Family in Ancient Israel." *BASOR* 260 (1985) 1-35.

Stanley, Christopher D. *Paul and the Language of Scripture: Citation Technique in the Pauline Epistles and Contemporary Literature.* Cambridge: Cambridge University Press, 1992.

Stark, Christine. *"Kultprostitution" im Alten Testament? Die Qedeschen der Hebräischen Bibel und das Motiv der Hurerei.* OBO 221. Fribourg: Academic Press, 2006.

Stern, Ephraim. *Archaeology of the Land of the Bible.* Vol. 2: *The Assyrian, Babylonian, and Persian Periods, 732-332 BCE.* ABRL. New York: Doubleday, 2001.

Stienstra, Nelly. *YHWH Is the Husband of His People: Analysis of a Biblical Metaphor with Special Reference to Translation.* Kampen: Pharos, 1993.

Stinespring, William F. "The Problem of Theological Ethics in Hosea." Pages 131-44 in *Essays in Old Testament Ethics (J. Philip Hyatt, in Memoriam).* Ed. James L. Crenshaw and John T. Willis. New York: Ktav, 1974.

Strawn, Brent. *What Is Stronger than a Lion? Leonine Imagery and Metaphor in the Hebrew Bible and the Ancient Near East.* OBO 212. Fribourg: Academic Press, 2005.

Stuart, Douglas K. *Hosea–Jonah.* WBC 31. Waco: Word, 1987.

Swaim, Gerald. "Hosea the Statesman." Pages 177-83 in *Biblical and Near Eastern Studies: Essays in Honor of William Sanford LaSor.* Ed. Gary Tuttle. Grand Rapids: Eerdmans, 1978.

Sweeney, Marvin. *The Twelve Prophets.* Berit Olam. Collegeville, MN: Liturgical Press, 2000.

Tadmor, Hayim. "The Campaigns of Sargon II of Assur: A Chronological-Historical Study." *JCS* 12 (1958) 22-40, 77-100.

———. *The Inscriptions of Tiglath-pileser III King of Assyria: Critical Edition, with Introductions, Translations and Commentary.* Jerusalem: Israel Academy of Sciences and Humanities, 1994.

Tångberg, K. A. "'I am like an evergreen fir; from me comes your fruit': Notes on the Meaning and Symbolism in Hosea 14,9b (MT)." *SJOT* 2 (1989) 81-93.

Tetley, M. Christine. "The Date of Samaria's Fall as a Reason for Rejecting the Hypothesis of Two Conquests." *CBQ* 64 (2002) 59-77.

Tomes, R. "The Reason for the Syro-Ephraimitic War." *JSOT* 59 (1993) 55-71.

Toorn, Karel van der. *Scribal Culture and the Making of the Hebrew Bible.* Cambridge: Harvard University Press, 2007.

Tov, Emanuel. *The Greek Minor Prophets Scroll from Naḥal Ḥever (8ḤevXIIgr).* DJD 8. Oxford: Clarendon, 1990.

Trotter, James M. *Reading Hosea in Achaemenid Yehud.* JSOTSup 328. Sheffield: Sheffield Academic Press, 2001.

Tucker, Gene M. "The Law in the Eighth-Century Prophets." Pages 201-16 in *Canon, Theology, and Old Testament Interpretation: Essays in Honor of*

Brevard S. Childs. Ed. Gene M. Tucker et al. Philadelphia: Fortress, 1988.

Ulrich, Eugene, et al. *Qumran Cave 4.* Vol. X: *The Prophets.* DJD 15. Oxford: Clarendon, 1997.

Utzschneider, Helmut. *Hosea, Prophet vor dem Ende: Zum Verhältnis von Geschichte und Institution in der alttestamentlichen Prophetie.* OBO 31. Göttingen: Vandenhoeck & Ruprecht, 1980.

Van Hecke, Pierre, ed. *Metaphor in the Hebrew Bible.* BETL 187. Leuven: Leuven University Press, 2005.

Van Leeuwen, Raymond. "Scribal Wisdom and Theodicy in the Book of the Twelve." Pages 31-51 in *In Search of Wisdom: Essays in Memory of John G. Gammie.* Ed. Leo G. Perdue et al. Louisville: Westminster John Knox, 1993.

Vuilleumier-Bessard, R. "Osée 13,12 et les manuscrits." *RevQ* 1 (1958) 281-82.

Walton, J. H. *Covenant: God's Purpose and God's Plan.* Grand Rapids: Zondervan, 1994.

Weems, Renita. "Gomer: Victim of Violence or Victim of Metaphor?" *Semeia* 47 (1989) 87-104.

Weinfeld, Moshe. *Deuteronomy and the Deuteronomic School.* Oxford: Clarendon, 1972.

Weippert, M. "Menahem von Israel und seine Zeitgenossen in einer Steleinschrift des assyrischen Königs Tiglath Pileser III. aus dem Iran." *ZDPV* 89 (1973) 26-53.

Wellhausen, Julius. *Die kleinen Propheten übersetzt und erklärt.* 1893. Repr. Berlin: de Gruyter, 1963.

———. *Prolegomena to the History of Israel.* Trans. J. Sutherland Black and Allan Menzies. Edinburgh: A & C Black, 1885.

Westbrook, R. "Adultery in Ancient Near Eastern Law." *RB* 97 (1990) 542-80.

Whitt, W. D. "The Divorce of Yahweh and Asherah in Hos. 2.4-7, 12ff." *SJOT* 6 (1992) 31-67.

———. "The Jacob Traditions in Hosea and Their Relation to Genesis." *ZAW* 103 (1991) 18-43.

Wijngaards, J. "Death and Resurrection in a Covenantal Context (Hos. Vi.2)." *VT* 17 (1967) 226-39.

Williamson, H. G. M. "Jezreel in the Biblical Texts." *TA* 18 (1991) 72-92.

———. "Tel Jezreel and the Dynasty of Omri." *PEQ* 128 (1996) 41-51.

Williamson, Paul R. *Sealed with an Oath: Covenant in God's Unfolding Purpose.* Downers Grove, IL: InterVarsity Press, 2007.

Winter, Urs. *Frau und Göttin: Exegetische und ikonographische Studien zum weiblichen Gottesbild im Alten Israel und in dessen Umwelt.* 2nd ed. OBO 53. Göttingen: Vandenhoeck & Ruprecht, 1987.

Wolff, Hans W. *Hosea*. Trans. Gary Stansell. Hermeneia. Philadelphia: Fortress, 1974.

———. "Hoseas geistige Heimat." *TLZ* 81 (1956) 83-94.

Yee, Gale A. *Composition and Tradition in the Book of Hosea: A Redaction Critical Investigation*. SBLDS 102. Atlanta: Scholars Press, 1987.

Younger, K. Lawson. "The Deportations of the Israelites." *JBL* 117 (1998) 201-27.

———. "The Fall of Samaria in Light of Recent Research." *CBQ* 61 (1999) 461-82.

Zenger, E. "'Durch Menschen zog ich sie . . . (Hos. 11,4)': Beobachtungen zum Verständnis des prophetischen Amtes im Hoseabuch." Pages 183-202 in *Künder des Wortes, Beiträge zur Theologie der Propheten: Josef Schreiner zum 60. Geburtstag*. Ed. L. Ruppert et al. Würzburg: Echter Verlag, 1982.

Zevit, Ziony. *The Religions of Ancient Israel: A Synthesis of Parallactic Approaches*. New York: Continuum, 2001.

Zimmermann, Ruben. *Geschlechtermetaphorik und Gottesverhältnis: Traditionsgeschichte und Theologie eines Bildfelds in Urchristentum und antiker Umwelt*. Wissenschaftliche Untersuchungen zum Neuen Testament 2/122. Tübingen: Mohr Siebeck, 2001.

Zobel, H. J. "Hosea und das Deuteronomium." *TLZ* 110 (1985) 13-23.

TEXT AND COMMENTARY

I. SUPERSCRIPTION (1:1)

1 *The word of YHWH that came to Hosea, son of Beeri, in the days of Uzziah, Jotham, Ahaz, and Hezekiah, kings of Judah; and in the days of Jeroboam, son of Joash, king of Israel.*

1 The initial verse of the book is a superscription, i.e., a heading to the work that indicates its historical setting and very likely the context for its editing. It thereby communicates several things to the reader. First, although the term "prophet" is not used to identify Hosea, he is described as the recipient of the Lord's *word,* which indicates his prophetic status. The Hebrew term *dābār* is singular and indicates a communication; it is not, of course, a literal reference to a single word. Three other books begin exactly the same way ("the word of YHWH came to . . ."), namely Joel, Micah, and Zephaniah.[1] Furthermore, with minor variation the phrase occurs in Ezek. 1:3, Jonah 1:1, Zech. 1:1, Hag. 1:1, and Mal. 1:1. All of these works are part of the prophetic corpus in the OT. The phrase in Hos. 1:1, therefore, marks Hosea as a prophetic book with two sources: (1) the Lord, who initiates communication with Hosea, (2) who in turn communicates with contemporaries through an edited version of his public activities and speaking.

Second, Hosea's father's name, *Beeri,* is given to identify further Hosea for readers. While this detail might have been significant for Hosea's contemporaries, it no longer indicates much to later readers, since the father's name is obscure.[2] Four other persons in the OT, however, are named

---

1. In the LXX Jer. 1:2 begins similarly, "the word of God came to Jeremiah," although the Hebrew text begins somewhat differently.

2. Esau's Hittite father-in-law was named Beeri (Gen. 26:34). Hebrew *b'r* means "well" or "pit."

Hosea. It was the earlier name of Joshua (cf. Num. 13:8), the name of the last king of Israel (2 Kgs. 15:30), the name of a leader in postexilic Jerusalem (Neh. 10:23 [MT 24]), and the name of a prominent Ephraimite leader (1 Chr. 27:20). It is formed from the Hebrew verb *yāšaʿ,* which means "help" or "deliver." The name Hosea means "he [YHWH] has saved" or something similar.

Third, the references to the kings provides the historical setting for the prophet's words. Four rulers from Judah (Uzziah, Jotham, Ahaz, and Hezekiah) and one from Israel (Jeroboam, son of Joash, i.e., Jeroboam II) are named.[3] Jeroboam II died ca. 750. Uzziah's long reign overlapped with that of Jeroboam, although the length of Uzziah's de facto reign and the year of his death are difficult to sort out.[4] The Judean list of kings in v. 1, however, continues with an additional three names, even though the book's prophecies are directed primarily to Israel. Hezekiah's accession is a difficult problem for chronological reconstruction, but his reign continued into the 7th century on almost any reckoning. The dates of the kings in 1:1, when taken in their entirety, cover approximately a hundred years. Moreover, the emphasis on the Judean rulers sits awkwardly at the beginning of a book addressed primarily to Israel, the nation whose capital was Samaria and whose political end came at the hands of the Assyrian rulers Shalmaneser V and Sargon II.

The chronological difficulties can be mitigated on the assumptions that Hosea's prophetic work began some time toward the end of Jeroboam's reign, ca. 755-750, and that Hezekiah's reign began in 728/727, if the synchronism in 2 Kgs. 18:10 is correct,[5] so that Hosea's public activity ran thirty

---

3. Amos 1:1 is the only other prophetic superscription that refers to rulers from both Israel and Judah. That book is introduced as "words of Amos . . . which he saw *(ḥāzâ)* concerning Israel in the days of Uzziah, king of Judah, and in the days of Jeroboam, son of Joash, king of Israel." This chronological indication makes Amos and Hosea contemporaries. Isaiah 1:1 has the same list of Judean kings as Hos. 1:1, which indicates that Isaiah and Hosea were also contemporaries.

4. Uzziah began his reign in the 27th year of Jeroboam II and reigned 52 years according to 2 Kgs. 15:2. He contracted leprosy and his son Jotham served as regent in his stead (2 Kgs. 15:5). The 52 years almost certainly describe the period in which he was king de jure, although Jotham was the de facto ruler during some of that time. Indeed, Jotham may have been elevated officially to the position of vice-regent or coregent. According to 2 Kgs. 15:32, Uzziah died in the second year of Pekah, son of Remaliah, king of Israel.

5. 2 Kgs. 18:10 is complicated by the reference in v. 13 that Sennacherib's assault on Jerusalem came in Hezekiah's 14th year. That assault is firmly dated to the year 701 B.C., which would place Hezekiah's first year in 715. For one explanation of the difficulty, see M. Cogan, "Chronology," *ABD* 1:1008, who thinks that Hezekiah indeed came on the throne in Jerusalem before the fall of Samaria. He suggests that the "14th year" in v. 13 originally belonged with the account of Hezekiah's recovery from illness in 2 Kgs. 20,

years or so. It is not clear from the book when Hosea's prophetic activity ceased. From the evidence in the book, one cannot discern whether Hosea actually witnessed the downfall of Samaria. Broadly speaking, therefore, the prophet's public work appears set in a fifty-year period, from 760 to 710 B.C., with the years 750-725 being the most likely setting.

There is still the question of the emphasis on the Judean kings rather than on those in Israel, where Hosea carried out his prophetic task. The majority of modern scholars regard Hosea as a prophet of northern origin, based primarily on the addresses to Israel, Samaria, and Bethel in the book, plus a number of lexical peculiarities in the text that may reflect a northern dialect. If this is the case — that is, if Hosea himself is of northern origin and not, like Amos, someone from the south who travels north to prophesy — then the Judean emphasis of the superscription probably indicates the context in which the book was edited and preserved. This is understandable, since the fall of Samaria meant the political end of Israel. Archaeological investigation indicates that the population of Jerusalem increased markedly toward the end of the 8th century B.C.; the primary reason was probably an influx of refugees fleeing turmoil in Israel. Hosea's words may have been preserved among various circles who survived the Assyrian onslaught, but the origins of the book we now have likely come from Yahwists who moved southward in the aftermath of Israel's demise. Whether these preservationists and editors included disciples of Hosea or simply people who passed along a prophetic tradition they valued we cannot now determine.

Other 8th-century prophets have similar lists in their superscriptions. Isaiah 1:1 lists the same four Judean kings as Hos. 1:1, but with no reference to a northern ruler. Micah 1:1 lacks the reference to Uzziah, but includes the other three. Micah, apparently a Judean, is credited with "seeing" *(hāzâ)* YHWH's word concerning Samaria and Jerusalem. Amos, a contemporary of Hosea's in Israel, also "saw" the words he communicated in the time of Uzziah and Jeroboam II. The similarities of the superscriptions of these four books suggest a common editorial effort in Judah to preserve their contents as witnesses to YHWH's (recent) past revelation of his word.

---

where Hezekiah is granted an additional 15 years of life. Hezekiah's reign was 29 years in duration (so 18:2). Another, more likely, possibility is that Hezekiah was a vice-regent with his father until 715, which would have been the first year of his sole rule.

II. HOSEA'S FAMILY (1:2–3:5)

INTRODUCTION AND HISTORY OF INTERPRETATION

When read together, chs. 1–3 have a basic theme: God's judgment in the historical process will come against a faithless Israel, sometime after which God will initiate a period of restoration. Hosea's marriage and children are rendered through literary devices to illustrate the theme, and the texts are thoroughly shaped with that goal in mind.[6] Indeed, each chapter — at least in English versification — gives a rendering of the same basic theme, moving from judgment to restoration.

Within the three chapters, readers encounter different literary forms in support of this basic theme. Hosea 1:2-9 is a succinct account, written in third-person prose, that describes Hosea's marriage to Gomer, a woman of harlotry, who subsequently bears three children with symbolic names. Both mother and children symbolize Israel in flagrant rebellion against the Lord. Hosea 2:2-13 (MT 4-15) covers the same theme in the form of a charge of faithlessness (adultery, harlotry) against the mother. Her actions disqualify her as a wife. As her promiscuity is described, it becomes clear that she symbolizes Israel. Hosea 3:1-5 is a first-person prose account, in which the prophet is commanded to acquire and love an unnamed adulteress. In her adultery she too symbolizes Israel. A time of disciplinary penance is described for her in her guise as Israel (and Judah).

Several decades ago H. H. Rowley wrote a masterful survey of scholarly opinions entitled "The Marriage of Hosea."[7] With his usual encyclopedic style, he surveyed the gamut of opinions on the subject of Hos. 1–3 and offered his own assessment. Rowley's essay is still a profitable read, since the options he then surveyed and evaluated remain relevant. Indeed, my own conclusions essentially follow his. In the intervening years, new directions in interpretation have come primarily in two categories: feminist concerns, and various forms of literary analysis such as deconstruction, canonical criticism, and intertextuality.[8] These categories influence, and at times even supersede, those approaches Rowley noted.

6. J. Mays, *Hosea* (OTL; Philadelphia: Westminster, 1969), pp. 23-24: "The narrative is kerygmatic, not biographical. Through it, as well as oracle, the word of Yahweh is known — and that is its sole purpose. The details of Hosea's family life are hidden behind the word-function of the narrative."

7. First published in *BJRL* 39 (1956-57) 200-233; repr. in Rowley's *Men of God* (London: Nelson, 1963), pp. 66-97. References below are to the reprinted version.

8. To see developments in the interpretation of Hos. 1–3, one should compare Rowley's survey and evaluation with those of Y. Sherwood, *The Prostitute and the Prophet: Hosea's Marriage in Literary-Theoretical Perspective* (JSOTSup 212; Sheffield:

One cannot stress too strongly that the interpreter must begin and end with the text of Hos. 1–3. This seems trite to express, but insistence on this principle should keep interpreters focused on the fact that the only source of information available on the topic (Hosea's marriage and family) comes in ancient literary form. Those who are interested in such matters as Hosea's feelings about his wife[9] or the nature of her infidelity pursue legitimate questions, but we must keep in mind that the literary composition we know as Hos. 1–3 may not adequately answer them. Readers must first attend to the literary properties of Hos. 1–3 before seeking what is "behind the text."

A reading of Hos. 1–3 raises a number of questions for interpretation that can be grouped essentially in three categories.[10]

1. *The Promiscuously Adulterous Female.* Is the Gomer of ch. 1 the mother of ch. 2 and also the unnamed adulteress of ch. 3? Put slightly differently, how many women are depicted in chs. 1–3?
2. *Narrative Sequence.* Do chs. 1–3 provide a basic sequence of events (marriage, marriage breakdown, reconciliation), or is the first-person account of ch. 3 the earliest presentation of the marriage, with ch. 1 a later, originally parallel, rendering? Regarding sequence, is the command to marry a "woman of harlotry" presented retrospectively (i.e., Hosea married normally, his wife's promiscuity developed subsequently), or did the command come initially to him as his sense of prophetic call, so that the woman he chose had already been involved in some form of sexual misconduct?[11]
3. *Symbol and Reality.* Should these chapters be read only as a symbolic

Sheffield Academic Press, 1994); N. Graetz, "God Is to Israel as Husband Is to Wife: The Metaphoric Battering of Hosea's Wife," in *A Feminist Companion to the Latter Prophets,* ed. A. Brenner (FCB 8; Sheffield: Sheffield Academic Press, 1995), pp. 126-45; T. J. Hornsby, "'Israel Has Become a Worthless Thing': Re-reading Gomer in Hosea 1–3," *JSOT* 82 (1999) 115-28; E. Ben Zvi, "Observations on the Marital Metaphor of YHWH and Israel in Its Ancient Israelite Context: General Considerations and Particular Images in Hosea 1.2," *JSOT* 28 (2004) 363-84. Macintosh, *Hosea,* pp. 113-26, has a detailed excursus on Hosea's marriage.

9. A striking example of the futility of asking this question is the analysis of O. R. Sellers, "Hosea's Motives," *AJSL* 41 (1924-25) 243-47. Francis Landy, *Hosea* (Readings; Sheffield: Sheffield Academic Press, 1995), pp. 23-24, has little more success in supposing what Gomer must have thought in being married to Hosea. The questions are not wrong; it is simply that the text (which must be the object of our concern) is not capable of assisting readers with the answers.

10. Readers may consult either Rowley or Sherwood for references to scholars representing the following viewpoints on Hos. 1–3.

11. The specifics of the misconduct portrayed are also a matter of debate. See appendix 6, "Sexual Infidelity in Hosea," for further discussion.

rendering of Israel's history (allegory, parable, vision, dream account), or in their symbolic import do they also reflect actual events in the life of Hosea, son of Beeri, and his family?

To begin with category 3, symbol and reality, is to begin properly with literary questions. What kind of literature makes up Hos. 1–3? As noted above, these chapters comprise more than one literary type, but the best parallels to the commands in 1:2 and 3:1 are with accounts of symbolic acts[12] performed by prophets, not with dream reports (e.g., Gen. 40:1–41:36), parables (e.g., Judg. 9:7-21), or vision reports (e.g., Jer. 4:23-28; Zech. 1:7–6:15). Not only do these commands give structure to the reading of Hos. 1–3 as a unit, but they have particularly close parallels with narratives about the prophet Isaiah and symbolic acts undertaken by him through his family. At least two of Isaiah's children have symbolic names, both of whom served to illustrate the prophet's message (Isa. 7:1-9; 8:1-4). The children are signs ('ôt, 8:18) from the Lord to Israel. In both cases the child's role is introduced by commands from the Lord to Isaiah: "Go . . . take your son" (7:3); "Take a tablet and write. . . . The Lord said to me, 'Name him Maher-shalel-hash-baz'" (8:1, 3). One encounters both third-person account and first-person report in these narratives, just as in Hos. 1:2-9 and 3:1-5. Apparently Isaiah's marriage (to a prophetess, Isa. 8:3) also served a symbolic role. At the command of the Lord, Isaiah went naked and barefoot for three years as a sign ('ôt) against Egypt and Cush (20:1-6). Bizarre behavior is thus not out of the question for prophetic signs!

Ezekiel 3–5 depicts a series of symbolic acts[13] to be carried out by the prophet to illustrate his message. A couple of these are so bizarre that some scholars wonder if they were literally carried out (e.g., lying on his side for 390 days; 4:4-15), but other commands (e.g., shaving his hair and beard with a sword, 5:1-4) indeed appear to be physical acts carried out as part of the prophetic task. It seems that being bizarre or offensive did not disqualify an act as a prophetic communication.

On the other hand, both Jeremiah and Ezekiel contain depictions of Israel and Judah as adulterous fornicators in language that is metaphorical and in instances even allegorical (Jer. 2:2-3, 20-37; 3:1-5, 6-14; Ezek. 16:1-

---

12. This is widely acknowledged among modern interpreters, irrespective of the importance they attach to the similarities in rendering Hos. 1–3. On these acts, cf. S. Amsler, "Les prophètes et la communication par les actes," in *Werden und Wirken des Altes Testament: Festschrift für Claus Westermann zum 70. Geburtstag,* ed. R. Albertz et al. (Göttingen: Vandenhoeck & Ruprecht, 1980), pp. 194-201; W. D. Stacey, *Prophetic Drama in the Old Testament* (London: Epworth, 1990), especially pp. 96-111.

13. Ezek. 3–5 is predominately composed in the first person, and 4:3 describes one of the acts as a sign ('ôt).

63; 23:1-49). In them the language of harlotry and family dynamics are used metaphorically to describe the faithlessness of Israel and Judah and/or that of Samaria and Jerusalem. These texts also have a number of parallels with vocabulary and metaphors employed in Hosea. It would seem, then, that the portrayal of Hosea's family is also an earlier example of literary presentation that owes as much to metaphor as it does to historical report.

Perhaps it is best to see Hosea's marriage, the naming of the three children, and the acquiring of an adulteress as public acts to illustrate a prophetic message, with the offensiveness, indeed the impurity and scandalousness of the report (see below), as integral to the prophetic sign. The Hebrew term *'ôt* ("sign") is not used to characterize these actions, but this is their function. At the same time, Hos. 1–3 does more than simply render these acts in literary form for public consumption. Mother and children are metaphorical symbols for Israel and the land. In metaphorical terms they are the vehicle (source domain) through which to interpret the tenor (target domain) of Israel and the land in dereliction of duty. The goal, therefore, is to render Israel and the land in breach of covenant with YHWH through sign-act and literary symbol, not to provide a simple digest of family history.

Nevertheless, if Hos. 1–3 interprets the prophet's actual family, as seems most likely, then a question from category 2 is raised: Should one interpret the command to marry a harlot retrospectively or as the initial step in a prophetic act? The thought that God would ask a prophet to do something immoral has caused consternation,[14] so that a number of interpreters have concluded that 1:2 is a retrospective presentation, produced by the prophet and his editors "after the fact," when the prophet had come to realize the spiritual relevance of his family turmoil over his wife's adultery. This would mean that Hosea married in acceptable fashion, only later to discover his wife's infidelities. After discovery, he came to see that his anger and disappointment mirrored that of God toward wayward Israel. According to this view, he presents his personal circumstances in literary form as originating with God, including a proleptic description of his wife's promiscuity.

---

14. Consternation over a literal interpretation of the command "to marry a prostitute" is perhaps the main reason that interpreters have seen Hos. 1–3 as an allegory, vision, or parable. Rowley cites several examples of those who take this point of view, but he does not cite Calvin, *Commentaries on the Twelve Minor Prophets,* vol. 1: *Hosea* (trans. John Owen; repr. Grand Rapids: Eerdmans, 1950), p. 44, whose conclusion puts the matter succinctly: "It seems not consistent with reason, that the Lord should thus gratuitously render his Prophet contemptible; for how could he expect to be received on coming abroad before the public, after having brought on himself such a disgrace? If he had married a wife such as is here described, he ought to have concealed himself for life rather than to undertake the Prophetic office. Their opinion, therefore, is not probable, who think that the Prophet had taken such a wife as is here described."

Such a retrospective view is plausible.[15] A charge of adultery against a woman presupposes her status as married and that her sexual activity is with someone other than her husband. Since Gomer is charged with adultery (2:2 [MT 4]), so the interpretation goes, her promiscuity began after her marriage. Some find the retrospective view difficult to square with 3:1 and the statement that "the Lord spoke to me again (*'ôd*)," issuing a command to go and love an adulteress. In this case, it is clear that the command to reacquire or to reconcile with an adulteress presupposes that Hosea enters the relationship already knowing of her infidelities.[16] A natural (but not necessary) corollary is that the same circumstances held for the first time that God commanded Hosea to marry a woman of harlotry (1:2). Nevertheless, one can neither find a beginning to her sexual history nor reconstruct much of her marital history from the command in 3:1. It is simply a claim that she had committed adultery prior to her (re)acquisition by Hosea. The difficulty comes in distinguishing a legal meaning for "adultery," as it might apply to Gomer in Israelite society, from its metaphorical meaning of faithlessness, with her representing Israel in breach of covenant fidelity. Gomer may, for example, have been married to someone else and subsequently divorced before her marriage to Hosea (cf. Deut. 24:1-4). She may have engaged in sexual relations with someone other than her husband. Her "adultery" could be related to one or more fertility practices or even commercial prostitution to support herself during her estrangement from Hosea.

One must deal with two related matters before one can reject the retrospective view on the basis of the "again" in 3:1. The first is whether Gomer is to be identified with the unnamed adulteress in 3:1, and the second is whether ch. 3 could still be interpreted as a parallel text to the command to marry in 1:2, rather than a sequel, as suggested here. The issue turns on the question of reading Hos. 1–3 as a unit and whether an editor has contrived a false sequence of events through the rendering of 1:2 and 3:1 and the adding of the third-person report in 1:2-9. Otherwise, is not the more natural reading of the unit one in which details from chs. 1–2 are presupposed in ch. 3, so that the latter serves as a sequel?[17] Interpreters who see ch. 3 as a parallel account to 1:2-9 could be correct, but it is a conclusion based on taking the two

---

15. The commentary by Andersen and Freedman, *Hosea,* is a sustained presentation from this point of view.

16. In terms of Hebrew grammar, the adverb *'ôd,* "again," in 3:1 can modify either the verb *wayyō'mer,* "spoke," or the imperatives *lēk,* "go," and *'ĕhab,* "love." Typically the adverb comes after the verb. The more natural sense is to read the adverb as modifying the preceding verb "spoke" and to interpret God's "speaking again" in light of the previous command to "go" and marry that opens the book (1:2).

17. If Hos. 3:1-5 is a summary of the marriage, i.e., a parallel to chs. 1–2, it is strange that it does not mention either the names of the children or the woman.

passages from their current contexts and drawing a historical judgment from a hypothetical reconstruction of their prehistory. Exegetes have offered several intriguing alternatives to reading ch. 3 as a sequel to ch. 1; but as Rowley has shown, they are forced either to accept a difficult literary-critical solution in 3:1 or otherwise to reject Hos. 1–3 as a coherent unit.[18] Moreover, whatever one concludes about the coherence of Hos. 1–3, one should acknowledge one thing about prophets and symbolic acts — the acts can be bizarre or offensive! Indeed, a bizarre or offensive act may effectively communicate the horror felt by the prophet (and by God!) concerning Israel's wretched state.

With respect to a sequence of events, Rowley makes a persuasive case that while Hos. 1–3 provides only a few details, it is a basic summary of Hosea's marriage and family life used as a comparison to the Israel/YHWH relationship.[19] He married a prostitute, however the term is defined; she bore three children; she and Hosea separated over her adultery; subsequently the two of them reconciled. Such a conclusion answers affirmatively one of the questions from category 1: Are Gomer, the immoral mother, and the unnamed adulteress the same woman?[20] One reads across the grain of Hos. 1–3, rather than with it, to conclude that Hosea married a second woman in ch. 3. That option seems open, since oddly Gomer is not explicitly named in 3:1, but neither are the children. Silence is not a persuasive argument to find in the unnamed woman a second wife of Hosea, any more than the silence with respect to children in 3:1 means that there were no children. The symbolic representation of Israel is better maintained if one spouse represents the corporate identity of the people from adultery to reconciliation.

Two matters remain from category 1: the nature of Gomer's prostitution, and the identity of the person(s) she symbolically represents. I treat her "harlotry" in appendix 6, where I conclude that the term is metaphorical and indicates primarily faithlessness in religious practice or social ethics. This is the most common use of the term in the OT, and it is too difficult to sort out from there the precise nature of Gomer's sexual offenses (which we may think were real enough). As we should remain cautious in reconstructing the sequence of Gomer's harlotry and her marriage to Hosea, so we must be cautious with any conclusion defining the nature of her particular sexual offense. Her representation of Israel is the primary matter in every aspect of her portrayal.

The increased attention given in recent years to the matter of gender

18. Rowley, "Marriage of Hosea," pp. 71-80.
19. Ibid., pp. 91-94.
20. Sweeney, *Hosea,* p. 39, is a recent interpreter who opts for the view that the unnamed woman is different from Gomer. He suggests that she is a prostitute whom Hosea purchased after his marriage with Gomer failed.

in biblical interpretation has resulted in a reexamination of her symbolic role(s).[21] One form of the reexamination comes in the interrelationship of gender, personification, and metaphor in Hos. 1–3, and more particularly how a female can or cannot symbolize a male. Since Israel is a masculine name, the masculine predominates in metaphor and personification in the OT. Some argue that Israel, where named or clearly presupposed, is exclusively symbolized through masculine imagery.[22] If this is correct, then Gomer cannot symbolically represent Israel — she must represent a female character. The obvious candidates would then be the city of Samaria or the land, since both cities and "land" in Hebrew are feminine in grammar and personification. Indeed, it is "the land" *(hā'āreṣ)* that metaphorically commits harlotry in 1:2, but this just transfers the question to that of the entity represented by the land. In context the land is a metonym, representing the nation of Israel. The character of the people is represented by the personification of a geographical and political term that happens to be female. Regarding the personification of Samaria, there is no overt reference to the city in Hos. 1–3 as there are to the entities Israel and Judah. Furthermore, the role and the personification of Samaria are slight elsewhere in the book of Hosea, especially when compared to the rich imagery for the capital cities of Samaria and Jerusalem in Isaiah, Jeremiah, and Ezekiel.[23] Nevertheless, royal cities, even when they are not city-states, can represent the polity of a whole people. And as Second Isaiah makes clear (50:1), they can be considered the "mother" of the people.

Some scholars see Gomer as representing a Canaanite goddess.[24] The proposal is more ingenious than persuasive. Its strength comes in the overlap between imagery for the fruitfulness of the land and the corresponding fertility roles of male and female deities in the various Canaanite pantheons. There is persuasive evidence that some Israelites and Judeans were polytheists and that one or more forms of their polytheism may have held

---

21. The bibliography on the subject is immense. For an introduction to some of the issues, see A. Brenner and F. van Dijk-Hemmes, *On Gendering Texts: Female and Male Voices in the Hebrew Bible* (BIS 1; Leiden: Brill, 1993); J. J. Schmitt, "Gender Correctness and Biblical Metaphors: The Case of God's Relation to Israel," *BTB* 26 (1996) 96-106.

22. J. J. Schmitt has several studies representing this viewpoint: "The Gender of Ancient Israel," *JSOT* 26 (1983) 115-25; "The Wife of God in Hosea 2," *BR* 24 (1989) 5-18; "Yahweh's Divorce in Hosea 2–Who Is That Woman?" *SJOT* 9 (1995) 119-32.

23. Cf. J. Galambush, *Jerusalem in the Book of Ezekiel: The City as Yahweh's Wife* (SBLDS 130; Atlanta: Scholars Press, 1992).

24. See H. Balz-Cochois, "Gomer oder die Macht der Astarte: Versuch einer feministischen Interpretation von Hos. 1–4," *EvT* 42 (1982) 37-65; W. D. Whitt, "The Divorce of Yahweh and Asherah in Hos. 2.4-7, 12ff.," *SJOT* 6 (1992) 31-67.

that YHWH had a female consort. Nevertheless, the difficulty with the proposal that Gomer represents a goddess is twofold. First, the root metaphor of Hos. 1–3 is that of family or household. As a female, Gomer represents Israel (people, land, Samaria) through that metaphorical model. Second, it is her masculine lovers, who do represent Canaanite deities, who have ruined the integrity of YHWH's house and rendered void the exclusivity of the covenant established with Israel. In this symbolism Gomer's gender and sexuality are not linked to a role in the divine world. Hosea is not trying to rid himself of a spouse, as if YHWH were divorcing Astarte or Asherah, but seeking to restore her.

It is the case that grammatical gender and personification are closely linked in Hebrew texts, and also that the link is important in Hosea, but it does not seem to be the case that female imagery is limited only to female gender (or vice versa). Regarding Hos. 1–3, this is best illustrated by the naming of Gomer's three children, each of whom symbolically represents the people or nation of Israel. The daughter named Lo-ruhamah (No Mercy) metaphorically represents the people, as do the two sons, Jezreel (God Sows) and Lo-ammi (Not My People). Likewise, the adulteress of ch. 3 represents Israel collectively, as the symmetry of address in 3:3-4 seems to indicate.

Indeed, Hos. 1–3 includes a variety of gender images and metaphors, all of which represent one or more aspects of Israelite character and identity. Three of them are introduced in 1:2-9 and set the tone for the first three chapters: woman engaged in prostitution (female), land engaged in prostitution (female), children derived from prostitution (male and female).[25]

A number of interpreters consider Gomer's rendering in Hos. 1–3 to be an unfortunate gender stereotype, ill at ease with feminine sexuality, as well as sexist and pornographic, if not misogynistic.[26] This interpretation illustrates both the power of metaphor and something of the divide between antiquity and modernity. On the one hand, there seems to be no way to avoid

25. Some have suggested that Hosea's children are literally "children of harlotry" in the sense that they are Hosea's through an extramarital liaison with a prostitute; so Scoralick, *Gottes Güte,* p. 150. Also Hornsby, "Israel Has Become a Worthless Thing," pp. 115-28, has raised the question whether Hosea actually married Gomer. Although the children, male and female, could represent Israel symbolically in its rebellion against YHWH through their status as children out of wedlock, the covenant YHWH made with Israel in the wilderness is better represented by the actual marriage of Hosea and Gomer.

26. E.g., T. D. Setel, "Prophets and Pornography: Female Sexual Imagery in Hosea," in *Feminist Interpretations of the Bible,* ed. L. Russell (Oxford: Blackwell, 1985), pp. 86-95; R. Weems, "Gomer: Victim of Violence or Victim of Metaphor?" *Semeia* 47 (1989) 87-104; G. Baumann, *Love and Violence: Marriage as Metaphor for the Relationship between YHWH and Israel in the Prophetic Books* (Collegeville, MN: Liturgical Press, 2003).

the offensiveness[27] of Gomer's portrayal and the command to marry a harlot, as well as the intent of Hos. 1–3 to portray Hosea (and thus the Lord) as an angry, wounded husband. On the other hand, Hos. 1–3 partakes of prophetic drama, not a universal rendering of adults or children of either gender. Its raw depictions are intended to wound Israel, but in hopes that the people will come to their senses. It represents God's prophet as completely caught up, enmeshed as it were, in Israel's folly. In an odd but compelling way, Hosea's family is the prophetic word made flesh, God's approach through the prophet in identification with Israel's circumstances, representing them in sordid detail while opposing their devastating effects, all in the cause of gaining them back again.

In the history of the book's interpretation, more attention has been given to the marriage of Hosea and Gomer than to the family dynamics. As noted in the introduction, it is better to see the family or household as the root metaphor in the book of Hosea as a whole, of which the marital relationship of the spouses plays the more prominent role in chs. 1–3 and that of household/children in chs. 4–14.

A. MARRIAGE, CHILDREN, AND JUDGMENT ON ISRAEL (1:2-9)

Verses 2-9 are in the third person, essentially a terse biographical account, and largely concerned with the symbolic employment of Hosea's family as a sign that judgment will fall upon Israel. The words that immediately follow about Israel and Judah indicate a future period in which the people are rightly related to God (1:10–2:1 [MT 2:1-3]). Taken together these verses provide both an overall tone and a basic pattern for the book as a whole: God's judgment of his faithless people has begun. It is a work in and through the histori-

---

27. On the offensiveness of the command to marry a prostitute in the ancient world, see R. D. Nelson, "Priestly Purity and Prophetic Lunacy: Hosea 1.2-3 and 9.7," in *The Priests in the Prophets: The Portrayal of Priests, Prophets and Other Religious Specialists in the Latter Prophets,* ed. L. L. Grabbe and A. Ogden Bellis (JSOTSup 408; New York: T & T Clark, 2004), pp. 115-33. Nelson rightly describes it as an "outrageous stereotypical act" of a prophet, comparable to Isaiah's nakedness (Isa. 20). He proposes to isolate the command and narrative in Hos. 1:2-9 from chs. 2–3, so that the sole comparison in ch. 1 is the comparison of Gomer to the sordid land. The comparison of Hosea and Gomer with the covenant relationship between Israel and YHWH is reserved for chs. 2–3. This proposed isolation unduly separates the first chapter from what is intended as a coherent unit, namely Hos. 1–3. Moreover, the name Lo-ammi (Not My People) and the declaration that YHWH is Lo-ehyeh (Not I AM) (i.e., no longer *'ehyeh;* see Exod. 3:14) are rooted in a covenantal context.

cal process. Restoration of the people will come in future times because God is merciful. Chapter 1, therefore, is a structured arrangement of different materials formed in the service of this fundamental theological purpose. Furthermore, ch. 1 is to be read in conjunction with chs. 2 and 3, so that a fuller perspective is gained on the symbolic significance of Hosea's family as a vehicle for prophetic proclamation. This appears to be the primary reason that ch. 1 exists: to introduce prophetic sign-acts based on the family metaphor as a means of public communication.

In some ways the third-person description in 1:2-9 is like a parable of Jesus, where the main actors and the situation set up the audience/hearers to think new thoughts about God's kingdom and claims upon them. In this case, the family itself becomes a sign or symbol of the message. As noted above, this is a communicative device employed by other prophets as well.

> 2 *The beginning of YHWH's speaking through Hosea: YHWH said to Hosea, "Go, take for yourself a wife of harlotry, and (have) children of harlotry, for the land commits great harlotry against YHWH."*
>
> 3 *Hosea went and took Gomer, the daughter of Diblaim; she conceived and bore a son for him.*
>
> 4 *And YHWH said to Hosea, "Name him Jezreel, because soon I will bring the blood of Jezreel upon the house of Jehu, and I will bring an end to the kingdom of the house of Israel.*
>
> 5 *It will happen on that day that I will shatter Israel's bow in the valley of Jezreel."*
>
> 6 *Gomer conceived again and bore a daughter. The Lord said to Hosea, "Name her Lo-ruhamah,[28] because I will no longer be merciful to the house of Israel, and I will certainly not forgive them.*
>
> 7 *But toward the house of Judah I will be merciful, and I will deliver them by means of the Lord their God. I will not deliver them with a bow, sword, or battle, or by cavalry!"*
>
> 8 *Gomer weaned Lo-ruhamah; then she conceived and bore a son.*
>
> 9 *And the Lord said, "Name him Lo-ammi,[29] because you[30] are not my people and I am Lo-ehyeh[31] for you."*

2 Verse 2 has three main elements: an introduction, a command from the Lord to Hosea, and an explanation of the command. The verse can be read at

28. The name means "no mercy."
29. The name means "not my people."
30. Both second person pronouns in 1:9b are plural (= you all).
31. The name means "not I AM."

least two different ways: (a) with the initial element — the beginning of God's speaking through Hosea — understood as an introduction or brief heading to what follows,[32] or (b) with the initial element as an adverbial phrase — "when the Lord began to speak through Hosea, he said. . . ." Both readings function similarly. The phrase *speak through* or "by means of" *(dibber bě)* has parallels in Num. 12:2, 6, 8; 2 Sam. 23:2; 1 Kgs. 22:28; and Hab. 2:1. In each case the significance seems to be that of divine communication through human agency. The writer wants it known that God initiated Hosea's prophetic work in Israel and that it began with a command to marry.

Go, take for yourself is a command for Hosea to marry (cf. 1:3). This is the second element of v. 2. The common verb *take (lāqaḥ)* is used elsewhere as a description of the act of procuring a bride.[33] Typically, after successful negotiations between the respective families, the bride-to-be is taken by the groom and becomes "his."[34] The shocking thing, of course, is not the command to marry but the person whom Hosea is commanded to marry. She is a woman of *harlotry (zěnûnîm)!* Whatever the term *harlotry* indicates in particular about Gomer's sexual history, it is a metaphor intended to indict Israel for breach of faith toward the Lord.[35] This is made clear by the third and last element in the verse: that the land commits harlotry by forsaking the Lord. Hosea's marriage to harlotrous Gomer is to signify this defection of Israel, personified in the actions of the land. Such personification also occurs in Lev. 19:29, where the noun "land" is the subject of the verb *zānâ,* "to act as a harlot" (cf. Lev. 18:25; Num. 5:3; Deut. 24:4).

The conclusion to v. 2 is thus a succinct statement of much that Hosea finds wrong with Israel. The indictment of the nation comes in a subtle combination of metaphor and metonymy. Within a single verse a sophisticated portrayal is presented through employment of symbolic vocabulary. *Land ('ereṣ)* is a metonym for the nation; but like most substitute terms, some aspect of the substitute helps to reimage the subject. The first step for readers is to take note of the relationship between grammar, personification, and gender that is part of Hebrew rhetoric. "Land" is not only a substitute for the nation, it is probably a personified ellipsis for "the land of Israel." In grammar the noun is feminine, so that "her" personification is consistent with that of the woman of harlotry.[36]

32. The LXX renders the beginning of the verse as a heading. The Hebrew verb *dibber,* "speak," in 1:2a is rendered as a noun *(logos),* so that the verse begins: "The beginning of the word of the Lord to Hosea. . . ."

33. E.g., Gen. 4:19; 6:2; 11:29; 12:19; 19:14; Exod. 6:20.

34. Cf. Gen. 24:3, 67; 34:4; and further, J. Andrew Dearman, "Marriage in the Old Testament," in *Biblical Ethics & Homosexuality: Listening to Scripture,* ed. R. Brawley (Louisville: Westminster John Knox, 1996), pp. 53-67.

35. See appendix 6, "Sexual Infidelity in Hosea."

36. Israel is a masculine name.

Both Hosea's spouse and the covenant partner of the Lord have transgressed a sacred boundary and violated an agreed-upon norm.

The personification of the land in v. 2 seems to indicate more than a clever poetic adaptation on the part of an ancient writer, no matter how odd the description may seem to modern sensibilities. A modern Western mode of thinking tends to depict nations or ethnic groups from an anthropocentric point of view. A nation is defined almost solely by people. Hosea's depiction of Israel as a personified land, however, represents a more holistic mode of perception. Just as a family unit in ancient Semitic society is understood collectively as people *and* their possessions/inheritance, so also a people or nation is understood collectively as the relevant human population, plus its divinely granted possessions (e.g., land, capital city, temple). This larger environmental context is a constituent element of Israel's identity in a holistic or synthetic way of thinking. The land can even be symbiotically defined vis-à-vis the people who inhabit it, so that the land reflects (almost "is") the life of the people. For example, Israel's sinfulness toward the Lord causes the land to mourn and be dry/ill (Hos. 4:1-3).[37] In a future restoration, the Lord will make a covenant with the animals so that all can dwell in safety (2:18 [MT 20]; see below). This is a restoration of a peaceable environment conducive to the health of all. The Lord will *respond* or "answer" (i.e., respond adequately to) the heavens and the earth (*'ereṣ*), and the earth correspondingly shall *respond* to the grain, wine, and oil (2:21-22 [MT 23-24]).

Gomer, the woman of harlotry acquired by Hosea, represents in this fuller sense a land in flagrant disobedience to the Lord. As a personified metonym, the land portrays the people named Israel. She and they are prostitutes, in that both have forsaken an exclusive intimate relationship with their spouse or covenant partner.

3-5 Verses 3-5 report that Hosea did as the Lord commanded, and they elaborate on the theme of judgment because of Israel's unfaithfulness. The woman of harlotry is named; she is Gomer, daughter of Diblaim.[38] Neither name is common, but there seems to be no symbolic meaning assumed

37. See Joel 1:8-12. Offerings in the temple have ceased, fields are destroyed, both priests and the land mourn (*'ābal*), and joy has withered away from the people. Ezek. 14:13-20 speaks of the "land that sins" (land is subject of the verb "to sin") and the devastating effects upon it. In Gen. 6:11-13 corruption is predicated of the "land" and "all flesh"; judgment comes, therefore, on both land and flesh because they are integrally related (i.e., understood holistically).

38. Gomer is formed from the root *gmr*, meaning "bring to completion." The OT also attests a male Gomer (Gen. 10:2) and a prominent Judean named Gemariah (Jer. 36:10), whose name is formed from the same root. Diblaim, as pointed by the MT, has a dual ending. This is odd for a personal name, but not for a place name (cf. Diblathaim, Jer. 48:22). The noun *dĕbēlâ* is a raisin cake.

91

in either case, as there is for the names of her three children. Nothing more is preserved about Gomer's family or religious persuasion. She was apparently an Israelite — at least her symbolic role in representing Israel seems to presuppose it — but even this we cannot confirm. Whether at some time she was a prostitute in the accepted commercial sense of the term we cannot know for certain either, but we cannot rule it out. After the marriage of Hosea and Gomer, she bears a son "for him." That explanation "for him" is not included in the description of the births of the next two children, leading some interpreters to speculate that Hosea was the father only of the firstborn. The terseness of the account precludes certainty on the matter, but the more likely conclusion is that the latter two children are also Hosea's biological offspring.

Jezreel, the name of the firstborn son, represents a divinely provided sign to illustrate the judgment of God to come. The name means "God sows," based on the common verb *zāraʿ.* It is the well-known name of the fertile valley in the heartland of the Israelite state. It is also the name of a prominent town during the Omride dynasty at the eastern end of the valley near Mt. Gilboa.[39] King Ahab had a palace there (1 Kgs. 21:1). Moreover, "Jezreel" is grammatically and phonetically similar to "Israel." This is a trademark Hosean pun, with the recognized similarity to "Israel" adding to the ominous significance of Jezreel's predicted demise.[40] "Jezreel" is not used elsewhere in the OT as a personal name, nor does its basic meaning communicate judgment. That God "sows" would be thought of primarily in terms of fruitfulness and prosperity, as is clear in Hos. 2:22-23 (MT 24-25), although when the verb is rendered as "scattered," it can communicate a judgment through forced dispersion (cf. Zech. 10:9). Here in Hos. 1:3 the child's name is a mnemonic device that draws attention to prior bloodshed perpetrated at Jezreel.

4 According to 1:4, God will *bring* (lit. "visit" or "inspect") *the blood of Jezreel upon the house of Jehu.* Modern translations often render the Hebrew phrase *pāqad ʿal* here and in similar texts as "punish" because the action conveyed in the Lord's visitation is understood to be judgment.[41] This is not wrong, but the rendering misses an important nuance. God's judgment in the coming historical process is the bringing of a negative effect on the ruling house, based on prior failures related to that dynasty. As discussed below, the phrase may indicate murder on the part of the Jehu dynasty, so that God's judgment brings back upon them what their crime set in motion, as it were

39. See H. G. M. Williamson, "Jezreel in the Biblical Texts," *TA* 18 (1991) 72-92; idem, "Tel Jezreel and the Dynasty of Omri," *PEQ* 128 (1996) 41-51.

40. Hos. 1:4b-5 preserves an intricate chiastic relationship between Jezreel and Israel: (a) blood of Jezreel; (b) kingdom of the house of Israel; (b′) bow of Israel; (a′) valley of Jezreel.

41. Cf. NRSV. For related texts in the OT, see Exod. 20:5; 32:14; 34:7; Num. 14:18; Jer. 36:31; Amos 3:2, 14; Hos. 2:13 (MT 15); 4:9; 8:13; 9:9.

linking cause and effect. On the other hand, the naming of Jezreel may be a matter of joining a well-known place of fighting (cf. 1 Kgs. 21) with the coming fall of the ruling dynasty.[42]

In preserving this prophecy, the narrator/editor reaches back to what must have been more extensively portrayed in public by Hosea early in his prophetic work, namely that judgment would come upon the house, or dynasty, of Jehu. Jeroboam II was the fourth member of that family to reign in Israel. Upon his death his son Zechariah became king and was assassinated after one month (2 Kgs. 15:8-12). Shallum, the usurper, was not a member of the Jehu dynasty. Even though it is not mentioned explicitly in Hosea, Zechariah's death could be seen as the fulfillment of Hosea's prophecy with respect to the house of Jehu. Furthermore, Hosea's prophecy is not the only scriptural text that concerns the end of the Jehu dynasty. In commending the founder of the dynasty, the historian of the kings records that God had limited the house of Jehu to only four generations of rule (2 Kgs. 10:28-31; 15:12).

Even in the terse account of Hos. 1:4-5, the link between the child's name and the prophecy of judgment upon the house of Jehu is clear; what remains unclear is the nature of the *blood of Jezreel* to which 1:4 refers. Is the focal point the requiting of blood spilled by the Jehu dynasty in Jezreel, or is the significance of Jezreel that of a place of battles where kingdoms and dynasties can be overthrown? *Blood* or "bloodshed" could refer to the slaughter of the ruling houses of both Israel and Judah that was carried out by Jehu (2 Kgs. 9–10; cf. 10:11). Jehu, an army officer, took the throne from the Omride dynasty through a military-backed coup. According to 2 Kgs. 9:1-10, Jehu's bloody purge of the house of Ahab fulfilled a prophetic command from the Lord. Does this mean that Hosea opposes what is elsewhere described as a divine command? Possibly so, but it would not be because Hosea supported the policies of Ahab and Jezebel or because he believed that death was too harsh a judgment for faithlessness toward God. Hosea too (along with the compilers of 2 Kings) is adamantly opposed to the religion and culture of Baal, and his prophecies also reckon with the possibility that his compatriots will forfeit their lives as a result of their faithlessness. Thus, if the bloodshed in Jezreel of 1:4 is a reference to Jehu's purge, it could refer more precisely to the murderous excess carried out by Jehu, such as the killing of Ahaziah, king of Judah (2 Kgs. 9:27), or the murder of 42 of Ahaziah's relatives (10:12-14). The reference might include acts perpetrated by the

---

42. In addition to the commentaries, see T. E. McComiskey, "Prophetic Irony in Hosea 1.4: A Study of the Collocation פקד על and Its Implications for the Fall of Jehu's Dynasty," *JSOT* 58 (1993) 93-101; S. A. Irvine, "The Threat of Jezreel (Hosea 1:4-5)," *CBQ* 57 (1995) 494-503.

Omrides (e.g., murder of Naboth, 1 Kgs. 21), but not sufficiently atoned for by the dynasty of Jehu, who were also finally judged as corrupt.[43]

Possibly the *blood of Jezreel* here in 1:4 refers not to a specific act of the Jehu dynasty, but to judgment to come at a particular place, a place widely known for military activity. This would mean taking "blood of Jezreel" as a description characteristic of the locale, as if to say, "I will bring the significance of 'bloody valley' on the ruling house."[44] If one reads 1:4 in this manner, then 1:5, with its reference to breaking the bow of Israel in the valley of Jezreel, would be a synonymous phrase. The "blood of Jezreel" would refer to military defeat and the end of the dynasty at the location long known for its fighting and bloodshed.

It is also possible that the *blood of Jezreel* is indeed a reference to acts carried out during the ninety-plus years of the Jehu dynasty, but it refers to acts otherwise not recorded in Kings or Chronicles. One gets just an inkling of how selective are the histories of the kings by considering the claims of extrabiblical texts for the period in question. The inscription of the Moabite king Mesha (cf. 2 Kgs. 3:4) narrates several battles with Israelite forces, none of which is mentioned in Kings or Chronicles. The so-called Tell Dan inscription narrates fighting between Israelite and Aramean forces and the murder of kings in the later 9th century B.C., narratives that are not easily correlated with the accounts in 1-2 Kings.[45] Indeed, elsewhere Hosea has obscure references to transgressions at Adam, Gilead, and on the way to Shechem (6:7-9), evil in Gilgal (9:15), sin in Gibeah (10:9), and slaughter in Beth-arbel (10:14). Thus the terse phrase "blood of Jezreel" may refer to any number of events.

5 However one understands the reference to the "blood of Jezreel" in 1:4, perhaps the most important point to keep in mind is the parallel phrase to it in 1:5, with its prophecy of the end of the kingdom[46] of the house of Israel. Thus the naming of the child is a prophecy indicating something more than the end of a ruling house; it is tantamount to an announcement that the nation of Israel itself will come to an end. The reference to a broken (war) bow in 1:5 portrays a military defeat for Israel in the valley of Jezreel. Such a defeat is something that would lead to the humiliation of Israel, if not eventu-

---

43. 2 Kgs. 10:31 notes that Jehu was disobedient to divine instruction. See Macintosh, *Hosea,* p. 17, with reference to the interpretation of medieval rabbis.

44. Andersen and Freedman, *Hosea,* p. 186: "The text tells us not *why* Jehu's house was punished, but *how* it is to be punished."

45. For the Mesha and Tell Dan inscriptions, including references to the publication of the Semitic texts themselves, see the translations of K. A. D. Smelik and Alan Millard, respectively, *COS* 2:137-38, 161-62.

46. Heb. *mamlākût* can be rendered either "kingdom" or more abstractly "domain" or "rule."

ally to its complete fall. Some scholars have opined that 1:5 is an editorial addition to the original prophecy of judgment on the house of Jehu and an attempt to extend the language of judgment more broadly to the nation itself. If so, it could be that Hosea added the comment sometime after Zechariah's death to account for the stripping away of Israelite territory by Tiglath-pileser III in 734-732 (2 Kgs. 15:29). If 1:5 is an editorial addition to an earlier prophecy, it could also be the work of an editor at some point after the death of Hosea, perhaps taking into account the fall of Israel to the Assyrians.[47]

Excursus: Sowing in Hosea

Hosea makes varied use of the root *zr'*, which in noun form refers to "seed" and as a verb refers to the act of "sowing/scattering." The term is the verbal element in the name Jezreel, which means "God sows." Hosea and Gomer's first child is named Jezreel (1:4-5). His name is a pun intended to signify Israel's judgment for/of the "bloodshed of Jezreel" that will come in the valley of Jezreel. The valley in question is the fertile division between the central hill country to the south and the mountains of Lower Galilee to the north. Moreover, Jezreel, a prominent city of the Omride dynasty, is located in the eastern half of the valley.[48] The judgmental aspect of the name is reversed in 1:10-11 (MT 2:1-2) and 2:21-23 (MT 23-25). In 1:10-11 the ancestral promises of descendants (Gen. 22:17; 32:12 [MT 13]) are brought to bear on the *great day of Jezreel,* when land and people are restored to wholeness. In Hos. 2:21-23 (MT 23-25) the people of Israel[49] are again "sown" *(zāra')* in the land. The fertility cycle of rain and crop production is mirrored in the multiple "answers" or "responses" *('ānâ)* initiated by YHWH between the heavens, earth, and Jezreel in 2:21-22 (MT 23-24).

Hosea is adept at the metaphorical use of the verb "sow" to indicate the relationship between act and consequence. Seed sown and plants reaped hold forth the interconnection between act and consequence. The consequences may be positive or negative, depending on the tenor (target domain) that the vehicle (source domain) "sow" represents. In 8:7 the people are charged with "sowing" wind, and they will be judged by "reaping" *(qāṣar)* a whirlwind or storm. The connection between sowing

47. See the discussion of Wolff, *Hosea,* pp. 19-20. Wolff accepts the secondary nature of 1:5, but suggests that it is more likely the work of Hosea in updating his own prophetic witness than that of a later editor.

48. The settlement is listed as part of the inheritance of Issachar (Josh. 19:18). The vineyard of Naboth coveted by Ahab was located near the royal quarter of the city according to 1 Kgs. 21. A massacre of kings and people took place there (2 Kgs. 9:14–10:11).

49. Both MT and LXX have "her" as the object of the sowing in the land in 2:23 (MT 25), referring either to "Gomer" or the capital city. The NSRV translates "him," based on the masculine name Jezreel for the son.

and reaping is also made by the relationship of the resulting nouns "wind" *(rûaḥ)* and "whirlwind" *(sûpâ).* In 10:12 the people are urged to "sow" righteousness and therefore to "reap" steadfast love. This is explained through employment of another (and related) metaphor, to break ground in the prospect of a future harvest after the rains. Both metaphors are employed to urge a "seeking" *(dāraš)* of YHWH, who may yet bless Israel.

Parallels to this metaphorical vocabulary are most frequent in the wisdom literature. On the "sowing of righteousness," see Prov. 11:18. The "sowing/reaping" metaphor, using "injustice/iniquity," occurs in Prov. 22:8, and a similar metaphor, which adds "plowing" to the expected verb pair, occurs in Job 4:8. Ecclesiastes has the verb pair in the context of observing wind and clouds (11:4). These data suggest that the prophet has an affinity not only for agriculture and the wisdom tradition in general, but also particularly for the latter's attention to act and consequence.[50]

6-7   The narration of family matters continues with the symbolism of the second child and her name. Hosea is commanded to give the daughter the Hebrew name *lō' ruḥāmâ,* which means *No Mercy* or "Not Pitied." The reason for this astounding name is given in the second half of v. 6. She shall be called No Mercy because God will no longer have mercy on Israel. Here 1:6 follows 1:3-5 in literary form and theme. The child's name symbolizes judgment to come upon Israel.

The last phrase of 1:6 is difficult in the MT, and the versions do not agree in their renderings. The verb *nāśā'* has the basic meaning of "to lift up," "to bear." One of its senses is "forgive," as in bear or take away sin and guilt. It is used with this meaning in Hos. 14:2 (MT 3) and elsewhere (e.g., Exod. 32:32; 34:7; Mic. 7:18), and that is its probable use here in v. 6. In the context of 1:6 it is judgment and not forgiveness that is at hand. Thus the rendering proposed assumes that the negative particle *lō'* in the previous phrase ("I will *no longer* be merciful") does double duty and modifies this last clause as well. The strength of this rendering *(and I will certainly not forgive them)* is the parallel with the divine self-disclosure in Exod. 34:6-7, where YHWH is defined as "merciful and gracious *(raḥûm wĕhannûn)* . . . one who forgives iniquity and transgression and sin *(nōśē' 'āwôn wāpeša' wĕḥaṭṭā'â).*[51] This self-disclosure of YHWH completes the theophany of 33:19ff., where YHWH had declared his freedom initially "to show mercy to whom I will show mercy [Piel of *rāḥam*]." YHWH's classical self-definition contains an adjective and verb from the root *rḥm* ("compassion, mercy") and the verb *nāśā'* with the nu-

50. A. A. Macintosh, "Hosea and the Wisdom Tradition," in *Wisdom in Ancient Israel: Essays in Honour of J. A. Emerton,* ed. J. Day et al. (Cambridge: Cambridge University Press, 1995), pp. 124-32.

51. See appendix 10, "YHWH's Self-Definition (Exod. 34:6-7) and Hosea."

ance of "forgiving." It is as if YHWH says through the naming of the daughter, "I am no longer the merciful one and I will not forgive them."[52] As Sweeney puts it, the daughter's name "clearly signifies the reversal of the relationship between YHWH and Israel as it is portrayed in the Mosaic tradition, the foundational tradition of Israel's existence and sense of identity."[53]

One should compare the daughter's name, with its intended reversal of identity, with the explanation of the name of the third child (see 1:9 below). The meaning of the son's name *Lo-ammi* (Not My People) is predicated on the claim that God is *Lo-ehyeh* (Not I AM) with respect to the Israelites. *Lo-ehyeh* is a pun on the tetragrammaton *(yhwh)* and depends on the account of the revelation of the divine name in Exod. 3:14. Put simply, YHWH is no longer *I AM* on behalf of Israel. As a result of Israel's faithlessness, YHWH's name is "reversed," i.e., changed to reflect the breaking of the relationship between him and Israel.

7 Verse 7 abruptly contrasts the judgment shortly to come on Israel with the surprising deliverance of Judah. Judah will be saved, but not by means of the instruments of war.[54] Already in the context (1:5) the Lord claims that he will shatter the war bow of Israel. This indicates the overcoming of Israel's military capability, if not the downright defeat of the nation's army. Deliverance for Judah, on the other hand, will not come through its military might, nor through the Lord's employment of that might.

The majority of modern commentators have interpreted v. 7 as an editorial comment, of Judean origin, that attempts to account for the different fates of Israel and Judah, vis-à-vis the Assyrian onslaughts in the region from the time of Tiglath-pileser III through Sennacherib.[55] Whereas Israel fell completely to the Assyrians, Judah was ravaged by them, though Jerusalem itself did not fall and the Davidic dynasty stayed on the throne. Indeed, both

52. One could also render the last phrase of 1:6: "I will certainly take [forgiveness] away from them." This rendering does not employ the negative from the previous clause and it interprets *lāhem* ("to them") as an indirect object. Yet another option would be, "I will certainly take them away [to judgment or to exile]." The verb is used again in 14:2 (MT 3) in the context of YHWH's forgiveness of "iniquity."

53. Sweeney, *Twelve Prophets,* p. 20.

54. That 1:7 contrasts the deliverance of Judah with the fall of Israel in 1:6 is disputed by Andersen and Freedman, *Hosea,* pp. 188-92, who suggest that the strong negation in 1:6b governs all subsequent clauses in 1:6-7. This results in the following: "Never again shall I show pity for the state of Israel . . . nor for the state of Judah will I show pity, or save them. I will not save them from bow and sword and weapons of war, from horses and horsemen" (p. 3). It seems better, however, with most scholars to see *wĕ'et-bêt yĕhûdâ* in 1:7a as an emphatic contrast: "But the house of Judah. . . ." It is awkward syntax to extend the negative particle in v. 6 to all clauses in v. 7.

55. See the discussion in Emmerson, *Hosea,* pp. 88-95. She thinks the verse is secondary, but is ambivalent about denying it to Hosea.

2 Kgs. 18:9–19:37 and Isa. 36:1–37:38 narrate the miraculous deliverance of Jerusalem and Hezekiah in 701 B.C. from an Assyrian siege during the reign of Sennacherib. The verse is often considered part of the Judean redaction of the prophet's work, carried out in Judah after the fall of Samaria, but before the fall of Judah and Jerusalem in 587/586.[56]

The evidence for v. 7 as an editorial addition is based primarily on literary analysis (i.e., style and genre). There is no evidence for its omission among extant Hebrew or Greek manuscripts. Admittedly, a prophecy of Judah's deliverance sits awkwardly in the context of judgment upon Israel portrayed through a family metaphor. Moreover, reference to God in the third person is also awkward in a divine speech (but cf. 1:2). These are reasons enough for most commentators to conclude that v. 7 is an addition. On the other hand, Judah's historical fate at the hands of the Assyrians was different from that of Israel in Hosea's lifetime, as well as after. A siege of Jerusalem on the part of Israel and Damascus failed (Isa. 7:1-9). Subsequently, Tiglath-pileser III devastated Damascus and ripped away much of Israelite territory from Samaria. Judah, however, and its king, Ahaz, survived essentially intact by the payment of tribute. Moreover, the emergence of Hezekiah in Judah may have been viewed favorably by Hosea and/or his early disciples.[57] Verse 7 could be a reflection of the deliverance of Jerusalem and Judah apart from military action on their own. The balance of probability is that v. 7 is an editorial addition to the account of naming the children as signs of divine judgment. YHWH dealt differently with Judah. Whether it originates with Hosea or one of his disciples, or whether it comes decades after that, is an open question.

8 The birth of the third child, a second son, is yet another means to portray judgment on Israel. That some time had passed between the second and third child is intimated by the terse report that Lo-ruhamah had been weaned before Gomer conceived and bore Lo-ammi. In traditional, preindustrial societies, a child may nurse for two years or longer. Thus for all the brevity of the account, the births of three children likely presuppose the passing of several years.

The name *Lo-ammi* (Not My People) in v. 9 communicates the status of sinful Israel and resulting consequences vis-à-vis YHWH as clearly as does the previous name *Lo-ruhamah* (No Mercy). Indeed, the two names are related; without divine mercy Israel could never remain God's people. Ho-

---

56. For example, Macintosh, *Hosea,* p. 26: "Hosea 1:7 . . . is a Judaean gloss of the seventh century BC." He associates its sentiments with the period immediately following Josiah's reform.

57. See the introductory section II.B, "Written Composition and Outline"; and the excursus at 3:5, "David Their King."

sea's proclamation is designed to show that there is, at least in the historical process, a limit to God's forbearance and thus also to his mercy in response to ingrained evil.

9   Several modern translations render 1:9 differently, presupposing an emendation of *'ānōkî lō'-'ehyeh lākem* ("I will not be yours/for you") to read instead *'ānōkî lō' 'ĕlōhêkem* ("I am not your God").[58] The NASB, NIV, and NRSV all render 1:9b as "for you are not my people and I am not your God." The strength of this rendering is the clarity with which it presents a reversal of the basic covenant formula, "I will be your God and you will be my people," and the related marital formula.[59] Interpreters following the emendation rightly see that the names of the children are signs indicating that Israel stands under judgment for breaking the covenant relationship with YHWH. The weakness is that the emendation itself has no textual basis and is unnecessary. Moreover, the symmetry and paronomasia in the Hebrew text are evident in the juxtaposition of Lo-ammi with Lo-ehyeh.[60] And it is the second symbolic name to be associated with God's self-revelation in the aftermath of deliverance from Egypt (see comments on 1:6 above).

The two names, Lo-ammi and Lo-ehyeh, both cancel a previous relationship. This is their symmetry. On the one hand, Israel is no longer God's people, as had been proclaimed in the Sinai/Horeb covenant, predicated on Israel's response to redemption from Egypt: "If you will keep my covenant *(bĕrîtî)*, then you will be my special possession . . . kingdom of priests . . . holy nation" (Exod. 19:5-6).[61] On the other hand, God had promised to be with Moses in responding to the cries of his people, instructing Moses to tell the people that *I AM* had sent him to them (Exod. 3:14).[62] The verbal form *'ehyeh,* "I am," is a pun on the personal name of God, YHWH, revealed to Moses at the burning bush. As a result of Israel's disobedience God was no

---

58. See *BHS.* For support of the emendation, see C. S. Ehrlich, "The Text of Hosea 1:9," *JBL* 104 (1985) 13-19.

59. For example, see Exod. 6:7; 19:4-6; Lev. 26:12; Jer. 24:7; 31:33; Ezek. 11:20; Zech. 8:8; and Rolf Rendtorff, *The Covenant Formula: An Exegetical and Theological Investigation,* trans. Margaret Kohl (Edinburgh: T & T Clark, 1998). In Rendtorff's judicious treatment, he does not give enough attention to the similarity of formulas of marriage with that for covenant. On this matter, see the introductory section IV.C, "Covenant and Marriage." The declaration "not my people" is not only similar to a divorce formulation, it functions like the reversal or negation of an adoption formula. See Melnyk, "When Israel Was a Child," pp. 256-58.

60. See the excursus below, "Wordplays on Names and Their Reversals in Hosea 1–2 and the New Testament"; and the comments in Andersen and Freedman, *Hosea,* pp. 198-99.

61. See also Exod. 6:7: "I will take you to be my people."

62. Note that in Exod. 3:14 the imperfect verbal form *'ehyeh* functions as a proper noun (i.e., a substitute for YHWH) and is the subject of the verb "to send."

longer "I AM" for them. The Hebrew *lō'-'ehyeh,* Not I AM, cancels the significance of the covenant name YHWH, rendering it null and void with respect to Israel. We might put the reversal language in the context of another polarity, that of presence and absence. Whereas YHWH signified his presence with Moses and the Israelites in the revealing of his name, the change to Not I AM represents his absence from Israel.

Finally, 1:2-9 opens not only the book of Hosea but also the Book of the Twelve, introducing a profound problem with the children of God. The last book in the collection notes in its final verse that Elijah will come to "restore the hearts of the fathers to their children and vice versa" (Mal. 4:6 [MT 3:24]). Thus not only does Hosea itself contain the promise of transformation for the wayward children (below), but it anticipates the other bookend of the Twelve as well.[63]

Excursus: Wordplays on Names and Their Reversals in Hosea 1–2 and the New Testament

The naming of the three children in 1:2-9 comes under the theme "children of harlotry" as introduced in 1:2. Each child (and their mother) represents Israel in its failures to maintain God's covenant standards. The names of the second and third children, Lo-ruhamah and Lo-ammi, contain a sufficiently clear negative connotation. This is not the case, however, with Jezreel, the name of the first child. While there were negative things in historical experience associated with the valley of Jezreel and the city of Jezreel (see comments on 1:4-5), the name itself typically carries a positive agricultural connotation that "God sows." The three names are first used to illustrate Israel's current failures; then, as part of a larger pattern of judgment and redemption in Hos. 1–3, the negative connotations of the names are reversed to represent a future restoration of Israel and Judah as God's people.

1. *Jezreel,* meaning "God sows," is elsewhere the name of a fertile valley and that of a royal city in the valley where blood had been shed. For grammatical and phonetic reasons the name Jezreel is also a play on the national name "Israel." According to 1:4-5, Israel's military strength would be broken in the valley of Jezreel as God judged the ruling house of Jehu. Jeroboam II and Zechariah, the last two rulers from the house of Jehu, were contemporaries of Hosea, but only the former is named in the book.

By way of reversal, 1:11 (MT 2:2) notes somewhat cryptically that great will be the "day of Jezreel." This is likely tantamount to saying that great will be the day of Israel. Similarly, 2:22 (MT 24) has promised agricultural blessings "answering" Jezreel. The repeated verb "to answer" in 2:21-22 (MT 23-24) probably has the connotation of "to respond positively." In 2:23 the Lord will "sow *(zāra')* her in the land." The "her" that is sown in the land could be Gomer, who represents Israel, or perhaps

---

63. See further the comments in Scoralick, *Gottes Güte,* p. 151.

the royal city of Samaria. In any case, the negative connotation initially given to Jezreel, the firstborn of Hosea and Gomer, is reversed with the affirmation of God's future "sowing."

2. *Lo-ruhamah* (No Mercy) is the second child and the one daughter among the three children. According to 1:6, she represents the judgment that the Lord will no longer have mercy on the house of Israel or forgive them. This ominous name and its explanation in 1:6 are a negation of the divine self-identification of God as *merciful and gracious . . . one who forgives iniquity* (cf. Exod. 34:6-7). Her negative name is reversed in 2:1 (MT 3), which depicts Israel as siblings collectively called Ruhamah, "Mercy." A second reversal comes in 2:23 (MT 25), with the declaration that in the future restoration God will show mercy to Lo-ruhamah (No Mercy).

3. *Lo-ammi* (Not My People) is the third child and second son. In 1:9 he represents Israel estranged from the Lord and reckoned as a covenant violator, a negation of the covenant declaration that Israel will be YHWH's people in Exod. 6:7. By way of reversal, in 1:10 (MT 2:1) Israel will become not only God's people (cf. 2:1 [MT 3], Ammi, "My People"), but "children of the living God." This latter term, which occurs only in Hosea, likely functions as a new collective name for the restored people. Similarly, in 2:23 (MT 25) the name Lo-ammi (Not My People) is changed to Ammi (My People).

4. *Lo-ehyeh* (Not I AM) and *YHWH,* the name of Israel's deity, are related "names," at least as presented in Exod. 3:12-15 and in Hos. 1:9. In the context of the revelation of the divine name at the burning bush, Exod. 3:14 preserves a wordplay on the tetragrammaton (= YHWH) that includes a finite verbal form as the subject of a sentence. When asked by Moses what his name is, "God" *('ĕlōhîm)* responds, "I am who I am"[64] *('ehyeh 'ăšer 'ehyeh). . . . You shall say to the Israelites, 'I AM ('ehyeh)* has sent me to you.'" The verbal form "I am/I will be" *('ehyeh)* is used like a proper name and is the subject of the verb "to send." The next verse has the tetragrammaton, YHWH (= Yahweh), as the subject of the same verb "to send," emphasizing that YHWH is the God who "will be" with Moses *and* who is "sending" him (3:12).

Many difficult issues are associated with this text in Exodus and the wordplay on the verb "to be" *(hāyâ/hāwâ)* as an indication of God's personal name. These are best left to another discussion.[65] One can say, however, that Hosea and his readers/hearers knew the wordplay on the verb "to be" and the tetragrammaton. Furthermore, the positive sense of the wordplay in Exod. 3:12, 14-15, is reversed in Hos. 1:9b. YHWH, who is the "I AM" for Israel in Hosea's narrative theology, becomes *Not I AM* for Israel at the historical moment because of the people's failures.

The double wordplay in 1:9b can be set out as follows:

You all are Not My People
  And I am Not I AM *('ehyeh)* for you all.

64. Another possibility is to translate "I will be who I will be."
65. See D. N. Freedman, M. O'Connor, and H. Ringgren, "*YHWH,*" *TDOT* 5:500-521, especially pp. 513-17.

The second person plural "you all" of 1:9b indicates that the audience is either the family of Hosea, whose members represent Israel, or Israel itself. This last clause of the verse is a negation of identities, where the names of both child and God are parallel. Previously in saving history, Israel had been YHWH's people and he, in turn, had been I AM for them as covenant Lord. Now, however, Israel is no longer the people of God as proclaimed in the covenant declaration. And God, in turn, is no longer "I AM" for them.

By way of reversing this negative connotation, Not I Am becomes the "living God" with children in 1:10 (MT 2:1). In 2:23 (MT 25) those children are reckoned as God's people and thus will call out to the Lord "my God."

New Testament Appropriation

Hosea 1:10 (MT 2:1) and 2:23 (MT 25) are employed in the apostolic witness of the NT. As part of his reflections on Israel, divine election, and the place of Gentile believers in Jesus Christ, the apostle Paul cites Hosea as evidence that God has called not only Jews but also Gentiles (Rom. 9:25-26):

> As he says in Hosea, "I will call Not My People, My People; and Not Loved, Beloved." And it shall be in the place where it was said to them, "you all are not my people," there they will be called "sons of the living God."

Verse 25 is an adaptation of Hos. 2:23 (MT 25), and 9:26 is a quotation of Hos. 2:1 LXX (Eng. 1:10). Whereas in Hosea's time both Not My People and My People refer to Israel, Paul also finds in the name Not My People a reflection of the traditional status of Gentiles before the God of Israel. Put another way, Gentiles and disobedient Israel would have the same status: neither was in covenant relationship with God. In God's magnificent reversal of status, the Gentiles (Not My People) are called by grace to be children of God.

Romans 9:27 refers to Isaiah as prophesying that though the number of Israelites be like the sand of the sea, only a remnant would be saved. This is consistent with what Isa. 10:22 states in the MT and in the LXX. The Greek of "number of Israelites be like the sand of the sea" in Rom. 9:27, however, is also word-for-word from Hos. 2:1 LXX (Eng. 1:10). Apparently the "Isaiah" citation in Rom. 9:27 is a mixture of the two texts, serving as evidence for Paul that OT prophecy supports his claim.

In 1 Pet. 2:9-10 the Christian recipients of the letter are defined in terms from the OT. As in Rom. 9:26-27, Hos. 2:23 (MT 25) and 1:10 (MT 2:1) are joined as evidence that the addressees are the people of God and recipients now of God's mercy. It does not seem the case, however, that Rom.

102

9:26-27 and 1 Pet. 2:10 draw on a common formulation. There is too much variation in the Greek rendering of the names from Hosea.[66] On the other hand, it seems likely that the name reversals in Hosea were part of a prior tradition in Jewish Christianity that affirmed God's power and freedom to call and to rename a people for himself. Two different writers appropriate the same textual tradition as scriptural warrant for their claim that Jews and Gentiles alike can be accorded the status of children of God on the basis of what God has accomplished through Jesus the Messiah. And as such, Hosea's name reversals play an important role in early Christianity's defining of its place in God's unfolding revelation.

B. REVERSAL OF THE JUDGMENT AND RESTORATION OF ISRAEL AND JUDAH (1:10–2:1 [MT 2:1-3])

> 1:10 (2:1) *The number of the Israelites shall be like the sand of the sea, which can be neither measured nor numbered. And in the place where it was said to them, "You are not my people," they will be told, "(You are) children of the living God."*
>
> 1:11 (2:2) *The Israelites and the Judeans shall gather themselves together. They shall appoint for themselves a single head and go up from the land because great is the day of Jezreel.*
>
> 2:1 (3) *Speak to your brothers, "Ammi,"[1] and to your sisters, "Ruhamah!"[2]*

The predictions in these three verses regarding Israel and Judah are a reversal of the judgment depicted in 1:2-9, expanded to include Judah in God's future saving restoration. The names of the three children are presupposed. These predictions are part of the pattern of reversals in chs. 1–3 and in the book as a whole, whereby God's historical judgment is reversed in a future act of restoration. The verses are not likely a unity in the sense of constituting a single

---

66. 1 Pet. 2:10   *ou laos, nyn de laos theou,*
                    "Not People, but now People of God."
    Rom. 9:25   *ou laon mou laon mou,*
                    "Not My People, My People."

    1 Pet. 2:10   *hoi ouk eleēmenoi, nyn de eleēthentes,*
                    "Those without mercy, but now they have received mercy."
    Rom. 9:25   *ouk ēgapēmenēn ēgapēmenēn,*
                    "Not Loved, Beloved."

1. The word means "my people."
2. The word means "mercy."

coherent prophetic utterance, but they are joined together because they indicate a common point: the restoration of God's people in the land of promise. The second person plural command to speak in 2:1 (MT 3) is a change from the prophetic announcements in 1:10-11 (MT 2:1-2).[3] For that reason some versions have placed 2:1 with 2:2, since the latter verse also begins with a second person plural command. The positive content of 2:1, however, is best situated with 1:10-11, just as the language of judgment in 2:2 is best understood as the beginning to an indictment that concludes in 2:13. The children of Hosea are to address their broader siblings (YHWH's future restored covenant people) with words indicating divine acceptance.

1:10 (2:1) The countless or measureless *sand of the sea* is a proverbial image of abundance in the OT (Gen. 41:49; Josh. 11:4; Judg. 7:12; 1 Sam. 13:5; 1 Kgs. 4:20). It is also an image associated with God's promised blessing to the covenant people articulated to the ancestors. Abraham and Jacob are promised that their descendants will be like the sand of the sea (Gen. 22:17; 32:12 [MT 13]).[4] Given Hosea's employment of Jacob traditions elsewhere (ch. 12), it may be that this terminology is rooted for him particularly in them. In addition to the phrase *sand of the sea,* which does occur in Gen. 32:12 (MT 13), there is the similar expression in the blessing given to Jacob at Bethel (28:14), where he is told that his descendants would be like the "dust of the earth."

In the days of Solomon, a narrator comments that Israel and Judah were as numerous as the sand of the sea (1 Kgs. 4:20), as if to say that God's promise to the ancestors of land, progeny, and blessing had reached a preliminary and provisional fulfillment. In the prediction of Hos. 1:10 it is likely that both proverbial expression and ancestral promise are in mind. The ancestors would have many descendants constituting both Israel and Judah. But this is not all. Whereas the ancestral promise concerned numerous descendants, this prophecy proclaims that the future Israelites and Judahites would be children of the *living God ('ēl-ḥāy).* This affirmation is at the same time part of the reversal of the declaration that Israelites were "children of harlotry" (1:2) and "not God's people" (1:9). One might say that the phrase *children of the living God,* which occurs only in Hosea, is a corporate reversal of the name Not My People. As a new name for the reconstituted people of God, it continues the family/household metaphor so important to Hosea. The term

3. Throughout the commentary, differences between MT and English versification will usually be noted; but in sections with extensive references to the same verses, repetition of the variations will be minimized.

4. The promise to Abraham in Gen. 22:17 is joined with another proverbial expression of abundance, the multitude of stars in the heavens. See Gen. 15:5; 26:4; Exod. 32:13; Deut. 1:10; 10:22; 1 Chr. 27:23.

living God is used elsewhere and likely contrasts the action of God present in Israel's history with the absence or inattentiveness of other deities. Elijah, for example, mocks the priests of Baal with the suggestion that perhaps Baal is gone or sleeping (1 Kgs. 18:27). The defeat of the Canaanites is explained as confirmation that YHWH is the *living God* (Josh. 3:10).[5] One encounters references to the living God in oaths, whereby God's efficacy to act and bring about a desired end or to judge human failure is assumed.[6]

1:11 (2:2) The prophecy of a restored future is that Israel and Judah shall be one. By Hosea's day the political division between Israel and Judah had lasted for two hundred years. The Niphal verb to describe this reunion is not politically precise: they shall simply *gather themselves* or *be gathered* together. The unity of the people, furthermore, will be symbolized by having *a single head (rō'š 'eḥād)*. Again, that term is not politically precise. It can refer to a tribal leader and is not inappropriate for a king (cf. Job 29:25). A related passage in Hos. 3:5 refers to "David, their king." Either Hosea or an editor indicated by this reference that the future hope of the people of God was with a descendant of David. Such conviction was part of a widespread prophetic hope about the future.

Just what is meant by the phrase that the restored people will *go up from the land* is not clear, especially since the future flourishing of Israel is apparently depicted as taking place in the land of promise. The verb *'ālâ* is often used in a spatial sense to refer to a departure. And when used with Israel as subject, it can refer to the exodus or departing from Egypt (e.g., Hos. 2:15 [MT 17]; 12:13 [MT 14]; Exod. 3:8, 17). Its employment here in 1:11, however, apparently refers to Israel's activity in its land. Note, for example, the formulation that Israel will be called children of the living God "in the place" where they were described as not God's people (1:10). God will "sow her [= Gomer = Israel] in the land" (2:23 [MT 25]). Moreover, Israel's *going up* makes great the *day of Jezreel,* which as either valley or city assumes a geographic setting in Israel. If Jezreel is a synonym for Israel in a collective sense, the same thing applies. It is the flourishing of Israel in its land that is consistently predicted in Hosea. That would be a great day for Jezreel. Thus the meaning "go up from" for the verb *'ālâ,* at least in the sense of "to depart," does not make sense in this context. The verb may be used here in an agricultural sense, however, as in "growing up" or "increasing/flourishing" (Deut. 29:23 [MT 22]), rather than in its

---

5. The other two references to the "living God" (*'ēl ḥāy*) are in Pss. 42:2 (MT 3); 84:2 (MT 3). A similar formulation using the plural (*'ĕlōhîm ḥayyîm*) is also translated as the "living God" (Deut. 5:26; 1 Sam. 17:36).

6. In the oaths one swears "as YHWH lives" (*ḥay-yhwh;* e.g., Ruth 3:13; 1 Sam. 14:39, 45; 19:6). In Num. 14:21 God swears by his own life.

more common geographical sense of departing.[7] A positive agricultural connotation would make good sense in this context. Israel will sprout and flourish in the land. Furthermore, the use of the verb may be yet another Hosean pun. It may well imply a "flourishing" for the people of an exodus-like scale.

The reference to the *day of Jezreel* is a way to reverse the judgment announced in the birth of the first child (1:4). Likely it plays on the positive significance of the name Jezreel ("God sows"), a sense made explicit in the similar formulation of 2:23. Therefore, one might paraphrase slightly 1:11b as follows: "Israel shall come up flourishing from the land, for great will be the day of God's sowing."

2:1 (3)   The command in 2:1 fits with the reversal theme in 1:10-11, but the plural imperative with which the verse begins does not seem integrally connected to the previous two verses. It is likely, therefore, that the positive content of 2:1, and particularly the reversal of two negative names, is the reason for placing the verse here. It may be a fragment of a larger communication not further preserved. The sense of it can be found also in 2:23. The addressees are not otherwise identified, but they are depicted as children (of Hosea and Gomer?) addressing their siblings with a status or name change. *Ammi* (My People) reverses the judgment portrayed in the name of the second son, and *Ruhamah* (Mercy) is the emphatic reversal of the daughter's name. YHWH intends to save, and the voice of siblings crying out "mercy" is an emphatic affirmation that YHWH intends to overcome his people's failures.

C. CHARGE AGAINST THE MOTHER AS A SIGN OF THE CASE AGAINST ISRAEL (2:2-13 [MT 4-25])

The bulk of chapter 2 (vv. 2-23; MT 25) is comprised of two sections or panels, with the portrayal of Hosea's family in promiscuous infidelity in its first part (vv. 2-13), and its promised future restoration in its second part (vv. 14-23; see D below). These two panels are fundamentally a rehearsal of 1:2–2:1 (MT 3),[1] which also portrays in two panels the family in infidelity and in res-

---

7. In Deut. 29:23 (MT 22) the Hebrew verb *'ālâ* is used in conjunction with the verbs *zāra'* ("sow") and *ṣāmaḥ* ("sprout"). The verse compares a cursed land of promise with the way the Lord treated Sodom and Gomorrah, Admah and Zeboiim. Hosea elsewhere demonstrates knowledge of the treatment of Admah and Zeboiim (11:8). In 1:11 (MT 2:2), therefore, the promise that the people will go up from the land may be a reversal of a covenant curse for disobedience and resulting infertility.
1. Since 1:10-11 in English versions are 2:1-2 in MT, English versification in ch. 2

toration. This summary statement about 2:2-23, however, does not begin to do justice to the complexity of the portrayal and the fact that the family members play more than one role in it. Gomer and the children still represent Israel, as Hosea represents the Lord, all in continuation of the symbolism in 1:2-9. But now there are other figures in the depiction. Gomer's illicit lovers also stand for those deities, the Baals, who have seduced Israel and prevailed upon the people to forsake the Lord. The land of Israel, which in the holistic understanding of Hosea is a metonym for the people, is personified and then also represented by nonhuman constituents such as animals and vegetation. The heavens too play a role by responding to their covenant partners, YHWH and the land. Hosea's perspective thus widens to include cosmic dimensions in which the family and people are embedded.

The two-panel portrayal in vv. 2-23 comes in speech and quoted speech, as well as prophecies about the future. It begins with the imperative to state a case or to contend with the mother. The speaker begins in 2:3 to use first-person speech ("I"). On more than one occasion the mother is quoted. The speaker/presenter also describes how other figures will respond to (lit. "answer") one another. What begins as family contention with charges of infidelity concludes with reconciliation and a transformed peaceful realm for the people of God.

Verses 2-13 contain the indictment of faithless Gomer (= Israel) by an angry and anguished Hosea (= YHWH), using the children to address their mother with his words. He describes a scenario based on her past and continuing infidelities and her seeming inability to comprehend the perilousness of her situation. Judgment will come upon her for her adulteries with her lovers (= Canaanite deities).

> 2 (4) *"Contend with your mother! Contend because she is not my wife and I am not her husband; (contend) so that she will put away her harlotry from her countenance and her adulteries from between her breasts.*
>
> 3 (5) *Otherwise, I will strip her naked and render her like the day of her birth, I will make her like the wilderness, I will make her like parched land and kill her with thirst.*
>
> 4 (6) *On her children I will not have mercy because they are children of harlotry.*
>
> 5 (7) *Indeed, she played the harlot with them; she who conceived them has acted shamefully. She said (to herself), 'I will go after my lovers, those who provide my bread, my water, my wool, my flax, my oil, and my drink.'*

varies from MT by two. In many cases in what follows, both numbering systems are noted. Where only one numbering system is given, it indicates the English versification.

6 (8) *For these things, therefore, I am impeding her[2] way with thorns and hedging her in so that she will not find her ways.*

7 (9) *She will pursue her lovers, but not catch up to them; she will seek them, but not find (them). She will say (to herself), 'I will go and return to my first husband because it was better for me then than now.'*

8 (10) *But she does not know that I gave to her the corn, wine, and oil, that I increased her silver — yet they made gold for Baal.*

9 (11) *Thus I will turn and take away my corn in season and wine at his time. I will take away my wool and flax (used) to cover her nakedness.*

10 (12) *Now I will uncover her folly in the eyes of her lovers and no one will deliver her from my hand.*

11 (13) *I will bring an end to her celebration, her festivals, new moons, Sabbaths, and appointed days.*

12 (14) *I will destroy her vines and figs, those of which she said, 'They are my payment that my lovers have given to me.' But I will make them a forest and the wild animals will eat them.*

13 (15) *I will bring upon her the days of the Baals when she burned incense to them, adorned herself with ring and jewelry, and went after her lovers. Me, however, she forgot," says YHWH.*

2 (4) The verb *rîb*, translated as *Contend* here, typically refers to contentions and struggles that surface in the public arena, where the issue of right and wrong is to be adjudicated in one way or another, rather than to private disagreements and rebukes. When employed as a noun it can mean "quarrel" or "struggle" (Gen. 13:7) and refer also to a legal dispute or something akin to a lawsuit (Exod. 23:2-3, 6; Deut. 17:8; 21:5). As a verb it can even depict a physical struggle, perhaps based on a disagreement (Exod. 21:18), or an argument based on a dispute (Num. 20:3; cf. Hos. 4:4). Both noun and verb are associated with representing the cause of widows who otherwise lack protectors and advocates (Isa. 1:17, 23). In the prophets God contends with the failures of his people by charging or indicting them with wrongdoing (Isa. 3:13; Jer. 2:9; Mic. 6:1-2). It is thus a term that fits with the prophetic task. Elsewhere Hosea preserves similar usage (4:1; 12:2 [MT 3]).

What the children do in contending with their mother is to charge her with a breach of family integrity, namely infidelity to her husband, their father. Why the children are employed in this role is not known. Perhaps it is part of a shaming mechanism, whereby members of a family represent its honor and the offender is humiliated by those closest to him or her. They rep-

2. Following the Greek and Syriac. Hebrew has "your" (fem. sing.).

resent "Israel" indicting Israel, and so the shaming mechanism may be a twice-wounding. It is also the case that the children represent the unfaithfulness with which their mother is charged, and there is something to be said for self-interest. Her condemnation would adversely affect them just as her restoration would impinge on their own restoration.

The assertion that follows — *she is not my wife and I am not her husband* — puts the status of the marital bond into illocutionary speech. Gomer's harlotry has severed the marital bond in practice, but it is unclear whether such a declaration also indicates a divorce in legal terms.[3] The declaration in 2:2 is similar to those in divorce documents from the ancient Near East, which either state that a man and woman are no longer married, or represent the status of divorce and reasons for it.[4] It is, furthermore, formally like the declaration in 1:9b, where the third child is named Lo-ammi (Not My People) "because you (all) are not my people." One might put the difficult question of legal status as follows: The marriage is broken de facto; has it also been severed de jure? On the basis of what follows (which is all we have to go on), it seems that for a time Hosea still engages Gomer in the hope that she can be convinced of the error of her ways. Again, the parallel with the naming of the children may be helpful. Hosea names a child Lo-ruhamah (No Mercy) or Lo-ammi (Not My People) to indicate that Israel has broken the covenant with the Lord, although apparently during this same time he continues to live with Gomer, just as Israel remains in its land and with a king for some years even as it continued in its dereliction of covenant responsibilities. Correspondingly, it seems that the children charge Gomer with adultery and declare certain consequences, even though a formal divorce has not been enacted. Having said this, one cannot be sure about the legal status of the marriage. If there was no divorce, Gomer's infidelities seemingly resulted in one or more (enforced) separations from Hosea.[5]

We should acknowledge that we know too little about the mechanisms of divorce in ancient Israel and the subsequent status of the parties to conclude confidently that Gomer and Hosea were not divorced. One might expect, for example, mention of a certificate of divorce (Deut. 24:1) since it plays a role in other prophetic adaptations of the marriage metaphor (Jer. 3:8;

---

3. For the view that 2:2 (MT 4) reflects an actual divorce between Hosea and Gomer, see Wolff, *Hosea*, pp. 32, 33.

4. See the introduction, section IV.C, "Covenant and Marriage."

5. Andersen and Freedman, *Hosea*, p. 222, put it this way: "From the wife's side (Israel's) the relationship was severed; from Hosea's (Yahweh's) it was not. In 2:4-25 the woman is treated as not his wife in practice and yet still his wife in principle. . . . It is as a husband who still has claims on his wife that he applies the various disciplines and makes the appeals."

Isa. 50:1). Presumably these functioned to provide proper evidence that the two parties were divorced, to quell potential legal charges that might otherwise arise between the two parties and their families, and to allow the former wife to remarry. Also, there are no citizens called as witnesses, no legal setting (court) or judge is mentioned, and no sanctions are carried out against Gomer by the community. Adultery, which could occasion divorce, was a capital crime (Lev. 20:10; Deut. 22:22), and public charges of adultery would almost certainly involve community sanctions in one form or another. We should not, however, suppose that infidelity, once proven, led automatically to execution. The conversations in Hos. 2:2-13 are all from the family sphere with the exception of the concluding phrase of v. 13 ("says YHWH"). This setting may mean that the matter is being kept confidential, except among the family. In any case, the family is where we see the sad drama of failure being carried out.

The goal of the children's contention is that Gomer put away the signs of her infidelity. Both harlotry and adultery describe her activities, which are symbolized with *her countenance* and *between her breasts*. The language of *putting things away* has suggested to some that jewelry, clothing, perfume, or something tangible is in mind (cf. 2:13). In the harlotry motif elsewhere, there are references to the "forehead of a harlot" (Jer. 3:3) and to details of physical appearance intended to attract lovers (Jer. 4:30). Perhaps jewelry or ornaments depicted fertility rituals and devotion to the cults of the Baals, or cultural markers in dress and appearance denoted a harlot. Apart from more explicit evidence, it is probably better to see the phrase as metaphorical, commanding Gomer to put aside all things that prompt or feed her infidelities.

3 (5) Here I translate the Hebrew particle *pen* as *Otherwise;* it is often translated as "lest." The judgments of stripping, making her like the wilderness or parched land, and killing her with thirst are the negative reinforcements of the children's contention with her. They are to engage their mother strenuously by first stating her dire situation — she is no longer the wife of Hosea — in the hope that she will put away the various inducements to her infidelities. The particle *pen* introduces the consequences of not responding positively to the contention of the children. The last phrase, *kill her with thirst,* is the final step of the judgment process. Without mitigation, nakedness and dehydration in an arid wilderness would lead to death.

The sequence of acts in 2:3 is the threatened response to continued failure. Should we understand the first act, *stripping,* as a judgment that could be literally carried out by the husband or the elders/judges in a community, forcing the disgraced wife to leave behind the clothing provided her by her husband (cf. Exod. 21:10) and thus shaming her? Possibly stripping was a judgment on an adulteress that was sanctioned by the community

110

upon proven guilt, or even part of a divorce ceremony in certain instances.[6] But proceeding to a public execution is not what the comparison to wilderness and parched land entails, even if *dying of thirst* is the conclusion to the sequence in 2:3. We are better off seeing the sequence in 2:3 as moving quickly from the person of Gomer to the portrayal of (the land of) Israel. Instead of the fruitfulness that results from God's sowing, the land of Israel will be like the wilderness, the forest (2:12), or the desert, none of which is sown.

The best parallels to the stripping and resulting nakedness elsewhere in the OT are in Ezekiel's involved symbolism of God's marriage to Jerusalem and Samaria (Ezek. 16:1-59; 23:1-49).[7] In the harsh judgment against Jerusalem for adultery and bloodshed, she will be given into the hands of those who will mistreat her (16:38-39). Historically these would be the Babylonians or others who wreaked havoc on Jerusalem.[8] Their assault is symbolized in the acts of "stripping" *(pāšaṭ)* Jerusalem naked and taking her jewelry (so also 23:26). Stripping people, naked or otherwise, is a charge against unscrupulous people (Mic. 2:8; Job 22:6; 24:7-10), perhaps reflecting the practice of taking garments in pledge (Exod. 22:26-27). Thus the stripping of Gomer is likely a metaphor for the humiliating punishment that Israel will suffer in the historical process rather than her literally being forced naked from the home.[9]

4 (6) The transition from the children as speakers to the children as objects of a declarative judgment is abrupt. The role of the children in contending with their mother is a literary device, and after the initial command in 2:2, that role fades into the background. The voice of the text is apparently that of Hosea, but the portrayal is also that of the prophet speaking for God and against Israel. That both children and mother represent Israel, roles clearly presented in 1:2–2:1, emerges again as the root metaphor of family/household momentarily takes center stage. Even as Gomer moves quickly to the foreground in what immediately follows, the family as metaphorical vehicle is still in mind. This will become clear in the way that ch. 2 concludes.

At one level, there is nothing new in v. 4. Hosea's daughter was named Lo-ruhamah (No Mercy) in order to make the point that faithless Israel is no longer the recipient of God's mercy. The attribution *children of harlotry* is synonymous with the opening command in 1:2 to have *children of harlotry.*

6. For evidence of the former in the ancient Near East, see the discussion in P. Kruger, "Israel, the Harlot," *JNSL* 11 (1987) 111-12. The latter proposal is from Wolff, *Hosea,* p. 34.

7. See the comments on nakedness in 2:9 below.

8. NASB and NIV have those who abuse Jerusalem as "your lovers." That is an inference from the context, not a rendering of the Hebrew text.

9. Isaiah's nakedness was a sign-act to symbolize defeat and exile in Isa. 20:1-5.

The offending term *harlotry* is the same *(zĕnûnîm)* in both, and there is no appreciable difference between *bānîm* here in 2:4 and *yĕlādîm* in 1:2.

5 (7) Gomer's actions as harlot come again to the foreground. She involved her children in her activities, since the metaphor of harlotry includes the children (1:2; 2:4). She and the children represent Israel as members of YHWH's faithless household. As mother, Gomer may also represent Samaria, since elsewhere in prophetic symbolism the capital city is portrayed as the mother of the people (Isa. 51:18; 54:1, 13; 66:7). The land too can play this role; its fruitfulness can be understood in terms of producing offspring (Isa. 62:4; cf. Hos. 1:2). For both entities, it is the combination of grammatical gender (city and land are female) and culturally rooted poetry.[10] Thus the antecedent of *them* in the description of "Gomer's" harlotry goes back to the children mentioned at the end of the previous verse. Gomer as representative has acted shamefully in involving her offspring in her activities. This does not mean that the children were objects of her harlotry, but rather that they are coparticipants.

On two occasions in 2:2-13, Gomer is represented as *speaking* (*'āmar;* 2:5, 7). This is likely comparable to such modern expressions as "she thought to herself" or "she said to herself." Classical Hebrew does not preserve a ready-made expression for "so-and-so thought." Action is the key to intention, and speaking is a primary indication of a point of view. It should be stressed that it is the prophet who presents Gomer in this light. We have no other access to Gomer's (or the children's) point of view. In this instance she intends to go after her lovers. The metaphor of "going/walking after" *(hālak 'aḥărê)* can be used in several senses, including that of religious devotion (e.g., Judg. 2:12, 17) or a man going after a prostitute (Prov. 7:22).

Gomer's partners in harlotry are now mentioned explicitly. They are her *lovers.* The Piel participle *(mĕ'ahăbîm)* is used four more times in this context (2:7, 10, 12, 13). These lovers are Canaanite deities *(ba'ălîm)* mentioned in 2:13, to whom Gomer wrongly attributes the commodities listed in 2:5, 8, 12. These goods are things the lovers *provided* or "gave" *(nātan)* her, just as paramours give payment for sexual favors rendered. Perhaps, however, we should not think of Gomer's (= Israel's) lovers as only Canaanite deities. Elsewhere, international suitors such as Egypt or Assyria, who make offers for Israel's allegiance, are objects of illicit love and were thus opposed by the prophet.[11]

---

10. On the comparison between wives and fertile land in the Ancient Near East, see the comments in Andersen and Freedman, *Hosea,* p. 288.

11. See appendix 4, "Love in the Prophecy of Hosea." In international suzerainty treaties, whose structural elements are similar to the Mosaic or Sinai covenant, "love" in the sense of devotion is expected of those bound by oath. See W. L. Moran, "The Ancient Near Eastern Background of the Love of God in Deuteronomy," *CBQ* 25 (1963) 77-87.

The lovers are those who gave her life-sustaining commodities, those things that a cultivated land blessed by the divine world can produce for its inhabitants. This implies that the "lovers" here are the Baals of the Canaanite world. Other and similar commodities are listed in the immediate context.

2:5	2:8	2:9	2:22
bread	grain	grain	grain
water	wine	wine	wine
wool	oil	wool	oil
flax	silver	silver	
oil	gold		

What Gomer thinks of as the payoff for her affections (the commodities) are actually gifts from her husband, as 2:8 makes clear. Here is a strong indication that the concern for fertility and blessing is not itself wayward — her error is only the means by which she pursued them and the deities to whom she wrongly attributed them.

6 (8)   The negative consequences of Gomer's following after or pursuing her lovers are behind the limiting actions taken by the husband. Since the imagery are intended to describe God's constricting or *impeding* of Israel, it is difficult to know what in the description, if anything directly, pertains to Hosea's actions toward Gomer. Indeed, the imagery is symbolism for God's frustrating of Israel in its attempts to secure itself through worship of other deities and perhaps foreign alliances.[12] These two efforts may be interrelated or simply different steps taken by faithless Israel.

The image of *hedging with thorns* in v. 6 is graphic and suggestive, but does not translate easily to readers at a cultural distance. It could be an animal husbandry metaphor, with the hedge of thorns as the vehicle or source domain to represent the tenor or target domain, which was divine constriction or limitation on Israel. Another possibility is that the imagery is an analogy with the siege of a city, such as occurred when Shalmaneser V came up against Samaria. Similar imagery is also used for the individual who laments God's judgments and limitations in the pathetic fall of Jerusalem to the Babylonians (Lam. 3:7-9).

7 (9)   Gomer's pursuit of her lovers will not bear the success she desires; therefore, she considers another option to attain security for herself: a return to a previous husband. In interpreting v. 7, we are better off concentrating from the outset on the relationship between Israel and God rather than seeking clues to the sequence of events in the marriage of Gomer and Hosea. The prophet confronts Israel through the symbolic depiction of a wayward

12. See P. Kruger, " 'I will hedge her way with thornbushes' (Hosea 2,8): Another Example of Literary Multiplicity?" *BZ* 43 (1999) 92-99.

spouse who now finds that she has very limited options. What she thought was a better arrangement, namely dependence upon her lovers, has proven illusory. There are no overt indications of remorse or repentance, only that a return to her first husband would be *better.* Such reasoning may also imply that Israel believed that her *first husband* (YHWH) had previously done a substandard job of supporting his own. Perhaps Israel's move into polytheism (and the related field of international diplomacy?) was based on the logic of safety in numbers or hedging one's bets.

If there are real-life elements in this portrayal of the relationship between Gomer and Hosea, particularly if there was a divorce because of her adultery, then one might see her impulse to return to her first husband as a hoped-for reunion (remarriage?) between them. The surviving evidence in the OT suggests that a remarriage would be illegal. Deuteronomy 24:1-4 states that when a man and woman divorce, if she then marries another man, remarriage to her first husband is not permissible, even if her second husband has died and she is otherwise not married. Jeremiah seems to depend on this reasoning in applying the marriage and covenant metaphor to Judah in 3:1: "If a man divorces his wife and she departs from him and becomes the wife of another, can he [= first husband] return to her? Will not the land be polluted? Yet you[13] have played the harlot with many companions, and you would return to me? Utterance of YHWH." Jeremiah's rhetorical question has the man "returning" to the former wife, whereas Deut. 24:4 states that the man is not permitted to take her again for a wife. The presumed answer to Jeremiah's rhetorical question is no, he may not marry the woman again. The second and related rhetorical question is whether the land is polluted. The answer to that question is apparently yes. It is instructive for interpreters of Hosea to see how quickly the subject at hand in Jeremiah went from wife to land. In terms of fertility both are entities that are "sown" in the hope of producing offspring. Offspring and family identity depend on clear lines of relationship, which in turn depends on exclusivity of use.

There is always the danger of pressing the details of symbolic expression too far. Thus it is probably safer not to insist that Gomer's response to frustration *(I will return to my first husband)* presupposes a prior divorce and suggests remarriage as mitigation of her problems. If indeed this is the sense of her expression, then it may be evidence of a certain naivete or misplaced musing on her part, a hope in spite of societal strictures against remarriage.[14]

---

13. The "you" is fem. sing.; it may refer to Jerusalem in her role as capital city and representative of Judah, or to Judah as a state. If the latter, it would be a rare instance in which a masculine entity is addressed directly as a female. In 3:6 Israel is addressed as a faithless female.

14. The line of interpretation proposed by Hornsby, "Israel Has Become a Worthless Thing," is significantly different. She understands Gomer's harlotry to be that of com-

Should it be the case that she is married to Hosea de jure, but de facto estranged and formally separated from him, then a return to him (= her first husband) would still be unlikely to succeed in reconciliation.

Thus Israel is in a bad way. After seeking security through polytheism and international deals, a return to YHWH and covenant fidelity seems like a quick fix. Once a marriage or covenant had been violated, however, there were no means to restore it from the violator's side. Indeed, it would be an exceptional move from the side of the one offended to restore the prior relationship. It is, nevertheless, part of the fundamental message of the book as a whole that such matters can be healed from the side of the offended, if that party is YHWH. But it will be a painful process all the way around.

8 (10)   The husband's sad response is at the same time a pitiful evaluation of the wife's depth of understanding and sincerity. What prosperity Israel had experienced was a gift from YHWH, the covenant Lord, but that had been and continued to be overlooked or unappreciated. The commodities of agriculture and precious metals reflect materials already named in context. Gomer has receded into the background and Israel has moved to the foreground. The concluding comment sits awkwardly at the end of the verse, as if it is an editorial addition or an impromptu remark. Gold, along with silver, was a precious commodity used for jewelry and a measure for exchanging goods and services. The comment that *yet they made [or used] gold for Baal* explicitly moves the portrayal from Gomer to Israel. The other plural antecedents in the context would be the children, who like their mother represent Israel, or the *lovers* pursued by Gomer. The last-named are unlikely as subjects of the verb. That Israel had used gold for Baal as an act of devotion, or even constructed figures of the deity in gold, reflects the belief that Baal had provided for the Israelites (so 2:5).[15]

9 (11)   The initial verb in v. 9 catches up Gomer's thought that she would go and return *(šûb)* to her first husband. The husband, recognizing the shallowness of Gomer's supposition, opts to turn *(šûb)* and take back things that he, not the lovers, had provided. The symbolism of spousal provisions is maintained by reference to the materials for clothing that cover the wife.

In terms of a sequential reading of 2:2-13, this verse begins the por-

---

mercial prostitution. Hosea and Gomer are related by sexual transaction, but not as husband and wife. Thus when she avers, "I will return to my first *ʾîš*," she means "man" as client, not man as "husband." This interpretation bypasses completely the difficulty of Hosea and Gomer's marriage, and whether or not they divorced or simply separated. As a persuasive interpretation it breaks down, however, because the terminology of marriage and covenant is explicit in 2:14-23 and is almost certainly presupposed in chs. 1–3. One reads against the grain of the portrayal in chs. 1–3 if Hosea and Gomer were not married. Having said that, it is possible (but quite unlikely) that in an attempt to formulate a literary simile, an editor has fabricated a marriage for the two where none formally existed.

15. See appendix 1, "Baal in Hosea."

trayal of judgment that is to emerge from the present circumstances and continue into the future. Part of the portrayal in 2:2-13 has been a sketch of the recent past, using the metaphor of Hosea and Gomer's marriage to signify ongoing difficulties in the relationship between Israel and YHWH. From this point on the consequences of Israel's defection loom larger and more ominous, and the figure of Gomer recedes even more behind the figure of Israel.

Reference to Gomer's *nakedness* in v. 9 is a metaphorical way to get at Israel's shame in forsaking YHWH. She has been indicted already in the context for acting shamefully (2:5). The polarities of shame and honor were central to ancient Israel, as they would have been among their neighbors, though they are less so in modern Western societies. In taking note of this distinction, modern readers should also be wary of interpreting the language of nakedness in psychological terms, especially in a Freudian sense. Nakedness is much more titillating than shameful in modern society, hence the popularity of revealing clothes and the appeal of nudity in pornography. Nakedness could have its erotic side in antiquity as well, but in Semitic society public displays of it were considered shameful (as is still the case in Orthodox Judaism and Islamic society). God's judgment on Israel will expose the people shamefully to observers.

Just how God would remove or take away the means of sustenance listed in 2:9 is not made clear. The covenant curses in Deuteronomy and Leviticus indicate that God's people will not prosper in disobedience (Deut. 28:1-68; Lev. 26:14-39). Prominent among the curses is the barrenness of the land, whether from disease or drought. Defeat by an enemy and exile from the land are other consequences of violating God's covenant statutes. The interplay between historical judgment and agricultural failure may be behind the judgmental language here in Hosea.

10 (12) The theme of exposing shame and folly continues. One of the most somber comments in the book comes in the declaration that no one can rescue the exposed Gomer from her sad state. Israel is under the judgment of YHWH. It is an instinctive reaction among virtually all societies to assist someone physically compromised and publically humiliated. Gomer's uncovering would be a painful thing and evoke a visceral reaction, whatever treatment of Israel is being signified by it. In context the symbolism of the portrayal suggests that Gomer had previously been uncovered in the sight of her lovers, but this time her exposure is for judgment rather than pleasure or commerce. We may find in her a play on the illicit trade of harlotry.

The word rendered *folly, nablût,* occurs only here in the OT and translations of it vary.[16] The term *nābāl,* whence *nablût* most likely derives, means

16. S. Olyan, "'In the Sight of Her Lovers': On the Interpretation of *nablūt* in Hos. 2,12," *BZ* 36 (1992) 255-61.

"fool/foolish." At its most basic it means to act inappropriately in a setting where wisdom and tradition provide guidance for proper behavior. The noun *nĕbālâ* refers to something foolish, which may be sexual in nature (Gen. 34:7; Deut. 22:21; Judg. 19:23; 2 Sam. 13:12), but the term is not limited to that. Translations that render *nablût* as "lewdness" do so because of the context, and perhaps because of the verb *uncover (gālâ)*.[17] In any case, Gomer's exposure is a public one with shameful consequences, indeed, life-threatening ones.

11 (13)   We might paraphrase the judgment here as bringing an end to Israel's cultic calendar and the collective identity it represents. The individual Gomer would not have festivals and Sabbaths; they are activities of the people. She would, however, participate in them. The terminology for cultic observance is general and can represent those practices that are national (i.e., state supported) and those of a popular, ethnic nature. One cannot tell, however, from the list whether the festivals include such things as Passover or Firstfruits; whether the Sabbaths are a once-a-week cessation of normal activities; or the extent to which this general list combines Yahwistic and non-Yahwistic rites. As part of the portrayal of judgment in 2:9-13, there are references to Gomer's *lovers* and to the *days of the Baals,* so it is very likely that the cultic celebrations include Yahwistic (baalized?) and other Canaanite rites.

The verb *hišbattî, "bring an end to,"* more literally means "cause to cease." It is the same verb used in 1:4 to announce the end of the rule of the house of Israel. Other prophets use the verb in representing first-person divine speech, where God declares an end to something, usually in the form of judgment upon iniquity, pride, or, as with 2:11, public celebration (cf. Isa. 13:11; Jer. 48:35; Ezek. 7:24; 23:27, 48). A parallel is found in Jer. 7:34, which comes at the end of the diatribe against the temple cult in Jerusalem: "From the cities of Judah and the streets of Jerusalem I will bring an end to the voice of gladness and joy, the voice of the groom and the bride, for the land will become a ruin." In this expression one finds public celebration, reference to people and capital city, and the ruin of the land, all of which are also part of Hosea's criticism of Israel.

12 (14)   Cultic practices associated with fertility had as their goal the increase of crops and flocks. The Canaanite deities, the Baals, were considered the masters of the fertility cycle, and in Israel's mind had provided them with needed produce. In 2:12 the produce of the land is represented more specifically as the *payment* from Gomer's *lovers.* Here the metaphor in the foreground is not marriage and covenant, but prostitution and payment. The term rendered *payment ('etnâ)* is unique, but it is almost certainly a variant of

17. So NASB and NIV. NRSV has "shame." The LXX has *akatharsia*, something unclean and immodest. A related Hebrew noun, *nĕbēlâ*, means "corpse." See Lev. 5:2.

the term *'etnan,* which is specifically the hire of a prostitute and is also used in Hos. 9:1.[18] Perhaps the variant form here in 2:12 is for assonance with the other words in context ending in *-â.*

The judgment is that the inhabited and cultivated land will become forest and the habitation of wild animals. This reversion of inhabited land to forest and wild animals is an image shared with other prophets and the curses of covenant disobedience in Leviticus (26:6, 22). Micah, for example, envisions Jerusalem as a heap of ruins and the Temple Mount a forest (3:12; cf. Jer. 26:18).[19] Amos depicts the roar of a lion in the forest as the announcement that the animal has found prey (3:4). In the postjudgment reconciliation, land and animals are brought back into harmony with the larger environment and the human community (Hos. 2:18).

13 (15) In v. 13 the identity between lovers and the Baals is made explicit. The language of *bringing upon* is that of judgment. It is not the festivals per se of Baalism that are to be visited upon Israel, but the consequences of involvement with them. Burning incense is cultic worship, here directed to the Baals. The verb *qāṭar* means to "burn on the altar with smoke" (Lev. 1:9, 13, 15, 17). Incense can be used to create smoke and a soothing aroma in the place of seared flesh and spilled blood, and smaller altars in the broader Iron Age culture were used solely for the burning of incense. The verb *qāṭar* in the Hiphil can be used for worship directed to YHWH (1 Kgs. 9:25) or to other deities (1 Kgs. 11:8). It also is used in the Piel with little or no difference in meaning. The two other uses of the verb in Hosea are in Piel and refer to the worship of other deities (4:13; 11:2). Jeremiah uses similar vocabulary to refer a number of times to sacrifices offered to Baal and other deities.[20]

The description of Gomer in v. 13 returns to the theme of her appearance. To honor the days of the Baals, she put on fine jewelry. The particulars are a sign of her devotion to them. In all of this description the theme in the foreground is Israel's worship of Canaanite deities.

The extended description of Israel's judgment to come concludes with the declaration that Gomer (= Israel) had *forgotten* YHWH. It seems awkward to have the claim underscored by the concluding phrase *says YHWH.* Perhaps this is an editorial comment designed to emphasize that just as Gomer really represents Israel, so Hosea represents YHWH. The dalliances with the Baals are a rejection of the covenant Lord.

---

18. Deut. 23:18; Isa. 23:18; Ezek. 16:31, 34, 41.

19. In Jer. 12:8 God complains that his inheritance *(naḥălâ)* is like a lion in the forest, and that she roars against him. This is another image of God's people personified as female.

20. Jer. 7:9; 11:12-13, 17; 19:4, 13; 32:29; eleven occurrences in ch. 44. All of these references are *qāṭar* in the Piel.

To *forget (šākah)* God is not the failure to remember, in the modern sense of the term. For example, Israel would not be in danger of forgetting God's name. Forgetting has the sense of not bringing into conscious thought and thus not allowing something to shape a response. The worship of the Baals had focused Israel's attention on them. In 2:17 the Lord declares that the names of the Baals shall no longer be invoked, using a verb associated with remembering *(zākar)*. YHWH, perhaps, was more and more overlooked or ignored in public rites and thus in public life. His name was less *remembered* and *invoked*. A telling sign of a broken relationship would be when YHWH's name is not invoked, but that of the Baals.

A divine complaint regarding Judah and Jerusalem in Jer. 18:15 may well reflect Hos. 2:13: "My people have forgotten me; they burn incense to worthlessness."

The metaphorical portrayal of Gomer and the children in 2:2-13 is primarily an indictment of Israel. The frustration and anger of Hosea represent a spurned YHWH, whose competency as head of the household has been spurned. It is the rejection of family members, who have gone elsewhere for affection and security. It is not clear from the description that the wayward members of the household can be shamed or brought to their senses. That will not stop YHWH from trying.

D. REVERSAL OF THE JUDGMENT AGAINST ISRAEL AND ITS TRANSFORMATION (2:14-23 [MT 16-25])

The second half of ch. 2 reverses the language of judgment in 2:2-13. It begins with a connecting particle *(lākēn)*, joining the new beginning proposed by YHWH to the uncovering of Israel's awful circumstances portrayed earlier in the chapter. One could translate *lākēn* as "therefore" or "thus," and in doing so would demonstrate the surprise of God's freedom in moving toward forgiveness and new life for the people in spite of their failures. Instead of "Israel has transgressed, therefore, I will punish them," the logic of the link is "Israel has transgressed, *even so,* I will. . . ." Where there was prostitution, adultery, and a kind of naive heedlessness, even so, or nevertheless, these things will be overcome with a renewed courtship, fidelity, betrothal, and covenant. Just as the judgmental language of 1:2-9 is followed by the promise of restoration in 1:10–2:1, so here the promised restoration of 2:14-23 follows the judgmental language of 2:2-13.

In addition to continuing the family/household metaphor established in 1:2–2:13, the second half of the chapter also draws upon a grand typology whereby the significance of Israel's earlier history, namely the exodus from Egypt, wilderness wandering, and settlement in the land of promise, gives structure to the depiction of betrothal and (re)marriage between YHWH and Israel. The link between metaphor and typology in these verses is the equation between marriage and covenant. Metaphor and typology are not just literary devices, but reveal a synthetic conceptual framework to Hosea's way of connecting Israel's history and identity with their divine Lord. Not only is it a grand typological schema, employing the events of saving history to portray a people once again redeemed and joined to YHWH; the expanse of the renewal is also grand, whereby the land and nonhuman inhabitants are part of the transformation to come.

14 (16) *Even so I will woo her and bring her to the wilderness and speak to her heart.*

15 (17) *From there I will give her vineyards to her, and the Valley of Achor[1] will be the Door of Hope. From there she will respond like the days of her youth, like the day when she came up from the land of Egypt.*

16 (18) *It will happen in that day, declares YHWH, that you will call me "my husband," and you will no longer call me "my Baal."*

17 (19) *For I will remove the names of the Baals from her mouth, so that they will no longer be invoked by their names.*

18 (20) *In that day I will make a covenant with the animals of the field, the birds of the sky, and the crawling things on the ground. I will remove the bow, sword, and warfare from the land and cause them[2] to dwell in security.*

19 (21) *I will take you in marriage for myself forever; I will take you in marriage for myself by means of righteousness, justice, devoted loyalty, and compassion.*

20 (22) *And I will take you in marriage by giving faithfulness, and you will know YHWH.*

21 (23) *It will happen in that day that I will respond, declares YHWH; I will respond to the heavens, and they shall respond to the land;*

22 (24) *and the land shall respond to the grain, the new wine, and the oil; and they shall respond to Jezreel.*

23 (25) *And I will sow her for myself in the land, and have mercy on*

1. The word means "trouble."
2. The antecedent of "them" is not certain and some translations vary as a result, e.g., NIV: "so that all may lie down in safety"; NRSV: "I will make you lie down in safety." In the immediate context of 2:18, it would seem that "they" are the animals mentioned elsewhere in the verse. Their security comes with the removal of warfare and its implements. From the broader context, "they" can refer to the children (= Israelites).

Lo-ruhamah;[3] I will say to Lo-ammi,[4] "You are my people," and he will say, "My God."

14 (16)   YHWH speaks to Israel in v. 14. Gomer has receded far into the background, and all that remains are the feminine pronouns. *Woo* (Piel of *pātâ*) can also be translated "seduce," "entice," or "court" in those contexts where a man or woman attempts to persuade a member of the opposite sex of their interest in or affection for them.[5] The verb is used in contexts both negative and positive, depending on the circumstances at hand. In the metaphor of remarriage and renewed covenant, God will *woo* Israel and *speak to her heart.*[6] This is not the depiction of a self-centered seduction, but a whole-hearted appeal based on personal commitment.

There is metaphorical geography in this verse associated with God's appeal to Israel. He will bring the people to the *wilderness.* In 2:3 the *wilderness (midbār)* has already been mentioned in a threat to "Gomer" to make her like *(kĕ)* the wilderness, an arid and difficult area to cultivate. But in the reversal of Israel's state of judgment in 2:14, the wilderness plays yet another role. It is the area where Moses mediated God's covenant to Israel and where God sustained Israel for years before bringing them to the land of promise. Hosea is not alone among his prophetic contemporaries in drawing upon an epic of national birth and early sustenance, but he is first among them in the number and range of his allusions.[7] And with his reference to the wilderness, he is not finished with the marriage/covenant metaphor. As the place of covenant making and divine guidance, where Israel needed to depend totally on the covenant Lord, the wilderness is also the place of marital beginnings. *Wooing* Israel, *speaking to her heart,* and *bringing her to the wilderness* are ways to reprise the national identity as a second bridal period.

Jeremiah also draws on the wilderness bridal metaphor in what is literarily his opening address to Jerusalem (2:2). In doing so he is very likely dependent on Hosea: "I remember the devotion *(ḥesed)* of your youth, your bridal love, your following *(hālak 'aḥăray)* me in the wilderness *(midbār),* in a land not sown *(zāra')."*

---

3. The words mean "no mercy."

4. The words mean "not my people."

5. Exod. 22:16 (MT 15; man to woman); Judg. 14:15 and 16:5 (wife to husband); Job 31:9, 27 (Niphal and Qal; woman to man). Jeremiah accuses God of persuading him to act in ways detrimental to his well-being (20:7).

6. For this phrase, which is an appeal to the rational faculties and the will of a person (= heart) based on the personal commitments of the speaker, see Gen. 50:21; Ruth 2:13; Isa. 40:2.

7. Hos. 1:11 (MT 2:2) perhaps; 9:10; 11:1; 12:9, 13 (MT 10, 14); 13:4-5; Amos 2:10; 9:7; Mic. 6:4-5.

Readers should be wary of two things in reading these comparisons of the wilderness to a bridal or honeymoon period. One is a kind of Western romanticism, an idealistically naive view of the desert as a solitary place of purity, where Israel originally developed its monotheism, only to lose it in the corruptions of Canaan. Neither the wilderness nor the desert proper is inherently more pure than the land of Canaan. The second matter is to beware of thinking that the traditions of Israel's wilderness period known to Hosea (or say Amos or Jeremiah) were all positive, as distinct from the pentateuchal narratives, which preserve several accounts of Israel's failures. If one includes the apostasy at Baal-peor as part of the wilderness tradition, then clearly Hosea does not think of the period as uniformly positive (9:10). It is the intimacy and ardor of the covenant initiation and the subsequent dependence upon God that are in the foreground of the wilderness simile.[8]

15 (17) Verse 15 reflects the simile of Israel in the wilderness, poised once again to enter the promised land. The *days of her youth* hark back (as in Jer. 2:2) to the period of Israel's birth in the wilderness in conjunction with the *day when she came up from the land of Egypt*.[9] Past saving history shapes typologically the blessing and transformation to come. And in this projection of future bliss, the prophet exercises his penchant for symbolic names taken from the national epic. *The Valley of Achor* is likely one of the rugged narrow entrances into the central hill country from the Jordan Valley (the corridor from Jericho through Ai to Bethel?).[10] It is the location of the execution of Achan after the defeat at the battle of Ai (Josh. 7:24-26), where the term "trouble" *('ākôr)* is a reminder of the trouble occasioned by his disobedience of the Lord's commands.[11] Now, in the recapitulation of the entrance into the promised land, the name is reversed and will be known as the *Door of Hope,* a name otherwise unknown. The term for "hope" is understandable in context as a reference not to impediment (trouble), but to the ex-

8. One might compare the positive rehearsal of the wilderness period in Ps. 105:37-45 with the negative rehearsal in Ps. 106:13-31. Both are selective in their appropriation of a larger national epic in which the period from the exodus to the promised land provided both positive and negative examples for instructing Israel and Judah.

9. The deliverance from Egypt is fundamental to defining who Israel is and who YHWH is (11:1; 13:4). The verb *'ālâ,* "to ascend, go up," is part of the confessional language that God had brought Israel up from Egypt (Exod. 3:8, 17; Josh. 24:17; Judg. 2:1; 1 Sam. 12:6; 2 Sam. 7:6; Jer. 2:6; 7:22; 11:7; Ezek. 37:12 [brought up from the grave for a new entrance into Israel]; Amos 2:10; 3:1; Mic. 6:4). On occasion it is Moses who brought them up from Egypt (Exod. 32:7, 23), or in the case of Hos. 2:15, Israel (lit. "she") is the subject.

10. The location of the valley cannot be identified with certainty. See Wolff, *Hosea,* pp. 42-43, for an extensive discussion.

11. See the pun on the valley's name and Achan's actions in Josh. 7:25. The area is mentioned also in Josh. 15:7 (boundary reference) and Isa. 65:10.

pectation of new life. It may also continue Hosea's wordplay from the national epic. Hebrew *tiqwâ*, meaning *hope* or "expectancy," has a homonym meaning "thread" or "string" (Josh. 2:18, 21). It is used in the account of Rahab, the Canaanite prostitute(!) of Jericho, who assisted the Israelites in the occupation of the land (Josh. 2:1-24). She was told to tie a scarlet thread in her window in the hope that her family would be spared. The details of past saving history come around again in the restoration of harlotrous Israel.

Israel also will get the *vineyards* that are part of the Canaanite environment and were included in the inheritance received by the ancestors who entered Canaan (Deut. 6:11). They are items threatened by Israel's disobedience to the covenant (Deut. 28:30, 39).

The prophet predicts in v. 15 that Israel will *respond ('ānâ)* in the wilderness. In context this response is likely part of the typology based on the first wilderness period. In the account of covenant making at Sinai (Exod. 24:3-8), Moses read to the people from the book of the covenant and the people "answered" *('āmar)* positively and promised obedience to the Lord. That is one instance in which Israel responded to the Lord's appeal to keep his covenant (Exod. 19:4-6). In the second wilderness, God will speak to Israel's *heart* (Hos. 2:14), and it is now affirmed that she will *respond* positively. This same verb *('ānâ)* is repeated five times in 2:21-22 as various elements of creation respond affirmatively to a process of blessing initiated by God. Here in 2:15 the verb has the connotation of accepting an invitation, and more particularly, responding to an invitation from a spouse. The term may well be rooted in the intimacy of the household.

16 (18) The metaphor of marriage and covenant emerges again to the foreground in v. 16, as prophetic imagination adds yet more to a future *day* (i.e., the time) of decisive change and blessing. To grasp the significance of v. 16 requires hearing it on at least two levels, one of which requires particular attention on the part of modern readers. The first level is that of the immediate literary context with its solemn declaration in 2:2 that Gomer is not Hosea's wife and he is not her husband. Whether this state of affairs is the result of a divorce (indeed possibly the declaration of divorce itself), or whether it sums up the status of their relationship, even though they may still be married, are open questions. The net effect is essentially the same, however. Husband and wife are no longer "husband and wife," just as Israel is no longer the covenant partner of YHWH. The affirmation for the future is that Israel will once more be graced by YHWH as the recipient of his covenant and his blessing. Thus 2:16 continues the pattern of projecting a reversal of Israel's current sad and humiliating circumstances.

The second level is that of vocabulary at home with Hosea and his audience but not so with modern readers. In classical Hebrew the familiar terms *ʾîš* ("man") and *ʾiššâ* ("woman") also express what modern readers understand by husband and wife. Thus in 2:2 one could translate quite literally: "She is not my woman and I am not her man." The noun *baʿal* means "owner, master, lord," and in certain contexts "husband."[12] Both senses of the word are presupposed here in 2:16. In the patriarchal, non-Western societies of ancient Canaan, a husband was the owner and master of his household, which included his wife. In a few instances in the OT the related verb *bāʿal* is used with the meaning "to marry, to take a wife." A wife, furthermore, could be described as *bĕʿûlâ,* a feminine passive form, meaning "possessed [by a husband]," i.e., married. And as a noun, *baʿal* also is used for Canaanite deities. They were masters of certain powers and possessors/owners of property and people. "Baal" is not a proper name, even though in reference to deities it often functions like one. A Canaanite god called upon as Baal would additionally have one or more names and perhaps some epithets. The same thing can be said for a goddess, if called upon as *baʿălâ/baʿălat.* A modern parallel is the invocation of a deity as "Lord."

The declaration in 2:16 that Israel will no longer call YHWH *baʿal* presupposes that some in Israel had called upon YHWH with this common noun, a term completely at home in the eastern Mediterranean, especially in the Phoenician-influenced areas. To call YHWH *baʿal* carried with it, at least in Hosea's eyes, an unacceptable form of syncretism with the broader Canaanite culture of which Israel was nevertheless a constituent part. YHWH was worshiped as a deity in the land of Canaan, but for Hosea not all attributes of the Canaanite deities could be applied to the one Lord of Israel.

YHWH should no longer be called *baʿal,* but it would be a sign of covenant intimacy to call him *husband (ʾîš).* It is a metaphor, signifying intimacy as well as indicating more mutuality between God and people than was found in the hierarchy and role specificity of a Canaanite pantheon. As the gracious giver of a covenant to Israel, YHWH is the father, husband, and owner of the people. These are his identities in his relationship to Israel, reflecting modes of his self-revelation. And in his household he can be known by the simplest relational term, *ʾîš.* Nevertheless, YHWH is no more *essentially* male than collective Israel or Samaria are female. In the comprehensiveness of his being, YHWH had attributes that belonged to various deities in the Canaanite world. These attributes were not uncritically assimilated to him, and as the comprehensive Lord for Israel, YHWH transcends a defining by gender.

17 (19) The plural noun *Baals* here indicates a broad critique of Israel's polytheistic and unacceptably syncretistic worship. Included in this critique would be the baalized forms of Yahwistic worship assumed in 2:16 and there rejected. Perhaps the plural term *Baals* is intended as a comprehen-

---

12. See further appendix 1, "Baal in Hosea."

sive term, essentially a synonym for "other gods" (cf. 3:1), since the (re)mar-
riage/renewed covenant is intended to be an exclusive one. No other deity is
allowed in YHWH's household. It may be also that the term *Baals* is chosen
particularly as an anti-Phoenician comment or as a rejection of those deities
who had mastered certain skills such as protection in childbearing or healing
from sickness. One might compare the account in 2 Kgs. 1:1-8 of the Israelite
king Ahaziah consulting Baal-zebub, the god of Ekron (a traditionally
Philistine town), about his illness and whether he would recover. Ahaziah is
castigated by the question, "Is it because there is no God in Israel that you are
sending to inquire of Baal-zebub, the god of Ekron?" Readers will naturally
understand this to be Elijah's criticism of Ahaziah for not trusting in YHWH,
but we might turn the question to the viewpoint of a polytheist in Israel who
observed the king's inquiry to a god in Ekron, for it is that worldview that is
being opposed in Hos. 2:17. Two responses might be forthcoming. A first
polytheistic response could be that indeed the reputation of Baal-zebub is
such that an inquiry to his shrine may prove beneficial. A second polytheistic
response, however, might be to provide a list of deities who are strong, who
are masters in the sphere of healing, and who could be sought (invoked) at
high places in Israel.

The Baals shall *no longer be invoked by their names,* that is, called
upon in cult service or other forms of worship.[13] It is not clear whether *invoke
by name* in v. 17 means to call upon the personal name of a Canaanite deity
(e.g., Resheph, Astarte) or simply to employ the epithet "master/mistress" to
seek their presence. The latter seems to be in mind, but either would be opposed by Hosea. In the Mt. Carmel contest Jezebel's priests "called on the
name of *habba'al*" (= "the baal"; 1 Kgs. 18:26), as if that were the deity's
name. In Yahwistic circles one actually "called on the name of YHWH"
(Gen. 4:26; Pss. 116:4, 13; 118:5). At the burning bush Moses was instructed
about the significance of God's name YHWH and told that this name would
be a "remembrance" for every generation (Exod. 3:15). His name was the
strong indication of identity and presence with Israel. Thus the Decalogue
forbids the misuse of YHWH's name (Exod. 20:7; Deut. 5:11), and prohibits
using or preserving the names of other deities (Exod. 23:32-33; Deut. 12:3;
18:20). These latter prohibitions are the outworking of the first commandment of the Decalogue: "You shall have no other gods before me" (Exod.
20:3; Deut. 5:7), a base text for Hosea in his critique of Israel.

18 (20) On the future day of transformation God will make a covenant with the nonhuman inhabitants of the land. In v. 18 is the first of five

---

13. The phrase is *zākar bĕ,* with the verb in Niphal imperfect. The subject of the
verb is implicit (third masc. pl.), but in context the "they" is likely the Baals. This would
make the Niphal passive: "The Baals will be invoked no longer by their names."

uses of the term *covenant (běrît)* in the book of Hosea. A covenant is a solemn promise based on an oath or some form of ratifying sign. This covenant is not called "new," but it is made in response to Israel's failure to keep the national (Mosaic or Sinai) covenant that YHWH had extended to their ancestors in the wilderness. The Pentateuch envisions judgments for breach of that covenant that include wild animals harmful to the human community (Lev. 26:22). YHWH's unilateral covenant with the animals is a way to overcome the judgment that would leave the land as a wilderness or forest with the animals eating the produce (Hos. 2:3, 12). The covenantal effects, moreover, are cosmic, bringing in security, peace, and prosperity for all.

The three categories of animals in 2:18 are related to the four mentioned in the Genesis account of creation (1:26-30). In Gen. 1:21 the *crawling (remeś)* creatures swarm in the water, while in 1:25 they move along the ground. The three primary categories of animals in Gen. 1:1-31 are those of the land, sky, and waters.

Judgment and not just strife is indicated by the presence of *bow, sword, and warfare* in the land. Each of these was already mentioned in Hos. 1:7 and will occur elsewhere in Hosea. Their removal is another of the reversals depicted in Hos. 1–3. Whereas in Hosea's day God would *break (šābar) Israel's bow* to signify its defeat (1:5), so in the future God will *remove the bow* that is employed (owner not specified) in the land so that security will prevail.

There are overtones in this prophecy not only of the creation account in Gen. 1, but also of the account(s) of flood and covenant making in Gen. 6:1–9:17. Human wickedness brought judgment upon the created order, including inhabitants. As the waters receded, Noah brought out the animals who represent all living creatures, namely, cattle, birds, and crawling creatures (8:17). The covenant that God then announced to Noah and his descendants in 9:8-17 is an *everlasting ('ōlām)* one containing a promise never to destroy the world again by floods. As such it is a covenant also made with "every living creature, birds, cattle, and every living creature of the land" (9:10). Similarly, Israel's betrothal in marriage to the Lord, which is portrayed next in Hos. 2:19-20, completes the restoration of the created order in 2:18 and is *forever ('ōlām)*.

Verse 18 projects an environment in which the various inhabitants of God's restored creation all dwell in security and harmony. It reflects a holistic approach to the concept of restoration and blessing. Although the judgmental language in Hosea is directed primarily at the sinful community of Israel (and Judah), the state of sinfulness extends to the land and all of its inhabitants (so 4:1-3). Just so, God's promised restoration extends comprehensively to the land and all of its inhabitants.

19-20 (21-22) In v. 19 the thrice-repeated verb for betrothal/engage

126

for marriage is *'āraś*.[14] It refers apparently to the proposal and the agreement for marriage in Israelite society. Once agreement is reached between the respective families, there are exchanges between them (bride-price; agreements about dowries/bride wealth, etc.) in the context of communal expectations that the marriage will soon be physically consummated. A signifying act for a betrothal includes at least the giving of gifts from the groom to the bride's family in order to effect the agreement between the two families. In betrothal a new family is instituted that remains related in various ways to the families of the groom and bride. And once a betrothal is enacted, there would be consequences if it is broken, such as the status of the gift made by the groom or his family to the bride's family, even if the union between groom and bride had not been consummated physically. The disposition of exchanged gifts and related matters depends essentially on who is the aggrieved party in the broken agreement.

The metaphorical betrothal language in 2:19-20 is closely parallel to that in 2 Sam. 3:14, where David demands the return of his "wife" as part of a negotiation that he become king over Israel. In the context of David's negotiation, it is clear that his rule over Israel would be more secure if his wife Michal, the daughter of Saul, is returned to him. His makes his claim, however, on what appears to be a legal matter that the Israelite tribes would understand: he and Saul had agreed that he would marry the king's daughter, and the betrothal was signified (legally enacted) by a gift. Since Saul had accepted the gift of a hundred Philistine foreskins, Michal was David's "wife." Both Hos. 2:19-20 and 2 Sam. 3:14 employ *'āraś* in the Piel, with the preposition *bĕ* governing the betrothal gift, and the preposition *lĕ* governing the groom and gift giver, who will possess the wife: "Give [me] my wife Michal, whom I betrothed *('ēraśtî)* for myself *(lî)* by means of *(bĕ)* one hundred Philistine foreskins" (2 Sam. 3:14).

In Hos. 2:19-20 the bridal gifts that YHWH provides go to establishing the family unit, the household that is made up of himself and Israel. These gifts are the basic building blocks of a covenant community. *Righteous(ness) (ṣedeq)* means essentially to be rightly related. It can refer to someone innocent or "in the right" in a legal dispute (Exod. 23:7). It represents integrity in communal life as defined through relationships based on solidarity and commitment. One can be in the right in the sense of a commitment to family and community, even if it brushes up against law and custom (so Gen. 38:26). *Righteousness* is often paired with *justice (mišpāṭ)*. The latter also can be related to legal matters. Justice would be the enactment of what is right in the community. That would include the restraining or punishing of vice and the

14. See the use of this verb in Exod. 22:16 (MT 15); Deut. 20:7; 22:23-29; 28:30; 2 Sam. 3:14.

protection of the righteous or the innocent (Gen. 18:25). For those matters that go beyond law or societal custom, but demonstrate the combination of justice and compassion, there is *devoted loyalty (ḥesed).* For example, from the human side it describes the commitment of Ruth to the well-being of Naomi that went beyond what was required by law or custom, demonstrating a loyalty in action (Ruth 1:8; 3:10; cf. Hos. 4:1; 6:4, 6). *Compassion (raḥămîm)* can also be translated "mercy/mercies." The term represents the tender side of commitment[15] to the well-being of someone or something, where failure or wrongdoing does not have the last word on a relationship.

These "gifts" are also attributes of YHWH. He is righteous, just, loyal, and compassionate. What he gives to undergird the relationship are things that characterize him in action. We should not press the metaphor too far and ask about the father and family of the bride to whom the "gifts" are given to complete a betrothal and confirm a marriage. The point of the metaphor is the creation of a marriage and a family, and the gifts will come along with YHWH to the entire household or broader kinship unit.

Faithfulness ('ĕmûnâ) in v. 20 is the constancy of commitment and compassion. It has the basic meaning of steadiness, constancy, supportiveness (Exod. 17:12). It is the beneficial effect of doing good (Ps. 37:3). It is the last of the five gifts that the Lord will bring to the *marriage* (= covenant) with Israel. These characteristics in Hos. 2:19-20 are indispensable for the flourishing of a community and relationships established within it, whether that community is the people of Israel or a family (household). All of these gifts are also characteristics of the Lord who gives them. In essence, in giving them to the marriage, the Lord is giving of himself to the covenant community created through his choosing of them.

The result of providing such magnificent bridal gifts is that the bride (= Israel) *will know YHWH.* In context, this is a bold declaration, for the verb *know (yāda')* can also have the connotation of sexual intimacy between husband and wife. Thus it is written that "Adam knew his wife Eve and she conceived and bore Cain" (Gen. 4:1). What such a gifted Israel will *know* is not additional facts or figures about her covenant Lord, but the significance of who he is on her behalf, and correspondingly who she is on his behalf. A marriage may produce knowledge of additional facts, but the primary gain is relational and personal intimacy. This prediction of *knowing YHWH* can be compared with the one of the revelations of the divine name to Moses in Exod. 6:2-7:

> God spoke to Moses and said to him: "I am YHWH. I appeared to Abraham, Isaac, and Jacob as God Almighty *('ēl šaddāy),* but by my

---

15. *Reḥem* as a singular noun can also mean "womb," and the maternal care for a fetus apparently undergirds the more abstract sense of "mercy" indicated by the term.

name YHWH I was not made known to them. . . . Therefore, say to the Israelites, 'I am YHWH, and I will bring you out from the burden of Egypt and I will deliver you from their [enforced] servitude. I will redeem you with an outstretched arm and with great judgments. And I will take *(lāqaḥ)* you as a people for myself, and I will be your God, and you will know *(yāda')* that I am YHWH your God, the one who brought you out from the burden of Egypt.'"

This is one of two accounts of the revelation of the divine name to Moses, the first being Exod. 3:1-15 (in classical source analysis, an account preserved originally by the Elohist [E], an anonymous Israelite writer/tradent). The second, in 6:2-7, is that of the Priestly writer (P), another anonymous writer/ tradent. Both the E and P writers, so the classical documentary hypothesis has held, understood that the divine name of God was not revealed until the time of Moses, whereas yet another tradent (the Yahwist, or J, a Judahite writer) understood that the personal name of God was used from the beginning (cf. Gen. 4:26). Whatever the validity of the documentary hypothesis as an explanation of the Pentateuch's origins, it is likely that the verb "know" in Exod. 6:7 is not used with regard to recognition of an unknown name, but in the manner of "recognize the significance" of God's personal name.[16] This emphasis can be seen in the emphatic declaration of Jer. 16:21, where the matter is not the learning of a new name, but the recognition of its significance: "Therefore, I will make them know this time; I will make them know my power and strength, and they will know that my name is YHWH." Hosea's terminology in 2:20 is similar and colored by the intimacy of the household metaphor. In the future transformation that YHWH will bring about, Israel will *know,* i.e., recognize and relate to, the Lord in a new and significant way.

It is even plausible that Hosea knew the elements of the revelation now included in Exod. 6:2-7. I noted earlier in the analysis of 1:9 that the prophet's reversal of God's name in describing him as Lo-ehyeh (Not I Am) played on the significance of his name YHWH as presented in Exod. 3:12, 14-15. Both Hos. 2:20 and Exod. 6:7 speak of Israel *knowing* the significance of YHWH as covenant maker and redeemer. The covenant declaration in 6:7, moreover, closely follows that of the marriage declaration.[17] One cannot say for certain that Hosea knew Exod. 6:2-7 in the form and setting in which it is now preserved (although that is possible), but it is clear that he

16. A better argument can be made that the verb "to know" *(yāda')* in Exod. 6:3 is used to convey the point that the ancestors did not know God's personal name, YHWH; but even there it is also capable of expressing the thought that it is the significance of the name YHWH that was not made known to them.

17. See further in the introduction, section IV.C, "Covenant and Marriage."

knew the covenant declaration formula, along with its connections to the marriage declaration.

21 (23)   The portrayal of a future blessing continues to unfold in v. 21. This and the next verse are linked by repetition of the verb *answer/ respond (ʿānâ)* as fruitful relations between Creator and land are described as right responses to each other. One may imagine the depiction in 2:21-22 as wholly consonant with a Canaanite worldview and its emphasis on fertility. YHWH initiates a series of actions resulting in the land's production of life-supporting commodities. Indeed, the description of YHWH as a "weather god" is accurate as far as it goes and should not be overlooked or rejected by readers conditioned to reject all things Canaanite.[18] YHWH is the Lord not only of history but of nature as well. Those duties typically parceled out in the Canaanite pantheons all accrue to YHWH. One should note also that YHWH's *answer* for the future is also indicated in 14:8 (MT 9): "I indeed have responded to [Ephraim] and watch for him." It may well be that the verb is also rooted in the intimate relationships between family members in a household as they respond to one another.

Agricultural production requires rain. Thus YHWH *answers* the heavens, prompting them in turn to respond to the earth. The proper response of the heavens to YHWH's initiative is to water the earth. The earth, in turn (see next verse), will have its own response. Some interpreters have assumed a Canaanite perception of the rain falling on the soil by analogy to heterosexual intercourse. Baal, rider of the thunderclouds, provides the fertilizing semen in the form of rain; the land as female receptacle absorbs the drops through its furrows. Whether a sexual analogy is presumed in 2:21-22 or not, there can be little doubt that the *answering* effects an agricultural fertility cycle that will nourish the inhabitants of the land. YHWH initiates it and intends to bring it to completion.

22 (24)   The land responds to what YHWH initiates through the heavens as the agricultural cycle of production gets underway. The land responds to rain by producing grain, (grapes) new wine, and (olives) oil, the commodities that Gomer mistakenly believed came as payment from her lovers (2:5, 8). The last-named response is that of agricultural produce to Jezreel. Like most things dealing with Jezreel, the connection is less clear than we would like. Is the reference here to the fertile valley of that name or the child of that name? A good case can be made that it is Hosea's firstborn, the child who represents Israel, in the foreground. After all, it would be the people who benefit from the agricultural production, plus the other two children are named explicitly in the next verse. We might then paraphrase the conclusion of 2:22 as: "the grain, new

18. See W. S. Boshoff, "Yahweh as God of Nature: Elements of the Concept of God in the Book of Hosea," *JNSL* 18 (1992) 13-24, especially 21.

wine, and oil will respond to the people of Israel." The whole cosmos responds as if its constituent parts are YHWH's household at work.

23 (25)   The reference to Jezreel in v. 22 is carried through in v. 23 with the declaration that God will *sow (zāra') her in the land.* The third feminine singular pronoun *her* is understandable in context as a reference to Gomer, i.e., the mother who represents the people, but "she" has not been mentioned since 2:19-20, and there she is referred to in the second feminine singular. Jezreel normally carries a positive connotation — God sows — and that connotation is seen in the claim that God will sow Gomer in the land.[19] She will prosper in the land granted her by the Lord of nature and history. This is a reversal of the negative *sowing* of historical judgment in 1:4-5.

To confirm the beneficent interpretation of *Jezreel,* the names of the other two children are also changed for the positive. God will have mercy on those he had formerly not shown mercy. And those characterized by the name Lo-ammi (Not My People) are declared again to be God's people. The third child's response is meant to be representative of the people, who will confess with thanksgiving that YHWH is *my God.*

Thus what began as a charge of infidelity, with resulting separation and punishment, is brought around to the renewal of the relationship between Gomer/Israel and Hosea/YHWH, and extending from the marriage to the fertility and the security of the land. Whatever details we can take about Gomer, Hosea, and the children from this portrayal, all are in service to the larger theme of depicting the transformed relationship YHWH will have with his household Israel. A time of restoration, renewal, and transformation is predicted and depicted. Israel, YHWH's human household, is set in a cosmic arena that also has responded to YHWH's restorative word. And none of this is predicated initially on Israel coming to its collective senses, but on God's resolve to overcome their failures and to transform them.

E. LOVE HER AGAIN AS A SIGN THAT YHWH LOVES ISRAEL AND JUDAH (3:1-5)

Chapter 3 is a first-person report and thus different from the third-person reporting that makes up the first two chapters.[1] Its five verses cover ground similar in theme to that in chs. 1–2, but the vocabulary varies between them. The

---

19. See the excursus at 1:4-5 on "Sowing in Hosea."

1. Wolff, *Hosea,* pp. 57-58, connects the literary form to what he calls a *memorabile,* where data are arranged to describe unique events. It is not clear from his description why this is significant, except that he (rightly) wishes to separate 3:1-5 from visionary reports or allegory and to link the chapter with the recounting of symbolic acts.

chapter begins with the broken marriage and moves to a reconciliation between Hosea and Gomer that takes place in stages, thus supplementing, as well as quickly rehearsing, some aspects of the material contained in chs. 1–2. Less plausibly, some interpreters have seen the first-person account as not only independent from, but originally parallel to, the marital history in chs. 1–2. Put another way, the third-person report and the first-person report are different portrayals of the same events. It is possible that the temporal indications in 1:2 ("beginning") and 3:1 ("again"), which seem intended to make the first-person report in ch. 3 a summary and supplemental conclusion of the portrayal contained in chs. 1–2, are editorial comments and do not render an accurate sequence of events. If this is the case, we can remove the editorial comments, but we will have no independent way to reconstruct what was "behind" the two versions of the marriage and separation. Overall, it is best to see ch. 3 as a text linked originally to Hosea himself, which does indeed provide supplemental information about the marital rupture and reconciliation. The compilers of the book then adapted and shortened the material to serve as the concluding unit of Hos. 1–3.

Some form of separation took place between Hosea and Gomer. This is presupposed in the two-part presentation of 2:2-23 (MT 4-25) as well as in 3:1. Apparently her circumstances became desperate. In reacquiring her, Hosea played a symbolic role for his audience that is made explicit in the initial verse of the chapter. He is to love her as God loves Israel. As the chapter unfolds, Gomer's full restoration is not accomplished immediately, and Israel's would not be either. The restoration of Israel in chs. 1–2 was qualified as coming about "on that day," which is a way to refer to future events of decisiveness, whose significance would continue. Chapter 3 will speak of restoration to come in *the latter days*. To the prediction in 1:11 (MT 2:2) that Israel and Judah will have one head, 3:5 adds that he will be a Davidic ruler.

> 1 *YHWH said to me again, "Go and love a woman who is loved[2] by a paramour and commits adultery, because YHWH loves the Israelites, though they embrace other deities and love raisin cakes."*
>
> 2 *So I acquired her for myself for fifteen shekels of silver and a homer and a lethek of barley.*
>
> 3 *I said to her: "You shall live as mine[3] for many days. You will neither play the harlot nor belong to[4] another man, nor I with you."*

2. The Hebrew participle is passive. The LXX has an active verb with a direct object: *gynaika agapōsan ponēra*, "a woman who loves iniquity."

3. NRSV renders the Hebrew prepositional phrase *lî* "as mine." The phrase apparently reflects or reinforces that she is now legally his.

4. The phrase *hāyâ lĕ* ("belong to, be for") is used in the context of both covenant

4 *For many days the Israelites shall live without king, without prince, without sacrifice, without standing stone, without ephod and teraphim.*

5 *Afterward the Israelites shall return⁵ and seek YHWH their God and David their king, and they will be in awe before YHWH and his goodness in the latter days.*

1 The initial verse of ch. 3 influences a number of matters regarding Hosea's family and the interpretation of Hos. 1–3. With regard to the family, readers are faced with the question: Is the unnamed woman Gomer? Although certainty is precluded, it is likely that she is Gomer.⁶ The commands to *Go and love* are parallels to the commands in 1:2 to *Go, take* a woman of harlotry in marriage. It also seems preferable to see the adverb *again (ʿôd)* as a modifier of the initial verb in the sentence. In grammatical terms it can modify either the verb it follows (which is the more common position for that adverb) or the verb that comes after it. The difference between the two options is minimal once one puts together 1:2 with 3:1:

The beginning of YHWH's speaking through Hosea: YHWH said to Hosea, "Go, take for yourself a wife of harlotry . . ." (1:2).

YHWH said to me again, "Go and love a woman who is loved by a paramour . . ." (3:1).

Whereas the communication in 1:2 is qualified as the *beginning* of the Lord's speaking, 3:1 qualifies the Lord's speaking as *again*. The content of the speaking is similar in both instances. Hosea is to acquire a woman of sexual infidelity. A straightforward reading of 3:1 indicates that Hosea knows her adulterous status and yet acquires her in obedience to the divine command. By analogy, this gives support to the interpretation that Gomer's sexual history was compromised in some fashion(s) before her marriage to Hosea and that the prophet knew it.

---

and marriage declarations. See the appendix listing texts in Rendtorff, *Covenant Formula,* p. 93. In the majority of cases the verb *hāyâ* is an infinitive followed by the preposition *lĕ.* It also occurs in the first person singular ("I will be . . ."), second plural ("You will be . . ."), and third plural ("They will be . . ."). The second feminine singular in Hos. 3:3 is direct address to the adulterous woman. The phrases *hāyâ lĕʾîš* and *hāyâ lî* are ways to indicate a woman "belongs to" a man in marriage (Gen. 20:12; Deut. 22:29). See Sohn, *Divine Election of Israel,* pp. 26-28.

5. Another possible way to translate the verb *šûb* is as an auxiliary to the verb "seek" that follows. It would indicate repetition, so that the verse would begin: "Afterward, the Israelites will again seek. . . ."

6. See the introductory section to ch. 1 on Hosea's marriage and family.

The description of the woman as an *adulteress* in v. 1 assumes that she is a wife who has violated her marriage commitments. This is the first occurrence of the verb *nā'ap* ("to commit adultery") in the book,[7] and it may bear as much metaphorical weight as the terminology for harlotry. That is, whatever the actual details of Gomer's marital infidelity, her *adultery* is that of Israel in turning to other deities. Adultery was punishable by death, although such a judgment was not inevitable. Once guilt was established, the question regarding punishment for the wife or her lover[8] would essentially depend on the disposition of the husband in choosing a response and in his appeal to the community. But whatever custom or precedent might be in Hosea's day, Gomer is in dire straits morally, legally, and, as 3:2 seemingly indicates, economically.

Israel has *embraced* (lit. "turned to," *pānâ 'el*) *other deities*. The same combination of verb and object also occurs in Deut. 31:18, 20, and Lev. 19:4 ("idols"). The verb has the basic meaning of turning toward or facing someone for the purpose of engagement or interaction.[9] Disengagement would be the act of turning away from *(pānâ min)*. In either case, the activity can be positive or negative, depending on the circumstances. Israel's embracing of other deities is tantamount to following after them (2:5 [MT 7]). It is probable that we should also connect Israel's *turning to other deities* in 3:1 with the first commandment of the Decalogue.[10] The phrase *other deities* is common to both, with the verb for *turning* derived from the same root as "face" in the first commandment.

Exod. 20:3/Deut. 5:7   "You shall have no other deities before me"
                        (*'ĕlōhîm 'ăḥērîm 'al-pānāy*).

Hos. 3:1   "They are turning to other deities"
                        (*pōnîm 'el-'ĕlōhîm 'ăḥērîm*).

As noted in the introduction, the essentials of the prologue and first two commandments of the Decalogue are a base text for Hosea, a fundamental part of his theological worldview and that of the particular community of which he was a prophetic member.

Gomer's love of *raisin cakes* is an intriguing conundrum. Such delicacies are mentioned elsewhere only in 2 Sam. 6:19 (parallel in 1 Chr. 16:3)

---

7. It is used also in 4:2, 13, 14; 7:4. The related noun *na'ăpûpîm* occurs in 2:2 (MT 4).

8. The word here for "paramour" is *rēa'*, a term that describes the relationship of the "neighbor" or fellow member of the community to the woman.

9. The ends of the earth are urged to "turn to" the Lord and thus be saved (Isa. 45:22).

10. So also Wolff, *Hosea,* p. 60.

and Song 2:5. The word for *cake* (*ʾăšîšâ*) occurs once by itself in Isa. 16:7, where it is predicted that Moab will wail for the *cakes* of Kir-hareseth.[11] There is nothing inherent to the contents of the food or the literary context of the references to indicate why loving raisin cakes is a cause for judgment. The context of Hos. 3:1 implies idolatry, as if such cakes illustrate the turning to other deities opposed by the prophet. There is scattered evidence for baked goods as religious symbols, which would support this interpretation for Hos. 3:1. For example, Jeremiah's critique of his contemporaries includes reference to baked goods of a certain type (shape?) intended to honor the goddess known as the Queen of Heaven.[12] Some interpreters have also suggested that the cakes were understood in the culture of the day to be an aphrodisiac.[13]

2 Just as God's commands in 1:2 were reported as carried out in 1:3, so it is with this report in 3:2 that Hosea purchased or acquired[14] Gomer in response to the commands in 3:1. The sense of acquisition is clear from the context, but the verb and some of the other commercial terminology in the verse are imperfectly known. To reacquire Gomer took both silver and barley. A *homer* is a substantial measure of grain. It is ten times larger than either an ephah or a bath (Ezek. 45:11-14). A *lethek*[15] is otherwise unmentioned in the OT, but in postbiblical times it was smaller than a homer. There are too many variables in this brief report to give an accurate accounting for the transaction or to discern more precisely the ramifications of Hosea's payment. Since at one point in Israel's history a male or female slave was worth 30 shekels of silver (so Exod. 21:32), it is possible that a homer and a lethek of barley combined was worth 15 shekels of silver, so that Hosea's acquisition of Gomer was literally a complete cancelling of her indebtedness and thus servitude. A cancelling of her indebtedness appears to be the point, whatever the combined silver equivalent of Hosea's purchase. One cannot tell from such a brief description, however, if what Hosea did was to purchase Gomer herself or to pay in full a debt she owed that had otherwise constricted her activities.[16] Readers would do well not to forget the parallel with

---

11. NASB and NRSV translate as "raisin cakes," even though the term for raisin/grape (*ʿēnāb*) is not present.

12. Jer. 44:19. The term for bread or cake is *kawwānîm*.

13. See Andersen and Freedman, *Hosea,* p. 298.

14. For *kārâ* as "acquire," "trade," or "purchase," see Deut. 2:6; Job 6:27; 40:30. The LXX renders it with the verb *misthoō,* "to hire." It is possible that instead of *kārâ,* the verb is *nākar,* "to recognize," in the sense of to gain recognition for the act of acquiring. See Macintosh, *Hosea,* p. 100.

15. Instead of a "lethek of barley" the LXX reads *nebel oinou,* "a nebel of wine." Wine could certainly be used as a commodity of exchange, but MT is the more difficult reading and likely to be original.

16. Wolff, *Hosea,* p. 61, tentatively suggests that she had become the slave or

Gomer's initial acquisition by Hosea. It would have required gifts on his part to her family in order to facilitate his taking of her in marriage.

3 Hosea's words in 3:3 both define Gomer's status and restrict her activities. Gomer will dwell for a period of time with Hosea during which she will refrain from the activities that had previously ruined their marriage. She will not engage in harlotry or be intimate with another man. Indeed, intimate relations with Hosea are apparently precluded as well by the last phrase of the verse. At first glance it seems grossly redundant to say: *nor belong to another man.* What else would one expect? Certainly not the continuation of infidelity. This expectation, however, raises the question of Gomer's state of mind and her disposition toward Hosea, neither of which is indicated in the terse account. One assumes at least that whatever debt or obligation that Hosea paid was good news to her.

The clue for understanding perhaps comes in the last phrase of the verse, but frustratingly it is somewhat unclear. In rendering *wĕgam 'ănî 'ēlāyik* as *nor I with you,* I understand the particle *gam* in the sense of "also" or "furthermore, in the same manner." A literal translation could be: "and also I with you." In context, therefore, the sense would be: "You shall refrain from sexual activities outside our marriage, and I also will refrain from intimate relations with you" (cf. NRSV). This rendering assumes a carryover (indicated by *gam*) of the negative particles from the previous clauses. Another possibility, however, is to see the last phrase simply as an affirmation that Hosea alone will live with her (so NIV: "And I will live with you").[17] In 3:4 comes a list of things that Israel will be forced to do without in the (near?) future. Since Gomer represents Israel, 3:4 lends contextual support for the view that a period of sexual abstinence and moral purification is indicated for her in 3:3. Hosea's abstinence is a continuation of the prophetic symbolic act initiated with his marriage. As the following verse indicates, Israel shall live for some time without the normal sociopolitical and religious institutions for a state. This is a period of its purification, a road to be taken along the way to restoration.

4 In 3:4 readers are given commentary that links explicitly the fate of Gomer with that of Israel, whom she represents. The particle *kî (For)* with which v. 4 begins indicates a link between Gomer's circumstances in 3:1-3 and those of Israel under elaboration here in 3:4 and in v. 5.

Repetition of the negative term *without* serves to emphasize Israel's future historical deprivation. For a time Israel will be without the sociopolitical and religious institutions that define a state. Their absence is a

---

property of someone else in the aftermath of her separation from Hosea. Sweeney, *Hosea,* p. 39, proposes that Hosea "bought himself a prostitute."

17. This seems to be sense of LXX *kai egō epi soi* as well.

sign of judgment and contributes to a period of purification for the Israelites in preparation for a better time to come. The parallel with Gomer's situation is instructive. The stricture to Gomer, that she not play the harlot (so 3:3), is intended to rid her of a debilitating vice. By analogy, Israel's lack of king, sacrifice, and so on represents the losses that have debilitated the people and led them astray. At the same time, the period of sexual abstinence for Hosea and Gomer (so also 3:3) illustrates the lack of an otherwise good and appropriate aspect of marriage. One can make the same analogy with king and sacrifice. There is nothing inherently wrong with either, and for good or ill they play significant roles in the life of an ancient people.[18] If the analogy with Gomer and Hosea's (re)marriage holds true, then Israel is deprived not only of things necessary to the functioning of a people, but things that, to one degree or another, were corrupt.

Elsewhere Hosea mentions Israelite kings (3:5; 5:1; 7:3, 5, 7; 8:4, 10[?]; 10:3, 7, 15; 13:10-11) and princes (7:3, 5, 16; 9:15; 13:10). With the exception of the future Davidic king in 3:5, the other references are negative or judgmental. What little is preserved about the kings of Hosea's day elsewhere in the OT does not encourage an alternative view. There is no compelling reason, however, to conclude that Hosea's political philosophy was antimonarchical any more than he was antimarriage because of certain bitter experiences. It seems, however, that he viewed both monarchy and its administrative apparatus as largely corrupt. The word for *prince (śār)* can be used more broadly than just to refer to a male member of the royal family. It has wider connotations of people in authority and can serve as a term for chief, leader, official, and officer (e.g., 2 Sam. 3:38; 1 Kgs. 4:2). There would be overlap, of course, since members of the royal house often served in such positions. The lack of a king or prince means military defeat for Israel (and perhaps exile) and the transfer of political sovereignty to someone else.

Sacrifice, standing stone (maṣṣēbâ), ephod, and *teraphim* are all connected to the cult. In predicting their absence we should think of the prophet thereby as opposed not to cultic forms of religion but just to their abuse. For Israel to do without sacrifice likely entails the absence of temples and high places where sacrificial rites are carried out. Thus *without sacrifice,* as *without king and prince,* is tantamount to describing a defeated (and perhaps exiled) people, lacking control over their own affairs.

Standing stones are unacceptably syncretistic according to Deuteronomy (7:5; 12:3; 16:22). They were employed by the Canaanite population of

---

18. Hosea elsewhere has negative things to say about monarch and sacrifice, both of which are (and in his day were) capable of corruption, but it is most likely a mistake to conclude that he envisioned a restored Israel without either monarch or sacrifice. If 3:5 is to be attributed to Hosea, then clearly monarchy is in Israel's future.

the land and should be destroyed rather than adopted in the worship of YHWH. That Deuteronomy has such a polemic against them strongly suggests that they were popular also in certain Israelite circles. Indeed, their employment in Israel is assumed in Hos. 10:1-2, where there is a polemic against the multiplication of altars and standing stones as examples of guilt before the Lord. They are, moreover, associated with the ancestral period in a more neutral way, particularly with Jacob. He erected a standing stone at an evening stopover where God had revealed himself, renaming the place Bethel (Gen. 28:10-22). The function of the pillar is not made clear; it might represent the ladder, the connection that Jacob had seen between heaven and earth, or commemorate a theophany (pedestal for an invisible deity?), or represent Jacob on holy ground while he is away. He also set up a pillar at the grave of Rachel (Gen. 35:20) and to commemorate an agreement with his father-in-law (Gen. 31:45-46), both of which may have had a different function from the stone erected at Bethel. Moses erected twelve stones as part of the covenant ratification procedure at Mt. Sinai (Exod. 24:3-8). Joshua erected a memorial stone as part of a covenant renewal ceremony at Shechem (Josh. 24:22-27).[19] There is no suggestion in the Genesis account that Jacob's act at Bethel (or that of Moses and Joshua) is unacceptable. Nevertheless, as with developments in any number of religious practices, standing stones became a snare in the cult of YHWH.[20] The general expression in 3:4 does not indicate whether the pillars in question were part of the (baalized?) Yahwistic cult or represented other deities.

The phrase *ephod and teraphim* suggests that the two implements go together. They are, furthermore, to be associated with divination or cultic means of ascertaining the will of the deity. In the Israelite cult, an ephod was part of a garment or a pouch that could be carried by cultic functionaries seeking to discern the will of the Lord (1 Sam. 23:6). The high priest wore an *ephod* to carry out his sacred tasks. It is associated with inscribed stones and

19. Jacob built an altar at Shechem (Gen. 33:20), as did Abram (12:6-7).

20. A good example of one such religious practice would be the bronze serpent Moses used in the wilderness (Num. 21:6-9) to remind the people that God had power over the serpents that afflicted them. The bronze serpent was part of the sacred collection of implements kept at the temple in Jerusalem. It became an idol and was subsequently destroyed in Hezekiah's reform (2 Kgs. 18:4). Another part of Hezekiah's reform was to smash sacred pillars set up in the Jerusalem temple.

There is considerable archaeological evidence for pillars at temples and high places in ancient Canaan and Israel. Three representative sites would be Late Bronze Gezer, Late Bronze Hazor, and Iron Age II Arad. The last-named had a temple shrine dedicated to the worship of YHWH with two carved standing stones associated with its holy of holies. See Ziony Zevit, *The Religions of Ancient Israel: A Synthesis of Parallactic Approaches* (New York: Continuum, 2001), pp. 256-62.

the Urim and Thummim (Exod. 28:1-43; cf. 1 Sam. 2:28). *Teraphim* are implements, perhaps statues or another type of representative figure, associated with "divination" (*qesem;* 1 Sam. 15:23; Ezek. 21:21; Zech. 10:2). They too can be a part of priestly paraphernalia and are mentioned together with an ephod at a shrine in the hill country of Ephraim (Judg. 17:5; 18:14-20). Teraphim are part of the corrupt cultic paraphernalia in the Jerusalem temple that Josiah later removed (2 Kgs. 23:24).[21] It is their role in concert with the ephod that Hosea has in mind.

5 *Afterward.* Verse 5 begins with an adverb indicating a next thing in a sequence of events. In context, v. 5 is also a conclusion of events set in motion as a result of God's command to Hosea to go and love an adulteress in v. 1. She stands for disobedient Israel; and her circumstances of purchase from debt, her reacquisition, and a subsequent period of judgment/purification symbolize those of the nation. In the typology of presentation, Israel is separated from God as a result of its sinfulness and will be restored after a period of judgment and purification. As a consequence, it will exist for a time without the political status of a sovereign people. This is a form of self-incurred punishment that functions also as a period of purification. *Afterward,* a return to the Lord is anticipated, at a time described as *the latter days* (*'aḥărît hayyāmîm*).[22] Whatever the phrase indicates about Hosea's concept of eschatology, the quality of life depicted in 3:5 is such that nothing else in the book of Hosea would supersede it. The perspective of judgment and then reversal in the latter days in 3:5 is similar to that expressed in Deut. 4:29-30, where the failure of Israel and its subsequent exile are anticipated as a painful prelude to a future return to the Lord:

> And you will seek (*bāqaš*) from there YHWH your God, and you will find [him] when you search [for him] with all your heart and soul. In

---

21. Apparently one of their functions concerns family identity and perhaps divine protection and oracular discernment. Rachel took away with her the teraphim belonging to her father Laban without his knowledge or permission. She was able to conceal them on the saddle of a camel upon which she sat. Their loss was a very serious matter to Laban (Gen. 31:19-45). One or more teraphim in David's house were used by Michal in a ruse to portray David as asleep under a layer of clothes (1 Sam. 19:13-16).

22. See the excursus at 6:1 on "Return to YHWH." The phrase "the latter days" essentially refers to what is coming in the future. Jacob, Balaam, and Moses use the phrase in this fashion to speak of what will happen after their deaths (Gen. 49:1; Num. 24:14; Deut. 31:29). As a noun the word *'aḥărît* can mean "latter part" or "end." The question is raised in prophetic contexts, therefore, whether the phrase "latter days" reflects an eschatological sense of "last days" or end of days. It approaches that sense in Isa. 2:2/Mic. 4:1; Ezek. 38:16 (cf. 38:8); Dan. 10:14 (cf. 8:19); and there are other references where it is difficult to tell whether the phrase means anything more than "in the future." See Jer. 23:20; 30:24; 48:47; 49:39.

your distress, when all these things have happened to you, [then] in the latter days *('aḥărît hayyāmîm)* you will return *(šûb)* to YHWH and listen to his voice.

As one can see, this passage shares with Hos. 3:5 not only a similar perspective on Israel's future, but also the vocabulary of God's people *seeking* him and *returning* to him.[23]

In 1:11 it is predicted that in the future Israel and Judah will appoint "one head" for themselves. Such a reconstituted political future is behind the reference to *David their king* in 3:5. Interpreters have raised the question whether a reference to David can have originated with a northern Israelite like Hosea, and a number of them have concluded that it is more likely the contribution of a Judean editor, updating, as it were, Hosea's predictions of Israel's future. This makes a certain amount of sense.[24] There is comparatively little elsewhere in the book to suggest a pro-Judean perspective on the part of Hosea himself, and where it exists it can be explained as the perspective of the book's editors, some of whom were quite likely Judeans. Such a conclusion may seem like begging the question or circular reasoning; where there is evidence of a Judean perspective, it is automatically assigned to an editor. If so, it is worthwhile to recall that Hosea lived among the descendants of those who had earlier exclaimed, "What portion do we have with David?" (1 Kgs. 12:16). On the other hand, much less "northern" perspective is preserved in the OT relative to that associated with Judah, so that we are hampered by a relative paucity of evidence. What survives does not indicate a pro-Judean or, better, pro-Davidic dynasty perspective in northern Israel. On the other hand, we must ask if a reference to a future Davidic ruler in Hosea, which is a frequent theme elsewhere in prophetic literature,[25] could originate only from a southern or Judean perspective. The answer to that question is surely no, even if a Judean editorial origin is favored. It is possible that the phrase *David their king* has a precise setting in the reign of Hezekiah, who sought to recapture the glory years of the united monarchy. In any case, in the final composition of 3:5 David is an elaboration on the prophecy that Israel and Judah shall have "one head" (1:11). It is consistent, furthermore, with the broader prophetic claims that the Davidic dynasty will once more reign over the assembly of Israel.

The final clause of 3:5 indicates that Israel will tremble or *be in awe (pāḥad) before the Lord*. It is difficult to find a precise equivalent in English

23. In Hos. 14:1-2 (MT 2-3) Israel is implored to "return" to the Lord in the confidence that he will accept and heal them.

24. For further discussion see the excursus below on "David Their King."

25. Note, for example, the reference in Jer. 30:9 to serving "YHWH their God and David their king." See the excursus below on "David Their King."

to a verb that runs the gamut from "fear" to "be awestruck," and can be used to describe both the positive and negative aspects of such feelings. One aid in interpretation comes in the addition of *and his goodness (ṭôb)*. Israel will present themselves to the Lord and his goodness, which suggests at least a positive apprehension on Israel's part of God's disposition toward them. Jeremiah 33:9 offers some parallels in perspective and vocabulary. Speaking of joy and praise that Jerusalem's future restoration will bring to the Lord among the nations, the prophet states that they "will be in awe *(pāḥad)* and tremble *(rāgaz)* concerning all the goodness *(ṭôb)* and all the peace that I am doing for her."[26]

With Hos. 3 the extended portrayal of Israel by way of Hosea's family comes to an end. Israel's future depends finally on the character of its electing Lord and his goodness, not on its own ability to come to its senses. However one renders the verb *pāḥad,* it represents the fundamental posture of a repentant people cautiously embracing the one who had faithfully pursued them. In 14:1-3 (MT 2-4) Israel will be enjoined to return to the Lord in repentance. In 14:4 (MT 5) YHWH declares that he loves them freely. These elements are commentary on and reinforcement of the claim that YHWH loves Israel, though they have turned to other deities.

Excursus: YHWH's Goodness

In Hos. 3:5 the people of God are described as coming in trembling fashion to YHWH and his "goodness" *(ṭôb)*. The root is used broadly in the OT as an adjective, noun, and verb. YHWH's goodness is his integrity in action on which the people's restoration in the "latter days" is dependent. It is a common confession in the Psalter that YHWH is good and acts accordingly (Pss. 25:7-8; 27:13; 31:19 [MT 20]; 34:8 [MT 9]; 85:12 [MT 13]; 100:5; 106:1; 119:68; 135:3; 145:7, 9). An affirmation repeatedly employed is to "praise YHWH, for he is good *(ṭôb),* his loving-kindness *(ḥesed)* is everlasting (106:1; 107:1; 118:1, 29; 136:1; cf. 1 Chr. 16:34). Jeremiah was likely influenced by this text in Hos. 3:5. He preserves references to YHWH's "goodness" in Jer. 31:12, 14, where the people are radiant and satisfied with YHWH's treatment of them; in 33:9 he also refers to "awe" *(pāḥad)* and "trembling" *(rāgaz)* concerning all the goodness *(ṭôb)* and all the peace that YHWH is doing for Jerusalem.

When Hosea accuses Israel of *rejecting the good* (Hos. 8:3), he has in mind YHWH himself, and his actions and his instructions for Israel's well-being. In context the prophet has accused the people of breaking covenant faith with YHWH and rejecting his instruction *(tôrâ),* to which they are represented as responding, *we know God!* (8:1-2). Hosea's charge in v. 3 undercuts their response, for if they knew

---

26. See further the excursus on "YHWH's Goodness" below.

YHWH, they would have followed a different course of action and their enemy would not be in pursuit of them.

In a theophany, YHWH promises to show Moses the significance of his name and cause his "goodness" to pass before him (Exod. 33:19-20). YHWH's self-definition signifies his freedom to show mercy to whom he will. In the theophany YHWH's goodness-in-action takes on tangible properties in order to instruct Moses in the aftermath of the golden calf episode. The theophany also contains the celebrated self-defining of YHWH as a God who "forgives[27] iniquity, transgression, and sin" (Exod. 34:7). Here YHWH's "goodness" and sovereign power to forgive are inextricably linked.

In Hos. 14:2 (MT 3) Israel is enjoined to return to YHWH and to ask that he "take away all iniquity *(nāśā' 'āwōn)* and receive good *(ṭôb)*." The "return to YHWH" envisioned is a heartfelt one that is set in a cultic context, and it presupposes words and deeds from Israel's side and the affirmation of forgiveness from YHWH's.

As with the account of theophany at Sinai (Exod. 33:19; 34:6-7), so the Psalter assists readers in grasping the context of the prophetic description in Hos. 14:1-3 (MT 2-4). In a prayer for deliverance and restoration (Ps. 86), YHWH is addressed directly as "good" and forgiving, and "great in loving-kindness" *(rab ḥesed)*.[28] In Ps. 25:7-8 YHWH is implored not to remember sins and transgressions, but "according to your loving-kindness *(ḥesed)* remember me, because of your goodness *(ṭôb)*, O YHWH. Good *(ṭôb)* and upright is YHWH; therefore he instructs sinners in his way." The psalmist joins the confession that YHWH forgives according to his goodness with the affirmation that in his goodness YHWH offers his errant people instruction in his way. The prophet Micah, similarly, answers the question of how to appear before YHWH (with a multitude of sacrifices?) by answering that YHWH has declared what is "good" (Mic. 6:6-8). Hosea's call to the people to return to YHWH is based on his conviction that YHWH's forgiveness and goodness work in tandem, and that YHWH has defined for the people what is good in accord with his integrity.

Excursus: David Their King

The reference to *David their king* in Hos. 3:5 is but one example of expectations in the OT prophets concerning the advent of a future glorious ruler from David's line. Hosea's 8th-century peers, namely, Amos (9:11-12), Isaiah (e.g., 9:1-7 [MT 8:23–9:6]; 11:1-9), and Micah (5:2-5a [MT 1-4a]), also contain such expectations. It is the same for Jeremiah (e.g., 23:5-6) and Ezekiel (e.g., 37:15-25) in the late 7th/early 6th century. The expectations about a Davidic figure underwent development over time and became one of the building blocks of what became known in Second Temple Ju-

---

27. The verb is *nāśā'*, used also in Hos. 1:6 and 14:3. Both Hos. 14:2 (MT 3) and Exod. 34:7 employ the phrase "take away iniquity" *(nāśā' 'āwōn)*. See also Exod. 32:32.

28. The phrase is used in the self-definition of YHWH in Exod. 34:6.

daism as the messianic hope.[29] In various ways the NT proceeds from this matrix and presents Jesus as the fulfillment of the promises to and about David.[30]

Researchers have debated the origins and the development of these expectations about David and his descendants. One school of thought sees them rooted deeply in ancient Near Eastern perceptions of royalty as refracted through Israel's sense of saving history and conviction that the Lord had promised support to the Davidic family (2 Sam. 7:1-16). Another sees the impetus for specific Israelite and Judean versions resulting from the tragic falls of Israel to the Assyrians and Judah to the Babylonians. This would also mean that some, if not all, of the references in the 8th-century prophets are the result of editorial activity stemming from a later time.

The closest parallels to Hosea's *David their king* come in Jeremiah and Ezekiel, two large prophetic books that emerge from the Babylonian exile. It is possible, therefore, that the reference in Hosea derives from essentially the same time period and is an editorial addition. Indeed, the reference to David in 3:5 is one of the most frequently cited examples of editorial additions to the book.[31] On the other hand, since a number of themes in Hosea were apparently taken over in Jeremiah and adapted for his audience, it is also possible that one of them was an expectation of the healing of the tribal rift under a future Davidic ruler.[32] Among the references in Jeremiah to David (= his descendant) as future king are the following:

"Days are coming, says YHWH, when I will raise up for David a righteous branch, and he will rule as king and be wise and do justice and righteousness in the land" (Jer. 23:5).[33]

"They will serve YHWH their God and David their king whom I will raise up for them" (Jer. 30:9).[34]

29. On the broader issues of messianism and expectations, see Joachim Becker, *Messianic Expectation in the Old Testament,* trans. David E. Green (Philadelphia: Fortress, 1980); R. Hess, G. Wenham, and P. Satterthwaite, eds., *The Lord's Anointed: Interpretation of Old Testament Messianic Texts* (Grand Rapids: Baker, 1995); J. Day, ed., *King and Messiah in Israel and the Ancient Near East* (JSOTSup 270; Sheffield: Sheffield Academic Press, 1998); R. Hess and M. Daniel Carroll R., eds., *Israel's Messiah in the Bible and the Dead Sea Scrolls* (Grand Rapids: Baker Academic, 2003); Stanley E. Porter, *The Messiah in the Old and New Testaments* (Grand Rapids: Eerdmans, 2007).

30. Matt. 1–2; 9:27; 21:9; Luke 1:26-38; 2:1-38; Acts 13:26-41; 15:12-21; Rom. 1:1-6; 2 Tim. 2:8; Rev. 3:7; 5:5; 22:16.

31. For a list of interpreters taking this position in the 19th century, see Harper, *Hosea,* pp. 223-24. Some eighty years later, see the discussion with bibliography in Yee, *Composition and Tradition,* pp. 57-63. She regards 3:1-5 as an editorial edition no earlier than the exilic period.

32. Isaiah too regarded the division of the kingdom after Solomon's death as a tragedy to be overcome (7:17; 9:1-7 [MT 8:23–9:6]) through the exalting of Zion and a future ruler from David's line (2:2-4; 11:1-9).

33. Similarly Jer. 33:15.

34. Note Jeremiah's reference to nations trembling or coming in awe to the Lord and his goodness in 33:9, using vocabulary similar to Hos. 3:5.

"David shall never lack a man to sit on the throne of the house of Israel"[35] (Jer. 33:17).

Ezekiel also has two references to a future David:

"And I will raise up for them one shepherd, my servant David, who will feed them" (Ezek. 34:23-24).

"My servant David[36] shall be king over them and one shepherd for them" (Ezek. 37:24-25).

Some interpreters have wondered whether the repeated references to David as a future king implies a David redivivus. This is unlikely. Already in Rehoboam's day a reference to "David" was understood to mean the Davidic dynasty (1 Kgs. 12:16). Similarly, Jeremiah's affirmation that David will not lack a descendant on the throne (Jer. 33:17) is the best interpretation of the claims elsewhere in the book that the Lord will raise up "David" (= dynastic descendants) as king and shepherd.

If the reference to David in Hos. 3:5 derives from the northern prophet, it would be unique in emerging from a member of one of the breakaway tribes, plus it would be one of the earliest prophetic predictions of the reunion of the tribal confederacy under a Davidic descendant (cf. 1:11 [MT 2:2]). It is possible that as a result of his thorough critique of the Israelite kingdom and kingship, Hosea saw an opportunity for political renewal with the Davidic dynasty.[37] A similar issue concerns the prophecy of the rebuilding of David's booth in Amos 9:11-12. Does this future restoration go back to the prophet of doom or is it also an example of Judean updating?[38]

If the reference to David in 3:5 is editorial and derives from Judean circles later than Hosea, then it reflects a type of canonical updating, whereby Hosea's own hope for the future is supplemented to present a fresh application of his conviction that Israel and Judah shall be gathered together under one head (1:11 [MT 2:2]). A

35. "House of Israel" is likely used here inclusively to signify the whole people of God.

36. "My servant David" is also used in Jeremiah (33:21-22, 26).

37. This is offered as a suggestion by Jacob, "Osée," p. 37, who acknowledges that the majority of interpreters have seen "David their king" as a Judean addition. See the cautious analysis of Emmerson, *Hosea*, pp. 101-13. She finds a number of references to Judah in the book to be redactional, but is open to the view that Davidic kingship was Hosea's preferred way for tribal reunion. Others who hold that Hosea was politically motivated and represented the Davidic dynasty as hope for the future include André Caquot, "Osée et la Royauté," *RHPR* 41 (1961) 123-46; and G. Swaim, "Hosea the Statesman," in *Biblical and Near Eastern Studies: Essays in Honor of William Sanford LaSor*, ed. Gary Tuttle (Grant Rapids: Eerdmans, 1978), pp. 177-83.

38. Amos, unlike Hosea, was from Judah. See the discussion in Max E. Polley, *Amos and the Davidic Empire: A Socio-Historical Approach* (New York: Oxford University Press, 1989), who proposes that one of the things that got him into trouble in Bethel and Israel was his pro-Judah convictions, which included an affirmation of the Davidic dynasty.

good candidate for the editorial setting would be the reign of Hezekiah in Jerusalem.[39] The city of Jerusalem expanded greatly in size during his reign, at least in part due to the refugees fleeing south from the Assyrian onslaught in Israel. Some of Hosea's disciples were likely among them, perhaps even the first editors of his prophecies in written form. Hezekiah promulgated religious reforms, a centralized cult, and made overtures to the northern tribes.[40] Hosea's prophecies of tribal unification and a glorious future for YHWH's household would have been one plank in a platform of centralization and renewal.

III. GOD AND HIS PEOPLE (4:1–11:11)

INTRODUCTION

Chapter 4 begins a second section of the prophetic book (chs. 4–11; 12–14). The extended portrayal of the prophet's family in Hos. 1–3 is left behind (though presupposed in what follows), and the remainder of the book is addressed to Israel and Judah, God's household. Chapter 4 itself breaks down into two sections: 4:1-3 introduces God's case against Israel for breach of covenant, and 4:4-19 elaborates upon it.[1] As an introduction, 4:1-3 likely serves not only what follows in ch. 4, but the second major section of the book.

It is possible that the indictments in 4:1-19 reflect an understanding of the Mosaic period and more particularly traditions now contained in Exod. 32–34 about idolatry and the breaking of covenant faithfulness. Given the allusiveness of Hosea's poetry, such a connection is difficult to demonstrate conclusively, but that they share vocabulary and themes is clear. Here are some points in its favor.[2] (1) Hosea 1–3 understands the covenant between YHWH and people by analogy with marriage. Thus the indictment in 4:1,

39. The editorial work could have been done by Hosea's own disciples or by Judean prophetic circles who supported the expansions of Hezekiah and his religious reforms.

40. Finkelstein and Silberman, "Temple and Dynasty," 259-85.

1. As proposed in the outline in the introduction, 4:4–5:7 can be taken as a unit of prophetic speech. The section is likely not an original unit of speech but an editorial arrangement. In any case, 5:1-7 continues the critique of priesthood and people with themes common to 4:1-19. Note the repetition of the phrase "spirit of harlotry" in 4:10 and 5:4. The call to listen and the address to the royal house in 5:1 are evidence of expanding the addressees from priesthood and people in 4:4-19.

2. The connection between Hosea's approach to idolatry and covenant breach and the narrative traditions in Exod. 32–34 is also made by Scoralick, *Gottes Güte*, p. 145. See further the introductory section on Hosea's narrative theology.

145

drawing on the tradition of covenant and fidelity, may also draw on the period of covenant making and the terminology established then. The Mosaic period is manifestly in view at points elsewhere in Hosea (12:9, 13 [MT 10, 14]; 13:4). (2) In Exod. 32–34 God's displeasure is shown against the people for their failures. The presenting issue is the golden calf, an example of idolatry. Idolatry is also a presenting issue in 4:12, 17, texts that elaborate on the indictment in 4:1. Psalm 106:6-39 is a poetic rendering of the wilderness period emphasizing the deceit of idolatry and the golden calf, and it has several parallels with the material in Hos. 4:1–5:7,[3] as well as with other texts in Hosea about an idolatrous calf (e.g., 8:5-6). (3) In Exod. 34:6-7 — what may be described as a divine self-portrayal — occur the word pair "loving-kindness" *(ḥesed)* and "faithfulness" *('ĕmet),* which are central to Hos. 4:1 and what YHWH desires from his people.[4] (4) The divine self-portrayal in Exod. 34:6-7 posits both abundant mercy for those who love YHWH and sure judgment on the guilty. The theme of Hos. 4:1-19 is judgment springing upon the guilty, who love something else rather than YHWH (4:18).

A. YHWH'S CASE AGAINST THE PEOPLE (4:1-3)

> 1 *Hear the word of YHWH, children of Israel: YHWH has a case against the inhabitants of the land. There is no faithfulness, no loving-kindness, and no knowledge of God in the land.*
>
> 2 *(Instead) swearing, lying, murder, stealing, and adultery break forth, and bloodshed follows bloodshed.*
>
> 3 *Therefore, the land mourns and all who dwell in it waste away; the animals of the field, the birds of the air, and even the fish of the sea are taken away.*

1 The prophetic summons or call to hear YHWH's case against the people in v. 1 begins the second major unit in the book of Hosea. The use of the noun *rîb (case)* suggests to some interpreters that the prophet plays the role of accuser in a lawsuit that God initiates with his people. The noun can indeed refer to a case someone wishes to press against an opponent (2 Sam. 15:2, 4), but it is not clear that the genre of Hos. 4:1-3 is precisely that of a (covenant) lawsuit.[5] More generally, 4:1-3 is an accusation and a dispute using terminol-

---

3. See appendix 5, "Psalm 106 and Hosea."

4. In the introductory section IV.A, "Hosea's Theology: Narrative and Community Identity," I have proposed that the tradition of YHWH's self-revelation in Exod. 34:6-7 is a base text for the prophet.

5. On the question of a specific prophetic lawsuit speech form, as opposed to the

ogy that reflects formal means of accusation and contains a summary of the evidence for the charge.

The case is against *the inhabitants of the land,* which for readers of the book will bring to mind the charge in 1:2 that "the land commits harlotry against YHWH." The addressees in 4:1 make explicit what was implicit in that earlier verse: the personified land represents the people of Israel. The inhabitants are also the descendants (lit. *children*) of Israel. Their identity is that of a covenant people, bound to YHWH by promise and by historical intervention.

The evidence for the case is summarized in the latter part of 4:1. As a summary it is devastating in what it claims. In essence, the charge is that among the people of God there is no conduct or character in accord with God's revealed will and consistent with his character.

Loving-kindness and *faithfulness* are a recognized word pair in ancient Israel. The word pair typically describes attributes of YHWH,[6] so that their dearth in Israel is a failure on the part of the nation to reflect an adequate *knowledge of God.* That, of course, is a prominent Hosean theme. Psalm 25:10 also effectively illustrates this point: "All the paths of the LORD are lovingkindness and truth to those who keep His covenant and His testimonies" (NASB).

Hosea elsewhere employs the noun *daʿat* ("knowledge," 4:6; "knowledge of God," 6:6), based on the common Hebrew verb *yādaʿ,* "to know." In those places the knowledge referred to is the correct apprehension of YHWH and his will for the life of the people in the historical moment. *Knowledge of God* would be covenant fidelity.[7] Two nuances of the phrase may be in the background. The first is a relationship between "knowing" and marriage, where the verb "to know" can indicate physical intimacy (cf. Gen. 4:1). Of course, the *knowledge of God* in Hosea does not refer to marital physical intimacy, but on the analogy of covenant and marriage it can connote the desired, wholehearted personal fidelity of YHWH's people. This is reflected in the betrothal gifts of Hos. 2:19-20 (MT 21-22), where the conclusion to

---

adoption of legal terminology, see Kirsten Nielsen, *Yahweh as Prosecutor and Judge: An Investigation of the Prophetic Lawsuit (Rîb-Pattern),* trans. Frederick Cryer (JSOTSup 9; Sheffield: JSOT Press, 1978). The term *rîb* is used in pressing YHWH's "case" against Israel in Mic. 6:1-2.

6. E.g., 2 Sam. 2:6; 1 Kgs. 3:6; Mic. 7:20; Pss. 26:3; 40:10-11 (MT 11-12); 57:3, 10 (MT 4, 11 [= 108:4]); 61:7; 69:13 (MT 14); 86:15; 89:14 (MT 15); 115:1; 117:2; 138:2. The two terms are also part of YHWH's self-definition in Exod. 34:6-7, a text suggested above as a base text for Hosea.

7. In Hos. 13:4-5 Israel's "knowing" God is predicated on his delivering act in Egypt. In sustaining Israel in the wilderness, God "knew" them. Unfortunately, Israel can have a false sense that it "knows" YHWH (8:2).

YHWH's lavish investment in the "marriage" will be that Israel "knows" him. The second nuance comes from the expectation that priests, in particular, possess "knowledge of God" (cf. Jer. 2:8)[8] and share that with the people whom they serve. "Knowledge" in this sense refers to apprehension of and fidelity to divine instruction, the maintenance of the covenant ethos. Chapter 4 contains a massive critique of priests for their failures.

Land (*'ereṣ*) is mentioned twice in v. 1. The verse initiates a case against the inhabitants of the land for the reason that there is no *knowledge of God* in the land. As noted above, the land is a metonym for the people. The disastrous consequences for the land are spelled out in the next two verses. Perhaps also the scattered references to "mother" (v. 5) and "her" later in ch. 4 (vv. 3, 19) have the land as their antecedent.

2 The accusations against the people continue. They are a summary of vices and crimes among the people. In essence, these transgressions are the negative reflex of loving-kindness, faithfulness, and knowledge of God. Where fidelity to YHWH's covenant is absent, social crimes are in the ascendancy, destroying communal life. The first five transgressions are all infinitives absolute, which function in this instance like nouns and serve as a general characterization of activity. The last clause of the verse lists a sixth transgression, but one that is repetitive and follows as a consequence of the others.

Three of the transgressions (murder, theft, adultery) are terms also used in the Decalogue, but the accusations in 4:2 are not limited to its strictures.[9] The first five transgressions are those that ruin human community and are an affront to the God of Israel. All five of them reappear elsewhere in Hosea. *Swearing* (*'ālōh*) is probably used in the context of swearing an oath in the form of a curse or imprecation. In that regard, it may be similar to the third commandment of the Decalogue, which forbids the use of the Lord's name "in vain." Isaiah 24:6 uses the term as a noun in the context of imprecation or curse (whatever its origin) with negative consequences for the land: "a curse (*'ālâ*) consumes the land; those who inhabit her are guilty." Much of the vocabulary in Isa. 24:6 is also contained in Hos. 4:2-3, including the connection between curse, guilty inhabitants of the land, and the debilitating circumstances for the land.[10] The connection reflects Hosea's holistic mode of thinking and its implication that negative acts influence communities as a whole.

Lying (*kaḥēš*) is also more broadly deceitfulness. Possibly the term

---

8. The books of Jeremiah and Ezekiel contain many references to ways in which the people of God either have not "known" God or will in the future "know" God. In several instances Jeremiah, who elsewhere follows a number of themes in Hosea, may well be reflecting Hosea's claim about "knowledge of God." See Jer. 4:22; 5:4-5; 7:9; 9:6, 24 (MT 5, 23); 24:7; 31:34.

9. See the excursus below on "Hosea and the Decalogue."

10. Cf. Jer. 42:18; 44:12.

approximates what is forbidden in the ninth commandment, false testimony
(Exod. 20:16). Lying is not only deceit, but can be part of defrauding and
condemning another person.[11]

Murder (rāṣōaḥ) is the unsanctioned taking of human life; the term is
used in the Decalogue with similar meaning. Context determines its specificity. The repeated use of the term *bloodshed (dāmîm)* at the end of the verse
would seem to indicate the gravity and perceived frequency of this crime and
the one that follows it. Hosea attributes it to a priestly band in 6:9.

Theft (gānōb) is also used in the Decalogue. It can be used in case law,
where it describes kidnapping a person and stealing possessions (Exod.
21:16-17). No guilt is attached to the homeowner who strikes and kills a thief
breaking into his property (Exod. 22:2 [MT 1]). The image of the "thief who
breaks in" is used in Hos. 7:1.

Adultery (nā'ōp) is a term that Hosea can use elsewhere in a metaphorical sense, referring to the faithlessness of the people toward God. In the
Decalogue it is used in its legal and covenantal sense to describe the breaking
of the marriage vow wherein a man has sexual relations with a woman married to another man. For a married woman to have sexual relations with a
man other than her husband is also considered adultery. The violation of marriage appears to be the charge in 4:2, as it occurs in the context of other social
transgressions.[12]

The verb associated with the list of vices indicates that they *break
forth (pāraṣ)* in debilitating influence. The term can indicate vigorous and
aggressive acts (Exod. 19:22, 24; 2 Sam. 5:20) and is also associated more
specifically with violence and theft. In noun form it represents a robber or
thief (Jer. 7:11; Ezek. 7:22). In Ezek. 18:10 a violent person *(pārîṣ)* is one
who sheds blood.[13] Hence the last clause of the verse follows naturally from
the description of a societal outbreak of vices.

The expression *bloodshed follows bloodshed* (lit. "bloodshed touches
bloodshed") characterizes societal dissolution as a result of the vices listed
previously.[14] Thus it may include various acts of violence and theft, includ-

11. Lev. 6:2-3 (MT 5:21-22); 19:11; Josh. 24:27; Job 31:28 = deal falsely with
God. This is a term that Hosea uses elsewhere in 7:3; 9:2; 10:13; 12:1.

12. "Adultery" seems to be used metaphorically to refer to political deceit in 7:4.
In 4:13-14 it refers to participation in cultic rites opposed by Hosea.

13. 4:10 has a play on the verb. Israel's harlotry will not result in "breaking out,"
which likely reflects the process of giving birth.

14. As discussed in appendix 5, "Psalm 106 and Hosea," the prophecy of Hosea
has a number of related themes and common vocabulary with the psalm. Bloodshed is
common to both of them (106:38). The reference in the psalm is to the innocent blood of
children, sacrificed to the gods of Canaan. Such activity could be included in the repeated
bloodshed of Hos. 4:2.

ing murder. In a parental polemic against thievery in Prov. 1:8-19 come repeated references to "blood" (*dām;* 1:11, 16, 18). The term indicates that the life of victims will be diminished, physically violated, or even taken away, in the act of theft. The polemic also warns that the company of thieves has its own built-in destruction. As Hos. 4:3 reinforces, that would be the assumption behind the accusations in 4:2. YHWH's judgment comes in seeing that disorder sown results in disorder reaped. Hosea paints with a broad brush in the sense that his list of social transgressions is a summary charge that Israel is fundamentally flawed in its communal ethos and thus in its relationship with YHWH.

Excursus: Hosea and the Decalogue

Hosea draws upon a narrative of Israel's history and certain base texts that interpret the meaning of that narrative for him. A base text does not have to be in fixed written form; the term may also apply to a tradition that is inherited and recognized as authoritative. At least in this sense the essential claims of the prologue and first two commandments of the Decalogue are a base text for Hosea. Much of his claims about Israel's identity and current failures relate point-by-point to that traditional material: YHWH brought up Israel from Egypt; Israel should worship no other deities; Israel's image/idols are an affront to YHWH.[15]

Three of the transgressions (murder, theft, adultery) listed in Hos. 4:2 are terms also used in the Decalogue. Does this not indicate that Hosea is employing a form of the Decalogue? Interpreters are not of one mind on this question, for the issue is wrapped up with the related question whether the Decalogue was even known in a stable written form in the 8th century BCE. One can argue, for example, that the Decalogue takes some of its shape and vocabulary from the incessant preaching of prophets like Hosea and thus its written form is later than the eighth century B.C.[16] If,

15. One may illustrate points of difference in Hosea by recourse to specific terminology. For example, Hosea uses the verb "brought up" (*'ālâ;* 2:15; 12:13 [MT 14]; cf. 13:4) to describe God's act of saving Israel from Egypt, whereas the prologue uses "brought out" (*yāṣā';* Exod. 20:2; Deut. 5:6). Hosea does not use the phrase "house of slavery" either. For both Hosea and the Decalogue — and this is the important matter — God's saving act is prior to the covenantal ethos extended to Israel as an expected national response. Cf. Gene M. Tucker, "The Law in the Eighth-Century Prophets," in *Canon, Theology, and Old Testament Interpretation: Essays in Honor of Brevard S. Childs,* ed. Tucker et al. (Philadelphia: Fortress, 1988), p. 204: "One of the clearest instances of prophetic reliance upon old legal tradition is Hos. 4:1-3, which has definite links with the decalogue."

16. Bernhard Lang, *Monotheism and the Prophetic Minority: An Essay in Biblical History and Sociology* (SWBA 1; Sheffield: Almond, 1983), p. 31, makes just this point. H. D. Neef, *Die Heilstraditionen Israels in der Verkündigung des Propheten Hosea* (BZAW 169; New York: de Gruyter, 1987), pp. 175-209, concludes that much of the

however, one reframes the question slightly and asks whether Hosea is citing recognized covenant standards that are rooted in his national narrative, then an affirmative answer seems likely. This way of putting the matter puts less emphasis on fixed written form (and the question of dating it) and puts more on tradition (which may exist in written form) and oral elaboration.[17] This point can be illustrated by considering the three transgressions cited by Hosea that are part of the Decalogue. Note the lack of consistent order and the presence of elaboration in a tradition that stretches nearly a millennium.

Here is the order of the three commandments in Exodus and Deuteronomy, which differs from that in Hosea. There is, furthermore, a difference in order between the MT and LXX of Exodus.

Exod. 20:13/Deut. 5:17	murder *(rṣḥ)*	20:13 LXX	adultery
Exod. 20:14/Deut. 5:18	adultery *(n'p)*	20:14 LXX	theft
Exod. 20:15/Deut. 5:19	theft *(gnb)*	20:15 LXX	murder

The same three transgressions occur in an accusation in Jer. 7:9, employing the infinitive absolute to characterize the acts, as in Hos. 4:2, but with yet a different sequence:

Jer. 7:9   theft *(gnb),* murder *(rṣḥ),* adultery *(n'p).*

This sequence in Jeremiah is followed by a charge that Judah worships Baal and other deities (cf. Exod. 20:3-6; Deut. 5:7-10).

In the Decalogue the three commandments are quite succinct (each is two words in Hebrew) and perhaps were joined together early on because they share this pattern. For ease of citation and preservation these brief prohibitions may have been bundled together. It is also the case that murder, theft, and adultery are social crimes and major impediments to communal life, and can thus be grouped together by cultural association.

However one explains the variety in sequence and common association in the Decalogue and the Prophets, similar characteristics of citation continue into the Greco-Roman period. One observes variable sequence in citation among the commandments proper, plus the use of additional terminology by way of elaboration, in the NT. Mark 10:19, for example, contains the sequence "murder," "adultery," and "theft," followed by a reference to defrauding, and then the commandment to honor one's parents. Matthew 19:18-19 also cites the sequence "murder," "adultery," and "theft," but then lists the commands not to bear false witness, the honoring of parents,

---

Decalogue material existed in Hosea's day as "a preliminary form," but reached its final form later than Hosea. Hosea would be an early witness to the authoritative tradition in which the Decalogue is rooted. In his view, that he does not mention the Sabbath or the honoring of parents may mean that those commandments were added later.

17. Note, for example, that in 4:2 the prophet also lists the transgressions of *swearing ('ālōh)* and *deception (kaḥēš).* The first may relate to the third commandment of the Decalogue (Exod. 20:7; Deut. 5:11), which forbids the misuse of YHWH's name. The latter is possibly related to "false testimony" in the ninth commandment (Exod. 20:16; Deut. 5:20). See the discussion in Neef, *Heilstraditionen,* pp. 196-99.

and finally a citation of Lev. 19:18. Luke 18:20 has the sequence "adultery," "murder," "theft," then no false witness and the honoring of parents, but no citation of Lev. 19:18. Romans 13:9 has "adultery," "murder," "theft," "covet," then a citation of Lev. 19:18.

When one puts Hos. 4:2 in the context of Exod. 20:3-17 (MT + LXX), Deut. 5:7-21, Jer. 7:9, Mark 10:19, Matt 19:18-19, and Luke 18:20, at least two patterns emerge. First, all have references to murder, adultery, and theft, but they are listed in five different orders as chart 1 shows. The Gospel citations show that a commandment in the Decalogue can be cited out of order (e.g., honoring of parents), even though one is safe in assuming that Exodus and Deuteronomy had achieved essentially fixed forms (Hebrew, Greek) by the first century A.D. Apparently the order of their listing in the Torah was not something fundamental in making reference to them. A second pattern is that Hosea, Jeremiah, Mark, and Matthew all refer to these particular transgressions in a context where material other than that specific to the Decalogue is also drawn upon. The context in the Gospel accounts is that of divine instruction, i.e., the commandments of God; and although the Decalogue has pride of place in such a context, it is not the sole collection drawn upon. There is a reference to defrauding in Mark and a citation of Lev. 19:18 in Matthew. Something similar is likely at work already in Hosea and Jeremiah, where the acts forbidden in the Decalogue are known as part of the covenantal ethos and are named, but in a way that draws in related matters for the instruction of an audience.

Chart 1: Sequence of Instruction in Decalogue Material

I. Exod. 20:13-15	murder	adultery	theft		
Deut. 5:17-19	murder	adultery	theft		
Mark 10:19	murder	adultery	theft	defrauding	honor parents
Matt. 19:18-19	murder	adultery	theft	false witness	honor parents	Lev. 19:18

II. Exod. 20:13-15 (LXX)	adultery	theft	murder		
III. Hos. 4:2	murder[18]	theft	adultery		
IV. Jer. 7:9	theft	murder	adultery	incense Baal	walk after other gods
V. Luke 18:20	adultery	murder	theft	false witness	honor parents
Rom. 13:9	adultery	murder	theft	covet	Lev. 19:18

18. These three transgressions are preceded by "swearing" and "lying" in Hos. 4:2.

3   Acts in v. 2 are joined to their consequences in v. 3 by the term *Therefore*. After a summary of the evidence is listed, God's case against the land and its inhabitants results in the dissolution of both the human and animal societies who inhabit the land. Indeed, the land itself is depicted as ill, just as the human community is rotten. This is Hosea's holistic analysis at work. The three categories of animals, birds, and fish here in 4:3 are those listed in Ps. 8:7-8 (MT 8-9), a psalm that celebrates the exalted place of humankind in God's good creation.[19] The environment depicted in Hos. 4:3 is the withering, physically weak and depleted land of Israel. If bloodshed is the lot of the human community, then weakness and loss infect the land's nonhuman inhabitants as well. This is tantamount to the reversal of creation and its good order, undone by human fallibility and culpability. Whereas the human community (and most certainly Israel) is designated collectively as God's stewards, intended to bring order and rule in a good creation, human failure permeates creation with disorder and debilitation.

Verse 3 employs a verbal word pair to describe the disorder and weakness of the land and its inhabitants. They are the verbs *'ābal ("mourn")* and *'āmal ("waste away")*, used together in eight other contexts.[20] Just as the land can be personified as harlotrous, so she can be depicted as mourning, weak, and sad. She is the matrix of life for the people and animals, and even when she is not, the fish of the sea are nevertheless similarly affected. In the holistic thinking of Hosea, the people and land (plants and animals) live in a symbiotic relationship. When YHWH and Israel live in a restored covenant relationship, as depicted at the conclusion of ch. 2, then the health and vitality of the land are everywhere apparent. The current failures of Israel, however, function like disease or a stain to produce an environmental debilitation.[21] Such is the predicament of YHWH's people and land (his household) in 4:1-3. It is a salutary reminder to readers that failures have consequences and that they cannot be compartmentalized and kept from permeating aspects of corporate existence.

---

19. Ps. 8, in turn, reflects aspects of the first creation account in Gen. 1:1–2:3. The latter subdivides the category of beasts of the field to include reptiles or "creeping creatures" (1:24-26). In the blessing extended by God to humankind in 1:28, they are to exercise dominion as God's stewards over the fish, birds, and everything that moves on earth (1:28).

20. Isa. 19:8; 24:4 (twice), 7; 33:9; Jer. 14:2; Lam. 2:8; Joel 1:10; cf. Katherine Hayes, *"The Earth Mourns": Prophetic Metaphor and Oral Aesthetic* (SBLAB 8; Atlanta: SBL, 2002). See also the excursus below on "Mourning Earth in Hosea 4:3."

21. See further Laurie J. Braaten, "Hosea's Land Theme in the Book of the Twelve," in *Thematic Threads*, ed. Redditt and Schart, pp. 104-32.

Excursus: Mourning Earth in Hosea 4:3

"Mourning" is one of several personifications and metaphors to describe the earth/ land in the Bible. The act is rooted in funeral practices, but takes on other roles in OT literature.[22] In Hosea's opening thematic verse (1:2), the land *('ereṣ)* is charged with harlotry in defecting from the Lord. Thus behind the depiction of Gomer in chs. 1–3 lies the land as a female metonym for the people. In the opening of the second portion of the book (4:1-3), the land is depicted as *mourning ('ābal)* and its inhabitants *languishing ('āmal)* as the consequences of Israel's sin are revealed. The harsh language of 9:11 and 14 functions as a reversal of family blessing and increase. No conception and no lactation reflect the heavy hand of judgment.

In the Genesis account(s) of the flood, there is a close relationship between the earth or land and the failure of the human community upon it. Note, for example, the criticism in Gen. 6:11-17, which begins *the earth ('ereṣ) was corrupt in God's sight and it was full of violence.* In the description of disorder that follows, there are overlap and variation in reference to the "earth" as well as to its inhabitants. God makes a covenant with Noah and his descendants that can also be described as a covenant that God makes with the "earth" (9:13).[23] Thus there is also a close relationship between the flourishing of human community and that of the earth. That the earth can be the recipient of God's covenant is both literary personification and recognition that God is intimately related to creation in ways difficult to describe.

Isaiah 24:4-6 is part of a visionary depiction of the earth laid waste through the judgment of God. Likely the depiction is part of the exilic or early postexilic additions to the book of Isaiah. In context not only the earth mourns and languishes but also new wine and the vine that produces it (24:7): "The earth mourns and withers, the world languishes and withers. . . . The earth is polluted by its inhabitants, for they transgress instruction, remove statutes, they violate the everlasting covenant. Therefore a curse consumes the earth and her inhabitants are guilty." In vocabulary similar to that of Hos. 4:1-3, a prophet depicts the symbiotic relationship between earth and inhabitants, particularly with regard to the failure of human community and its broader consequences. It is, like the depiction in Hosea, a sickness unto death.

It is possible also to see in creation's "mourning" one of the sources for Paul's description of creation groaning and mourning in Rom. 8:19-22.[24] In 8:22 creation "mourns together" *(systenazō).* Forms of the cognate verb *stenazō* are used in the LXX for mourning, including Isa. 19:8 and 24:7, where the Hebrew verb *'ābal* is employed. Both creation and the children of God "mourn/groan" *(stenazō)* according to Rom. 8:23. Interpreters have typically seen Paul's description as a reflection of the

---

22. Saul M. Olyan, *Biblical Mourning: Ritual and Social Dimensions* (Oxford: Oxford University Press, 2004); see also Hayes, *Earth Mourns.*

23. In Gen. 9:9-17 God's covenant is established with Noah and his descendants, every living creature with them, the earth, and every living creature on the earth. In Hosea's depiction of a restored Gomer/Israel (2:18 [MT 20]), God also makes a covenant with the creatures of the land.

24. I owe much of what follows to Professor Laurie J. Braaten.

fall, but perhaps the vocabulary is just as connected to the disordered mourning of creation as a result of the ongoing sinfulness of the human community.

Another OT source for Rom. 8:19-22 may be the book of Ecclesiastes. According to 8:20 the creation has been subjected to "futility" *(mataiotēs)*. The Greek term is also used in the translation of Eccl. 1:2, "vanity of vanities."

These various texts, taken together, assume a holistic assessment of the cosmos, i.e. inhabited space, where there is interdependence of constituent parts. Moreover, God is related variously to the cosmic community. It can be personified and is capable of reflecting negatively or positively its roles in the divine economy. As the book of Hosea makes clear, cosmic community can respond to the healing, restorative word of its creator, and like its human inhabitants, can be transformed (Hos. 2:21-23 [MT 23-25]).

B. "SPIRIT OF HARLOTRY" (4:4–5:7)

1. Priesthood and People (4:4-19)

This section contains several shifts in address along with some textual difficulties (4:4, 16-19) without clear solutions. These two characteristics, combined with the remarkable allusiveness of Hosea's poetry, make for a number of tentative proposals for interpretation. Overall, 4:4-19 elaborates on the charge against the people in 4:1-3, with the priesthood initially a major focus of attention (cf. 5:1). The spirit of harlotry mentioned in v. 12 is Hosea's characterization of the priesthood and the people in this section. The addressees are a priest (4:4-6), the priesthood (4:7-10), and the people (4:11-19).

4 *Indeed, let no one [else] charge or anyone [else] make a case; with you is my charge, O priest.*[1]

5 *You will stumble today, and also the prophet will stumble with you tonight. And I will destroy your mother!*

6 *My people are destroyed from lack of knowledge. Because you have rejected knowledge I will reject*[2] *you from priestly service for me. You have forgotten the instruction of your God; so I too will forget your children.*

7 *The more they increased, the more they sinned against me. Their glory I will replace with dishonor.*[3]

1. In place of the difficult MT, the translation assumes *'immĕkā rîbî kōhēn*. See *BHS*.

2. The verb *'m's'k* ("reject") has a superfluous *aleph* in it before the suffix. The *aleph* is possibly a dialectical variant of northern Hebrew or a copyist error.

3. A medieval scribal tradition (one of the 18 *Tiqqune Sopherim*, "corrections of the scribes") holds that the conclusion to the verse earlier read "they exchanged my

8 *They eat the "sin" of my people and desire their iniquity.*

9 *And it will be like people, like priest; I will visit upon them their activities, and their deeds I will return to them.*[4]

10 *They will eat but not be satisfied, engage in prostitution but not be fruitful. For they have rejected YHWH to maintain*

11a *harlotry.*[5]

11b *Wine and new wine take away understanding.*

12 *My people inquire of a piece of wood, and a staff instructs them! They have lost their bearings because of a spirit of harlotry; they play the harlot in place of (reliance on) God.*

13 *On hilltops they sacrifice, and on heights they burn offerings with incense, under oak, poplar, and terebinth, for their*[6] *shade is good. Therefore, your daughters play the harlot and your daughters-in-law commit adultery.*

14 *I will not punish (only) your daughters because they play the harlot, and your daughters-in-law because they commit adultery; for they [men, males] are going off with harlots, and with prostitutes they sacrifice. A people who do not discern will come to ruin.*

15 *Though you play the harlot, O Israel — let not Judah become guilty! — do not go to Gilgal, do not go up to Beth-aven, and do not swear "as YHWH lives."*

16 *Like a recalcitrant cow Israel has been stubborn. Now will YHWH pasture them like sheep in open range?*

17 *Ephraim is united with idols; leave him alone.*

18 *Their liquor finished, they play the harlot even more. They dearly love*[7] *dishonor more than her pride.*[8]

---

glory for dishonor." If this is correct, then the verse concluded with a complaint from YHWH through the prophet that the people exchanged YHWH's glory for that which dishonors.

4. The Hebrew text has 3rd masc. sing. suffixes in 4:9, probably in reference to the term "people" (*'ām,* which is masc. sing.). The verse reads lit., "I will visit his ways upon him, and his deeds I will return to him."

5. This last term (harlotry) is the first word of 4:11 according to the division of the MT; I follow LXX and most translations in taking it with 4:10.

6. Hebrew has a third-person singular possessive.

7. *Dearly love* is an interpretation of the difficult phrase *'āhăbû hēbû* in the MT. It has a parallel clause in 4:18a, where an infinitive absolute and finite verbal form of *zānâ* occur. My suggestion is to read *'āhăbû hēbû* similarly, based on the verb *'āhab* ("to love"). It is possible that the biconsonantal *hab* is a dialectical variant of *'āhab* or an abbreviation rather than a corrupted form. A reduplicated form *habhābay* occurs in 8:13. The LXX renders it with the participle of *agapaō.*

8. The final word in the MT is *māginneyhā,* "her shields." Interpreters have made several suggestions to change the third feminine singular suffix and/or the plural noun. The

19 *A wind has wrapped her in its wings, and they are ashamed because of their sacrifices.*

4 The translation of v. 4 presupposes a textual reconstruction in the final clause of the verse and includes bracketed terms to bring out perceived intention. A literal rendering of the Hebrew, similar to the NASB and NRSV, is as follows: "Indeed, let no one find fault, and let no one reprove another; for your people are like those who contend with the priest." The MT is awkward and obscure as is, but not unintelligible. Verses 5 and 6, however, are better interpreted as a direct address to a priest, and so a number of interpreters have taken a clue from the final term in v. 4 *(priest)* and reconstruct a direct address to a priest in v. 4 as well. That is the interpretation of v. 4 represented here. The prophet is addressing a priest on behalf of YHWH. Without the influence of the two verses that follow, it is more difficult to discern the speaker and intention.[9]

A (high?) priest is addressed and charged (a form of the word *rîb* is used) with dereliction of duty. This is a continuation and elaboration of the charges against Israel in 4:1-3, where the noun *rîb* is employed in v. 1. In the context there will be further critique of priests and the priesthood, so the singular address and the individual here may be representative in nature. It is also possible that a part of a heated exchange between the prophet and a representative priest is allusively preserved in these verses. If so, there is a parallel in the give-and-take between Amos and Amaziah, priest at Bethel (Amos 7:10-17), or that between the prophets Hananiah and Jeremiah (Jer. 28).

The prophet denies the necessity of anyone else besides YHWH addressing the priest. As a mediator of YHWH's will, it is the task of the prophet to speak for the Lord of the covenant and to accost the priest with charges of failure.

5 Continuing the address, the priest is told that he will *stumble,* as will the prophet. The latter figure is likely a representative one as well, indicting whatever prophet cooperates with priests in leading Israel astray. It is worth noting that the dual indictment presupposes that prophet and priest have worked together. This should not be surprising, given that prophets and priests can be found together in service to central institutions such as the royal court or a state-sponsored sanctuary.[10] It makes sense from many things in the book

translation proposed here maintains the suffix, but follows a commonly suggested emendation (cf. *BHS*) to read *miggĕ'ōnāh,* "more than her pride."

9. Andersen and Freedman, *Hosea,* pp. 346-50, have a long discussion on the difficulty of 4:4. They too conclude that 4:4b is a direct address to a priest, but understand that 4:4a is the priest's rebuke to Hosea.

10. As examples, note the priestly functions of the prophets of Baal sponsored by Jezebel in 1 Kgs. 19, the Yahwistic prophets that accompanied Ahab in 1 Kgs. 22, and

that Hosea opposed (and was opposed by) cultic prophets in service to the central institutions of Israel. Hosea opposed them not because they were "cultic prophets," but because they served corrupt institutions upon which YHWH had announced judgment. They, on the other hand, would undergird the legitimacy of those same institutions through the agency of their prophetic tasks. Hosea opposed priests for similar reasons, not the priesthood as such.

Stumbling (kāšal) is a metaphor for failure to achieve success along a path of action. The term is used also in 5:5; 14:1, 9 (MT 2, 10). A curse for covenant disobedience is that God's people will collectively stumble (Lev. 26:37). And in Mal. 2:8 priests are accused of diverting many from the way, causing them to stumble by their (false) instruction, and perverting the covenant with Levi.

Reference to the priest's *mother,* who will be destroyed, is likely metaphorical and not biological.[11] Readers have already been introduced to a mother in chs. 1 and 2 who represents the nation through the feminine characters of Gomer, the land, and perhaps Samaria. In v. 3 the land is represented as mourning and lacking in inhabitants. Now she or a royal city who nurtured the priesthood has destruction on her horizon.[12]

6 The first charge here is similar to 4:1, where the charge was lack of the knowledge of God among the inhabitants of the land. One of the channels for the knowledge of God is the *instruction (tôrâ)* from priests. This is recognized in the succinct formulation of Jer. 2:8, where the charge is made on YHWH's behalf that priests did not ask "where is YHWH," and the parallel phrase is that "the handlers of torah did not know me." Similarly, Jer. 18:18 attributes "torah" to the priests, "counsel" to the wise, and a (divine) "word" to the prophet. The failure of the priesthood is linked directly to that of the people, who like the "mother" of the previous verse will be *destroyed (dāmâ).*[13] The priesthood failed in their task as mediators of divine instruction, and the ripple effect permeates the community.

The charges against the priest relate act to consequence. In rejecting *knowledge* (= apprehension of YHWH's will as revealed in covenant instruction), the priest sets in motion the response of God, who rejects him from priestly service. The *instruction of your God* is likely interchangeable with

---

the connections to the royal court of Hilkiah, the priest, and Huldah, the prophetess, in 2 Kgs. 22.

11. In spite of commentators like Wolff, *Hosea,* pp. 76-80; and Andersen and Freedman, *Hosea,* pp. 350-52, who take the reference literally to a priest's mother.

12. Margaret Odell, "Who Were the Prophets in Hosea?" *HBT* 18 (1996) 79, suggests that the "mother" refers "to an archaic female cultic role that did not survive the battle against syncretism in the Yahweh cult." This seems less likely than the metaphorical representation of land or city, since both entities are personified elsewhere in the book.

13. In 4:5 the verb is Qal; in 4:6 the verb is Niphal.

"knowledge/knowledge of God." Both *forgetting (šākaḥ)* and *remembering (zākar)* in Hebrew have assumed elements of proper response in their meaning. To forget does not necessarily mean to be unable to recall something, as if a priest is unable to make reference to divine instruction and covenant stipulations. To forget something means to fail to bring something to conscious focus or to ignore its significance, so that it no longer guides a person to the proper response. Correspondingly, if one remembers, then the matter is brought to mind in such a way that a proper response then ensues.

Act and divine response correspond in the conclusion of v. 6. The children of the priest are not likely his biological offspring, unless the reference is narrowly to his family and their hereditary role in the priesthood. And that is plausible. More likely options are that the "children" in question could be his brethren and associates in priestly service, which would also include any male descendants, or a reference to the people as a whole, over whom a priest has a fatherlike role. Those who forget will be forgotten.

7 Now the priesthood is the object of discussion, progressing from the attention directed to an individual in the previous verses. The "children" mentioned at the end of 4:6 likely represent the priesthood, and *they* are the subject of the first sentence.

Tragically, with the increase of priestly service comes an increase in the affront to God. The accusation that the increase of numbers and activities means the increase of sin is a play on priestly activity and more particularly a wordplay on the senses of the verb *ḥāṭā'*, which means both "to sin" and "to expiate sin." Hosea makes a similar point in 8:11, using the same verb and noting there that the increase of altars to deal with sin has led to the increase of sinfulness on the people's part: "When Ephraim increased altars (in response) to sinning, they became for him altars for sinning!"[14] Priests deal with means to expiate sin and they officiate at sin offerings. That is their vocation. So at one level all priests are involved with "sin." The cutting edge to the charge, however, is that instead of expiating sin through divinely approved means and engaging in holiness of life, the priesthood itself is corrupt and thus contributes to the sinful state of the people. And in these failures, they sin against YHWH.

God himself is the greatest *glory* of the Israelite priesthood and the nation it was called to serve. Similarly, the land, royal cities, temples, and so on are divine gifts and reflect divine glory. Priestly service, therefore, is a glorious responsibility assigned by God for the instruction and edification of his people. Sadly, the failure of the priesthood will be judged by giving them over to *dishonor.* The term *(qālôn)* also has elements of shame attached to it and is used again in 4:18. This is in keeping with the importance in ancient

---

14. A similar point is made in 10:1-2, where the increase of fruitfulness leads to the increase in altars and a negative reaction from YHWH.

Mediterranean and Semitic cultures of the honor/shame dichotomy. Dishonor and shame go together. In Jer. 13:26 and Nah. 3:5 the term is used to describe the shame of lifting a skirt and exposing genitalia. In Isaiah's judgment upon the high official Shebna, the term is used to contrast the glory of his chariots with the dishonor/shame he has incurred (22:18).

The Hebrew text of v. 7 represents God saying, *Their glory I will replace (mûr) with dishonor.* As noted previously, a medieval scribal tradition has it that the text earlier read *they exchanged my glory for dishonor,* using the same verb, but with a continuation of the subject *they* and a third person plural suffix for *glory.* The change was intended to protect God's glory and to thwart the implication that it could be lost. Whether or not this accurately reflects the textual history of v. 7, Jeremiah has a similar critique of Judah in 2:11b, reflecting a charge that the people "exchanged its glory": "my people have exchanged [*mûr,* Hiphil] its glory for that which does not profit." Psalm 106:19-21 also links the exchange of glory with idolatry: "They made a calf in Horeb and worshiped an image; they exchanged *(mûr)* their glory for the image of an ox who eats grass. They forgot [*šākaḥ;* see Hos. 4:6] God their savior, who did great things in Egypt."

The difference between the text of Hos. 4:7 and these related verses in Ps. 106 is the grammatical subject of the verb *mûr* ("exchange" or "replace"). Otherwise, the vocabulary and point of view are similar. In Hos. 4:7 the verb implies an act of judgment on God's part, whereas its employment in Ps. 106 apparently implies the folly of the people, which led to divine judgment. Perhaps the sense of 4:7 is that God is acting through something that Israel has done in giving away its glory. God will judge Israel by letting the people's glory depart, as similarly in the judgment of the tribal alliance when Shiloh and the ark of the covenant fell to the Philistines (1 Sam. 4:1-22; cf. especially vv. 21-22).

8 The feeding on or *eating of sin* is a further play on priestly service. Priests ate portions of the sacrifices and offerings brought by people to the sanctuaries. The charge is that the priesthood has become greedy for their portions and has encouraged sacrificial worship as a way to enrich themselves.[15] It is possible that the noun for *sin (ḥaṭṭa't)* also has the more specific sense of "sin offering,"[16] which was a common element in the sacrificial cultus. In light of Hosea's propensity for puns, it may best be taken as a double entendre, meaning that the priests are affected by the sins of the people in the act of enriching themselves on the sin offerings they have encouraged.[17]

---

15. Cf. 1 Sam. 2:12-17 and the greedy activity of Eli's priestly sons.

16. The term often means "sin offering" in sacrificial contexts. Cf. Exod. 29:14 and especially Lev. 4:1–5:13, where details of the "sin offering" *(ḥaṭṭa't)* are presented.

17. So Eidevall, *Grapes in the Desert,* p. 58.

The second half of v. 8 uses a parallel term to the noun "sin," namely *iniquity ('āwōn)*. At this point in the description of priestly failure, there is no charge of idolatry or polytheism, although both could be implicit (but see below). The charge is godlessness and greed in the guise of divinely sanctioned religious practice.[18] Such a critique presupposes a full course of religious practices and a busy priesthood at work. Readers may question whether this explanation goes far enough, and wonder instead if it is not a critique of the legitimacy of the priesthood and sacrificial practice as social institutions. While the question is plausible, it is more likely priestly failure and abuse that is in mind, not a judgment that the social institutions themselves are obsolete. The same can be said for Hosea's critique of the monarchy. His critique of Israelite social institutions, however, goes to the root of their viability and their place in Israelite society.

Hosea's critique continues his concern to uncover act and consequence. In 4:4-6 the corruption of the priest leads to the corruption of the priesthood and thus the people they serve. Now in 4:7-10 Hosea elaborates on the corruption of the priesthood. If the priesthood deals corruptly with "sin" by encouraging sacrifice and by desiring a show of *guilt/iniquity ('āwōn)* that prompts additional sacrificial practice, then what they bring upon themselves and their people is the consequences of actual sin/iniquity.

9 The proverbial clause that begins v. 9 is an ancient version of the modern Western saying: "like father, like son" or "like mother, like daughter." With regard to status and culpability, both priesthood and people are similarly estranged from YHWH and will incur the same judgment. The relationship between sinful act and its inbred consequence was indicated in v. 8. It is made explicit in this verse through an exquisite poetic chiasm. The two clauses in 4:9b can be depicted as follows:

> A I will visit upon them
>   B their activities,
>   B′ and their deeds
> A′ I will return to them.

Within the chiasm are corresponding terms in parallelism. The verbal phrase *visit upon (pāqad 'al)*[19] is paired with *cause to return (šûb lĕ, Hiphil)*, while the noun and modifier *their activities (dĕrākîm)* is paired with *their deeds*.

In this case, literary artistry does not conceal a somber judgment behind clever words, but allows it to be heard. Punishment is announced with YHWH in the role of facilitator. Careful consideration of the grammar shows

---

18. 4:8b uses an idiom of desire, *to lift the throat/appetite (nāśā' nepeš)*, which also occurs in Deut. 24:15 and Pss. 24:4; 25:1; 86:4; 143:8.

19. See Hos. 1:4; 2:13 (MT 15).

that it is the activities (lit. "ways") of the people that YHWH will bring back upon them. Judgment is self-incurred for its results are homegrown.

Amos 3:2 has a parallel to this announcement of judgment: "You only have I known of all the families of the earth; therefore, I will bring *(pāqad)* your iniquities *('āwōn)* upon *('al)* you."[20] The *you* is Israel whom YHWH has *known,* i.e., chosen, and to whom he extended a covenant and a homeland. Precisely because of Israel's election came responsibility toward their electing Lord. Judgment comes in the form of YHWH's visiting or bringing the substance of their iniquities upon Israel, who should have known better (at least, the priests should have ensured that they knew better).

10-11a Verse 10 represents an ironic reversal of the theme "sowing and reaping" (act and consequence), but maintains the theme of judgment from the previous verses. Whereas in the previous announcing of judgment the emphasis was on the coming to fruition of the seeds of the faithless deeds, here the judgment is that there will be no such connection between act and consequence. In literary form the verse begins with a double proverb or saying in reinforcing parallelism: Eat, but no filling; sex, but no breaking forth with child. The act of "eating" plays on the same term used in 4:8. Perhaps the saying is a metaphor for repetitive activity that cannot satisfy because it is not in accord with God's will for his people. The charge of harlotry is typically metaphorical in Hosea in that it represents infidelity to the Lord, but it may also presuppose illicit sexual activity of a cultic nature, since that is a topic in context (4:14).[21] Perhaps, therefore, we should also think of eating in cultic contexts and what that activity might signify for the people. The prophet's polemic may be directed against ritual activities of eating and reproduction that were intended to secure fertility, but that YHWH's judgment will override.

In the MT v. 10 ends oddly with an infinitive construct of the verb translated *maintain (šāmar;* lit. "to keep"). A number of interpreters, beginning with the Greek translators, have found the object of this verb in *harlotry,* the first word of v. 11. Grammatically this is permissible and it makes tolerable sense, but nowhere else in the OT does this verb have harlotry as an object. On the other hand, the verb is frequently used in Deuteronomy with objects like "statutes" or "commandments," and the positive connotations of keeping them may be reversed here in v. 10. In Jer. 16:11b the verb "main-

20. Amos also has several instances of the verb "turn/return" *(šûb)* in the Hiphil with YHWH as subject (1:3, 6, 9, 11, 13; 2:1, 4, 6).

21. The charge in 4:10 is *leaving/forsaking/rejecting ('āzab)* the Lord. Deut. 28:20 records a curse that Israel's activities will be frustrated when they "forsake" the Lord (cf. 29:22-28 [MT 21-27]; 31:16-18). Ezekiel records that Samaria did not "forsake" her harlotries *(taznût)* and that her paramours poured out their harlotries on her (23:8). See appendix 6, "Sexual Infidelity in Hosea."

tain" is used in conjunction with the verb "forsake" *('āzab)*, which is also used here in 4:10. In the context of a charge against the people for following other deities, Jeremiah states on behalf of YHWH: "They have forsaken me, and my instruction they have not kept" (Jer. 16:11).

11b As ch. 4 unfolds there is first the indictment of the land and people, followed by accusations against priest and priesthood, concluding with the failures of the people as a whole. Verse 11b exposes the sins of the people with a proverbial saying that indicts them for senseless behavior. It is a cross-cultural truism that the consumption of alcoholic beverages can impair mental faculties. Hosea's assertion may have the context of festival celebration in mind, so that the consumption of celebratory wine contributes to impaired judgment when seeking YHWH's will.

The MT (followed by LXX) of v. 11b uses "heart" for the seat of the human will and understanding, stating literally that wine and new wine "take away the heart." Hosea refers several times to the heart as the location of understanding and volition, from which motives and emotions proceed (2:14 [MT 16]; 7:6, 11, 14; 10:2). Two of these in particular represent sentiments similar to the saying at hand: "Ephraim is like a silly dove, without sense *('ên lēb)*" (7:11); "Their heart is divided, now they are guilty" (10:2).

12 Forms of divining and oracle seeking (and magic?) are apparently behind the sarcasm of inquiring of and listening to a piece of wood. Hosea is at one with other prophets who make fun of idolatry, particularly the seeking of divine guidance from something made by human hands (Isa. 44:9-17; Jer. 10:1-16). The term for wood is a general one, but that for *staff (maqqēl)* is used for a piece of wood that can be carried by hand (Gen. 32:11; Exod. 12:11; Num. 22:27). The prophet Zechariah gave names to two pieces of wood and used them as symbols of his prophetic message (11:7-14).

It is a *spirit of harlotry* that leads the people astray (cf. 5:4). The charge of harlotry is familiar. Perhaps its *spirit* is the opposite of the knowledge of God that Hosea enjoins upon Israel elsewhere. The latter indicates being rightly related to God through obedience to the ethos of the covenant. The former separates the people from being rightly related to God. In a provocative pun the prophet charges the people with playing the harlot *in place of,* or more literally "from under," God. For the meaning *in place of* see Gen. 30:2 and 50:19. The use of the term *under* in a sexual context occurs in the next verse (cf. Jer. 2:20; 3:6, 13). Verse 12, therefore, brings to the forefront religious practices that are incompatible with the worship of YHWH.

13 Sacrificial worship on hilltops and associated with trees is seen as defective and finally perverse. The object of the worship is not named. It is difficult, therefore, to discern whether the reference is to misguided worship of YHWH in some unacceptably syncretistic forms or to outright polytheism. Both are probably in mind as a general critique. The reference to a variety of shrines likely assumes a variety of rites. The sacrificial terminology used in v. 13 is common in both Yahwistic and polytheistic settings, and the geographic references to hills and trees are also used elsewhere.[22] The initial verb *(zābaḥ)* is the general term for the sacrifice of animals, used eleven times in Hosea alone. The second verb *(qāṭar)* also occurs elsewhere in Hosea (2:13 [MT 15], sacrifice to/for the Baals; 11:2, sacrifice to idols) and is commonly used in the contexts of sacrificial practice where incense is used.

Excursus: Geography of Sacrifice

Hills and trees are associated with sacrificial practice and cultic worship in Hos. 4:13-14. The terminology is shared with other writers in the OT,[23] where the setting is occasionally either a hilltop (Jer. 13:27; Ezek. 18:6-17) or an altar with a tree (Deut. 16:21). In several instances the two elements are combined (e.g., Jer. 2:20; 17:2; Ezek. 6:13; cf. Isa. 57:5-8). Jeremiah 3:6 succinctly combines the two, along with the terminology of harlotry also present in Hosea: "Have you seen what faithless Israel did? She went to every high hill and under every green tree and played the harlot!"[24]

Hosea contains some of the earliest, and perhaps the earliest securely dated, texts combining these two elements and the charge of harlotry. Jeremiah, in particular, is Hosea's heir in using vocabulary. In a collection of charges against Judah, Jeremiah accuses Jerusalem of lying down like a prostitute on every high hill and under every green tree (2:20). She is also charged with pursuing the Baal deities in the valley (2:23), which is likely a reference to the Valley of Hinnom (cf. 7:32; 19:4-6; 32:35). Members of the house of Israel (= Judah) say to a tree, "you are my father," and to a stone, "you gave me birth" (2:27). The parental roles of trees and stones may be Jeremiah's sarcastic reversal of popular polytheism, for there is considerable evidence for trees as symbols of goddesses and the divine power of fertility. Correspondingly, standing stones have long been interpreted as phallic symbols among other representative traits in cultic settings.[25]

A term that some interpreters will associate with hilltops and worship is the so-called high place *(bāmâ)*, a term for shrines opposed particularly by the compilers of 1–2 Kings.[26] The Hebrew term refers primarily to a shrine, which will have an al-

---

22. See the excursus at 4:13-14 on "Geography of Sacrifice."

23. S. Ackerman, *Under Every Green Tree: Popular Religion in Sixth-Century Judah* (HSM 46; Atlanta: Scholars Press, 1992).

24. On the basis of the Hebrew grammar in Jer. 3:6, it is hard to avoid the conclusion that Israel is personified as a female, in spite of the claims of some interpreters that Israel is always masculine in personification.

25. O. Keel, *Goddesses and Trees, New Moon and Yahweh: Ancient Near Eastern Art and the Hebrew Bible* (JSOTSup 261; Sheffield: Sheffield Academic Press, 1998); Keel and C. Uehlinger, *Gods, Goddesses, and Images for God in Ancient Israel,* trans. Thomas H. Trapp (Minneapolis: Fortress, 1998).

26. The Hebrew term occurs in both the singular and plural. See W. Boyd Barrick,

tar and perhaps even a house (= temple). It may be on a hill, like the shrine built for Moabite Chemosh by Solomon (1 Kgs. 11:7), or in a valley, like those attributed to Baal in the Valley of Hinnom (Jer. 32:35). Thus there may be overlap between the hilltop-and-tree shrines opposed by Hosea and Jeremiah and what is called elsewhere a "high place," but this must be determined on a case-by-case basis.

Hosea once refers to "high places," indicating the location of multiple altars for sacrifice in and around Bethel (10:8). The city boasted of connections back to the ancestors (Gen. 12:8; 13:3-4; 35:1, 6, 8), and the volume of clients it would serve, particularly during festival days, might necessitate multiple altars. It is also possible that multiple shrines in and around Bethel might serve more than one deity. Once the sanctity of Bethel became widely recognized, then it may have attracted a variety of cultic practices.

Daughters and *daughters-in-law* (or possibly "brides") in v. 13 are accused of harlotry and adultery. This is a context in which it is possible that the charge is not only metaphorical for infidelity toward YHWH, but that some of the cultic activities under trees and on hills included sexual rites for fertility and/or sacred prostitution. In recent years there has been a strong reaction against this line of interpretation.[27] Since the wording here is allusive, and evidence for cultic sexual rites in Canaan is elusive, caution is necessary. The charge, however, is explicitly directed at women and one is hard-pressed to read the criticism of them here and of men in the following verse and not conclude that sexual activities are, at least in part, behind the criticisms of the prophet.

14 A basic translation of 4:14a is straightforward; it is the nuance that is difficult. The MT reads literally that YHWH "will not punish your [masc. pl.] daughters . . . and your daughters-in-law. . . ." The *only* inserted in my translation above is an interpretation of the sense of the text in context. A straightforward meaning could be that although the women are guilty, YHWH will overlook their transgression, since men too are engaged with prostitutes in sacrificial activity. The reason for the qualification proposed here is that nowhere else in the immediate context is forgiveness offered or transgression overlooked. Indeed, the overwhelming direction of ch. 4 to this point has been the link between guilt and consequence for all parties. The

---

"On the Meaning of *Beth-Ha/Bamoth* and *Bate-habamoth* and the Composition of the Kings History," *JBL* 115 (1996) 621-42; John Emerton, "The Biblical High Place in Light of Recent Study," *PEQ* 129 (1997) 116-32; Matthias Gleis, *Die Bamah* (BZAW 251; Berlin: de Gruyter, 1997).

27. See appendix 6, "Sexual Infidelity in Hosea," for further discussion. To illustrate the change in assessment one can compare the comments by Wolff, *Hosea,* p. 14, with those of Keefe, *Woman's Body,* pp. 36-103.

Hebrew text can thus be read emphatically to reinforce this point, and that is the option proposed here.

There are two different terms for prostitute or harlot in this verse. The first, *zōnâ*, is familiar to readers of Hosea. The second *(qĕdēšâ),* however, is used only here in Hosea. It can be used interchangeably with *zōnâ* (as Gen. 38:15, 21-22 suggest) as another term for prostitute. Perhaps readers should leave it at that and also assume a synonymous relationship between the two here in 4:14. Yet the etymology of the word *qĕdēšâ* ("holy," "set apart") has long suggested to interpreters that some form of sacred prostitution or fertility rite is indicated by the term at some points in its employment.[28] The injunction in Deut. 23:17 (MT 18), where the term is used, can certainly be read that way for both men and women, as can the use of the use of the term for men in 2 Kgs. 23:7. The term *qĕdēšâ* here in v. 14 could refer to personnel set apart for cultic practices of a nonsexual nature, but if this is the case, we know nothing of the cultic roles represented by these women. We should take the language of harlotry in v. 14 as primarily metaphorical in the sense that it indicates faithless activity on the part of both men and women. They may well have included forms of prostitution ("sacred" or otherwise) associated with public places and shrines. A sexual component to the rites opposed seems likely.

Verse 14 concludes with a proverb cited to illustrate that a heedless people will come to ruin. It is corporate judgment portrayed for a nation without discernment. The verb *discern (bîn)* is twice used in the editorial epilogue of the book (14:9 [MT 10]) and is rooted in the vocabulary of the wise. The conclusion in v. 14 reflects the somber judgment that a people who do not recognize their perilous circumstances in ignoring YHWH's pleas will pay a heavy price.

15 Here Israel collectively plays the role of a harlot.[29] This is a claim that readers of the book have variously encountered since 1:2. Here the prophet builds sarcastically on the claim, with advice that even if Israel has taken on this persona, it should not go to the shrines at Gilgal and Beth-aven ("Wicked House"), Hosea's nickname for Bethel. This is intended as a slap at both shrines, as if to say even a prostitute will be corrupted at such places!

The precise location of Gilgal is unknown, but its general setting and profile can be surmised from scattered references in the biblical text. It was the first place encountered by the Israelite tribes on the west side of the Jordan River (Josh. 4:1-24), not far from Jericho. The etymology of the name is

28. See appendix 6, "Sexual Infidelity in Hosea."

29. For those who believe that the charge of harlotry is gender-based, it is worth noting that the participial form of "harlot" *(zōneh)* in 4:15 is masculine singular because Israel is grammatically masculine.

played upon in the narratives of Josh. 4–5. It is the location of the twelve stones symbolizing the Israelite tribal confederation and the site of the circumcision of Israelite males at the end of the wilderness journeys. These two elements imply a sacred or cultic identity for the site in later Israel, perhaps some type of outdoor shrine and pilgrimage site with an altar for sacrifice, but not necessarily a temple or much of a permanent population.[30]

Bethel's founding by Jacob/Israel is narrated in Gen. 28:10-22 (cf. 35:1-7). The first king of breakaway Israel, Jeroboam I, built a shrine there with an altar and idolatrous calves (1 Kgs. 12:25-33). It was intended as a place of pilgrimage for Israelites. In Hebrew the name Bethel means "house of God," thus giving occasion to Hosea's slur on the place as *Beth-aven* ("Wicked House" or "House of Iniquity").[31]

Yet another religious practice is proscribed in v. 15, although in itself the oath ratification *as YHWH lives* is neither a negative act nor forbidden elsewhere in the OT. It is used on a number of occasions (e.g., Ruth 3:13, by Boaz; 2 Sam. 14:11, by David; 2 Kgs. 2:2, by Elisha). Apparently the oath ratifier is of no significance when the one who swears is in flagrant disobedience to the covenantal ethos of Yahwism.

Hosea's strictures on Israelite religious practices are interrupted by an interjection, *let not Judah become guilty.* This is probably an addition to the sarcasm the prophet directs toward Israelites in 4:15. As an addition, it may be traced back to the prophet himself, who added it for those Judeans who might be involved in pilgrimage to Bethel or Gilgal, or it may be the work of later disciples, who lived in Judah and wanted to update the prophetic tradition for a wider audience.

16 Animal similes are part of Hosea's repertoire.[32] Here Israel is a stubborn or recalcitrant cow. The simile switches gender so that grammatically male Israel is compared to a cow or heifer. Attention to the Hebrew text also reveals a wordplay on the name Israel. The terms in question are *śārâ,* a part of the name Israel, and *sārar (stubborn),* used twice in this verse.[33] Literary art and poetic license are used to prick Israel and to further the critique of

---

30. Heb. *gālal,* on which the noun Gilgal is based, signifies "round." In Josh. 4:19-20 the campsite is named Gilgal for the first time in the narrative and described as the place of the stones. In 5:9 after the circumcision of the Israelite males, Joshua is told that the reproach of Egypt has now been "rolled away." See further appendix 9, "Worship Centers in Hosea."

31. Heb. *'āwen* means "empty," "false," "iniquity."

32. See appendix 3, "Flora and Fauna Metaphors in Hosea."

33. The wordplay is echoed (continued?) in 4:18 with the verb *sār.* The name Israel is given an etiological and etymological explanation in Gen. 32:24-32 (MT 25-33), when Jacob wrestled with a nocturnal visitor, an account that Hosea knew in some form (Hos. 12:3 [MT 4]).

its identity. Rather than identified as one who is tenacious in striving *(śārâ),* Israel is simply stubborn and exhibits little by way of understanding. A similar critique of Israel is given in Ps. 78:8, describing them as a *stubborn (sōrēr)* and *rebellious (mōreh)* generation.

Israel's stubborn stupidity with regard to YHWH means that the rhetorical question with which the verse concludes has a negative answer. Take a stubborn cow to an open pasture? How could she then be controlled? Although the feeding opportunities would be good for the cow (she needs it to produce milk and to bear calves), her recalcitrance would make it a disaster. Context is the clue that the verse concludes with a rhetorical question; there is no grammatical marker such as an interrogative *h*. This seems preferable to interpreting the shepherding imagery in a pasture as somehow judgmental.[34]

17 Ephraim, a major tribal component to the northern kingdom of Israel, is sometimes used as a synonym for the people as a whole. In v. 17 the people are joined to physical evidence of their infidelity, namely *idols ('āṣāb).* Hosea uses the same term elsewhere in 8:4; 13:2; and 14:8 (MT 9). This is a general critique of Israel's religiosity. Who and what the idols represent are not mentioned. Following on the charge of animal-like stubbornness, that of being joined to idols results in the frustrated side comment — *leave him alone.* Readers should not take the comment as evidence that Ephraim is being let off the hook, but more to the point that the people are given over to their own devices and consequences.

18 A reconstruction and translation of v. 18 can only be suggested. The MT is difficult, and the LXX translators apparently had difficulties with the text that they received. Although the general sense of v. 18a is tolerably clear, the sense of the verse as a whole is obscured by the difficulties of the latter half. The noun translated *liquor (sōbe')* refers to a strong alcoholic beverage. When the drinking of it has *finished,* literally "turned aside" *(sār),*[35] then infidelity toward YHWH increases. Whereas 4:11 notes that wine takes away understanding, a related problem is in view here: the loss of good sense is frequently joined to the loss of inhibitions and an engagement in risky activity.

So what was the result of the strong drink? The people increased their harlotry (a common Hosean trope) and loved *dishonor* or shame *(qālôn).*[36] Note that the charge of harlotry applies to the people as a whole and is not

---

34. Cf. P. Van Hecke, "Conceptual Blending: A Recent Approach to Metaphor, Illustrated with the Pastoral Metaphor in Hos. 4, 16," in *Metaphor in the Hebrew Bible,* ed. Van Hecke (BETL 187; Leuven: Leuven University Press, 2005), pp. 215-31.

35. The verb continues the play on the sound *sr,* related to *yiśrā'ēl,* "Israel," and *sārar,* "stubborn," in 4:16.

36. See the comments on this term in 4:7, where it is juxtaposed to "glory."

gender-based. The translation of the end of the verse is, however, a guess. *Pride (gā'ôn)* could refer to YHWH; the phrase "pride of Israel" occurs in 5:5 and 7:10, likely with this meaning (cf. Mic. 5:4 [MT 3]). If the possessive pronoun *her* is to be retained, then it would go back to the "land" of 4:1-3, the "mother" of 4:5, or the "stubborn heifer" of 4:16.

19 Perhaps v. 19 continues the metaphor (theme?) of drunkenness. A *wind* has wrapped up the befuddled people (= fem.).[37] The term *rûaḥ (wind)* can also be translated *spirit,* and it is also possible that the action being described plays on the term and its association in context with the *spirit* (of harlotry) in 4:12 that has deluded the people. The feminine pronoun *her* occurs again in v. 19. This is a reason not to delete or emend it in the previous verse. The wind/spirit has wrapped up the land or the mother (royal city) in its tumult. Her inhabitants (= the people) are, or should be, ashamed because of their cultic activities that offend YHWH. The sad contrast with sober and upright behavior continues.

In v. 19 the LXX and other versions presuppose the term *altars* (Heb. *mizbĕḥôt*) for MT *sacrifices* (*zibḥôt,* the only occurrence of this fem. pl. form). They may be correct. In Hebrew the difference in spelling between the two nouns is slight, and correspondingly the difference in meaning is small. As part of his institutional critique, Hosea engages in sustained polemic against both sacrifices and altars.

2. Government and People (5:1-7)

> 1 *Listen to this, priests; pay attention, house of Israel; house of the king, give ear! The judgment is yours. You have been a snare at Mizpah, a spread net on Tabor,*
>
> 2 *a pit at Shittim*[38] *they dug deep; but I will chastise all of them.*
>
> 3 *I know Ephraim, and Israel is not hidden from me; but now, Ephraim, you have played the harlot, Israel has defiled itself.*
>
> 4 *Their deeds do not allow a return to their God. For a spirit of harlotry is in their midst, and they do not know YHWH.*

37. The *her* in the rendering of v. 18 is based on the feminine suffix on the last word of the verse.

38. The Hebrew of 5:2a is difficult. The initial word, *šaḥăṭâ,* is a hapax legomenon, a feminine noun derived from the root for "slaughter." The second word, *śēṭîm,* is a plural noun based on the verb "swerve" or "revolt." How these two terms relate to one another and to the verb *he'mîqû,* "dig," that follows is the problem. The LXX is of no assistance, as clearly the translators were puzzled. The emendation proposed here, *šaḥat haššiṭṭîm,* has been adopted by a number of interpreters, e.g., Wolff, *Hosea,* p. 94; Rudolph, *Hosea,* p. 116. Cf. *BHS* and NRSV. The verb *šāḥat* is used with the verb *'āmaq* ("dig") in Hos. 9:9.

5 *The pride of Israel*[39] *testifies against him; Israel and Ephraim stumble in their iniquity; and Judah also stumbles with them.*

6 *With their flocks and herds they go to seek YHWH; but they will not find (him); he has withdrawn from them.*

7 *They have dealt treacherously with YHWH; they have borne strange children. Now the new moon will eat them with their portions.*

Those addressed in 5:1-7 follow easily from the train of thought in the previous chapter. The phrase *spirit of harlotry* (4:12; 5:4) is commonly used. Priesthood and people in 4:4-19 are followed in 5:1 by a call to attention directed at priests, state administration, and even the royal house. These are central institutions that define and shape the people called Israel. Some of Hosea's most structured and conventional poetry occurs in these seven verses.

1-2 When vv. 1 and 2 are read together, then the emendation proposed in the translation for v. 2a has a setting in which it at least makes textual sense. This, of course, is different from claiming to have solved the textual difficulties of v. 2a. The translation and resulting arrangement of clauses in vv. 1 and 2 has a 3 + 1 structure. Put another way, a tricolon communication is followed by a single clause (a colon) in each verse. That structure depends on linking the last two cola of v. 1 with the two of v. 2. In outline form the structure is as follows:

Call to attention:	(a) priests,	3 entities
	(b) house of Israel,	
	(c) house of the king.	
Judgment:	Judgment is yours.	+1
Charge:	(a) snare at Mizpah;	3 entities
	(b) net on Tabor;	
	(c) pit at Shittim.	
Judgment:	I will chastise them.	+1

Three entities are addressed in v. 1, all representing aspects of the national identity of Israel. Structurally they are easy to set out, as each is associated with an imperative. The next clause is a wordplay (see below) that expresses judgment to come on them. Two charges are made at the conclusion of v. 1, each of which is associated with a place name. The first reconstructed clause

---

39. This same phrase occurs also in 7:10, and some (e.g., *BHS*) propose *gĕʾôn,* "pride," also as an emendation in 4:18, on the basis of LXX. Note the similar phrase, "pride of Jacob," in Amos 6:8 and 8:7; and "pride of Judah" and "pride of Jerusalem" in Jer. 13:9. In each case such pride resides under the judgment of YHWH.

of v. 2 is understood also as an accusation with a place name (Shittim). When joined with the concluding bicolon of v. 1, there is a second three-part communication, each of which is associated with a place name. The second and final clause of v. 2 is an announcement of judgment, parallel to that following the three administrative entities in v. 1. In structural outline, therefore, we have a 3 + 1 followed by a second 3 + 1 arrangement.

Good parallels to v. 1 in address and vocabulary occur in Mic. 3:1; Jer. 21:11-12; and 22:1-9. In these parallels state leaders (and in Jeremiah the royal house explicitly) are addressed and reminded that "justice" *(mišpāṭ)* is their responsibility. In a sense justice belongs to them, as it is their responsibility to administrate affairs of state with equity. With respect to the phrase *house of Israel* in 5:1, one might think that it is a reference to the nation as a whole. In context, however, it is more likely a reference to representatives of the royal house and the national administrative apparatus related to it. Priesthood and the monarchy are constituent parts of the state administration and central institutions of Israelite society. They have a responsibility to discern what is right for the life of the people in their respective spheres of influence and to dispense "justice" by seeing that what is right is done.

"Justice" and "judgment" (justice enacted) are the same term in Hebrew *(mišpāṭ)*. The term is used for "judgment" here and in 5:11; 6:5; and 10:4. It is likely that the confrontative address to the leaders in v. 1, *mišpāṭ is yours,* should be understood as an ironic pun, a sarcastic double entendre, on a recognized phrase describing their social responsibilities. A paraphrase of the pun would run something like: "Yes, responsibility for *mišpāṭ* resides with you and your respective offices, but the *mišpāṭ* of YHWH upon you is forthcoming."

The irony that judgment is coming upon so-called dispensers of justice continues with the imagery of hunting and trapping of animals. A *snare (paḥ), spread net (rešet pěrûśâ),* and *pit (šaḥaṭ)* are means by which animals are trapped, and they are also recognized metaphors for the work of evildoers who prey upon the righteous.[40] In this case, however, the national leaders are themselves the snares, spread net, and pit, overcoming the good and the right with their corrupted power. Such sentiments surely set Hosea over against powerful forces, just as the announcement of the end of the Jehu dynasty (1:4-5) would have exposed him to the ire of many. But why name Mizpah, Tabor, and Shittim?[41] It is best to begin by acknowledging the limitation of the evidence and the textual uncertainty of 5:2a. At the same time, we may

---

40. The image is frequent in the Psalter: snare, 119:110; 124:7; 140:5; 141:9; net and pit, 9:15 (MT 16); 35:7; 57:6 (MT 7); net and snare, 140:5 (MT 6); pit, 7:15 (MT 16); 94:13. In Hos. 7:12 YHWH will cast his net upon his foolish people.

41. In addition to what follows, see appendix 9, "Worship Centers in Hosea."

suppose that the geographic references meant something more specific to the prophet's contemporaries than they do to later readers.

More than one place with the name *Mizpah* had a role in Israel's history. Two of them would be options for the place named in v. 1, either a place of assembly in Gilead or another town and place of assembly located in Benjamin. The latter hosted cultic/judicial activities.[42] Either place may have been involved in some form of political (?) intrigue that provoked the prophetic outburst in 5:1-2. A threat to the territory of Benjamin is voiced in 5:8. That concern may be a clue that the Mizpah of 5:1 is also located in Benjamin. On the other hand, there is a distinction drawn in 5:5 between Ephraim and Israel (see below), where "Israel" might refer to the political entity led by Pekah, son of Remaliah, who was allied with Rezin and the Arameans of Damascus. It is frequently asserted that Pekah was a Gileadite, since men from Gilead assisted him in his coup (2 Kgs. 15:25). Thus the Mizpah of 5:1 could be the city in Gilead and represent the intrigue between Israel and Ephraim.

Less is known about *Tabor,* a majestic mountain in the plain of Jezreel, but it too was a place of assembly (Judg. 4:6). Quite possibly its summit had a shrine to a Canaanite (Baal) deity.

Shittim, located on the plains of Moab near Nebo and Pisgah, may be a regional name rather than a single settlement (Num. 25:1). What role the leaders of Israel might have had at Shittim is perplexing, but there are at least a couple of clues to consider. First, Shittim is located near Baal-peor, a place known to Hosea as the location of an earlier disaster in Israel's history (9:10). Nearby there was likely a shrine to YHWH at Nebo (a rival to Baal-peor), as the Mesha inscription seemingly indicates.[43] Thus something of the area and its influence is known to Hosea. According to Micah (6:4-5) Shittim is the last-named place on the itinerary of divine guidance to the promised land. Second, Shittim is in Transjordan. Perhaps the area was also a staging ground for Israelite tribal elements across the Jordan (like Gileadite Mizpah?).

Whatever the regional intrigues and violations represented by these places, the conclusion is clear enough: YHWH stands over against them and

42. For Gilead see Judg. 10:17; 11:11. For Benjamin and the role of Samuel as judge see Judg. 20:1, 3; 1 Sam. 7:6, 16; 10:17. Mizpah of Benjamin is likely located at Tell en-Nasbeh, ca. 7.5 miles north of Jerusalem. Mizpah of Gilead is not conclusively identified, but is likely northwest of Amman. For discussion of the various Mizpahs, see Patrick Arnold, "Mizpah," *ABD* 4:879-81.

43. *COS* 2:138, lines 14-18. The inscription indicates that Nebo belonged to Israel in the mid-9th century B.C. and that the attacking Moabites dragged "th[e ves]sels of YHWH . . . before Kemosh." If the word "vessels" is rightly restored, it suggests a shrine or altar for YHWH located at Nebo (Khirbet el-Muhayyat). See appendix 8, "Transjordan in Hosea."

will judge the perpetrators of injustice. The last clause of 5:2 has no verb, reading literally, "I a chastiser/chastisement to all of them." Some interpreters, therefore, have proposed repointing the Hebrew noun *mûsār* ("chastiser") to make a participial form or to supply a verb.[44] Although such an interpretation is possible, despite its awkwardness, the Hebrew text is intelligible as it is.

3 The judgment exposed and expressed in 5:3 comes in exquisite poetic form. A chiastic formulation in v. 3a declares that God's knowledge of Ephraim/Israel's deeds is complete. One wonders if there were some in Israel who thought otherwise, i.e., that they might escape YHWH's vigilance with secret activities. Another possibility is that v. 3 simply employs conventional imagery in poetic parallelism, saying in effect: "You cannot hide from me!" The terms *know (yādaʿ)* and *not hidden (lōʾ kāḥad)* occur together elsewhere in Ps. 69:5 (MT 6) and suggest conventional imagery in poetic parallelism. The chiasm of 5:3a is structured as follows:

A   B   B′   A′

know — Ephraim   Israel — not hidden

In 5:3b the prophet employs two verbs from his stock of charges. *Play the harlot (zānâ)* and *defile (ṭāmēʾ)* are also used together in 6:10. This is language that elaborates on the critique made in 4:12-19 and is applied corporately to the people.[45] The language is that of judgment, generally speaking, and more particularly accusations of what is wrong with the people. Judgment in the sense of punishment is announced elsewhere.

4 The accusations in v. 4 continue the task of judgment through description of the people's failures. What separates them from God in the first instance is their actions. *Deed (maʿălāl)* is also from Hosea's stock vocabulary, used typically in the negative sense of inappropriate or treacherous actions.[46] They have driven a wedge between God and people and do not allow a *return (šûb)* on the part of the people to him.[47] A return to God, finally, only God can bring to pass, and it will not come to pass until Israel has experienced the error of its ways.

As indicated previously, harlotry in Hosea is primarily a metaphor for faithless activity toward God. The *spirit of harlotry* (cf. 4:12) mentioned in v. 4 seems to reflect a related mind-set that both produces and feeds such activities. Such a mind-set is the opposite of knowing YHWH, a knowledge

---

44. Cf. *BHS;* Wolff, *Hosea,* pp. 94, 99; Andersen and Freedman, *Hosea,* pp. 588-89.

45. On *ṭāmēʾ* see also 9:3-4. The two verbs *zānâ* and *ṭāmēʾ* are also paired in a description of Israel in Ps. 106:39. See further appendix 5, "Psalm 106 and Hosea."

46. 4:9; 7:2; 9:15; 12:2 (MT 3). Cf. Ps. 106:39.

47. See the excursus at 6:1 on "Return to YHWH."

that produces different deeds (cf. 4:1). The accusation of having such a spirit in their midst is a biting wordplay on the widespread notion that YHWH is present *in the midst* of his people. In Jerusalem such an understanding was attached first to the temple on Mt. Zion. Conceptually, however, divine presence goes back to the tangible symbols of the tabernacle/tent of meeting and the ark of the covenant.[48] In Hosea's accusatory description, it is not YHWH who is in the midst of his people, as he has withdrawn (so 5:6), but his polar opposite, a treacherous way of perceiving reality that is leading the people to destruction.

One wonders about the setting in Hosea's prophetic actions that gave rise to the charge that the people do not *know YHWH.* In 8:2 the public cry is precisely that Israel "knows" YHWH. It appears to be a phrase under dispute. As the national deity, surely many in Israel would claim that they know and serve YHWH. For Hosea, however, such knowledge is made apparent and effective by adherence to the covenant ethos. There is a logic to the unfolding of 5:4 that is central to the understanding of Hosea's critique. It starts with what Israel does, not what it says. Israel's failure is not an innocent mistake, but proceeds from a mind-set that fundamentally misleads them. They cannot, therefore, know YHWH adequately because that knowledge is both relational and based on obedience to YHWH's expressed will.

5 God himself is the *pride (gāʾôn)* or "majesty" (Exod. 15:7) of Israel. This is a positive use of the term, based appropriately on the divine gifts of covenant and land that set Israel apart (Isa. 4:2; Nah. 2:2 [MT 3]). In a negative sense, pride can reflect a nationalistic arrogance, a heedless sense of self-importance, and a related stubbornness of will. The last two senses would fit the term in v. 5a. When pride leads Israel astray from covenant and commandments, God promises to judge the people (Lev. 26:19). The process of judgment is depicted as *stumbling (kāšal),* an activity that is self-generated because it proceeds from debilitating pride. Stumbling describes an individual who cannot traverse successfully a path. When used corporately, as here, it is a metaphor that indicates neither Israel nor Judah is successfully on the pathway that YHWH has marked out for them to follow, but are stumbling along a route of their own choosing. Hosea presses this point on his hearers by using a phrase rooted in public discourse and the judicial system: the people's pride *testifies against* them.[49]

The last clause of v. 5 repeats the verb *stumble,* but the tense is changed from imperfect to perfect. For some interpreters the mention of Ju-

---

48. Exod. 8:8; 17:7; Num. 11:20; 14:14; Deut. 6:15 ("a jealous God is YHWH your God in your midst"); Jer. 14:9; Mic. 3:11; Zeph. 3:5, 15, 17; Joel 2:27.

49. "Testify" or "answer against" seems to be the nuance of *ʿānâ bĕ* in 5:5a. See Gen. 30:33; Exod. 20:16; Deut. 19:16, 18; Isa. 3:9.

dah here is evidence of an editorial insertion; if so, the shift in verbal aspect could be attributed to the editor.[50] The rendering above coordinates the verb of the last clause with that of the preceding clause since the verbal repetition intends to link Judah's stumbling to that of Israel and Ephraim. The clause referring to Judah may well be an editorial update to include that state in the prophet's critique. Whether it goes back to the prophet's own updating of his work or to one of his disciples at a later time cannot be determined.[51]

Ephraim and *Israel* are listed as separate entities in v. 5, rather than as synonyms, as is typically the case in Hosea. This is apparent from the statement that *they* stumble in *their* iniquities, and also from the concluding prepositional phrase, where Judah stumbles *with them*.[52] Why they are listed separately is not apparent. Their failure is described as *iniquity ('āwōn)*, a general term for violating divine standards, and thus offers no specific insight into the separate nature of their roles. Ephraim is the central Cisjordanian tribe, the heartland of the west bank of the Jordan, and closely related to the city of Samaria. It serves well as a synonym for Israel, but that role is not a given at all times in Israel's history. Israel, the old name for the tribal kingdom, may represent the polity centered in Samaria, but that role is not a given at all times either. There are, furthermore, plausible occasions in Hosea's day when internal political tensions might be defined by tribal or regional forces. Ephraim may represent essentially the city-state of Samaria, while Israel may stand for a tribal union centered elsewhere, such as Gilead. The ongoing dynastic instability following the death of Jeroboam II is evidence for tension, whether related to Ephraim or to Israel. One possibility for consideration is the coup of Pekah, who deposed Pekahiah, the king in Samaria (2 Kgs. 15:25). Pekah toppled the monarchy using men from Gilead. Perhaps he represented a disaffected group who viewed the monarchs since the death of Zechariah as interlopers and who represented themselves in continuity with the Israel of old.[53] In any case, Hosea's terminology suggests internal

50. So, for example, Wolff, *Hosea,* p. 95; Macintosh, *Hosea,* p. 186.

51. See further the discussion in Emmerson, *Hosea,* pp. 65-68.

52. It is interesting to note that *BHS* proposes to delete the name Israel and to emend the following clause to read, "Ephraim will stumble in his iniquity." This would remove the difficulty of having Ephraim and Israel as separate entities, but emending the text is too drastic, given that the versions offer no significant support for the change.

53. Gilead was the location of Ish-bosheth's rule, with Mahanaim as his base of operations. Note how Ish-bosheth's rule is described in 2 Sam. 2:8-9: he was king over Gilead, the Ashurites, Jezreel, Ephraim, and Benjamin. The last phrase of v. 9 is an epexegetical comment that he was really king over "all Israel." The geographic/tribal entities in the list, however, show something of the component parts that made up "all Israel" and that could serve as catalysts for regional tensions in the future. See further the discussion on the historical background to Hosea's prophecy in the introductory section.

divisions of some kind that have resulted in a corporate stumbling of the people. Judah too follows suit. Even if the comment is editorial, it is a recognition that the stumbling of Israel and Ephraim would eventually catch Judah as well.

6 Perhaps the seeking of YHWH under critical scrutiny in 5:6 is that associated with cultic service, since the parties in question are accompanied by animals that can be used as sacrifices and offerings. When the verb *seek* (Piel of *bāqaš*) takes YHWH or an attribute like his "face" as an object (cf. 5:15), the basic sense is the seeking of God's will and blessing, whether in a cultic setting (Exod. 33:7) or more broadly (Deut. 4:29).[54] The prophet has already described other actions of Israel as iniquity, so their seeking will go unanswered. This is made explicit by the last clause in v. 6, which states that YHWH has *withdrawn* or "removed" himself from them (cf. 5:15). YHWH's withdrawal is directly related to the prophet's announcing of judgment to come. One seeks the presence of God, at least in part, for blessing, support, and defense. Divine absence means no aid or protection and thus disaster is on the horizon.

7 Those who are seeking YHWH (v. 6) are characterized by Hosea in v. 7 as dealing *treacherously with* him. That same phrase *(bāgad bě)* is used elsewhere to describe the breaking of the covenant with YHWH (6:7; cf. Mal. 2:10). It can also be used to describe disobedience to a royal command (1 Sam. 14:33), treachery among nations (Ps. 59:5 [MT 6]), faithlessness between spouses (Jer. 3:20; Mal. 2:14-16), and the "harlotry" of Judah (Jer. 3:8). The nuances of infidelity and harlotry are likely included in this accusation of treachery, since it continues with a charge of bearing *strange (zārîm) children*. Likely the phrase is complementary to "children of harlotry" in Hos. 1:2. In both cases the terminology is metaphorical and shockingly indicts the people for their defection from YHWH. Hosea uses *zārîm* as a noun twice ("strangers," 7:9; 8:7) and once more as an adjective to qualify an instruction as "foreign," indicating something peculiar and not accepted (8:12). Perhaps there is also some assistance to be gained from Mal. 2:14-16, where priests are accused of being "faithless" *(bāgad)* toward their wives with whom they have a covenant. Malachi 2:15 is an obscure and difficult text, but it may indicate that God seeks "godly offspring"[55] from the priestly covenant of marriage. In any case, Hos. 5:7 draws another connection be-

---

54. The phrases "seeking YHWH" or "seeking his face/presence" occur several times in the Psalter: 27:8; 40:16 (MT 17); 69:6 (MT 7); 83:16 (MT 17); 105:3-4. Note the expansion of the phrase in Zech. 8:21-22, where those who seek the Lord will seek "favor" from him *(lěḥallôt 'et-pěnê YHWH;* lit. "to stroke/caress the face").

55. The MT of Mal. 2:15 has *měbaqqēš zeraʿ 'ĕlōhîm*. The adjective *zār* is also used for deities other than YHWH (Deut. 32:16; Ps. 44:20 [MT 21]). See further the excursus below on "Strangers in Hosea."

tween act and consequence for the people as a whole: faithless activity against YHWH bears not fruit, but *strange* offspring instead.

Excursus: Strangers in Hosea

Hosea employs the term *zār* meaning "strange(r)/foreign(er)" four times (5:7; 7:9; 8:7, 12). As an adjective it is applied to portions of written instruction that Israel is accused of regarding as "strange" (8:12) and metaphorically in 5:7 to "illegitimate/ alien" children produced in rebellion against YHWH. As a noun it is used twice to refer to foreigners who will eat or devour something belonging to Israel.

> 7:9 Strangers consume his [Ephraim's] strength
> 8:7 Strangers will swallow it [flour, meal]

The context for both sayings is Israel's engagement in international affairs. In 7:8 Ephraim is described as *mixed (bālal) among the nations.* In 8:8 Israel is *swallowed up* among the nations, repeating the verb "swallow" *(bālaʿ)* from 8:7.

The description of those who would consume Israel as "strangers/foreigners" is an indication of Hosea's suspicion of outside forces and their deleterious effect on the covenant people. They may also be the "enemy" *('ôyēb)* pursuing Israel in 8:3. Elsewhere in the OT a "stranger" can be a basic description of an outsider, someone who does not fit in a sphere of activity or belong in/with a group of individuals. Thus in the sphere of clan identity, a widow is encouraged not to marry an "outsider" while her brother-in-law is encouraged to take her as a wife (Deut. 25:5). An outsider defines someone whose heritage is not in a community of contact and whose ethics are not necessarily bound to it (Job 15:19; 19:15; Prov. 6:1-3; 11:15). In defining priestly duties and sacred space, a nonpriest is an interloper or nonauthorized presence (Lev. 22:10; Num. 1:51; 3:10, 38; 16:40), even if an Israelite. Aaron's sons Nadab and Abihu offered "strange" or unauthorized fire and were punished for it (Lev. 10:1; Num. 3:4). A concern for holiness, therefore, excludes the presence of foreigners/ outsiders and unauthorized actions.

In the sphere of sexual ethics, the sages argued against the influence of a "strange" (as in unauthorized?) woman (Prov. 2:16; 5:1-23; 7:5). She will bring a man to ruin. An adulterous woman receives "strangers" rather than her husband, a comment that comes in Ezekiel's portrayal of Jerusalem as an unfaithful wife (16:32; cf. Jer. 2:25; 3:13). In cultic terms, Israel is to avoid "strange" deities (Deut. 32:16; Pss. 44:20 [MT 21]; 81:9 [MT 10]) in preference for YHWH, who brought them into existence.

In the sphere of international relations, "strangers/foreigners" is a collective term for the powerful who overrun Israel or Judah. Thus, in the aftermath of the Babylonian destruction of Jerusalem, a poet laments and a prophet accuses: "Our inheritance has been turned over to strangers *(zārîm),* our houses to foreigners *(nokrîm)*" (Lam. 5:2); "You stood while strangers *(zārîm)* looted his [Jacob's] strength and foreigners *(nokrîm)* came to his gates" (Obad. 11).

The book of Hosea does not always identify the strangers who are threatening to devour Israel, but at least some of their names are known. Assyria and Egypt are two of them. Damascus and Phoenicia may be two other entities who sought to expand their influence at Israel's expense. And each of these entities had their advocates in Israel. While it may seem initially that the prophet is narrowly tribal and suspicious, perhaps even xenophobic, this is not necessarily the case. The matter has less to do with the status of outsider or alien and more to do with the effects of the outsider on the community's identity. Thus Israel is enjoined to have compassion toward the "sojourner" *(gēr),* who is in some sense a stranger or outsider by heritage, but who lives in Israel (Exod. 22:21 [MT 20]; 23:9; Lev. 19:33-34; Deut. 10:19) and who is not viewed as a subverter of the community. In Ezekiel's vision of a renewed temple area, there is a place for the sojourner (47:22-23). Moreover, a foreigner *(nēkār)* who joins himself to the Lord has a place in the covenant community and the temple (Isa. 56:3-8). It is better to put the matter in the context of election, holiness, and exclusive fidelity to the national deity rather than in the categories of ethnic suspicion or chauvinism. Election and holiness are the elements that should define Israel in Hosea's viewpoint. None of the foreigners, and none of their deities, are authorized to hold sway over Israel, the people of God. Just as an outsider was forbidden to encroach on the sphere of priestly activity or the adulteress on family sanctity, so the international powers were not welcome to violate YHWH's sovereignty over his "kingdom of priests" (Exod. 19:6) or subvert his "household" (Hos. 8:1).

The enumeration of consequences for treachery continues with the announcement that the *new moon will eat them* and their portions/possessions. The description is itself strange enough to suggest to some that an emendation is necessary in order to make sense.[56] Celebrations of the new moon are mentioned in Hos. 2:11 (MT 13) as well as Amos (8:5) and Isaiah of Jerusalem (1:13-14). The proposal here is that Hosea speaks metaphorically about judgment, with the cultic celebration (a time of sacrifice and feasting) doing the consuming rather than the people themselves consuming food and drink in celebration. The syntax of the Hebrew may also indicate that the term *new moon* is a concrete reinforcement for "soon," as in "next month."[57] The clause begins with *now (ʿattâ),* a Hebrew particle indicating something current or on the horizon.

56. So Wolff, *Hosea,* p. 95, who reads "locust," based on the LXX.
57. See the discussion in Macintosh, *Hosea,* p. 190.

C. ALARM OVER ISRAEL AND JUDAH (5:8–7:7)

Introduction

This subsection is not a literary unity, but comprised of materials related by key words and themes. The cry of alarm in 5:8 is the beginning of a prophetic address in three parts (5:8-15; 6:1-3; 6:4-6) using three speakers: the prophet in 5:8, YHWH in 5:9-15, the people in 6:1-3, with YHWH again in 6:4-6. A number of scholars have concluded that the subunit should end at 6:6 (see below), but it is also the case that YHWH's first-person judgmental speaking continues through 7:7. One might qualify this description of voices by merging the voices of the prophet and YHWH in 5:8-15, so that in effect the speaking sequence is YHWH, people, YHWH. The theme of Israel (and Judah) stumbling is continued.

The subsection 5:8–6:6 is often associated with a time during or at the end of the Syro-Ephraimite War. This setting, and more particularly the war's conclusion, was proposed by A. Alt in an influential study, suggesting that Judah claimed Benjaminite territory after Tiglath-pileser III had devastated Israel and left Samaria as a rump state.[1] The clues are the alarm for the towns in the tribal inheritance of Benjamin in 5:8 and the comparison of Judah's officials to reprobates who move boundary markers in 5:10. His proposals have left their mark on subsequent interpreters, even when they have correlated 5:8ff. with different aspects of the Syro-Ephraimite War or the subsequent devastation in Israel by Tiglath-pileser III.[2]

It is difficult, although not necessarily wrong, to sustain a military-historical reading of 5:8-10. E. M. Good has argued that the blowing of the trumpet in 5:8 has a cultic setting in regional shrines, so that cultic practices and liturgy give shape to what follows in 5:8–6:6, rather than military campaigns.[3] A cultic setting for 6:1-3 is certainly plausible, and in any case the

---

1. The basis for this interpretation goes back to A. Alt, "Hosea 5,8–6,6: Ein Krieg und seine Folgen in prophetischer Beleuchtung," *Kleine Schriften zur Geschichte Israels* (3 vols.; Munich: Beck, 1953-59), 2:163-37. Alt's study was originally published in 1919. See further the excursus on Gibeah at 5:8.

2. One can see this influence in the historical reconstructions of Wolff, *Hosea,* pp. 110-12; Andersen and Freedman, *Hosea,* pp. 402-5; Macintosh, *Hosea,* pp. 194-98. Related historical interpretations include that of P. Arnold, "Hosea and the Sin of Gibeah," *CBQ* 51 (1989) 457-60, who proposes that 5:8 represents Hosea's alarm to Benjamin and his opposition to the coalition forces of Pekah and Rezin moving south against Jerusalem; and John Hayes, *Amos, the Eighth-Century Prophet: His Times and His Preaching* (Nashville: Abingdon, 1988), pp. 76-77, who proposes that 5:8 is Hosea's alarm to Benjamin over the advance of Pekah from Gilead in his bid to topple Pekahiah in Samaria.

3. E. M. Good, "Hosea 5:8–6:6: An Alternative to Alt," *JBL* 85 (1966) 273-86. An encounter with Assyria is presupposed as part of the background to the passage (5:13).

encounter with God is the prominent element in this subsection. The faith-lessness that is underscored in 5:1-7 is assumed and explicated in 5:8-11, 13, with the anger of YHWH and his withdrawal (cf. 5:6) taking center stage in 5:12, 14-15. Perhaps it is best to see this subsection as concentrating on the people's encounter with YHWH against the backdrop of the Syro-Ephraimite War and its immediate aftermath. In the foreground is an angry YHWH confronting Israel for breach of covenant. In the subsection are textual echoes of covenant curse language embedded in Deut. 27–28. Moreover, there is an explicit parallel between the Song of Moses (Deut. 32:39) and the defining of YHWH as one who "tears" and who "kills and makes alive" in 5:14 and 6:1-2. The historical details reflected in 5:8–6:6 are in the service of describing a covenant rupture and a divine response.

1. A Lion against Ephraim and Judah (5:8-15)

8 *Blow the horn in Gibeah, the trumpet in Ramah. Raise an alarm in Beth-aven. Behind you, Benjamin!*

9 *Ephraim shall become a wasteland in the day of reckoning; in the tribes of Israel I make known what is sure.*

10 *The officials of Judah have become like boundary movers; I will pour out my wrath on them like water.*

11 *Ephraim is oppressed and crushed in judgment; he was determined to go after worthlessness.*[4]

12 *Therefore, I am like a moth to Ephraim and rottenness to the house of Judah.*

13 *When Ephraim saw his sickness, and Judah (saw) his wound; then Ephraim went to Assyria, and sent to the great king;*[5] *but he is unable to heal you or cure your affliction.*

---

4. The rendering here follows the lead of the LXX, which has *mataiōn,* meaning "vain" or "worthless." The meaning of the Hebrew term *ṣāw* in this context is unclear. It normally represents a word or command, from the root *ṣwh.* Note the myriad of proposals listed already by Harper, *Hosea,* p. 276. An Arabic cognate has been proposed *(ṣww)* meaning "empty"; see the discussion in Macintosh, *Hosea,* pp. 204-5.

5. As a number of interpreters have proposed, *melek yārēb* (also in 10:6) is likely the equivalent of the Assyrian royal title *šarru rabū* ("Great King"), although there is a difference of opinion whether the Hebrew consonants have been misdivided in the transmission of the text; cf., e.g., *BHS,* which suggests *malkî rāb.* An Aramaic equivalent *(mlk rb)* of the royal title occurs in the 8th-century Sefire treaty (I.B.7). Compare the comments by Andersen and Freedman, *Hosea,* pp. 413-14, with those of Macintosh, *Hosea,* pp. 209-10. A different (Judean) rendering of the Assyrian phrase is in 2 Kgs. 18:19. Given Hosea's penchant for wordplay, Macintosh's suggestion that *yārēb* is a pun on *yārîb* ("he will contend") is interesting.

14 *For I am like a lion to Ephraim, and like a young lion to the house of Judah. Indeed, I myself will tear and depart, bear away and there will be no deliverer.*

15 *I will go and return to my place, until they acknowledge their guilt; then they will seek my face, and in their distress they will eagerly seek me.*

8   Gibeah, Ramah, and Beth-aven (= Bethel) are towns in Benjamin in the southern region of Israel, just north of Jerusalem and Judah (Josh. 18:11-28). Beth-aven literally means "wicked house" or "house of iniquity" (cf. 4:15; 10:5) and is intended as a polemical denunciation of Bethel, modern Beitin, some 11 miles north of Jerusalem. Gibeah (Tell el-Fûl) and Ramah (er-Ram) are approximately halfway between Bethel and Jerusalem. The Benjaminite inheritance is a border area in which inhabitants may be drawn into conflict by competing polities. Some Benjaminites, for example, fought on the side of Judah and Jerusalem (1 Kgs. 12:20-21), although Benjamin itself was reckoned as part of Israel in the division of the kingdom. Ramah was seized by Baasha, king of Israel, to put pressure on Jerusalem (1 Kgs. 15:17-22), only to have his hold there reversed. A subsequent struggle between Israel and Judah likely solidified the control of Israel over most of Benjamin (2 Kgs. 14:8-14).

The effect of calling for the horn and trumpet in v. 8 is intended to be startling, for these were means to grasp public attention for important information and to evoke a response (cf. 8:1). One assumes that Benjamin is singled out, at least in part, because of its location between Judah and Ephraim, since both of them are also mentioned in the context (5:9-10). As noted above, Benjamin could be the location of an assembled army, the object of expansion by Judah, or the designs of a Pekah and Rezin. Whatever the historical threat, the primary matter is that YHWH's judgment is underway in the historical process.

Excursus: Gibeah

The Hebrew term *gib'â* has the basic meaning of hill/hilltop. In Hosea the term occurs twice in the plural (4:13; 10:8) in this generic sense. In the singular it occurs in three places as a proper name. It is the name of a site in the tribal inheritance of Benjamin (5:8), where it is mentioned in context with Ramah and Beth-aven (= Bethel). The name appears twice in the phrase "days of Gibeah" (9:9; 10:9), which is a reference to earlier sinful activity. It is likely that this Gibeah is the same site as that named in 5:8, perhaps to be identified with modern *Tell el-Fûl.*[6]

6. William M. Schniedewind, "The Search for Gibeah: Notes on the Historical

Blowing a shofar in Gibeah (5:8) seems to refer to sounding an alarm for the populace. The context may be that of the turmoil that broke out with the Syro-Ephraimite War and its aftermath. A number of interpreters have been influenced by the reconstruction of Albrecht Alt, who found in 5:8–6:6 the results of Judah's countermove against Israel after the threat against Israel failed to dislodge Ahaz (Isa. 7:1-9).[7] The cities of Benjamin, which lie immediately to the north of Jerusalem, are in the path of the countermove. In contrast to Alt, Patrick Arnold proposed that Hosea opposed the military alliance of Pekah and Rezin that prompted the hostilities, and that 5:8 is the prophet's depiction of danger approaching the Benjaminite cities as the coalition forces move south.[8] John Hayes has proposed that the warning of danger in 5:8 comes from a slightly earlier time when the Gileadite Pekah came to the central hill country of Israel and fomented a coup against Pekahiah.[9] One thus has options for relating a threat to Gibeah in 5:8 as well as assessing the prophet's take on it.

It is possible that the threat to Gibeah depicted in 5:8 could be related to the prophet's references to Israel's past sins during the "days of Gibeah" (9:9; 10:9), but those "sins" are most naturally understood as having taken place sometime before Hosea's own day. Most scholars, therefore, have looked elsewhere for the historical referent in those two texts, and two basic options have commended themselves:

1. Judges 19–21 records a sexual outrage and murder in Gibeah that evoked a response from other Israelite tribes to strike the city and those Benjaminites who were complicit in the crime. The account has some overtones of the Sodom and Gomorrah outrage and destruction in Gen. 19, which is a story that Hosea knows in some form (Hos. 11:8). Given the prophet's use of sexual imagery to critique Israel's failures, a number of scholars have seen Hosea drawing on a form of the Judges account in his reference to the "days of Gibeah."[10] The evidence for this association, however, is not persuasive to all. The canonical account has other Israelite tribes acting in judgment upon Gibeah and Benjamin. One can see how Hos. 9:9 could compare the current corruption of Israel to that earlier in Gibeah, but 10:9 charges Israel *itself* with sin during the "days of Gibeah."[11]

Geography of Central Benjamin," in *"I Will Speak the Riddles of Ancient Times": Archaeological and Historical Studies in Honor of Amihai Mazar on the Occasion of His Sixtieth Birthday,* ed. A. M. Maeir and P. de Miroschedji (2 vols.; Winona Lake, IN: Eisenbrauns, 2006), 2:711-22; Patrick Arnold, "Hosea and the Sin of Gibeah," *CBQ* 51 (1989) 447-60. Arnold reviews interpretations for Gibeah's sin in 9:9 and 10:9, and opts for a different site (Geba) as the location of Benjaminite Gibeah.

7. Alt, "Hosea 5,8–6,6."

8. Arnold, "Hosea," pp. 458-60. On this view it is not clear how the reference to Judah's aggrandizement in 5:10 fits the context. Arnold opines that "Judah" may be an editorial insertion for an earlier "Israel."

9. Hayes, *Amos,* pp. 76-77.

10. So, e.g., Wolff, *Hosea,* pp. 158, 184; Rudolph, *Hosea,* pp. 179-80, 199-200; Macintosh, *Hosea,* pp. 357-58, 412-13.

11. Garrett, *Hosea,* p. 196, interprets Hos. 9:9 as a reference to the outrage of Judg. 19–21, and Hos. 10:9 as a reference to the sin of the people in 1 Sam. 8 who sought human kingship in place of YHWH's rule (p. 214). Arnold, "Hosea," proposes that Hosea

2. Saul, the first king over Israel, was a Benjaminite with a home in Gibeah (1 Sam. 10:26; 11:4). Given Hosea's severe criticism of the monarchy in Israel, some have proposed that the "days of Gibeah" refer to Israel's false step of seeking a king (cf. 1 Sam. 8:1-22).[12] The evidence for this interpretation, however, is not persuasive to all either. Apart from its location as Saul's home, mentioned a couple of times in passing, Gibeah does not play a prominent role in the canonical traditions of Saul's rise to power in 1 Sam. 9–11 (cf. 1 Sam. 10:10). The people ask Samuel for a prophet in Ramah (1 Sam. 8:4; cf. Hos. 5:8). He is anointed king in Mizpah (1 Sam. 10:17). Gilgal is an assembly point for sacrifice after Saul has been made king (1 Sam. 10:8; 11:14-15). And subsequent references to Saul and Gibeah are not linked to any Israelite offense (13:2, 15; 14:2, 16; 15:34; 22:6; 23:19).

Hosea has a penchant for citing disturbing events by reference to a geographic locale (4:15; 5:1, 8; 6:7, 9; 9:6, 10b; 12:11 [MT 12]), assuming that his contemporaries know enough of previous national history to understand his references. Several of these towns and events are now obscure references, given the historical distance between Hosea and modern readers. This is the broader interpretive context in which to put his references to the "days of Gibeah." They are two more examples of his tendency to illustrate his point by reference to the past, as they are for his preference for the preposition kě to portray a simile or to employ a typological comparison. Hence it is entirely possible that the "days of Gibeah" refer to something not preserved in the OT, but still well-enough known to the prophet's contemporaries. Of the options discussed above, the events of Judg. 19–21 seem more likely to portray the events upon which Hosea draws. We would do well, however, to recognize the wisdom of Rudolph's comments for modern readers: The event(s) behind the "days of Gibeah" references would have to be better known to his contemporaries; otherwise, Hosea fails as a prophet.[13]

9   There is in v. 9 an intriguing pair of references, first to Ephraim and then to the tribes of Israel. Although the terminology differs from that used in 5:5, it is possible that a distinction is also being made between Ephraim and some of the other tribal entities that made up the kingdom of Israel. The *tribes of Israel* is kinship terminology, with Israel as the common ancestor of a confederation of descendants. Possibly Ephraim had arrogated to itself certain decisions or had acted independently. Judah had been accused of favoritism during the rule of Solomon and Rehoboam, so it is at least plausible that Ephraim had the major influence over the affairs in Sa-

knew a somewhat different account than that now contained in Judg. 19–20 in which Ephraim attacked Benjamin. The account of the sexual outrage in Judg. 19 was later added to the story to account for Ephraim's attack.

12. Jacob, "Osée," p. 69, sees Saul and his rule as the referent behind 9:9; similarly, J. Wellhausen, *Die kleinen Propheten übersetzt und erklärt* (1893; repr. Berlin: de Gruyter, 1963), p. 125, in his comments on 10:9.

13. Rudolph, *Hosea,* p. 180.

maria and may have incurred suspicion or jealousy as a result. On the other hand, *Ephraim* may well be used here as a synonym for Israel, similar to the use of Joseph and Isaac in the prophecies of Amos (5:6, 15; 6:6; 7:9).

The vocabulary here in 5:9a indicates judgment upon land and people. The Hebrew term for *wasteland* or "horror/destruction" *(šammâ)* is part of the list of curses to fall upon the people of God for covenant disobedience in Deut. 28:37 (cf. 2 Kgs. 22:19). Jeremiah uses the term similarly.[14] In Isa. 13:9 the earth is made a "wasteland" when judgment comes on the "day of YHWH." In Hos. 5:9 the phrase *day of reckoning* indicates something quite similar — a day or time of YHWH's decisive act — although the precise phrase occurs only here in the OT. The term *reckoning (tōkēḥâ)* is associated with a day of judgment in 2 Kgs. 19:3, and it is used in parallel with "vengeance" *(nĕqāmâ)* in Ps. 149:7. The prophetic point is clear: YHWH's judgment is underway in the events depicted.

According to v. 9, the communication of judgment depends on the veracity of YHWH. Thus the prophet declares on YHWH's behalf that what has been made known is *sure* or "true" *(ne'ĕmānâ)*. The term is a Niphal participle, used as an adjective elsewhere to modify God's edicts, decrees, covenant, and witness (Ps. 19:7 [MT 8]; 89:28, 37 [MT 29, 38]; 93:5; 111:7). In v. 9 there is no noun for the participle (if used as an adjective) to modify. It may function, therefore, more like a noun. If so, it would be seen as the object of the verb and the final phrase could be translated as "to make known that which is truth."[15]

10 Judah's leadership comes under withering critique with the simile that they are *boundary movers*. It is possible that the charge is literal and that Judah has expanded northward at Israel's expense. Benjamin was, after all, a border area in which political control was part of the ebb and flow of regional history. It may, however, be rhetorical and proverbial rather than indicating a particular military endeavor, a metaphorical way to charge Judah with being treacherous in that they are *like* such criminals. The moving of a family or clan's boundary marker is a crime in the Deuteronomic code and resides under a collective curse (Deut. 19:14; 27:17). The wisdom tradition likewise regards the practice as heinous (Prov. 22:28; 23:10; cf. Job 24:2). It is an affront to the ancestors, a threat to the inheritance and livelihood of a family, and strikes at the heart of a community's life. If the accusation in 5:10

---

14. Jer. 2:15; 4:7; 5:30; 18:16; 25:11, 18, 38. In 2:15, 4:7, and 25:38, Jeremiah joins the roaring of lions with the wasting of the land. In 25:38 YHWH is the lion who brings devastation. Perhaps the language of wasteland in Hos. 5:9 is linked also with YHWH as lion in 5:14.

15. In Hos. 11:12 (MT 12:1) the masculine singular participle *ne'ĕmān* modifies Judah and refers to its relationship with the holy one(s).

is influenced by the ethos of the Deuteronomic code, then it is tantamount to saying that Judah resides under a curse overseen by YHWH. Such an understanding certainly fits the concluding clause of v. 10. The simile of YHWH's *wrath being poured out like water* is unique in the OT. Perhaps the declaration stands in the tradition of floods as the chaos of judgment (Amos 5:8; 9:6). Floods are also part of treaty curses in the ancient Near East, which may well link this threat of judgment to violation of YHWH's covenant ethos.[16] Although YHWH had promised never again to destroy the earth with a flood (Gen. 9:8-17), the overwhelming nature of his judgment will nevertheless hit Judah. Does this mean that Judah's iniquity is comparable to that of the legendary flood generation?

An ambiguity resides in the term for *official (śār)*. It can refer to someone in the administrative system of the royal house or national government, but it can also mean more narrowly "prince," a descendant or offspring of a monarch. Hosea uses the term frequently (3:4; 7:3, 5, 16; 8:10; 9:15; 13:10) as part of his institutional critique of Israel and Judah.

11 Ephraim, like Judah, is in a sad state, the result of self-incurred judgment. The word pair *oppress ('āšaq)* and *crush (rāṣaṣ)* also appears in 1 Sam. 12:3-4 and Amos 4:1, where they represent the negative effects of social crimes upon the fabric of society. Such a context can fit the debilitated state of Ephraim, but a more likely nuance for the word pair comes in Deut. 28:33 in the list of curses for covenant disobedience: "A people whom you do not know shall eat up the fruit of your ground and of all your labors; you shall be continually abused and crushed" (NRSV). If this passage in Hosea is set in the aftermath of the Assyrian onslaught on Israel in 733/732, then the application of the covenant curse is a somber judgment indeed, but stated clearly enough for his contemporaries to grasp. Judah is included in the judgment, which could be the prophet's take on Ahaz's submission to Assyria.

12 YHWH is at work through the historical process to bring about his judgment. The similes for his judgment in v. 12 are the *moth ('āš)* on the one hand and *rottenness (rāqāb)* on the other. The two terms are used together in Job 13:28, in reference to one who is "like a rotten thing, consumed like a moth-eaten garment." Elsewhere "moth" is associated with garments (Isa. 50:9; 51:8), and "rotten" is applied to bones and wood (Prov. 12:4; 14:30; Hab. 3:16; Isa. 40:20). Perhaps Hosea's description of YHWH is an adaptation of a proverbial saying about things in decay and no longer fit for service.[17] Similar

16. Hillers, *Treaty-Curses,* pp. 70-71.

17. Wolff, *Hosea,* p. 104; and Macintosh, *Hosea,* p. 207, think that *'āš* does not refer to a moth, but to a homonym meaning "pus" (so Wolff) or "emaciating disease" (so Macintosh). The primary reason is one of context. The description of sickness and wound in 5:13 better accords with a physical ailment rather than a scourge that consumes clothing.

language is also used in the curse tradition for treaty violation.[18] In any case, Hosea's simile is a bold application of the work of YHWH among his people: God is the source of their decay, brought on by their following a futile pathway.

13 The prophet refers to external political history and apparently some form of an embassy sent by Ephraim to the Assyrian king. Since Israel paid tribute to Assyria on more than one occasion, and other forms of contact and submission may have occurred as well, one cannot determine the precise context of the prophet's reference. As noted previously, a number of elements in 5:8–6:6 can be associated with the tumultuous period from the outbreak of the Syro-Ephraimite War through the campaign of Tiglath-pileser III in the region and its immediate aftermath (ca. 736-731). At the conclusion of this period, Israel had been truncated with Samaria left as a rump state; Pekah had been killed and Hoshea placed on the throne by Assyrian agreement; and Judah, under Ahaz, had also submitted to Assyrian control.[19] The reference to both Ephraim and Judah in v. 13a fits attractively as an accusation in 732/731, when both states were made Assyrian vassals. It is the case, however, that Menahem paid tribute at least once several years earlier, and there were embassies back and forth after Tiglath-pileser III died in 727 and was succeeded by his son Shalmaneser V.

Hosea states that the Assyrian great king cannot *heal (rāpā')* the illness that afflicts Ephraim and Judah. He speaks metaphorically, comparing the treachery and pursuit of futility on the part of the people also to a *wound.* Physicians can assist in the healing process, but only YHWH, the cosmic king, can heal this wound of his people (cf. 6:1).[20] It is impossible, even for the resources at the disposal of the Assyrian great king, to provide what Hosea understands by YHWH's healing. Assyria's great king has no political cure for what ails Israel. In this instance YHWH's cure would mean removing Israel's dependence on other deities and the power of Assyria, restoring them to fidelity and sole dependence on him, and then granting them the blessings promised in the covenant.

14 In yet another simile Hosea indicates in 5:14 just how far the cosmic king YHWH is at the historical moment from being a healer. In response to the political and theological rebellion against him, YHWH represents himself as a lion. The parallelism of v. 14a with v. 14b is synonymous. Ephraim and Judah are placed on an equal and rebellious footing. The actions in v. 14b describe the stages of a lion's successful hunt: capture, killing, and dragging away with impunity. The poetry is exquisite, the content frightful.

---

18. Hillers, *Treaty-Curses,* p. 56.

19. For further details, see the introduction, section III, "Historical Background to Hosea's Prophecy."

20. The terms "heal" and "wound *(māzōr)* occur together in Jer. 30:13.

A	B
lion — Ephraim	young lion — Judah
tear, depart	carry away, no deliverer

At one level of presentation, the language is formulaic, culturally specific, and perhaps even proverbial.[21] For example, some of the same imagery and vocabulary is employed in Mic. 5:8 (MT 7), where a lion *tears (ṭārap)* its prey with *no one to deliver ('ên maṣṣîl)*. The application, however, is to the future resurgence of the people of God among the nations — a point far removed from that described by Hosea. Similar imagery can be found elsewhere (Isa. 5:29; Ps. 7:2 [MT 3]; 50:22).

There is a close parallel to Hos. 5:13–6:2 in Deut. 32:39, part of the Song of Moses. It lacks, however, a lion simile for YHWH. "See now that I myself am he and there is no other God except me. I kill and make alive; I smite and heal, and there is no deliverer from my hand." Apart from the explicit lion simile, this formulaic identification of the covenant Lord relates quite directly to the representation of YHWH in Hos. 5:14 and also the confessional language about YHWH in 6:1-2.[22] They share the emphatic first person pronoun (*'ănî*, twice), the verb *rāpā'* ("heal," 5:13; 6:1), the Piel of the verb *ḥāyâ* ("to make alive," 6:2), and the phrase *no deliverer* (5:14).

The lion simile in v. 14 and elsewhere (11:10; 13:7) may be a play on Assyrian royal propaganda. In their public sculpture and boastful annals, the Assyrian kings are represented as fierce hunters of the king of beasts, even as each of them presented himself as the *great king,* a supreme monarch subjugating other peoples and kingdoms. Nahum's oracle against Nineveh depicts Assyrian might in the guise of lions, who nevertheless will be conquered through God's judgment (2:11-13 [MT 13-15]). Although the peoples of the ancient Near East had plenty to fear from Neo-Assyria, Hosea insists that Ephraim and Judah have more to fear in a theological and historical sense from YHWH. In Hosea's mind YHWH is the real king and the only lion that Ephraim should fear.

15 Verse 15 concludes the representation of YHWH speaking that began in 5:9. After YHWH's self-presentation as an attacking lion, there really is little else that can be said at such a somber time. With the affirmation that he will go away to his *place (māqôm),* a reader might well think that the lion simile continues, with YHWH returning to his lair. This is likely in accord with

---

21. Ravaging lions and wild beasts are also part of the treaty curse tradition of the ancient Near East; see Hillers, *Treaty-Curses,* pp. 55-56. For further details on lion imagery, see Brent Strawn, *What Is Stronger than a Lion? Leonine Imagery and Metaphor in the Hebrew Bible and the Ancient Near East* (OBO 212; Fribourg: Academic Press, 2005).

22. For additional details see appendix 2, "The Song of Moses and Hosea."

Hosea's intention, but a *place* for YHWH is more than a comparison with a lion's lair. Deuteronomy indicates that there is a "place" *(māqôm)* among the tribes where YHWH "causes his name to dwell" (12:5, 11), a place that is eventually identified with Jerusalem, but that is potentially applicable to other places that YHWH may designate. Thus even in his absence, the divine lion-king is not far removed from his people. It is also the case that YHWH's place cannot be limited so easily to geography, so that even the heavens themselves cannot contain him (1 Kgs. 8:27, 30, 39, 43). Yet even in such transcendence YHWH can hear and act. Thus later readers are confronted with some unsettling implications of the divine abode. YHWH may return to his *place,* but wherever that is, it is not too far from his people. That can be good news when they acknowledge their *guilt,*[23] but terrifying news if they do not.

The poetry of v. 15 employs vocabulary used elsewhere in the context and reinforces the implications of YHWH's departure:

A	B
They bear their guilt [cf. 4:15],	they seek [cf. 5:6] my face.

In his *return to his place,* YHWH awaits the *return* (6:1) of his people to him. In the historical process, he has *torn* (5:14; 6:1), but he is capable of *making alive.*

2. Failed Repentance and Failed Relationships (6:1-11a)

> 1 *Come, let us return to YHWH; for he has torn, but he will heal us; he struck,*[24] *but he will bandage us.*
>
> 2 *He will revive us after two days; on the third day he will raise us; and we shall live before him and*
>
> 3 *know him.*[25] *Let us move forward to know YHWH; like dawn his appearance*[26] *is sure; he will come forth like the rain to us; he will water the earth like the spring rains.*

23. Hosea uses the root *'šm,* "to be guilty, incur guilt," elsewhere in 4:15; 10:2; 13:1; 13:16 (MT 14:1).

24. With *BHS* and a number of interpreters one might anticipate a prefixed *waw* with the shortened imperfect form *yak.* Its absence could be the result of haplography, but in poetry the imperfect form can follow a previous perfect verb (like *ṭārap,* the verb "to tear") with a past meaning. The poetic parallelism between the two verbs assumes a past deed for the imperfect form.

25. Andersen and Freedman, *Hosea,* p. 417, also include the first word of 6:3 with the final clause of 6:2.

26. The noun translated "appearance" *(môṣā')* is derived from the verb *yāṣā',* "to go out/forth." The noun is used in Ps. 19:6 (MT 7) in reference to the rising of the sun. On occasion the noun is used with the terms "mouth" or "lips" (e.g., Deut. 8:3; 23 [MT 24])

4 *What shall I do about you, O Ephraim; what shall I do about you, O Judah? Your loyalty is like a morning cloud, like dew disappearing early.*

5 *Therefore, I have cut them up through the prophets, killed them with words of my mouth; my judgments have gone forth like light.*[27]

6 *For I desire steadfast love and not sacrifice, the knowledge of God rather than burnt offerings.*

7 *But as at Adam they transgressed the covenant; there they acted treacherously against me.*

8 *Gilead is a city of evildoers with tracks of blood.*

9 *And as a band of robbers lies in wait for someone, so a band of priests murder on the way to Shechem; they have done wickedness.*

10 *In the house of Israel I have seen a horrible thing; there is Ephraim's harlotry, Israel is defiled.*

11a *Also Judah, a harvest is set for you!*

1-3   The voice in 6:1-3 is that of the people whom Hosea represents as having encountered judgment and who recognize that it comes from YHWH. *Tearing, healing,* and *returning* in v. 1 are all terms from the immediate context of YHWH's prior speaking in judgment (5:13-15); moreover, the language of being bandaged also follows naturally from the prior reference to "wound" in 5:13. Thus the cohortative *let us return* in v. 1 would seem to be Israel's response to the declaration in 5:15 of YHWH's own "return"[28] to his place until the offenders recognize their betrayal, i.e., their guilt, and sincerely seek him.

Excursus: Return to YHWH

In 6:1 the people are represented as saying, *let us return to (šûb 'el) YHWH.* The verb in question is a common one in the OT, with the basic meaning of turning/returning. In combination with another verb, it can also indicate doing something a second time (so Hos. 11:9). In certain contexts it has the connotation of "repenting," i.e., turning

---

to refer to an utterance. Possibly Hosea is using ambiguity to express the certainty of divine appearance and speaking.

27. This rendering follows a number of interpreters who have proposed that the MT *ûmišpāṭeykā 'ôr* be redivided to read *ûmišpāṭî kā'ôr.* This is also in accord with the rendering of the LXX. The redivision of the Hebrew text makes for a smoother reading (which in itself is not a compelling reason to adopt it), plus it continues the use of similes established in preceding verses.

28. Both YHWH and Israel's "returning" are first-person cohortatives of the verb *šûb.* See further the excursus below, "Return to YHWH."

from an action or attitude and embracing YHWH himself and his covenant ethos. Hosea uses the term 21 times (2:7, 9 [MT 9, 11]; 3:5; 4:9; 5:4, 15; 6:1, 11; 7:10, 16; 8:13; 9:3; 11:5, 9; 12:2, 6, 14 [MT 3, 7, 15]; 14:1, 2, 4, 7 [MT 2, 3, 5, 8]).[29] The subjects include Gomer, YHWH, and the people (Ephraim, Israel, Judah). YHWH himself is the object of the people's return in 2:7 (MT 9) (metaphorically as Gomer's first husband); 3:5 (indirectly); 6:1; 7:10; 11:5; 12:6 (MT 7); and 14:1-2 (MT 2-3).[30] When YHWH or God is an object of a preposition in these texts, the preposition typically is ʾel, meaning "to/toward." One exception is 14:1 (MT 2), which has ʿad, meaning "to/unto." Since this single exception is in proximity to 14:2 (MT 3), where YHWH is again the object of ʾel, it seems that the two prepositions are used with the same nuance in reference to "returning to YHWH" (cf. Joel 2:12-13). Another exception is 12:6 (MT 7), where the governing preposition is bĕ, and the phrase can be translated "you should return with your God." In this instance the phrase is likely reflecting elements from Jacob's life (Gen. 28:15, 20-21) that Hosea applies to Israel.

As one might surmise, the closest parallels to Hosea's "return to YHWH" come in Jeremiah (3:7, 20, 22; 4:1; 24:7) and Deuteronomy (4:30; 30:2-3, 10).[31] Furthermore, Jeremiah prefers the same construction as Hosea, using the preposition ʾel with YHWH as object, while Deuteronomy uses ʿad twice and ʾel once. In 3:7 Jeremiah uses the terminology of "return" in the context of a comparison between the divorce and possible remarriage of a couple, on the one hand, and the consideration of faithless Israel's "return to YHWH," on the other hand. This context and choice of vocabulary show how deeply indebted the book of Jeremiah is to portions of Hosea. In Deut. 30:2-3 and 10 the author places a future "return to" the Lord in the context of the people's realization that they have sinned against the Lord and have been sent into exile. Chapter 30 comes after the extensive list of curses for covenant breaking in chs. 27–28. Here too Hosea and Deuteronomy share not only similar vocabulary but similarity of perspective on matters related to covenant and corporate fidelity.[32] On the other hand, Hosea's employment of "returning" has YHWH as the object, but not the land.[33] Hosea has much to say about a future transformation of Israel and Judah, but comparatively little explicitly about a return from exile. Both Deuteronomy and Jeremiah share with Hosea (6:11) the idiomatic phrase to "restore the fortunes" of the people (šûb šĕbût).[34] Whereas it is employed by Deuteronomy in the context of a return from exile, in Hosea it is used more generally in the sense of turning the circumstances of Israel for the better.

Hosea also uses the verb in ways to signify the opposite of returning to YHWH. In one instance, the people turn to that which does not profit (7:16; cf. com-

---

29. In 6:11 the verb is used with a cognate accusative to form the phrase šûb šûbût, which means idiomatically "to turn the turning," i.e., "to restore the fortunes."

30. 7:10 and 11:5 actually state that Israel has refused to return to YHWH.

31. See also Pss. 22:27 [MT 28]; 126:4; Zech. 1:3; Mal. 3:7.

32. See Weinfeld, *Deuteronomy and the Deuteronomic School,* pp. 366-70. See also H. J. Zobel, "Hosea und das Deuteronomium," *TLZ* 110 (1985) 13-23.

33. Hos. 11:10-11 has Israelites coming from Egypt and Assyria to be "settled" (yāšab) in their homes.

34. Deut. 30:3; Jer. 30:3, 18; 31:23; 32:44; 33:7, 11, 26. Cf. Amos 9:14; Zeph. 2:7; 3:20.

mentary there). Three times those who refuse to return to YHWH are threatened with a "return to Egypt" (8:13; 9:3; 11:5). In 9:3 Hosea employs a pun on the verbs "dwell" *(yāšab)* and "return" *(šûb)*. Disobedient Israel will not be able to "dwell" in YHWH's land, but will "return" to Egypt.

The saying in Hos. 6:1 is rooted in cultic practice as the context intimates. Hosea declares in 6:6 a preference for loving-kindness/loyalty and knowledge of God rather than sacrifice and burnt offerings. And there are other places in Hosea in which a cultic setting may be discerned for the vocabulary. For example, the magnificent turning to the Lord in 14:2-3 (MT 3-4) has several characteristics of liturgical-based language. Perhaps Hos. 3:5 also reflects cultic practice in the prophecy that the disciplined people will "(re)turn and seek YHWH in the latter days."

These texts in Hosea are evidence for the personal and the particular in the covenant YHWH established with Israel. When Israel offends against the covenant ethos, it is preeminently an offense against the covenant giver. This is highlighted in the metaphorical designation of covenant with marriage. Obedience to instruction is a sign of fidelity, as are proper sacrifices and offerings, but the emphasis on Israel's returning in Hosea is upon the people's return *to YHWH*. It is personal and not simply a matter of obedience to instruction. Moreover, a return to the Lord is not based on Israel's strength to change, but on the resolve of the offended Lord to enable and to accept them. In 11:10 the trembling people return to one who has internally resolved to forego a killing blow (11:8-9) in order to beckon and to lead them home. In 14:1-3 (MT 2-4) Israel is encouraged to return to Yahweh. A successful return, however, is not determined by measuring the sacrifices or the prayers, but by YHWH, who has mercy on the orphan (prodigal son?).

The question is whether 6:1-3 is the speech of the people that the Lord longs to hear while waiting in his place (5:15), and is thus composed by Hosea to represent true repentance (if only Israel would embrace it!); or whether 6:1-3 is something that Israel is proposing but in an inadequate way.[35] A decision between the options is difficult. With regard to the witness of the book, the result is crystal clear: whether repentance is inadequately expressed or offered as advice to Israel, the people failed the loyalty test.

The poetry in 6:2 is best interpreted as a chiastic reflex of 6:1. A comparison of the six clauses of the two verses bears this out.

(6:1A) return to YHWH//(6:2A) we shall live before him and know him
(6:1B) torn, but he will heal us//(6:2B) third day he will raise us
(6:1C) struck, but he will bandage us//(6:2C) revive us after two days

35. Macintosh, *Hosea,* pp. 216-19, does a good job of setting out these alternatives and opts for 6:1-3 as the prophet's composition of what YHWH would like to hear from his people. The alternative, that 6:1-3 is taken from a repentance ritual engaged in by the people, has a possible parallel in Jer. 14:1-10, where the people's approach to the Lord in prayer and confession is deemed insufficient.

The poetry in 6:2 also has a type of a numerical formula that is at home in prophetic address and proverbial wisdom. Amos's formula "for three transgressions and for four" (1:3–2:8) indicates a series of transgressions perpetrated by various nations, but it does not necessarily indicate either three or four transgressions in each cited instance. The formula indicates that the series of transgressions, however many in actual number, have tried God's patience and will usher in a response of judgment. The sayings of Agur refer several times to "three, even four" of something (Prov. 30:15-31), where four is the actual number in the sage's mind. Since the saying here in Hos. 6:2 is not precisely parallel, the question is raised: do the phrases *after two* and *on the third* refer literally to a three-day period, or is it a reference to a short period of time? The poetic parallelism with 6:1 does not provide an answer. Moreover, the time element is complicated by history-of-religion parallels to the motif of a "dying and rising" deity and to the language of recovery from illness.[36] The expression of hope thus derives from a culture where this language of a quick healing and renewal has multiple literary and social roots. Likely the difference that modern readers assume between recovery from illness and resurrection from the dead was understood more synthetically by the ancients. Sickness could be the intrusion of the powers of death, and recovery could be understood as a new gift of life. There should be no doubt, anyway, that the language of 6:2 rests its hope for the health of the people in their acceptance by YHWH. This would mean his turning from the activity of a lion (5:13-14) to that of a healer and restorer of life.

3 Israel's voice continues in v. 3 with an expression of confidence and an affirmation of YHWH's life-giving presence. Two factors from the people's corporate experience are employed as similes. YHWH is *like the appearance of the sun at dawn and like* the periodic rains that come in a Mediterranean climate during winter and early spring. Sun and rain are necessary to the agricultural cycle, which undergirds Israel's existence. YHWH is the agent of fertility, not the Canaanite or Phoenician pantheons. In citing these two components, Hosea confirms that the life sought by Israel is not divorced from the legitimate concerns over health and fertility. They are rooted, however, in exclusive fidelity to YHWH and the covenant ethos, not in the supposed safety of polytheism or the coercion of sacrifice (6:6).

The OT contains a number of comparisons between YHWH and the sun, since both are agents of light and blessing. Some interpreters have even seen an identification between the two, but that presses the poetic imagery too far (e.g., Ps. 84:11 [MT 12]). The sun is a creation of the Creator, and even when personified (Ps. 19:1-6) the distinction between Creator and creation is maintained. The sun is, however, a powerful illustration of the work

36. See the excursus below, "Being Raised on the Third Day."

and presence of YHWH in his world (Pss. 19:1-6 [MT 2-7]; 72:17; 113:1-4; 136:8; Isa. 45:6; 60:19-20). It is not mentioned by name in Hosea, but the term "dawn" signals its approach in this passage. Rain and dew (Hos. 14:5 [MT 6])[37] are other examples of YHWH's provisions for the life of the earth and its inhabitants. A general term for precipitation is mentioned first *(gešem),* and in the last clause comes a term that indicates the latter or spring rains *(malqôš).*

The affirmation of YHWH as eager responder and benevolent sustainer is true, but sadly not applicable to Israel's present situation. Their continuing faithlessness is reflected in the rhetorical questions and the charge of 6:4. There is nothing per se in 6:1-3 that demonstrates the inadequacy of Israel's confession that YHWH judges and makes alive, if these verses are part of a liturgy of repentance. If they represent what Judge YHWH wishes to hear, then it is obvious from what follows that he did not hear it from his people. Thus at the historical moment depicted in 6:1-3, Israel's redeemer has become Israel's judge and remains so.

Excursus: Being Raised on the Third Day

Cryptic phrases in Hos. 6:2 refer to YHWH "reviving us after two days" and "raising us up on the third day." The "us" indicates the people who propose a return to the Lord who has judged them. There are a number of questions that come with the phrases. For the purposes at hand, we will briefly examine two matters. One is that of the vocabulary in its primary literary context in Hosea. The other is the history-of-religions context of Hosea's audience in which language of being *made alive* and *raised up* occurs.

Vocabulary and Context

Hosea 6:1-3 comes between two passages where YHWH is represented as speaking in the first person (5:8-15; 6:4-6). The three verses propose a return on Israel's part to the Lord, who according to 5:14-15 has been like a lion to his people in judgment, and who in 6:4-6 reflects exasperation with the inadequacy of their commitment. The terms "live/make alive" *(ḥāyâ,* Qal/Piel) and "raise up" *(qûm)* in 6:2 are common terms in the OT. It is their use as a word pair, however, that is of primary interest. As a word pair, the closest parallel to these verbs in 6:2 comes in the context of life and death and the return to life from the grave.[38]

37. The "dew" *(ṭal)* of YHWH is compared to his ability to give life to the dead in Isa. 26:19.

38. See the discussion in Philip S. Johnston, *Shades of Sheol: Death and Afterlife*

"The dead will not live *(ḥāyâ);* the shades [of the departed] will not rise *(qûm).* Isa. 26:14

"Your dead will live *(ḥāyâ),* [your] corpses[39] will rise *(qûm).* Isa. 26:19

This nuance of the recovery of life fits the word pair well in the context in Hos. 6:1-3. The question, however, is whether in 6:2 it depicts a type of corporate "resurrection" for the people, perhaps similar to the restoration of the exiles depicted in Ezek. 37:1-14, or instead that of a healing by the Lord and subsequent recovery of health. "Resurrection" from the dead, therefore, can be a metaphor for restoration from the powers of evil. With respect to the timing of healing, there are some parallels in Neo-Assyrian texts and elsewhere to the recovery from sickness on a second or third day using similar language.[40] Since the power of sickness and the power of death are related in the minds of many, it is difficult to choose between the two options. Indeed, Hosea's own poetic allusiveness may intentionally include both.

History-of-Religions Background

A number of scholars earlier in the 20th century proposed that the motif of the "dying and rising god" (Baal, Melqart, Eshmun, Adon[is]) from the Canaanite and Phoenician cultures influenced the renewing language of 6:2.[41] Israel may well have known a seasonal pattern in Canaan in which a deity dies in the fall and then in the spring rises again. Such a divinely engendered "turnaround" could be the basis for the language of the people expressing hope of being made alive and raised by YHWH. Others in recent years have disputed whether there is a "dying and rising deity" motif[42] in the ancient Near East before the inception of the Christian faith, preferring to see in the corporate voice of 6:2 either the language of human recovery from sickness or perhaps a cultic life-setting in which the relationship is renewed by the Lord with the

---

in the Old Testament (Downers Grove, IL: InterVarsity Press, 2002), pp. 112-14, 221-27. Another related text is 1 Sam. 2:6, "YHWH kills and makes alive *(ḥāyâ),* brings down to Sheol and raises up." The last verb is *'ālâ* rather than *qûm,* but it is used in a similar way to express the overcoming of Sheol and the powers of death.

39. The LXX preserves the plural "graves." Readers would anticipate a plural noun as a parallel to the plural ("dead") with which the verse begins. Thus the MT, which has "my corpse," should likely be emended to a plural. Perhaps the final *yod* is a dittography and comes from the initial *yod* of the following verb.

40. Michael Barré, "New Light on Hos VI 2," *VT* 28 (1978) 129-41. Hosea 6:2 can be read as a reference to raising up/recovery on a literal third day or as a reference to vindication after a short period of time.

41. This interpretation, which stresses the language of overcoming the powers of death through YHWH's "raising," is argued by Andersen and Freedman, *Hosea,* pp. 415-25.

42. Mark Smith, "The Death of 'Dying and Rising Gods' in the Biblical World: An Update, with Special Reference to Baal in the Baal Cycle," *SJOT* 12 (1998) 257-313.

people. Thus Eidevall, in reference to several recent commentators, states: "the vehicle field [for the metaphor in 6:2] is most probably that of a sick person, expecting to be cured and able to rise from the bed."[43]

In an important review of the evidence for "dying and rising" deities in the ancient Near East, T. N. D. Mettinger has questioned whether the more recent skepticism of the motif is justified.[44] In his brief references to Hos. 6:2, Mettinger does not insist that the "dying and rising deity" motif has influenced the language of Israel's *being made alive* and *raising up,* but that is the way he cautiously leans. For him the language represents a fundamental conviction that YHWH is the living God who is able to heal and restore the people, including life from the dead, and in this he is likely correct. The point finally at issue is Israel's ruptured relationship with YHWH and how the recovery/resurrection language was understood.

"Dying" and "being raised to life" are also themes in relationships between suzerains and vassals.[45] Indeed, a transfer of this terminology from treaties to Israel's relationship with YHWH is easier to comprehend than that used in Phoenician cults for deities. Examples from treaty texts indicate that the terminology for death and killing is applied to the deposing of a ruler or the prevention of a rightful claimant from being elevated to the throne. Correspondingly, the installation of a vassal or a confirming of his rule is compared to "raising to life." In one instance the king of Hatti claims to have raised the land of Mitanni to life through his benevolence. This language of (political) restoration may have a counterpart in the covenant relationship between Israel and YHWH. Hosea used the terminology of "covenant" *(bĕrît)* in reference to Israel's relationship with YHWH as well as for political agreements made by Israel that he opposed (10:4). The repentance language of 6:1-2 holds forth the hope that Israel will be raised, i.e., made alive through restoration of the covenant blessings under the aegis of YHWH. Some support for this understanding occurs in 6:3b, where YHWH's approach is like that of life-giving rain.

Christian interpreters have rightly asked whether Hos. 6:2 is one of the texts in the mind of Paul when he claims that the resurrection of Christ on the third day is in accord with the Scriptures (1 Cor. 15:4). That the apostle made such a connection between Hos. 6:2 and the Easter event is possible, and perhaps even likely, but Tertullian appears to be the first Christian writer to cite Hos. 6:2 explicitly as scriptural proof of Christ's resurrection.[46] It is also possible to see the motifs of the "dying and rising god" and that of "corporate resurrection" (as with Ezek. 37:1-14) as tradition-history links, first of all to Hos. 6:2 and then to the proclamation of Christ's resurrection.

4-6   God's response to the people's continuing faithlessness comes in 6:4-6. The two rhetorical questions in 6:4 are literally identical except for

43. Eidevall, *Grapes in the Desert,* p. 95.

44. *The Riddle of Resurrection: "Dying and Rising" Gods in the Ancient Near East* (ConBOT 50; Stockholm: Almqvist & Wiksell, 2001).

45. See J. Wijngaards, "Death and Resurrection in a Covenantal Context (Hos. Vi.2)," *VT* 17 (1967) 230-36.

46. See Macintosh, *Hosea,* pp. 222-23, and the discussion there.

the change between Ephraim and Judah as different addressees (cf. 11:8). The word translated *loyalty* is *ḥesed,* often translated as "loving-kindness." It appears here in a simile in the context of a charge of fickleness against the people. During the dry summer months early morning clouds and dew appear periodically along the coast and into the hill country, but the clouds disappear quickly and the moisture from the dew goes soon after. On the one hand, the dew is life-giving and sustains certain fruits and vegetables from the end of the spring rains until harvest (Hos. 14:5 [MT 6]). On the other hand, the dry summer season dominates, and the morning clouds and dew are fleeting. This latter characteristic stands behind the simile of loyalty like the morning cloud and defines the fleeting commitment of Ephraim and Judah to YHWH (cf. 13:3).

5 One form of YHWH's response to Israel's failures and fickleness has been the employment of prophets. They uncover iniquity, announce judgment, and call for repentance. In this verse readers encounter one aspect of that profile, namely, that they announced judgment against God's people and that it came to pass in the historical process. Such a description fits the work of an Elijah or Micaiah, and doubtless others known to the audience, but whose words are not preserved in the OT as a book. Hosea's contemporary Amos reminded Israel that prophets were part of YHWH's means of instructing them in the aftermath of the settlement in the land, even if what the prophets said at times was unpalatable (Amos 2:11-12). And Hosea's successor Jeremiah reminded a prophetic opponent that it was the task of a prophet to announce and thereby to interpret disasters (Jer. 28:7-9).

The last clause of Hos. 6:5 is another simile, as well as commentary on the claim that YHWH had killed through the prophetic word. Just as light pierces the darkness, so divine judgment has come forth in Israel's history. The term used for *judgment (mišpāṭ)* is the same one as in 5:1, although here it occurs in the plural, perhaps indicating a series of chastisements or representing YHWH's corrective actions as repetitive.

6 YHWH's poetic affirmation is also proverb-like in form, i.e., a wise saying that can be applied in a variety of circumstances.[47] It is employed that way, as a saying apart from its Hosean context, in the Gospel of Matthew (9:13; 12:7). We lack the requisite data to know if it is a saying originating with Hosea or one known to him. The hierarchy of values that the saying represents, however, resonates with other claims in the prophetic book. Elsewhere Hosea uses the Hebrew terms for *steadfast love* or "loyalty" (*ḥesed,* 2:19 [MT 21]; 6:4; 10:12; 12:6 [MT 7]) and *knowledge of God (daʿat*

---

47. Eberhard Bons, *"Car c'est l'amour qui me plaît, non le sacrifice . . .":* *Recherches sur Osée 6:6 et son interprétation juive et chrétienne* (JSJSup 88; Leiden: Brill, 2004).

'ĕlōhîm, 4:6). They are paired with "faithfulness" in 4:1 as pillars of the covenantal ethos that the Lord desires from his people.

The proverbial form is an absolute contrast of entities, but it presupposes nuanced commitments. The first commitment is to the love and knowledge of God; sacrificial worship, rightly understood, plays a supporting role to the first commitment. It is unlikely that Hosea represents God as rejecting the efficacy assigned to sacrificial practice elsewhere in the OT; rather, he represents a prophetic critique of an overreliance on sacrifice, coupled with an insistence on the basic claim of the first commandment: "You shall have no other gods [or cultic practices] before me." Sacrificial practice, rightly understood, is neither magic nor coercive of its divine author, but is rather a gift to the covenant community intended as a means to greater ends. As with the disciplinary period portrayed in 3:4, there are fundamental practices more important than sacrifice. It is the lack of love and knowledge of God among the people that is tragic, not the presence of burnt offerings and other sacrifices. Hosea offers here a critique of sacrificial ritual when it is not rooted in a covenantal ethos and where it is seen as a means of inducing a deity to act. In this way of speaking, Hosea joins other prophets and voices that see sacrifice and the public cultus as divinely given gifts to be used with gratitude, not as ritual coercion.[48]

7 The prophet illustrates Israel's ongoing faithlessness by reference to an incident at a place named Adam and wickedness in Gilead. Some interpret *Adam* as a personal name and thus as a reference to Gen. 3 and the disobedience in the garden.[49] According to this view, Israel was repeating the error of the first man's disobedience to divine command. Another possibility is to take *'ādām* as a collective reference to "people" acting disobediently.[50] The Hebrew particle *šām ("there")* in the verse, however, marks a geographical reference, and Adam is the likely antecedent (see below). In Hos. 10:9 a similar syntactical expression occurs, with an initial reference to Gibeah followed by the particle "there" in the next clause. *BHS*, followed by a number of commentators, suggests that the *kĕ* ("like/as") prefixed to *Adam* be changed to a *bĕ* ("in/at"), so that the phrase would read "but they transgressed the covenant in Adam." Given Hosea's propensity for similes and comparisons employing a *kĕ*, the use of the *kĕ* to compare an action at a place is not unexpected.

As noted, *at Adam* in v. 7 is the likely antecedent for the particle *there,* although the particle possibly anticipates the reference to Gilead in v. 8. According to Josh. 3:16 a city on the east bank of the Jordan River is named

---

48. Amos 5:21-26; Isa. 1:10-20; Jer. 7:1-15; Pss. 50; 51.
49. A defense of this view can be found in McComiskey, "Hosea," p. 95.
50. So the JPS translation of 1917. The LXX reads the singular, "like a man."

Adam (modern Tell Damiyeh), not far from Zarethan and the joining of the Jabbok River with the Jordan. The settlement was located along a route between Ephraim and Gilead, which would makes geographical sense, given the reference to the city of Gilead in v. 8. There are, furthermore, indications elsewhere in the broader historical context for political intrigue in Gilead that this obscure reference may reflect, such as the murder in Samaria of Pekahiah, king of Israel, by Pekah, who was accompanied by fifty men from Gilead (2 Kgs. 15:25).[51] This event took place ca. 738, during the public activity of Hosea.

The phrase *transgress the covenant* in v. 7 occurs elsewhere in Hosea (8:1) and in the OT (2 Kgs. 18:12; Jer. 34:18), but the nature of the covenant transgressed at Adam is unclear. Should we think of it as the Mosaic covenant, as seems likely in 2 Kgs. 18:12 (and probably in Hos. 8:1); as the violation of a self-commitment, such as that indicated in Josh. 24:16ff.; as a reference to some solemn commitment, like that of Jer. 34:18 (a solemn agreement to free slaves); or even to some agreement made with another state that infringes on YHWH's sovereignty? In context the critique of Hos. 6:7-11a is that of Israel's rebelliousness against YHWH; so that whatever particularities are to be associated with place and precipitating event(s) there, it is YHWH's covenant that has been transgressed.[52] Perhaps a parallel might be that of the "covenant of brothers" (Amos 1:9), where the city-state Tyre is judged for breaking a solemn relationship by engaging in the slave trade or some other form of violence against a group of people.

8 The city of *Gilead* in v. 8, where the result of violence is underscored with the phrase *tracks of blood* or "bloody footprints," could well be Jabesh-gilead, a prominent city east of the Jordan River. This is not certain, as the phrase *Gilead is a city of evildoers* could refer to other settlements in the region of Gilead. Indeed, it could be a further reference to the city of Adam. In any case, the city's inhabitants (leaders) are described as *evildoers,* a phrase used frequently in the Psalms to refer to persons who oppose YHWH and/or the psalmists.[53]

9 The critique of Israel for heinous activities continues with another simile, this time a murderous group of priests arrayed like bandits against travelers. *Shechem* is an old city located in a narrow valley in the heartland of Israel's hill country. It was a place to gather for assemblies

51. See the introduction, section III, "Historical Background to Hosea's Prophecy," and appendix 8, "Transjordan in Hosea."

52. See the careful weighing of options in Nicholson, *God and His People,* pp. 179-86, and his conclusion that *bĕrît* in 6:7 is genuine to Hosea and a reference to YHWH's covenant.

53. E.g., Ps. 5:5 (MT 6); 6:8 (MT 9); 14:4. Hosea 7:1 preserves a reference to those who work falsehood, using the verb *pā'al* as in 6:8.

(Josh. 24:1; Judg. 9:6-7), and it served early on as the capital for the break-away state of Israel (1 Kgs. 12:1, 25). Political intrigue, treachery, and robber bands were part of Shechem's history during the tumultuous period of the judges (Judg. 9:1-57).

The priests acted in *wickedness (zimmâ)*. The noun can refer to wanton acts of desire and violence. It indicates sexual depravity (Lev. 18:17; 19:29; 20:14; Jer. 13:27; Ezek. 16:27), and in the wisdom literature it has connotations of folly and devising wickedness (Prov. 21:27; 24:9; cf. Ps. 119:150). In Ps. 26:9-10 *zimmâ* describes sinners who are "bloodthirsty" or "men of bloodshed."

For all of their obscurity to modern readers, the comparisons to Israel's folly in Hos. 6:7-9 suggest political treachery with religious motivations, violence, and murder with the collusion of priests. It is a picture of the society coming apart. And one of the intriguing factors is the reference to Adam and Gilead. These places (and perhaps also the mention of Shechem) may represent a type of sectionalism, regional tensions, or geographic specificity to the dissolution of Israel. Parallels with 5:1-7 include allusions to treachery and wrongdoing at specific places (Tabor and Mizpah), charges against central institutions (house of the king), and the language of harlotry to describe the rebellion (see also 6:10).

10   The description of failure serves as a summary statement regarding the people's folly. It contains the noun *harlotry (zĕnût)* to describe Ephraim, joining the depiction of failure with that portrayed in the family history of Hos. 1–3, and the verb *defiled* (Niphal of *ṭāmēʾ*) in reference to Israel. They are both ritually unclean and morally impure. The verbs "to play the harlot" and "to be defiled" are used similarly in 5:3.

11a   With 6:11a comes a sudden brief shift to *Judah*. The MT apparently assumes that the reference to a *harvest* for Judah is positive and part of the reversal of fortunes for the people expressed in 6:11b. This is plausible, for there are prophecies elsewhere that hold forth positive change and deliverance for Judah (e.g., 1:7). On the other hand, a plausible case can be made on the basis of poetic balance that 6:11b is the first clause in a charge against Israel and Ephraim that continues in 7:1. This, in turn, links 6:11a to 6:10 and the possibility that v. 11a represents a charge against Judah, i.e., an announcement that Judah too would reap the results of failure. The short sentence in v. 11a seems to stand alone, almost as an ejaculatory cry: "You too, Judah!" As such it may be an editorial update, added later by Hosea or an editor. Surprisingly, the LXX does not preserve the name Judah in this verse. It does, however, link the activity of the people's turning in 6:11 with the negative acts described in 7:1.

3. Their Deeds Encompass Them (6:11b–7:2)

6:11b *When I would turn the fortunes of my people,*

7:1 *when I would heal Ephraim, then the iniquity of Ephraim is re-vealed, and the evil deeds of Samaria. They indeed deal falsely; the thief enters in and a band marauds in the street.*

2 *But they have not taken to heart that I have remembered all their evil. Now their deeds encompass them; they are before my face.*

6:11b–7:1 The first four clauses of 6:11b and 7:1a are poetically balanced and related in thought. Note the parallelism:

A	B
When — turn	when — heal;

A′	B′
iniquity — revealed	evil — uncovered.

The perfidy uncovered or *revealed (gālâ)* in 7:1a is explained by way of analogy with thieves and marauders in 7:1b, employing vocabulary used else-where in Hosea. Theft *(gnb)* is also the charge against Israel in 4:2. Robbery, and more specifically a marauding band *(gĕdûd),* is found in 6:9. These are crimes intended to portray violations of YHWH's household by his own people.

2 The conclusion in 7:2 is somber, indeed chilling. Israel has not considered the consequences of their iniquity, although God *remembered* their deeds. Implicit in the verb "to remember" *(zākar)* is the bringing of something to mind in a conscious fashion, so that the matter is in some sense "before" or "with" a person, and then he or she is prepared to respond to it. To remember is tantamount to perceiving something and then reacting to it, whereas the nuance of "forgetting" is not thinking of a matter consciously. And since the matter is not present, a person is not prepared to respond to it. The connection between "remembering" and "reaction" is depicted in 7:2. Tragically Israel has not *taken to heart* (lit. "said in their heart") that God re-members. One could paraphrase the expression by saying that Israel does not remember that God remembers. The matter is one of act and consequence: Israel's deeds are "before" God, who is prepared to react in judgment and oversee the reaping of consequences.

There is perhaps significance to the portrayal of Israel's deeds as *en-compassing (sābab,* lit. "surrounding") them. It is likely a way of describing the inner connection between act and consequence. Israel's "evil deeds" pro-duce the seeds of an outcome commensurate with the deeds.[54] Evil begets

54. There is essential correspondence in 7:2 between the phrases "all their evil"

200

evil. In stating that Israel's iniquity surrounds them, the prophet implies that the judgment YHWH will bring upon them grows out of the transgressions themselves. In essence, what surrounds Israel is homegrown judgment.

4. All Adulterers and the Kings Have Fallen (7:3-7)

The text of 7:3-7 has several obscurities, and it is difficult for readers to follow the thread of presentation and not be sidetracked by lists of clarifying options. By way of summary one can say that a pair of images and related metaphors run through the verses. With them readers can at least begin the process of interpreting 7:3-7 in the context of Israel's attempts at political intrigue and control. The images are a "hot oven" and the "heat" of political intrigue. The word "oven" *(tannûr)* occurs three times, and the verb "to consume" *(bāʿar)* is used twice with it. Together they indicate a burning or hot oven. The verb "to bake" *(ʾāpâ)* is also used twice in the MT, but obscurely, and various scholars have emended one or the other occurrence. Finally, the noun "king" occurs once in the singular and once in the plural. The depiction seems to be the comparison of political trickery and resulting chaos with heated ovens and drunken plots. The political machinations apparently included the demise of one or more regimes.

During Hosea's day the demise of monarchs at three points in Israel's history was recorded. One came about 750 after the death of Jeroboam II and the resulting end of the Jehu dynasty. It was actually a series of three deaths in less than a year's time, the last two of which were assassinations. Jeroboam's son Zechariah was assassinated by Shallum, who in turn was assassinated by Menahem. Menahem, furthermore, committed mass murder in Tiphsah (2 Kgs. 15:8-21). A second time came with the assassination of Pekahiah by Pekah, the son of Remaliah (2 Kgs. 15:23-25), ca. 738. A third occurrence was the killing of Pekah and the (Assyrian) appointment of Hoshea as king (2 Kgs. 15:29-30), ca. 732/731.[55] The summary statement in Hos. 7:7, that "all their kings have fallen," could be a retrospective comment from the time of Hoshea.

---

and "their deeds." The former YHWH remembers, and the latter are before him. YHWH's remembering of them leads to his overseeing the process of judgment by which the deeds themselves surround Israel. The phrase "all their evil" occurs again in 9:15, where it is lodged in Gilgal.

55. See the introduction, section III, "Historical Background to Hosea's Prophecy."

3 *With their evil they make the king glad, and princes with their lies.*

4 *All of them are adulterers, like a burning oven;*[56] *a baker ceasing to stoke (it), from the kneading of the dough until it is leavened.*

5 *(On the) day of our king the princes became sick from*[57] *the heat of wine. He stretched out his hand to mockers.*

6 *They set*[58] *their heart (fired) like the oven with their ambush; every night their anger*[59] *sleeps; in the morning it burns like a flaming fire.*

7 *All of them are heated up like the oven, and they have devoured their judges. All their kings have fallen, and there is no one calling to me.*

3-4 Verse 3 is a bicolon in reinforcing parallelism:

A	B
evil . . . king	princes . . . lies

The indefinite subject *they* (responsible for *evil* and *lies*) is further defined in what follows. As v. 4 indicates, "they" are adulterers (metaphorically speaking) and involved in political machinations. It is not clear how or why the king is pleased with their evil or the royal administration is taken in by their lies. Hosea's strong use of symbolism and puns suggests the possibilities of sarcasm and/or subterfuge on the part of the evildoers, and that the king was taken in by devious plotting. The ill-defined "they" are best understood as plotters, whose deception results in the toppling of a monarch and his extended family, which would make up much of the national administration.

56. Poetic balance and grammatical agreement suggest that MT *kĕmô tannûr bō'ĕrâ mē'ōpeh* be divided and read as *kattannûr bō'ēr hēm 'ōpeh*. Cf. *BHS*. This gives agreement between the participle "burning" and the masculine noun "oven." It means, however, that the next clause begins awkwardly with the anarthrous term "baker."

57. The preposition *min*, "from," is attached to the noun *yāyin*, "wine," not to the term *ḥămat*, "heat." This is atypical syntax, but it does occur elsewhere (GKC §130a).

58. The verb is *qārab* in the Piel. The basic meaning of the verb is "draw near," and in the Piel it can be a transitive verb. In this instance the noun "heart" is the object of "set." Perhaps the meaning is akin to "gathering one's resolve" or "drawing together one's plans in readiness."

59. A number of interpreters have assumed an original *'appĕhem* ("their anger") for the MT *'ōpēhem* ("their baker"). The phrase in the MT, "their baker sleeps," does not fit the context well. In itself, this is not a reason to reject it, but the repointing of the consonants to read "their anger" is a cautious emendation, it fits the context better, and the Syriac version can be adduced in support of this reading (see *BHS*). Possibly the term "baker" here in v. 6 came by way of influence from v. 4.

But who are the plotters? Most interpreters agree that the "plotting" in 7:3-7 represents one or more of the regicides of the mid-8th century. The difficulty comes in discerning who was in league with Menahem, Pekah or Hoshea, in fomenting the various regime changes during Hosea's day.[60]

Depicting lies and treachery as *adultery* is one of Hosea's stock metaphors. He is not the only prophet to use the comparison (Jer. 9:2 [MT 1]). The plotters of v. 4 are collectively *adulterers,* using the participle form to describe ongoing deception. They are also *like a burning* (or heated) *oven.* The simile has an analogy to modern English slang, where one can speak of a group of people "cooking something up," i.e., conceiving a plan of action. But more than hatching a plot is indicated. The "heat" of the oven suggests energy and excitement, if not anger, behind the intrigue.

The second half of v. 4 is obscure and interpreters would be wise not to found a particular view solely on it. A time element is part of a comparison, which reflects the period from kneading dough to the completion of the leavening. That much is relatively clear. The difficulty comes in the subject ("baker") and the verbs ("cease" and "stoke/rouse/stir up"). In context, the latter verb, a Hiphil participle (from '*ûr*), would seem to refer to the oven and its fire. Hence the rendering *stoke (it).* The verb is used to describe the awakening from sleep, a stirring up to action, and even the arousal of affection.[61] One wonders if the term is chosen here to play on the charge of adultery, or if that is to read more into it than the poet intends. In any case, readers are left with the questions of the identity of the "baker" and the reason for "ceasing" to stir up. Possibly, the term "baker" is not intended in the simile to represent a particular figure. "He" is simply mentioned as part of the baking process. If, on the other hand, the "baker" represents someone (e.g., the leader of a coup), his action of "ceasing" does not help identify him.

Wolff's interpretation is perhaps the most helpful.[62] He concentrates on the baker's task, which is to refrain from stoking a fire for a period of time in order to maintain an acceptable level of heat. This is even the case before the bread is placed in the oven. Both heat and energy are maintained until the time for baking is at hand. To use a modern phrase, the "hatching of the plot" takes some time to develop.

5 The actions represented here come in condensed, allusive language. Again, it would be wise not to found a particular interpretation of

---

60. Andersen and Freedman, *Hosea,* pp. 447-61, make a case for priestly involvement in the political plotting. Their proposal is based, in part, on the references to priestly corruption and violence in ch. 6.

61. Ps. 7:6 (MT 7); Isa. 41:2, 25; Song 2:7; 3:5; 4:16; 5:2; 8:4-5.

62. Wolff, *Hosea,* p. 125.

events solely on this verse. One would expect the sentence to begin explicitly with the preposition *bĕ* ("on" or "in"), and although it does not, it seems best to assume it in the terse reference to *day*. One assumes, furthermore, that the *day of a king* is a coronation, a birthday (?), or some other day of royal significance and public celebration. *King* can also refer to a deity, but that is not likely here. On that day the *princes became sick*. Perhaps these are the same princes mentioned in v. 3. The verb *ḥālâ* is literally "to be sick," and in the Hiphil can have an intransitive meaning, which is the one adopted here. Interpreters differ, however, over the subject of the verb. The compressed nature of the text is such that *princes* could also be the object of the verb, with the subject an indefinite "they." Moreover, the verb in the Hiphil typically has a causative force, so that the subject could be the plotting "adulterers" mentioned earlier in v. 4, i.e., those "heated up like an oven." On this reading, the "princes" are the object of the verb, i.e., they are "made sick." One can argue the point either way: the princes became sick or were made sick.[63]

The *heat* of wine apparently describes the effects of overconsumption, an understandable situation in the context of feasting and celebrations. Likely the term is chosen to blend with the heat of the plotters in 7:4, 6-7. "Heat" and "sickness" may also elaborate on the deception of the princes noted in 7:3.

The subject of the verbal clause to *stretch out the hand* at the end of v. 5 is also ambiguous. The meaning of the gesture is also unclear. In context, the explicit choices for the subject are the "king" mentioned earlier in this verse or the "baker" of 7:4. If the subject is implied, then at this distance from Hosea's historical context, it is difficult to know who it is. Perhaps the best option for the subject is that of the king. The king (Zechariah? Pekah? Pekahiah?) stretched out his hand to engage or to embrace his contemporaries. Possibly the term is idiomatic or it has a political nuance. The verb *māšak* is used only one other time in Hosea (11:4), where it means "to draw along" or "to lead."

The term *mockers* in v. 5 could refer to the inebriated princes, who under the influence of wine are rude and scornful. The term, however, might be another reference to the plotters, whose designs on the kingdom are revealed through this characterization. Verse 6, which follows, begins with the actions of those who are compared to an oven, as were the plotters in 7:4. The king sought to engage the plotters politically or in some related fashion, but their stance toward the monarch was scornful or mocking.

63. For the intransitive interpretation, see Macintosh, *Hosea,* p. 259. For the causative interpretation, see Andersen and Freedman, *Hosea,* pp. 457-58. The latter, however, have the king as the object of the verb: "By day they made our king ill. . . ."

6 There are yet other obscurities for modern readers in v. 6, no matter how clear and pointed the communication may have been to the prophet's contemporaries. Tolerable sense can be made of the verse in context, but as noted in the translation above, this depends in part on a proposed emendation, reading "their anger" for the similarly formed "their baker" of the MT. The term *like the oven* sits awkwardly in the first clause and could be deleted without detracting from either parallelism or basic meaning. The term may be an explanatory gloss, since the imagery of the heated oven runs through the passage. Whether added or not, the reference to an *oven* provides specificity to the burning flame of the last clause of the verse. The comparison seems to be that of political intrigue to a fire that smolders at night and heats up in the morning. This is apparently the depiction of the plotters and their designs, which get further elaboration in v. 7.

7 Here the end results of political intrigue and forced regime changes are summarized. However one interprets the previous difficulties in vv. 4-6, their subject matter leads to this: rulers have fallen to plotters and no one calls to YHWH. The terseness of the latter claim precludes certainty of interpretation, but it seems to represent a chaos that the perpetrators have brought into being, but that was not authorized by YHWH. It is possible, but unlikely, that the charge "no one calls to YHWH" is literally the case. It is more likely that the fomenters of regime change made several claims in the name of the national deity. Most rebels claim a higher authority than personal gain for their actions. YHWH himself, however, repudiates them through the voice of Hosea. We should assume that those responsible for regime change had their own prophetic support.

A *judge* is someone in administrative authority, whether as military leader (as in the book of Judges), political leader, or in judicial affairs. The comment that "they" have devoured judges and that kings have fallen indicates that Israel's central administration has come to an end. None of the remaining leaders have a mandate from YHWH, since none of them have called upon him.

Of the various options for interpreting the regime change depicted in 7:3-7, perhaps the best is the assassination of Pekah and the resulting appointment of Hoshea as ruler by the Assyrians. Hosea would not represent the imposing of Hoshea by the Assyrians as YHWH's will, except as further punishment for the people's faithless activity. The tone of 7:3-7 is not one of support for the plotters, but acknowledgment of the intrigue and vigor associated with their work. Furthermore, the comment in v. 7 implies the loss of more than one king in the past and a somber future in which YHWH is not acknowledged. That comment may reflect the Neo-Assyrian hegemony that came with Pekah's murder and Hoshea's appointment.

D. ISRAEL IS MIXED AND SWALLOWED UP AMONG THE NATIONS (7:8–9:9)

Introduction

A new subsection, 7:8–9:9, comes after the comment in 7:7 that the kings have fallen and none have called on YHWH. An emphasis on divine first-person speech continues in the next subsection, revealing the folly of Ephraim/Israel among the nations. The outward folly of dangerous diplomacy is matched by internal sickness, characterized as the breaking of covenant (8:1, 12), regime change (8:4), and idolatry (8:4b-6).

Failure and folly among the nations is a theme running through 7:8–9:9, with the metaphor of Ephraim as a "half-baked cake" in 7:8 serving as a sarcastic opening metaphor. In this subsection political activities, and more particularly international relations, are the primary subject.[1] Imagery and poetic expression abound in this subsection. Hosea's analysis is thoroughly theological, characterizing Israel's attempts to make itself secure through diplomacy as stupidity and a rejection of YHWH.

1. Calling Egypt and Assyria (7:8-16)

8 *Ephraim has mixed himself among the nations; he has become a half-baked[2] cake.*

9 *Strangers have eaten his strength, but he does not know (it); his gray hair is apparent,[3] but he does not know (it).*

10 *The pride of Israel testifies against him. They have neither returned to YHWH their God nor sought him for all this.*

11 *Ephraim has become like a silly dove, lacking sense, calling to Egypt and going to Assyria.*

12 *As they go, I will cast my net upon them; like birds of the air I will bring them down. I will chastise[4] them according to the word to their assembly.*

---

1. See the excursus on "Similes and Metaphors for Political Actions in Hosea 4–14" in the introduction, section II.A.

2. Hebrew *bĕlî hăpûkâ* means lit. "not flipped." The verb *(hāpak)* is used in 11:8 to refer to the "overturning" of YHWH's heart.

3. The MT reads lit., "gray hair is sprinkled upon him."

4. Some interpreters follow a slight emendation of the MT to read *'e'esrēm,* "I will bind them," on the assumption that the verb "bind" *('āsar)* better continues to the imagery of the net over birds than does the verb *yāsar.* See Rudolph, *Hosea,* pp. 150-51. In light of other examples of Hosea's paronomasia, a deliberate play on the two verbs is possible.

13 *Woe to them, for they have strayed from me; devastation to them, for they have rebelled against me! I would redeem them, but they speak lies against me.*

14 *But they have not cried out to me with their heart; they are howling on their beds. They cut themselves[5] for grain and wine, but they turn away from me.*

15 *I trained and strengthened their arms, yet they are devising evil against me.*

16 *They turn to "No Profit,"[6] they have become like a faulty bow; their princes will fall by the sword because of the cursedness[7] of their tongue. This[8] will be their mockery in the land of Egypt.*

8   The charge of debilitating political relationships comes with comparison to the baker's task. Perhaps this is a (redactional?) link to the descriptions of 7:3-7, where baking is part of the poetic symbolism. Whereas internal intrigue is described in 7:3-7, international relations with Egypt and Assyria are part of 7:8-16. Perhaps the treacherous international situation portrayed in the latter half of ch. 7 is the flip side to the previously described internal intrigue.

The verb *mix (bālal)* is used frequently to describe grain offerings

---

5. The MT is difficult (*gārar* Hithpoel or *gûr* Hithpolel) and its meaning obscure. Some render the verb as "assemble" (so JPS, NASB). Other interpreters, however, have followed a minority manuscript tradition in Hebrew to read *yitgôdĕdû*. This assumes a confusion in transmission between *dalet* and *resh* and that the root is *gādad* ("cut/gash"). The NRSV translates accordingly, and the LXX rendering would be consistent with this. In 1 Kgs. 18:28 the worshipers of Baal cut themselves (*yitgōdĕdû*) in order to attract the deity's attention and to secure rain.

6. Heb. *lō' 'āl* ("not above/higher") is difficult, and no consensus exists for its rendering or emendation. Andersen and Freedman, *Hosea,* pp. 477-78; and Macintosh, *Hosea,* pp. 284-85, accept the MT as intelligible. The former understand *'āl* as a reference to a deity ("High") and render the phrase "no god." Macintosh takes *'āl* as indicating "height" and the phrase as indicting Israel for not setting its mind on what is above. Other proposed emendations include *labba'al* ("to Baal"), *labbĕlîya'al* ("to worthlessness"), *lō' yō'îl* ("to no profit"). This last emendation has a parallel with Jer. 2:8, where the prophet criticizes Jerusalem's leaders as going after that which does not profit. It is cautiously adopted here, as it fits the comparison with a faulty bow that follows and is consistent with Hosea's polemic against turning to other deities.

7. The Hebrew noun *za'am* has the basic meaning of "indignation." In verbal form it is associated with verbs for cursing people in Prov. 24:24 (*qābab*) and Num. 23:7-8 (*'ārâ, qābab*).

8. The Hebrew particle *zô ("This")* is feminine, and the antecedent *za'am ("cursedness")* is masculine. The reason for this disparity is not clear, but it is not finally a detriment to the translation. See Macintosh, *Hosea,* p. 287.

mixed with oil. It is also a pun on the prophet's similar expression in 8:7, that Israel is "swallowed up" *(bālaʿ)* among the nations. Ephraim, or at least aspects of its political leadership, has thrown itself into the volatile field of international relations, engaging in activities that are fraught with peril. In context Ephraim's mixing among the nations is viewed with alarm and as a cause for judgment to come in the historical process.[9] Unfortunately, the state is like an unflipped pancake on a skillet, a product easily recognized as unserviceable and inedible. It has, furthermore, an interesting profile, cooked on one side and raw on the other. No one starts the task of cooking pancakes with such a result in mind; a badly cooked cake is the result of something going awry in the cooking process. This is apparently what the simile of the cake intends to say about the diplomatic processes in which Ephraim is mixed up.

We may be guided by Hosea's basic theological convictions in seeking the source of his opposition to the international diplomacy undertaken in his day. His opposition appears rooted in the theological conviction that the covenant ethos granted Israel by YHWH required them to be a holy people. This is likely the logic of his "mixing" metaphor. Israel's holiness before YHWH was threatened by the compromise (even treachery) of diplomatic intrigue. Engagement with Egypt or Assyria was also an affront to YHWH's sovereignty as head of his household, for the process may well have required recognition of Egyptian and Assyrian deities as partners in treaty agreements, and so on.

9 Two familiar points are made. First, Ephraim is in bad straits. Second, the nation does not recognize its dire circumstances. This is further comment on the negative consequences of being mixed up among the nations in the previous verse. *Strangers* indicates essentially non-Israelites. Since Egypt and Assyria are mentioned in the context, they are likely examples of the strangers the prophet has in mind. The Hebrew term for "strange/stranger" *(zār)* occurs elsewhere in Hosea (5:7; 8:7, 12). In 8:7 Hosea depicts a possible condition of strangers devouring Israel's grain. This is the same vein of thinking as expressed in 7:9.[10]

Gray hair can represent a variety of circumstances. In 7:9 it appears to represent old age and the proximity of death. What is apparent to observers — in this case gray hair and the consequences of old age — is not apparent to

9. The verb *bālal* is used twice to describe God's "mixing" of languages upon the earth as a judgment on the tower of Babel (Gen. 11:7, 9). Is it possible that Hosea's "mixing" is an echo of that tradition?

10. Isa. 1:7 refers to strangers devouring Judah's land, using the same vocabulary as Hos. 7:9. See also Jer. 2:25; 3:13; 5:19; and the judgment of foreigners upon Judah in Ezek. 7:21; 11:9.

the senior citizen Ephraim. The repeated charge that Ephraim does not know its own dire straits must have originated at a time in which the nation's leaders were enmeshed in multiple relationships of a sensitive and ultimately threatening nature. Since both Egypt and Assyria had designs on the territory of Israel, perhaps the Israelite leadership sought to play one off against the other or to hedge their bets by currying favor with both rather than one or the other. It is difficult to be more precise about the historical and political circumstances behind Hosea's stinging critique. From the time of Tiglath-pileser III's accession (745 B.C.) until the fall of Samaria over two decades later, Israel had been in the midst of diplomatic turbulence and international intrigue. Moreover, the Assyrian campaigns of 734-732 resulted in the loss of much of Israel's traditional territory. It is possible that the description of Ephraim as advanced in age reflects the view that the next step after the loss of its former territories will be death.

10   Israel's *pride* is similarly addressed in 5:5. The verbal phrase *'ānâ bĕ* has the nuance of *testify* or "answer *against* someone." In context it seems that Israel's pride in seeking to secure itself through foreign alliances is at the same time the evidence of its folly. Such activities are incompatible with a return to YHWH[11] and a seeking of his will for national health. Does this make Hosea an isolationist, someone who finds the inevitable compromise of diplomatic relationships reason to reject them? This is a possible way to read these expressions and the overall tone of the book, but it is not certain. As noted above, Hosea apparently regarded the diplomacy of his day as a compromise of Israel's holy identity and an affront to YHWH's sovereignty over his people. It is not clear that Hosea was opposed *in principle* to the political give-and-take with Egypt and Assyria, but that may have been the case. He is convinced that YHWH has not endorsed the actions and they are thus a betrayal of the covenant between people and Deity.

We cannot know for certain either what forms of "rejecting YHWH" were taken by Israel. One of them is obvious: Israel's leadership did not accept Hosea's prophetic word as YHWH's instruction to them. Otherwise, all that we have are the literary hints provided by Hosea and his editors for the forms of rejection. They may have included swearing by the deities of Egypt or Assyria, gifts from Samaria's treasury to Egypt and Assyria (cf. 12:1 [MT 2]), or priestly divination and prophetic oracles from official circles alleging that YHWH approved the courses of action underway. There is no mention in the immediate context of the influence of non-Yahwistic elements. Nevertheless, their influence may have contributed to Hosea's description of "rejecting" YHWH.

---

11. See the excursus at 6:1, "Return to YHWH." In 7:16a the prophet denounces Israel for returning to that which is not God.

In the ebb and flow of the past, Egypt had included much of the eastern Mediterranean in its imperial designs. During the 8th and 7th centuries Egypt played various roles in the affairs of the region. Hoshea, the last king of Israel, made entreaties to Egypt, while withholding tribute from Shalmaneser V (2 Kgs. 17:4),[12] and we may be confident that Hoshea was not the only king during Hosea's lifetime to seek agreements and support from Egypt. Assyria was heavily involved in the region in the 9th-7th centuries B.C., including campaigns in Israel and Judah during the 8th century that resulted in the incorporation of two-thirds of Israel into their empire in 734-732 and a successful conclusion to a siege of Samaria that commenced ca. 724. The references that survive in historical documents to diplomatic flurries between the states are likely only the tip of the iceberg.

11-12 In v. 11 the prophet uses an image from Israel's cultural life as a metaphor for the folly of Ephraim's diplomacy. It continues the contextual theme of Israel's clueless mental state. Doves were common in the area and were trapped for food. When baited, doves tend to be single-minded in their pursuit of food and will remain near a ready source of food in spite of suspicious activity. Other birds (and animals) may not be so heedless of potential threat, hence the description of the dove as *lacking sense* (lit. "without heart"). What Hosea refers to as YHWH's *net* in v. 12 is part of a trap that could be sprung in an area where doves feed on the ground. The net was held in tension and the trap sprung in order to cast the net over the birds. Thus the dove, whose security in the air is given up in the pursuit of food on the ground, is likened to heedless Israel, which has embarked on a fruitless search to Egypt and Assyria to try and ensure its security apart from dependence upon YHWH.

The last part of v. 12 is obscure to modern readers. Chastisement will fall upon Israel according to the *word* or "report"[13] to their (= Israel?) assembly. We may ask, what assembly? Unfortunately, there is no answer forthcoming, and at such a historical and cultural distance from Hosea, we have less understanding upon which to proceed than the prophet's first audience. An assembly might refer to the ratification of agreements between Israel and one of its international suitors. Perhaps actual covenant ceremonies binding Israel to Egypt or Assyria were enacted, complete with self-imprecations for failure. The verb for *chastise* or "discipline" *(yāsar)* is also used in 7:15 and in 10:10. In all three cases it is employed with YHWH as the subject and Israel as the recipient of instruction or disciplinary action akin to punishment. It is a term used in various circles in Israel.

---

12. See the introduction, section III, "Historical Background to Hosea's Prophecy."
13. The Hebrew term is *šēma'*, which refers to something heard.

Excursus: Discipline and Correction in Hosea

Since schooling in the modern senses of that term was lacking for most Israelites, what we might call education in Israel came largely from parents and the elders of the clan or village.[14] Teachers appealed to tradition and experience, urging children and younger adults to listen, observe, and learn. Hosea's concept of Israel as the family/ household of YHWH also carries with it convictions that Israel's covenant ethos contains the necessary discipline for life of the people. That ethos was defined by YHWH, the divine head of the household.

On three occasions the book employs the verb *yāsar,* which carries the connotations of teach, discipline, and chastise (7:12, 15; 10:10). The verb is used elsewhere in the OT in various literary contexts in which the contributions of parents, elders, and experience all play a formative educational role. Deuteronomy contains several examples set in the context of Israel as YHWH's covenant community. In 4:36 Israel is reminded that they heard the commanding voice at Mt. Horeb in order that YHWH might "instruct/discipline" *(yāsar)* his people. Elsewhere in that chapter, the commanding voice is linked with YHWH's covenant *(běrît),* which Israel is to observe (4:13). Regarding the health of the community, when a stubborn and rebellious son will not listen to his parents, even when they "discipline" *(yāsar)* him, then the consequences for this entail community judgment and are severe (21:18-21). For the communal infraction of slandering his wife (22:13-19), a man is "disciplined" *(yāsar,* v. 18) by the elders. The context strongly implies that the term carries with it a chastising of the individual, indeed a punishment, that deals with the infraction and makes way for his restoration in the community. With respect to the relationship between YHWH and his covenant people, the analogy of father and son is explicit in Deuteronomy: "Know in your heart that as a man *disciplines* his son, so YHWH your God is disciplining you" (8:5). The shared conceptual world with Hosea is apparent with respect to the importance attached to the covenant ethos and the analogy between parent and child for the divine-human relationship.[15]

The wisdom traditions of Israel make ample use of the term *yāsar* in the contexts of training and discipline. Hosea is likely an heir to sapiential modes of thinking as well. Of the five occurrences of the verb in the book of Proverbs, three are used for parental teaching and discipline (19:18; 29:17; 31:1; cf. 9:7; 29:19; Job 4:3). A related pattern is revealed in the piety of the Psalter through the employment of the verb. God is repeatedly seen as the one who "teaches," "disciplines," and "corrects" through chastisement (Pss. 6:1 [MT 2]; 38:1 [MT 2]; 39:11; 94:10, 12; 118:18). Divine instruction extends even to the kings of the earth, who are enjoined

14. James L. Crenshaw, *Education in Ancient Israel: Across the Deadening Silence* (ABRL; New York: Doubleday, 1998). More formal aspects of education may have been located at a royal court or in an urban setting.

15. See also Lev. 26:18-23 for repeated uses of the verb in the context of a chastising discipline on Israel for infractions of the covenant. The imagery of parental training can be found in Hos. 7:15 and 11:1-7. It is presupposed also in the metaphor of Hosea's children representing Israel in Hos. 1–2.

in 2:10 to be "wise" *(śākal,* Hiphil) and to be "instructed" *(yāsar,* Niphal), lest they be judged by YHWH.

The three occurrences of the verb in Hosea are congruent with the covenant ethos of Deuteronomy and the insights of wisdom and piety. In 7:12 YHWH promises to "chastise them according to the word to their assembly." The last phrase is obscure, but the context of judgment for folly committed is not. In the same context, 7:15 reports that YHWH had "trained" and strengthened Israel, but in return they had reckoned evil against him. In 10:10 YHWH promises to "chastise" the people.[16] In context the reference appears to indicate judgment in the historical process, similar to that in 7:12.

13 Verse 13 is one of two places in the book where a cry of *woe* is pronounced upon Israel (the other is 9:12). It is a rhetorical device used by prophets to call attention to calamity and to lament, and such a cry fits a situation in which a heedless Israel stands culpable before YHWH. The initial basis for Hosea's "woe" is explicated in the first two bicola of the verse:

A	B
woe . . .	devastation *(šōd)* . . .
they have strayed *(nādad)*	they have rebelled *(pāšaʿ).*

In the bicola the "woe" is reinforced by "devastation," and the verbs "stray" and "rebel" play the same role.

The use of the verb *rebel* may have political nuance. It can be used for those who revolt against a political overlord (1 Kgs. 12:19; 2 Kgs. 1:1; 8:20). The connotation of rebelling against an authority or breaking faith with someone carries over to its use in the theological sense of spurning God or rejecting divine instruction. This is the way the term is used in 8:1.[17]

Verse 13 concludes with a colon expressing a supposed condition (that YHWH would redeem Israel) that sadly will not come to pass. The people are portrayed yet a third time in v. 13 in negative terms as speaking "lies" *(kĕzābîm).* It is also a word that Hosea uses elsewhere (12:1 [MT 2]).[18]

14 The initial charge in v. 14 follows the critique of the preceding verses, indeed of ch. 7 as a whole. The people have not turned to YHWH or sought him in sincerity in spite of vigorous activity intended to secure blessings. This devastating criticism is likely related to the charge that the people

---

16. In 10:10 the prophet employs a pun, using the verbs *yāsar* and *ʾāsar* ("constrict").

17. The plural participle is used for "transgressors" in 14:9 [MT 10]. The root *pšʿ* is a favorite of Amos, Hosea's contemporary (e.g., Amos 1:3, 6, 9, 11, 13; 3:14; 4:4).

18. As a reinforcing term to *kāzāb,* 12:1 (MT 2) uses *šōd* ("destruction, devastation").

have lied against YHWH (7:13). In form, the accusation in v. 14 is a chiasm: (A) not crying to YHWH wholeheartedly; (B) howling on their beds/ (B′) seeking grain and wine; (A′) turning away from YHWH.

The imagery of 7:11 compares Ephraim to a dove lacking sense (= heart). In v. 14 the cry to the Lord has been either absent or (more likely) superficial, lacking in commitment and understanding. All this points to a continuation of the clueless theme from the immediate context. The verb for *cry out (zāʿaq)* is, however, deeply embedded in various OT traditions as the vocal call to God in times of trouble. It is a recognized means of approaching God, as a psalmist (Ps. 142:1) and prophet (Joel 1:14) make clear.[19] Hosea uses the verb elsewhere in a quotation put in Israel's mouth (8:2). Perhaps Hosea's critique is similar to that of Joel, who called upon those in Judah "to return to YHWH with all their heart, with fasting, weeping, and mourning, and to rend their hearts and not simply their garments" (2:12-13).

Here in Hos. 7:14 the language of *howling* or moaning *(yālal)* indicates that there are those in Israel who cry out for assistance, but it is not in a context, physical or theological, that induces YHWH to act. In the guise of Gomer, Israel was resolute in seeking the payments of commodities such as grain and wine from her lovers (2:5, 8 [MT 7, 10]). Here in v. 14 Israel is keenly seeking grain and wine.[20] This may be a reference to idolatry and polytheism, where Israel seeks blessings wherever they can be found (i.e., from other deities), or it may refer more specifically to the kind of inducements that Israel's leaders might receive to enter into an agreement with Egypt or Assyria.

15 Perhaps we have in v. 15 a reflection on YHWH's past dealings with Israel using the metaphor of the parent training a child, along with the language of judgment in the historical process that comes as a result of rebellion against such parental guidance. YHWH provided guidance and training for those in his household, yet their response is to spurn that advantage. The description of Israel rejecting God and bringing judgment upon themselves also continues the theme of Israel's foolishness among the nations. They should know better! There is similar language in 11:1-7, where Israel brings judgment upon itself for rejecting YHWH's parental love and guidance. Moreover, the verb translated *trained (yāsar)* is part of the immediate context (7:12), employed in its nuance of "discipline" or "chastise." The verb carries the connotation of both education and discipline. Here in v. 15 the verb is used in parallel with another verb, *ḥāzaq,* meaning *strengthen.* Both verbs are transitive (Piel) and have the plural noun *arms* as a common object. They are

19. On the cry to YHWH see Exod. 2:23; Judg. 3:9, 15; 6:6; 10:10; Ps. 22:5.
20. On occasion Neo-Hittite kings praised the "Grain-God" and the "Wine-God" as providers of blessing. See J. D. Hawkins, *COS* 2:123 §7; 124 §9; 126 §§53, 55.

used similarly as a pair in Job 4:3, where Eliphaz describes Job's former standing in the community as someone who "instructed many and strengthened weak hands."

There is an interesting comparison between what is stated here in 7:15 and Jer. 2:19. The logic of Hosea's expression is that Israel *is devising evil* (ḥāšab rāʿ) against YHWH by rejecting divine instruction or training (yāsar). That Israel has devised evil is Hosea's interpretation of their actions, but certainly not the self-understanding of Israel's leadership. Jeremiah's logic in 2:19 runs in a complementary direction. The evil (rāʿâ) that Judah has done will instruct/chastise (yāsar) them. Again, it is Jeremiah's assessment of Judah that results in the diagnosis of "evil" activity, not the self-understanding of Judah's leadership. Both prophetic expressions employ common vocabulary and the application of an act-consequence diagnosis to the failures of God's people. There are also parallels in thought and vocabulary with Nah. 1:11, which charges that arrogant Nineveh has "devised evil" (ḥāšab rāʿâ) against the Lord's plans. As Nahum's further prophecy makes clear, YHWH will turn that evil against Nineveh.

16 The concluding verse of ch. 7 is textually difficult at the beginning and obscure at the end. The thrust of the communication, however, is intelligible and makes sense in context. Criticism of Israel continues for being mixed among the nations and for engaging in activity that will lead to its ruin.

One can only guess at the meaning of the initial phrase. The verb *turn* or "return" (šûb) is common and capable of bearing a range of related meanings; here the people have (re)turned to something that threatens their well-being and their relationship with YHWH. The difficulty comes in discerning more precisely what is the object of the turning. The rendering *No Profit* is an emendation, reading a form of the verb yāʿal for the enigmatic ʿāl of the MT.

Israel is *like a faulty bow*. Hosea's love of simile draws on a recognizable problem in threatening circumstances, i.e., a weapon that does not work when it is employed. Indeed, a malfunctioning weapon endangers the one who wields it. The term *faulty bow* occurs one other time in the OT in a poetic evaluation of failure in Israel's history (Ps. 78:57). A psalmist notes that the people were faithless (bāgad) toward the Lord and were overturned/twisted (hāpak) like a *faulty bow*. The imagery assumes that when an arrow is mounted and drawn and the bowstring then released, a bow, typically the result of careful crafting, should be able to send the arrow forward. A faulty bow can lose its tensive spring and go slack, or it can twist and snap and injure the archer. Like a modern firearm that misfires, this bow does not complete the task for which it was made. Correspondingly, Israel's efforts will misfire and be injurious because it has pursued that which does not profit.

Perhaps related to the simile of the faulty bow and injury is the humiliation of military defeat. The princes (those who lead the nation have a role in leading the army) would perish by the sword.

What Israel's leaders said is a *cursedness of their tongue*. It is not easy to determine the content or the context of their speaking, but it may assume spoken commitments that the prophet believes will lead to their demise. For example, a treaty ratification with Egypt or Assyria would fit the context satisfactorily. A related term for speech, *la'ag,* meaning *mockery* or "derision," is used in the concluding phrase of v. 16. It too has the possessive suffix *their,* as does the word "tongue" in the previous phrase. The suffixes are linked to the princes who will fall to the sword. One wonders if these references to their failed speech are related to the obscure phrase "word to their assembly" in 7:12 and the chastisement that God will bring about because of it. Perhaps the princes or officials had been emissaries in the back-and-forth of diplomacy. It is also possible that the imagery of the faulty bow includes an implication that the words of Israel's leaders are like arrows that will not reach their mark.[21]

In context, Hosea had spoken of "calling" upon Egypt (7:11) and elsewhere speaks of a "return to Egypt" (8:13; 9:3; 11:5). Perhaps the reference in v. 16 to Israel's *mockery in the land of Egypt* is a sarcastic reversal of the exodus motif of Egyptians urging the Israelites to leave and giving them valuable articles in their departure (Exod. 12:33-36; Ps. 105:37-38). Egypt shall see YHWH's judgment upon Israel this time! And Israel thought itself clever to negotiate with Egypt in hopes of preserving its status! Admittedly, both the syntax and the referent of the final clause of the verse are difficult. One cannot tell if the mockery also assumes a defeat of Israel by Egypt with a literal return of some to the land of the Nile, or if it is a poetic expression of derision about Israel's demise at the hands of the Assyrians that will be proclaimed in Egypt. Whatever its meaning for Hosea's first audience, it presupposes yet one more consequence of Israel's failed policy of international diplomacy. The mixing of Israel among the nations would lead to defeat (falling to the sword) and derision for Israel in Egypt, once the land of its enslavement and also the place where YHWH previously declared himself Israel's God (12:9 [MT 10]; 13:4).

21. Andersen and Freedman, *Hosea,* pp. 478-79, propose this understanding of the faulty bow and arrow.

2. Broken Covenant and Shattered Calf (8:1-6)

1 *(Put) to your lips the ram's horn! (One) like an eagle is upon the house of YHWH because they have violated my covenant and transgressed my instruction.*

2 *To me they cry out, "My God, we (Israel)²² know you!"*

3 *Israel has rejected good, (so) an enemy will pursue him.*

4 *They have made kings, but not from me; they have appointed officials, but I have not known (it). With their silver and gold they have made idols, with the result that it (Israel)²³ will be cut off.*

5 *Your calf is wretched,²⁴ O Samaria! My anger is against them. How long will they be unable to maintain innocence?*

6 *Indeed, (it) is from Israel; a craftsman made it. It is not divine; indeed, Samaria's calf shall be shattered.*

1 Verse 1 begins with two compressed expressions. This is indicated in the translation by the two parenthetical words, which do not render a particular Hebrew term but are included to complete the intent of the expressions. The *ram's horn (šōpār)* or shofar is a means of public communication. It can be blown for a variety of reasons, one of which is to signal approaching danger. The bird presupposed by the Hebrew term *nešer* in the second expression cannot be precisely identified; it can refer to an eagle or a vulture. Perhaps the eagle is more likely, since it is a predator, not a carrion eater like the vulture, and the blowing of the *šōpār* better represents the danger signal for an attack by a human predator. The eagle (predatory) image also better fits the aggression of Neo-Assyria or other aggressive states in the region.²⁵ In literary-symbolic terms, the predatory eagle de-

---

22. The noun "Israel" sits awkwardly in the sentence and may be a dittography from v. 3 or a later explanatory gloss of the subject "we." Neither the LXX nor the Peshitta presupposes it.

23. The subject is an unnamed masculine singular (an understood "he" or "it"). Most of the early versions interpret the subject as a plural, apparently with the view that the aforementioned idols are in mind.

24. The verb *zānaḥ* typically means "reject," as it is rendered in 8:3, but it can have the sense of "be rancid/stink/abominable" in the Hiphil (Isa. 19:6). The latter meaning for the Qal also fits 8:5 and its context well, and is consistent with the MT pointing of the verb as 3rd masc. sing., which would give the verb a stative aspect. The NEB translates the verb as "stink," and a number of 19th-century critical commentators render similarly, as Harper, *Hosea*, p. 315, documents. *HALOT* (1:276) proposes a *zānaḥ* I ("to become foul-smelling"; Hiphil) and II ("reject"). Should this be correct, then 8:5 could be *zānaḥ* I, but in Qal, and 8:3 would be *zānaḥ* II. Perhaps we should see in *zānaḥ* a pun on the verb *zānâ*, "to play the harlot."

25. Eidevall, *Grapes in the Desert*, p. 127, has proposed that the eagle was a rec-

scending on YHWH's house reverses the imagery of YHWH as the eagle who bears Israel from Egypt to himself (Exod. 19:4) and who supported the people through the wilderness like the mother eagle hovering over the nest (Deut. 32:10-12). This reversal may be intended in Hosea's depiction, since he refers explicitly elsewhere to the exodus and wilderness traditions.

It is interesting that Deuteronomy itself also contains a reversal of the "saving eagle" tradition in a list of curses to come for disobedience to the covenant (28:49). As a consequence of Israel's disobedience, YHWH will bring upon them "a nation from afar, from the end of the earth, swooping down like an eagle *(nešer)*." The covenant curse imagery fits the context of Hosea particularly well, and its expression in Deut. 28:49 is likely a fuller form of the tradition compressed in Hos. 8:1.

The reversal tradition of the "predatory eagle" assists, furthermore, in interpreting the *house of YHWH* under threat for covenant transgression. Some would see in Hosea's phrase a reference to YHWH's temple in Samaria or even Jerusalem,[26] but this is unlikely. Just as the curse in Deut. 28:49 is directed against the people as a whole, including its land, so too the "house" in Hos. 8:1 is probably a reference to Israel (land and people) as YHWH's household.[27] Interpreting the *house* as a national reference is consistent with other places in the OT where the predatory eagle is a metaphor for an enemy attack. Jeremiah's oracles against Moab (48:40) and against Bozrah (49:22; an Edomite city), where national devastation is to come upon the Transjordanian peoples, depict the approach of an eagle. That the eagle is not otherwise named by Hosea perhaps adds to the ominous nature of the proclamation. It most likely represents the (imminent?) threat of Assyria, but like his contemporary Amos and his heir Jeremiah, Hosea's prophecies of judgment often leave the specific identity of the threat to the imagination of the audience.

Judgment is announced on YHWH's household through a beautifully structured parallel charge of *violating covenant ('ābar bĕrît)* and *transgressing instruction (pāša' tôrâ)*. The vocabulary can be found elsewhere in Hosea (6:7, "violate covenant"; 4:6 and 8:12, "instruction"; 7:13, "rebelled against me"; 14:9, "transgressors"). Some scholars, however, see in 8:1b an example not of Hosea's thinking but that of a redactor, who supplemented the emerg-

---

ognizable symbol of Assyria. That is likely, but the eagle was a potent symbol and source of imagery in a variety of ancient contexts.

26. For the former see Eidevall, *Grapes in the Desert,* p. 127. For the latter see Yee, *Composition and Tradition,* p. 288. She regards 8:1-4a as a Deuteronomically influenced editorial addition, as is the reference to transgressing the covenant in 6:7. See further the commentary discussion of 9:4.

27. On the centrality of the concept "house of YHWH," see the comments in the introduction, section IV.A, "Hosea's Theology: Narrative and Community Identity."

ing book of Hosea with an understanding of a national covenant in line with the book of Deuteronomy (which, in their view, emerged no earlier than the reign of Josiah and reached final form no earlier than the Babylonian exile).[28] The problem with this reasoning is the conclusion that the proposal of a national covenant with YHWH is a Deuteronomic (and late-7th-century) innovation.[29] Since Hosea was from the previous century, so the reasoning goes, he could not have conceived of the Israel-YHWH relationship as a *běrît*, though the marriage metaphor may be his innovation. Such an accounting for 8:1b is possible, but less likely than that Hosea employed the fully developed marriage metaphor because he also knew the term *běrît* in the context of YHWH's election and calling of Israel to be his people. There is no compelling reason to posit a Deuteronomic *origin* for the vocabulary of 8:1b as opposed to the conclusion that Hosea and Deuteronomy (or the Deuteronomist) shared the term *běrît* and some of the vocabulary of 8:1b.[30]

The first person possessive suffix -*î* (*my* = YHWH) in v. 1 is attached to the nouns *covenant* and *instruction.* The two nouns are not synonyms but complements. The covenant is God's gracious establishment of Israel as his people, and his *tôrâ* proceeds from this gift as the instructive ethos by which Israel can maintain its status as his people.[31] Together *covenant* and *torah* are a major part of the inheritance YHWH granted to his adopted household, even though Hosea describes them as spurned and ignored in his day. Indeed, that the people have not responded adequately to YHWH's prior gracious acts of deliverance, covenant making, and blessing lies at the heart of the prophet's judgment language.

2 On a first reading, the description of the people *crying out* to God

---

28. See, e.g., Perlitt, *Bundestheologie,* pp. 146-51.

29. See the introduction, section IV.C, "Hosea's Theology: Covenant and Marriage."

30. The phrase "violating the covenant" *('ābar běrît)* occurs twice in Hosea (6:7; 8:1), but only four times in all the Deuteronomistic History (Deut. 17:2; Josh. 23:16; Judg. 2:20; 2 Kgs. 18:12), which employs several other verbs for rejecting or breaking YHWH's covenant. In Hos. 8:1b the parallel phrase, "transgressing instruction" *(pāša' tôrâ),* does not occur at all in the Deuteronomistic History, and the verb *pāša'* with Israel as subject and YHWH as object occurs just once in it (1 Kgs. 8:50). The combination is more frequent in the prophets (e.g., Hos. 7:13; Zeph. 3:11; Jer. 2:8, 29; 3:13; 33:8; Ezek. 2:3; 14:11; 20:38), who may have adopted the verb from the political realm, where it is often used in the context of rebellion against authority. In Ps. 78:10 the poet writes that Israel "did not keep the covenant of God and they refused to walk according to his instruction," using *běrît* and *tôrâ* in parallel phrases. See J. Day, "Pre-Deuteronomic Allusions to the Covenant in Hosea and Psalm lxxviii," *VT* 36 (1986) 1-12. These data do not support the case for Hos. 8:1b as a Deuteronomistic redaction.

31. Note the expressions "my covenant" and "my voice" (Exod. 19:5) in the introduction to the Sinai pericope.

seems to contradict the charge in 7:14 that they do not "cry out" to the Lord. Consideration of the context of 7:14, particularly the charge that the appeal to God is "not from the heart," shows that a similar communication is given in two different formulations. No doubt many Israelites called upon YHWH, even if some conceived of him as one among several deities to be venerated. Hosea's charges have to do with their understanding and intention in calling upon YHWH. Surely, many in Israel would claim precisely that they "know" YHWH and recognize his work in the formation and support of the nation.[32] The issue turns on whether Hosea has correctly grasped the inadequacies of his contemporaries and whether he was prompted by YHWH to proclaim them in judgmental language. That subsequent generations preserved the book attests to the belief that Hosea was so prompted.

3   The good that Israel is charged with rejecting is, broadly speaking, an obedient, life-giving path that YHWH would have them take in the historical moment.[33] *Good (ṭôb)* is what God had promised Israel (Num. 10:29), if they would follow his lead. Deuteronomy employs the term several times in the context of the good from YHWH that comes with obedience (5:33; 6:24; 10:13; 12:28; 26:11). Particularly poignant is the Mosaic injunction to choose life and good over death and evil (30:15). Hosea charges the people with rejecting what YHWH has defined as *good* for them in his day. Two basic charges are leveled throughout the book that illustrate *rejecting good:* the embrace of idolatry and polytheism on the one hand, and involvement with international suitors on the other hand.

Even more personally, YHWH himself is *good* for Israel (Exod. 33:19). Thus Israel's rejection of certain actions (which are good) and embrace of others (which are bad) is at the same time a rejection of the nation's covenant Lord and his revealed will. There is a prediction in 3:5 that in the latter days Israel will come trembling after YHWH and his "goodness." Their current status, however, is not good: they are being pursued by an enemy who serves at YHWH's design as judgment to come upon them. For connections in Hosea's vocabulary, we suggest that his charge of Israel *rejecting good* is tantamount to its "devising evil," a theme that he underscores in 7:15.

The *pursuit (rādap) by an enemy* is another phrase of reversal in the book. According to 6:3 Israel should "pursue" *(rādap)* YHWH — a good thing if they would only do it! Since they have not done it adequately, pursuit is thus literally on the other foot, that of an enemy. The enemy is not named, but it could be Assyria, Egypt, or Damascus, all of whom sought to seize and control Israel.

---

32. See the discussions on "knowing" and "knowledge" in the commentary on 2:20 (MT 22); 4:1; and 6:6.

33. In addition to what follows, see the excursus at 3:5 on "YHWH's Goodness."

4 The first two clauses of v. 4 are poetically parallel. Clause A, the making of kings (note the plural), and clause B, the appointing of officials, are actions that YHWH has not approved. The verb *know* in the second clause is not intended to represent YHWH as unaware of the political process that produced the officials; it is a relational term used in this context as a parallel to the prepositional phrase *(not from me)* in the first clause. The prophet represents YHWH as not related to, and thus not approving, the appointment of kings and officials. Such a criticism cuts to the heart of Israel's political legitimacy and is tantamount to the declaration that the monarchy and its officials do not represent YHWH's will for his people.

The making of kings was a sacral act in the ancient world; it thus required divine approval.[34] Thus prophets and priests must proclaim the investiture as divinely willed, and the designated king would be anointed and invested in his office. Hosea offers his prophetic perspective that the kings (and related officials) have not been YHWH's designees, whatever the official steps undertaken in Israel.

It is difficult to extrapolate the prophet's view of monarchy from such heated and pointed criticism here and elsewhere (e.g., 13:9-11).[35] One could conclude from the scattered references in the book to the current rulers, since without exception they are negative, that *in principle* Hosea had an opposition to the institution of monarchy in Israel, or that his thorough institutional criticism had to do simply with royal failure to perform effectively. Is it the case that Hosea thinks of the kings as illegitimate because they were designated by corrupted members of the priesthood and court prophecy? It is partly a question of how far back in history does the denial of divine support for the kings go. Is the comment that Israel made kings, but not through YHWH's approval, applicable to the circumstances in Israel from the end of the Jehu dynasty? Does it include all the kings of the northern kingdom, beginning with Jeroboam I? Could such a comment include the beginnings under Saul and everything subsequently (cf. 1 Sam. 8:1-22; Judg. 8:22-27), as if to say that the institution itself is an aberration?

In the book of Hosea the only positive references about the leadership of the people are for the future (1:11 [MT 2:2]; 3:5).[36] If these prophecies of a

---

34. Cf. 1 Sam. 10:17-25; 1 Kgs. 1:28-35; 2 Kgs. 9:1-9. The last text represents the anointing of Jehu as a prophetic act after which he kills the Israelite king Joram and rules in his place.

35. Cf. André Caquot, "Osée et la Royauté," *RHPR* 41 (1961) 123-46; A. Gelston, "Kingship in the Book of Hosea," *OTS* 19 (1974) 71-85; P. Machinist, "Hosea and the Ambiguity of Kingship in Ancient Israel," in *Constituting the Community: Studies on the Polity of Ancient Israel in Honor of S. Dean McBride Jr.,* ed. John T. Strong and Steven S. Tuell (Winona Lake, IN: Eisenbrauns, 2005), pp. 153-81.

36. See the excursus at 3:5 on "David Their King."

future ruler over a reunited Israel derive from Hosea and not his editors, then he did not regard the institution itself as a usurpation of YHWH's kingship over his people, but as a failed source of leadership, perhaps analogous to the failures of the priesthood. There is no reason to think that the harsh criticism of priests in the book means that the prophet believed the institution of the priesthood was an aberration. He was certainly not against the institution of prophecy, even if he opposed much that proceeded from court prophecy in his day. If the reference to "David their king" in 3:5 goes back to the prophet, then he not only believed that monarchy could reflect the will of YHWH for Israel, he was also committed to the view, expressed elsewhere in the OT, that YHWH had promised rule over his people to the Davidic family. This is certainly the view represented by the *book* of Hosea as well as that of the book of Amos.[37] Possibly Hosea had reservations about any monarch in Samaria who ruled over only a portion of YHWH's household.

The second half of v. 4 is a criticism of Israel's crafting of images in silver and gold. These are representations of the Divine and break both the letter and the spirit of the covenant ethos (*tôrâ,* "instruction," in 8:1) and the exclusivity of the relationship between YHWH and Israel. It is not clear whether the charge of idolatry in 8:4b-7 continues and elaborates upon the critique of the house of YHWH in 8:1-4a, or whether it is another passage now incorporated in a secondary collection of prophecies against Israel in ch. 8. Although one can argue that 8:1–9:6 is a single poetic critique, even on the assumption of a collection of separate oracles, the material is now presented together. If the critique of idolatry in v. 4b is integral to the critique of the royal administration in v. 4a, then we may have a clue to Hosea's rejection of Israelite monarchy: the priests and prophets who proclaim divine favor toward the monarchs are practitioners of idolatry and are thus illegitimate representatives of YHWH.

With respect to idolatry, similar charges were lodged against Gomer in her representation of Israel (2:8 [MT 10]), and the term *idols* (ʿăṣabbîm; lit. "crafted images") employed here in 8:4b is also used in 4:17. Hosea draws upon the covenant ethos from Israel's past as still relevant, and from his standpoint, authoritative. Israel's past, with its charter as God's household, is also its only viable future. This is the way to read the critique of idolatry in 4:4-19. It follows the programmatic statement of 4:1-3, which draws

---

37. The question with regard to Amos and the book by his name is very similar to that of Hosea and his book, namely, whether the prophecies about a future rule for David's dynasty (Hos. 3:5; Amos 9:11-12) are editorial additions to the books or reflect the view of the prophets themselves. For Amos see the discussion in Max Polley, *Amos and the Davidic Empire: A Socio-Historical Approach* (New York: Oxford University Press, 1989).

directly upon the fundamental tenets of the covenant ethos. This is the better way to read 8:4b-7. It follows the charge that YHWH's house had broken the covenant and disregarded divine instruction in 8:1. How else would Hosea have known or come to believe that the making of images as depicted in vv. 4b-6 was a form of idolatry and an offense to Israel's divine founder, if not from a tradition that he inherited and that he was convinced was still authoritative? Image making was, after all, a dominant form of religious expression in the Semitic world, and it would require a community with a different history for some of its inhabitants to argue against the dominant culture.

The last phrase of v. 4 is syntactically and grammatically difficult. The particle *lĕma'an* typically introduces a result clause ("therefore," "with the result that"), and that is the way I render it in v. 4. It is unlikely that idols were intended by their Israelite makers as reason for someone or something to be cut off, unless they were execration figures representing enemies to be crushed.[38] More likely, the intent of the images is to secure blessing and security for those who possess them. Hosea's charge is that the intended outcome is reversed through YHWH's historical judgment. As the prophet represents it, there is cause and effect here, though intended not by the idol makers but by YHWH. The idol makers have brought on failure and destruction for Israel through their actions, even if it was blessing and security that they intended to secure by them.

There remains the question of the subject of the last clause. Who is to be *cut off* (*kārat*, Niphal)? The subject in Hebrew is third person masculine singular, but indefinite (= "he" or "it"). The subject may be the state or people as a single entity, since Israel is the subject of the criticism in previous verses. Another possibility is that the subject is a proleptic reference to the idolatrous calf explicitly mentioned in the next verse[39] or a reference to the current king, who will be cut off as a result of YHWH's anger.

5 The rendering of the initial clause in 8:5 differs from most modern translations, all of which wrestle with the best way to render the verb *zānaḥ*. The MT points the text as a Qal perfect verb with "your calf" as the subject, but this makes the typical translation inexplicable ("your calf, O Samaria, has rejected . . ."), since the verb takes an object and none is provided. Options include repointing the text to be an imperative or infinitive, repointing as a passive, or emending to make the text first person, either perfect or imperfect.[40]

38. An execration figurine representing an enemy or rival typically had a curse written on it. See *ANET*, 328-29; *COS* 1:50-52.

39. As if to say, "that one, in particular, will be cut off." Cf. Andersen and Freedman, *Hosea*, p. 493, who propose that the calf of 8:5 is the object (the "he") to be cut off in 8:4.

40. For the first see Wolff, *Hosea*, p. 132: "Throw away your calf, O Samaria!" The imperative that he proposes, however, is 2nd masc. sing., whereas Samaria is personi-

The versions assume some form of rejection is described, but they are not consistent in their rendering. On the one hand, any of these solutions is a plausible response to a difficulty. One is not compelled to maintain either the Hebrew text or its Masoretic pointing in the face of difficulties when satisfactory solutions present themselves. On the other hand, the MT can be satisfactorily rendered if one gives a stative interpretation for *zānaḥ* rather than a transitive one. Moreover, it has the intriguing characteristic of a Hosean pun on *zānâ* ("to play the harlot"). In 8:3 Israel is accused of *rejecting (zānaḥ)* the good. Perhaps, then, in 8:5 Samaria holds onto a divine image that is *wretched* or "stinks" *(zānaḥ).*[41]

The prophet's representation of divine anger in v. 5 includes a rhetorical question. How long can Israel remain guilty? A major claim of the book is that Israel cannot remain guilty forever. Israel must repent or suffer the consequences. Moreover, the time of judgment is at hand in the historical process. That is the unspoken conclusion to the question of 8:5.

6 One aspect of the prophetic critique of idolatry in the OT is predicated on the simple fact that divine images are made by humans (Jer. 10:1-5; Isa. 44:6-20). That basic but devastating critique is briefly presented in 8:6. A worker made the calf, so Hosea's logic goes, which means that the calf is *not divine (lōʾ ʾĕlōhîm)* and hence is unworthy of the attention (veneration?) it is given. Perhaps Hosea's expression is influenced by the ways in which Israel addressed the calf and conceived of it as representing deity. According to the somewhat different formulas of Exod. 32:4 and 1 Kgs. 12:28, a calf represented the "gods" *(ʾĕlōhîm)* who brought Israel up from Egypt. Hosea's terse dictum of *not divine* simply reverses that description. His polemic also reinforces the critique of idolatry as confusing true Deity with others things that are "not gods" (2 Kgs. 19:18; Isa. 37:19): "and he becomes a priest for 'Not Gods' *(lōʾ ʾĕlōhîm)*" (2 Chr. 13:9); "Can someone make gods for himself, when they are not gods *(lōʾ ʾĕlōhîm)*?" (Jer. 16:20).

Both Aaron (Exod. 32) and Jeroboam I (1 Kgs. 12:28) could envisage a calf as an acceptable divine symbol in Israel. This reflects not only the power of the bovine image in the ancient Semitic world, but also its particular influence in some Israelite circles, including the priesthood. So strong was the calf image in Israel that some interpreters would argue that the criticism of it here in 8:5-6 could not have originated as early as the prophet Hosea, who would have found the calf an acceptable representation of YHWH,

---

fied as female. For the second see Rudolph, *Hosea,* pp. 156-57: "Rejected is your calf. . . ." For the last, reading either "I have rejected . . ." or "I will reject . . . ," see Davies, *Hosea,* pp. 200-201; cf. Stuart, *Hosea,* pp. 126, 128.

41. See the excursus below on "Hosea and the Calf."

as did his contemporaries.[42] Only later was criticism of representing YHWH as a calf written into Israel's national traditions. That the aniconic requirements of the Decalogue (Exod. 20:4; Deut. 5:8) arose after Hosea seems less likely than that the aniconic traits of Yahwism were older than Hosea and accepted by him as normative, but still in dispute among Israelites who worshiped YHWH using the symbol.[43] Hosea's strictures against idolatry are consistent with the Decalogue's requirements, just as his understanding of Israel's origins are consistent with the prologue to the Decalogue (cf. Hos. 13:4; 11:1 with Exod. 20:2; Deut. 5:6). For him, the aniconic principle is rooted in his understanding of the covenant.

The prediction in v. 6 is that the calf will be *shattered (šĕbābîm)*. The Hebrew term occurs only here and may mean "splintered" or "smashed to pieces."[44] Whatever the nuance of the term, the fate of the calf will demonstrate that it is *not divine*. Hosea says nothing about who is responsible for the destruction or when it will happen. According to 10:5, the calf at Bethel will be taken to Assyria, presumably as a trophy of war. Samaria's calf in 8:5-6 may be the calf located at Bethel. If so, then Hosea made more than one prediction about the fate of a national religious symbol.

Excursus: Hosea and the Calf

Hosea contains references to a bovine figure *('ēgel)* in three places (8:5-6, twice masc. sing.; 10:5, MT fem. pl.; 13:2, masc. pl.). The references in 8:5-6 come in the context of judgment against Israel because of its "idols" *('ăṣabbîm,* 8:4). Idols are also mentioned in 13:2 with "calves." The plural reference is possibly to smaller, individual images, rather than to a state-sponsored statue in a shrine. In 10:5 (MT) the feminine plural "calves" of Beth-aven is odd, since the other references in Hosea and the pronouns in 10:5-6 refer to a singular calf. Moreover, most early versions of 10:5 refer to the calf itself in the singular, and thus most modern translations do so as well. Nevertheless, the feminine plural in 10:5 is not likely to be a textual error; it is more likely a polemical slur on the calf figure.[45]

42. This view is represented by Lang, *Monotheism,* pp. 32-33. Gomes, *Sanctuary of Bethel,* p. 165, thinks that the critique is Hosea's, but concludes: "Hosea had no problems with the calf icon *per se.* It was the misuse of this legitimate icon, perhaps worshipped as more than a symbol . . . that led him to reject the calf-cult."

43. See the balanced discussion by T. Mettinger, *No Graven Image? Israelite Aniconism in Its Ancient Near Eastern Context* (ConBOT 42; Stockholm: Almqvist & Wiksell, 1995). Possibly the measures instituted by Jeroboam I resulted in the disenfranchising of forms of Yahwism from which Hosea derived his commitments. See the introduction, section IV.A, "Hosea's Theology: Narrative and Community Identity."

44. See Macintosh, *Hosea,* pp. 308-10, for an extensive discussion of options.

45. Interpreters are not of one mind just how the feminine plural demeans the

The calf of 8:5 belongs to "Samaria," and this attribution could be geographical in the particular sense that the calf is located in the royal city of Samaria. Samaria may, however, represent the royal city and state administration, but not the physical location of the crafted figure, since 10:5 has the inhabitants of Samaria fearing for the calf of Beth-aven (= Bethel). Some interpreters have been persuaded of the Bethel venue for Samaria's calf, but it is based in part on the odd silence of the OT with regard to a temple for YHWH in Samaria, where a calf figure would likely be kept.[46] According to 2 Kgs. 10:21 there was a "house of Baal" in Samaria, but no textual reference to a Yahwistic temple in Samaria exists. The house for Baal was turned into a latrine by Jehu (10:27), who left untouched, however, the golden calves at Bethel and at Dan made by Jeroboam I (10:29). The latter were to represent the "gods" who brought Israel out from Egypt (1 Kgs. 12:28, 32; 2 Chr. 13:8).

It is not clear from the texts themselves what/whom the calf represented.[47] Most interpreters see Hosea's references in light of the polemical references to the making of calf images in Exod. 32 and 1 Kgs. 12:28-32. This is most likely correct, but the meaning(s) attached to the images in those sources is also not clear. A major divide among interpreters is whether the calf should be associated with the worship of YHWH or with another deity (e.g., Baal/Hadad). Since bovine symbolism for deity was widespread in the ancient world, the figure could represent a variety of deities. And in any case, the question of function remains. Does the calf represent the deity himself or does it represent some aspect of the deity's cult such as a pedestal or attendant? In terms of Hosea's polemic, the calf can represent YHWH (which can be understood as a violation of the second commandment)[48] or a Canaanite deity (which would be a violation also of the first commandment). But if one must choose, then the balance of probability favors the view that the bovine figure(s) represents YHWH himself or one of his divine characteristics in material form. Jehu is represented as a severe persecutor of Phoenician baalism in the 9th century B.C. (2 Kgs. 9–10). If the golden calves of Dan and Bethel had been associated with one or more of the Baal cults, then one assumes they would have been destroyed like the temple of Baal and its worshipers in Samaria (2 Kgs. 10:18-29). The calf, or calves,

---

calf. Rudolph, *Hosea,* p. 195, suggests that the MT be repointed as *'eglût* and be translated abstractly and polemically as "calfhood." So similarly Macintosh, *Hosea,* pp. 399-400. Andersen and Freedman, *Hosea,* p. 555, suggest the possibility that the feminine plural form is a polemical parallel to the plural of majesty as a reference to deity.

46. Various archaeological excavations at the site of Israelite Samaria have not turned up the remains of an Iron Age temple either. Absence of evidence is not necessarily evidence of absence, but the lack of material remains for a Yahwistic temple in Israelite Samaria is odd.

47. For detailed discussions see Koenen, *Bethel,* pp. 95-110; and Gomes, *Sanctuary of Bethel,* pp. 163-66.

48. A number of interpreters have suggested that the calves were intended as pedestals for the invisible YHWH, not unlike ark/cherubim appurtenances in Jerusalem. For bibliographic references see Gomes, *Sanctuary of Bethel,* p. 25. If this is correct, Hosea's criticisms presuppose that the "pedestals" had become venerated in their own right or were adopted for other cultic purposes that detracted from YHWH's sovereignty.

in Hosea's assessment would then be examples of a syncretistic or baalized cult of YHWH.

Elsewhere in the OT, a calf is associated with idolatrous Israelite worship (Exod. 32; Ps. 106:19; 1 Kgs. 12:28). The one crafted at Mt. Sinai was a molten object *(massēkâ)*, and it, like the golden calves of Jeroboam I, was proclaimed as the god(s)[49] who brought Israel up from Egypt (Exod. 32:4, 8). The relationship between the golden calf episode at Mt. Sinai and the golden calves of Jeroboam I is not clear, although the biblical writers viewed both accounts similarly as examples of Israelite-generated idolatry. That the calf is associated with Israel's beginnings, even by its detractors, strongly implies that it struck a resonant chord with many Israelites.

In material terms the calf of Samaria is a crafted figure, perhaps made of silver and gold (8:4). It will be shattered/broken because it is not divine (8:6). Possibly the calf was carved of wood and then overlaid with precious metal. The explanation of the calf in 8:6b (not divine) may be a polemical reversal of the phrase in 1 Kgs. 12:28: "Behold your gods, O Israel. . . ." According to 10:6, the calf of Bethel will be carried away to Assyria. Does this indicate a different fate than that predicted in 8:6, or that the calf of Bethel is to be distinguished from that in Samaria? The sources do not allow for a clear answer. The "calves" of 13:2 are apparently understood by Hosea to be idols, since "molten images" *(massēkâ)* are mentioned in the same verse. It is the same term used for the molten calf in Exod. 32:4 and Deut. 9:12. These "idols" (*'ăṣabbîm;* so 13:2) may be smaller forms that are acquired and kept by individual worshipers.

3. Calling Egypt and Assyria (8:7-14)

7 *For they sow the wind and will reap the whirlwind. There is no standing grain, (so) the sprout will produce no flour; (but) even if it produced, strangers would devour it.*

8 *Israel is swallowed up; now they are among the nations, like a vessel no one desires.*

9 *For they have gone up to Assyria; Ephraim is a solitary wild ass; they have paid for love.*

10 *Even though they hire among the nations, I will gather them; the king and princes will writhe*[50] *soon because of the burden.*[51]

---

49. Exod. 32:4, 8; 1 Kgs. 12:28 all refer to the calf (calves) as the "gods" who brought Israel from Egypt.

50. Repointing MT *wayyāḥēllû* ("they begin") from *ḥll*, as *wayyāḥîlû,* from *ḥyl.* So NRSV, ESV, and a number of interpreters (e.g., Wolff, *Hosea,* pp. 133, 143-44).

51. Most interpreters take the phrase "king and princes" as *nomen rectum* in the expression "burden of king and princes," although it is awkward syntax. The nouns could be, however, the subject of the verb "writhe," as proposed here. See Andersen and Freedman, *Hosea,* pp. 506-8; and ESV. The LXX renders 8:10b: "And they shall cease for a little while anointing a king and princes." The translators may have read the adverb *ma'aṭ* as

226

11 *When Ephraim increased altars (in response) to sinning, they became for him altars for sinning!*

12 *If I write a multitude*[52] *of my instructions,*[53] *they would be reckoned as strange.*

13 *My sacrificial gifts they offer in sacrifice and they eat flesh. YHWH does not accept them. Now he will remember their iniquity and punish their sin. They will return to Egypt.*[54]

14 *Israel has forgotten his maker and built palaces, and Judah has increased fortified cities; but I will send fire on their*[55] *cities, and it will consume their large buildings.*

7 Here a summary statement of proverbial wisdom, based on the connection between act and consequence, is employed to portray the folly of Israel's self-destructive activities. "What you sow, you shall reap,"[56] is a familiar, cross-cultural saying. Instead of seed for food, Israel has sown the *wind (rûaḥ),* a folly that turns even worse with payback. They will reap a stronger blowback, a storm or *whirlwind (sûpâ).* The term is used elsewhere of destructive meteorological phenomena (Job 21:18; 27:20; 37:9), but more to the point, it can signify God's approach in judgment (Amos 1:14; Isa. 29:6; 66:15; Nah. 1:3) and the terror of a foreign army (Jer. 4:13). The *wind,* therefore, is Israel's foolish casting about in the international arena; the *whirlwind* is the catastrophe that such endeavors will bring about. In modern colloquial terms, Israel was stirring up trouble for itself.

A second analogy regarding the production of grain is offered to reinforce the metaphor of sowing and reaping. It too is formulated in proverbial form and represents the consequence of misapplied or misguided cultivation: no mature grain and thus no growth to produce the sought-after flour. There is alliteration in Hebrew (*qāmâ* = standing grain; *ṣemaḥ* = sprout; *qemaḥ* =

---

the verb "to cease" and the noun *maśśā'* ("burden") as *māšaḥ* ("anoint"), or may have had a different text before them.

52. Following the Qere *rubbê,* rather than the Kethib *ribbô,* "myriad/ten thousand."

53. The MT is pointed as a sing., *tôrātî* ("my instruction/law"). This is the same as the reference to YHWH's instruction in 8:1. The difference in meaning is slight, if any. The sense seems to be multiple instructions, whether the Hebrew text is configured as singular or plural. The reference does not seem to be to many copies of a single instruction.

54. The LXX has "and eat unclean food in Assyria." This is a repetition of Hos. 9:3.

55. The MT reads lit., *her* cities and *her* large buildings. The reason is unclear, since both Israel and Judah are masculine entities. Cities, however, are feminine, and possibly the pronoun "her" refers to the capital cities of Samaria and Jerusalem.

56. See an application of the proverb in Gal. 6:7-9. See also the excursus at 1:4-5 on "Sowing in Hosea."

flour). The proverbial saying is followed by a sarcastic *even if.* Even if the agricultural process develops to the point of harvest time and production, i.e., the mature grain stands ready for reaping and the making of flour is at hand, someone beside the farmers will consume it (cf. Isa. 17:10-11). That someone is collectively described as *strangers* or "foreigners" *(zārîm),* a term Hosea uses elsewhere to describe non-Israelites who will abuse the nation in the political-historical process.[57]

8 The verb *swallow (bālaʿ)* represents something other than a literal consuming here, perhaps something like the verb of mixing *(bālal)* in 7:8, whose sound it approximates. *Bālaʿ* is also the verb used in the previous verse to describe strangers "devouring" Israel's produce. Israel's political involvement has made it not stronger but weaker.

The simile in v. 8b is that of a vessel (e.g., a terra-cotta pot) that has no value and is thus undesirable. Clay vessels were ubiquitous in ancient societies, and the comparison between people and vessels was culturally understandable (cf. Jer. 18). More particularly, the Hebrew phrase in v. 8b, *a vessel no one desires (kĕlî ʾên-ḥēpeṣ bô),* is apparently a traditional phrase. King Jehoiachin is described as a broken "pot no one desires" and as a man to be hurled into exile (Jer. 22:28). His fate would certainly illustrate being "swallowed" by another nation. That same phrase is also used to describe the people of Moab after YHWH's judgment has struck: they too are a broken "pot that no one desires" (Jer. 48:38).

The prophet's characterization of Israel as *a vessel no one desires* is probably not the judgment of nations like Assyria and Egypt, but the prophet's shaming mechanism. Either nation will be pleased to take Israel as its own. Indeed, Hosea's saying may reflect the initial conscription of portions of the Israelite population in the aftermath of Tiglath-pileser III's campaigns in 734-732. Babylon, for example, kept Jehoiachin for decades as a prized prisoner of conquest. Hosea's cutting description reflects a divine assessment and resulting judgment of the people. They will be used and abused as a result of their failures. As pawns and servants of either Assyria or Egypt, Israel's self-worth will plummet, and they will be compared to a marred pot.

The depiction of Ephraim mixed among the nations in 7:8-16 has a number of thematic parallels to Israel swallowed among the nations in 8:8-14. Both have internal intrigue and failure on the part of the nation's rulers. Both, moreover, combine references to idolatry as one of the practices leading the people astray and contributing to their coming downfall.

9 Verse 9 provides an example of being mixed or swallowed among the nations. The description is apparently that of an embassy to Assyria and the example is a wild ass. For Hosea's first audience, embassies to Assyria

---

57. See the excursus at 5:7 on "Strangers in Hosea."

would have been well known, since there were certainly several of them during the reigns of Tiglath-pileser III (745-727) and Shalmaneser V (727-722). For later readers (and interpreters), a precise identification of the situation under evaluation is considerably more difficult.[58] Hosea regards the enterprise as an affront to YHWH's sovereignty, whether it means recognition of the influence of Assyria's gods or the loss of political autonomy for Israel.

Ephraim is compared to a solitary wild ass. This kind of comparison is a trademark of Hosea. It employs both metaphor and pun, playing on the similarity of the name *'eprayim* (Ephraim) with *pere'* ("wild ass"). The political connotation of the comparison has been taken in more than one way.[59] The Asian wild ass is not a solitary figure; it lives in herds as a sociable animal. Like the zebra, however, it does not take to domestication. Ishmael, for example, is compared to the wild ass (Gen. 16:12), although the mobile desert dwellers descended from him were tightly organized in clans and tribes. Perhaps the related characteristics of independence and stubbornness are the vehicle (source domain) of the metaphor to render the tenor (target domain) of a laughable and pitiful Israel overwhelmed in the diplomatic arena. Elsewhere Hosea describes the people as a stubborn heifer (4:16). A wild ass hiring love is a metaphor of cutting sarcasm, intended to shame Ephraim and its diplomatic frenzy. Here is a solitary wild ass (which still has plenty of opportunities to mate in its own herd) out paying for lovers![60] The *love* in this case would be the goodwill or favors offered by the Assyrian suzerain. Ephraim, however, is going to pay for them.

There may be a cultural factor in the comparison of the wild ass and finding love, although one not so apparent to modern readers. Jeremiah, for example, uses a similar comparison in 2:24-25, citing a female wild ass who sniffs the wind and finds a mate, while excoriating Judah, who loves strangers. Hosea's comparison may have been like an inside joke that takes root in a community or particular culture, or a proverbial saying that takes on a life of its own in political circles. Perhaps it is the wonder from the human perspective that a stubborn, irascible creature like the wild ass can reproduce so prolifically. Just so, Israel, a stubborn idolatrous people, are going to get affection, but from an uninviting source.

10 Verse 10 should be read as a continuation of the sarcasm expressed in the immediate context, but the text and syntax of the last clause are

58. See the reconstruction of Israel's diplomatic missions in Stuart Irvine, "Politics and Prophetic Commentary in Hosea 8:8-10," *JBL* 114 (1995) 292-94.

59. See the discussion in Eidevall, *Grapes in the Desert,* pp. 133-36.

60. "Pay for" or "hire" is a common way to translate the rare verb *tānâ* (here in the Hiphil), which is also used in the next verse in the Qal. The plural noun *'āhābîm,* "lovers," from *'āhab,* is uncommon and not the same as the plural Piel participle *(mĕ'ahăbîm)* of the term used elsewhere in Hosea (2:5, 7, 10, 12, 13 [MT 7, 9, 12, 14, 15]).

difficult to interpret. In this verse Ephraim is a "they" who are out bargaining and purchasing among the nations, using the same verb *(tānâ)* as in 8:9b. YHWH's *gathering (qābaṣ,* Piel) of the people, therefore, has a negative, judgmental connotation, like Egypt's "gathering" of them for their subsequent burial in 9:6. They will be gathered in order to work or to be used. One wonders if the imagery is an oblique reversal of the status of a solitary wild ass. Ephraim will no longer be independent. They will be gathered together and will be afflicted by the *burden* that involvement among the nations will bring upon them. If it is correct that the phrase *king and princes* is the subject of the verb *writhe,* then they are Israelite royalty afflicted by their subservient status. No longer the head of the nation, the king and princes are menial servants to other kings like everyone else. If, on the other hand, the phrase *king and princes* should be joined to the noun *burden,* then it is probably Assyrian royalty that is in mind as a burden to Ephraim. Ephraim would *writhe* under the burden of the Assyrian king and princes. In either case, the conclusion is that Ephraim/Israel will suffer.

11 The subject matter of Israel's folly shifts back to internal sickness. In one sense it is a shift back to the subject of cultic sin described in 8:4-6, and more particularly Ephraim's cultic practices and sin before YHWH.

Verse 11 is a terse elliptical saying with repetitive vocabulary. As a result the versions differ somewhat, and modern interpreters have proposed various emendations.[61] The MT is intelligible, however, as ironic sarcasm, and it represents a thought complementary to 4:7-8. One way to deal with angst and guilt is to increase religious practice. That is the essence of 8:11a. Ephraim increased sacrificial practice in order to effect atonement and expiation. But according to 8:11b the altars themselves became the occasion for sinfulness and thus provide no atonement at all. There are at least two possibilities why Hosea connected the increase in altars and the increase in sinfulness, which, of course, was the opposite of Ephraim's intent in building them. One is a charge of polytheism, with Ephraim following the logic of polytheism in offering sacrifice to a number of deities in hopes of securing its well-being. Modern proverbial analogies would be "covering all the bases" or "hedging one's bets." The other possibility is a critique of perceived syncretistic and baalized forms of Yahwism that usher forth from those who do not "know YHWH" (8:2). If 8:13 continues the charge of inadequate cultic service to YHWH, then syncretistic, baalized forms of Yahwism are likely in mind in v. 11. The brevity of Hosea's expression makes it difficult to choose between these options for increased sacrificial activities, and it is quite possible that the broad-based charge includes examples of both.

61. Cf. *BHS;* Macintosh, *Hosea,* pp. 323-25; Andersen and Freedman, *Hosea,* pp. 508-9.

12   An increase in written instructions seems to be no more effective in bringing Israel closer to YHWH than the multiplication of altars described in v. 11. The point is not that having written instructions is strange — if anything, the assumption is the opposite. There is nothing strange or un-Israelite about YHWH's will being expressed in written form. After all, that is the reason the book of Hosea was compiled in written form: to preserve an expression of God's will from a historical moment and to employ that material as instruction for later readers. Perhaps 8:1 assumes that there is a written component to the covenant and instruction being rejected in the house of YHWH. In v. 12 it is the supposed condition that is exasperatingly odd, not the fact of written instruction. To paraphrase: no matter how much guidance might be provided in written form, it will not be accepted by Ephraim, but regarded as *strange*. The term *zār* means out of place and thus unacceptable.[62] It has an echo in the context at 8:7, where in another conditional sentence "strangers" would eat Samaria's grain, should it reach maturity, rather than Israelites (cf. 7:9). That is not what should be the case, but unfortunately what would be the case. The expression in 8:12 functions similarly.

Hosea's expression is meant to charge Israel with failure to know YHWH and his will at this crucial stage in their history. It is a charge that is made repeatedly in various ways in the book. The function of the instruction would be to provide Israel with what it needs to respond adequately to YHWH's leading in the time of crisis. Since Israel has been told that it has failed with its altars and cultic practices (8:11, 13), one might suppose that the content of the written instructions would be about the covenant ethos and the application of faithfulness and loving-kindness (4:1-3).

One cannot tell from the expression of a supposed condition *(if I write . . . instructions)* whether there are, in fact, written collections of Yahwistic instructions widely recognized among the people in Israel. The essential point seems to be that even if such a collection existed, Israel would not recognize its authority. If there were one or more written collections known among the people, they might well be a form of the Covenant Code in Exodus, the Deuteronomic Covenant Code, the Holiness Code now in Leviticus, or even a collection of Hosea's prophecies, but these are all simply guesses. In any case, Hosea expresses frustration on YHWH's behalf that even an authoritative text would be seen as *strange*.

13   Verse 13 begins awkwardly and employs a rare noun in the first phrase translated here as *gift* (*habhab,* from *yāhab,* "to give"). As with a number of expressions in ch. 8, interpreters have suggested emendations for the initial phrase, all of which assume some form of corruption in the MT. For the most part, however, modern translations have sought to stay with the

---

62. See the excursus at 5:7 on "Strangers in Hosea."

MT in spite of its difficulties, which Rudolph said are severe enough to result in "the splitting of heads!"[63] One possible reconstruction of the text is to see in the rare word *habhab* either a corruption or a dialectical variant of the word *'āhab* ("love") and to render the first clause: "They love sacrifice, so they sacrifice and eat flesh."[64] This may claim partial support from the LXX. In essence this emendation clarifies what is likely the logic of the MT, though expressed more obscurely. Israel has multiplied altars and offers numerous sacrifices (cf. 8:11), enjoying the eating of meat as one by-product of its cultic practices.

However one renders the opening phrase, the rest of the verse is clear with its ominous claim: YHWH does not accept the cultic service being offered to him and there will be consequences. There is a time element in the expression *Now he [YHWH] will remember* that perhaps should be coordinated with the adverb *mĕʿāṭ* ("soon") in 8:10. Judgment is on the horizon. The prophet can visualize it taking shape as Israel continues down a destructive path of internal sickness and international folly.

Each of the last three phrases in v. 13 elaborates on the consequences when YHWH does not accept the sacrifices offered by Israel. The first two phrases are coordinated with one another: YHWH *remembers iniquity (zākar ʿāwōn)* and *punishes sin (pāqad ḥaṭṭāʾt)*. Hosea's listeners might well catch the ominous echo in these two phrases with the confessional language about YHWH (Exod. 34:6-7; 20:5), who forgives *iniquity (ʿāwōn) and sin (ḥaṭṭāʾâ)*, but *visits iniquity (pāqad ḥaṭṭāʾâ)* on those who hate him. Although the vocabulary is common, the combination of expressions is chilling in what it evokes. YHWH *remembers,* not to forgive but to institute judgment. Israel, which had declared that it *knows YHWH* (8:2), is declared by the prophet to be YHWH's enemy and thus liable for judgment.

The people will *return to Egypt.* This final clause is one way that YHWH visits iniquity on guilty Israel through the historical process. It is also another example of the manner in which Hosea draws on a narrative that defines both God and Israel. The people's *return to Egypt* assumes a prior presence there, and the grand narrative upon which Hosea depends has Israel's ancestors in Egypt when YHWH called them and brought them out (11:1; 12:13 [MT 14]). Hosea's vocabulary and thought patterns are infused with the traditions now contained in the book of Exodus, from the confession

---

63. Rudolph, *Hosea,* p. 160.

64. See *BHS;* Wolff, *Hosea,* p. 133; Davies, *Hosea,* p. 208. This rendering assumes other slight changes from the MT. The LXX appears to have read the rare term this way, although it puts the phrase "beloved sacrifices" at the end of v. 12. See also the odd phrase in 4:18, *'āhăbû hēbû,* which may reflect a derivation of *hab* from *'āhab.* The verb *'āhab,* "to love," occurs elsewhere in the context in 9:1.

of divine justice to the memory of a servile sojourn in Egypt. Moreover, he predicts Israel's future based on his understanding of its past. If Israel breaks the national covenant, which YHWH made with Israel in bringing them from Egypt, then a return to Egypt is poetic justice, even if the return is a metaphorical expression for another form of punishment. This mode of expression fits Hosea's narrative-based typology and his propensity to portray reversals in poetic turns of phrase. The announcement of the return, therefore, may be a threat to be taken literally or, since it carries the symbolic weight of an end to Israel's calling from Egypt, it may represent more generally the fate that comes with being "mixed" or "swallowed up" among the nations (7:8; 8:8). A projected return to Egypt also occurs in 9:3, where it is coupled with the announcement that the people will eat unclean food in Assyria. The parallelism there may simply represent the future reality of displaced Israelites in the locations where they sought to curry favors (12:1 [MT 2]), with Egypt as the symbol for slavery and Assyria the location of exile and servitude.

14 Here one encounters what is almost a semantic field representing large architectural features. These would be the result of royal building projects, all in the name of national security and certainly dynastic pride. But they will meet destruction sent by YHWH. This is in keeping with the larger theme of judgment on the horizon. Very similar judgmental language predicting consuming fire on urban buildings is found in Hosea's contemporary Amos (1:4, 7, 10, 12, 14; 2:2, 5).

For many modern readers v. 14 seems somewhat anticlimactic after v. 13. That sense, the parallels with Amos, the mention of Judah, and the unexpected reference to YHWH as Israel's "maker," where the best parallels are with Deutero-Isaiah, suggest to some that the whole verse is an editorial addition. Possibly the material is Hosea's and was simply transferred to this literary context, but it may well have been added at a later time by Judean editors in the transmission of the book.[65] Catchwords in the verse do find resonance with the immediate context and expressions used elsewhere by the prophet. If v. 14 is an addition, the verse's editor has fitted it to the contents of the book. For example, Hosea elsewhere speaks of Gomer and Israel "forgetting" God (2:13 [MT 15]; 4:6; 13:6). In the immediate context, YHWH remembers Israel's iniquity (8:13), while they "make" idols and a calf (8:4, 6), yet "forget" their own "maker." Judah has "increased" fortified cities, using the same verb in the charge that Ephraim has "increased" altars (8:11). Is-

---

65. By 1905 Harper, *Hosea,* p. 324, could produce an impressive list of interpreters who concluded that 8:14 was a later addition, either whole or in part. Yee, *Composition and Tradition,* pp. 195-97, is a more recent interpreter who follows this line of analysis. Wolff, *Hosea,* p. 146, is among those who think that 8:14 is an anticlimactic addition, but that the contents go back to Hosea.

rael "eats" meat from the sacrificial cult (8:13), while YHWH's fire "consumes" (same verb) large buildings. Furthermore, the parallel with Amos and the announcement of divine judgment upon peoples and cities are explained easily enough as part of a shared tradition among early prophets.

There is also poetic balance, but not balanced length, in v. 14's two pairs of clauses.[66] Israel and Judah, respectively, are the subjects of the first two clauses. Each has expended energy to make themselves more secure through building. As noted above, this follows the contextual theme of multiplying problems. Israel had increased altars (8:11). Even if YHWH increased written instructions, it would only lead to Israel's rejection (8:12). Now Israel has forgotten his maker and built palaces,[67] and Judah has increased its fortified cities. Using the term *maker (ʿōśeh)* for YHWH relativizes the expensive building projects attributed to Israel and Judah. No matter what they have made, the charge of forgetting the divine *maker* can only lead to disaster.

One may set out the parallels as follows:

A	B
Israel . . .	built palaces
A′	B′
Judah increased	fortified cities
A	B
fire	on cities
A′	B′
consume	large buildings

There is also a chiasm in the semantic field of building projects that connects all four clauses.

A	B
palaces	fortified cities
B′	A′
cities	large buildings

66. See the reconstruction by Andersen and Freedman, *Hosea,* pp. 511-12, who suggest five clauses of unequal length but with poetic features. They do not think the verse is an addition. I suggest four clauses in descending size and see no compelling reason either to see the verse as an addition.

67. The term *hêkāl* can also refer to a temple, but this is less likely in comparison to the other type of buildings mentioned in the verse: *ʾarmĕnōt,* which are large public buildings such as storerooms or fortifications; and *ʿārîm bĕṣurôt,* lit. "cities with walls."

The reference to Judah in v. 14 is surprising in the context. One could, for example, delete the clause with Judah as the subject, or keep the clause and reconstruct an original "Ephraim" for Judah as its subject. Either results in a plausible communication and neither should be rejected out of hand as editorial revision unworthy of a prophetic book. (All of them had editors.) The parallels above, however uneven the length of the clauses, do show a relationship between them that is understandable. And as a viable communication in its received form, we are obligated to deal with it. "Judah" has pursued its security in ways similar to Israel and will be judged similarly.

4. Days of Punishment Have Come (9:1-9)

In 9:1-9 comes a shift back to a theme used more frequently in chs. 1–2, 4–5, namely the metaphor of "playing the harlot" and its severe consequences. Harlotry is here associated with the theme announced in 7:8 that Israel had mixed itself among the nations, so it has a political connotation. Judgment is now at hand, similar in that regard to the way that ch. 8 presents a foreign threat upon the house of YHWH as imminent. There are references to YHWH's land and house (9:3-4), plus suggestive indications that this prophecy had a setting during a festival season (v. 5). Verses 7-8 are quite difficult to interpret, but the give-and-take they suggest between Hosea and an opponent would fit plausibly in a festival setting.

> 1 *Do not rejoice, O Israel, do not celebrate like the nations;*[68] *for you have committed harlotry against your God; you have loved a harlot's wage upon every threshing floor.*
>
> 2 *A threshing floor and wine vat will not feed them, and new wine will deceive them.*[69]
>
> 3 *They will not dwell in YHWH's land! Instead Ephraim will return to Egypt, and in Assyria they will eat unclean (food).*
>
> 4 *They will not pour out offerings of wine to YHWH, for their sacrifices will not be pleasing to him. Like mourners' bread to them, everything eaten is unclean. Their bread is for their life; he [Ephraim] will not enter YHWH's house.*

68. The MT has *'el-gîl kā'ammîm,* lit. "to a celebration like the nations." Following the LXX, most translations opt for a slight emendation to read *'al-tāgēl kā'ammîm* (see *BHS*). Macintosh, *Hosea*, p. 337, makes tolerable sense of the MT: "Don't give yourself, Israel, to exuberant rejoicing like other peoples."

69. Reading *bām* as assumed by LXX and other early versions. The MT has *bāh* ("her"). If this more difficult reading is correct, then it likely refers to Samaria as national representative.

5 *What will you do on the day of the festival, on the day of YHWH's feast?*

6 *For behold, they will go from destruction; Egypt will gather them, Memphis will bury them. Their precious silver? Thistles will possess them, briars will be in their tents.*

7 *The days of punishment have arrived; the days of recompense have come. Let Israel know! A fool is the prophet, demented is the man of the spirit; abundant is your iniquity, great is (your) hostility.*

8 *A prophet is a watchman over Ephraim with my God; a bird-catcher's net is upon all his ways. Hostility is in the house of his god.*

9 *They have corrupted themselves completely*[70] *as in the days of Gibeah; he will remember their iniquity and punish their sins.*

1 Here Hosea employs one of his staple criticisms of the people. Israel has committed harlotry against God (cf. 4:12-15). In 9:1 Israel is addressed corporately, using masculine singular references, unlike the extended portrayal of Israel in chs. 1–3, where Gomer and the land are both feminine. The terminology used, however, is complementary because the charges are the same:

1:2   the feminine land (of Israel) commits harlotry *mē'aḥărê yhwh*
4:12 the people commit harlotry *mittaḥat 'ĕlōhêhem*
9:1   Israel commits harlotry *mē'al 'ĕlōheykā*.

There is another link between 9:1 and the portrait of the wayward wife in 2:5, 12 (MT 7, 14), using the terminology of harlotry and wages. The specific term for a prostitute's *wages* is *'etnān*.[71] It is used in 9:1 in the accusation that Israel has loved the wages of a harlot. According to Deut. 23:18, prostitutes were specifically forbidden to bring *'etnān* into the house of YHWH. A similar conviction may be behind the announcement that Israel the prostitute will be exiled from YHWH's land in 9:3. It is not clear whether sexual rites are implied by the *'etnān*. In either case, sinful pay (= Israel's faithless activities) will not be allowed in YHWH's temple or his household.

In 2:5, 12 (MT 7, 14) "Gomer" goes after her lovers who have provided her with sought-after commodities; the latter verse refers to the products as *'etnâ*, apparently a variant form of *'etnān*. The connection that Hosea draws between fertility concerns and harlotry is seen in the charge that Israel has loved its harlot's wage on every threshing floor. Harvest season and

---

70. The MT has two verbs side-by-side without a conjunction, lit. "They have dug deep/they have corrupted." Such asyndetic phrases are awkward, but not grammatically suspect. No object is expressed, but a location is given. A reflexive element is assumed (with NRSV) by the presence of the prepositional phrase *as in the days of Gibeah*.

71. Deut. 23:18 (MT 19); Isa. 23:17; Ezek. 16:31, 34; Mic. 1:7.

threshing activities provided a good setting for cultic practices associated with fertility. More specifically the reference in v. 1 is to threshing floors of *grain (dāgān)*, a commodity that elsewhere Gomer wrongly attributed to her lovers (2:8-9 [MT 10-11]; cf. 7:14). As Gomer was ultimately frustrated by the false road of the fertility cults, so Israel will not be satisfied by threshing floor and wine vat (9:2).

The injunction against *rejoicing* is related to a subject in the immediate context, namely, an appointed festival for the worship of YHWH (9:5). Israel is not to celebrate just like other inhabitants of Canaan. Moreover, the harvest that it will reap is judgment, not blessing. Hosea has announced in various ways that judgment is on the horizon. In what follows, judgment proceeds from the description of harlotry in 9:1.

2 Verse 2 provides reasons why Israel should not rejoice. The grain and wine that they sought as their "harlot's wage" will not *feed* (satisfy) them.[72] Instead, they will be *deceived (kāḥaš)*, a term that Hosea employs elsewhere as both noun and verb to describe Israel's internal sickness (4:2; 12:1 [MT 2]) and the deceiving of princes (7:3). The noun in 10:13 is used similarly to the verb in 9:2: the deception is the fruit or consequence of Israel's sinful activity.

Threshing floors and wine vats are joined together in a Deuteronomic reference to the celebration of the Festival of Booths, the great autumn festival (Deut. 16:13). The immediate context of Hosea's prophecies has additional indications of a festival season in 9:4-5. It is possible, therefore, that the prophet confronted an audience at one of the sacrificial centers during the Festival of Booths in a city like Samaria or Bethel.[73]

3 A clever pun unfolds from the first clause in v. 3. It is the play on the similar sounding verbs *dwell (yāšab)* and *return (šûb)*. With the play on words comes also the reversal of saving history and, sadly, Israel's identity. They were once rescued and brought to dwell in YHWH's land. Now they will be overtaken and returned to Egypt.

The land of Israel is YHWH's property, an integral part of his household. As such, it has sanctity and cannot continue to support the people's defection from the covenant ethos and from their covenant Lord. In 4:3 the land is portrayed as ill and in mourning, as if it suffered from the effects of Israel's moral and cultic pollution. Part of the punishment depicted for Israel in 9:3 is

---

72. The verb is from *rāʿâ*, "lead to pasture/care for/shepherd." Some interpreters have proposed instead that *rāʿâ* II, a verb meaning "to accompany" someone, is the verb used here. Utzschneider, *Hosea,* p. 155, discusses options and opts for this latter meaning in 9:2.

73. Sweeney, *Twelve Prophets,* pp. 94-95, 103, sees the Festival of Booths as a background to Hos. 9–10.

that they will be thrust from the land and forced to eat unclean food in Assyria, thereby defiling themselves. The term for *unclean (ṭāmē')* in 9:3 is an adjective. In 9:4 it is employed as a verb. Hosea's line of thought converges with a basic claim of the pentateuchal Holiness Code: the land belongs to YHWH. While living in it Israel is but an alien or a sojourner with him (Lev. 25:23), and there are instructions to avoid defiling activities in it.[74] Much of what makes up the instructions for holiness in the Pentateuch is concerned not just with Israel relating rightly to God, but also with Israel attending to that task, in part, by efforts to sanctify time and space. Even Deuteronomy, which concentrates on "all Israel" rather than emphasizing priestly sanctification, states repeatedly that the land is YHWH's gift to Israel. From that perspective it contains instruction so that the land is not defiled (Deut. 21:23). Hosea's logic runs thusly: If the people profane the covenant and engage in harlotrous activities against YHWH, they will be expelled from his land, a constituent element of his household, and be forced to live in a defiling situation.

Related matters in Amos and Jeremiah deserve comment in this context. Hosea's contemporary Amos announces to Amaziah, priest of Bethel, that his property will be parceled out to someone else, that he will die in an unclean land *('ădāmâ ṭĕmē'â),* and that Israel will go into exile (Amos 7:17). Amos's equation of unclean land and life in exile is clear enough. Jeremiah employs the narrative-based theology known to Hosea in setting Judah up for judgment to come (Jer. 2:2-13). YHWH acquired Israel with a bridal period in the wilderness. Israel was thereby "holy" to the Lord. The people were brought to a fruitful land, but defiled YHWH's land by their faithless actions. They are charged with "forsaking" *('āzab,* v. 13) YHWH. The vocabulary and logic of this indictment are almost point-by-point with that of Hosea. This is the case particularly with Jer. 2:7 when compared with Hos. 9:3-4: "I brought you to the fruitful land to eat her fruit and good produce, but you entered and defiled *(ṭāmē')* my land and made my inheritance an abomination."

Hosea names the place of expulsion for Israel: Egypt and Assyria. Not coincidentally, these are two foreign powers with whom Israel was involved in diplomatic exchanges (Hos. 12:1b). They are paired again as locations of expulsion in the LXX of Hos. 8:13.[75]

4 The train of thought from 9:3 continues with elaboration on what life will be like outside YHWH's land, when YHWH's judgment is made manifest. The first cultic act listed is the pouring out of a drink offering to YHWH. Like other sacrifices, it will not be pleasing to him. Indeed, Hosea may not have reckoned with the possibility of making a drink offering to

---

74. Heb. *ṭm',* indicating "defilement/uncleanness," is used over 130 times in Leviticus.

75. On the phrase "return to Egypt," see the comments on 8:13.

YHWH outside YHWH's land. Perhaps the reference to *mourners' bread* is an oblique and somewhat hyperbolic indication that outside the promised land YHWH's judgment upon them is like death itself.[76] Food will keep them alive when away from the land, but it has no holy properties to help sustain a covenant ethos in exile.

The last phrase of 9:4 appears straightforward at first glance. An unnamed subject will not come/go into YHWH's house. Since the last-mentioned masculine noun was *lehem* ("bread/food"), it appears a likely subject for the phrase *he/it will not go* and is so rendered in most modern translations. The primary meaning of *YHWH's house* in the OT is the temple in Jerusalem. Thus the last phrase of 9:4 may be understood to say that profane food will not go into the temple. Upon reflection, however, the identities of the unnamed subject and YHWH's house are not obvious in this context. Moreover, sorting out other options has implications for interpreting Hosea that reach beyond the last clause of a single verse. Here are two aspects of the problem that the interpretive process must sort out.

1. Typically when a person is the subject of the verb *bô*', he or she "goes (Qal) with/in/to/after," depending on the preposition associated with the verb. Objects such as bread can be "brought" (*bô*', Hiphil) to a location. Admittedly there are cases in which Hosea's grammar and syntax are not typical, and v. 4 may be another one. The question is raised, nevertheless, about the unnamed subject of the verb *go* in 9:4b and whether a human subject is available in the context for *yābō*', the verbal form in question. Verses 3-4 offer three possibilities of human subjects for the verb, all of which are related: "Ephraim," "they/theirs" (= Ephraim), and "all" (= all in Ephraim). "They" is masculine plural and is thus most likely ruled out as the subject in the Hebrew text. Two plausible subjects then remain for the expression *will not go* in 9:4: "Ephraim" and "all."[77]

2. The other references to YHWH's house in Hosea (8:1; 9:8, 15) are problematic if they indicate the temple in Jerusalem.[78] Macintosh states the matter succinctly:

   Mention of "Yahweh's House" in 4b has generally led to the conclusion that the words [in 4b] are a later gloss. There can be no doubt that *byt*

---

76. Later Ezekiel will develop a related theme that Judah's exile is like corporate death and a return from exile is like resurrection from the dead (Ezek. 37:1-14).

77. In consideration of what they call consistent usage of the verb *bô*', Andersen and Freedman, *Hosea,* pp. 528-29, suggest that either of these is the subject of the verb.

78. "House of his God" in 9:8 may not be a reference to YHWH's house, but it is proper to consider it nevertheless.

yhwh denotes the temple and that Hosea, knowing a multiplicity of open-air sanctuaries, could not have spoken of any one in such terms. Elsewhere (8.1; 9.15) Hosea uses the phrase to denote Yahweh's land, but this meaning can hardly be said to fit the context here.[79]

First, it is an arduous task to document what Macintosh states is generally the conclusion about 9:4b as a later gloss. Suffice it to say that this conclusion can be found in a number of critical commentaries from the 19th century onward.[80] Second, there are those who do not think that 9:4b is a later gloss,[81] and their reticence has less to do with their stance toward historical criticism and more to do with a disagreement over the identity of YHWH's house. It does seem unlikely that a northern prophet such as Hosea would forbid Ephraim to frequent the temple in Jerusalem. Thus the issue turns, as Macintosh states indirectly, on whether in any given reference in Hosea the phrase "YHWH's house" stands for the temple in Jerusalem or for Israel as YHWH's property. One may take each reference in Hosea individually, as Macintosh prudently does, and in his view the conclusion that YHWH's house in 9:4 equates to the Jerusalem temple also results in a judgment that it is a Judean gloss.

In the context of 9:3-4, particularly in light of the parallels in Amos 7:17 and Jer. 2:7 cited above, YHWH's "house" is better understood as a parallel reference to his "land." Hosea announces in 9:3 that Ephraim will be expelled from YHWH's land, and symmetry suggests that Ephraim will then not be able to enter YHWH's *household*, i.e., come home because of his defilement. For a time Ephraim will be without the sustaining resources of life in YHWH's land (household), perhaps analogous to the period of discipline depicted in 3:4-5, until YHWH makes a return possible.[82]

5 Israel or Ephraim is addressed directly in v. 5 with a rhetorical question in a continuation of the theme of cultic and moral impurity. The *you* of address is second person plural and the verb from the first clause does dou-

79. Macintosh, *Hosea,* pp. 345-46.

80. E.g., Rudolph, *Hosea,* p. 176; Wolff, *Hosea,* p. 150; Yee, *Composition and Tradition,* p. 198.

81. E.g., Andersen and Freedman, *Hosea,* pp. 528-29; Utzschneider, *Hosea,* pp. 178-85. For the latter scholar, YHWH's house in 8:1; 9:4, 15 is a synonym for the more primary concept, YHWH's land, referred to in 9:3.

82. It is not clear how 3:4-5 might be coordinated with 9:3-4 in Hosea's thinking, even though the two passages have in common a period of discipline/judgment to come that is quite apart from life as Israel has known it in YHWH's land. Indeed, they may better be coordinated on the supposition that both are editorial (so Yee, *Composition and Tradition,* pp. 129-30, 199). According to this view, a Judean redactor posits in 3:5 a return in the latter days to YHWH and "David their king." In 9:4 the same redactor notes that until the period of defilement is complete, Ephraim cannot enter YHWH's temple (in Jerusalem).

ble duty, as it is presupposed in the second and last clause of the verse. At least a partial answer to the rhetorical question in v. 5 is given in v. 6. There will be or should be no celebration at one of YHWH's festivals because destruction is imminent.

Two terms are used in parallelism, both of which occur elsewhere in Hosea (2:9, 11 [MT 11, 13]; 12:9 [MT 10]). A *festival (mô'ēd)* is, generally speaking, an appointed time or season. In this context it is a reference to a sacred festival (Gen. 1:14; Exod. 23:15; Lev. 23:2; Isa. 1:14). A *feast (ḥag)* can be a synonym for an appointed festival (Exod. 34:22), as well as a general reference to an occasion for feasting and celebration (Exod. 10:9). And as with 9:5, the two terms can be used together in reference to events in Israel's cultic calendar (Exod. 23:15-16; Lev. 23:4). One cannot tell from the context in Hos. 9:1-9 whether the rhetorical question intends a particular festival or simply refers to Israelite cultural festivals more generally. A number of interpreters favor the autumn festival, and this is certainly plausible.[83] The term *mô'ēd* is used with reference to living in tents in Hos. 12:9 (MT 10). In Deut. 16:13 the Festival of Booths is associated with the produce from "threshing floors" and "wine vats," the two terms also used in Hos. 9:2. If an autumn festival in Hosea's day celebrated the wilderness tradition of YHWH's sustenance of the people (cf. Lev. 23:39-43), or more generally was a time in which Israel reflected on God's promises for the future, then perhaps Hosea's language about judgment and life outside of the promised land is intended to reverse popular understanding of a bright future.[84]

6 Instead of celebration at a national festival, the Israelites will go from *destruction* to some form of exile. The term *šôd* in v. 6 is used by Hosea elsewhere to refer to what will come upon Israel as a result of its rebellion against YHWH (7:13). It describes the result of warfare in 10:14 and is associated with the negative results of diplomacy with predator nations (12:2 [MT 3]). Here in 9:6 Egypt is the historical agent of violence who will gather them, and one of its prominent cities will bury them. This is threat language, an announcement about corporate death on the horizon at the hands of a neighboring predator. It is a further illustration of life outside YHWH's land.

The last two clauses in v. 6 are in synonymous parallelism. *Thistles* and *briars* are a word pair used elsewhere to portray a sedentary existence gone awry as a result of divine judgment. A human community that seeks to

---

83. E.g., Wolff, *Hosea,* p. 156; Utzschneider, *Hosea,* pp. 178; Macintosh, *Hosea,* p. 347. Another possibility for a northern prophet would be the yearly feast in Shiloh (Judg. 21:19; cf. 1 Sam. 1:3), which may or may not be one form of an autumn festival.

84. Landy, *Hosea,* p. 111, plausibly suggests that Hosea is developing an "anti-pilgrimage" theme in 9:1-9.

settle down will also seek to eradicate them (Job 31:40), not grow them in their fields or make their home among them. When they reappear where towers and cities were once located, then the inhabitants will be not human but jackals and loathsome creatures (Isa. 34:1-15, especially v. 13). This language is another example of Hosea's employment of a reversal motif. If Gomer seeks the fertility cults for her life and blessing, then she will be made like a wilderness, her way hedged in with thorns, and her fruit trees will become a forest with wild beasts (2:3b, 6, 12 [MT 5b, 8, 14]). The language of threat in 9:6 functions similarly for Israel. On the other hand, when God ushers in a transformed future, then the earth will respond with grain, new wine, and oil (2:22 [MT 24]).

The reference to *their silver* in v. 6 can be taken in several ways. I render the terse phrase as an ironic question, as if the subject is first raised only to denigrate it with what follows. It might refer to idols made with silver (cf. 2:8 [MT 10]; 8:4; 13:2) or the value of the offerings made at the appointed festival in 9:5 that will not save them. It might refer more generally to Israel's wealth (again as something that will not save them) or more specifically to silver used in diplomacy to purchase a good standing with Egypt. If it is reference to a tribute or diplomatic gift, then the sentiments expressed belong in the same category as 7:8-13; 8:8-10; 12:1 (MT 2).

7 The past-tense verbs in the first two clauses of v. 7 are almost certainly to be understood as prophetic perfects, i.e., so certain is the depiction of the future that the prophet announces it in past tense (action completed). In the Hebrew text the same verb *bô'* is used twice and the subjects correspond to one another, indicating that the two clauses are essentially parallel announcements. Days of *punishment* and *recompense* not only reinforce each other, but serve as summary terms for the judgment contained in 9:1-6: Israel should not rejoice, for it will lose its land and live an unclean existence in exile.

Related vocabulary is found elsewhere in Hosea. The noun *punishment (pĕquddâ)* occurs only here in Hosea, but the prophet uses the related verb "visit/punish" *(pāqad)* in 1:4; 2:13 (MT 15); 4:9, 14; 8:13; 9:9; 12:2 (MT 3). A forceful comparison comes in 2:13 (MT 15), where the aggrieved husband (YHWH) will visit upon Gomer the "days of the Baals."[85] The noun *recompense (šillūm)* occurs only here in Hosea. Its closest parallel is with the "day of vengeance" in Isa. 34:8 (cf. Deut. 32:35; Ps. 91:8).

In the structure of v. 7, the phrase *Let Israel know* sits awkwardly.[86]

---

85. For prophetic parallels with Hosea's "day of punishment" see Mic. 7:4 and Isa. 10:3. One should note also the related phrases "year of punishment" in Jer. 11:23; 23:12; 48:44; and "time of punishment" in Jer. 8:12; 10:15; 46:21; 50:27; 51:6.

86. A number of interpreters have proposed to emend the verb *yĕdĕ'û* to *yārē'û*, so that Israel "cried out." See Wolff, *Hosea*, pp. 150, 156. This suggests that the phrase intro-

Without it the verse would have three pairs of synonymous parallel phrases (see below). It may well be an explanatory gloss to emphasize that Israel is being addressed, whether it is intended to clarify 9:7a or 9:7b-c. It may have been added by the prophet himself in the transition from spoken word to written word, or by an editor at a subsequent point. Perhaps it functions to clarify the audience of 9:7b-c as Israel, who should know that the prophets (or a prophet) have misled them and should bear their guilt.

A popular interpretation of 9:7b has been to see it as a quotation of the people, who react negatively to Hosea and describe him as a demented fool.[87] This is possible, but it requires textual emendation or a changed speaker who is unidentified. A more straightforward reading sees in 9:7b-c the continuation of Hosea's critical voice. Who, then, is the crazy prophet(s) condemned by him? That prophet would be one who is blind to the imminent danger announced by Hosea, someone who has announced blessing and security for Israel. Such prophets would have been Hosea's opponents.[88] If one interprets 9:7b as an indictment of Hosea's prophetic opponent(s), then it fits in a larger context of inner-prophetic debate, of which there are several instances elsewhere in the OT (see below). Here is a structural outline of 9:7 following the Hebrew text:

Punishment has come	Recompense has come
Let Israel know!	
A fool is the prophet	Demented is the man of the spirit[89]
Abundant is your[90] iniquity	Great is (your) hostility

---

duces the bicolon that follows: "Israel may cry out: 'A fool is the prophet; crazy is the man of the Spirit.'" The NRSV follows this proposal. The emendation is not necessary. See the excursus below on "Hosea 9:8."

87. This interpretation has been argued influentially by Wolff, *Hosea,* pp. 150, 156-57. He is forced by his conclusion to accept an emendation for the previous clause (see n. 86 above) and places a lot of weight on a particular reading of 9:8, which is one of the most difficult texts in the book of Hosea. Furthermore, since he thinks that all authentic references to prophets in the book are to opposition prophets like Hosea, Wolff is forced to regard the criticism of a prophet in 4:5 as an editorial addition.

88. Stuart A. Irvine, "Enmity in the House of God (Hosea 9:7-9)," *JBL* 117 (1998) 648, lists other interpreters who propose that 9:7b is a description of a prophetic adversary or adversaries.

89. The poetic parallelism indicates that "man of the spirit" is a synonym for "prophet." It is not a common term for a prophet, but spirit possession is a characteristic of prophetic activity, and it is probable that the term describes prophetic activity as such. Odell, "Who Were the Prophets," p. 85, suggests that it is a pejorative term for Hosea. That is possible, but Micah identifies himself as someone "full of the Spirit of YHWH" (3:8), which indicates that another prophetic figure would find the description itself positive.

90. The possessive pronoun *your* (2nd masc. sing.) could refer either to the demented prophet or to Israel.

One can see from this arrangement that the phrase *let Israel know* sits awkwardly with three pairs of bicola. This does not mean it is a gloss — though it may well be one — but the arrangement shows that it likely functions as an emphasis to a spoken audience or as a clarifying comment about the audience.

Interpreters are on safe ground in assuming that Hosea was opposed by at least some of the Israelite prophets of his day, just as Elijah and Amos were opposed by Israelite religious authorities and Jeremiah and Ezekiel by those in Judah (cf. Mic. 3:5-8). If the setting for Hos. 9:1-9 is a national festival, then priests and prophets would have extolled the goodness of YHWH and prophesied continued blessing. Amos was confronted by a priest in Bethel, perhaps during a festival; why not Hosea as well by one or more prophets? In 4:5 Hosea charges that a prophet will stumble with the disobedient people. This would be an example of a prophetic figure who would have opposed Hosea and his platform and who was associated with priests. It is claimed that the prophets of 6:5 spoke judgment as coming from YHWH's mouth, but that does not mean that all prophets and priests of Hosea's day spoke judgment or agreed that Hosea was correct when he did. The foolish prophet, according to 9:7, is one who does not recognize the presence of the time of judgment. The interjection, *Let Israel know,* was a plea that the people would recognize it and not listen to the (court?) prophets of weal. The witness of the book is that they were confronted but did not *know* (4:1, 6; 6:6; cf. 8:2), i.e., recognize and respond adequately to, divine instruction. In Hosea's assessment, however, Israel's perfidy would work as a spur to the prophets of prosperity.

Jeremiah offers an instructive parallel in the conflict between him and some of the religious leaders of his day, including prophets: "They heal the wound of my people in a trifling manner, saying, 'Peace, peace,' and there is no peace" (6:14; 8:15). The significance of the quotation is seen elsewhere in the book (14:13; 23:17; 28:9). Ezekiel reflects a related situation (Ezek. 13:10, 16). One wonders if Hosea's employment of the phrase *days of recompense (šillūm)* is intended as a cutting pun on his counterparts who cried "peace" *(šālôm).*

The final two clauses of v. 7 speak of great iniquity and *hostility (maśṭēmâ).* To whom are these negative characteristics attributed? A second masculine singular pronominal suffix is attached to the term *iniquity,* but the antecedent is not clear from the context. It might refer to the demented prophet or to the people, both of whom are mentioned explicitly in the verse. The rare word *hostility* occurs again in the following verse.

8 The Hebrew text of v. 8 is terse and difficult, and these characteristics are compounded by an overall allusiveness to matters better understood (one assumes) among Hosea's contemporaries. One should not base any far-reaching claims on this verse, and in all humility an interpreter should hope that his or her proposals for clarification do not inadvertently mislead.

The translation offered for v. 8 follows the Hebrew text, although the proposed syntactical analysis is intuitive and largely a guess. Hosea's criticism of his opposition continues from the previous verse. Both 9:7 and 9:8 contain the term *prophet (nābî')*, which is not merely a catchword but is the basis of a continuing line of thought about the prophetic task. The same may be said for the term *hostility (maśṭēmâ)*, which occurs in each verse. Verse 8 begins with Hosea's self-understanding of a prophet as a watchman/sentinel over Ephraim with God. Perhaps this is an accepted definition that Hosea employs and then turns on his detractors. Human communities need a *watchman (ṣōpeh)* to look out for approaching danger (2 Sam. 13:34; 18:24-29; 2 Kgs. 9:17-20; Isa. 52:8). It is a uniquely prophetic task not just to warn the people as their *watchman,* but also to point out the consequences of the approaching danger. That task of bearing bad news does not make a prophet like Hosea the enemy of Israel, but at a deeper level someone who is concerned to point out self-destructive behavior. Both Jeremiah (6:17) and Ezekiel (3:17; 33:2-7) apply the role of watchman/sentinel to the prophetic task. If it is a divine calling, then it is carried out in conjunction with God. This, in essence, is the first clause. We might expand its terseness by rendering it: "A prophet is *supposed to be* a watchman over Ephraim with God." If in 9:7 Hosea excoriates a prophetic opponent as demented, here in 9:8 he begins with a definition of who/what a prophet should be.

The second clause describes what is wrong with his opponent(s). A net or snaring trap is upon all *his,* i.e., the prophetic opponent or Ephraim's, *ways (děrākāyw)*. Hosea employs the same term and its related imagery in 5:1 (cf. 7:12). The *net* elsewhere is a device employed by the wicked to trap their human prey (Pss. 119:110; 140:5; 141:9; 142:3). It is also a metaphor for foreign nations that will overrun disobedient Israel (Josh. 23:13) and for judgment sent upon Moab by God (Jer. 48:44). In proverbial wisdom it is the metaphorical disruption in the *way (derek)* of the perverted person (Prov. 22:5). This last text is closely related to the sense proposed for Hos. 9:8b. A frustrating, inhibiting judgment is upon the (prophetic?) opponent of Hosea. We might expand its allusive terseness as follows: "*yet* a snare *from God* is upon all his ways."

Hostility is another term repeated from 9:7. What unfortunately was rampant in Israel or with the prophetic opponent in 9:7 extends to the house of *his* god. The term fits as judgment upon Hosea's opponent, but the identification of the "house of god" remains obscure. It probably refers to a temple (in Bethel?). The suffix, however, is crucial. *My God* is mentioned in v. 8a, which should be contrasted with 9:8c and *his god* and a hostile temple. Whatever the phrase represents, it is the opponent's *god,* not that of Hosea.

It is worth a moment's reflection to compare 9:8 with 8:1 (cf. 5:8). The shofar or trumpet in 8:1 is an instrument for warning of approaching danger, an imminent threat to YHWH's *house*. Hosea's prophecies take on the role of a verbal shofar, but as 9:1-9 indicates, the sound falls mainly on deaf ears.

Excursus: Hosea 9:8

Odell describes 9:8 as part of "the most difficult passage [9:7-9] in the entire book of Hosea," and such sentiments about the verse or the passage can be found among other interpreters.[91] There are two basic problems, each of which can be "solved" in a variety of ways. On the one hand, the text of v. 8a is difficult, giving rise to a number of reconstructions and suggested emendations.[92] The textual difficulties of v. 8a extend to the noun *prophet* and whether it should be part of the first clause of the verse, or whether it should go with the following clause (so MT, LXX). On the other hand, it is not clear if 9:8a is a statement about Hosea, Ephraim, or a representative prophet (demented or otherwise). A survey of interpretations is an instructive lesson in the exegetical enterprise, as was demonstrated over a century ago by Harper.[93] Below I briefly examine two different interpretations to illustrate the difficulty of the passage. In conclusion, I repeat some elements from the commentary section in order to compare with these other data.

1. Wolff's interpretation has proved influential in recent decades.[94] He understands the description of the foolish prophet in 9:7b as a condemnation of Hosea by the people (= Israel), who are fed up with his preaching of judgment. In reply Hosea asserts that he is a prophetic watchman over Israel with God, using a third-person self-description, who faces persecution and hostility in the land/area of his God. Wolff's rendering can be set out as follows:

> 9:7 Israel may cry: [emending the MT to *yārîa'* or *yārî'û;* from *rw'*]
> The prophet [= Hosea] is a fool! The man of the spirit is mad!
> . . .
> 9:8 The watchman of Ephraim [= Hosea; *ṣōpēh* in construct with Ephraim][95]
> is with God [suffix "my" in Hebrew text is secondary], prophet [an explanatory gloss].
> A trap lies upon all his paths.
> Hostility rages in the house of his God.

91. Odell, "Who Were the Prophets," p. 83. See also Harper, *Hosea,* p. 332: "almost hopelessly confused"; Wolff, *Hosea,* p. 156: "8a is one of the most difficult passages in Hosea"; Rudolph, *Hosea,* p. 173: "8a is a difficult *crux interpretum.* The versions provide no further assistance."

92. R. Dobbie, "The Text of Hosea 9:8," *VT* 5 (1955) 199-203; Irvine, "Enmity in the House of God," pp. 645-53.

93. Harper, *Hosea,* pp. 331-34.

94. *Hosea,* pp. 150-51, 156-58.

95. The MT, where *ṣōpeh* is pointed as an absolute form, is more likely rendered "a watchman is Ephraim with my God."

The emendation of *yd'* ("know") in v. 7 to a form of *rw'* ("cry out") is not implausible, and Wolff notes that others have made this suggested change (so NRSV). It is not necessary, however, and one cannot help but think that it is proposed by him and others because it makes the proposal more coherent that 9:7b is a quotation of the people. Possibly the phrase in the MT ("let Israel know") is itself a gloss, intended to clarify for readers who is speaking and who is being addressed. That would leave the verse in three paired clauses before this later clarification. Whether 9:7b is a gloss or not, one may still interpret it as a quotation of the people, but one that is not explicitly introduced as such.[96] Nevertheless, the MT of 9:7, as it is now constituted, reads more coherently as an address to the people.

Wolff's rendering of the first clause of 9:8 is a plausible solution for a difficult Hebrew text. The question is the relationship between three entities: watchman/sentinel, Ephraim, prophet. In order to make the text a self-reference to the speaker Hosea, Wolff concludes that the prophet speaks about himself in the third person; that the phrase "my God" in the MT must be changed, since it is first person; and that the noun "prophet" is an explanatory gloss.[97] He recognizes, furthermore, that the odd phrase "house of his God" would not likely be Hosea's reference to a temple, so he interprets it as a reference to land or area: hostility is in the land/area of Hosea's God.

2. Odell's interpretation departs markedly from that of Wolff. She proposes that the people cry out in frustration against the prophets who have misled them. Beginning with 9:7c, Hosea offers criticism of Ephraim and recognition that a prophet receives opposition in various forms, including in the temple of his God. Her rendering is as follows:

9:7b Israel cries:
      The prophet is a fool,
      The man of the spirit is mad!
      [Hosea replies]
      Because your [Israel's] guilt is great,
      (your) hostility is great.
9:8   Ephraim lies in wait[98] against[99] my God.
      A prophet is a snare against all his [Ephraim's] ways.
      Opposition is in the house of his [a prophet's] god.

96. So Andersen and Freedman, *Hosea*, p. 515: "Let Israel know — (they say) 'The prophet is a fool. . . .'"

97. Even an interpreter as cautious as Macintosh, who departs rarely from the MT to accept a gloss or emendation, interprets the noun "prophet" as a gloss (*Hosea*, p. 355).

98. Odell, "Who Were the Prophets," pp. 84, 94 n. 28, translates *ṣōpeh* by analogy with its occurrence in Ps. 37:32, where the wicked "lie in wait" for the righteous. It is by no means self-evident that the verb *ṣāpâ* has this nuance in 37:32, which it carries nowhere else in the OT. It can also be rendered "on the lookout for" in 37:32, which is consistent with its primary usage.

99. Odell, "Who Were the Prophets," pp. 84, 94 n. 29, renders the preposition *'im*, which typically means "with," in an adversative fashion, "against," appealing to Gen. 26:29; Ps. 94:16; Hos. 4:1; 12:2 (MT 3). See also *IBHS* §11.2.14b.

Her interpretation of Ephraim as an opponent of God in 9:8 depends wholly on an unlikely rendering of the participle *ṣōpeh,* plus an atypical rendering of the preposition *'im.*[100] Her rendering places the noun "prophet" with the clause that follows it. This accords with the MT punctuation and the LXX translation, and it makes the initial clause of 9:8 less cumbersome. She understands the last phrase in the verse to refer to a temple and provide evidence for prophets participating in the cult. In this she draws another distinction with the interpretation of Wolff, who sees the true prophets of Hosea's day as disengaged from the cult and critical of it.

3. I briefly propose another interpretation. The two interpretations sketched above illustrate the difficulty of reconstructing a conversation in 9:7-8 between the prophet and people. My position is that 9:7b is a charge by Hosea against prophets who mislead the people, that a prophet should be known as a *watcher of Ephraim* along with God (9:8a), and that the snare and opposition in 9:8b-c are what results from criticizing a prophetic watchman like Hosea and the God who sent him. For ease of comparison, the rendering is set out as follows:

9:7   *The days of punishment have arrived; the days of recompense have*
            come. Let Israel know!
        [Hosea describing "false prophets"] *A fool is the prophet, demented*
            is the man of the spirit;
        abundant is your ["false" prophet's] *iniquity, great is (your) hostility.*

        [Hosea defining a prophet]
9:8   *A prophet is* [indeed, supposed to be] *a watchman over Ephraim with*
            my God;
        [*therefore*] *a bird-catcher's net is upon all his* ["false" prophet's] *ways.*
        Hostility is in the house of his ["false" prophet's] *god.*

This proposal has problems. It assumes, for example, that part of the reason that the people remonstrated with Hosea is that they had the backing of other prophets who proclaimed that peace and blessing were on the horizon and that no lasting danger was imminent. Another is that the difficult first clause of 9:8 seems overloaded.[101] A third is the antecedent of the possessive pronouns in 9:8b-c. Little difference in meaning, however, would result from interpreting the possessive pronouns as a reference to Israel/Ephraim rather than to a false prophet. Because the prophet is a sentinel and announces the danger to the people, a net is indeed upon the people and hostility in the house of God.

9 The subject of the initial clause in v. 9 is an unidentified "they," different, at least grammatically speaking, from Ephraim (3rd masc. sing.) in 9:8. It is likely, however, that the "they" is simply another way to render

100. Support for her rendering is offered by Ben Zvi, *Hosea,* p. 193.
101. It is, nevertheless, essentially the NRSV rendering.

Ephraim or the people in their self-destructive activities. The references to Gibeah and "their" iniquity/sins all point to this conclusion.

Verse 9 concludes a unit of speech (9:1-9) in a somewhat anticlimactic way. One wonders if it is not a saying of the prophet that has been brought to this literary context as an editorial decision. The second half of the verse is repeated verbatim in 8:13 and is made up of vocabulary used elsewhere in the book. In any case, the thrust of the verse is that the people have corrupted themselves in a manner similar to a previous event in Gibeah and that God will see to their judgment in the historical process.

Hosea's reference to Gibeah has his trademark comparison "like/as" *(kĕ).* His exact phrase is *like/as the days of Gibeah,* using a time element that has an ominous echo in 9:7, with its reference to the *days of punishment/recompense.* Unfortunately, there is no other indication in either the phrase in question or its use elsewhere (10:9) to further identify the event(s) at Gibeah.[102] If the reference is to something recorded elsewhere in the OT, then the sexual outrage and subsequent warfare at Gibeah is the best option (Judg. 19–21). The rape and murder of a concubine evoked the declaration that "such a thing has not occurred or been seen since the day that Israel came up from Egypt" (Judg. 19:30). Perhaps the comparison that Hosea makes to the *days of Gibeah* is that between Israel's current wanton folly and the earlier sexual violence of the Benjaminites in Gibeah, in both cases leading to destruction.

As noted above, 9:9b also occurs in 8:13. The two verbs employed ("remember," *zākar;* "visit/punish," *pāqad ['al])* are used elsewhere in Hosea.[103] The second verb is associated with one of Hosea's base texts (traditions), that YHWH, who is gracious and compassionate, is nevertheless jealous for his own and will not overlook the guilty among them, but punish/visit upon them their transgressions (Exod. 20:5; 34:6-7). There is a sense in which the subunit Hos. 9:1-9 is brought to a conclusion with the application of a traditional affirmation about divine character.

E. THE PAST PRESSES JUDGMENT ON THE PRESENT (9:10–10:15)

The second half of ch. 9 (9:10-17) begins a collection of prophecies comparing Israel to fruitful plants and terrain that continues through ch. 10. These

102. See the excursus on "Gibeah" at 5:8.

103. "I will remember their evil" (7:2); YHWH will "punish/visit upon the people" the "bloodshed of Jezreel" (1:4), "the days of the Baals" (2:13 [MT 15]), "their ways" (4:9; 12:2 [MT 3]). See further appendix 10, "YHWH's Self-Definition (Exod. 34:6-7) and Hosea."

metaphorical comparisons are the basis for highlighting Israel's coming demise. Hosea draws on the national tradition in 9:10 to make his case against Israel. He will draw repeatedly upon various historical traditions through ch. 13.

1. Grapes in the Wilderness to No Fruit (9:10-17)

10 *Like grapes in the wilderness, I found Israel; like the first fruit of the fig tree (in its initial season), I saw your ancestors. They came to Baal-peor and devoted themselves to Shame; they became vile like the thing they loved.*[1]

11 *Ephraim's glory will fly away like a bird; thus no*[2] *birth, gestation, conception!*

12 *Even if they raise children, I will make them childless!*[3] *Woe indeed to them when I leave*[4] *them!*

13 *Ephraim, as I have seen, (was) a palm*[5] *transplanted in a meadow, but now Ephraim (is destined) to bring out his children to slaughter.*

14 *"Provide for them, YHWH; what will you provide? Give them a womb that miscarries and dry breasts!"*

15 *All their evil is in Gilgal; indeed, there I have come to hate them. Because of their evil actions I will drive them out of my house! I will not continue to love them; all their officials are rebellious.*

16 *Ephraim is struck, their root is dried up. They will not produce fruit. Indeed, if they bear children, I will put them to death.*[6]

1. The last term, *'āhăbām,* is punctuated in the MT as an infinitive construct. With minimal repointing it could be a noun, *'ōhăbām,* "their lovers." See, e.g., Stuart, *Hosea,* pp. 148-49. The sense expressed is essentially the same.

2. The repeated preposition *min* in 9:11b has a privative force; see *IBHS* §11.2.11e.

3. Lit. "I will bereave them from people."

4. The MT *běśûrî* is pointed as an infinitive construct and is a hapax legomenon. The verb is either a dialectical form of *sûr* ("turn away from") or *šûr* ("depart").

5. The MT has *ṣôr,* the term for "rock" and also the name for the Phoenician city of Tyre. The NASB renders: "Ephraim, as I have seen, is planted in a pleasant meadow like Tyre." See further J. K. Kuan, "Hosea 9.13 and Josephus, *Antiquities* IX, 277-287," *PEQ* 123 (1991) 103-8. A number of interpreters have proposed that the term is better taken as a cognate to Arabic *ṣawrun,* "young palm tree." The Qal passive participle that follows, *šětûlâ,* is used elsewhere to refer to plants. It is not clear, however, why the feminine participial form is used in 9:13a.

6. The last clause translates lit.: "I will put to death the precious things from their belly." In a metaphorical sense Ephraim collectively has a belly or womb.

17 *My God will reject them because they have not listened to him.*
They will become wanderers among the nations.

10 Here Hosea combines metaphor and historical typology. The metaphor is a comparison of Israel to the delightful surprise of finding fruit in the wilderness. It is important to underscore the historical typology in Hosea's expression and not simply to note the literary simile. Israel is not "like" delectable fruit, except in the sense that their ancestors were found by YHWH in the wilderness and joyfully made his own. In metaphorical terms "fruit in the wilderness" is the vehicle (source domain), and the tenor (target domain) is YHWH's wondrous acquisition of Israel's ancestors. Perhaps the best explanations of why Hosea cites the comparison come in 13:4-5, which links Egypt and Israel's sustenance in the wilderness together, and 2:14-15 (MT 16-17), where Israel is a youthful bride in the wilderness.[7] They are all reflections of the authoritative narrative of Israel's past from which he draws and from which he finds points of correspondence with circumstances in his own day. In v. 10 the metaphor of delight in discovery is a prelude to the disgust of subsequent defection, intended to contrast Israel's shameful activity with the divine grace of its origins (cf. Jer. 2:1-3).

Poetic parallelism puts grapes and early figs together as delightful surprises in the wilderness. Part of the surprise is simply the presence of the fruit in such an infertile region. To the extent that the wilderness is equated with the desert, fresh fruit is an impossibility apart from an oasis. The wilderness can be a rugged area with little or no cultivation, but not necessarily the desert. To find a grapevine or a fig tree in a sheltered crevice or hidden valley in a rugged, semi-arid region would be quite surprising, but not impossible. Delectable fruit, a real joy when passing through a wilderness, puts YHWH's acquisition of Israel in personal and emotive terms. He took delight in them.

There may be also a metaphorical hint in the choice of the *figs* for comparison. Hebrew *bikkûrâ* is the early ripe fig, which is a delicacy (Isa. 28:4; Mic. 7:1). Related terms for "firstborn child" are *bākîr, bĕkîrâ,* and *bĕkōr;* the last is used once elsewhere to describe Israel collectively as YHWH's "firstborn son" (Exod. 4:22). With Hosea's explicit reference to Israel as God's son in Egypt (11:1), it seems almost certain that the metaphor in 9:10 plays on the privilege of Israel's adoption as firstborn and heir in YHWH's household.

The verse makes an abrupt transition from fruit to Israel's shameful behavior at Baal-peor. The site is the location of an infamous account of Is-

---

7. Some interpreters have seen in the claim that YHWH "found" *(māṣā')* Israel in the wilderness evidence for an independent "finding tradition." See appendix 7, "Terms for Election in Hosea," for discussion and bibliography.

251

rael's sexual dalliance with Moabite women and engagement with a deity venerated there known as the Baal of Peor (Num. 25:1-11; Deut. 4:3-4).[8] The account in Num. 25 describes Israel's engagement with Moabite women as "playing the harlot" *(zānâ)*, using the verb with Israel as subject in a metaphorical manner similar to Hosea (4:15; 5:3; 9:1). In the transition from delectable fruit to shame at Baal-peor, Hosea continues his historical typology. In calling Israel's attention to a remembered transgression of their ancestors, the prophet is defining his contemporaries by comparison with them.

According to the prophet, the ancestors *devoted themselves (nāzar,* Niphal) to *Shame (bōšet)* at Baal-peor. The verb has the related connotations of "consecrate for" and "separate from" (Ezek. 14:7). It is used, along with a related noun form, in the instructions for nazirite service and vows (Num. 6:1-21). Other descriptions of the shameful episode describe Israel as "yoked" to the Deity (Num. 25:3, 5; Ps. 106:28), using a simile for the joining of animals in a common task.[9] Perhaps the choice of another verb is Hosea's or part of an independent account that he inherited.

The object of Israel's devotion is *Shame,* a polemical slur on the Baal of Peor. Readers should compare this allusive historical lesson with the polemical language elsewhere against Baal in Hosea.[10] Hosea's theology is that like begets like. In consecrating themselves to a Baal deity, Israel became *vile (šiqqûṣîm),* like the shameful object of its love.[11]

11-12 The Hebrew text of 9:11-12 is almost staccato in expression, conveying what may be pent-up emotions in terse declarations. Hosea has elsewhere compared Israel to a senseless dove that will be brought down by YHWH's net (7:11-12). Here the comparison with birds in flight is different. Ephraim's *glory* will depart abruptly, leaving behind devastating consequences. Indeed, it is YHWH himself, Ephraim's true glory, who is leaving. The terminology in 9:11 is a reversal of the nation's fertility. There will be no conceiving and bearing of children, but even if parents raise children, they will become childless. Perhaps there are two related trajectories of thought in these disturbing declarations. One is part of the nature/nurture synthesis expressed elsewhere by Hosea. In the fundamental indictment of 4:1-3, the prophet indicates that Israel's failure leaves the land itself in sickness and mourning. In the projection of future bliss, however, YHWH speaks to the

---

8. For further details see appendix 8, "Transjordan in Hosea."

9. The verb, also Niphal, is *ṣāmad.* The term in noun and verb forms is used for the yoking of animals (2 Sam. 20:8; 1 Kgs. 19:19-21).

10. For further details see appendix 1, "Baal in Hosea."

11. The term for *vile things (šiqqûṣîm)* is used for idols (Deut. 29:17; 2 Chr. 15:8) and for foreign deities (1 Kgs. 11:5, 7). It is used repeatedly with similar meaning in Jeremiah (4:1; 7:30; 13:27; 16:18; 32:34) and Ezekiel (5:11; 7:20; 11:18, 21; 20:7-8, 30; 37:23). It is a vivid contrast with delectable fruit.

heavens and the process of reproduction and fertile increase is brought about (2:21-23 [MT 23-25]). The lack of conception and birth in 9:11 fits the connection between failure and fertility portrayed in 4:1-3 (cf. 9:14).

The prediction of *no birth* in v. 11 is also part of the hyperbole of judgment to be heaped upon the people. This is the second and related trajectory of thought in Hosea: judgment to come in the historical process will deny Ephraim children, either literally or in the symbolic sense that exile and servitude truncate the hopes that parents have for their children. Thus 9:12 elaborates on the chilling declaration: No fertility! Even if (or when) children are brought up, the result will still be bereavement, an allusion to destruction and devastation in the historical process. A cry of *woe ('ôy)* is the ejaculatory response when one faces devastating distress and destruction (1 Sam. 4:7-8; Isa. 3:9-11; Jer. 4:31). It was also the cry of Isaiah in response to an overwhelming vision of YHWH's enthroned holiness (Isa. 6:1-5), where his own predicament comes into view precisely because he has glimpsed it and intuitively senses his own undoing. Here in Hos. 9:12 a *woe* is pronounced upon Ephraim by a furious YHWH. The anthropopathism is stunning: YHWH is leaving the people of his household. It is a grim declaration, brought on by an ingrained recalcitrance to correction on their part. Thankfully the departure is only temporary on his part, but its full force falls on Hosea's contemporaries.

In Israel's previous history there is an account of the departure of Israel's "glory" (1 Sam. 4:10-22). The Philistines defeated the Israelites and captured the ark of the covenant. In response, the newly born son of a slain Israelite is named Ichabod ("Where is the glory?") because "the glory has departed from Israel" (v. 22). A similar dynamic is at work in Hosea's compressed declaration. The ark of the covenant represented divine presence. Its loss to the Philistines was tantamount to the loss of divine presence in Israel and the resulting devastation of the people. In 9:12 it is YHWH himself, Israel's true glory, on the way out. He is not captured, but nevertheless takes his leave.[12]

13 The first clause of v. 13 is a jumble, and there is no consensus among interpreters for sorting out either misunderstood terms or errors in the text's transmission.[13] Verse 13b is somewhat better understood. I assume that the two clauses in the verse are another of Hosea's elliptical and allusive contrasts, with 9:13a an affirmation of Ephraim and 9:13b an indication of com-

---

12. One might compare also the account of the "glory of YHWH" departing the Jerusalem temple and the subsequent fall of the city (Ezek. 11:22-23). As prophetic books, both Hosea and Ezekiel report YHWH's departure from his sinful people, along with prophecies that he will find a way to reconcile the people. In the case of Ezekiel, the departure of God's glory from the temple is overcome by a vision of the complete remaking of Jerusalem, with a new temple in its center (Ezek. 40–48). The last line of the book reports that the new name of the city will be "YHWH is there" (48:35).

13. Macintosh, *Hosea,* pp. 370-72, provides a good summary of options.

ing disaster. The contrast appears to contain a pun: *in a meadow (bĕnāweh)* sounds like *his children (bānāyw)*, both of which are the last word in their respective clauses. One may draw on 9:10-14 for contextual support in interpreting this difficult verse. As 9:10 has a contrast between delectable fruit and vile things, so here is one between a pleasant planting and the death of children. Verse 13b may well be an elaboration on 9:11-12. They have in common a declaration that there will be no future for children. Verse 14 continues the theme of no fertility and nourishment from 9:11-12.

The term used for *slaughter* in 9:13b is an active participle *(hōrēg)* and can refer either to the gruesome task of "killing" or to an executioner, i.e., "one who slaughters." Hosea uses the verb in one other instance, describing the judgmental words of prophets as "killing" the people (6:5). Some matters of detail are left to the imagination in the terse declaration of 9:13b, in spite of the gruesome vocabulary. With the support of the terrifying language in the context, however, the near-term fate of the people is sadly not a matter of doubt.

14 The prophet speaks to YHWH, apparently in frustration over hostile treatment and the lack of receptiveness to his public preaching. Hosea says nothing here that is not part of the judgmental message he has consistently represented to a disobedient people, but one wonders about the tone of voice. Is it bitterness or sarcasm, like that of Job or Jeremiah; grim resignation that judgment is inevitable, or perhaps a harsh parody on a festival liturgy? If the context of this communication is the autumn festival, then the terminology of *providing* is understandable as echoing the liturgy, whatever else might be discerned about a tone of voice. The festival celebrated the later agricultural harvests (such as grapes and figs; cf. 9:10) that came after the Festival of Firstfruits and the dry summer season. It is also a time in which the coming fall rains are eagerly anticipated. Perhaps the *dry breasts* are a retort for a thirsty land and people?

Israel's concern is security and blessing, the increase of families, flocks, and crops. That was clearly indicated in the portrait of Gomer, who sought commodities from her "lovers." In a polytheistic environment the gods were implored to "give," and the worshipers offered sacrifices and sometimes engaged in sympathetic magic to bring about the desired fertility. The blessings sought, however, are not in themselves wrong. In the patriarchal blessing extended to Joseph (the tribe of Joseph was divided into Ephraim and Manasseh; Gen. 49:25), Jacob seeks for his offspring the blessings of "breasts" and "womb," using the same two nouns as Hos. 9:14. That prayer is answered according to the account of Israel's increase in Egypt (Exod. 1:7). Nonfunctional wombs and breasts, therefore, represent a future with no children. That future is the substance of 9:11b-13, with 9:14 simply a reiteration in a different voice.

A popular artistic representation in ancient Near Eastern culture is the female body, including at times accentuated breasts and a pubic triangle. The motivation, however, is not pornographic, but either the inducement or celebration of the powers of fertility. In the territory of Israel, the naked portrayal of the feminine is part of inscribed pendants used as jewelry and molded plaque figurines in the Late Bronze (ca. 1550-1200) and Early Iron Age (ca. 1200-1000), while terra-cotta pillar figurines with accentuated breasts are the norm in Iron Age II (ca. 1000-586).[14] Scholars debate whether the female figurines represent the divine world (one or more goddesses) or that of humans. The emphasis on fertility is obvious in either case, with the pendulous breasts on the pillar figurines almost certainly representing lactation. Such material culture provides a telling backdrop to the reversal language in 9:14. Instead of overseeing the process of birth and nursing, blessings associated with the national covenant, YHWH's judgment will usher in the curses of infertility and childlessness associated with covenantal disobedience.[15]

15 The terms for *evil (rā'â, rōa')* here are general and could refer to political rebellion, social unrest and violence, or cultic impurity. The last phrase may provide some clarification, or at least an indication of an evil action, with the indictment of rebellious officials. It is another of Hosea's puns. The term translated here as *officials (śārîm)* is employed several times by Hosea and can also mean "princes" in reference to descendants of royalty who have administrative duty in a kingdom.[16] Whatever the nuance, the term is modified by the similar sounding plural participle for *rebellious (sōrĕrîm)*. Isaiah of Jerusalem (1:23) used the same two terms in an indictment of Jerusalem's leaders for venality and corruption: "your officials are rebels, friends with thieves! Every one of them loves a bribe and pursues a gift. They do not adjudicate for the orphan; the widow's case does not

---

14. The bibliography on this subject is large. See U. Winter, *Frau und Göttin: Exegetische und ikonographische Studien zum weiblichen Gottesbild im Alten Israel und in dessen Umwelt* (OBO 53; Göttingen: Vandenhoeck & Ruprecht, 1987); R. Kletter, *The Judean Pillar-Figurines and the Archaeology of Asherah* (Oxford: Tempus Reparatum, 1996); Izak Cornelius, *The Many Faces of the Goddess: The Iconography of the Syro-Palestinian Goddesses Anat, Astarte, Qedeshet, and Asherah c. 1500-1000* BCE (OBO 204; Göttingen: Vandenhoeck & Ruprecht, 2004); William G. Dever, *Did God Have a Wife? Archaeology and Folk Religion in Ancient Israel* (Grand Rapids: Eerdmans, 2005), pp. 176-251.

15. D. Krause, "A Blessing Cursed: The Prophet's Prayer for Barren Womb and Dry Breasts in Hosea 9," in *Reading Between the Texts: Intertextuality and the Hebrew Bible,* ed. D. N. Fewell (Louisville: Westminster John Knox, 1992), pp. 191-202.

16. Hos. 3:4; 5:10 (princes of Judah); 7:3, 5 (mentioned in conjunction with a king), 16; 13:10 (with king).

come to them." Hosea uses the verb *sārar* elsewhere to describe a "stubborn" cow (4:16). In family law the same term describes a stubborn/incorrigible son (Deut. 21:18-21). As a description of a people, it refers to those who follow a course of action "that is not good" and who have been told as much (Isa. 65:2).

Perhaps the best indication for Hosea's contemporaries of the evil deeds the prophet deplored comes in the reference to Gilgal. His description is emphatic: *all* their evil is *in* Gilgal, and this may reflect something quite particular in his day. What cannot be known now is whether the comment reaches back into Israel's history, for example, as a reference to Saul's failed kingship or to political activity in the previous century.[17] The singling out of officials/princes suggests that (seditious?) political activity is at least part of the "evil actions." Elsewhere Hosea mentions Gilgal in conjunction with Beth-aven (House of Iniquity = Bethel) and in a context in which cultic transgressions play a primary role (4:15; cf. 4:4-19).[18] As a cultic center Gilgal may have been a staging ground for one or more of the regime changes fomented in Hosea's day.

The language of *hate (śānā')* in v. 15 carries a range of both emotion and action. In the second commandment YHWH declares that he will visit judgment upon those who *hate* him (Exod. 20:5; Deut. 5:9). Hate describes the attitude and actions of an enemy. That God *hates* the perpetrators of evil in Gilgal means that they are considered his foes and that he rejects them.[19] The term is also used in familial relationships, where it refers to severe sibling rivalry (Gen. 37:4-8), extending ultimately to murderous intent (2 Sam. 13:22), and even to relations between husband and wife, where the term describes a less favored (Gen. 29:31-33) or ignored (Judg. 14:16) wife. "Hatred" among spouses can have the nuance of not favored, overlooked, or unfairly treated, but not necessarily the connotation of a visceral rejection (Deut. 21:15-17).

In the instructional code of Deuteronomy, when a man "hates" his wife, she can be given a certificate of divorce and sent "from his house" (Deut. 24:1-4). In this context the verb seems to represent the ending of a marriage for stipulated reasons (cf. Deut. 22:13-21), not necessarily an emo-

17. Gilgal is associated with Saul's kingship and rejection (1 Sam. 11:14-15; 15:12), and a number of interpreters have seen in 9:15 an allusion to his failed leadership and an institutional criticism of the monarchy. Cf. Wolff, *Hosea,* p. 167. Gilgal is also associated with Elijah and Elisha and a band of prophets (2 Kgs. 2:1; 4:38).

18. In 12:11 (MT 12) Hosea refers contemptuously to Gilgal as a place of sacrifice with multiple altars. Amos also criticizes Gilgal in conjunction with Bethel (Amos 4:4; 5:5). See appendix 9, "Worship Centers in Hosea."

19. For the verb "hate/reject" with God as subject in prophetic rhetoric, see Isa. 1:14; Jer. 12:8; Amos 5:21; 6:8; Zech. 8:17; Mal. 1:3.

tive detesting of the wife. It is possibly a technical term for divorce, as it appears in Jewish contracts of the Persian period.[20] In Hos. 9:15 YHWH's declaration that he will *drive* the evildoers in Gilgal from his *house* and no longer *love* them portrays the dynamics of a failed marriage, not just the rejection of an enemy.[21] The household metaphor is here at work. YHWH is *driving* family members from the house. The verb *drive (gāraš)* is used elsewhere in connection with a divorced woman (e.g., Lev. 21:7, 14) as well as with Hagar, when she is expelled from Abraham's family (Gen. 21:10).

16 Three linked terms for destruction are used in 9:16. They are *strike* or "smite" *(nākâ), dry up* or "wither away" *(yābaš),* and *put to death* or "kill" *(mût;* Hiphil). The first and third occur in descriptions of warfare and its destruction (Jer. 43:11; 52:27). Withering is the result of being *struck* (Jonah 4:7; Zech. 10:11). Hosea employs a pun on the name *Ephraim* in speaking about the lack of fruit *(pĕrî)* production (cf. Hos. 10:1; 14:8 [MT 9]). That pun, furthermore, is in the service of the metaphor of children as fruit.[22] Beginning with 9:10 the prophet has played on the comparison between the people of God as delectable fruit from the wilderness and the awful judgment of childless bereavement, a fruitless future because of Ephraim's mortal folly. The death of the future, which comes here at YHWH's hand, grows out of Ephraim's persistent rejection of YHWH's guidance. Fortunately, this devastating announcement of disaster is not the last word in Hosea about the *root (šōreš)* of the people of God. In an envisioned future transformation the "root" of the people shall take hold like the majestic forests of Lebanon (14:5 [MT 6]).

17 Hosea speaks again, as if offering commentary on the previous verses that announced destruction on Israel. Those threats to the people as a whole, while real enough, also partake of the hyperbole of warfare imagery and attendant disasters. Here in 9:17 YHWH's *rejection (mā'as;* cf. 4:6) is predicated on Israel's rejection, and more particularly the refusal to hear and obey their covenant Lord. One wonders if the biting comment *My God* adds insult to announced injury. YHWH is still Hosea's God, even if temporarily he is not Israel's. Note the contrast in 9:8 between the prophet who is to be a watchman with *my God* and a prophetic opponent of Hosea's, where the house of *his god* has hostility in it.

Stubborn Israel is thus condemned to be scattered among the nations

20. See the remarks in the introduction, section IV.C, "Hosea's Theology: Covenant and Marriage."

21. This is suggested by Sweeney, *Twelve Prophets,* pp. 101-2, but he does not note the parallel between the husband's "house" in Deut. 24:3 and YHWH's house in Hos. 9:15.

22. Note the "root" and "fruit" of the Amorites that YHWH destroyed in order to provide a promised land for Israel (Amos 2:9).

where they have been currying favor and seeking diplomatic advantage. Hosea uses the verb *wander (nādad)* in another context to refer to the people who have "strayed" or departed from YHWH (7:13). Although he does not use the term "go into exile" *(gālâ)* in v. 17, as he does in 10:5, this is what is meant by the combination of YHWH rejecting the people and their subsequent wandering among other peoples.[23]

2. Luxuriant Vine to Thorn and Thistle (10:1-10)

1 *Israel is a luxuriant vine, making fruit for himself. According to the increase of his fruit, he has increased altars. According to the goodness of his land, he has done well by standing stones.*[24]

2 *Their heart is false; they are guilty. Now he will break down their altars; he will destroy their standing stones.*

3 *Certainly now they will say, "We have no king. We do not fear YHWH! And the king, what can he do for us?"*

4 *They offer promises,*[25] *utter false oaths, make covenants. Justice sprouts like a poisonous plant in the furrows of the field.*

5 *Samaria's inhabitants*[26] *fear for*[27] *the calf*[28] *of Beth-aven. Its*

23. Hosea's contemporary Amos used the verb "to go in exile" *(gālâ)* several times. Cf. Amos 1:5; 5:27; 6:7; 7:17.

24. The last two clauses contain a pun on the noun *good (ṭôb)* with the verb *make good* (*yāṭab;* standing stones as object). Both clauses are governed by the preposition *kĕ* to constitute a simile.

25. Lit. "They speak words." The expression is not a trite statement, but in context apparently represents a specific form of speaking. In conjunction with oath and covenant, perhaps the best option is to see the phrase in a technical sense as offering promises; so Andersen and Freedman, *Hosea*, p. 554. There may be a similar use of the term "words" in 14:2 (MT 3), where Israel is enjoined to take "words" and return to YHWH.

26. The construct form *šĕkan šōmerôn* represents a collective entity, whether it is a general reference to the city's population or more specifically a reference to the ruling class. Only the latter would live in the city itself, where space for housing was at a premium. Most of the general population would live outside the city in houses and tents, though entering the city proper on a regular basis.

27. Macintosh, *Hosea*, p. 399, proposes that the verbal phrase *gûr lĕ* is best rendered "to fear for/be in dread concerning." Different prepositions are used with the verb for the rendering "to be in fear/awe of."

28. The fem. pl. form *ʿeglôt*, lit. "heifers," apparently represents the calf figure in Bethel. The pronouns in the verse that refer back to the figure are masculine singular, and so most translations translate the plural form as a singular. The fem. form is anomalous for the calf figure elsewhere in the OT, which is mentioned in 8:5 and 13:2 (masc. pl.). It may be a slur on the virile young bull figure, but just how the fem. pl. form accomplishes that task is not clear. See further the excursus at 8:5-6 on "Hosea and the Calf."

people have mourned on its behalf, and its priests[29] tremble[30] over its glory. Indeed, it [= glory] has departed from it.

6 Just so, the calf itself[31] will be carried off to Assyria, a gift for the great king. Ephraim brings shame upon himself, and Israel is ashamed because of his plan.

7 Samaria's king[32] is gone, like foam on the face of the waters.

8 The high places of iniquity (Israel's sin) shall be destroyed; thorns and thistles shall grow up on their altars. And they will say to the mountains, "Cover us," and to the hills, "Fall on us!"

9 From the days of Gibeah you have sinned, O Israel; there they stood. Will not war overtake them in Gibeah? Against evildoers

10 I have come,[33] and I will discipline them. Nations will be gathered against them when they are bound for their double iniquities.[34]

1   The thrust of v. 1 is made clear in its second half. The comparison of Israel to a *luxuriant vine (gepen bôqēq)* in v. 1a is another of Hosea's trade-

---

29. Heb. *kōmer* is used elsewhere for idolatrous, non-Yahwistic priests (Zeph. 1:4; 2 Kgs. 23:5). Its cognate forms are used as a general term for priests in Syriac and Aramaic texts. According to 2 Kgs. 23:5, this class of priests were royal appointees to officiate at various high places, but were removed as part of Josiah's reforms.

30. The verb *gîl*, which typically means "rejoice," appears to have a different nuance here. It represents an emotional response such as excitement or fear/dread in Ps. 2:11, and that better fits the context here. Hosea has employed a pun with *gîl* and *gālâ* ("depart; go into exile").

31. The accusative *'ôtô* in 10:6a can be rendered with a passive verb as a subject, perhaps in an emphatic sense; so most modern translations. One must take care, however, to separate the various indefinite third person pronouns in 10:5-6. The last clause can be paraphrased, "the glory has departed from the calf." The calf, therefore, is that which is carried to the great king. Cf. Isa. 18:7.

32. The MT reads lit. "Samaria, her king," which is not the usual syntax for a construct phrase. There are, however, other attested examples of a noun in absolute form followed by another with possessive suffix (Eccl. 2:14; Jonah 2:7). The phrase is also unusual. There are no other references to a king of Samaria, and it may be a contemptuous term.

33. The MT is pointed as a noun with a pronominal suffix, *bě'awwātî*, "in my desire." This rendering is intelligible, particularly if it is not associated with the preceding prepositional phrase and it begins a new sentence. So, for example, the NASB, "When it is my desire, I will chastise them"; and similarly Macintosh, *Hosea*, pp. 414-15. The LXX has the verb *ēlthon*, "go/come," which apparently presupposes *bā'tî*. Cf. *BHS*. This proposal is the basis of the rendering offered here. The NRSV follows the LXX and joins the previous prepositional phrase to the verb to read: "I will come against the wayward people." So similarly Garrett, *Hosea*, p. 213.

34. Following the Qere *'ăwōnōtām* and most interpreters; the Kethib, *'ēnōtām*, "their eyes," does not fit the context well.

mark metaphors, which serves to ground the description of cultic excess in v. 1b. In v. 1b a twice-expressed simile with two poetically balanced clauses invokes a relationship between the general prosperity of the land and the increase of the paraphernalia used in cultic worship.

> According to the increase . . . he has increased *altars*
> According to the goodness . . . he has done well with *standing stones*.

Hosea refers elsewhere to both altars and standing stones, two elements employed in cultic worship in Israel and the surrounding cultures (3:4; 8:11; 10:8; 12:11 [MT 12]). Hosea viewed their presence, indeed their increase over time, not as positive but as evidence for Israel's religious folly and defection from an acceptable Yahwistic standard. One cannot tell from this reference if the cultic paraphernalia are dedicated solely to the worship of YHWH or are also employed in the veneration of other deities.[35]

The thought expressed in 10:1b has a basic parallel elsewhere in Hosea: "When Ephraim increased *(rābâ)*[36] altars (in response) to sinning, they became for him altars for sinning!" (8:11). The correlation in both texts is between an increase in cultic worship (potentially a good thing) and an increase in estrangement from YHWH. Israel's worship of YHWH does not depend on repetitive cultic acts, although these are a constituent element of the covenant ethos, but more fundamentally on a correct apprehension of YHWH's will for them as a holy people (4:1; 6:6). As the next verse puts it, the issue at hand is a matter collectively of Israel's heart, not the matter of cultic worship per se.

The description of agricultural increase in 10:1b assists to discern the meaning of 10:1a, which is more obscure. The matter is not that of textual corruption, but of terms used atypically. Scholars have a history of appealing to classical Arabic cognates for their translations. This assumes that Hosea has used agricultural imagery with nuanced terminology that has not survived elsewhere in classical Hebrew. The verse begins with the description of Israel as a *luxuriant vine;* at least *luxuriant* is the sense of the adjective *bōqēq* as translated by the LXX. The term's basic meaning is "to pour out" or "to be empty." It is clear from another use of the term that it can be applied to plants (Nah. 2:2 [MT 3]), but its use there is of no assistance in the present context.

---

35. See the comments on 3:4. In pentateuchal instruction Israel is commanded to tear down and destroy the altars and the standing stones of the Canaanite inhabitants of the land (Exod. 34:11-16; Deut. 7:5; 12:3).

36. In 10:1b Hoses uses the noun *rōb* ("increase") and the same form of the verb *rābâ* ("to increase") with altars as the object. Note also the pairing of *rābâ* with *yāṭab* in Deut. 30:5 in the claim that YHWH would "increase" the people in the promised land and make them "prosperous."

Possibly the sense of "spread out" with the meaning of "fertile" or "productive" is intended by the prophet in his metaphorical description.[37] In metaphorical terms, the tenor of the comparison is Israel's increase of (unacceptable) worship and the vehicle is a *vine (gepen)* that produces *fruit.*[38]

Either Hosea himself or an editor has put together a sequence of the prophet's agricultural comparisons in 9:10, 13, and 10:1.[39]

9:10 grapes in the wilderness
9:13 a palm
10:1 a luxuriant vine

The pattern of presentation is clear, regardless of the difficulty of individual details. There is an affirmation of goodness and fertility, followed by an indictment of the people for their transgressions.

2 The first clause of v. 2 depends on characterizing the people as a willful individual. Israel's folly is rooted in the center of its being, *their heart (libbām)*. The religious defection depicted in the increase of altars and so on is a symptom of their basic disorientation, which is rooted in a core flaw (cf. Jer. 17:9). Literally, the phrase in v. 2 is "their heart is smooth" *(ḥālaq)*.[40] Perhaps the opposite profile is that of a "wholehearted" response to YHWH such as that commanded in Deut. 6:5. Israel's heart-based deception is contrary to the covenant ethos and thus the people are declared *guilty* and liable for punishment.

In the destruction to come upon the cultic paraphernalia, YHWH is not mentioned explicitly, but the indefinite subject (*hû'*, meaning "he" or

37. Another possibility is that *bōqēq* has an Arabic cognate that means "to be fertile." Among the commentators, Macintosh, *Hosea,* pp. 383-85, has a thorough discussion of translation options, although his own conclusion is to read the participle in its primary sense of "empty," or as he renders it, "damaged."

38. The verb employed (*šāwâ,* Piel) for "producing" fruit is not common either with respect to agricultural production, but it is used in conjunction with providing things and a rightful return or response (Job 33:27; Pss. 21:5 [MT 6]; 89:19 [MT 20]). Rudolph, *Hosea,* p. 191, plausibly suggests that it means "to make ripe," based on an Arabic cognate. The term *pĕrî* ("fruit") is used elsewhere in the context as a pun on *'eprayim* (Ephraim; 9:16).

39. For other comparisons of Israel or Judah to agricultural plants, including a "vine," see Ps. 80; Isa. 5:1-7; Ezek. 17.

40. There are two possible roots (homonyms) for *ḥālaq,* one meaning "divide" and the other "be smooth/slippery," and thus two basic ways to translate the phrase in 10:2. Macintosh, *Hosea,* pp. 394-95, opts for the latter and translates: "they have dissimulated in their hearts." Rudolph, *Hosea,* p. 191, is an example of one who translates it as "their heart is divided" *(zerteilen).* Difference over which is the better translation goes back to the early versions, and one can line up a list of interpreters for either option, as already made clear by Harper, *Hosea,* p. 344.

261

"it") of the verbs is certainly the divine Lord of the covenant and the land. The verb *'ārap ("break down")* is denominative, from the noun *'ōrep,* "neck." Elsewhere the verb is used in the context of breaking the neck of an animal (Exod. 13:13, donkey; Deut. 21:4, heifer; Isa. 66:3, dog). It is not, however, the term used to refer to the destruction of Canaanite altars in Exod. 34:13; Deut. 7:5; 12:3. This may reflect nothing more than Hosea's independence from the pentateuchal vocabulary, or it may indicate that the destruction of the altars is likened to the execution of an animal.

3 Here Hosea represents the people speaking. Their speaking is coordinated with the previous verse through the repetition of the particle *now.* In doing so, he may quote them accurately according to the political situation at hand. From the dynastic instability during Hosea's day, we can certainly extrapolate the repeated rejection of royal rule on the part of one or more factions (cf. 1 Kgs. 12:16; 2 Kgs. 9; 15:1-31). It is also possible that the prophet represents the people speaking on an occasion when there was no king. If it is the latter, there are several options from which to choose, such as the assassinations of Zechariah, Shallum, Pekahiah, and Pekah, or the capture of Hoshea by Shalmaneser V. At the same time, one imagines only with difficulty that Israel en masse would deny that they *fear YHWH.* What is more likely in such a quote is the depiction of Israel's "false" heart (noted in v. 2) as the prophet has discerned it. It is he who interprets their actions as denying the efficacy of YHWH and that of a king. Through various attempts to find security for themselves, they have rejected human and divine rule. It is also the case that one cannot discern an implied tone of voice so easily at this distance from the prophet and the presenting circumstances. Perhaps the prophet was using sarcasm to shame the people, saying in effect that they had no confidence in either YHWH or the monarchy. If Hosea speaks at the time when Shalmaneser V took Hoshea captive and took the calf image from Bethel (see below on 10:5-6), then the prophet represents the people's response to the loss of their monarch and a popular cult image for YHWH.

An alternative to the interpretation offered above is to consider the references to a king as divine references, more particularly as contemptuous references to YHWH, again with the prophet interpreting the heart of the people for them.[41] A prominent rendering of YHWH in the OT is that of cosmic ruler.[42] Moreover, it is the case that no king is named in 10:3 except YHWH. On the other hand, elsewhere Hosea refers a number of times to kings and kingship (e.g., 7:3, 5, 7; 8:4, 10), including the immediate context

41. So Andersen and Freedman, *Hosea,* p. 553.
42. See Marc Z. Brettler, *God Is King: Understanding an Israelite Metaphor* (JSOTSup 76; Sheffield: JSOT Press, 1989). Cf. Isaiah's statement that he had seen "the king, YHWH of hosts" (Isa. 6:5).

(10:6-7), and a persuasive case can be made that without exception they are references to human rule. One may even split the difference in these two options for interpreting v. 3: Hosea may employ a pun on the term "king," saying in effect that the people have no king (= YHWH), that they do not reverence him, and the king (human ruler) in Samaria is of no help either.

4 The indictments in 10:4 are a continuation of the theme of Israel's false heart, which plays itself out in various ways. On the one hand, there is contempt for king and national deity (10:3). On the other hand, it manifests itself in forms of political activity that do not lead to justice. The terminology of v. 4a is that of political agreement, whether that between king and subjects or that of a treaty between nations. Hosea uses the term *bĕrît,* which can represent either option (Gen. 14:13; 1 Sam. 11:1; 2 Sam. 5:3; 1 Kgs. 5:12; 15:19), just as it represents the national covenant YHWH made with Israel's ancestors. In Hos. 12:1 (MT 2) the prophet refers to "making a covenant" with Assyria, likely the same kind of agreement expressed here in v. 4a, whereas in 6:7 and 8:1 he employs the term for the national covenant extended by YHWH to Israel.

Perhaps we draw a false distinction in v. 4a if we insist on too rigid a separation between the internal matter of an agreement put in place by a king with his subjects and an external matter of a treaty with another king. If one must choose, the more likely object of Hosea's wrath is an agreement between Israel and Assyria, similar or identical to that in 12:1;[43] but one must keep in mind that whatever treaty a Menahem or Hoshea made with Assyria (or Egypt or Damascus), it would have ramifications for the people. In some cases a national assembly might be called (cf. Jer. 36:9), and the consequences for the populace could be quite severe. For example, when Menahem paid tribute to Tiglath-pileser III, he levied a tax on "Israel" (2 Kgs. 15:19-20). Those who paid the tax may have been bound by oath to the Israelite king to support the aims of the dynasty.

There are thus matters of consequence to the political terminology of *oaths* (infinitive of *'ālâ*) in 10:4a. An oath is properly part of a covenant.[44] When the latter term refers to a matter of God's initiation with a party, then God may offer an oath or solemn promise to undergird his choice (e.g., Gen. 9:8-17). The national covenant extended by God to Israel, in which a response of the people was required, included a ritual sealing with blood and a voiced commitment of obedience on their part (Exod. 24:3-7). An oath, therefore, is a promise and can be a form of self-imprecation. The blood of the animals sacrificed in the ritual represented a life given to seal the cove-

---

43. See the detailed discussion in Utzschneider, *Hosea,* pp. 110-19.
44. See the introduction, section IV.C, "Hosea's Theology: Covenant and Marriage."

nant and to confirm the obligations of those who made vows of obedience. A quasi-secular form of this obligation is reflected in Jer. 34:8-20, where Judean officials and slave owners made a covenant to free their slaves and then reneged. Part of the agreement included passing between the divided carcass of a calf, thereby obligating themselves to a course of action based on the sanctity of a life given (34:18).[45] Jeremiah announces that those who reneged would be given into the hand of those who seek their life. His announced judgment would be predicated on their self-imprecation for noncompliance, which was part of the covenant ratification ceremony.

The international treaty tradition of the ancient Near East often included a section of blessing and curses jointly acknowledged by the respective parties. These were to be overseen by the deities of the parties involved. The curses spelled out a publicly acknowledged fate for noncompliance. For example, in Israel's case any vassal treaty imposed by Assyria on it would likely invoke the support of YHWH (and other deities?) for Israel's obligations. And, of course, the deities of Assyria would be party to the treaty. In the Pentateuch, the curses associated with disobedience in the national covenant have a similar function to those included in the international treaties. No other deities are represented in the pentateuchal curses, but the structure of defection followed by announced disaster is the same. YHWH had the sole role of covenant maker and covenant enforcer. As is clear from 10:4, Hosea roundly opposes the offering of promises, the uttering of oaths, and the making of agreements/covenants in the political realm. He sees them apparently as an infringement on YHWH's sovereignty and more specifically as a violation of the prior national covenant with YHWH (6:7; 8:1).

The book of Hosea is replete with language related to treaty curses and covenant violations directed at Israel. Perhaps one reason for this is that the prophet has two related traditions from which to draw. One comes from the political agreement(s) entered into by Israel (i.e., the northern kingdom) to which Hosea was opposed. The second comes from the curses for disobedience rooted in the national covenant.

The second half of 10:4 returns to Hosea's employment of botanical similes. *Justice*,[46] the task of a government and the expectation of the covenant ethos, is thwarted as a result of Israel's unwise political activity. The comparison is to a *poisonous plant (rōʾš)* that *sprouts in a field.* No term for "plant" is explicit, but the modifying phrase assumes some form of poison-

45. Jeremiah refers to "keeping the *words* of the covenant" in 34:18. Perhaps the use of "words" in Hos. 10:4a is related to this expression.

46. Heb. *mišpāṭ* can be translated as "justice" or "judgment" (i.e., justice enacted against an offender). The same ambiguity exists in Hos. 5:1, where the latter nuance seems more probable. The prophet may be playing on both senses of the term in 10:4.

ous plant that can ruin a future harvest. It is possible that we have here an intersection between the prophecies of Amos and those of Hosea. Consider the following indictments of Israel from Amos: "You who turn justice to wormwood, who bring righteousness to the ground" (5:7); "You have turned justice to poison, the fruit of righteousness to wormwood" (6:12b). In 6:12 Amos has the same two terms as Hosea, and his employment of the term "fruit" *(pĕrî)* also shows the metaphorical connection between social rectitude and agricultural production that Hosea uses. There is no compelling reason to affirm or deny a line of dependence between the two prophetic figures. It is just as likely that they draw upon similar material in their critique of Israelite society. Both prophets offer a thorough, institutionally based critique of Israel. The lack of *justice* is evidence that the institutions of king, regional administration, and judicial redress had failed.

5   Verse 5 is a textbook illustration of Hosea's allusive style, atypical vocabulary, and alternation of perfect and imperfect verbs. Virtually every term invites comment. The interpretation proposed here is that Hosea describes the emotions attached to the idolatrous calf figure, which, as 10:6 makes clear, will be taken by the Assyrians. One cannot tell from the alternating verbs whether the departure of the calf is depicted as imminent or accomplished. In either case, a crisis is described for the prophet's contemporaries. The very last clause of 10:5 is understood to go directly with the following verse.[47] Thus I render 10:6 together with 10:5 and comment on it accordingly.

There is also polemic against Samaria's calf in 8:5-6. Although Samaria is mentioned again in 10:5, the calf itself is associated with *Beth-aven* ("House of Iniquity"), a polemical term that Hosea elsewhere uses for Bethel (4:15; 5:8). A reference to Bethel is probably also intended here in v. 5, although one can imagine Hosea describing Samaria as an iniquitous place. By linking Samaria's inhabitants with the calf figure at Bethel, including the holy site there whose history reaches back to Israel's ancestors, Hosea reflects indirectly how central a symbol the calf figure was for Israelite identity. That is the way the calf figure is depicted in Exod. 32 and 1 Kgs. 12, as a representative of the God(s) who brought Israel from Egypt, even while the writers polemicize against it. Hosea, indeed, also stands in the tradition that regards the calf as idolatrous (and syncretistic?), but his fierce opposition to it is a backhanded admission of its place within the Israelite Yahwistic cult.

The calf's glory is under threat, and the non-Levitical priests tremble in fear for it. Hosea's other use of the term is in 9:11, where Ephraim's glory was to depart like a bird. The glory of the calf may simply represent the sanctity of the figure itself as a divine representative, just as the ark of the covenant (a pedestal like the calf?) represented the glory of YHWH among his

---

47. So also Garrett, *Hosea,* p. 210.

people. Perhaps it was covered in silver or gold and thus its "glory" was a tangible thing in terms of beauty and value.[48]

The verb for *depart (gālâ)* is also employed for going into exile. Amos, Hosea's contemporary, frequently employs the verb *gālâ* in the sense of "be taken away, go into exile" (1:5, 6; 5:5, 27; 6:7; 7:11, 17). The experience of exile is described by Hosea in 9:17, but the verb itself is used only in 10:5. In 1 Sam. 4:22 the capture of the ark is described as the *carrying away (gālâ)* of Israel's "glory."

6 According to the first clause of 10:6 the calf was taken to Assyria. The ruler of Assyria is not named, but the title accorded him, *great king (melek yārēb)*, reflects an Assyrian epithet that Hosea also uses in 5:13.[49] Bethel's calf is the Assyrian monarch's present or prize. It could have been carried away by the forces of Tiglath-pileser III in 732, but there is no independent confirmation of that. It is also possible that Bethel's calf was taken away by his son, Shalmaneser V, as he sought control over Israel in the aftermath of his father's death, perhaps at the time that he took Hoshea prisoner. This setting could provide clarity on the comments in 10:3 that *we have no king* (cf. 10:7) and that the people no longer feared YHWH. If his cult statue or pedestal had been taken, some would think that YHWH had been vanquished by Assyrian power.

The last two clauses of 10:6 preserve a trademark pun in parallel expressions. Both the noun *shame (bošnâ)*, which occurs only here in the OT, and the verb *be ashamed (bôš)* are employed to underscore the humiliation of the people. The correspondence of the clauses is as follows:

Ephraim brings *shame* upon himself

Israel is *ashamed* because of his plans.

Israel's *plans* had negative results, indeed catastrophic ones. The term "plans" *('ēṣâ)* is used similarly in Ps. 106:43, a poetic text with a number of connections to Hosea.[50] In both places the term refers to plans undertaken by Israel in rebellion against YHWH's leading. In the context of describing God's anger and the resulting exile of his people (vv. 40-43), the psalmist notes, "Many times God delivered them, but they rebelled with their counsel *('ēṣâ)*, they sank down because of their iniquity *('āwōn)*." Hosea could not agree more.

7 The simile of v. 7 contains a word whose meaning is obscure. The verb of the initial clause of the verse is clearer, indicating that the monarch in

48. So Wolff, *Hosea*, p. 175.
49. In addition to the excursus at 8:5-6 on "Hosea and the Calf," see the discussion of the Assyrian epithet at 5:13.
50. See appendix 5, "Psalm 106 and Hosea."

Samaria *is gone* or will cease to be (*dāmâ,* Niphal). Indeed, the forces that will bring this about may already be underway. Two primary options are apparent for the simile, either taking the noun *qeṣep* as a chip of wood, a piece of flotsam, or as *foam,* the frothy part of roiled waters that quickly dissipates. In favor of the first option is the LXX, which is followed by the NRSV and a number of commentators.[51] These translators assume that if *qeṣep* is a chip of wood,[52] then it is a homonym for the better-attested noun for "anger" or "wrath" (e.g., Josh. 9:20; Isa. 34:2). The latter option of *foam,* cautiously adopted here, takes the noun in its better-attested sense, but with the nuance of "agitation."[53] The phrase "foam on the water" allows for a subtle pun on the word "anger," and can be readily related to Hosea's expression in 13:11 that YHWH had given Israel a king in *anger ('ap)* and taken him away in *wrath ('ebrâ).* The intent of the simile differs little in either case. In metaphorical terms the tenor is the sudden disappearance or end of Israel's king. The vehicle is the fleeting life of a wood chip on water or that of the foam on water produced by movement.

8 A *high place* is not inherently a place of idolatry. It is a term for a shrine, often located on a high point (cf. 4:13), with an altar and other cultic paraphernalia.[54] In plural form, as here in v. 8, it is used commonly to refer to idolatrous, syncretistic, or non-Yahwistic places of worship.[55] One cannot discern for certain whether the term *iniquity ('āwen)* is a short form of Beth-aven, i.e., Bethel, or is used as a common noun. In view of the fact that Beth-aven is named in 10:5, the former view seems preferable.[56]

Hosea announces destruction is coming upon the various cultic shrines in and around Bethel. There are multiple *altars* because there are various shrines. Their dissolution continues the fearsome trouble that comes with the loss of the calf figure and Israel's king, figures mentioned in previous verses. The altars, platforms of stones, will be overgrown with thorns and other wild plants because they are no longer in use. All this is due to divine judgment. Only one other text in the OT has the word pair *thorns* and *thistles* (*qôṣ* + *dardar*), Gen. 3:18, where it is part of the cursing of the ground because of Adam's disobedience. The intertextual echo between the two is instructive, whether or not Hosea draws intentionally upon the curse tradition in Gen. 3. The future desolation of the high places will show that they reside under a curse similar to the ground outside Eden.

Verse 8 concludes with a corporate cry of dereliction and a plea for

---

51. E.g., Wolff, *Hosea,* p. 171.
52. The fem. noun *qĕṣāpâ* in Joel 1:7 may refer to a splinter or the bark of a tree.
53. Macintosh, *Hosea,* pp. 406-7.
54. See the excursus at 4:13-14 on "Geography of Sacrifice."
55. 1 Kgs. 13:33; 14:23; 2 Kgs. 17:9; 23:8; Jer. 7:31; 19:5; 32:35.
56. See appendix 9, "Worship Centers in Hosea."

the end of suffering. It also brings to an end a literary subunit going back to 9:10. Better to be covered by the hills than to be further subjected to such anguish and humiliation as depicted for the people in the last few verses. It may or may not have been a traditional cry of woe and fearful resignation in Hosea's day. It has a different tone than the voice of the people in 10:3. Later writers pick up the cry to illustrate the horror of a defeated populace facing the wrath of their conqueror (Luke 23:30; Rev. 6:16).

9-10 These verses have several incongruities of expression, and no interpretation of them is free of difficulty. Perhaps we have disparate sayings in these two verses; if so, then attempting to read them together as a brief reflection on Gibeah and Israel's sinfulness is a frustrating exercise. The interpretation proposed is that 10:9-10, 11-12, and 13-15 are three units of speech joined together by an editor. Perhaps they originated at the same time in the prophet's public outcry against Israel. If they are to be linked historically with 10:1-8, then they likely offer commentary at the time of strong Assyrian pressure and the capture of King Hoshea.

In 9:9 Hosea uses past events at Gibeah to refer to a time when Israel was corrupted. He does the same thing in 10:9, even using the same phrase, *days of Gibeah.* His reference is probably related to the sexual horror and resulting warfare in Judg. 19–21,[57] but his allusions are difficult to correlate with the account in Judges. Hosea may well have had different source material upon which to draw than now contained in the other biblical account.

The events at Gibeah are cited to confirm that Israel continues to sin in a familiar pattern. That point is clear, whatever past events are in mind. The comment that an unnamed group *stood there* is obscure.[58] The second half of v. 9 is usually taken by interpreters as a rhetorical question and understood as a pointed claim that warfare is coming upon the people, as it did during the previous *days of Gibeah.* This makes tolerable sense, is consistent with what follows in 10:10, and is permissible grammar. Questions in Hebrew are not always marked with the interrogative *h,* and context guides their identification.

The concluding prepositional phrase of v. 9 apparently refers to the earlier culprits in Gibeah in a way that joins them by analogy to Israel's current crisis, but it too is obscure. The phrase *běnê 'alwâ* is almost certainly pejorative and is so taken by most early versions. There are good contextual reasons for this, but since the noun *'alwâ* does not occur elsewhere, the question is raised, "sons/children" *(běnê)* of what? The LXX, for example, trans-

---

57. See the excursus at 5:8 on "Gibeah."

58. It may refer to the combatants who stood their ground and engaged in fighting (Judg. 20) or to Benjaminite resolve to stand their ground in the face of their opprobrium. Sweeney, *Twelve Prophets,* pp. 107-8, offers a detailed attempt to correlate 10:9 with Judg. 19–21.

lates the phrase as the "children of unrighteousness" *(adikias).* Hebrew *'alwâ* is probably a copyist's error, a metathesis, for *'awlâ,* a term for "violence" and "injustice." The term *běnê 'awlâ,* meaning "reprobates" or "violent men," occurs in 2 Sam. 3:34; 7:10, and it fits the context of Hos. 10:9-10. Indeed, the noun *'awlâ* is used in 10:13. The concluding phrase of 10:9 can be interpreted as an elaboration on the rhetorical question: "Will not war overtake them in Gibeah, (war, that is) against evildoers?" The phrase reads more smoothly, however, if it is joined to the initial verb in 10:10, as proposed in the rendering above (so NRSV). YHWH announces that he has come to judge (as previously at Gibeah) the reprobates and that he will *discipline* them, a verb also used in 7:12, 15.[59]

The gathering of peoples around sinful Israel is a motif for war and subsequent destruction. Israel has been described as mixed, swallowed, and wandering among the nations (7:8; 8:8; 9:17). In 10:10 the people are *bound*[60] by a double portion of their *iniquities*[61] and vulnerable to predators.

In summary, the distance in time and culture for modern readers makes much of 10:9-10 difficult to interpret. Perhaps two points can be made with some confidence. First, the reference to the *days of Gibeah* can be compared with the same phrase in a different context in 9:9. In the latter context, past problems are a clue to Israel's current crisis and a harbinger of judgment to come. Something similar is indicated in these two verses. Second, the mention of *warfare (milḥāmâ)* and the gathering of predator nations fits the context of violence and destruction as portrayed in 10:2, 8. A third observation offers some assistance with the broader context: Gibeah is the fourth of four cities to be singled out for comment. There is shame in Baal-peor (9:10), evil in Gilgal (9:15), fear and mourning in Samaria (10:5), and now sin in Gibeah (10:9).

3. From Trained Heifer to Fruit of Lies (10:11-15)

> 11 *Ephraim was*[62] *a trained heifer who loves to thresh; I passed by her delightful neck.*[63] *I will harness Ephraim; Judah will plough, Jacob will harrow for himself.*

59. See the excursus at 7:12 on "Discipline and Correction in Hosea."

60. The verb is *'āsar,* a pun on *yāsar,* "discipline."

61. Note the claim in Isa. 40:2 that Jerusalem had received "double" *(kiplayim)* from the hand of YHWH for her sins.

62. As often in translating Hebrew into English, the verb must be supplied, as the initial clause of the verse is verbless. The perfect form of *'ābartî* ("I passed by") in the second clause sets the time aspect.

63. This is a rendering of the MT. A common alternative is "I yoked her delightful neck," by reading the verb *'ābar* as Piel or Hiphil and the term "yoke," *'ōl* (lost through haplography), before the preposition *'al.*

12 *Sow for yourselves righteousness; reap steadfast love. Till the fallow ground; (it is) a time to seek YHWH until he comes and sends forth righteousness for you.*

13 *You have plowed wickedness; you have reaped injustice. You have eaten the fruit of falsehood. You have trusted in your way, in your numerous warriors.*

14 *So the noise of battle shall rise among your populace, and all of your fortified cities will be destroyed; like Shalman's destruction of Beth-arbel on the day of fighting — mother(s) and children dashed to death.*

15 *It will certainly happen to you, O Bethel, because of your surpassing wickedness. At daybreak the king of Israel will be undone.*

11 Verse 11 begins with another of the prophet's animal metaphors.[64] A *trained heifer* is one that has learned the task of threshing and is obedient to the guidance of the farmer. The Hebrew participle *mĕlummādâ (trained)* and participial phrase *'ōhabtî lādûš (who loves to thresh)* thus reinforce one another. This comparison of Ephraim with a heifer well illustrates the range of Hosea's analogical thinking and his historical typology of Israel's various identities, for he can also describe Israel as a "stubborn cow" (4:16). In the case of 10:11a, the *trained heifer* is the Israel of divine election and recipient of the covenant ethos. She is the same entity as the grapes in the wilderness (9:10), the bride in the wilderness (2:14-15 [MT 16-17]), and the beloved son in Egypt (11:1), a people who were at one time well-related to YHWH.

In *passing by her neck,* YHWH appears to be in the role of the farmer who could appreciate her work and did not need a goad or a tight rein. It is difficult to know just what is fair or *delightful* about the neck of a heifer, but the clue may be less in the impression of the body part and more in the verbal phrase "to pass by." Good synergy between animal and ploughman allows for the latter to move from behind the animal and not to exert undue force on the shoulders and neck of the animal. With 10:11b, however, the guidance increases — Ephraim needs a harness.[65] Preparing the land for cultivation takes related steps. *Judah will plough, Jacob will harrow,* i.e., smooth the ground, for the planting of seeds.[66]

The range of subjects in 10:11b is somewhat unexpected. *Ephraim is*

64. See further appendix 3, "Flora and Fauna Metaphors in Hosea."
65. The verb *rākab* means "to ride" and is associated with chariots, where horses are yoked and reined for guidance. The Hiphil employed in v. 11 likely includes the tasks of preparing the animal for the task of fieldwork.
66. The last two verbs of 10:11, *ḥāraš* and *śādad,* are paired in Isa. 28:24. The verb *ḥāraš* is also used in Hos. 10:13.

named initially, but *Judah* has played no role in the context, and *Jacob,* a term for the tribal kingdom, has not been mentioned either. Some interpreters, therefore, hold that Judah is an editorial insertion for an original "Israel," or that by the simple deletion of Judah, Jacob and Ephraim function as parallel terms in v. 11b, each with a verb associated with it.[67] This proposal has some appeal. The name Judah may well be an editorial update, given the final editing of the book in Judah and the apparent intrusiveness of Judah in the context. On the other hand, the question depends in part on Hosea's own historical horizon and whether his metaphor of the people as farm animals represents constituent elements of the broad tribal kingdom before its division. If so, then both Judah and Jacob are appropriate referents. We might ask the question differently: Is Judah part of YHWH's election in Hosea's understanding? The answer to this is affirmative (1:11 [MT 2:2]), so a reference to Judah is thus plausible in Hosea's prophecies. Perhaps Hosea's historical retrospective has Judah and Ephraim/Jacob yoked together. There are, furthermore, two other citations in Hosea that may be related to 10:11. In 5:5 *Israel, Ephraim,* and *Judah* occur together as three related entities in rebellion against YHWH. *Jacob* occurs only once more as a reference to the people of Israel (12:2 [MT 3]), and there it is also paired with *Judah.*[68]

Essentially 10:11 is historical typology through metaphor. Ephraim, Judah, and Jacob owe their identity to YHWH. Past favor has given way to the need for stronger guidance. Verse 11 is not the voice of imminent judgment, however. It is the language of past identity and future task.

12 If we read v. 12 as a continuation of v. 11, then we have in the two verses yet another brief metaphorical portrayal of Israel's identity. They are YHWH's possession, trained to produce for the household. The animal simile is set aside in v. 12, however, even as the agricultural tasks of the household are continued, with Israel exhorted to fulfill their tasks of sowing, reaping, and tilling. Israel's real work is fidelity to the covenant ethos and the Lord of the household. *Righteousness* and *steadfast love* constitute the essence of the covenant ethos (4:1; 6:6). They are essential elements also of the bridal gifts that YHWH will provide in the restored covenant (2:19 [MT 21]).

---

67. So Harper, *Hosea,* pp. 354-55; Macintosh, *Hosea,* pp. 418-19. Wolff, *Hosea,* p. 185, argues for the originality of Judah here.

68. The ancestor Jacob is named once, in 12:12 (MT 13). Both Israel and Jacob are names for the broad tribal kingdom and also for the northern state after the division of the kingdom. Isaiah of Jerusalem and Micah use the terms in both senses, and only context can discern the difference — if it can be discerned at all. They may even address Judah and Jerusalem as Jacob and Israel. Note Isaiah's use of the "house of Jacob" in 8:17 and the reference to the temple in Jerusalem as the "house of the God of Jacob" in 2:3. Micah 1:5 refers to the sins of Jacob and the house of Israel, which include Judah and Jerusalem. Cf. Mic. 3:1, 8, 9.

Implementing the covenant ethos (i.e., *sowing* and *reaping*) is preparation for the real harvest: YHWH sends forth righteousness as if it was the life-giving rain. The blessings of the covenant are depicted in language similar to the manner in which YHWH speaks to the heavens to begin a chain reaction of corporate blessings in 2:21-23 (MT 23-25). All of this, however, assumes obedient members of the household and their intentional *sowing and reaping,* but that is not the identity of historical Israel in Hosea's day. The gap between the people's calling and their performance was enormous.

It is difficult initially to see how 10:11-12 fits between 10:9-10 and 10:13-15, both of which are passages bearing a judgmental tone toward the people. I am suggesting that 10:11-12 should be seen in essentially the same vein as 9:10; 10:1; and 11:1, all of which are positive metaphorical portraits of Israel in the service of severe criticism of their current activities. Israel's household identity and tasks remind the people first of their historical relationship with YHWH. That they do not live up to their high calling is the basis for the announcements of judgment to come.

13   The metaphors of *ploughing* and *reaping* continue from the previous verses, but they depict Israel not as they are called to be by YHWH, but as they are in a historical moment of rebellion and faithlessness. One should note carefully the contrasting word pairs in vv. 12 and 13, for they indicate clearly the sad contrast between sacred call and current crisis.

v. 12 sow righteousness   v. 13 plough wickedness
v. 12 reap steadfast love   v. 13 reap injustice

Moreover, the theme of fruitfulness continues from the broader context. What Israel consumed was not the produce of either righteousness or steadfast love, but the fruit of *falsehood (kāḥaš),* a favorite term of Hosea's to describe the social rot of lying and deceit.[69]

Verse 13 concludes with an indictment that the people *trust* in themselves, particularly in their warriors. Hosea does not otherwise use the verb *bāṭaḥ,* but its employment here resonates with some other prophetic contexts. Isaiah, for example, warns against going to Egypt and trusting in horses and chariots, rather than in YHWH (Isa. 31:1). Jeremiah similarly speaks against trusting in the false security of fortified cities (Jer. 5:17). And in his celebrated temple sermon, he warns against a misplaced trust in YHWH's temple in Jerusalem (7:4, 14), as if YHWH were somehow bound to defend his sanctuary from outside threat in spite of Judah's repeated violations of the covenant ethos (7:9). Elsewhere, Hosea makes relatively little mention of Israel's military readiness. In 8:14 he refers to the public buildings and specifically

---

69. Hos. 4:2; 7:3; 9:2; 11:12 (MT 12:1).

Judean fortified cities, and in 10:14 there is a collective reference to *all your fortified cities.* Although it may seem naive or unrealistic, he follows the line of other (now) biblical prophets in regarding military might as yet another useless distraction in the face of the larger issue of fidelity to YHWH.

14-15   These verses have a somber word for the cities of Israel and particularly for Bethel. The spur to righteousness in 10:12 was a hope, but not apparently a reality. That *fortified cities* would be destroyed implies a military campaign against Israel. Both Tiglath-pileser III and Shalmaneser V carried out campaigns in Hosea's day, and the destruction contemplated in these verses could reflect the work of either king.

By way of ominous announcement, Hosea cites the devastation of a previous onslaught against Beth-arbel, likely a city in Gilead where the modern Jordanian city of Irbid is now located.[70] The historical setting of that horrible event, however, is elusive. The horror of the attack against Beth-arbel included the slaying of women and children (cf. 13:16). Sad to say, but that much is clear.

The reference to *Shalman* is obscure for later readers. One possibility is that Shalman is Shalmaneser III, the 9th-century Assyrian ruler who campaigned in the region and accepted tribute from the Israelite king Jehu in 841 B.C. A material reminder of Jehu's capitulation is carved on the famous Black Obelisk, an Assyrian propaganda monument now in the British Museum.[71] There is no explicit reference to Shalmaneser's campaign in the OT, but Israel's memory of an earlier destruction at the hands of the Assyrians could serve Hosea's message effectively.

There are other possibilities for Shalman's slaughter. It might refer to a reprisal or some such action on the part of Shalmaneser V that is otherwise unknown. If so, it dates no earlier than 727, the year of his accession to the throne. There is also a Moabite ruler named Salamanu, known from Tiglath-pileser III's annals,[72] who may have perpetrated an atrocity against an Israelite city in Gilead. Whatever the historical referent of the slaughter, Hosea projects more of the same for his contemporaries.

Bethel comes under particular scrutiny for its *surpassing wickedness.* Even Israel's king will be gone when the judgment rolls through the land. One cannot tell from these terse references whether it is the cultic sins of Bethel (e.g., the calf located there) or its support for a political option that qualifies as exceedingly wicked.

These last two verses conclude a subsection of the book. Their somberness reflects its dominant tone set in 9:10 with Israel's waywardness. His-

---

70. For bibliography and added details, see appendix 8, "Transjordan in Hosea."
71. See the translation by K. L. Younger Jr., *COS* 2:269-70.
72. See the translation by A. Leo Oppenheim, *ANET,* p. 282.

torical judgment, however, will not be the last word. The historical resume and divine soliloquy that follow in ch. 11 show YHWH to be at work not only in judgment, but also in redemption.

F. A PRODIGAL SON RETURNS HOME (11:1-11)

Chapter 11 makes a transition from the topic immediately preceding it.[1] The retrospective element in vv. 1-4 is not itself new, as some of the materials in the previous chapters also look back at Israel's prior history, but the sustained presentation of YHWH as divine father[2] marks out the chapter as a new pericope. Israel was addressed directly at the end of ch. 10. Beginning in 11:1 the prophet presents YHWH as reflecting on Israel as an incorrigible child called "my son." It continues the theme of drawing on historical tradition begun in 9:10 with the metaphor of Israel like grapes in the wilderness. Divine speech runs through 11:1-9, with a depiction of Israel's eventual return from dispersion and exile making up vv. 10-11. Verse 12 in English versions is 12:1 in the MT. That verse's contents clearly go with the material that follows rather than serving as a conclusion to 11:10-11.

Hosea 11:1-11 also concludes a second major section of the book (chs. 4–11), which thus ends with YHWH's resolve to maintain Israel as his own in spite of the historical judgment to fall upon them and in spite of his anger at their intransigence. There are parallels with 3:1-5 and 14:1-9 (MT 2-10), chapters that conclude major sections of the book on a hopeful note. Virtually everything in chs. 4–10 serves to support judgment on the people and to underscore that any forgiveness is an act of grace. Chapter 11's rehearsal of failure and recognition of judgment at hand are at the same time a reiteration of what preceded it. But the suffering love of a father for his family is also a reiteration of the wounded husband and father in chs. 1–3. In ch. 11 Israel is offered chastened hope for the future, not un-

---

1. For a thorough study of the chapter, see Kakkanattu, *God's Enduring Love.*

2. Just as Israel is metaphorically God's son, so YHWH is father, the head of the household and the agent who can adopt and convey inheritance. One can also say that the imagery of 11:1-4 is more broadly parental, with YHWH's tender mercies like those of a mother. The interpretation of YHWH as mother, however, cannot be sustained for the metaphor, in spite of the efforts by H. Schüngel-Straumann, "God as Mother in Hosea 11," in *A Feminist Companion to the Latter Prophets,* ed. A. Brenner (FCB 8; Sheffield: Sheffield Academic Press, 1995), pp. 194-218. See the comments below on v. 4. The analysis of B. Seifert, *Metaphorisches Reden von Gott im Hoseabuch* (FRLANT 166; Göttingen: Vandenhoeck & Ruprecht, 1996), pp. 198-202, is sound: "Without doubt in Hos. 11 YHWH does what a mother does according to the rule [in ancient Near Eastern cultures]; however, he does it not as a female divinity" (p. 200).

like the way ch. 3 concludes the first major section of the book or ch. 14 the third and final section.

Unfortunately, the textual transmission of ch. 11 has resulted in several difficulties for the translator. Most modern translations have resorted to one or more emendations of the MT and/or the adopting of a rendering supported by one or more of the Greek versions. The translation offered here is no exception.

1 *When Israel was a youth I loved him, and from Egypt I called my son.*[3]

2 *The more that I called them, the more they went from before me.*[4] *They offer sacrifice to the Baals; they burn incense to idols.*[5]

3 *Yet I brought Ephraim along the way,*[6] *taking*[7] *them upon my*[8] *arms; they did not know that I healed them.*

4 *With human cords I drew them, with bonds of love (I drew them); I was to them like those who lift a yoke*[9] *from their jaws; I stretched out to him and fed (him).*

3. The LXX has "his children" *(ta tekna autou).* The MT is preferable. The sing. *son* is a metaphor for the people (cf. Exod. 4:22-23).

4. Verse 2a varies among the ancient versions. The translation offered here follows the LXX and is similar to the rendering of NRSV and NIV. The MT can be rendered: "The more they called them, thus they went from before them." The LXX maintains the first-person voice from v. 1. The initial "they" of the Hebrew could refer to the work of prophetic figures who called Israel (the initial "them") back to YHWH. The Hebrew text is accepted by McComiskey, "Hosea," p. 184, who finds in it a depiction of YHWH's prophets calling Israel back to covenant fidelity.

5. The verbs in v. 2b are both imperfects. They could be narrative preterites or represent activities still underway in Israel.

6. The verbal form *tirgaltî* is an anomaly. It appears to be a Tiphel conjugation, perhaps a denominative form derived from the root *rgl,* which indicates a foot/feet and locomotion. It is possible that the verb has the nuance of guiding or leading individuals along a way.

7. Heb. *qāhām* is also an anomaly. It appears to be an infinitive absolute of the verb *lāqah* ("take" or "receive") with the 3rd masc. pl. suffix. Perhaps *qāh* is an abbreviation or defective form of *lāqah,* as seems to be the case in Ezek. 17:5, or possibly it is a textually corrupt form of *'eqqāhēm,* "I took them" (so Syriac). The LXX has "I took him."

8. The MT has "his arms." The LXX, Syriac, and Vulgate have the 1st person pronoun "my."

9. The MT is *'ōl* ("yoke"), which is followed by Syriac and Vulgate. This gives rise to the interpretation that in v. 4 the metaphor is that of care for and training of an animal. So also ESV, NIV, NASB. The LXX oddly has the simile "like a man striking (someone) on his cheek." An emendation of *'ōl* to *'ûl* ("infant") is followed by NRSV, "I was to them like those who lift infants to their cheeks," and by a number of modern commentators, e.g., Wolff, *Hosea,* p. 191.

5 *They*[10] *shall not return to the land of Egypt; instead Assyria —
he shall be their king because they refuse to return (to me).*

6 *And the sword shall whirl in his cities and bring an end to his
gate bars*[11] *and consume (them) because of their schemes.*

7 *My people are twisted, turning from me; they call him to the
Most High*[12] *as one; he will not raise (them).*

8 *How can I give you up, Ephraim? (How)*[13] *can I hand you over,
Israel? How can I make you like Admah? (How) can I treat you like
Zeboiim? My heart is overthrown against me! Altogether my compassions are kindled!*

9 *I will not carry out my fierce anger; I will not again destroy
Ephraim; for I am God and not mortal; in your midst (is) the Holy
One. And I will not come in wrath.*[14]

10 *After YHWH they will come; like a lion he will roar. Indeed he
will roar, and children*[15] *will tremble (coming) from the west.*

11 *Like a bird they will come trembling from Egypt, and like a*

10. The MT has the singular, both here and as the pronominal suffix on "king" in
v. 5b. As often in Hebrew, the singular can serve as a collective. Cf. Andersen and Freedman, *Hosea,* p. 584.

11. A number of proposals have been offered for Heb. *bad,* but as Macintosh,
Hosea, p. 453, notes, none of them is as plausible in context as the well-attested meaning of "bars," understood here in v. 6 as metonym for a city gate with "bars" used in its
defense.

12. This is a possible rendering of the noun *'al,* although it is not the typical formulation of the phrase "Most High," which is [*'el*] *'elyôn.* A related meaning of the noun
would be the more abstract "above." Perhaps it is a corrupted form of *'elyôn.* See
Macintosh, *Hosea,* p. 285, for discussion of options. There is variety already in the
Greek versions. The LXX has *theos epi,* a literal rendering of *'el-'al,* while Aquila,
Symmachus, and Theodotion have *zygos* ("yoke"). Taken together, this evidence suggests the accuracy of the Hebrew consonants *'l,* but divergence in how to render the text.
Wolff, *Hosea,* pp. 192-93, proposes that the Hebrew text originally had *ba'al,* and that
the object "him" of the verb "call" is actually the subject of the following verb "raise up"
(so also *BHS*). Thus he renders: "to Baal they call, (but) he by no means raises them up."
His reconstruction requires other emendations as well. It should be noted that *'al* is also
used oddly in 7:16.

13. The two parenthetical interrogatives are provided to indicate that they are the
continuation of the expressed "how" in the first and third clauses of the verse.

14. The last phrase in the MT, LXX, and Vulgate is "I will not come into a/the
city." Some modern translations and interpreters have seen in Heb. *b'yr* a reference to "in
terror" (cf. *'yr* in Jer. 15:8) or "consumption" *(b'yr),* as in consuming anger. I follow this
last option. An emendation in the Hebrew text perhaps can make better sense of the context, but the decision is not clear-cut.

15. Heb. *bānîm* can be translated either "children" or "sons." It refers metaphorically to Israelites as members of the Lord's family.

dove (trembling) from the land of Assyria. And I will settle[16] them in their houses, says YHWH.

1 In the first chapter of the book, each of Hosea's three children is presented as representing Israel in its relationship with YHWH, along with their mother. Here in v. 1 the familial metaphor is attached collectively to Israel as YHWH's *son.* Chapters 1 and 11 thus have complementary angles of vision on the same subject: Israel is YHWH's household, bound to him in electing love and brought from slavery in Egypt to live in YHWH's land. The matters of inheritance and family identity are likely behind the description of the people as *my son,* a term that occurs elsewhere only in Exod. 4:22-23.[17] Israel's willing obedience to the covenant ethos should come from the privilege of being YHWH's adopted son. This is the same dynamic associated with the marriage metaphor from Hos. 1–3, but rendered using another metaphor.

The term *youth (naʿar)* for Israel likely has the connotation of a young(er) person. It can also refer to someone in a subservient or dependent relationship of any age, but the youthful element in the term contributes to the narrative behind the description of Israel in 11:1 and is primary.[18] In her role as Israel in the wilderness, Gomer also came up from the land of Egypt in the days of "her youth," *nĕʿûreyhā* (2:15 [MT 17]), a plural form derived from the noun *naʿar.* Both Jeremiah (2:2) and Ezekiel (16:22, 43, 60) use the same plural term to describe YHWH's prior dealings with Jerusalem, who personifies and thus represents his people. As with Hosea and the portrayal of Gomer, the prophetic texts in Jeremiah and Ezekiel are based on a narrative of God's choice of Israel, entering into a covenant relationship with "her" like that of a marriage, and bringing her to the promised land. What sets 11:1 apart from these other references is the gender of Israel as metaphorical son. Both Gomer and Jerusalem are female. The exodus and wilderness traditions being rendered, however, are essentially the same. The basic data are as follows:

Hos. 2:14-15 (MT 16-17)	Jer. 2:2	Ezek. 16
I will woo her, bring her to the wilderness, and speak to her heart . . . she will answer as in the days of her *youth*	the loyalty *(hesed)* of your *youth,* the love of your betrothals, your following after me in the wilderness	days of your *youth* (vv. 22, 43; cf. vv. 6-7). I will remember my covenant with you in the days of your *youth* (v. 60).

16. Here the LXX uses *apokatastēsō,* "restore." The translator may have understood MT *hôšabtîm,* the Hiphil of *yāšab,* to have been *hăšîbōtîm,* the Hiphil of *šûb.*

17. See the excursus below on "Israel and Sonship."

18. The term "infant" used by Kakkanattu, *God's Enduring Love,* p. 39, does not quite fit the context. It is unlikely also that *naʿar* represents Israel's slavery in Egypt, as Rudolph, *Hosea,* p. 214, and Macintosh, *Hosea,* p. 437, have suggested.

YHWH's *love* and *calling* of youthful Israel are terms associated with his choice of the people to be his own.[19] The calling is a summons and may reflect also the imagery of naming or designating Israel ("I called [him] 'my son'"). The verbs interpret each other as do the nouns *youth* and *son*. They also interpret the significance of the grand narrative, so influential on Hosea, that YHWH made Israel his own people at a historical moment in the past, along with the understanding that Israel owed its continuing existence to divine forbearance. This latter element is behind the training metaphor in 11:3-4.

With the affirmation that YHWH *loved ('āhab),* and thus called, Israel, Hosea employs a term at the root of divine discretion and character.[20] In this the prophet is like Deuteronomy (7:6-8), which also bases YHWH's choice *(bāḥar)* of a small and insignificant Israel on divine love and commitment *(ḥāšaq, 'āhab).* In Deuteronomy there is also acknowledgment that the rescue from Egypt is based on YHWH's prior sworn oath to Israel's ancestors (to make of their descendants a people). Such an oath is not mentioned in 11:1; but mentioned or not, the promise simply moves the mystery of divine commitment further back in the narrative.[21]

Excursus: Israel and Sonship

In 11:1 Israel is described as a *youth (na'ar)* and called YHWH's *son (ben).* The former term can represent both youth and dependence/subservience, while the latter is an indication of family identity. The two nouns reinforce each other with respect to Israel's relationship to YHWH. The employment of familial imagery for Israel is central in Hosea, but this is the only explicit reference in the book to Israel collectively as YHWH's "son."[22]

In fact, Exod. 4:22-23 is the only other passage in the OT where Israel is explicitly described in divine speech as *my son.* In 4:22 Israel is also described as YHWH's "firstborn" *(běkōr).*[23] These two verses come in the context of the larger motif of sonship in chs. 1–13, where Israel's sons are killed (1:15-22), Egypt's firstborn sons are killed (4:23; 11:4-7; 12:29-32), and YHWH is honored with the substi-

19. See appendix 7, "Terms for Election in Hosea."

20. See appendix 4, "Love in the Prophecy of Hosea."

21. Hosea certainly knows some traditions about Israel's ancestors, as evidenced by his presentation of Jacob in 12:2-4, 12 (MT 3-5, 13). In 1:10 the description of future Israel like the "sand of the sea" may reflect the ancestral promise of increased descendants (Gen. 22:17).

22. In Hos. 1 "Jezreel" and "Lo-ammi" (Not My People) are male children that represent Israel.

23. There are close parallels in Jeremiah regarding the language of sonship, just as there are in the marriage metaphor. Ephraim is YHWH's "firstborn" in 31:9 and in a divine speech in 31:20 "a precious son to me *(bēn yaqqîr lî)."*

tute sacrifice for that which opens the womb (13:2, 11-15). The firstborn son carries the family tradition, bears a special responsibility to maintain it, and is thus granted a double portion of the family inheritance (Deut. 21:17). Hosea may draw on the traditions of Exod. 4, or vice versa. Of the two options, the former is more likely, given the numerous connections elsewhere between Hosea and the narrative portions of Exodus. Yet another option is that both texts draw on prior traditions, but are independent of each other. Whatever his narrative sources, Hosea almost certainly conveys the confession of Israel as YHWH's son out of them rather than inventing it.

There are other places in the OT where the people of Israel, Ephraim, or Judah are described as YHWH's children *(bānîm)*. There are even references to them as "sons and daughters." Some examples are as follows:

1. "son" (Ephraim)	Jer. 31:20
2. "children" *(bānîm)*	Hos. 11:10; Deut. 14:1; 32:5; Isa. 1:2; 30:1, 9; 45:11; 63:8; Jer. 3:14, 19, 22
3. "sons" and "daughters" *(bānîm, bānōt)*[24]	Deut. 32:19; Isa. 43:6

The Davidic monarch in Jerusalem is also understood as YHWH's adopted son and vice-regent. The *locus classicus* for this understanding is 2 Sam. 7:13-14, where YHWH confirms David's descendant on the Jerusalem throne and declares that the two will be "father and son" (cf. Ps. 2:6-7; Isa. 9:6-7 [MT 5-6]). The filial metaphor is part of the larger ancient Near Eastern world, where divine procreation is sometimes assumed in designating someone as the son of a deity. This is not the case in Israel. The procreation language in a text like Ps. 2:7 is metaphorical and apparently associated with coronation rather than birth. As a collective metaphor, Israel's sonship almost certainly assumes adoption as the means by which Israel became "family" when called from Egypt.[25] Israel's metaphorical adoption by YHWH is parallel with the metaphorical marriage to YHWH. Since YHWH is the cosmic king, Israel's adoptive sonship may carry with it a democratizing element regarding royal status. The people collectively have it. Royal imagery would also undergird the privilege of "firstborn status."[26]

This imagery of Israel's sonship is adapted in the NT to portray Christians (Rom. 8:14-39).[27] Collectively they are "sons/children of God" (8:14, 16, 19, 21).

---

24. In Hos. 1 Lo-ruhamah (No Mercy) is a daughter of Hosea and Gomer who represents Israel.

25. Melnyk, "When Israel Was a Child," pp. 245-59.

26. In Ps. 89:27 (MT 28) the Davidic king is metaphorically YHWH's "firstborn" *(bĕkôr)* and thus preeminent over other kings of the earth. See also the collection of oracles from Neo-Assyria regarding the king as child and protege of the deity in Nissinen, *Prophetie Redaktion,* pp. 280-94.

27. The Greek term for "sonship/adoption as sons" and thus the status of "heirs" is *huiothesias,* used in Rom. 8:15 for Christians and 9:4 (in reference to the privilege of Israel). Cf. Gal. 3:26; 4:5; and Trevor J. Burke, *Adopted into God's Family: Exploring a Pauline Metaphor* (Downers Grove, IL: InterVarsity Press, 2006).

Their ingrafting into Christ by the Spirit results in their "adoption" (8:15, 23) and a status as "heirs" of God and "joint heirs" with Christ (8:17).

Matthew's Gospel cites Hos. 11:1 to explain the significance of Jesus' descent to and subsequent departure from Egypt (2:15). More particularly, the author cites the reference in Hosea to say that Jesus' return to Nazareth from Egypt "fulfills" the prophecy of Hos. 11:1.[28] The reference to God's son being called from Egypt in 11:1 would not have conveyed this sense to Hosea's own generation. Matthew's application of Hos. 11:1, therefore, is best understood as an example of typology, which portrays a fundamental historical correspondence between two entities. In this case the two entities are Israel as God's Son and Jesus as God's Son, with Jesus as the recapitulation of Israel in dramatic, salvific mode. Hosea himself employs typological readings of his base texts in applying the historical significance of Israel's past to its then present time. The terminology of "fulfillment" used by Matthew in 2:15 can be understood essentially as an extension of that hermeneutic, portraying a different significance for 11:1 than that intended by Hosea for his generation, but demonstrating a coherence to divine activity in the historical process. Matthew seeks to show that eschatological and messianic aspects of Israelite history are revealed in God's Son Jesus and that this is in accord with Scripture and God's prior activity in and through his corporate son Israel.[29]

2 YHWH's *calling* of Israel in vv. 1-2 was not simply a one-time event, even though it is founded on the historical redemption from Egypt. The term also characterizes an ongoing relationship between Deity and people, not simply the moment of choosing and acquisition. YHWH continued to call, i.e., to claim and to instruct, Israel. No precise moment is indicated in this historical summary for a beginning to Israel's waywardness, but clearly Hosea's generation is not the first to engage in disobedience. The phenomena of calling and subsequent disobedience are likely telescoped in Hosea's brief rendition of past generations leading up to the present crisis. Seen from the angle of v. 2, the divine claim upon Israel led almost immediately to Israel's defection, although the metaphor of marriage in the wilderness (see above) assumes at least positive beginnings to the relationship. As with the presentation of Gomer and the children in chs. 1–2, the purpose of v. 2 is to demonstrate failure on Israel's part to respond faithfully to YHWH. The canonical narrative of the wilderness events includes more than one instance of Israel's early disobedience (e.g., the golden calf episode in Exod. 32 and the dalliance with Moabite women and the Baal of Peor in Num. 25). A lineal unfold-

28. The citation of Hos. 11:1 in Greek in Matt. 2:15 follows more closely the Hebrew text than the LXX.

29. For further discussion see John H. Sailhamer, "Hosea 11:1 and Matthew 2:15"; and a response by Dan McCartney and Peter Enns, "Matthew and Hosea: A Response to John Sailhamer," *WTJ* 63 (2001) 87-96, 97-105, respectively.

ing of the national narrative is subsumed under the metaphor of sonship and rebellion, and there is nothing pro or con in its imagery to compare to an initial honeymoon period as depicted in the marriage metaphor. Israel's defection from YHWH in the parent-child metaphor may depict the people along the lines of an incorrigible son destined for corporate judgment.[30]

The verb *went (hālak)* is a common term for moving in a particular direction and can represent human activity. Israel *went from before* YHWH.[31] Movement for God's son here reflects motive and deed. Israel's defection is a conscious choice and results in actions deplored by YHWH.

Verse 2b has two parallel phrases to describe the waywardness of Israel. They *offer sacrifice to the Baals* and *burn incense to idols.* This description functions as a summary statement of Israel's defection, defining ways in which Israel moved away from YHWH. The verbal pair *sacrifice (zābaḥ)/ burn incense* or "offer in smoke" (Piel of *qāṭar*) also occurs in 4:13. The verb *qāṭar* in the Hiphil occurs in 2:13 (MT 15) in reference to the Baal deities. The terminology of sacrifice in Hosea is primarily used in descriptions of illegitimate worship, as here in v. 2, but the terms themselves do not, by definition, indicate forbidden cultic acts. As noted above, the primary criticism of "Gomer," that she had sacrificed to the Baals (2:13 [MT 15]), is here directed against Israel. Just as Gomer committed treachery against her spouse, so Israel violated its sonship through similar activities. Thus, whether it is treachery against marriage and covenant or rebellion against rescue and adoption, Israel is a serial offender against YHWH.

The term *Baals* is probably to be interpreted broadly as a reference to other deities.[32] The parallel term in v. 2, *idols* (sing. *pāsîl*), indicates a crafted material form. Such images belonging to the non-Israelite inhabitants of the land are of particular concern to Deuteronomy (7:5, 25; 12:3). If the plural term *Baals* is to be limited to a particular class of deities, which is possible but less likely than a broader usage, then the corresponding *idols* may also refer more particularly to calf images.[33] Hosea does not use this term for *idols* elsewhere, although he makes several other references to images for deities (4:17; 8:4; 13:2; 14:3, 8 [MT 4, 9]).

3   Hosea's presentation of divine speech has YHWH contrast his ef-

---

30. Wolff, *Hosea,* p. 194, suggests that Hosea's description of Israel's continuing waywardness in vv. 2-7 is modeled on the father's accusations of an incorrigible son in Deut. 21:18-21. So also Sweeney, *Twelve Prophets,* p. 113.

31. In 1:2 the land was characterized as committing harlotry "against" *('aḥēr)* YHWH. In 2:13 (MT 15) Gomer "goes after" *(hālak + 'aḥēr)* her lovers.

32. See appendix 1, "Baal in Hosea." Andersen and Freedman, *Hosea,* p. 578, do not put much stock in the plural form in v. 2, and raise the question whether a reference to Baal Hadad or to Baal of Peor is in the prophet's mind.

33. Rudolph, *Hosea,* p. 213, thinks of the idols as "calf figures" *(Stierbildern).*

forts with those of defecting Israel, which remained the recipient of his care. The *Yet* of v. 3a could also be rendered "But." Like any good parent, YHWH sought to keep Israel on the right path in spite of the waywardness depicted in v. 2. The difficulties of the second clause of the MT preclude certainty of interpretation, but the proposed rendering assumes the continuation of the parental metaphor of guidance and comfort. Possibly the verbal imagery of "walking as guidance" more specifically interprets YHWH's providential care of youthful Israel in the wilderness.[34] This would fit the context as elaboration on the claim that YHWH had called them "from Egypt" in v. 1. Reference to YHWH's parental *arms (zĕrôaʿōt)* evokes a rich assembly of images regarding YHWH's strong or outstretched arm (cf. Exod. 15:16; Deut. 4:34; 11:2) that also interpret the preservation of Israel from Egypt and the entrance into the promised land.

The tasks of instruction and nurture are described metaphorically as divine *healing (rāpāʾ)*. This is one of five uses of the term in Hosea (5:13; 6:1; 7:1; 14:4 [MT 5]). In the first two instances, the physical aspect of healing is primary. In the third and fourth, YHWH's intended healing seems to apply to the alienated state of relations between himself and Israel. This usage is in view here in 11:3.[35] The shift of names from Israel in v. 1 to *Ephraim* in v. 3 may have the benefit of a play between *ʾeprayim* and *rāpāʾ*. The two names for the people are used synonymously in vv. 1-3, but Ephraim allows for a memorable connection with the term for healing. Hearers, furthermore, may discern yet another reflection/allusion of the exodus and wandering narrative in this reference. In Exod. 15:26 YHWH declares that if Israel heeds his instructions, none of the afflicting diseases of Egypt will be put on them, for "I, YHWH, am your healer."[36]

4 Interpreters have split over the training metaphor of v. 4. Some have seen a change from the parental imagery to a complementary one of farming and the training of animals.[37] That is the interpretive conclusion of-

---

34. So Andersen and Freedman, *Hosea,* p. 579.

35. See the discussion in D. F. O'Kennedy, "Healing as/or Forgiveness? The Use of the Term רפא in the Book of Hosea," *OTE* 14 (2001) 458-74; and Seong-Hyuk Hong, *The Metaphor of Illness and Healing in Hosea and Its Significance in the Socio-Economic Context of Eighth-Century Israel and Judah* (Studies in Biblical Literature 95; New York: Peter Lang, 2006).

36. Cf. Deut. 32:39, where YHWH is self-defined as a healer, in the context of a song with a number of connections to Hosea's prophecy. See appendix 2, "The Song of Moses and Hosea."

37. Good summaries of the interpretational issues with bibliographic references can be found in Eidevall, *Grapes in the Desert,* pp. 172-74, who opts for the farming/animal husbandry metaphor in v. 4; and in Kakkanattu, *God's Enduring Love,* pp. 57-63, who finds a consistent parental metaphor in 11:3-4. It is particularly interesting to compare the

fered here. The shift in imagery is consistent with the MT, which vocalizes the crucial lexeme *'l* as *'ōl,* "yoke," and apparently has Israel in the role of a plow animal and YHWH compared to those who lift a yoke (probably with harness) from the animal. The other option, which employs a slight emendation of the term to *'ūl,* "infant," also requires the image of lifting a child to the face. This option does keep the parental metaphor consistent, although its popularity among interpreters is a modern phenomenon. The choice between the two options is difficult, with interpreters lined up to support either option. In favor of the animal husbandry image is the MT, along with the Latin and Syriac versions. In addition, the change in imagery is more a change in semantic field (from parent to animal husbandry) than in basic metaphor, which is that of care and training in the broader household. The animal husbandry metaphor is not inconsistent with, or out of place in, the context. In favor of the parental metaphor is first and foremost a consistency with the designation of Israel as "son" in v. 1. The plausible emendation from "yoke" to "child," while it has no support among the early versions, is essentially a change in vocalization.

There are three reasons finally that favor the MT and the resulting animal husbandry imagery. The first is the limited parallels with Isa. 30:28, which refers to "a harness on the jaws of the people" *('al lĕḥāyê 'ammîm),* and Hos. 10:11, where Ephraim is referred to as a trained heifer. The former text shows the employment of similar vocabulary and imagery applied to God's people, albeit in a mode of judgment rather than nurture, and the latter text provides a metaphor of Ephraim as a trained plow animal as a positive image. The second reason is the awkward parallel between YHWH and *those who lift (mĕrîmê,* Hiphil pl. participle) an infant, if the imagery is parental. One would expect a parallel in the singular, perhaps even a reference to a father or mother embracing an infant, and the imagery of embracing to the jaws/face is not otherwise attested in Hebrew. Given the animal husbandry imagery *(yoke),* the comparison with those who care for an animal is more straightforward. The third reason follows from the first two: cords and bonds are also better understood as devices for animals, even when used metaphorically for people.

The initial phrase in v. 4, *human cords,* does not occur elsewhere in the OT. Its interpretation is best understood in comparison with the corresponding phrase *bonds of love* and is thus a further illustration of divine love for Ephraim/Israel. YHWH loved Israel as a youth and his constraining and training activities were on behalf of the people's education and upbringing.

---

analysis of Seifert, *Metaphorisches Reden,* pp. 183-98, with that of Eidevall, since the primary concern of both is the identification and explication of the metaphorical field in 11:1-7. Seifert, who opts for "infant" in v. 4, regards the parental imagery as stronger.

The cords or bonds used in training are *drawn (māšak)* by YHWH. While such language fits the tasks of animal husbandry, assisting animals to fulfill their appointed tasks, it is also used for the divine-human relationship. Perhaps the closest parallel to v. 4 is the affirmation in Jer. 31:3, where YHWH says to either Israel or Jeremiah himself:[38] "With an everlasting love I have loved you; therefore, I have drawn *(māšak)* you with loving-kindness *(ḥesed)*." As in many texts, Jeremiah is here an interpreter of Hosea. In 31:3 readers encounter the same combination of *love* and *drawing* as found in Hos. 11:4, and in a similar context of divine action toward a human figure. Whether the "you" (masc. sing.) in 31:3 indicates Israel or the prophet himself, YHWH's redemptive work in history is set forth in 31:1-3 as a restoration of the covenant relationship[39] with Israel and the rebuilding of the nation in 31:4-6. In Hos. 11:4 the emphasis appears to be on the efforts expended by YHWH in nurturing his people.

Does the phrase *human cords* give any indication of the actual means by which YHWH trained and cared for Israel? More specifically, the question concerns the relationship between the construct noun *cords* and the noun *human ('ādām)*. Does *'ādām* mean human in the sense of "humane," and function as an adjective to define the cords? Another possibility is that *'ādām* defines the cords; or put another way, the "cords" employed by YHWH to guide Israel were human beings. In light of other references in the book, such people would likely be prophets (6:5; 12:10 [MT 11]), with Moses numbered among them (12:13 [MT 14]).[40] This makes good sense of scattered references elsewhere to prophets in Hosea and likely undergirds Hosea's own conception of his prophetic task.[41]

The last two verbs of v. 4 are difficult to interpret for both grammatical and functional reasons. The term *'aṭ*, translated here as *stretched out*, appears to be a Hiphil imperfect first person singular form of *nāṭâ*. It may be a shortened form of the phrase to "incline an ear toward," i.e., to hear and to take notice of someone. In context the verb should be taken with the next verb, apparently a Hiphil imperfect first person singular form of *'ākal* ("to feed"). The basic sense would be that YHWH responds and feeds his charge,

38. Jer. 31:3a in Hebrew has "YHWH appeared to me . . . ," while the LXX, which is followed by the majority of modern translations, has "the Lord appeared to him. . . ." The "him" has an obvious antecedent in Israel in v. 2.

39. "I will be the God of all the clans of Israel and they shall be my people" (31:1). See the introduction, section IV.C, "Hosea's Theology: Covenant and Marriage."

40. Note the concluding phrase in 12:13 (MT 14): Israel was "kept/guarded" *(šāmar*, Niphal) by a prophet. The interpretation of "human cords" in this sense has been proposed by Zenger, "Durch Menschen," pp. 183-202.

41. See the introduction, section IV.A, "Hosea's Theology: Narrative and Community Identity," and the comments there about prophets and prophecy.

assuming from context that the actions are describing a relationship, not indicating future actions. One problem with this interpretation is that the verb "to feed" would typically have an explicit object. An option is to regard an object as implicit. Another is to follow the LXX, which has "him."[42] This latter option, however, has implications for the rendering of v. 5 (see below).

In summary, v. 4 completes the portrayal of YHWH's love and calling of Israel begun in 11:1, along with the subsequent sketch of filial failure against the background of divine guidance and care. The training metaphor serves the purpose of defining Israel as prepared from an early stage in the household to serve YHWH faithfully. The portrait underscores the personal, parental commitment of YHWH to them and thus the depth of their familial betrayal. YHWH's portrayal of the people continues on in what follows, but the subject matter for the moment turns to the impending consequences of Israel's failure.

5 My rendering of v. 5 follows the MT, although a number of interpreters have opted for alternatives. The problem, briefly stated, is the initial *lō'* of the sentence. As noted above, some have proposed to read *lō'*, a negating particle, as the homonym *lô* ("him") and to join it with the previous sentence. This would result in the claim in v. 5 that Israel would be returning to Egypt (so NRSV). There is partial precedent for this option in the rendering of vv. 4-5 in the LXX, and it comports with statements elsewhere in the book that Israel would, metaphorically or literally, return to Egypt (e.g., 8:13; 9:3). Another possibility for the beginning of v. 5 is to read Heb. *lō'* as an asseverative ("indeed"), reinforcing the statements elsewhere that Israel would return to Egypt.[43]

If one follows the MT, then one of three claims is likely being made. One option is to see the claimed "return to Egypt" elsewhere in Hosea as a metaphor for slavery or the loss of autonomy, with Assyria as the actual location of upcoming exile. The second is to see this statement as originating at a time when the Israelite king Hoshea had appealed to Egypt for help (2 Kgs. 17:4). His request resulted in a decisive response by Shalmaneser V. A third possibility is to see the whole verse as a rhetorical question: "Will they not return to Egypt and will not Assyria rule over them because they refuse to repent?" (so NIV). Such a rendering also allows for consistency with other statements in Hosea about Israel returning to Egypt.

---

42. LXX has the dative form of *autos* ("him" or "that one") following the verb *dynamai* ("to have power, to prevail"). Apparently the translator read Heb. *'wkyl* as first person of *yākal*. The dative of *autos* would represent Heb. *lô*. The first word of 11:5 in Hebrew is a homonym, *lō'*, which some commentators think is a mishearing of *lô*. So Harper, *Hosea*, p. 364; and Wolff, *Hosea*, p. 191.

43. So Andersen and Freedman, *Hosea*, pp. 583-84.

However one assesses Israel's status with Egypt, an important wordplay is at work in v. 5. The verb *šûb* can mean both "return" and "repent," and it is used twice in this verse. Israel's dealings with Egypt and Assyria are such that they have refused *to return to YHWH,* a cardinal error in Hosea's judgment.[44] Indeed, Israel's failure to return to YHWH is the essential point of v. 5, however the first part of the verse is rendered. The following verse, then, continues this train of thought, indicating that military defeat, and not simply exile, will be the result of Assyria becoming Israel's king. Furthermore, in v. 7 the noun *mĕšûbâ* ("turning one"; from *šûb*) is used to describe Israel as a people intent on "turning from" YHWH.

6 Israel's defection from YHWH and its schemes in the international arena will result in military action against the nation. Verse 6 is another twist on a common Hosean theme, in this instance employing the imagery of a spinning or *whirling* sword among Israel's cities. That indeed would be fierce fighting. The deadly sword work is indicated by the common verb *'ākal, consume* (lit. "eat"). A sword is not the instrument to break the bars of a gate nor does it literally eat them. Warfare and siege, however, which the military sword represents, are the primary powers at work.

Such sentiments might come from the cusp of the Assyrian invasion under Tiglath-pileser III in 734-732 or somewhat later during the reign of Hoshea. If from Hoshea's reign, then this message would be particularly chilling. Hoshea had been put on the throne by the Assyrians, perhaps working in concert with disaffected members of the Israelite state. He replaced Pekah, who was an opponent of the Assyrians, and in whose reign Tiglath-pileser III had invaded Israel and taken some two-thirds of the country as his own. Hoshea's appointment had been a way to conclude the hostilities and to bring the city of Samaria under Assyrian control. Now the rump state of Israel, technically a vassal of Assyria, would face the wrath of Assyria again. If, on the other hand, this prophecy should date a decade or so earlier, on the eve of Tiglath-pileser's campaign in the region, then it underscores the difficulties brought on by Israel's folly.

7 YHWH charges his people with being *twisted.* Two terms are employed to make this point. The first is the passive participle of *tālā'* ("to hang"). Although it is plural, it may still modify the singular noun "people." YHWH's people are "hung up" in the schemes noted in the previous verse. The second is a noun *mĕšûbâ,* formed from *šûb,* which indicates Israel's *turning away from* YHWH. It is the second part of the verse, however, that is obscure and difficult to interpret in light of this charge against Israel. Some interpreters have simply given up on the possibility of translating it.[45] An un-

---

44. See the excursus at 6:1 on "Return to YHWH."
45. See Eidevall, *Grapes in the Desert,* p. 177, for references.

named plural subject *(they) call him* (Israel apparently). These heralds may be prophets, but are they good or bad? Earlier in the chapter YHWH had lamented that the more he had called Israel, the more they had departed from him and his expressed will (11:2). The means by which he had drawn and nurtured Israel (v. 4) likely included prophets. Here the indefinite "they" (= prophets) are in accord with YHWH's will, intending to point the people to the Most High, a possible rendering of *'al,* which is more likely, however, to be a corrupted form of *'elyôn.* Because of Israel's failure, he (YHWH) will not raise the people up.

In facing difficulties such as v. 7, it is important to place the emphasis on what can be secured from the immediate context, and not to make fundamental claims on the basis of the obscure. The context is that of Israel's defection from YHWH in spite of his actions on the people's behalf. That is the primary subject of the immediately preceding verses, and it is still on YHWH's mind in the soliloquy that follows.

8   The poetry of v. 8 has six clauses, structured in three consecutive pairs (bicola) of parallel expressions. The first two pairs are questions, but they are not rhetorical questions in the modern sense of that term. YHWH is not asking questions with expected or obvious answers, but making a statement in interrogative (or even exclamatory) form. That is one of the gifts of the prophet's presentation — the freedom in which YHWH declares his resolve to exercise compassion in spite of the expected and deserved judgment. In formal terms v. 8 is a soliloquy. Hearers and readers are invited to listen to a presentation. In metaphorical terms, YHWH is an anguished parent, asking profound questions of himself, with the future of his people at stake. YHWH has historical experience in handing out punishment to the disobedient, but the matter of deserved punishment is overwhelmed by commitment to restoring the repeatedly offending child, whom we might call a "prodigal son."[46]

YHWH's self-directed questions receive a personal reply (from the heart), but as noted above, the reply is intended for the hearer and reader. To paraphrase another writer (1 Cor. 10:11), these things are written for Israel's instruction. The way YHWH's parental anguish is presented is also a parade example of Hosea's theological approach. He combines historical analogy and metaphor, which for him are primarily ways of thinking. The historical analogy, furthermore, illustrates the kind of material in the narrative of God's historical acts known to Hosea. When it comes to YHWH, however, analogical comparison is at best partial. In the final analysis YHWH's assertion to be God (and not limited to human choices) is both an explanation and a mystery proceeding from divine discretion and freedom.

The historical analogy offered in v. 8 is that of Israel's historical situa-

46. So also Mays, *Hosea,* p. 156.

287

tion during Hosea's day compared to Admah and Zeboiim, two towns near Sodom and Gomorrah, that had previously acted in concert with their better-known neighbors (Gen. 10:19; 14:2, 8; Deut. 29:23 [MT 22]) and were destroyed. In the book of Genesis, it is Sodom and Gomorrah who are explicitly destroyed by God because of their wickedness (18:20–19:25), and they are employed as examples of wickedness by other prophets (Amos 4:11; Isa. 1:9-10; 13:19; Jer. 23:14). In addition a narrator notes that the district around the cities was also destroyed (Gen. 19:25, 28), but no other cities are named. Thus Hosea's brief allusion to past judgment does not employ the city names used in Gen. 18–19 and in the prophetic tradition, even though it is virtually certain that all refer to the same cataclysmic event(s). Apparently the narrative known to Hosea about this act of divine judgment is similar to that drawn upon by the compiler(s) of Deuteronomy, who indicates that Admah and Zeboiim were destroyed along with Sodom and Gomorrah. In an elaboration on the implementation of curses for breach of covenant, it is stated in Deuteronomy: "Its [Israel's] land is brimstone and salt, a burned territory, not sown and nothing growing in it, like the overthrow *(mahpēkâ)*[47] of Sodom and Gomorrah, Admah and Zeboiim, which YHWH overthrew *(hāpak)* in his anger and wrath" (29:23 [MT 22]). In naming the four cities, the better remembered Sodom and Gomorrah are listed first (cf. 32:32). Hosea alone of the biblical writers names only Admah and Zeboiim when referring to divine judgment on the ancient cities on the plain.

In summary, there are two types of connection between Hos. 11:8 and the references in Genesis and Deuteronomy regarding the destruction of these ancient cities. The connections (common elements) are as follows:

1. Admah and Zeboiim occur together five times in the OT. In four of the five occurrences they are mentioned in conjunction with Sodom and Gomorrah. The fifth occurrence is in Hos. 11:8, where the language assumes that some form of divine judgment fell upon Admah and Zeboiim, as does the description in Deut. 29:23 (MT 22).
2. Genesis 19:25, 29, and Deut. 29:23 (MT 22) use various inflected forms of the root *hpk* to describe the overthrow of the sinful cities (though only the last text names the cities). Significantly, Hos. 11:8 also uses the verb *hāpak* to describe YHWH's change of heart from

---

47. The noun *mahpēkâ* is derived from the verb *hāpak* ("to turn over"). A related form of the noun and the verb are used in Gen. 19:25 and 29 to describe the overthrow of Sodom and Gomorrah. Both noun and verb forms are used to describe the overthrow of Gomorrah and/or Sodom in Amos 4:11; Isa. 13:19; Jer. 49:18; 50:40; Lam. 4:6. The verb is also used in Hos. 11:8 to describe the "overthrow" of YHWH's heart in considering the fate of sinful Israel.

anger to compassion for wayward Israel, not to describe the fate of Admah and Zeboiim. Almost certainly the verb is chosen in v. 8 because it is part of the judgment tradition associated with Admah and Zeboiim.

The depiction of YHWH in v. 8 is anthropomorphic, and more particularly anthropopathic. Not only is the verb *hāpak* an integral part of the judgment tradition on the four ancient cities, it is also part of a recognized metaphor to describe emotional change and/or change of mind (Exod. 14:5; Ps. 105:25).[48] Regarding Saul (1 Sam. 10:9), it is reported that in departing from Samuel, God "gave him another heart" *(hāpak + lēb 'aḥēr)*. Personified Jerusalem describes herself as having an "upset" or "overthrown heart within me" *(hāpak* [Niphal] + *lēb bĕqirbî)* at the consequences of her rebellion against YHWH (Lam. 1:20).[49]

YHWH's "change of heart" also means that his *compassions* arise within him. The root *nḥm* has a range of meanings, but the plural noun *niḥûmîm* used here indicates comfort and compassion (cf. Isa. 57:18; Zech. 1:13). Given the poetic structure of Hos. 11:8, with its three pair of clauses, we would do well not to read the last pair in a linear fashion, as if a dramatic change of heart comes first, followed by the rise of compassion. One could just as easily say that the rise of compassion in YHWH led to his change of heart (mind). The two matters reinforce each other. They will result, furthermore, in YHWH's actions on behalf of Israel.

9 Verse 9 continues the evocative self-expression of YHWH in v. 8. It is structured in five clauses, as indicated by the punctuation of the translation. The first and second are a poetic pair, and the third and fourth are also poetic parallels. The last clause is a reinforcing conclusion to the first bicolon that YHWH will not execute his anger or destroy Ephraim.[50]

---

48. The phrase may describe the "conversion" of a person's mind and commitments according to the analysis of D. Ritschl, "God's Conversion: An Exposition of Hosea 11," *Int* 15 (1961) 286-303.

49. The phrase in Hos. 11:8 differs from that in Lam. 1:20 only in the preposition employed. Zion's heart is overthrown "within" *(qereb)* her, while YHWH's is overthrown "upon" or even "against" *('al)* himself. Perhaps there is no discernible difference in meaning, given that these are the only two close examples, but Wolff, *Hosea,* p. 201, sees the preposition in v. 8 having a hostile sense. This would indicate God in self-struggle as his compassion wins out.

50. If one follows the MT ("I will not come into a city") instead of the emendation in the proposed translation, then the interpretation of Garrett, *Hosea,* pp. 228-29, is intriguing. He suggests that the account of overthrowing the wicked cities of Admah and Zeboiim is in mind, so that in turning from his wrath, YHWH will not enter a city for judgment as was done previously.

That God will not carry out his anger presupposes that anger is something that he has and with which he must come to grips. This is daring anthropopathism, although consistent with the thrust of 11:1-8 that YHWH must engage a history of Israel's faithlessness. His resolve not to make an end of Israel proceeds from the description of YHWH in v. 8 as having a change of heart (mind) and a corresponding rise of compassion to define his assessment of the people. YHWH will not, therefore, carry out a judgment that from a human point of view is expected and deemed necessary.[51] He is divine, not human, and thus free to act in ways that transcend human limitation (and also human points of view).[52]

The parallel phrase for *I am God, not mortal,* is: *in your midst (is) the Holy One.* God's holiness sets him apart from creation and his people, and is an attribute that accrues to deity. In contrast, holy places and people have only a derivative holiness (Lev. 19:2), and Israel collectively has failed miserably to be the kingdom of priests and holy nation that the Sinai covenant intended for them. The paired clauses are remarkable in their respective defining of YHWH and Israel. They can be seen as follows:

Divine = YHWH   Human = Israel
Holy = YHWH   Midst = Israel

On the one hand, YHWH is not human and Israel is not divine. In Hosea's assessment Israel is not only finite, but also fallible and indeed culpable before YHWH. Moreover, a constituent part of YHWH's otherness, his deity, is holiness, a characteristic that separates him from Israel (cf. Isa. 6:1-5). On the other hand, YHWH is the holy one in the *midst* of Israel. His holiness is not an aloofness, for even in their recalcitrance Israel is YHWH's people and he is their God. In his holiness he cannot condone Israel's rebellious failures, but neither does he opt to end the dilemma by simply handing out a corporate death sentence. Thus the statement that YHWH is the *Holy One* in Israel's midst reinforces not only that he is divine but that even in his holiness there is no permanent divorce, no final judgment upon the rebellious son, and no covenant curse that is irreversible from the divine side.

The fifth and last clause of v. 9 is somewhat obscured by not having a corresponding clause for reinforcement, and by its odd last word. Its intent,

---

51. Andersen and Freedman, *Hosea,* pp. 589-90, conclude that YHWH keeps his anger, and they render the three negative particles *(lō')* in v. 9 as asseveratives. Thus YHWH "will indeed carry out his anger and turn to destroy Ephraim. . . ." They note that this decision about how to understand *lō'* cannot be made on the basis of grammatical analysis, but on context. As I have tried to indicate, however, the context is not in their favor. Subsequent interpreters of 11:9 have not followed their suggestion.

52. See the excursus below, "Divine, Not Human."

however, is relatively certain. It reinforces the previous two pairs of clauses and confirms the significance of the historical moment that YHWH will not carry out the fullness of his anger.

Excursus: Divine, Not Human

In 11:9 YHWH declares himself to be God *('ēl)* and not human *('îš)*. It is made in the context of the claim that judgment upon Israel will not be fully carried out, even though the people are guilty. In human terms, so the logic runs, the offended party would be intent on carrying out punishment and protecting the larger community. Indeed, the inevitableness of this logic is what drives even the parents of a dangerously incorrigible son to bring him to the elders of a city for execution, so that evil may be purged from Israel's midst (Deut. 21:18-21).

Thus the claim of "divine, not human" is in the service of the freedom of God. It is not a defense of mere whimsy, but an affirmation of the mystery of divine integrity in action. From the side of Israel, YHWH's forgiveness cannot be presumed upon, manipulated, or coerced. From YHWH's side, however, it can be granted. This is the case whether YHWH is portrayed in the role of offended husband or parent or covenant Lord. While there is no provision for healing a broken marriage, a violated family, or ruptured covenant from the side of the offenders, nothing prevents YHWH from renewing a broken relationship. Renewal proceeds solely (if at all) from the side of the offended.

Perhaps the dilemma of 11:8-9, in which YHWH displays a self-struggle, is related to one of Hosea's base texts, namely, YHWH's self-definition as one "slow to anger and abundant in loving-kindness," but who will nonetheless judge the guilty (Exod. 34:6-7). YHWH's compassion prevails at this crucial moment and so he will not execute his fierce anger and bring the full weight of the covenant curses upon Israel. Even if this means that all can be forgiven, not all the consequences of Israel's failure have been mitigated. It is clearly the case elsewhere in Hosea, as it is in the self-definition of Exod. 34:7, that YHWH is committed to deal justly with iniquity. The severity of Israel's treatment at the hand of the Assyrians is understood to be judgment brought about by YHWH in the historical process. That is a primary reason that the book of Hosea is preserved: to explain the fall of Israel and Samaria. It is not, however, a death sentence. And that is also a reason why the book is preserved.

At other places in the OT the freedom of YHWH to act is rooted in his deity and is contrasted with human limitation or pretension. Here are four examples:

1. "Indeed, the eminence of Israel [= YHWH] will not lie or change his mind; for he is not a man *('ādām)* that he should change his mind"[53] (1 Sam. 15:29).

---

53. The verb is the Niphal of *nāḥam,* which means "to be sorry" and thus to change one's mind and respond to a matter. The declaration comes in the context of Samuel's declaration that God has torn the Israelite kingdom from Saul and will not be "changing his mind."

2. "God *('ēl)* is not mortal *('îš)* that he should deceive, nor human *(ben-'ādām)* that he should change his mind"[54] (Num. 23:19).
3. "You have said, 'I am a god *('ēl)* . . . but you are a man *('ādām)* and not divine *('ēl)*" (Ezek. 28:2).[55]
4. "The Egyptians are human *('ādām)* and not divine *('ēl);* their horses are flesh and not spirit *(rûaḥ)*" (Isa. 31:3).[56]

In light of the first two examples, it is important to note that YHWH is also described elsewhere as being grieved and changing his course of action, using the lexeme *nāḥam* (Gen. 6:6; Jonah 3:9; 4:2). This is a confirmation of divine freedom at work as well, depicted in anthropomorphic language, where YHWH acts in response to changed situations. His involvement in the life of his people cannot be characterized as either fickle (Num. 23:19) or detached and unresponsive. Both the affirmation of and the denial of a changed mind and course of actions serve the cause of divine freedom. YHWH is free to act on the basis of his integrity.[57]

Three of the four examples cited above use the generic term for deity *('ēl)*, contrasting "deity" with some aspect of humanity, just as in Hos. 11:9.[58] It has been suggested that the employment of *'ēl* in Hos. 11:9; Num. 23:19; and Ezek. 28:2 is influenced by traditions of the Canaanite high deity El, whom Hosea was particularly keen to identify with YHWH, over against the religious traditions at Bethel, which maintained that El was the deity who brought Israel from Egypt.[59] This fascinating proposal is speculative, particularly in reconstructing a Bethel liturgy, and does not account for the use of *'ēl* in a text like Isa. 31:3. It is better to see the use of *'ēl* there and in Hos. 11:9 and so on, simply as generic, a reference to deity. Perhaps the formulation in 11:9 follows the pattern of Exod. 34:6, where YHWH is *'ēl raḥûm wĕhannûn,* "God gracious and merciful." YHWH's integrity and freedom are grounded in his divinity, traits that humankind can recognize, and in the case of Hosea, anchor a future hope.

54. The verb is the Hithpael of *nāḥam,* which in this context bears the same meaning as the Niphal formulation in 1 Sam. 15:29. The declaration comes in Balaam's reply to Balak's request to curse the Israelites. According to Num. 23:16-17 YHWH instructed Balaam to describe him thusly.

55. The second half of 28:2 is repeated in 28:9. It is a critique of the pretentiousness of the Tyrian king and comes in the context of judgment announced against him by YHWH.

56. The parallelism has "deity" and "spirit" contrasted with "humanity" and "flesh." The statement comes in Isaiah's critique of those who would trust in the power of Egypt but not that of the Holy One of Israel (31:1).

57. See the discussion in R. W. L. Moberly, "'God Is Not a Human That He Should Repent'" (Numbers 23:19 and 1 Samuel 15:19)," in *God in the Fray: A Tribute to Walter Brueggemann,* ed. T. Linafelt & T. Beal (Minneapolis: Fortress, 1998), pp. 112-23.

58. See also Isa. 51:12, where God's comforting *(nāḥam,* Piel) of Zion is incomparably greater than men whom she fears, men who will die and are like grass.

59. R. Scott Chambers, "Who Is the Real El? A Reconstruction of the Prophet's Polemic in Hosea 12:5a," *CBQ* 68 (2006) 611-30.

10-11   Verses 10-11 follow upon the declaration of YHWH's resolve
not to make an end of Israel. They presuppose a dispersion of Israelites in
Egypt and Assyria — a foregone conclusion, but still in the future, according
to v. 5 and elsewhere. Verse 10, furthermore, refers to YHWH in the third
person, breaking the first-person speech that extends back to 11:1, although
v. 11 picks up the first-person speech again. It is thus likely that the place-
ment of these two verses is redactional, offering commentary on the result of
YHWH's change of heart and bringing a major subsection of the book to a
positive conclusion. The thought is Hosean, whether its actual formulation is
his or that of the editor who placed the verses here.[60]

The animal similes for YHWH and people are vintage Hosea. A leonine YHWH in 5:14 and 13:7 indicates judgment upon his people. In 11:10
YHWH roars as one who stakes out his territory and provides food for his
pride (cf. Amos 1:2). The verb *tremble (ḥārad)* is used twice, once in reference to children and once for a bird. It is typically used to express fear. The
people "trembled," for example, at the dramatic approach of YHWH at Mt.
Sinai (Exod. 19:16).[61] It is an appropriate response to the lion's roar, even if
one is a member of the pride. A similar verb is used in Hos. 3:5, where in the
future people will come "trembling" *(pāḥad)* to the Lord.[62]

As noted, vv. 10-11 presuppose a dispersion to Egypt and Assyria.
The Assyrians took Israelites into exile after Tiglath-pileser III's campaign in
733-732 and also in the years associated with the fall of Samaria and its aftermath. There was, furthermore, dislocation to go with the political upheaval.
Egypt, on the other hand, was a potential ally against the Assyrians (2 Kgs.
17:4) and a place to flee in response to the Assyrian invasions. The people
are depicted as children and as fowl. Neither represents much for the people
by way of strength, and both require care in treatment. The language of restoration is clear. They will be resettled in their homes.

Thus ends a second major section of the book. Hosea 11:1-11 paral-

---

60. A number of interpreters assign some (particularly v. 10) or all of 11:10-11 to
a later redactor. They differ on dating, some of whom will see a preexilic setting while
others a later, postmonarchical one in Judah. Macintosh, *Hosea,* pp. 466-71, provides a
good summary of views. For a postexilic setting for the two verses, see Yee, *Composition
and Tradition,* pp. 153-56. Macintosh is surely correct that Hosea must have given expression to the fate of Israel based on YHWH's declaration to refrain from complete destruction. Thus whatever later elements are included in vv. 10-11, they connect with Hosea's
own conclusion about restoration.

61. The term, as used here, may have overtones of response to a theophany. Cf.
Amos 1:2 and Eidevall, *Grapes in the Desert,* pp. 181-82.

62. It is worth noting that 3:5 concludes the first section of the book and that
11:10-11 concludes the second section of the book. Both contain a "trembling" approach
to YHWH after a period of discipline.

lels 3:1-5, the conclusion of the first section. Hosea 3:1-5 presupposes failure on the part of the adulterous woman; 11:1-11 that of the recalcitrant son. Discipline and restoration are depicted for woman and child. In neither case does the impetus for restoration come from the offenders, but from YHWH, who cannot let them go.

IV. GOD AND HIS PEOPLE (11:12–14:8 [MT 12:1–14:9])

The third and final major section of Hosea is 11:12–14:8 (MT 12:1–14:9). It begins with a programmatic statement in 11:12–12:2 (MT 12:1-3), not unlike 1:2 and 4:1-3, which begin the first and second sections, respectively. Chapters 12–13 contain texts critical of Israel, while employing traditions about Israel's past as part of the critique. This follows the pattern of ch. 11. The last chapter calls Israel to return to YHWH, who loves Israel freely.

A. YHWH'S CASE CONTINUED (11:12–12:14 [MT 12:1-15])

This section offers challenges to the reader. Not only are there problems in translation (e.g., 11:12b; 12:4a, 11),[1] but the two references to Judah (11:12; 12:2) and the separating of the allusive Jacob traditions (12:3-4, 12) add to the difficulties of continuity for readers. Nevertheless, a basic theme for the chapter is set by the programmatic charge in 11:12 that the house of Israel surrounds YHWH with deceit, a theme that one should keep in mind when dealing with grammatical or literary problems in it. One must deal with these, but they should not be allowed to divert matters unduly so that Hosea's critique is hindered. YHWH's case against his people comes in 12:2-14, where the chapter concludes with similar words about Ephraim's failures. The material in 12:2-14 does not have the formal properties of a court case, but more that of a didactic presentation, alternating between various descriptions of Jacob/Israel, past, present, and future (vv. 3-4, 7-8, 11-12, 14), and references to YHWH, past, present, and future (vv. 5-6, 9-10, 13). In his critique the prophet employs traditions about Jacob as a means to define and to instruct that ancestor's descendants (his namesake Israel!), along with references to YHWH's act in bringing them to the promised land (12:9, 13).[2] He

---

1. To avoid needless repetition, in this section only English versification will be generally given for references to Hos. 12.

2. Interpreters have debated whether the portrayal of Jacob in ch. 12 is positive (a role model) or negative (an example to avoid). Perhaps the better option is that Jacob is an

interprets the fate of Israel in his own day by recourse to the past. As v. 14 has it, Israel's future resides under the negative consequences of its deceit and bloodguilt. Its fate, therefore, appears more somber than that of its ancestor. The references to Judah in 11:12 and 12:2, whether redactional or not, show concern to interpret divine activity in relation to the full covenant community.

11:12 (12:1) *Ephraim surrounds me with deception; the house of Israel (surrounds me) with deceit. Judah roams with God, is faithful with the holy one(s).*[3]

12:1 (2) *Ephraim shepherds the wind and follows the east wind all day long. He multiplies lies and violence. They make a covenant with Assyria; they*[4] *carry oil to Egypt.*

2 (3) *YHWH also has a case against Judah; [. . .]*[5] *to punish Jacob according to his ways; he will repay him according to his deeds.*

3 (4) *In the womb he supplanted his brother; and in his maturity he strove with God.*

4 (5) *He struggled*[6] *with an angel and prevailed; he wept and sought his mercy. He found him at Bethel, and there spoke*[7] *with him.*[8]

5 (6) *Indeed,*[9] *YHWH God of hosts, YHWH is his memorial.*

---

ambiguous figure in Hosea's representation of him; so Eidevall, *Grapes in the Desert,* pp. 186-87. One can make a similar claim about him in the Genesis accounts; there he is a person with obvious flaws and negative consequences, yet someone with whom YHWH is engaged for transformative and redemptive purposes.

3. The Hebrew term is plural, *qĕdôšîm.* It could be a plural of majesty and a reference to God in the previous clause, so Macintosh, *Hosea,* pp. 473-74; or a reference to the holy people of God (LXX *laos hagios*), so Wolff, *Hosea,* p. 210.

4. The verb in the MT, *yûbāl,* is singular. On the basis of parallelism with the verb in the previous clause, the plural is expected. A number of interpreters have suggested that the initial *waw* of v. 2 is better taken as the plural ending of the verb *yābal* (see *BHS*).

5. The brackets represent the possibility that a parallel to the initial colon of the verse has been lost in transmission. See comments below.

6. Reading *wayyiśśar* (from *śrh*) for MT *wāyyāśar,* "he reigned" (from *śrr*). See the explanation in the commentary.

7. The last two verbs are imperfect in form. They interpret past events, however, and are either old narrative preterites or have an iterative function.

8. The last prepositional phrase (*'immānû*) is lit. "with us." The parallel with the suffix "him" on the verb "find" would suggest third person singular. It is possible that *'immānû* intends the third person singular (a contraction of *'immānēhû*). The LXX has *pros auton.* If Hosea alludes to traditions about Jacob celebrated at Bethel, the reading "us" may indicate the way that the ancestral stories were appropriated there: God blessed our ancestor Jacob and spoke through him to us.

9. The initial *waw* can serve as an emphatic marker, as well as link the naming of YHWH here with the Deity revealed to Jacob at Bethel.

6 (7) *But you should return with your God, observe loyalty and justice, wait for your God continually.*

7 (8) *A trader, in whose hands are false balances, he loves to oppress.*

8 (9) *And Ephraim has said, "Indeed, I have become rich, I have found wealth for myself; all my gain does not find iniquity in me that is sin."*

9 (10) *But I am YHWH your God from the land of Egypt; I will cause you to dwell in tents again, like the appointed days.*

10 (11) *I spoke to the prophets; indeed, I multiplied visions, and by the hand of the prophets I am providing comparisons.[10]*

11 (12) *If there is iniquity in Gilead, now they have become nothing. If[11] in Gilgal they sacrifice bulls,[12] now also[13] their altars are like piles of stones along the furrows of the field.*

12 (13) *Jacob fled to the land[14] of Aram, and Israel worked for a wife; indeed, for a wife he kept (flocks).*

13 (14) *And by a prophet YHWH brought Israel from Egypt, and by a prophet he was kept.*

14 (15) *Ephraim has provoked bitterly;[15] his Lord will leave his bloodguilt[16] upon him and bring back his reproach to him.*

11:12 (12:1)   Ephraim's *deception (kaḥaš)* repeats a term used elsewhere in the book (7:3; 9:2; 10:13), including the opening of the second section of the book in 4:2. The corresponding phrase in 11:12 is the house of Israel's *deceit (mirmâ)*, which also occurs elsewhere in 12:7. In the latter reference it describes a dishonest merchant whose scales are false, i.e., "deceitful." Its repetition in this context could be influenced by its association with Jacob. Isaac reports to Esau that Jacob had come in "deception" *(mirmâ)* and taken his

---

10. The Hebrew verb is *dāmâ* II in the Piel imperfect, meaning "to intend, to resemble, to liken" (cf. Isa. 40:25; 46:5). Another verb, *dāmâ* I ("to destroy"), is used by Hosea in 4:5 (Qal), 6; 10:7, 15 (Niphal). Some interpreters, therefore, think that *dāmâ* I should be read here. Cf. NRSV: "through the prophets I will bring destruction."

11. Reading the conditional particle *'im* from the first clause as a double-duty modifier; so also Macintosh, *Hosea,* p. 504.

12. The MT has a strange pointing for "bulls" (*šĕwārîm* for an expected *šôrîm*), but the animals are a perfectly logical term as the objects of sacrifice and there is no compelling reason to seek an emendation.

13. The particle *gam* serves as a reinforcing agent or to offer emphasis.

14. Lit. "the field" of Aram.

15. The Hebrew is a plural noun, *tamrûrîm,* "bitterness(es)."

16. The Hebrew is a plural noun, *dāmāyw,* lit. "his blood(s)," or better "his bloodshed."

blessing (Gen. 27:35). A third related term is that for *lies* or "lying" *(kāzāb)*, which is used in Hos. 12:1. These three set the tone for the larger context of the chapter, which sets out the nation's plight before YHWH, and they are interesting also to consider in light of the ancestor Jacob and the prophet's depiction of Israel's commercial identity in 12:7-8. Perhaps these negative characteristics describe Israel's efforts at diplomacy and treaty noted in the following verse, efforts that YHWH regards as false.

The speaker in 11:12 is not named, but it appears to be YHWH. One could make the case that the speaker is Hosea,[17] who is beset by the lies of his contemporaries; after all, the second half of the verse refers to God in the third person. It would be a stronger case if v. 12 is understood as a detached saying and placed here editorially. Otherwise, opposition to Hosea plays no role in the context, whereas Israel's deception of YHWH is a central matter at hand.

For two reasons the reference to *Judah* in v. 12b has raised questions. The first is that of context. What is the purpose of naming Judah in a context where the subject matter seems to be Ephraim or the house of Israel? The second is the difficulty of the text itself in describing Judah.[18] Interpreters have differed over the sense of Judah's description, finding it both negative (NIV) and positive (NRSV).[19] A negative sense could be implied from the description of Ephraim, based on poetic parallelism.[20] For those interpreters who see the description of Judah as positive, which is the more natural sense of the Hebrew text, most also believe v. 12b to be an example of Judean editing.[21] Once v. 12b is removed, 11:12–12:2 represents an earlier, consistent critique of YHWH's people Israel. Nevertheless, v. 12b recognizes that Judah was related differently to the Lord, perhaps reflecting that Judah did not fall as did Samaria, and that with Hezekiah Judean affairs were more in accord with prophetic sensibilities.

12:1 (2) No one can shepherd the wind. It is folly, for the wind can-

---

17. So Wolff, *Hosea*, p. 209.

18. The verb *rûd* ("roam") has the basic meaning of to "be free" (Gen. 27:40; Ps. 55:2 [MT 3]; Jer. 2:31), which can be construed either positively or negatively. The Niphal participle *ne'ĕmān*, which also describes Judah, has the primary sense of "faithful, reliable." This is the sense of the Niphal participle in Hos. 5:9.

19. See chart 2 for various renderings.

20. This is the conclusion of Rudolph, *Hosea*, p. 221, who also points to the critique of Judah in 12:2. He emends the text significantly, however, to produce a negative assessment of Judah. Andersen and Freedman, *Hosea*, pp. 601-3, understand the reference to the *qĕdôšîm* to whom Judah is loyal to be the Canaanite pantheon, making the description of Judah negative. So essentially Garrett, *Hosea*, p. 230, who translates: "Judah still wanders with deity and is faithful with holy gods."

21. Macintosh, *Hosea*, pp. 473-76, offers the complicated explanation that v. 12b was originally a criticism of Ephraim and the house of Israel, that a redactor added "Judah," and that it is unclear whether the redactor understood the text as negative or positive.

not be controlled or guided. That apparently is one point of the prophetic sarcasm in v. 1a.[22] It is just as stupid to follow the east wind, which all people in the eastern Mediterranean hope to avoid, since it comes off the desert as a hot and dry scourge. So much for the good sense of Ephraim! Modern proverbial sayings such as "she is playing with fire" or "he has a tiger by the tail" are intended, like Hosea's *shepherds the wind* (cf. 8:7), to indicate fruitless and potentially harmful activity. Indeed, "lies and violence" are the product of Ephraim's efforts, which are further identified with political engagements.

Israel's leaders are engaged in a *covenant (běrît)* with Assyria. The imperfect verb *yikrōtû, They make,* in v. 1 (MT 2) seems to indicate a current activity with immediate consequences. The book thus presents readers with two aspects of the term "covenant." On the one hand, it is used for a binding agreement in the realm of political and international relations.[23] Neo-Assyrian kings bound a number of vassals to themselves with treaties. From Israel's side their "binding" to Assyria is described as a covenant. On the other hand, the term represents Israel's relationship with YHWH, founded on election and deliverance from Egypt (12:13; 13:4), and guided by divine instruction (8:1). From Hosea's perspective, the exclusivity of the covenant instituted by YHWH precludes the making of a covenant with Assyria. This is not stated in so many words, but it is consistent with the claim that YHWH alone is Israel's savior (13:4). More to the point is the metaphor of covenant and marriage in chs. 1–3, a concept that also underlies the theology of chs. 4–14. A vassal treaty with Assyria would be a denial of YHWH's sovereignty over Israel in the same way that a wife's pursuit of "lovers" (8:8-9) is an affront to her husband and a violation of their marriage.

In a coordinated activity,[24] *oil* is also taken to Egypt. As a parallel phrase to covenant making, the activity is likely political as well. It may be one of the constituent acts in making a treaty, or it functions similarly as an inducement to Egypt for political support.[25] The type of oil is not otherwise defined, but it is likely olive oil, a staple product in the region and prized for its multiple uses. Hosea's criticism of entanglement with Assyria and Egypt essentially follows that in 7:11 and 8:8-10, including the themes of folly and incongruity of actions found there. One cannot tell, however, whether 12:1

---

22. Ecclesiastes repeatedly describes human pretentiousness or attempts at mastery of circumstances as "striving after wind" (e.g., 1:14; 2:11; 4:4).

23. For making a covenant *(kārat + běrît)* in the context of political relations, see 1 Sam. 11:1; 18:3; 2 Sam. 3:12-13; 1 Kgs. 5:12 (MT 26). See also the introduction, section IV.C, "Hosea's Theology: Covenant and Marriage."

24. The Hebrew syntax and poetic parallelism of 12:1b (MT 2b; *waw* prefixed before both clauses; imperfect verbs) indicates simultaneous or coordinated activity.

25. On the possible treaty connections, see D. J. McCarthy, "Hosea XII 2: Covenant by Oil," *VT* 14 (1964) 215-21.

comes from the same time as the harsh criticisms in chs. 7–8. Explicit involvement with Assyria, at least during Hosea's day, goes back years before the campaign of Tiglath-pileser III in 733-732, to the reign of Menahem and the receipt of tribute payment from him (738 B.C., if not earlier). Involvement continued in various ways until the fall of Samaria. Egypt's ties to Israel (and Judah) were the result of proximity and shared concerns, as well as Egypt's historic role in the affairs of Syria-Palestine. At a point in the reign of Hoshea (2 Kgs. 17:4), the Israelite king appealed to Egypt for aid as a counterweight to Assyrian pressure from Shalmaneser V (726-723 B.C.). And these are matters whose mention has survived in ancient sources. There may well have been others in the period 740-720 B.C. that have not survived in extant literature.

2 (3)   YHWH's *case against* his people employs the same phrase *(rîb 'im)* as in 4:1. Although the terminology is essentially the same, the formulation of the case here in v. 2 is considerably different. The prophet will draw on traditions about the national ancestor Jacob in the following verses to make YHWH's case that judgment on the people is the just response to their nefarious *ways/deeds*.

Judah is named again (cf. 11:12 above), this time as the object of YHWH's charge. As with the reference in 11:12, interpreters have been divided about its function. For a number of them the mention of Judah in the context of a criticism of Israel is an example of an editorial addition, replacing an original "Israel" as a way to update Hosea's message for a later, Judean audience.[26] This is possible, for a substitution of "Israel" for the current "Judah" in v. 2 makes for a smoother flow with what follows in 12:3-14. "That 'Judah' is secondary here is indicated by the fact that Ephraim is clearly the focus of the entire passage. The parallelism with Jacob both here and in v. 13 [Eng. 12] further supports this view."[27] Dwight Daniels's judgment to this effect must be made on contextual and thematic kinds of evidence, since there is no textual evidence for "Israel" as an earlier recipient of YHWH's charge.

Judah is included in the criticism of Israel/Jacob as a member of the disobedient covenant community. That is the witness of the extant textual tradition, even if one of the prophet's editors offered it as an update for a Judean audience. On the other hand, if "Judah" is considered original to Hosea, one should acknowledge that the particulars of Judah's circumstances are explicitly addressed in what follows.

Poetic structure offers at least two perspectives to the mention of Ju-

26. So, for example, Wolff, *Hosea,* p. 206. In addition to the discussions among commentators, see Emmerson, *Hosea,* pp. 63-65. Cf. chart 2.

27. Dwight R. Daniels, *Hosea and Salvation History: The Early Traditions of Israel in the Prophecy of Hosea* (BZAW 191; Berlin: de Gruyter, 1990), p. 34.

dah.[28] Verse 2 is a tricolon and is related to v. 1, which has five clauses. The criticism of Ephraim (= Israel) is the common element in the two verses, with v. 1 providing the particulars of the ways and deeds to be judged. The first clause of v. 2 (MT 3) begins with a *waw,* meaning *also.* One option is to see the initial clause as yet another complaint about international entanglements followed by a full sentence stop. In the context of international entanglements, YHWH also has a case to prosecute against Judah. The second clause in v. 2, which also begins with a *waw,* is difficult to square with a full sentence stop, as the *waw* is most naturally taken to indicate continuation of the case against Judah. Nevertheless, one can argue that the second clause is a continuation of the critique from v. 1.[29] Verse 2, then, could be rendered as follows: "YHWH also has a case against Judah. And so Jacob will be punished for his ways, and repaid according to his deeds."

If v. 2 originally had four clauses, and more specifically a pair of bicola, then the abrupt transition from Judah back to Israel is lessened somewhat. A second colon in v. 2, naming Israel explicitly in a parallel expression, could have been lost in textual transmission. Such a colon would offer a transition back to the northern kingdom in v. 2b. According to this suggestion, an earlier form of 12:2 would reflect the following:

A	B
YHWH also has a case	[e.g., against Israel
against Judah;	is his charge]

A′	B′
to punish Jacob	he will repay him
according to his ways;	according to his deeds.

There is no evidence for this suggestion in the textual history of the verse, however, and it is thus hypothetical at best. Nevertheless, one can point to 8:14 as an analogy, where "Israel" and "Judah" are paired in the context of a judgment saying.[30] Given the play on the name Israel here in vv. 3-4, it is likely that Israel, as well as Jacob, is also explicitly named in v. 2. Those who have concluded that "Judah" is a substitute for an original "Israel" would certainly agree to this point.

As noted above, the case that YHWH has against his people (whether

28. The first explanation that follows is similar to that of Rudolph, *Hosea,* pp. 220-21.

29. This explanation of the second clause of v. 2 is the weak point of Rudolph's reconstruction.

30. See also the grouping of house of Israel, Ephraim, and Judah in 6:10-11a. As noted in the commentary, 6:11b is better taken with 7:1.

Judah is originally included or not) emphasizes deceit and lying. These things are used to describe the people corporately, or at least their leaders. In Hosea's presentation there is a history of deceptive practices in Israel that reaches back before the monarchical period (cf. 9:10). What has been said so far about national identity is now put in the context of the ancestor Jacob/ Israel.

Excursus: Judah in Hosea 11:12 and 12:2 (MT 12:1, 3)

Interpreters demonstrate considerable uncertainty about the two references to Judah in 11:12 and 12:2. One or both have been seen as examples of editorial activity, supplementing the traditions received about Hosea in order to instruct a later audience. Additional details can be found in the commentary above. What follows is a bird's-eye view of the references in context, using three columns, the first of which has the two references to Judah removed and "Israel" substituted for "Judah" in 12:2. Each of the other two columns has a different option for including them, differing primarily on the translation of 11:12b. The second column is the NRSV, the third is NIV.

Chart 2: Hosea 11:12–12:2

11:12	NRSV	NIV
Ephraim surrounds me with deception; the house of Israel (surrounds me) with deceit. [*11:12b deleted*]	Ephraim has surrounded me with lies, and the house of Israel with deceit; *but Judah still walks with God, and is faithful to the Holy One.*	Ephraim has surrounded me with lies, the house of Israel with deceit. *And Judah is unruly against God, even against the faithful Holy One.*
12:1		
Ephraim shepherds the wind and follows the east wind all day long. He multiplies lies and violence. They make a covenant with Assyria; they carry oil to Egypt.	Ephraim herds the wind, and pursues the east wind all day long; they multiply falsehood and violence; they make a treaty with Assyria, and oil is carried to Egypt.	Ephraim feeds on the wind; he pursues the east wind all day and multiplies lies and violence. He makes a treaty with Assyria and sends olive oil to Egypt.
12:2		
YHWH also has a case against *Israel,* to punish Jacob according to his ways; he will repay him according to his deeds.	The LORD has an indictment against *Judah,* and will punish Jacob according to his ways, and repay him according to his deeds.	The LORD has a charge to bring against *Judah;* he will punish Jacob according to his ways and repay him according to his deeds.

12:3	NRSV	NIV
In the womb he tried to supplant his brother; and in his maturity he strove with God.	In the womb he tried to supplant his brother, and in his manhood he strove with God.	In the womb he grasped his brother's heel; as a man he struggled with God.

3-4 (4-5) These verses contain several allusions to the ancestral figure Jacob. One can discern connections with narrative material now incorporated into the book of Genesis. Nevertheless, Hosea's portrayal of Jacob is compressed as well as allusive, sharing vocabulary and themes with that material, but not made up of citations from it.[31] It is likely that Hosea also reflects interpretive elements about Jacob that are independent of the Genesis materials.

Chart 3: Jacob in Hosea and in Genesis, Shared Vocabulary

Hosea (English versification)	Genesis (English versification)
12:3a Supplanted/deceived *('āqab)* his brother in the womb	25:26 holding the heel *('āqēb)* of Esau. 27:36 Jacob has cheated *('āqab)* Esau.
12:3b Struggled *(śārâ)* with God	32:28 Struggled *(śārâ)* with God and men and prevailed *(yākal)*
12:4a Struggled (reading *wayyiśar,* from *śārâ*) with an angel and prevailed *(yākal)*	32:28 Struggled *(śārâ)* with God and men
12:4a Wept *(bākâ)* at meeting Esau (?)	33:4 Jacob and Esau wept *(bākâ)* upon reunion.
12:4b Encountered God at Bethel	28:11-22; 35:6-15
12:12a Fled *(bāraḥ)* to Aram	27:43 Advised to flee *(bāraḥ)* to Haran 28:2 and to go to Paddan-aram
12:12b served *('ābad)* for a wife; kept (flocks; *šāmar)* for a wife	29:15, 18, 20, 25 served *('abad)* Laban for a wife 30:31 kept (flocks; *šamar)* for a wife

31. Cf. chart 3. For a discussion of the relationship between Hosea and the Jacob traditions in Genesis, see H. D. Neef, *Die Heilstraditionen Israels in der Verkündigung des Propheten Hosea* (BZAW 169; New York: de Gruyter, 1987), pp. 15-49; W. D. Whitt, "The Jacob Traditions in Hosea and Their Relation to Genesis," *ZAW* 103 (1991) 18-43. Whitt proposes that 12:3-4 and 12 (MT 4-5, 13) are quotes or near quotes from the cult at the Bethel sanctuary taken over by Hosea, and that the accounts in Genesis are later in written form.

Jacob's life is encapsulated but not exhausted in the brief bicolon of v. 3. The first clause begins where the longer account of his life in Genesis begins, interpreting the circumstances of his birth. In the womb Jacob attempted to "supplant" *('āqab)*[32] his brother Esau, who was born first (cf. Gen. 25:21-26). Thus Esau was the rightful heir to Isaac's blessings as his firstborn son, a fact with enormous influence in the traditions about Jacob. In the Genesis account, a noun form of *'qb* is used in 25:26, and the name Jacob itself is explained as a play on the circumstances of his birth: "Afterward, his brother emerged with his hand holding on to Esau's heel *('āqēb),* so he called his name Jacob *(ya'ăqōb)."* Later in the narrative Isaac informs Esau that his brother Jacob had "deceived" *('āqab)* him into granting him his patriarchal blessing (27:35). It is likely that Hos. 12:3a is an interpretation of the birth account, based on its capacity to foreshadow later circumstances. Jacob did not literally supplant Esau in the womb in the Genesis account, at least regarding the circumstances of birth order, but in that same account the future significance of Jacob is noted in the poetic oracle granted Rachel from the Lord (25:23). One brother shall be stronger than the other, and the elder will serve the younger. Thus from the perspective of divine intent, Jacob was the stronger from the beginning (cf. Jer. 1:5). The initial clause of Hos. 12:3 likewise projects Jacob's life based on the circumstances of his beginnings. It employs the verb *'āqab* in fidelity to the tradition defining Jacob's name and something of his character, perhaps playing on both its nuances of "supplant" and "deceive."

The second clause contains a double wordplay and similarly interprets Jacob's life. According to the narrative account in Genesis, Jacob wrestled with a nocturnal visitor near a ford of the Jabbok River named Peniel (32:22-32 [MT 23-33]). The summary statement addressed to Jacob in 32:28 (MT 29) is: "Your name shall no longer be Jacob but Israel *(yiśrā'ēl),* for you have striven *(śārâ)* with God *('ĕlōhîm)*[33] and with men and prevailed *(yākal)."* The terse clause in Hos. 12:3b assumes the tradition of the wordplay on the change of name to Israel. Jacob *strove with God (śārâ 'et-'ĕlōhîm).* It also employs a second, more involved play in the description of Jacob's *maturity ('ôn),* a term that represents strength and wealth (Gen. 49:3; Deut. 21:17) and characterizes Jacob in his adulthood. Hosea uses the root *'wn* twice more in the chapter, once to describe the "wealth" that Ephraim had acquired (12:8) and once in a difficult phrase to

---

32. The verb *'āqab* in Qal has two related meanings: "follow/supplant" and "deceive."

33. In Gen. 32:30 (MT 31) an etiology for the name Peniel ("countenance of God" or "face of God") is given, based on the fact that in the exchange with his opponent, Jacob had "seen God face to face."

describe the "worthlessness" *('āwen)* of Gilead (12:11). In its negative formulation, the term *'āwen* is used in the polemical nickname of Bethel as
Beth-aven ("Wicked House," "Worthless House").[34] Bethel is named in v. 4
in reference to another event in Jacob's life.

In the bicolon that makes up v. 3, Jacob's life is interpreted in vocabulary chosen with great care. On the one hand, the manner in which his actions
are described is drawn from traditions about him known to Hosea and presumably to his intended audience. On the other hand, in his deceit and
strength, he also encountered God. These two points are held together as the
prophet develops YHWH's case against his people Israel, Jacob's namesake.
They too have a deadly combination of deceit and strength and will be confronted by God in their historical experience.

4 (5) A continuation of allusions to the ancestor Jacob is set forth
in a pair of bicola. To summarize: the initial clause reiterates essentially the
concluding phrase of v. 3, which states that Jacob strove with God. The Hebrew text is difficult and the subject of numerous suggested emendations.[35]
If Jacob remains the subject of the verbs in the second clause (as seems
likely), he seeks mercy from either the angel or Esau. With the second
bicolon, a shift is made to Bethel, where Jacob encounters God. Since the
subject of the verbs is not named, either Jacob found God at Bethel, or God
found Jacob there.

The Hebrew text of the initial clause in v. 4 is either corrupt or an example of poetic license in expression. The latter fits the involved wordplay of
the previous verse and is the option I propose here. First, the verb is ambiguous and combined with a preposition in apparently ungrammatical fashion.[36]
The Masoretic pointing derives the verb from either *śôr* or *śārar,* indicating a
sense of "be dominate" or "in charge." This corresponds to the LXX rendering, which employs a form of the verb "to strengthen," and is consistent also
with the use of the verb *śôr* (Hiphil) in 8:4, which refers to the appointing of
officials. One advantage of this reading is that the verb has a clear seconding
in the parallel verb *prevail (yākal).*[37]

Some have suggested that the ungrammatical phrase in the initial
clause of v. 4 is in service to a wordplay, elaborating on Jacob's struggle with

34. See appendix 9, "Worship Centers in Hosea."
35. Macintosh, *Hosea,* pp. 483-84, has a helpful overview of suggestions. See
also below.
36. The preposition *'el* appears awkward with the verb. In 12:3b the verbal phrase
is *śārâ 'et.* Thus some interpreters read *'ēl* for *'el* here in v. 4a; e.g., Wolff, *Hosea,* p. 206,
thus makes "God" the subject of the verb. Macintosh, *Hosea,* p. 483, makes "God" the object. Both regard the noun *mal'āk* as a gloss.
37. Peter Ackroyd, "Hosea and Jacob," *VT* 13 (1963) 248, translates: "he lorded it
over the angel and prevailed."

God.[38] This seems the most plausible interpretation in context. With a slight change in pointing, the Hebrew verbal phrase (*wayiśśar 'el*) approximates the name Israel (*yiśrā'ēl*). A wordplay on "Israel" in v. 4a not only elaborates on v. 3b, introducing *mal'āk, angel,*[39] for the previous *'ĕlōhîm,* it also corresponds to the wordplay on the name Jacob and "supplant" (both from the root *'qb*) in v. 3a. The verbal phrase *strove with* in v. 3b is modified to approximate more closely the name Israel. As in Gen. 32:28 (MT 29), Hosea employs the wordplay between the verb *śārâ* and the name *yiśrā'ēl, Israel;* but unlike his counterpart in Genesis, his medium is poetry and he is able to approximate *'ēl* ("God") in his version by using the preposition *'el* in unexpected fashion.[40]

Here are some of the ways scholars have translated v. 4a:

Wolff:
"But (God)[41] [angel][42] proved himself lord[43]
and prevailed.
He (Jacob) wept and made supplication to him."[44]

Andersen and Freedman:
"He contended[45] with God.[46]
He overcame the angel.
He (likely the angel) wept and implored him."[47]

Yee:
"But God[48] ruled and (the) angel prevailed.
He wept and sought his favor."[49]

---

38. So, with difference in details, Macintosh, *Hosea,* pp. 483-84; Garrett, *Hosea,* p. 237.

39. The noun *mal'āk* means "messenger," hence the Greek translation *angelos,* "angel." The MT and LXX in Gen. 32:23-33 (Eng. 22-32) do not use the term to describe Jacob's nocturnal visitor.

40. See n. 36 above.

41. Wolff repoints *'el* as *'ēl* and understands it as the subject of the verb.

42. He considers *mal'āk* a gloss.

43. MT *wāyyāśar,* derived from *śārar.*

44. Wolff, *Hosea,* p. 206.

45. Andersen and Freedman apparently repoint MT as *wayyiśar,* derived from *śry* (as in 12:4b; *Hosea,* pp. 607-8). Jacob is the subject of the verb.

46. They repoint *'el* as *'ēl* and treat it as the object of the verb (*Hosea,* p. 608).

47. Ibid., p. 593.

48. Yee, *Composition and Tradition,* p. 234, repoints *'el* as *'ēl* and understands it as the subject of the verb *śārar.*

49. Ibid., p. 232.

Macintosh:
"But ISRA-EL[50] [i.e. God gained the ascendancy] and prevailed; he [Jacob] wept and implored the favour of him who[51] encounterd him at Bethel."[52]

Garrett (part of a chiasm):
B   "In the womb Jacob tripped up his brother;
   C   In his manhood he struggled with God" (vs. 3).
   C′   "And Israel struggled with[53] the angel and prevailed;
B′   He wept and sought his (Esau's) favor."[54]

As noted above, the subject of the verbs in the second clause of v. 4 is ambiguous. Did Jacob weep and seek mercy from the angel, over whom he prevailed in struggle, or from his brother Esau?[55] The former option is not part of the account in Gen. 32, although Hosea's description could be his interpretation of Jacob's request for a blessing (32:26 [MT 27]).[56] In the Genesis account Jacob and Esau meet immediately after the event at Peniel, and at that time they weep together at their reunion (33:4-5). Either option is plausible in Hosea's context. The latter has the advantage of shared vocabulary *(bākâ, weep; ḥānan, seek mercy)*. We should not assume a strict correspondence between Hosea and the Genesis material, even though the two share vocabulary and common themes. Hosea here (and elsewhere) offers his own application of the traditions that he inherited and may well draw on other traditions of the ancestor's life not included in the Genesis accounts.

The bicolon in v. 4b presents yet another point in Jacob's life. In the Genesis accounts Jacob twice encounters God at Bethel (28:11-22; 35:6-15). One cannot tell if God or Jacob is the subject of the verbs in Hos. 12:4b, so terse is the formulation, but almost certainly it is the Deity. This would also be the assumption of hearers/readers, if they are familiar with the Genesis materials. It is, however, a shift of subject from the previous clause. On the

50. Macintosh slightly emends MT in order to approximate the name Israel. He deletes *mal'āk* as a gloss (*Hosea,* pp. 483-84).
51. He understands the last two clauses of v. 4 as relative clauses (ibid., 485).
52. Ibid., p. 483.
53. The unusual grammar of *wysr 'l* is a wordplay on *yśr'l,* "Israel."
54. Garrett, *Hosea,* p. 237.
55. The difficulties of this text have led to various implausible views. For example, Whitt, "Jacob Traditions in Hosea," p. 33, takes the clause to mean that Jacob was the loser in the struggle. He suggests that the account in Gen. 32 is formulated later than the time of Hosea and portrays a different result of the struggle. Sweeney, *Twelve Prophets,* p. 122, proposes that it was the man or angel over whom Jacob had prevailed (i.e., lasted the night in struggle) who wept and sought mercy.
56. So Neef, *Heilstraditionen,* p. 232.

other hand, v. 5 presents YHWH as the God of hosts, apparently to affirm his finding[57] of and speaking to Jacob.

The verb *find (māṣā')* in v. 5 is not used in the Genesis accounts of the Bethel theophanies. In both accounts (Gen. 28:13-14; 35:11-12; cf. Hos. 1:10), God blesses Jacob/Israel and indicates that he will give him numerous descendants in the land. Hosea may presuppose something similar in his reference to *Bethel* in v. 4b. He had passed over any geographic reference in describing Jacob's struggle with God, but the reference to Bethel in v. 4b is made clear by *there (šām)*. In v. 8 Ephraim describes himself as *wealthy ('ôn)*, a term that Hosea associates with Bethel (Beth-aven; see appendix 9, "Worship Centers in Hosea"). The theological traditions preserved at Bethel in Hosea's day were quite likely focused on Jacob and the blessings that he represented for his descendants.[58] Hosea seems to have appropriated them and framed them in the context of *struggle with* God and the weeping request for reconciliation with his brother whom he had deceived. Jacob is a flawed figure whom God nevertheless sustained, and is thus an appropriate figure with whom to compare and contrast his descendants. The emphasis of Hosea's retelling of the story is that in his life's struggles, Jacob is also the recipient of divine care and blessing and not simply the recipient of negative consequences for his transgressions. These elements in the retelling of the ancestor's story would represent, at least in part, YHWH's "case" *(rîb)* against the people and the deception of their own day (v. 2).

5 (6) The naming of YHWH in v. 5 is intended to identify him with the Deity revealed to Jacob at Bethel. In the Gen. 28 account, YHWH is explicitly identified as the God of Abraham and Isaac in 28:13, although both *'ĕlōhîm* and *'ēl* also occur (28:17, 19-20). In the Gen. 35 account, the name YHWH does not occur, but *'ēl bêt-'ēl, 'ĕlōhîm,* and *'ēl šadday* are present (35:7, 9-11). Thus, according to classical source analysis, the traditions in Gen. 28 would have components from the Yahwist (J) and Elohist (E), and those in Gen. 35 would have components of the Elohist and the Priestly writer (P). Hosea 12:5 is emphatic: YHWH is the Deity's memorial name.

Verse 5 is also a formulaic expression with parallels in Amos 4:13; 9:5-6. The expressions have been called doxological and seen as editorial insertions.[59] Both conclusions may be true, but the formulaic expression in Hosea relates specifically to the Jacob/Bethel traditions in ways that would dif-

---

57. In Hos. 9:10 YHWH is the subject of the verb "find," which appears in that context to be part of the tradition of Israel's election by YHWH.

58. See further Whitt, "Jacob Traditions in Hosea"; and Jules F. Gomes, *The Sanctuary of Bethel and the Configuration of Israelite Identity* (BZAW 368; New York: de Gruyter, 2006), pp. 170-78.

59. See Wolff, *Hosea,* p. 213.

fer from its purposes in Amos. Nevertheless, the three expressions are indeed related, as the following texts demonstrate:

YHWH, God of hosts, YHWH is his memorial *(zēker)*	12:5
YHWH, God of hosts is his name *(šēm)*	Amos 4:13
Lord YHWH of hosts . . .	Amos 9:5-6
YHWH is his name *(šēm)*.	

First, a common emphasis of the three lies in the centrality of the tetragrammaton and that it is the name of the Deity confronting Israel.[60] Second, the term *zēker* ("memorial," "remembrance") functions similarly to the noun *šēm,* "name," as an identity marker. Is there any particular significance to the choice of *zēker* in Hosea? I suggested in the comments on Hos. 1:9 that the prophet knew of the tradition now formulated in Exod. 3:12-14, where the tetragrammaton, God's name YHWH, is defined through a wordplay on the verb *hāyâ,* "to be." In 3:15 the tetragrammaton is defined specifically as his *zēker,* "remembrance." In light of the theophanic language associated with the Bethel traditions in Gen. 28:13-15 and 35:11-12, where YHWH and *'ēl šadday,* respectively, identify themselves as the God of blessing, it is worthwhile to note the formulation of divine identity in Exod. 3:15. Moses is instructed to tell Israel: "'YHWH, the God of your fathers, the God of Abraham, the God of Isaac, and the God of Jacob has sent me to you.' This is my name *(šēm)* forever, and this is my memorial *(zēker)* from generation to generation." It is likely, therefore, that the employment of *zēker* in Hos. 12:5 is intentional and not the reflexive citation of a liturgical formula, and that it draws on the theophany to Moses where the significance of the divine name is revealed. In 12:13 Hosea will have occasion to remind his hearers that "YHWH brought up Israel from Egypt by a prophet." The exodus event also had particular significance for Bethel, at least according to 1 Kgs. 12:28-29. Thus Hosea draws together Jacob and the prophet Moses as past figures through whom YHWH has worked. On a related matter, the identification of God as *YHWH of hosts* may interpret the reference to the *angel (mal'āk)* in v. 4. Jacob's opponent was a messenger who represented God.

6 (7) A tricolon is addressed to Israel. They should *return with God (šûb bē'lōhîm)*. The ancestor Jacob may be the model in mind here, where

---

60. Important also is the epithet *hosts (ṣēbā'ôt)*. Scholars continue to debate the origin and significance of the term. For a recent discussion see Siegfried Kreuzer, "Zebaoth — Der Thronende," *VT* 56 (2006) 347-62. The basic meaning of *ṣābā'* is "company," "host," or "army"; and the plural term likely indicates that YHWH is the owner or master of host*s*, both human and divine. In time of sacred war, the people of Israel arrayed for battle would be a portion of YHWH's hosts, as would angels (cf. Josh. 5:13-15) and the company of heaven (Judg. 5:20).

similar terminology is used in the theophany at Bethel: "I am with you and will keep *(šāmar)*[61] you wherever you go, and bring *(šûb 'el)* you back to this land" (Gen. 28:15). Jacob, in turn, made a vow that if God indeed would provide for him and "keep" *(šāmar)* him on his way (28:20): "I will return in *(šûb bĕ)* peace to my father's house, then YHWH will be my God" (28:21). The verb *šûb* is common to the Genesis account and the didactic lesson offered Israel in Hos. 12 (vv. 2, 14), including the particular phrase *(šûb bĕ)* used in 12:6.[62]

Israel is instructed to *observe* *(šāmar,* imperative) loyalty and justice, and wait continually on God. *Loyalty/loving-kindness/steadfast love (ḥesed)* and *justice (mišpāṭ)* are fundamental to personal relationships and social order (cf. Mic. 6:8). They are an antidote to the deceit, lies, and violence with which Israel has been charged.[63] The instruction is not offered as a quick fix, however. Israel's *return with God* can also be characterized as waiting on God in anticipation. One wonders if this "waiting" is also Hosea's characterization of Jacob's life that he applies to his contemporaries.[64]

7-9 (8-10)   The noun *kĕna'an, trader,* derives from the word "Canaan." It is not a reference to a Canaanite or to the land of Canaan, but to the trading, mercantile culture of Canaan and to one who represents it, namely a merchant or trader (Isa. 23:8; Zeph. 1:11). The trader is Ephraim, who speaks in v. 8 in a self-confident manner. Canaan is Israel's home, a culture and geographic setting in which Israel now finds itself in crisis. As v. 9 makes clear, however, YHWH has a history with them that precedes Canaan.

The terminology for balances or scales is a recognized part of the commercial landscape. Hosea's false balances *(mō'zĕnê mirmâ)* are referred to elsewhere (Prov. 11:1; 20:23; Amos 8:5), as are *mō'zĕnê ṣedeq,* their "just" or "right" counterparts (Lev. 19:36; Job 31:6; Prov. 16:11). The term translated *false (mirmâ)* is the one used for the "deceit" of the house of Israel in 11:12. The verb *oppress ('āšaq)* is another recognized term for defrauding and injustice.[65]

8 (9)   In a double wordplay, Ephraim boasts that he had found *wealth ('ōn)* for himself, employing the same term used for Jacob, when he struggled with God in his *maturity* (v. 3). This is another point of contact

---

61. Note the use of *šāmar* in Hos. 12:12-13 (MT 13-14).

62. See the excursus at 6:1, "Return to YHWH."

63. "Loyalty/loving-kindness/steadfast love" *(ḥesed)* and "justice" *(mišpāṭ)* are two of YHWH's gifts for the restored Israel of the future (Hos. 2:19-20 [MT 21-22]).

64. Daniels, *Hosea and Salvation History,* pp. 45-46, interprets 12:6 as a report of God's address to the ancestor Jacob, drawing on a variant tradition of the theophany at Bethel in Gen. 28:10-22.

65. Lev. 19:13; Deut. 24:14; Ps. 72:4; Prov. 14:31; Amos 4:1; Mic. 2:2; Jer. 7:6; 21:12.

with the Jacob story and evidence that the description of Ephraim is still governed by comparison and contrast with Jacob. It is also a term to be associated with Bethel, as it is used polemically to refer to the city's shrine(s).[66] In his confidence, Ephraim denies that his gains are the result of *iniquity* (*'āwōn*), a similar-sounding term that also contributes to the critique of Bethel.

The verb *find (māṣā')* describes aspects of Ephraim's riches twice in v. 8. It too is used of Jacob, when God found him, i.e., encountered and addressed him, at Bethel (v. 4; cf. 9:10). Ephraim's boastful self-confidence is to deny that there may be a connection between his present possessions and any judgment to come because of iniquity. That boast, however, has overtones of the life of Jacob. And as Hosea indicates through his allusions to the ancestor, God will be involved in bringing matters to a head.

9 (10) Verse 9 reminds readers that YHWH's history with Ephraim precedes national life in Canaan. Not only was Jacob the object of God's care, both in and out of the promised land, but the fundamental dictum of Israelite identity goes back to their covenant with YHWH, who brought them up from Egypt. The self-presentation of YHWH here (and in 13:4) is like that of the prologue to the Decalogue (Exod. 20:2; Deut. 5:6), what has been proposed as a base text for the prophet.[67] YHWH's self-presentation is Hosea's answer to Ephraim's mistaken sense of identity. The covenant Lord who brought the ancestors from Egypt to Canaan will exercise his discipline of Ephraim in pursuit of a wholehearted return of the people. They will again *dwell (yāšab,* Hiphil) in tents. This is a metaphorical tent life, playing on the similar-sounding verb "return," and continuing the connection between redemption from Egypt and YHWH's subsequent guidance of the people in the wilderness. There may also be connections with the fall festival known as Sukkot, where booths were built during the harvest season and the historical memory of guidance in the wilderness was celebrated. A festival could be indicated by the terse simile *like the appointed days,* since the term *mô'ēd* refers not only to particular set times of a year (Exod. 13:10), but is commonly used of national festivals (Lev. 23:2, 4, 44).[68] At harvest time Israel was reminded again of its

66. Amos 5:5. See appendix 9, "Worship Centers in Hosea."

67. See the introduction, section IV.A, "Hosea's Theology: Narrative and Community Identity"; and also the comments at 13:4.

68. The connection between Israel's wandering in the wilderness and the fall festival is made explicit in Lev. 23:43. Some interpreters (e.g., Wolff, *Hosea,* p. 215) think that the fall festival developed this connection later than the 8th century, so they think more generally of the wilderness period as a time previously determined by God in his work through the people. Others note that "booths" are not tents, and that if something more specific than the wilderness period is indicated, it could be Passover plus Unleavened Bread. See Daniels, *Hosea and Salvation History,* p. 47.

past and that its present enjoyment of the fruits of the land is the result of divine blessing. The festival was an important part of Jeroboam I's cultic program in Bethel (1 Kgs. 12:32-33), a setting that also fits Hosea's time and audience. Thus the prophet contrasts Ephraim's declaration of its wealth with a declaration that the nation's future contains another wilderness.

10 (11) What gives Hosea the right to portray Israel's past history and to draw such conclusions as he has done with the Jacob, Egypt, and wilderness traditions? The continuation of YHWH's speech in v. 10 indicates that it is precisely his prophets through whom he communicates and instructs his people. There is no further qualification of *the prophets,* as if they belonged to a certain group, much less an indication of a prophetic office. It is more likely the institution of prophecy itself as something inherent to the people in their history with YHWH that is in view. Thus Hosea's prophetic work is a time-honored and sacred task. Yahwism and prophecy go together. As noted in 12:13, YHWH brought Israel up from Egypt by a prophet and preserved them by a prophet. Hosea apparently includes himself in the train of prophets employed by YHWH, whether or not his audience could accept his judgmental words as YHWH's own criticism of them.

One of the means by which YHWH communicates is through a *vision (ḥāzôn).* This is the only occurrence of the term in Hosea, but noun and verb forms of the root *ḥzh* are common in the prophetic books. The noun is used to describe a particular depiction for a prophet to convey to his audience (Hab. 2:2-3) and it can characterize a prophetic book as a whole (Isa. 1:1; Obad. 1; Nah. 1:1). The verb *ḥāzâ* ("to see, to behold") is used in the superscriptions of Amos, Micah, Isaiah, and Habakkuk to indicate the source of their respective contents. The prophets "saw" their oracles. This was apparently a recognized claim to authority for those who wished to mediate revelation from the divine world, for opposing prophets could also claim visionary experiences (Jer. 23:16; Ezek. 13:6-9, 16; 22:28).

It is probable that the last clause in v. 10, which employs the unusual term *dāmâ* ("to liken"), is an elaboration on the claims that YHWH spoke and multiplied visions. A vision can be more than words and include various perceived depictions, but just how the verb represents visionary depiction and subsequent prophetic presentation *(by the hand . . .)* is not clear. Hence interpreters offer an interesting range in translation. Among them are:

NIV: "told parables through them."
Daniels: "through the prophets I will perform symbolic actions."[69]
Sweeney: "by the hand of the prophets I spoke in metaphors."[70]

---

69. Daniels, *Hosea and Salvation History,* p. 34.
70. Sweeney, *Twelve Prophets,* p. 125.

The interesting element in Daniels's rendering is the possibility of joining the description of divine revelation ("multiplying visions") with communicating through prophetic actions and not simply through oral presentation. The rendering *provide comparisons* is intended to leave the matter open for oral interpretation and the possibility of physical representation as well.

11 (12)   The represented speaker here is Hosea, who offers criticism of Gilead and Gilgal. The text is difficult, particularly in v. 11a, though it may reflect on matters well recognized in Hosea's day, but less so for modern readers. *Iniquity ('āwen)* is predicated of the city of Gilead in 6:8 and is used to describe Bethel elsewhere. Its corresponding term *šāw', nothing,* in the second clause is used in 10:4 to describe empty or worthless oaths. Gilgal is also mentioned elsewhere (4:15; 9:15) in the context of its failures. The vocabulary, therefore, is Hosea's, and the tone of judgment fits the context, even though the description of Gilead (particularly) and Gilgal is obscure.

It is possible that the odd description of altars as *piles of stone (gallîm)* in v. 11 assists readers somewhat in catching a play on terms. A covenant-making ceremony between Laban and Jacob took place in the hill country of Gilead (Gen. 31:23, 25, 44-54). In it a pile *(gal)* of stones was used as a witness *('ēd)* to their mutual covenant and expected behavior, and perhaps also to establish boundaries (vv. 46-48). Sacrifice, moreover, was a constituent part of their meeting (v. 54). The pile and the witness are used as an etiological pun to explain the name Gilead *(gal'ēd;* vv. 46-47). Furthermore, the noun *gal* serves as a play on Gilgal.

With regard to Hos. 12:11, there are good grounds in the context for seeking connections with Jacob traditions in the verse's vocabulary. The problem is the cultural and chronological distance of modern readers, so that without further information on the particulars of Hosea's day, the nuances now escape us. We might wonder, for example, had Gilead and the sacrificial place been overtaken or destroyed, making them now a pile of stones and a witness to failure? The region was taken over by Tiglath-pileser III in the aftermath of his 733-732 campaign and became an Assyrian-administered province. In the case of v. 12, it is not so much the comparison of Jacob's life that is in the foreground, but more the defining of Gilead and Gilgal in ways that nevertheless have allusions to Jacob's life. Whereas Gilead is defined by the etiology of witness and covenant, its present circumstances are a far cry from that. Gilgal, moreover, shares in this judgment. It sacrifices bulls, but its altars are piles of stone, perhaps indicating a witness against them or that they had been toppled and put out of commission.

12 (13)   As a result of Jacob's devious actions, family tensions were such that he fled to an area settled by his mother's family in Aram, today the country of (northern) Syria. There he married women from his clan (so Gen. 27–29). Verse 12 alludes to these circumstances. Every verb used in Hosea's terse description can be found in the Genesis accounts. This is not conclusive evidence that Hosea draws explicitly on the Genesis accounts, but it suggests that his sources are similar to those incorporated in Gen. 27–29. The third and last clause of v. 12 concludes abruptly with a verb *(šāmar)*, and thus I supply the object of his keeping parenthetically in the translation according to the sense of the passage.

13 (14) The lessons to be learned from this summary statement about Jacob are not immediately apparent. In the verse that follows, however, some connections between ancestor and descendants are suggested. One is made between Jacob and later Israel on the basis of common terminology, namely, that just as Jacob *kept (šāmar)* the flocks in order to acquire a wife, so through a prophet YHWH *kept (šāmar,* Niphal) his people. One might translate the Niphal verb "they were preserved." A second connection may be a geographic analogy. Jacob fled to serve and subsequently returned to the land. Israel served in Egypt and returned to the land. A third connection may consist of the metaphor of marriage, joining this point in Hosea's didactic lesson with the presentation in chs. 1–3. Jacob served for his spouses; YHWH redeemed his spouse Israel.[71]

Jacob served for Leah	A prophet brought up Israel from Egypt
Jacob kept flocks for Rachel	A prophet preserved Israel

Hosea employs narrative details to construct a historical typology in vv. 12-13. YHWH was at work in the life of Jacob through years of labor and time spent away from his homeland. His departure, of course, was due to his deception of his brother and the latter's desire to end Jacob's life. The people Israel descended into Egypt in order to preserve life, only to be placed eventually in servitude. YHWH then employed historic means to bring them out of Egypt and into the promised land.

So why compare the Jacob and Exodus traditions in a context in which the people are being criticized? A likely reason is the historical predicament in which both Jacob and his descendants found themselves, difficulties in which YHWH worked to preserve them. The Israel of Hosea's day, which thinks of itself as wealthy and innocent, is actually in historical difficulty and will not survive intact unless it acknowledges its failures and "returns" *(šûb)* to YHWH. On his journey to Aram Jacob encountered God at Bethel and was told that he would be restored *(šûb)* to the land. His journey and efforts, however, took years. In Egypt YHWH raised up Moses and used him to bring the people from servitude to the wilderness and ultimately to the promised land.

71. So also R. B. Coote, "Hosea XII," *VT* 21 (1971) 401; Utzschneider, *Hosea,* p. 206.

Although Moses is not named in v. 13a, he is the prophet whom YHWH called to bring the people up (*'ālâ,* Hiphil) from Egypt.[72] It is an interesting question whether v. 13b also refers to Moses, employing poetic parallelism to reinforce his prophetic tasks, or whether it refers to one of his successors (Joshua, Samuel, Elijah?).[73]

YHWH's saving and preserving of Israel through prophets is the clearest statement in the book to the institutional importance of prophecy and prophetic mediation for the life of Israel. Prophecy is not a marginal factor in maintaining national identity, and Hosea's didactic typology is itself a prophetic act through which he implicitly places himself in a historic lineage. Interpreters have discussed whether texts like 12:13 and Deut. 18:15 reflect the acceptance of a "prophetic office," following in the train of Moses:

> The fact that Hosea speaks generally of a prophet(s) rather than specifically Moses (and Samuel) indicates that the emphasis is on the prophetic office as such. Combined with v. 11 [MT], this verse demonstrates the extreme importance of the prophetic office in Hosea's thinking. The prophets are the only true and faithful agents of Yahweh's protective guidance for his people. This care began with Moses as the prophet *par excellence* and, whether Hosea also referred to Samuel or not, he certainly viewed the office as continuing down to his own day (6:5). So crucial are the prophets that Hosea cannot conceive of a future renewal without them (v. 11 [MT]).[74]

One may agree that too much can be made of the phrase "prophetic office," as it is ambiguously used by interpreters.[75] Who, for example, defined the office in Israel? Was it sufficiently defined that certain people were appointed to it? Instead of a prophetic office, perhaps it would better to think of prophecy itself as a central Israelite institution with strong historical roots. Both Hosea and his detractors recognized it as an influential social phenomenon, even when they differed over who represented the divine world in their own day and time.

It may be also that in his basic understanding of prophecy as rooted in God's saving history, Hosea has a counterpart in Amos, his prophetic con-

---

72. In Exod. 32:7 YHWH speaks to Moses about "the people whom you brought up [*'ālâ,* Hiphil] from the land of Egypt."

73. Andersen and Freedman, *Hosea,* p. 621, propose that two different prophetic figures are intended, the first being Moses, and the second possibly Samuel or Elijah. Another possibility, should Hosea's poetry indicate two different figures, is Joshua, who was Moses' immediate successor (so Deut. 31:14-23).

74. Daniels, *Hosea and Salvation History,* p. 49.

75. See the discussion in David L. Petersen, "The Ambiguous Role of Moses as a Prophet," in *Israel's Prophets and Israel's Past,* ed. Brad E. Kelle and Megan Bishop Moore (London: T and T Clark, 2006), pp. 311-24.

temporary. In a longer indictment of Israel's transgressions, Amos 2:10-12 refers to YHWH's prior history with the people and the role of prophets: "I brought you up from the land of Egypt, and I guided you in the wilderness forty years (in order) to possess the land of the Amorites. I raised up prophets from your sons and nazirites from your young men. Is this not so, Israelites? (declares YHWH). Yet you made the nazirites drink wine, and you commanded the prophets saying: 'You should not prophesy!'" The logic in Amos's indictment has points of contact with Hos. 6:5 and 12:13, starting with YHWH's *bringing up ('ālâ)* Israel from Egypt as a fundamental datum point of the people's identity. Moreover, the rhetorical question regarding YHWH's provision for prophets assumes that Amos's audience would agree that prophets had played a decisive role in Israel's prior history. It is unlikely, however, that they would agree that they had forced nazirites to betray a vow or the implication that YHWH's current prophets are being silenced as had happened previously. From his brief rehearsal of prior history, it seems that Amos's specific reference to prophets fits in the period of Israel's settlement in Canaan (the land of the Amorites), rather than in Israel's time in Egypt, as with Hosea.

14 (15)   The didactic lesson of Hos. 12 concludes in v. 14 with both truth and consequences. Ephraim has provoked YHWH, and unlike Jacob shows no signs of transformation. Perhaps the fact that Ephraim is not more like Jacob in the sense of waiting expectantly on God and in working toward reconciliation is the essential case that YHWH makes in 12:2-14. Thus the last two cola of v. 14 give expression to an act-and-consequence continuum, reaching back for reinforcement to 12:1 and the charge of lies and violence, and more particularly to 12:2, which announces that YHWH will judge Jacob. The correspondence between v. 2b + c and 14b + c can be set out as follows:

2b punish Jacob according to his ways	14b leave his bloodguilt on Ephraim
2c repay him according to his deeds	14c bring back his reproach to him

Verse 14 is a somber conclusion to an intricately developed case against Ephraim/Israel. What is set forth as a transformative possibility in v. 6 simply hangs there in the midst of a didactic lesson that comes to the sad conclusion that Ephraim's guilt and reproach will come back upon him.

B. DEATH BEFITS THEM (13:1-16 [MT 13:1–14:1])

Chapter 13 is the second of two historically oriented prophetic lessons in 11:12–13:16 (MT 12:1–14:1). The first and last verses of this section frame the presentation with references to guilt and death. Ephraim's past, present,

315

and future are briefly indicated in 13:1-3, with a historical résumé in vv. 4-8 that demonstrates why YHWH is angry with the people. Their destruction is at hand; their leaders cannot save them (vv. 9-11). The people's rebellious folly and YHWH's righteous anger together signal a deadly disaster for Israel (vv. 12-16 [MT 13:12–14:1]).

13:1 *When Ephraim spoke in agitation,*[1] *he lifted up (his voice)*[2] *in Israel; but through Baal he became guilty and died.*

2 *And now they add to their sinning! They have made for themselves molten images, from their silver idols according to their understanding;*[3] *everything the work of craftsmen. To them they are saying "sacrifice,"*[4] *men who kiss calves!*

3 *Therefore, they will be like the morning cloud, like the dew that disappears early, like chaff wind-driven from the threshing floor, like smoke from a window.*

4 *Yet I am YHWH your God from the land of Egypt; you know no God but me, and there is no savior except for me.*

5 *I knew you in the wilderness, in the land of drought.*

6 *According to their pasturage they were satisfied; they were content and lifted up their heart; therefore, they forgot me!*

7 *So I will be to them like a lion; like a leopard I will keep watch along the way.*

8 *I will confront them like a bear bereft of her cubs, and I will rip*

---

1. In the OT *rĕtēt* is a hapax legomenon, but the root *rtt* is used in a psalmic text from Qumran (1QH 4:33) in conjunction with the term *r'd* ("to shake," "shaking"). Perhaps it indicates something like "with emotion" or "feeling" in Hos. 13:1.

2. The MT *nāśā' hû' bĕyiśrā'ēl* does not follow conventional grammar, as the Qal perfect verb is transitive. A number of interpreters have proposed a change in vowels to read the Niphal participle *niśśā'* (NRSV "he was exalted in Israel"). This is a plausible suggestion. The translation offered above is based on a recognized phrase *nāśā' qôl*, "to lift up the voice" (Judg. 9:7; 2 Kgs. 19:22; Isa. 24:14; 42:2; 52:8; and several other times in the context of lifting a voice and weeping), with ellipsis of *qôl*, as Andersen and Freedman, *Hosea*, pp. 629-30, point out, although they understand YHWH to be the speaker.

3. The MT has *tĕbûnâ*; the LXX has *eikona*. Some interpreters (e.g., *BHS*) have therefore suggested an emendation to *tabnît*.

4. The MT and its syntax in v. 2c are difficult. The translation proposed emends MT *zōbĕḥê 'ādām* to *zibḥû 'ādām*, reading *'ādām* with the clause that follows (cf. LXX, Vulgate; so NRSV). The MT has been understood to refer to human sacrifice ("sacrificers of men/people"), so Wolff, *Hosea*, p. 25; Andersen and Freedman, *Hosea*, p. 632; ESV: "It is said of them, 'Those who offer human sacrifice kiss calves!'" Cf. Ps. 106:37. Others understand the phrase *zōbĕḥê 'ādām* with *'ādām* as the subject of the participle (an awkward but grammatically understandable rendering); NASB: "They say of them, 'Let the men who sacrifice kiss the calves!'"

open their chests; and there I will eat them like a lion, (like) a wild beast will rip them.

9 *It is your destruction[5] Israel, indeed from me, from[6] your helper.*

10 *Where[7] is your king now that he will deliver you in all your cities, and your rulers[8] of whom you said, "Give me a king and princes"?*

11 *I gave you a king in my anger, and I took (him) in my wrath.*

12 *Ephraim's iniquity is bound up; his sin is stored up.*

13 *The pains of childbirth are coming to him; he is not a wise son, for[9] at the time (of delivery) he is not present at the opening of the womb.*

14 *Will I ransom them from the hand of Sheol, redeem them from death? Where[10] are your plagues, O Death; Sheol, where is your destruction? Compassion is hidden from my eyes.*

15 *Though he may flourish among brothers,[11] the east wind will come, YHWH's wind coming up from the wilderness; and his fountain shall dry up[12] and his spring be dry; it will plunder his treasury of every precious item.*

16 (14:1) *Samaria is guilty, for she has rebelled against her God. Her inhabitants will fall by the sword; their children will be dashed in pieces and her pregnant women ripped open.[13]*

---

5. Reading *šiḥetkā* as a noun. The versions show variation in rendering. One option is to read a first-person verb, "I will destroy you," following the Syriac. See Wolff, *Hosea*, pp. 220-21.

6. The preposition *bĕ* can bear this meaning. See the similar form *bĕʿezrî* in Exod. 18:4, where it is in apposition to the term "God of my father."

7. *'ĕhî* is a variant or dialectical form of an interrogative. It occurs here and in 13:14.

8. Although *šōpēṭ* more commonly refers to a "judge," it can have the more general sense of "ruler"; see *HALOT* 2:1624.

9. The particle *kî* introduces the explanation or reason for the previous declaration.

10. The same interrogative particle is used in 13:10.

11. The initial clause in Hebrew makes no sense and is commonly emended on the basis of the LXX. Thus I read the preposition *bên* for the noun *bēn*, "son." Some also emend the following word *'aḥîm* to *'āḥû*, producing "he will flourish among rushes" (NRSV; so Wolff, *Hosea*, p. 222). For a full discussion of translation possibilities, see Stuart Irvine, "Relating Prophets and History: An Example from Hosea 13," in *Israel's Prophets and Israel's Past*, ed. Kelle and Moore, pp. 158-66.

12. Reading *wayyābaš* or *wĕyōbîš* (so *BHS*) for the similar *wĕyēbôš* of MT. The parallel verb *ḥārab* supports the emendation.

13. The possessive pronoun on the subject is lit. "his" and the verb *yĕbuqqāʾû* is masculine plural, even though the subject is feminine plural. Such inconsistencies happen occasionally in Hebrew, particularly with feminine subjects and objects. Cf. GKC §§135o, 145u.

1 Chapter 13 begins a unit of prophetic speech with a new thought, but not a new topic. It is a new thought in that vocabulary heretofore unused for Ephraim is employed and a historical observation is made that separates it from the previous verse and prepares for a shift to the present in v. 2. It is not new in that the announcement in 12:14 of judgment to come upon Ephraim receives further explanation.[14]

The first half of v. 1 is difficult to place in a historical reading of the text. There are no clues for defining Ephraim's *agitation* or the *lifting up* of its voice. A plausible interpretation is that these matters refer to a corporate sense of threat or a reaction to negative circumstances. In any case, the result is that Ephraim *became guilty and* (in some sense) *died.*

Most interpreters have looked for a time (a nexus of events) in the nation's history in which Ephraim's actions violated YHWH's covenantal ethos and the people subsequently paid a price. The matter is complicated by two basic issues, plus the usual difficulty with Hosea's syntax. First, does Ephraim serve here as a synonym for Israel or does it represent the tribe of that name (or similarly the central hill country of Israel)? Second, in what sense did Ephraim die? Could this refer to a military setback, loss of life or territory, or defection from the covenant with YHWH through the veneration of Baal? It has been proposed, for example, that the reference to becoming guilty through Baal is an allusion to the encounter with the Baal of Peor in Transjordan (cf. 9:10b), where idolatry took place and thousands died (Num. 25).[15] Such an interpretation assumes that Ephraim is used anachronistically to refer to the nation as a whole. Another possibility is that it refers to the golden calf episode in Exod. 32–34.[16] This interpretation has the difficulty of explaining why "Baal" is predicated of the golden calf in Hosea, but not in Exod. 32. On the other hand, such an allusion fits with the critique of calf idolatry that follows in v. 2. With regard to Israel's settlement in the promised land, Macintosh has proposed that v. 1 concerns the circumstances of the formation of the breakaway kingdom of Israel under Jeroboam I and the advancement of Baal veneration under the Omride dynasty.[17] Moving closer to Hosea's own day, Wolff suggested that Ephraim's exalting of itself led to di-

---

14. Because v. 1 addresses events in Israel's past, it has been seen as a continuation of the historical lesson in ch. 12 and more particularly further commentary on the "apostasy of the wilderness generation"; so Kelle, *Hosea 2,* p. 162. This makes the most likely occasion for "guilt" incurred through Baal to be a reference to the idolatry at Baal-peor (Num. 25). Most interpreters rightly think that Hos. 13:1 begins another unit of prophetic speech, rather than directly continuing ch. 12.

15. In addition to Kelle, *Hosea 2,* p. 162, see Rudolph, *Hosea,* p. 242; Andersen and Freedman, *Hosea,* p. 630.

16. So Sweeney, *Twelve Prophets,* pp. 129-30.

17. Macintosh, *Hosea,* pp. 520-21.

saster and the assaults of Tiglath-pileser III in 733-732 in which both people and land were taken by the Assyrians.[18] In 722/721 came the fall of Samaria, and Robinson suggested that the "death" incurred by Ephraim is best interpreted in light of the siege and fall of the city.[19] This last option requires that Hosea was still alive at the fall of Samaria, which is possible but unlikely, or that 13:1 is a redactional comment, which is also possible but unlikely.

On the one hand, a historically based reading of v. 1 seems required initially by the vocabulary itself, however difficult it may be to identify one or more portions of the national history with it. Hosea's hearers are told that Ephraim's previous acts had brought guilt upon them and even death. The summary is intended to explain to them why the prophet offers judgment in the current historical hour. On the other hand, its terseness paints with a broad brush and almost certainly depends on material elsewhere in Hosea or used elsewhere by him in oral presentation. It is intended to underscore what has been claimed elsewhere in more detail. Thus, of the suggestions noted above, perhaps that of Macintosh is preferable, for it sets the national history in the monarchical period broadly in the context of self-aggrandizement and idolatry.[20]

Whatever Hosea means with Ephraim's "death" by Baal, it did not refer to the actual demise of the state of Israel. That end he announces in 1:4 as coming in the future, and the book elaborates on it in various ways. Indeed, he addresses Ephraim in the very act of reminding them of "death." Perhaps the prophet means essentially that Ephraim is "as good as dead." The expression may also indicate that the circumstances of Ephraim's death have been apparent for some time and that the transition to present circumstances in the following verse is evidence that the national death is on the horizon.[21] This would fit the somber statement in 12:14 that Israel's bloodguilt will be brought upon him.

2 A transition is made from past description to present crisis and critique. The particle *now* functions less as a time indicator and more for present emphasis. The present circumstances are indicated by the imperfect verbs of the first and last clauses.[22] Sarcasm, which is associated with the cri-

18. Wolff, *Hosea*, p. 225.

19. Robinson, "Hosea," p. 49.

20. See also Neef, *Heilstraditionen*, pp. 189-90, who proposes that in v. 1 Hosea represents broadly Israel's history in "decline, beginning with its entry into the land of Canaan." He compares v. 1 with 9:10-11; 11:1-7; and 13:4-8 in this regard.

21. One might compare in this instance the Pauline teaching of humankind "dead" in its sinful estate (Eph. 2:1, 5; Col. 2:13) apart from the revelation of God in Christ.

22. The narrative preterite *wayya'śû* ("have made") in v. 2b is coordinated with the imperfects by rendering it as a description of a completed task with continuing influence.

tique of idolatry in the OT, is apparent from the beginning of the verse. Who in their right mind would increase activities associated with their demise, as if the description of "death" at the hands of Baal in the previous verse was not enough to convince hearers of the continuing threat posed by idolatry? In his sarcasm Hosea draws on the essentials of the first two commandments of the national covenant (Exod. 20:3-6; Deut. 5:7-10), both of which are violated by the description of Israelite religious practices here in Hos. 13:1-2.

The crafting of *molten images (massēkâ)* is expressly forbidden in pentateuchal texts (Exod. 34:17; Lev. 19:4) and resides under a curse (Deut. 27:15). Perhaps Hosea draws also on the curse associated with crafting these images in his description of incurring guilt and dying in v. 1. The term *massēkâ* in v. 2 is the same used to describe the molten calf constructed at Sinai/Horeb (Exod. 32:4; Deut. 9:12, 16; Ps. 106:19), and is almost certainly chosen for that reason. It is likely that the *silver idols* are a type of the molten images opposed by the prophet. Idolatrous *calves* are mentioned in the final clause in the context of an obscure practice of (cultic?) kissing, perhaps a sign of veneration carried out in Bethel at the national shrine and/or a personal practice with household figurines. The polemic here should be compared to 2:8 (MT 10) and the harsh comments in 8:5-6.[23]

According to the reconstruction of the text of v. 2 proposed here, sacrifice is one of the constituent acts associated with idolatry. Because of its idolatrous frame of mind, Ephraim encourages sacrificial practice along with the employment of divine images. This would fit Hosea's polemic elsewhere against sacrificial practice, whether given to Baal (11:2), a syncretized form of YHWH (8:13), or a deity not identified (4:13-14; 6:6).

3 Verse 3 is an exquisite literary formulation, with four similes presented in a pair of bicola. In literary expression it is vintage Hosea. The first bicolon is used elsewhere in 6:4 to describe the fleeting loyalty of Israel. Here it serves to explain the fleeting existence of those engaged in the idolatrous practices described in the previous verse. Judgment — in this instance a quick departure — is the consequence of their actions. The simile of the *chaff (mōṣ)* is widely used in the OT. The term occurs with a variety of verbs to portray dust dissipating in the wind (Job 21:18; Ps. 1:4; 35:5; Isa. 29:5). Taken together, the two bicola represent things commonly visible, but quick to depart in the face of wind.

morning cloud	dew
chaff	smoke

23. Isa. 44:9-20 contains an extended polemic against idolatry. Note the use of sarcasm and the references to the "craftsmen" *(ḥārāš)* in vv. 11-13, the same term used in Hos. 8:6 and 13:2.

The two bicola in v. 3 serve to reinforce each other and the conclusion that idolatry and idolaters will come to an end. This conclusion builds on the previous two verses. Verses 1-3, therefore, can be outlined according to their presentation of Ephraim's identity past, present, and future.[24]

Past: (v. 1) Ephraim's sin: guilt through Baal and death
Present: (v. 2) They sin more: idolatry
Future: (v. 3) They will disappear like common elements driven by the wind.

4-5 YHWH's self-presentation as Israel's God in v. 4 is also given in 12:9 (MT 10). It is similar to the self-presentation in the prologue of the Decalogue.[25] Moreover, the exclusive nature of the relationship that began in Egypt finds similar expression here in v. 4b, which follows the particulars of the first commandment (Exod. 20:3; Deut. 5:7). As noted previously, the concerns of the prologue and the first two commandments are a base text for Hosea in whatever form he knew them, giving support to his convictions of YHWH's identity and expressed will for Israel. Hosea's expression of YHWH's exclusive claim to Israel resonates with other like-minded expressions such as Deut. 32:12: "YHWH alone guided him; no foreign god was with him."[26]

Hosea's emphasis on YHWH's election of Israel comes in the repetition of the verb *know (yāda‛)* in vv. 4-5. Israel is to know no other deity, a stricture designed to protect the intimacy of the national covenant, just as it would the exclusive intimacy of a marriage. Israel's knowledge of YHWH is a human reflex of what YHWH himself first brought to pass in *knowing,* i.e., claiming, Israel for himself.[27] Amos, Hosea's prophetic contemporary, uses the verb *yāda‛* in the sense of "choose and enter into a relationship" (3:2; cf. Hos. 9:10).

Along with the formulation of YHWH's exclusive claim upon Israel, comes Hosea's affirmation of the uniqueness of YHWH. It is expressed in terminology shared with other OT writers:

24. In essence I follow the structural observations of Mays, *Hosea,* pp. 171-73.

25. See chart 4 in appendix 10.

26. This affirmation comes in the context of YHWH "finding" *(māṣā’)* Israel in the wilderness (32:10-11). Cf. Hos. 9:10; 12:4 (MT 5). See also appendix 2, "The Song of Moses and Hosea."

27. Some interpreters have seen reason to emend MT *yĕda‛tîkā* to *rĕ‛îtîkā,* based on the LXX and Syriac. So Rudolph, *Hosea,* p. 238; Wolff, *Hosea,* p. 220; Jeremias, *Hosea,* p. 159. The conclusion of 2:20 (MT 22) speaks against the emendation. See appendix 7, "Terms for Election in Hosea." It may be, however, that "to know one's flock" is part of the metaphorical field of shepherding and used accordingly in v. 5; so Eidevall, *Grapes in the Desert,* p. 196.

"I am YHWH and there is no other, except me there is no God; I will strengthen you, though you have not known me" (Isa. 45:5).

"Am I not YHWH? And there is no other God apart from me; a righteous God and savior, there is no one except me" (Isa. 45:21).

"There is no holy one like YHWH, no one besides you; there is no rock like our God" (1 Sam. 2:2).

It is in the *wilderness (midbār)* where YHWH knew Israel, an event that is also indicated in 9:10, where YHWH found the people like grapes in the wilderness. In the other citation of YHWH's self-presentation in 12:9 (MT 10), mention is made of a return to tents, which is a reminder that the wilderness is a harsh environment apart from divine sustenance. These three texts (9:10; 12:9 [MT 10]; 13:4) join Gomer's symbolic world of the wilderness as the place of judgment and new beginnings (2:3, 14 [MT 5, 16]; cf. Amos 2:10), and provide one tie-in for the various parts of the book. YHWH's election and care are also the foundation for the criticism of Israel that follows in the next verse.

6 Both the theme and vocabulary of v. 6 are found elsewhere in the book. Hosea speaks of Israel not being *satisfied (śābaʿ)* because they have forsaken YHWH (4:10), and of circumstances where they have *forgotten (šākaḥ)* YHWH (2:13 [MT 15]; 4:6; 8:14). Moreover, the term *pasturage (marʿît)* is derived from the semantic field of shepherding, a theme that is also part of Hosea's perception of divine activity (4:16). Here satisfaction and subsequent forgetfulness come as a result of the people's perceived self-sufficiency and pride. The logic of Hosea's charge is that YHWH's formation of Israel and the setting of them in the promised land had been submerged or otherwise shunted aside in Israel's public life. One should note in particular the sharp contrast between the covenantal "knowing" of the previous verses (13:4) and the charge of forgetfulness here. Among the OT writings, Deuteronomy is particularly emphatic on the danger of becoming satisfied, lifting one's heart (in pride), and being forgetful, employing the same vocabulary as Hosea in the form of a warning:

"You shall eat and *be satisfied (śābaʿ)* and bless YHWH your God for the good land that he has given you. Take care that you do not *forget (šākaḥ)* YHWH your God, by failing to keep his commandments, his ordinances, and his statutes, which I am commanding you today. When you have eaten and are *satisfied (śābaʿ)* and have built fine houses and live in them, and when your herds and flocks have multiplied, and your silver and gold is multiplied, and all that you have is multiplied, then your *heart is lifted up (rôm + lēbāb), forgetting (šakaḥ)* YHWH your

God, who brought you out of the land of Egypt, out of the house of slavery." (Deut. 8:10-14)

This is Deuteronomic prose, while Hosea's sentiments are given in a poetic tricolon, where Israel's sequential steps of satisfaction and pride (the first two clauses) are linked by the particle 'al-kēn (therefore) to the third step (a charge) of forgetting YHWH.[28]

7-8 The four similes of Israel's fickleness (v. 3), coupled with the charge that they had forgotten YHWH (v. 6), are matched with five similes of theriomorphic attacks to come in vv. 7 and 8. Four of the five similes are explicit, formulated with the kĕ of comparison. The fifth simile is the last clause, where the kĕ is assumed. YHWH will attack the prideful, forgetful people!

There is a logic to the train of thought in vv. 4-8 that Hosea's first hearers would recognize, namely the activity of the shepherd.[29] As Israel's divine shepherd, YHWH knew Israel in the wilderness and cared for his flock in the land of drought. One of the tasks of a shepherd in a wilderness area is to protect the flock from predators. David's response to Saul, that he had killed both lion and bear in the protection of his father's flock, makes just this point (1 Sam. 17:34-35). The frightening element here is that YHWH has changed from defender of the flock to predator. His theriomorphic portrayal is a way to represent judgment to come in the historical process. The actual predator will be Assyria. Indeed, Hosea's choice of verb in v. 7b may be a clever wordplay on the name Assyria. The leopard will *keep watch, 'āšûr,* a term that sounds virtually identical to *'aššûr,* "Assyria."

This is not the only place in Hosea in which YHWH is depicted as a wild animal.[30] In 5:14 he is the lion who will fall upon Ephraim and Judah, employing imagery similar to 13:7-8, although the terms for lion vary. In 11:10 YHWH roars like a lion and his children follow him home.

> 5:14   *šahal; kĕpîr*
> 11:10   *'aryēh*
> 13:7-8 *šahal; lābî'*

---

28. Wolff, *Hosea,* p. 226, notes the close relationship between this verse and Deut. 6:12-19; 8:11-20, with the comment that Hosea is "one of the fathers of the early Deuteronomic movement."

29. Eidevall, *Grapes in the Desert,* pp. 196-99, with references to other interpreters who have noted the shift from shepherd to predator.

30. See also Lam. 3:10-11, where YHWH is a lion and a bear. The attack by wild animals is a prophetic motif (Ezek. 22:27; Zeph. 3:3; Hab. 1:8). See also the commentary on Hos. 5:14, where I note that attacks by wild animals are part of the treaty curse tradition in the ancient Near East.

The comparison of YHWH to a bear is expressed in conventional terms. He is like a "she-bear separated (from her cubs)." Hebrew *dōb šakkûl* literally indicates a "childless bear" and is a proverbial expression used to express a ferocious attack (2 Sam. 17:8; Prov. 17:12). A human interloper who separates a mother from her cubs will face a mother keenly aroused to protect her own. YHWH's aggression, therefore, is not simply the reflex action of a predator who kills to eat, but a rage over loss.

9 Verse 9 is tersely formulated and difficult to render, but its basic sense is determined by the context. It refers to the destruction attributed to YHWH in 13:7-8. Hosea uses the root *šḥt* ("to destroy") elsewhere in 9:9 and 11:9. It is difficult to render the term in 9:9 as well, but in all three instances it refers to the corrupting dissolution or destruction of the people. It is a term with some currency in describing Israel's failures. For example, the verb is used in Exod. 32:7 in reference to the corrupt activity of the people in constructing the golden calf. The verb is used similarly in Deut. 32:5 in a difficult initial clause, and is followed by the statement that the people are "not his children." It is possible that here and in v. 13 Hosea draws on the Deuteronomic song of judgment against Israel.[31]

One should compare the term *helper* (*ʿēzer*) here in v. 9 with that of *savior* (*mōšîaʿ*) in 13:4. Both terms indicate the work of YHWH in bringing Israel out of Egypt, through the wilderness, and to the land of promise. YHWH is the one who helped Israel in Egypt (Exod. 18:4). He helps and delivers (*yāšaʿ*) Israel (Deut. 33:29; Ps. 79:9). The chilling claim is that Israel's helper is now the agent of the people's demise.

10-11 The rhetorical question in v. 10 is addressed to Israel and presupposes a time in which the king is either gone or appears helpless in the face of trouble. Given the turnover in rulers from the death of Jeroboam II until the capture of Hoshea, it is not so easy to determine a particular instance where YHWH's searching question best fits. Perhaps the best option for a historical-contextual reading is the time in which Hoshea broke his vows to Shalmaneser V and was subsequently captured by the Assyrians (2 Kgs. 17:1-4). The Deuteronomistic historians describe Hoshea as having done evil in YHWH's sight, and given Hosea's negative evaluation of Israelite kings (Hos. 8:4), he would certainly have agreed with this assessment. The ineffectual, if not corrupt, government includes rulers or officials and not just the king himself. Hosea employs the three primary political categories for administrative rule: *king (melek), ruler* or *judge (šōpēṭ),* and *prince* or official *(śār).* The fate of *cities* is at stake, indicating a strong threat. The description of governmental failure would fit the presence of a strong external threat to national identity such as Assyria in

31. See further appendix 2, "The Song of Moses and Hosea."

which the extended royal family and its associates were unable to secure the nation's sovereignty.

One should be cautious in extrapolating a systematic viewpoint on monarchy from these brief references.[32] Clearly Hosea's institutional critique of Israel included various failures of the monarchy (7:3-7; 8:4; 10:3, 7), along with other political and religious institutions. His assessment of the Israelite monarchy was likely no different than his assessment of priesthood, sacrifice, or the national temple at Bethel. They all had failed in the historical moment and resided under YHWH's judgment. At the same time, all were gifts from YHWH in due season that had become corrupted. The book offers hope for a future reunited Israel and Judah under one head, a Davidic ruler (1:11; 3:5).

Hosea quotes the people in v. 10 to the effect that they had sought kings and princes. This is reminiscent of a request centuries earlier to the prophet Samuel, where representatives of the people requested the appointment of a king (1 Sam. 8:4-20). According to the narrative, both YHWH and the prophet reacted negatively. More particularly, the people state: "Indeed, a king shall be over us. And we will be like all the nations and he will rule over *(šāpaṭ)* us and fight our battles" (8:19-20). Nevertheless, monarchy as an institution is not rejected in 1 Sam. 8. YHWH accedes to the request for a king, but the text assumes the pretensions and excesses that accompany it (cf. Judg. 9:7-15), as well as the presumptuous nature of the people's request for a king. From their perspective, the need for strong leadership in threatening circumstances is a powerful motivator to opt for centralized leadership. In the case of the 11th century B.C. and Israel's historical context, the threat of the Philistines was one factor in the request for a king ("to fight our battles," 1 Sam. 8:20). During Hosea's day the external pressures came from Assyria, Damascus, and Egypt, complemented by their various supporters within Israel. In the crises confronting Israel in the second half of the 8th century, undoubtedly there were cries for strong political leadership and for an alliance with one or more foreign ruler. All claims to kingship and for alliances would have to be addressed to Israel's religious institutions to seek the will of YHWH. With regard to Hosea, there is nothing in the book to suggest his support for alliances with any of the above. In the case of King Hoshea, his rise to rule was ratified by Tiglath-pileser III in the aftermath of the Assyrian campaign in the region (733-732 B.C.) and the removal of Pekah, a stalwart anti-Assyrian. The king's investiture would also have required a Yahwistic blessing by the appropriate priests, but Hosea may well have seen in all of this an example of YHWH's anger. Hoshea's subsequent capture by Shalmaneser III would qualify as YHWH's *taking away in wrath.*

---

32. See the commentary on 8:4 and the excursus at 3:5 on "David Their King."

12 The point of the brief bicolon in v. 12 appears to be the collecting of Ephraim's failures with the result that their effects will be felt all at once. Nouns and verbs reinforce one another in this communication:

Ephraim's iniquity *('āwōn)*   bound *(ṣārûr)*[33]
his sin *(ḥaṭṭā't)*   stored *(ṣĕpûnâ).*

The word pair *iniquity* and *sin* occurs elsewhere in Hosea (4:8; 8:13; 9:9; 12:8 [MT 9]). These terms represent the essential failure of Israel vis-à-vis YHWH, but v. 12 is not the context in which to define their failures. This is the place to indicate that the force of Israel's failure, defined elsewhere in the book, is currently stored up and waiting to be released with negative results. It is thus the verbs that carry nuance for his hearers. It has been suggested, for example, that the two verbs together reflect the image of a document bound and secured for a future revealing.[34] This is possible, but the two verbs are not used elsewhere in tandem specifically to indicate the wrapping and the storing of a document. Nevertheless, the verb *ṣāpan* is used for concealing treasures, and important documents would certainly qualify for a secure concealing. The following verse, however, suggests that another metaphor is in the foreground, that of binding/storing associated with pregnancy. That the two verses are linked is confirmed by Ephraim being named here in v. 12, but in v. 13 only pronouns being used of the unwise son at the time of birth. Verse 13 then reveals that "stored" indicates pregnancy. In metaphorical terms, a stored fetus is the vehicle and the tenor is the future strong "delivery" or "birth" of Ephraim's iniquity, with devastating consequences.[35]

At the present time the consequences of Ephraim's iniquity have not yet shown themselves. Perhaps behind Hosea's comparison we can catch something of his detractors among the people. They insist that their actions are not necessarily iniquitous (cf. 12:8 [MT 9]), and in any case have not yet shown the disastrous consequences that Hosea has announced.

13 The metaphor of *childbirth* is applied to Ephraim's circumstances, following the poetic description of stored iniquity in v. 12. The pronouns *he* and *him* also have their antecedents in the "Ephraim" of v. 12. It is not clear whether the birth pangs are coming upon him, as if Ephraim himself is metaphorically pregnant, or whether Ephraim is the fetus who is affected by the

---

33. The verb is used in 4:19.

34. R. Vuilleumier Bessard, "Osée 13:12 et les manuscrits," *RevQ* 1 (1958) 281-82; so similarly Macintosh, *Hosea*, p. 542. One "binds up" *(ṣārar)* a written document for later presentation (Isa. 8:16).

35. The verb *ṣārar* is used of labor pains in Jer. 48:41 and 49:22. Labor pains are the vehicle to express the sense of pain and panic that strikes male warriors.

birth pangs that come upon the mother.[36] The latter is the option offered here, but Ephraim's role in the metaphor is both remarkable and complicated.[37]

At issue is the declaration that *he*[38] is an unwise son. What makes Ephraim so? Verse 13b offers the explanation that he does not recognize the time *('ēt),* i.e., the appropriate moment or due date, for the coming forth from the womb. Among other things, wisdom is concerned with recognizing the right time for an action. We should set aside any objection that a fetus cannot have such an understanding. The issue at hand is to portray the culpability of Ephraim, not awareness of fetal senses or lack thereof. Just as Jacob can be typified in the circumstances of birth (12:3a [MT 4a]), so too can Ephraim. More to the point is the potential danger of childbirth, including especially recognition that once labor begins, a proper sequence of actions is necessary for safe delivery. Ephraim is unwise because he does not present himself at the opening of the womb at the proper time. Hosea employs an idiom for the birth of a child; his phrase is literally the "breaking of children" *(mišbar bānîm),* apparently referring to the crucial moment when the head crowns and the child is ready to break forth from the birth canal. When a child is not in the proper position to exit the birth canal, then an extended, painful labor is the least serious result. In antiquity a breech baby or one with other obstructions to clear passage through the birth canal might not survive. As devastating as that would be, complications with the child can lead to danger for the mother's life as well.

Ephraim as an unwise son should be compared to other metaphorical descriptions of stupidity and heedlessness in the book. In 7:9 Ephraim is devoured by strangers and possessed of gray hair (= old age), yet he recognizes neither. In 7:11 he is a dove, lacking sense about his surroundings. The conclusion to the book (14:9 [MT 10]) enjoins those who are wise to understand the truth of the prophet's oracles, as if their import could be missed. Here in 13:13 the theme seems to be one of culpability. A stillborn child (Ephraim's "death") could well be the result of a mistimed birth. That, or something similar, appears to be the point of the labor pains that come to Ephraim. It is also possible that Hosea draws upon the song of judgment in Deut. 32 for some of his imagery. In 32:6 reference is made to a foolish and unwise people, who are in rebellion to YHWH their father. The relevant vocabulary can be set side-by-side:

36. For the latter option see Wolff, *Hosea,* p. 228; Andersen and Freedman, *Hosea,* p. 638. For the former option see Macintosh, *Hosea,* p. 543. He rightly notes with regard to gender roles that there is nothing wrong with the metaphorical portrayal of masculine Ephraim as pregnant. Cf. Jer. 30:6. His awkward rendering of v. 13b, however, speaks against his conclusion of a pregnant Ephraim ready to give birth.

37. Eidevall, *Grapes in the Desert,* pp. 201-2, 205, links the metaphor here with the indications of childlessness and bereavement, both of which he finds elsewhere in the chapter.

38. The pronoun *hû'* is emphatic.

Deut. 32:6 a foolish and unwise people *('am nābāl wĕlō' ḥākām)*
Hos. 13:13 he is an unwise son *(hû'-bēn lō' ḥākām).*

The metaphor of Ephraim as an unwise fetus in v. 13 supports the primary tenor of ch. 13, which is about the demise of Israel, whether it is the result of guilt with Baal (13:1), YHWH's animal-like employment of hostile forces (13:7-8), the power of Sheol (13:14), or Samaria devoured by the sword (13:16). One might push the metaphor and say that Ephraim should have known better and thus avoided the dismal conclusion depicted for him. If so, it became a moot point, as Ephraim maintained its folly to the bitter political end of the state.

14 Interpreters differ over the intention of v. 14. Should the first bicolon be rendered as a declaration ("I will ransom them . . .")[39] or as a pair of rhetorical questions? I propose the latter option. YHWH will not step in and save Israel. The last clause of the verse is best taken as a devastating declaration that YHWH will not exercise *compassion*[40] toward his people in the historical moment. It is a somber conclusion to which v. 14a + b offers support. Verse 14a is best taken as a pair of rhetorical questions, which is consistent with the word order of the bicolon. The rare *'ĕhî* of v. 14b is understood as a rhetorical particle and translated the same as in its other occurrence in 13:10 *(Where).* Thus the first four clauses are rhetorical questions, with the fifth and last clause an explanatory conclusion. YHWH can say such harsh things because at the moment compassion or pity is hidden from him. This is, furthermore, the train of thought from the chapter's beginning.

The poetic structure of v. 14a + b is precise and contains a high percentage of vocabulary not used elsewhere in Hosea.[41] It is possible, therefore, that Hosea employs material already in existence and adapts it for his presentation of judgment. The chiastic structure of the first four clauses (following the Hebrew word order) is as follows:

A	B
Sheol ransom	**death** redeem
B′	A′
plagues **death**	destruction Sheol

39. So LXX; NIV; Andersen and Freedman, *Hosea,* pp. 639-40; Garrett, *Hosea,* pp. 264-65.

40. Heb. *nōḥam* is a hapax legomenon derived from the root *nḥm.* It may have the nuance of "pity" and is related to the "compassions" *(niḥûmîm)* kindled in YHWH in 11:8.

41. The terms include: Sheol, redeem *(gā'al),* plague *(deber),* destruction *(qōṭeb),* compassion *(nōḥam),* to hide *(sātar).*

We have three recognized word pairs in Hebrew poetic parallelism: the nouns *Sheol* and *death* (Pss. 6:5 [MT 6]; 18:5 [MT 6]), *plague* and *destruction* (Ps. 91:6), and the verbs *ransom* and *redeem* (Ps. 69:18 [MT 19]; Jer. 31:11). While each term has its own nuance, when used in the recognized word pair it reinforces its counterpart and serves primarily as a synonym. The literary effect of the sequence is to undergird the inevitability of judgment.

There is a sense in which 13:14 is the negative counterpart to, or even a reversal of, 11:8-9. Both employ rhetorical questions and both have YHWH speaking about *compassion* (root *nḥm*). In 11:8-9 YHWH, as it were, speaks to himself, and the rhetorical question of 13:14 may also be taken as self-directed. Indeed, both passages reflect an aspect of the historical context in which the book takes shape. Samaria did fall, accompanied by death and dislocation for segments of the Israelite population. These are tragic events that the prophecies of judgment interpret. Yet YHWH did not make a complete end of the people, and the somber conclusion to an independent northern kingdom became a building block for future renewal. Chapter 13 contains some of the harshest language in the whole book of Hosea, with v. 14 a prominent example. Finally, however, while a negative counterpart to 11:8-9, 13:14 is not its overriding reversal. With 14:1 (MT 2) Israel's stumbling is confronted, and no longer is compassion hidden from YHWH's eyes (14:4 [MT 5]). The judgment of 13:14 focuses on the moment of disaster, the judgment soon to come in the historical process, but it is not the last word on YHWH's compassion.

Excursus: Hosea 13:14 LXX and 1 Corinthians 15:54-55

From the hand of Hades I will deliver them, and from death I will redeem them. Where is your judgment, O Death; where is your sting, O Hades? Comfort is hidden from my eyes. (Hos. 13:14 LXX)

Will I ransom them from the hand of Sheol, redeem them from death? Where are your plagues,[42] O Death; Sheol, where is your destruction? Compassion is hidden from my eyes. (Hos. 13:14 MT)

A comparison of the two translations will show that a main difference between the two is the declaratory nature of the first two clauses of the Greek,[43] whereas the Hebrew is rendered as questions. It is possible also to render the first two clauses of the Hebrew as declaratory, but the majority of interpreters take them as rhetorical questions in parallel with the third and fourth clauses, as is done here.

In his discussion of the resurrection of the human body in 1 Cor. 15:50-57,

---

42. The Syriac has *zkwtk,* "your victory."
43. This is the case also for the Vulgate and Syriac versions.

Paul claims that resurrection is the overcoming of death, a mystery in which the perishable puts on that which is imperishable. When this will come about — and except for Jesus, it has not yet happened — then the truth of what is written (quoted in vv. 54-55 below) will also come to be. Verses 54-55 combine elements of Isa. 25:8 and Hos. 13:14, which share the terms *death* and *victory*. Paul's text is neither a literal rendering of the Hebrew of Isa. 28:5a nor a quotation of the LXX version. He uses a passive form of the verb ("is swallowed up") whereas the same verb is aorist active in the LXX. In the Hebrew text God will *swallow up death*. In Paul's rendering, death will be swallowed up in *victory (nikos),* using a term that occurs in the Greek versions of Aquila and Theodotion.[44] The citation of Hos. 13:14 is close to the LXX text, with *victory*[45] in place of *judgment (dikē)*.

> When the perishable will have put on the imperishable, and mortality puts on immortality, then will come to pass the word that is written, "Death is swallowed up in victory *(nikos)*. O Death, where is your victory *(nikos)*? O Death, where is your sting?" (1 Cor. 15:54-55)

From this brief examination one can see that the textual history of the traditions cited by Paul is quite complicated. With respect to his interpretation of them, Paul has combined texts from Isaiah and Hosea in 1 Cor. 15:54-55 in analogous fashion to his more extensive citations in Rom. 9:24-27. Perhaps his source materials (selections of prophetic texts?) had already combined texts on the basis of key terms or common topics. In any case, Paul's intent is to show that prophecy is in accord with the gospel about God's Son that he preached. In the case of 1 Cor. 15, Jesus' resurrection is the evidence for and the basis of (cf. "firstfruits" in v. 20) the prophetic hope for the defeat of death and its eventual realization in those who believe. In the transformation to come (vv. 51-53) death will be swallowed up (vv. 54-55). In good rabbinic fashion he has seen that the key term *victory* over *death* is indicated by prophecy, as these are the two terms repeated in his quoted materials.[46] Hosea 13:14b is interpreted in light of the leading affirmation from Isaiah that death has been swallowed up in victory.

In the interpretation offered above, Hos. 13:14 was originally part of Hosea's prophecies of judgment in the historical moment in which YHWH employed Assyrian aggression against faithless, guilty Israel. With the LXX comes the possibility of

---

44. See the textual evidence as arranged by Hans Conzelmann, *1 Corinthians,* trans. James W. Leitch (Hermeneia; Philadelphia: Fortress, 1975), p. 292; and C. D. Stanley, *Paul and the Language of Scripture: Citation Technique in the Pauline Epistles and Contemporary Literature* (Cambridge: Cambridge University Press, 1992), pp. 210-11. Neither Aquila nor Theodotion has the verb "swallow." For the rabbis Isa. 25:8 was scriptural evidence to be cited for the conviction that death would be abolished in the age to come. See the discussion and references in Roy E. Ciampa and Brian S. Rosner, "I Corinthians," in *Commentary on the New Testament Use of the Old Testament,* ed. G. K. Beale and D. A. Carson (Grand Rapids: Baker Academic, 2007), p. 747.

45. A few LXX manuscripts have *nikē,* "victory," but they may be influenced by the citation in 1 Cor. 15:55.

46. Note the repetition of "victory" in 1 Cor. 15:57.

reading 13:14, or at least the first four clauses, in a more positive light. Paul is apparently influenced by this, as his citation serves to reinforce the prophecy of Isaiah that death will be swallowed up. The gospel based on Jesus' resurrection does indeed reverse the death sentence common to humanity and portrayed in Israel's folly. Whatever Hosea's intention in 13:14, his words live on in transmitted forms. They are reframed in light of other prophetic announcements, and most crucially in light of cross and resurrection. Since in his own day Hosea was an articulate spokesman of God's no to sin and yes to forgiveness and new life, he would rejoice at the ways in which a no could be swallowed up in a future transformation.

15 Chapter 13 began by characterizing Ephraim's past as an exalting of himself and yet dying by means of Baal. A similar critique of Ephraim's activities is portrayed in the initial clause of v. 15, at least with regard to Ephraim's intent at self-promotion. The difficult Hebrew text appears to have a characteristic Hosean wordplay, this time on the name Ephraim, using the verb *pārā'*, a variant form of *pārâ*, "be fruitful." The noun "fruit" *(pĕrî)* is the subject of a play on the name Ephraim in 9:16 and 14:8 (MT 9), and the verb is associated with the significance of Ephraim's birth in Gen. 41:52.[47] It is worth remembering that this way of portraying Ephraim may have some parallels with Jacob. Like Jacob before him, Ephraim surpasses his older brother, Manasseh (Gen. 48:9-20). Jacob's blessing of Ephraim in v. 19 includes the statement, "that his seed [descendants] shall become a multitude of nations." Thus the cryptic phrase that Ephraim is fruitful among his brothers[48] may reflect on tribal and sectional rivalry in the dissolution of the Israelite nation.[49] Ephraim may have achieved fruitfulness (political influence, numerical superiority?) among the northern tribes, but YHWH's judging wind will strike them and their advantages will disappear.

An attractive alternative to the proposed wordplay on "fruitful" is the suggestion that the verb *pārā'* is a denominative from *pere'* ("wild ass").[50] It is clear that Hosea has made the connection between Ephraim and *pere'*, as

47. Ephraim's name is interpreted as God making Joseph "fruitful" (*pārâ*, Hiphil).

48. Irvine, "Relating Prophet and History," pp. 162-66, takes "brothers" in the sense of political allies sought by Ephraim in the aftermath of Samaria's surrender and Shalmaneser V's death (721-720 B.C.). This is an interesting proposal, but it neglects the role of Ephraim among his brothers as typified in the ancestral stories.

49. While "Ephraim" is often a synonym for the northern kingdom of Israel in Hosea, texts like 5:5 and 13:1 indicate that "Ephraim" may also refer more particularly to a tribal identity or perhaps the central hill country of Cisjordan and the region of greater Samaria.

50. Andersen and Freedman, *Hosea*, pp. 625, 640; Macintosh, *Hosea*, pp. 550-51.

331

he uses the similarity of the noun with the tribal name to make a cutting pun on Ephraim's political machinations in 8:9. Two options for translating the initial clause with the verb *pārā'* ("be a wild ass") are as follows: Andersen and Freedman: "He became the wild one among his brothers"; Macintosh: "He is the one who behaves wilfully among brothers." Macintosh even proposes that the denominative verb *pārā'* is a pun on the traditional wordplay *(pārâ; 'eprayim)* given in Gen. 41:52. Given Hosea's propensities for paronomasia, one must take seriously the possibility that the prophet has adapted a noun to criticize Ephraim with a pun on a pun. Two points, however, should be kept in mind. First, the initial clause in v. 15 is but a setup for those that follow, underscoring YHWH's intention to reverse Ephraim's current sense of control. YHWH's coming judgment represents the main point, following the tenor of the chapter as a whole. Second, Ephraim's activity is among his brothers. As noted above, that detail should push the interpreter to see the activity in light of other references to Ephraim's brothers (kin), following the references to national traditions of an earlier time in chs. 12–13.

YHWH's judgment is like the *east wind (qādîm)* blowing from the wilderness. Hosea employs the term elsewhere in 12:1 (MT 2) in the sarcastic description of Ephraim as shepherding wind and following the east wind. No one in their right mind would follow the hot dry wind. It dries up things in its path, as v. 15 indicates. In 12:1 (MT 2) Ephraim's foolish pursuit is put in the context of international relations with Assyria and Egypt. Perhaps here in v. 15 YHWH's east wind is the consequence of Ephraim's failed diplomacy. They foolishly followed it and now it (i.e., YHWH) is about to hit home. A political reading also makes sense of the final clause. The treasury is a secure storeroom used by kings and temples (1 Kgs. 7:51; 2 Kgs. 12:9; Ezek. 28:4). When monarchs and cities are vanquished, then their treasuries are looted by the victors. What Ephraim intended as political maneuvering will result in the desiccating wind of a victor from the east and the loss of the nation's valuables.

16 (14:1) Verse 16 asserts that Samaria *is guilty ('āšam)* before YHWH her God. The verb is used by Hosea elsewhere and applied to the people generally (5:14), Israel (10:2), and Ephraim (13:1).[51] Surprisingly, the verb is uncommon among other 8th-century prophets. Moreover, there are few explicit references to Samaria in Hosea. Perhaps in Hosea's mind there is little difference between Samaria and Ephraim (cf. 7:1). Ephraim is the central tribe of Israel and is often by metonymy used to refer to the national entity. As with any capital city, Samaria too can stand for the nation or its government. However, Samaria is not cited explicitly with the frequency in Hosea that Jerusalem, her counterpart in Judah, is cited in Judean prophetic

51. Judah is enjoined not to become guilty in 4:15.

collections like Isaiah or Jeremiah.[52] Nevertheless, metaphorically speaking, "she" is related by covenant to God (cf. Ezek. 16, 23). Hence, in her representation of the people, she can be held in violation of her covenantal responsibilities and described as guilty and *engaged in rebellion (mārâ)*. The verb occurs only here in Hosea, but it is used several times in Deuteronomy to describe Israel in times of its rebellion (9:7, 23-24; 31:27)[53] and for a stubborn, incorrigible son (21:18, 20).

The gruesome description of the city's inhabitants is part of a recognized trope for the treatment of conquered peoples who have resisted takeover or who have broken solemn agreements. The *dashing of children* is described elsewhere in Hosea in a battle at Beth-arbel (10:14; cf. Nah. 3:10). In 2 Kgs. 8:12 Elisha weeps at the thought of the Aramean Hazael and his cruelty toward Israel, and names the deadly triad of killing by the sword, dashing infants, and ripping open pregnant women. While Hosea charges that Samaria *has rebelled against her God,* the predictions of death would come as a result of an assault on the city by a hostile army. Samaria endured a three-year siege at the hands of the Assyrians before finally falling to them (2 Kgs. 17:5-6). It is not clear whether v. 16 anticipates a tragic conclusion or reflects back on it. The former is the more natural reading. Samaria's fate is the same as that of the unwise son. A missed opportunity will result in death.

Thus concludes the last verse of the judgment texts in ch. 13. Samaria's coming demise, based on her guilt, reinforces the beginning of the chapter, where Ephraim is declared guilty for past failures and declared dead. Verses 1 and 16 bracket some of the harshest language in the book of Hosea. Thank God they are not the prophet's last words.

C. ISRAEL'S REPENTANCE AND YHWH'S HEALING POWER (14:1-8 [MT 2-9])

The last chapter of the book divides into three parts. The first is the prophet's call to the people to return to YHWH in penitence, including instruction to them on what to say (vv. 1-3).[1] YHWH speaks in the first person as a response (vv. 4-6, 8). A conclusion to the book follows (v. 9). Apart from the plant and

52. If Gomer represents Samaria in Hos. 1–3, then the frequency of references to the city increases markedly.

53. Deut. 9:7 and 23-24 refer to rebellion in the wilderness wandering (cf. Num. 20:24; 27:14). Deuteronomy 31:27 is Moses' statement that Israel will be rebellious in the future.

1. To avoid needless repetition, English versification will be used generally in this section.

geography metaphors in vv. 5b-8, a good percentage of the chapter's vocabulary is found elsewhere in the book. Some of the data are as follows:

vv. 1-2	return to YHWH	6:1
vv. 1, 9	stumbling (in iniquity)	5:5
v. 3	Assyria cannot save or heal	5:13
v. 3	YHWH is compassionate	2:23 (MT 25)
v. 4	YHWH can heal	6:1; 7:1; 11:3
v. 4	YHWH loves Israel	11:1
v. 4	YHWH's anger	8:5; 11:9; 13:11
v. 5	dew in Israel	6:4; 13:3
v. 8	idols	4:17; 8:4; 13:2
v. 8	YHWH answers	2:21 (MT 23)
v. 8	Israel's fruit	9:16; 10:1
v. 9	wise person	13:13 = unwise son.

There are few clues in this material for a particular setting in Hosea's life. I suggested above that ch. 13 likely comes from the 720s and the reign of King Hoshea, perhaps even reflecting the siege of Samaria. Chapter 14 is not necessarily from that same time or later, simply because it comes next. As the conclusion to the book, however, it reflects a number of terms and themes from the book and frames them in the future light of repentance and forgiveness.[2] More particularly, it serves as a reversal of Israel's eminent demise as depicted in ch. 13.[3] These characteristics suggest that ch. 14 is one of the latest compositions in the book. It could well be Hosea's own studied conclusion to the dilemma presented by Israel's failure or that of the book's editors. If it is the latter, then they had absorbed deeply the thought processes and theological analysis of the prophet. In either case, the conclusion is a witness to the conviction that the fall of Israel and Samaria was not the end of YHWH's work with this portion of his covenant people. Forgiveness, restoration, and transformation are projected for the future. A later generation looking back at Israel's history through the lens of ch. 14 would see in it a prophecy pointing to an eschatological future in which past failures and their consequences are overcome by YHWH's will to redeem.

2. See Paul A. Kruger, "Yahweh's Generous Love: Eschatological Expectations in Hosea 14:2-9," *OTE* 1 (1988) 27-48.

3. Note that Israel's "iniquity" (13:12) will be taken away (14:2); neither king (13:10) nor Assyria will "save" Israel (14:3); Israel will not deify the "work" of their hands (13:2; 14:3); YHWH's "anger" (13:11) will be removed (14:4); YHWH will be the "dew" (13:3; 14:5) to sustain Israel.

1 (2) *Return, O Israel, to YHWH your God, for you have stumbled in your iniquity.*

2 (3) *Take words with you and return to YHWH. Say to him, "Take away all (our) iniquity[4] and receive good, and we will present the fruit[5] of our lips.*

3 (4) *"Assyria will not deliver us. We will not ride horses; and no longer will we say, 'Our God,'[6] to the work of our hands, for with you the orphan finds mercy."*

4 (5) *I will heal their apostasy, I will love them freely. My anger has turned from them.[7]*

5 (6) *I will be like the dew to Israel, he will be like the lily. And he will strike[8] his roots like Lebanon.*

6 (7) *His shoots shall spread out; his splendor will be like the olive tree, and his fragrance like Lebanon.*

7 (8) *Those who live[9] in his shadow[10] will again raise grain, and they will sprout like the vine; his renown will be like the wine of Lebanon.*

8 (9) *Ephraim, what more do I[11] have to do with idols? I indeed have responded and watch for him. I am like a luxuriant cypress; from me comes your fruit.*

4. The Hebrew phrase *kol-tiśśā' 'āwōn* is a grammatical anomaly, as the adjective "all" should be attached or placed with the noun "iniquity." Andersen and Freedman, *Hosea,* p. 645, rightly describe the phrase as a "discontinuous construct chain," of which there are other examples in the OT.

5. Following LXX *karpon,* which would suggest Heb. *pĕrî* ("fruit"). The MT has *pārîm* ("bulls"). The final *mem* is considered an "archaic Canaanite case ending" on the noun *pĕrî* by Wolff, *Hosea,* p. 231, what others identify as an enclitic *mem;* so Andersen and Freedman, *Hosea,* p. 645. Macintosh, *Hosea,* p. 561, accepts the plural noun "bulls" and renders: "with our confession as if with young bulls"; also McComiskey, *Hosea,* p. 228: "our lips as bulls."

6. The LXX has *theoi hēmōn,* "our gods," which is also an acceptable rendering of Heb. *'ĕlōhēnû.* So also NIV and Macintosh, *Hosea,* p. 565.

7. The MT has *mimmennû,* "from him," apparently a collective reference to Israel.

8. The form *wĕyak* is an abbreviated imperfect of the verb *nākâ.*

9. Some interpreters read *yēšĕbû* ("they will dwell") for *yōšĕbê* ("inhabitants of"); so Wolff, *Hosea,* p. 232; Rudolph, *Hosea,* p. 248. Although awkward, the MT is coherent. The initial verb of the verse, *yāšūbû,* functions as a support to the next verb signifying repetition ("again"), as it does in 11:9 and perhaps in 3:5.

10. In order to maintain the continuity of first-person speech from the context, some interpreters emend *bĕṣillô,* "in his shadow," to *bĕṣillî,* "in my shadow"; so NRSV and Wolff, *Hosea,* p. 232. This makes good sense and is a viable option, since the difference in the final letter, -*ô* or -*î,* in Biblical Hebrew script was often slight.

11. The LXX has *autō,* "him," which would presuppose *lô* for MT *lî.* Some interpreters adopt the LXX as more plausible; so Wolff, *Hosea,* p. 233; Yee, *Composition and Tradition,* p. 137. This, in turn, assumes that it is Ephraim who is associated with idols. That

1 (2) Israel is called to return to YHWH in v. 1, and it is repeated in v. 2, although with slight variations.[12] It is a jarring call, but also a relief, to set beside the somber account of destruction with which ch. 13 ended. The call to *Return (šûb)* is the language of repentance, with YHWH as the object. It is extended by the prophet to the people.[13] There is likely a cultic context in mind as well, with rites of repentance and corresponding actions to be carried out. This is at least the implication of v. 2. As the context makes clear, YHWH expects some things of Israel in its return, but the goal is not a list of things but finally a return to YHWH himself.

The language of *return to YHWH* is employed similarly in 6:1, where it is spoken by (or attributed to) the people whom YHWH had struck. There the context was YHWH's death-dealing attack as a lion (5:14), and the proposed "return to YHWH" was expressed in light of his "healing" *(rāpā')*, reviving, and raising abilities. A cultic context for the language of healing and reviving is plausible for 6:1-3.[14] With 14:1, ch. 13 is the immediate backdrop, with its description of YHWH's death-dealing attack as a lion (v. 7) and the fall of Samaria to the sword (v. 16). In 13:10 the Israelite king was unable to "deliver" *(yāša');* in 14:3 Assyria will not "deliver" *(yāša')* either. YHWH's work of *healing (rāpā')* is also noted in 14:4. The repentance set forth in 6:1 did not happen, or it was not accepted. That the call in 14:1 comes from the prophet and is backed in 14:4 by YHWH's declaration of healing and love offers yet another opportunity for the people after the historical death sentences expressed elsewhere in the book.

Much of the criticism of Israel in the book can be summed up in v. 1b. The terminology is vintage Hosea. *Stumbling* is attributed to priests and people (4:5), as well as to Israel, Ephraim, and Judah (5:5).[15] Moreover, the term *iniquity,* which is also used on a number of occasions, occurs with the verb *stumbling* in 5:5. The phrase *stumble in iniquity (kšl b + 'wn)* appears to encapsulate an act-consequence relationship in which the iniquities have within them the cause of stumbling. We might, therefore, translate the phrase as

---

assumption makes sense, for the people have been charged with idolatry in 8:4b-6 and 13:2. Although he does not accept the proposed emendation, Macintosh, *Hosea,* pp. 576-77, opts to see v. 8a as a quotation attributed to Ephraim. His reconstruction of the verse has three changes of speaker.

12. The preposition differs (*'ad,* v. 1; *'el,* v. 2), and Israel is represented with singular pronouns in v. 1 and plural pronouns in v. 2. See the excursus at 6:1, "Return to YHWH."

13. Macintosh, *Hosea,* pp. 558-59, proposes that 14:1-3 is Hosea's prayer for Israel.

14. See the excursus at 6:3, "Being Raised on the Third Day." Note also the parallels in language with 11:5, "he refused to return *(šûb)* to me"; and 11:3, "they did not know that I healed *(rāpā')* them."

15. The verb is also used in 14:9 to describe what happens to transgressors who encounter God's "ways."

"stumble by means of iniquity," and v. 1b more expansively as "you have stumbled through the agency of your iniquity."

2 (3)   Verse 2 continues the call to the people, here addressed in second person plural, to return to YHWH. The second imperative, *Take words,* is intended to guide their approach to him, as the third imperative, *Say to him,* makes clear. The content of the words to be presented before YHWH then follows.

An appearance before YHWH in a cultic setting had certain expectations. Worshipers are instructed elsewhere not to appear before YHWH "empty-handed" (Exod. 23:15; 34:20; Deut. 16:16). They are to be prepared to offer what is necessary and appropriate in context: prayer, sacrificial gifts, vows, and so on. Thus, while repentance and the request for forgiveness are in the foreground, the people's prayer to YHWH also contains the request that he receive[16] from them what is *good (ṭôb).* The noun is common and used in a variety of settings, rather than being limited to a cultic context. It is a given in the hymns and prayers of the Psalter, where YHWH's self-revelation in the cult is acknowledged, that YHWH himself is good and defines what is good.[17] Thus in v. 2 he is asked in prayer to receive what he has declared elsewhere to be appropriate to the occasion of repentance (e.g., confession, vows, sacrifice).

The final phrase of v. 2 continues the goal of presenting to YHWH what is good and appropriate. The verb *present (šālam,* Piel) is one of returning or paying what is necessary. It is frequently associated with vows because they are first expressed and then fulfilled by carrying them out, often in the context of sacrifice.[18] A textual problem in the object of the verb is usually solved by recourse to the LXX ("fruit" in place of "bulls"). The *fruit of the lips* is apparently a metaphor for saying what is appropriate. Lips are used metaphorically in proverbial wisdom especially as vehicles (source domain) to convey the tenor (target domain) of right speech and character or their opposite.[19] The fruit of Israel's lips in v. 2 is best defined by the confession that follows in v. 3.

---

16. The common verb *lāqaḥ* is used for both "taking" and "receiving." In v. 2 the people are to "take words" and they are to ask YHWH to "receive good." Note the use of the verb in Exod. 22:11 (MT 10), where a property owner is asked to "receive" *(lāqaḥ)* a vow of a neighbor so that the neighbor does not have to "make restitution" *(šālam,* Piel). Both verbs are used in Hos. 14:2.

17. See the various uses of the term in 2:7 (MT 9); 3:5; 4:13; 8:3; 10:1, and the excursus at 3:5, "YHWH's Goodness."

18. In the Psalter the fulfilling of vows is often associated with sacrifice and other acts of worship. See 22:25 (MT 26); 50:14; 56:12 (MT 13); 66:13; 116:14, 18.

19. For example, Prov. 10:13, lips of discernment; 10:18, lying lips; 12:19, lip of truth; 16:21, sweetness of lips. Isa. 57:19 has the phrase "fruit *(nûd)* of the lips" as something that YHWH will create for mourners when he heals *(rāpā')* them.

In this context, readers might consider also the language of Ps. 51:14-17 (MT 16-19), with its plea for forgiveness from bloodguilt and the request that YHWH would:

> open my lips, that my mouth can declare your praise;
> for you have no desire in sacrifice *(ḥāpaṣ zebaḥ)*, or I would present it.
> You are not pleased with a burnt offering. God's sacrifices are a
>   broken spirit;
> a broken and humbled heart O God, you will not despise.

For his part, Hosea avoids the actual mention of sacrifice in his call to the people to return to YHWH in v. 2 and make restitution with the fruit of their lips. On the one hand, sacrifice itself does not bind YHWH to the will of the worshiper who presents it. YHWH remains free in his disposition toward cultic service. Hosea repeatedly criticizes the institution of sacrifice else-where as syncretistic, a reflection of the people's corruption and misunder-standing of YHWH's will, and their attempt to manipulate him. Indeed, YHWH's lack of "desire for sacrifice" (Ps. 51:16 [MT 18]) is expressed in Hos. 6:6a, where YHWH declares that he desires *ḥesed* ("loving-kindness, loyalty"), not sacrifice. On the other hand, sacrifice is an appropriate act in the worship of YHWH in the pentateuchal codes, and it is difficult to think of Hosea as suggesting that it is inadequate, in principle, to offer YHWH sacri-fice. In the disciplinary period of the future, Israel will be without cultic para-phernalia, but the implication of 3:4-5 is that sacrifice itself would be accept-able to YHWH when the people come trembling to him in the latter days. While it may be true that Hosea represents a spiritualizing of sacrifice in the metaphor of providing a *fruit of the lips* offering to YHWH, it is unlikely that he opposed sacrificial practice in principle.[20]

In essence, the plea for forgiveness in vv. 2b-3 is a way of presenting oneself to YHWH in sincerity of heart (as the psalmist indicates) and in the hope of a merciful response. Whatever is vowed before God is essentially in the form of a promise for change in the future.

3 (4) The book of Hosea states in several ways that *Assyria* is not the solution to Israel's dilemma. Now at the end of the prophecy, the people themselves are asked to confess it. Assyria cannot *deliver* or save *(yāša')* them, and neither could their own rulers (13:10). YHWH is the one who will deliver Judah (so 1:7) and who was Israel's savior from Egypt (13:4; cf. Exod. 14:30).

20. See the discussion of this point in Eidevall, *Grapes in the Desert*, p. 211, along with references to interpreters who emphasize the nonsacrificial aspect of Hosea's thought. The phrase *fruit of the lips* as a metaphor for the spiritualizing of sacrificial wor-ship of God is used in Heb. 13:15.

The significance of the reference to *horses* is unclear. Two options, however, commend themselves. One is to see them as representing Israel's military power. If this is correct, then Israel is to confess that neither the power of Assyria nor that of their cavalry or chariots will deliver them. The second option is related to the first, but sees the reference as a backhanded indication of Egypt, which was active in the horse trade with Israel and others (Deut. 17:16; 1 Kgs. 10:28-29; Ezek. 17:15). Egypt and Assyria are paired in Hosea elsewhere as diplomatic entities to be avoided (7:11; 12:1 [MT 2]), and King Hoshea, in particular, appealed to Egypt (2 Kgs. 17:4). Isaiah polemicized against those who go to Egypt and rely upon horses and chariots (31:3).[21]

Israel is also to forswear idolatry. This picks up another theme from the book, particularly the polemic against things made by hand, yet foolishly associated with the divine (8:6; 13:2). Hosea's language represents an ambiguity, for one may translate *'ĕlōhēnû* as "our God" or our gods."

YHWH's *mercy* or compassion[22] is indicated by the reference to his care for the *orphan*. In Hosea's day one's basic social identity came from the extended family with its patriarchal head. An orphan (more specifically, someone who is fatherless) would be without the support and guidance of a father and thus a relatively easy subject for exploitation and entrance into debt slavery. The psalmist praised YHWH as the "father of the fatherless" and "judge for widows" (68:5 [MT 6]; cf. Deut. 10:18). Widows, like orphans, were often at the mercy of greedy and unsavory elements in society. Recognition of their needs was explicit in pentateuchal instruction (Exod. 22:22 [MT 21]; Deut. 14:29; 24:17-21; 27:19). But why note YHWH's compassion toward the fatherless at this point? Perhaps the best answer is that Israel had effectively become an orphan rather than a son in its rejection of YHWH's covenant and instruction (8:1-3; 11:1-2). As a penitent, a prodigal son who has squandered his inheritance, Israel found itself in the position of an orphan.

4 (5) YHWH speaks as if he has accepted every word of the proposed prayer of repentance from the previous verses. The verse is a classic tricolon in which each clause (colon) interprets the others. In v. 1 Hosea summarized Israel's plight as stumbling in iniquity. Here in v. 4 their predicament is encapsulated in the term *apostasy (měšûbâ)*. It is a noun formed from the

---

21. Macintosh, *Hosea*, p. 566, suggests that the reference to horses continues the thought that Assyria will not save them and refers specifically to dispatching riders of horses as messengers to either Assyria or Egypt. Perhaps he presses the distinction between the phrase "riding horses" and Israel's reliance on chariots too far.

22. The verb is from the root *rḥm*, which is the basis of the name Lo-ruhamah, "No Mercy," in 1:6-7 and the verb in 2:23 (MT 25).

root *šwb* and has the basic meaning of "turning" or "turning one." Hosea also employs the term in 11:7 with the nuance of Israel as "turning" from YHWH. It is a favored term with Jeremiah, who uses it to describe both Israel and Judah as backsliding, treacherously turning, and faithless (2:19; 3:6, 8, 11, 12, 22; 5:6; 8:5; 14:7). The appeal of YHWH through Jeremiah to Israel[23] in 3:22 is likely dependent upon Hosea's prophecies: "Return *(šûb)* faithless children, I will heal *(rāpā')* your apostasies *(mĕšûbōtêkem)*." The connection in Jer. 3:22 is explicit between the return to YHWH and the exercise of his forgiveness as "healing." This follows Hosea's point of view. YHWH's healing has been active since Israel's youth, even if Israel did not acknowledge it formerly (Hos. 11:3).[24] And YHWH will heal Israel's corporate failures when they turn to him. Apparently some of Hosea's contemporaries believed that Assyria could heal them in the complexities of their historical predicament, although the prophet strongly contradicted them (cf. 5:13).

The second clause in v. 4 reinforces what YHWH's healing of Israel entails. It is an uncoerced love.[25] The root *'hb* ("love") plays a significant role in the book, but nowhere a more important one than in YHWH's own speech in v. 4.[26] In 9:15 YHWH declared that he would drive his people out of his house and love them no longer. That declaration and its subsequent effects are reversed by YHWH's declaration in v. 4. YHWH's love will be freely extended to a penitent Israel. The adverb *nĕdābâ* refers to giving that is spontaneous and/or voluntary. When used as a noun, the term represents a "freewill offering" (Exod. 35:29; 2 Chr. 31:14). It is sometimes used with the noun "vow" *(nēder;* Num. 15:3; Lev. 22:18; 23:38) and the verb "to make a vow" *(nādar;* Deut. 23:23). As an adjective it indicates abundance or voluntariness (Pss. 68:9 [MT 10]; 110:3). Perhaps the term *nĕdābâ* is employed here as an echo of the vow language in v. 2. The confession that Hosea urges on Israel is that they will "present [*šālam,* Piel] the fruit of their lips" to YHWH. The Piel of *šālam* is often used in the paying or carrying out of vows. In YHWH's response in v. 4, it is as if he makes a freewill vow of his own.

The third clause of v. 4 also contains a wordplay. In Israel's invited *return* to YHWH, there is also a divine counterpart in the *turning (šûb)* of YHWH's *anger ('ap)* from them. That fierce anger is mentioned explicitly in 13:11, and its *turning* from Israel here in 14:4 is a reversal of its deadly effects.

23. Jeremiah appeals to the house of Israel and to Israel in 3:20-21. These terms may well represent elements from the former northern kingdom in distinction from Judah (cf. 3:11-14).

24. Oestreich, *Metaphors,* pp. 57-87, suggests that the healing activity of YHWH in Hosea here and elsewhere (5:12-13; 6:1; 6:11b–7:1; 11:3) is rooted in the metaphor of YHWH as father and king.

25. No "hiring of lovers" is involved (8:9; 9:1; cf. 2:12 [MT 14]).

26. See appendix 4, "Love in the Prophecy of Hosea."

Thus v. 4 reinforces the compassion that is predicated of YHWH at the conclusion of v. 3. The tricolon is made up largely of terms used elsewhere in the book. They are employed here as YHWH's already-given response to the repentance urged upon Israel.

5 (6)   Twice Hosea employs the related metaphors of morning cloud and dew to portray the fickleness of Israel (6:4; 13:3). In v. 5 the sustaining presence of YHWH as *dew (tal)* reverses the fickleness, dryness, and unfruitfulness attributed to the people elsewhere in the book. Dew is associated with the morning clouds and early mist of the summer in ancient Israel, a season that is otherwise dry. A Mediterranean climate typically offers very little rain from April through October. Without the dew, the agricultural season is cut short, and ripening fruits will be stunted in development or not survive. Given the use of Jacob traditions elsewhere, it is also possible that the blessing of Isaac upon Jacob contributes to the comparison of YHWH to dew. In Gen. 27:28 Isaac's blessing seeks that "God give you the dew of heaven and from the fatness of the land much grain and new wine."[27]

Verses 5-7 all end with a reference to *Lebanon,* providing a metaphorical field or source domain for the imagery in them.[28] Lebanon refers to the mountainous area of northern Galilee and modern-day Lebanon, a fertile and at times fragrant region. Ezekiel 17:3-10 and 22-24 contain a parable about an eagle who plucked a twig from a cedar in Lebanon and planted it in good soil with abundant waters. The description is intended, among other things, to say that the transplanted twig became a large fruitful vine with roots and shoots. Such fecund images also inform Ps. 80:8-19 (MT 9-20), where Israel is depicted as a vine YHWH removed from Egypt that took root in the land where he planted it until wild animals consumed it. Both texts, furthermore, show the interlocking imagery of plant metaphors and the involved literary forms that employ them.

If YHWH is like dew, then Israel will be like the *lily* nourished by him. It is important to note the sequence. Without the moisture, there is no lily. With YHWH's nourishing presence, there are not only the wild flowers but the *striking of roots* in the soil for plants and trees.

6 (7)   Israel will branch out under YHWH's care. The *shoots (yôneqet)*[29] of v. 6 are the sign of flourishing and growth when a vine or tree has the proper water and soil. Olives are a staple of the region, providing food and

---

27. See the analysis of the "dew" traditions in Hosea in Oestreich, *Metaphors,* pp. 157-89.

28. Some interpreters and translations regard the noun Lebanon as a metonym for the forests or the cedars of Lebanon in vv. 5-6; so NRSV; NASB; Wolff, *Hosea,* p. 232; and Macintosh, *Hosea,* p. 570. This seems to unduly restrict the source domain for the variety of images in the two verses.

29. The same term is used in Ps. 80:11 (MT 12) and Ezek. 17:22.

oil and commodities for trade. The term *splendor (hôd)* is typically associated with divine majesty (Ps. 8:1 [MT 2]; 96:6; 104:1; Isa. 30:30; Hab. 3:3) and human royalty (Ps. 21:5 [MT 6]; 45:3 [MT 4]; Jer. 22:18). Hence Israel's future blessedness is portrayed not just as fruitful, but as also partaking of royal splendor. Even the sense of smell is involved, with the people having a pleasing fragrance. The same simile is used to describe the magnificence of the bride in the Song of Songs (4:11), who is called to journey with her lover from Lebanon (4:8; cf. 5:5), who is compared to a lush garden with water from Lebanon (4:12-15), and who is a lily sitting in the shade of her lover (2:1-3). Given these connections with the amorous Song of Songs, some interpreters have proposed marital imagery for Israel here in v. 6.[30] We should not reject this suggestion simply because Israel is portrayed throughout 14:5-7 as masculine.[31] If Israel can be portrayed as masculine and committing prostitution (*zānâ;* 4:12), a commercial role for women, then possibly the allusion to Israel as beloved spouse (3:1) can be seconded in 14:5-7. Perhaps we should also see Israel's future blessedness in terms of paradise, an Eden-like existence. In a metaphorical depiction of Assyria as a cedar in Lebanon, the great beauty of the tree is compared to those in "God's garden, Eden" (Ezek. 31:1-14).

7 (8) For understandable reasons, some interpreters would emend the text of v. 7 so that YHWH remains the speaker, as is the case in the previous two verses. The emendation entails reading "my" for "his" shadow. The emendation is relatively minor. Nevertheless, there are other occasions in the book where the speaker changes abruptly, and the MT can be understood as the prophet's comment on future Israel's security and fruitfulness vis-à-vis YHWH, the great tree of the verse that follows. The second "his" of the verse is probably a reference to Israel in third person singular, a switch from the third person plural. Such switches are also typical of Hosea.

The agricultural imagery in v. 7 has connections elsewhere in the book. Hosea referred to Israel as a luxuriant vine (10:1), but one with self-incurred problems (cf. Ps. 80). In the historical judgment of Hosea's day (Hos. 8:7) the nation's grain would be lost. Here in v. 7 the grain is renewed,[32] and the simile of the sprouting vine leads to that of wine from Lebanon. Perhaps we have the continuation of the comparison of YHWH with dew (v. 5) and an allusion to the ancestral blessing on Jacob (Gen. 27:28), with its references to dew, grain, and wine.[33]

---

30. So A. Feuillet, "'S'asseoir à l'ombre' de l'époux," *RB* 78 (1971) 391-405; Yee, *Composition and Tradition,* p. 138.

31. So Eidevall, *Grapes in the Desert,* p. 213.

32. The use of the Piel of *ḥāyâ* is odd. The verb typically means "to make alive," used for people and animals. It is so used in 6:2.

33. For wine Gen. 27:28 has *tîrōš,* whereas Hos. 14:7 has *yayin.*

8 (9)   Verse 8 is best taken as a pair of bicola in which the first colon is a rhetorical question, if not a soliloquy. Rhetorical question and soliloquy are combined in 11:8, also with regard to Ephraim. YHWH refused to give Ephraim up in that instance and in 14:8 wants nothing to do with divine images made by hand. This is made clear also in 13:2. In 14:3 Israel is urged to confess the error of employing idols.

The second colon of v. 8 can be taken in a variety of ways. The first matter is that of tense or aspect. Is the response an aspect of the future, as translated with NIV, "I will answer him and care for him"? The Qal perfect and imperfect (*waw* "conversive") verbs do not lend themselves readily to this rendering. Many translations render in the present as a statement of YHWH's present disposition toward Israel, which can be coordinated with the opening question. In effect, "I have nothing to do with idols, past or present," and "it is I who answer and look after you"[34] (so NRSV). A past aspect to the verbs can be coordinated similarly, as if to say that YHWH has responded and that his disposition remains in effect, just like the rejection of idols.

The second matter has to do with the nuance of the verbs. The LXX apparently takes the verb *ʿānâ* in the Piel as "afflict." The verb is Qal in the MT, which is the pointing in all other occurrences of the verb in Hosea. In the restoration passage of ch. 2, YHWH "answers" the heavens and begins a chain reaction of fertility and blessing (2:21-22 [MT 23-24]). This is the likely sense of YHWH's answer here in v. 8. It is a positive response open and ready for Israel. With respect to the second verb, it seems best to take it as the Qal of *šûr* ("to watch for, to wait in anticipation"). This is the sense of the verb in 13:7, where the leopard (YHWH) waits for its prey. Using the same verb here in v. 8 is a nice reversal of that image.[35]

Over a century ago Wellhausen suggested that the second clause of v. 8 be rendered, "I am his Anat and his Asherah."[36] One wonders if this is not too clever, even for Hosea, as there are no other clear references to goddesses in the Hosea materials. In light of recent interest in goddesses and new inscriptional references to them, other interpreters have accepted his proposal in toto, or at least the view that the assonance of the clause alludes to the goddesses.[37] On balance, the allusions in v. 8 to vocabulary used elsewhere in Hosea outweigh the more strained proposal to find Anat and Asherah in the verbs *ʿānâ* and *ʾāšar*.

In the second bicolon of v. 8, YHWH presents himself as a luxuriant

---

34. The "you" of the NRSV is an emendation to fit more closely the address to Ephraim in 14:8.

35. The Vulgate rendering seems to presuppose the Piel of *ʾšr*, "to lead." Stuart, *Hosea*, p. 211, emends to the Qal of *ʾšr*, "to bless."

36. Wellhausen, *Kleinen Propheten*, p. 134.

37. For references see Eidevall, *Grapes in the Desert*, p. 218.

tree and the provider of Ephraim's *fruit*. The wordplay on the name *'eprayim* (Ephraim) and *pĕrî* ("fruit") is found elsewhere in the book (9:16), plus the mention of fruit here is a nice reinforcement of the praise directed to YHWH as the "fruit of the lips" in v. 2.

Nowhere else in the OT is YHWH compared to a tree. This does not make the simile in v. 8 inappropriate, just unique. It fits the metaphorical style of Hosea, as well as the close connection drawn between YHWH, the natural world, and fertility in the immediate context. In the critique of Gomer (Israel) and her engagement with the Baal deities in ch. 2, Hosea represented YHWH as a Deity capable of providing all that she mistakenly attributed to them. That same theological conclusion undergirds the close link between YHWH and fruitfulness here. YHWH is the Lord not only of history but also of nature.

Other deities are compared to and represented by trees.[38] YHWH is *like* the great Lebanese cypress or juniper in his majesty and presence for Ephraim.[39] Of course, there are ways in which he is unlike such a tree or should not be so compared.

The book began with the charge that the land committed harlotry in disobedience to YHWH (1:2). The charge of Israel's faithlessness continued, including the description of the land ill and in mourning (4:1-3). Now the book comes to a penultimate conclusion here in 14:4-8 with an eschatological projection of Israel healed and loved, fruitful in the land under YHWH's shadow and secure in the provisions of his care.

V. THIS IS WISDOM:
YHWH'S WAYS ARE RIGHT (14:9 [MT 10])

9 (10) *Whoever is wise let him consider these things; (whoever is) discerning, let him know them. For the ways of YHWH are right, and the righteous will walk in them, but transgressors will stumble in them.*

---

38. Majestic trees are also symbols of royalty. On the symbolism of the tree, see K. A. Tångberg, "'I am like an evergreen fir; from me comes your fruit': Notes on the Meaning and Symbolism in Hosea 14,9b (MT)," *SJOT* 2 (1989) 81-93.

39. It is not clear which of the great trees in northern Galilee or Lebanon is in mind. Part of the issue relates to the adjective *ra'ănān* and whether it indicates an "evergreen" tree or one of extensive size and foliage. In addition to the discussion in Tångberg, see also Oestreich, *Metaphors,* pp. 192-95. Oestreich opts for juniper but notes that it is not a fruit-bearing tree, so that the reference to "fruit" in v. 8 would have to be an extension of the metaphor of YHWH as tree, not something inherent in the tree itself. Oestreich, *Metaphors,* pp. 223-24, agrees with Tångberg that YHWH as "tree" is a royal metaphor.

9 (10)   This epilogue is sage counsel to readers of Hosea, formulated as proverbial instruction in both form and content. The prophecies within the book *(these things)* require wisdom and insight for their interpretation and may not reveal much to superficial inquiry. Indeed, one way to define a wise person[1] is if he or she is motivated to ponder the mysteries within the book and to learn from them. YHWH's *ways (dĕrākîm)* with Israel, nature, and the historical process are revealed in it. Those ways are *right (yĕšārîm),* an adjective indicating something that is straight, upright, or correct, and a term associated with YHWH in various contexts in the OT (see below). The matter at hand in v. 9 (MT 10) is not just the wisdom associated with *discerning (bîn)*[2] something of YHWH's modes of action and instruction, but also the wisdom of a patterned, disciplined response to the ways revealed. Hence the final antithetical parallelism of the verse between the righteous and transgressors. The former would be rightly related to YHWH and his ways by *walking (hālak)* in them.[3] YHWH's ways become the ways of the righteous who follow them properly. The *transgressors (pōšĕ'îm),* however, will *stumble (yikkāšĕlû)* in those same ways.[4] A transgressor is one who rebels against the guidance provided in YHWH's ways, and in doing so does not reach the goal of blessing and security. Sage observations elsewhere offer parallels in form and content to the antithetical conclusion:

> The one who walks in uprightness *(yāšār)* fears YHWH, but he who is devious in his ways *(dĕrākîm)* despises him. (Prov. 14:2)

> YHWH knows the way *(derek)* of the righteous, but the way *(derek)* of the wicked shall perish. (Ps. 1:6)

One can readily see that the terminology of v. 9 (MT 10) echoes the contents of the prophecy, with an emphasis on the ways in which the people of Hosea's day missed the mark.[5] This is an editorial viewpoint, recommending that readers learn from the missteps of Israel. It is also a viewpoint thoroughly conversant with and committed to the perspectives of the prophecy. One might think of members of Hosea's prophetic community who transmit-

---

1. Cf. 13:13: Ephraim is an unwise *(lō' ḥākām)* son.

2. Cf. 4:14, "a people without discernment *(lō'-yābîn)* will come to ruin."

3. The corrupted "ways" of the people are variously depicted: 2:6 (MT 8); 4:9; 10:13; 12:2 (MT 3); they "walk" or go after things that are to their detriment: 2:5, 13 (MT 7, 15); 5:11; 11:2. Cf. "walking in YHWH's ways" and doing what is "right *(yāšār)* in his eyes" (1 Kgs. 11:33, 38).

4. On *pš'* see 7:13; 8:1, "they have rejected my instruction." On *kšl* see 5:5; 14:1 (MT 2).

5. C. L. Seow, "Hosea 14:10 and the Foolish People Motif," *CBQ* 44 (1982) 212-24.

ted his work as plausible sources for this concluding comment. Similarly, the notice that Hezekiah's scribes put forth an edition of proverbs (Prov. 25:1) provides another plausible setting for the wisdom hermeneutic of Hos. 14:9 (MT 10). As noted in the introduction, a penultimate version of the book likely took shape during Hezekiah's reign in Judah.[6]

One can also see from the terminology in v. 9 (MT 10) that the emphasis is not only to set forth the folly of Israel as a negative example from which to learn, but also to confess the integrity of YHWH in his ways of dealing with his world. Here are some echoes for this theme, keyed to the adjective *yāšār* ("right/upright") and the noun *derek* ("way").

> Deut. 32:4   The rock, his work has integrity *(tāmîm),* and all his ways *(děrākîm)* are just *(mišpāṭ).* A faithful God, without deceit, he is just *(ṣaddîq)* and upright *(yāšār).*

> Ps. 92:15 (MT 16)   Upright *(yāšār)* is YHWH my rock

> Ps. 25:8   Good *(ṭôb)* and upright *(yāšār)* is YHWH; therefore he instructs sinners *(ḥaṭṭā'îm)* in the way *(derek).*

YHWH's "ways" are the primary indication of his integrity and a primary source of his instruction to Israel. There is a sense in which YHWH *is* his ways. Note, for example, that the adjective *yāšār* modifies YHWH himself in the three examples cited above, rather than his *ways,* as in Hos. 14:9 (MT 10). The adjective applies in either case. That YHWH is *yāšār* undergirds his work in instructing sinners in his way. It is this element in particular that v. 9 (MT 10) has in mind in recommending the prophecy of Hosea to readers. From this perspective, the prophecy of Hosea reveals YHWH to be *yāšār* in judgment. Later readers have a history lesson set before them regarding the failure of their ancestors. For their own guidance they may take instruction from the critique of Israel (i.e., what they should avoid) and from what was enjoined on Israel (i.e., what they should embrace as YHWH's ways). For the future, they could take comfort in the various promises that God would restore his household in ways more glorious than the time in which he took them from Egypt and planted them in the promised land.

---

6. See the introduction, section I, "Origins and Transmission."

APPENDICES

APPENDICES

1. Baal in Hosea

The noun *ba'al* occurs seven times in Hosea (2:8, 13, 16, 17 [MT 10, 15, 18, 19]; 9:10; 11:2; 13:1). Three of those are plural (2:13, 17; 11:2). In Hebrew the root *b'l* is also used as a verb meaning to "own" or "possess," and thus to represent the act of marriage in which a man acquires a wife. As a common noun it represents an owner or master, hence its application to Canaanite deities, who can be owners of holy places[1] and possessors of powers. The noun can refer to a husband (Gen. 20:3), an owner of a commodity (Exod. 21:28), and leaders of a community (Josh. 24:11). It is not a personal name.

A standard interpretation of the references in Hosea has been that both the plural and the singular terms are references to Canaanite deities other than YHWH, the sole exception being 2:16 (MT 18), where Israel is no longer to call YHWH by this term. With the discovery of the Ugaritic texts and their representation of a powerful Baal named Hadad, Lord of heaven and earth, some interpreters emphasized the singular references in Hosea and interpreted the plural ones as synonymous for "other deities," based on the assumption that Hosea's contemporaries were tempted to worship one primary Baal.[2] One alternative to this debate over the nature of Canaanite deities is the suggestion that the term *ba'al* is a cipher for syncretistic worship of YHWH as Baal.[3] Another alternative is to attribute some of the references in Hosea not to deities but to kings and political leaders with whom Israel has concluded entangling political alliances.[4]

---

1. J. Andrew Dearman, "Baal in Ancient Israel: The Contribution of Some Place Names and Personal Names to the Understanding of Early Israelite Religion," in *History and Interpretation,* ed. Graham et al., pp. 173-91.

2. For more details see J. Andrew Dearman, "Interpreting the Religious Polemics against Baal and the Baalim in the Book of Hosea," *OTE* 14 (2001) 9-25.

3. J. Jeremias, "Der Begriff 'Baal' im Hoseabuch und seine Wirkungsgeschichte," in *Hosea und Amos: Studien zu den Anfängen des Dodekapropheton* (Tübingen: Mohr, 1986), pp. 86-103.

4. See Kelle, *Hosea 2,* pp. 137-66.

Hosea 9:10 is in some ways the easiest of the references to interpret. There the term is part of a place name and refers to the apostasy committed by an earlier generation of Israel with the Canaanite deity who gave his name to the site. It represents an account reflected elsewhere in the OT (Num. 25:1-13; Deut. 4:3; Ps. 106:28-31). Two other references in the plural have cultic terminology associated with the term, and these are best interpreted as representing sacrificial overtures to deities:

> ". . . they sacrificed to the Baals and burned incense to idols" (Hos. 11:2)

> "I will bring upon her the days of the Baals when she burned incense to them . . ." (Hos. 2:13 [MT 15])

In 2:16 (MT 18) the prophet represents YHWH as saying that Israel will no longer call him Baal. This strongly implies that some in Israel understood YHWH as a Canaanite Baal and referred to him explicitly with this term. Following directly from this denial is the promise in v. 17 (MT 18) that YHWH will remove the names of the Baals from her (= Israel) mouth and that they will be remembered no more. Contextually this suggests a continuation of the usage of the term for deities in v. 17, not foreign leaders. The natural counterpart to YHWH would be a deity or deities, but the matter is not certain.[5] Since the other two instances of *ba'al* in the plural are deities, this is an additional reason to see the plural term in 2:17 as a polemic against polytheism.

The remaining references to *ba'al* are 2:8 (MT 10) and 13:1, both in the singular. In 2:8 a list of commodities and precious metals is followed by the awkward comment that "they made for the Baal *(labba'al)*." The definite article[6] with the singular noun indicates specificity and that *ba'al* is an epithet, not a personal name. The list is made up of things that can be given in tribute or as offerings. The majority of interpreters have seen the last comment of the verse to refer to the crafting of an idol in silver and gold or otherwise making an offering. In 13:1 comes the claim that Ephraim became guilty by means of the *ba'al* and died. The next verse contains a polemic against idolatry and the making of images with silver. Contextually, the better interpretation of *ba'al* in 13:1 is that of a deity. Furthermore, the refer-

---

5. To "remember a name" *(zākar šēm)* can apply to human names or to divine names in the OT. Perhaps the verb in 2:17 (MT 19) means more specifically to "invoke" (cf. Exod. 23:13).

6. The definite article is indicated by the Masoretic punctuation. The earlier consonantal text is ambiguous with respect to the definite article. The LXX also employs a definite article (feminine!) with the noun: *tē Baal*.

ence in 13:2 to people making for themselves *(lāhem)* an idol from silver suggests that essentially the same thing is in view in 2:8. While much remains unclear about the references to Baal(s) in Hosea, they are all best interpreted as references to deities other than YHWH, even if their veneration in Hosea's day may be partially due to alliances concluded by Israel's leaders with other states.

The related proposal by Brad Kelle (and others) that international alliances, not a polemic against Canaanite deities, are behind the "harlotry" and "lover" language in Hosea is plausible, at least in certain texts,[7] and also a helpful correction to an overemphasis on polytheism in the interpretation of the book. Whether those alliances are the primary element behind the metaphorical language in ch. 2 (the Syro-Ephraimite War according to Kelle), and more to the point, whether any of the references to the Baal(s) in it are metaphorical and represent foreign rulers, seem less likely. Kelle proposes that the references to Baal/Baals as a deity/deities in 9:10; 11:2; and 13:1 are all to the sinfulness of a previous generation and that the *baʿal* references in ch. 2, when applied to Hosea's own generation, could have human counterparts. He admits that the usage of *baʿal* for human political leaders is not well established in Hebrew for the 8th century; and that fact, when compared to the established usage elsewhere in the book for deity/deities, is damaging to the proposal for reinterpreting *baʿal* in ch. 2. Baal as a human figure in 2:16 (MT 18) is quite unlikely, and that conclusion should have its influence on the related use of the term elsewhere in the chapter.[8] Furthermore, the religious polemic against *baʿal* in Jeremiah, who is Hosea's closest interpreter in the OT, is primarily a polemic against other deities (Jer. 2:8, 23; 7:9; 9:14 [MT 13]; 11:13, 17; 12:16; 19:5; 23:13, 27; 32:29, 35). This is not to deny that the root in noun or verb form can have the metaphorical nuance of overlord or suzerain in Jeremiah (or Hosea) when applied to YHWH (3:14; 31:32),[9] but that is different than an application of the term *to* a human overlord. It is doubtful whether the term is applied to human political figures in either book.

---

7. For example, the reference to "loves/lovers" in 8:9 is likely a polemic against foreign alliances.

8. Peggy Day, "A Prostitute Unlike Women: Whoring as Metaphoric Vehicle for Foreign Alliances," in *Israel's Prophets and Israel's Past*, ed. Kelle and Moore, p. 167, concludes that Kelle's case for Baal(s) in Hosea as having an implicit tenor in political overlord(s) is unpersuasive. She demonstrates, however, that the language of love and lovers can play this role in both biblical (Ezek. 16, 23) and extrabiblical texts.

9. One can make a good case, however, in both texts for the familial metaphor of husband, owner, and head of the household. Jeremiah does use the language of "love" in contexts where entangling alliances may be in view (30:14). Internal political supporters of Pashhur are his "lovers" (20:4, 6). Jehoiakim's "lovers" will go into exile with him (22:20, 22), but their identity is obscure.

Interestingly, Deuteronomy, another book related thematically to Hosea, does not refer to a *ba'al* deity in its polemics against the worship of other deities. It does, however, refer to the apostasy at Baal-peor (Deut. 4:3). It is the book in the OT most closely related to the international treaties and their vocabulary, yet it does not use the root *b'l* as either a verb or a noun to refer to political leaders of neighboring peoples who should be avoided. Deuteronomy does, however, have several references to the verb "to love" *('āhab)* in common with Hosea. Even if the semantic background to the term in Deuteronomy is the international treaty and loyalty oath, the term is used primarily in the context of Israel's love for YHWH and YHWH's love for Israel. When used for humans otherwise, it refers to the sojourner loved by YHWH and to be loved by Israel (Deut. 10:18-19), and to familial love (21:15-16). The only occurrence of the term in the context of other deities is in the instruction to reject a prophet or dreamer who urges the worship of other deities. Israel is to love YHWH instead (13:1-11; "love" in v. 4).

2. The Song of Moses and Hosea

The Song of Moses (Deut. 32:1-43) is a poetic instruction to Israel that portrays the people in their history as objects of YHWH's fatherly affection and judgment.[10] In Deuteronomy the song is described as Moses' hymnic composition *(šîrâ),* presented to the people by him and by Joshua (32:44).[11] It is likely an independent, preexilic composition that has been incorporated into the book of Deuteronomy, representing "prophetical thoughts in a poetic dress."[12] It has a number of literary-thematic connections to Hosea.[13] These connections can be (and have been) explained in at least three different ways. One is to see a partial dependence of the song on Hosea's prophecies, and more broadly, to see the song as an heir to preexilic and exilic prophets. A second is the reverse: Hosea and other prophets drew upon the song. The third is that both drew upon some common traditions. Depending on the forms of the traditions in common, there may be little difference between the second and third options. A decision on this matter is not crucial for the task of noting the parallels, but the third option seems the more likely one, given

10. See Paul Sanders, *The Provenance of Deuteronomy 32* (OTS 37; Leiden: Brill, 1996), for a thorough investigation of the song and the history of its interpretation.

11. The MT has *hôšēaʿ,* "Hosea," son of Nun, an abbreviated form of *yĕhôšūaʿ,* "Joshua."

12. So S. R. Driver, *Deuteronomy* (ICC; Edinburgh: T & T Clark, 1902), p. 345. One can see the force of this observation in the details provided by Sanders, *Provenance,* pp. 354-424.

13. Umberto Cassuto, "The Song of Moses (Deuteronomy Chapter xxxii 1-43)," and "The Prophet Hosea and the Books of the Pentateuch," in *Biblical and Oriental Studies,* vol. 1: *Bible,* trans. Israel Abrahams (Jerusalem: Magnes, 1973), pp. 41-46 and 79-100. Cassuto posits a direct relationship between the song and Hosea and proposes that the song was written first, at some point in the period of the judges. See also the details in Willibald Kuhnigk, *Nordwestsemitische Studien zum Hoseabuch* (BibOr 27; Rome: Biblical Institute Press, 1974), pp. 34-39.

the general nature of the parallels and the period of oral transmission typical of poetic compositions.

Hosea and the Song of Moses poetically render and evaluate Israel's history, sharing literary style (poetry), some vocabulary, and similar angles of vision on the significance attached to Israel's early history. Two elements in particular are held in common and suggest that the song and the prophet engaged the same matrix of traditions: a basic metaphor for the divine-human relationship, namely Israel as YHWH's children[14] (no. 2 below), and an election narrative of YHWH's finding Israel in the wilderness (no. 5 below). The sharing of vocabulary is not in itself persuasive evidence of dependence of one on the other, but there is enough of it to support the conclusion drawn above about access to a common matrix of traditions *and* similar points of view.

1. "Act corruptly *(šāḥat)* toward YHWH": Deut. 32:5; Hos. 9:9; 13:9.
2. Israel depicted as YHWH's children: Deut. 32:5, 18-20; Hos. 1–3; 11:1; 13:13.
3. Israel as "unwise people" *(lō' ḥākām):* Deut. 32:6; Israel as "unwise son" *(lō' ḥākām):* Hos. 13:13.
4. YHWH as Israel's "maker" *('āśâ,* Qal perfect): Deut. 32:6, 15; YHWH as Israel's "maker" *('ōśēh,* Qal participle): Hos. 8:14.
5. YHWH "found" *(māṣā')* Israel in the "wilderness" *(midbār):* Deut. 32:10; YHWH "found" *(māṣā')* Israel like grapes in the "wilderness" *(midbār):* Hos. 9:10; cf. 2:14-15 (MT 16-17).
6. Israel provoked YHWH by involving themselves with "strangers" *(zārîm):*[15] Deut. 32:16; Israel engages with "foreign" *(zārîm)* nations: Hos. 7:9; 8:7.[16]
7. Israel "provoked" or "vexed" *(kā'as)* YHWH: Deut. 32:16, 21; Ephraim "provoked" *(kā'as)* YHWH: Hos. 12:14 (MT 15).
8. Israel sacrificed to deities who are "not god" *(lō' 'ĕlōah; lō'-'ēl):* Deut. 32:17, 21; Israel made an idol that is "not god" *(lō' 'ĕlōhîm):* Hos. 8:6.
9. Israel worshiped deities they have not "known" *(yāda'):* Deut. 32:16; in its confused rebellion Israel does not "know" *(yāda')* YHWH: Hos. 5:4; cf. 13:4.
10. Israel's foreign oppressors are a "vine" *(gepen)* like Sodom: Deut. 32:32; Israel was a luxuriant "vine" *(gepen)* that went bad: Hos. 10:1.

---

14. The metaphor of the "apple of the eye" in Deut. 32:10 is used in the context of election and inheritance, and thus should be added to the terminology for family in 32:5, 18-20. Could it also have a marital nuance?

15. In context the "strangers" are likely foreign deities (cf. 32:12, *'ēl nēkār).*

16. Israel will also have "strange children" (Hos. 5:7), perhaps a metaphor for the result of engaging "strange" peoples and "foreign" deities.

11. "See now that I myself *('ănî 'ănî)* am he": Deut. 32:39; "I myself *('ănî 'ănî)* will tear": Hos. 5:14.

12. "There is no other God except me *('immādî)*": Deut. 32:39; "There is no savior except me *(biltî)*": Hos. 13:4.

13. "I kill and make alive; I smite and heal *(rāpā')*": Deut. 32:39; "he has torn, but he will heal *(rāpā');* he has struck, but he will bandage": Hos. 6:1.

14. "There is no deliverer *('ên . . . maṣṣîl)* from my hand": Deut. 32:39; "There will be no deliverer *('ên maṣṣîl)*": Hos. 5:14.

The narrative context in which the song is set also relates to the concerns of the book of Hosea. In describing Moses' impending death, YHWH commands him to write the words of the song and to teach it to the Israelites, so that it will be a "witness against" *('ēd bĕ)* them in the future (Deut. 31:19). What function a poetic "witness" might have for the people is at least partially explained by the instruction that Moses should compose the song because: "this people will arise and play the harlot after foreign gods in the land where they are going; they will forsake me and violate the covenant I have made with them" (Deut. 31:16). The "witness" is an explanation of future difficulties for Israel. In this regard the "prophetic" element is also central.

The prose explanation in Deut. 31:16 contains lexical data in common with Hosea, including the verbal phrase "to play the harlot after" *(zānâ 'aḥărê,* Hos. 1:2) and to "forsake" *('āzab,* 4:10) YHWH. The dalliance with other deities is a major theme in Hosea, although the odd phrase in Deut. 31:16 *('ĕlōhê nēkar-hā'āreṣ)* does not itself appear in Hosea.[17] Similarly, the violation of the covenant *(bĕrît)* is explicit in Hos. 6:7 and 8:1, but the verb used *('ābar)* by the prophet differs from that in Deut. 31:16 *(pārar,* Hiphil).

The book of Deuteronomy and the book of Hosea share a number of related concerns and vocabulary. The commonalities with Hosea are particularly numerous in Moses' Song (Deut. 32). Both compositions are poetic, represent judgment upon the covenant people for their faithlessness, and are associated with the Mosaic tradition (Hos. 12:13 [MT 14]).

---

17. Hos. 3:1 refers to "other gods" *('ĕlōhîm 'ăḥērîm).* The references to the "Baal deities" *(ba'ălîm)* and those to Gomer's "lovers" should be included in Hosea's terminology for Canaanite deities.

3. Flora and Fauna Metaphors in Hosea

There is no single category for all the metaphors (and similes) in the book of Hosea, but two prominent and related categories are those of flora and fauna. These metaphors have both negative and positive tenors (target domains) and vehicles (source domains). Negative and positive are not necessarily moral categories, though they can be. They are more impressionistic and intuitive judgments; furthermore, the impression of a "positive" vehicle may indicate a "negative" tenor and vice versa. For example, that Israel is a luxuriant vine (10:1) is intuitively positive, since a vine that produces edible fruit is positive. The tenor, however, is negative, since the comparison is that of Israel's increased agricultural productivity (intuitively positive) resulting in increased cultic paraphernalia (altars, standing stones) of a suspect nature, which is negative. To cite another example, YHWH will roar like a lion (11:10-11), a negative vehicle typically from a human point of view, but his victory is not that of a predator bringing home a kill, but of one who brings home trembling subjects, a positive image for exiles.

Lion metaphors illustrate another point for interpreting the book of Hosea: Vehicles and tenors are particular, but not immutable or comprehensive. Their particularity allows for variety and overlap. YHWH is a lion in judgment on his people (5:14), but he also roars in victory in prevailing over forces to bring them home. Two cow metaphors, one where Israel is a stubborn cow (4:16) and the other where Ephraim is a trained heifer (10:11), further illustrate this point. These are not contradictory comparisons, but particular to time and action. In continuing disobedience to YHWH, Israel is a recalcitrant cow. At a different time in its history, Ephraim took its instruction seriously and was productive.

Flora and Israel/Ephraim
9:10   Israel, like grapes in the wilderness, early figs on the tree
9:16   Ephraim is stricken, their root is dried up

10:1   Israel is a luxuriant vine, producing fruit
13:3   (Israel) like chaff from the threshing floor
14:5-6 (MT 6-7) (Israel) will bloom like a lily, take root like Lebanon and
       sprout
14:6 (MT 7) (Israel's) splendor will be like the olive tree, fragrance like
       Lebanon

Flora and YHWH
14:8 (MT 9) I (= YHWH) am like a luxuriant cypress

Fauna and Israel/Ephraim
4:16   Israel is a stubborn cow
7:11   Ephraim has become like a silly dove, without sense
8:9   A lone wild donkey, Ephraim has hired lovers
9:11   Ephraim's glory will fly away like a bird
10:11 Ephraim is a trained heifer that loves to thresh
11:11 They will come trembling like birds from Egypt and like doves
       from the land of Assyria

Fauna and YHWH
5:12   I (= YHWH) am like a moth to Ephraim
5:14   I (= YHWH) will be like a lion to Ephraim and like a young lion
       to the house of Judah
11:10 He (= YHWH) will roar like a lion
13:7   I (= YHWH) will be like a lion; like a leopard I will watch along
       the way
13:8   I (= YHWH) will meet them like a bear bereft of cubs
       And I will devour them like a lion
       (Like) a beast of the field will tear them

4. Love in the Prophecy of Hosea

Various passions run deep in the poetic prophecies of Hosea. In a literary sense these are embedded in the text. They are also likely part of the historical prophet whose family becomes a metaphorical vehicle to bring readers to understand the great passion of YHWH for Israel, his "family/household." It is thus the witness of the book that such love runs deep in the character of YHWH.

A Hebrew root for "love" (*'hb*) occurs 18 times in the book. While frequency alone does not make a word central to a document, there can be little doubt that *'hb* is central to Hosea's prophecy.[18] A cluster of references comes in the description of Gomer's harlotry in 2:2-13 (MT 4-15), where the Piel participle is used for her "lovers" (2:5, 7, 10, 12, 13 [MT 7, 9, 12, 14, 15]). The lovers are not otherwise explicitly identified, but contextually their identity as Canaanite deities is firm. In 2:13 (MT 15) the "days of the *ba'alîm*" will be visited upon Gomer, who has bedecked herself with jewelry and gone after her lovers. The phrase "to go/walk after" is used in the context of following after, i.e., worshiping, a deity.[19] The terminology can be used in political relations as well. In 8:9 the prophet complains that Ephraim has hired "lovers" (*'ăhābîm*). In context this clearly refers to intrigue in interna-

---

18. According to Wolff, *Hosea,* p. 197, "Hosea was the first to use the word 'love' (*'hb . . .*) as an interpretation of the election of God's people." Although plausible, it is also possible that Hosea simply emphasized the term along with the metaphor of marriage and family, without being the first person to discern that God's election of Israel was based on love.

19. The phrase occurs several times in the Deuteronomistic literature. In Judg. 2:12 Israel "went after other deities" to their detriment. A parallel phrase in 2:17 has Israel "playing the harlot after other deities" (*zānâ + 'ahărē*). In 1 Kgs. 11:10 Solomon was diverted by following other deities. In 1 Kgs. 18:18 Ahab is charged with "following after the Baals." Hezekiah, on the other hand, is praised for "not diverting from following YHWH" (2 Kgs. 18:6).

tional relations. The Piel participle, therefore, may be the indication of polytheism on Israel's part, while the plural noun in 8:9 indicates political allies purchased through diplomatic means such as bribery, gifts, or treaties.

Recent interpreters have pointed to the use of the terminology of love in the sphere of international relations and more particularly in suzerain treaties and loyalty oaths from the Hittites (Late Bronze Age) and the Neo-Assyrians (Iron Age IIB-C; 9th-7th centuries B.C.) as influences on the way the terminology is used in the OT. Deuteronomy, for example, is a book whose form and structure adapt elements from international treaties. Its commanding of love for YHWH (6:5) is likely rooted in this sphere, with its overtones of loyalty and obedience.[20] Since Hosea, like Deuteronomy, portrays God's electing love of Israel in covenantal terms, it is probable that the language of love and the maledictions for disloyalty in the prophecy are also influenced by this cultural understanding.

The root metaphor for the prophecy of Hosea, that Israel is the "household of God," is able to reflect both the corporate aspects of faithfulness (Israel's religious fidelity to YHWH; rejection of international entanglements) and the personal aspects of love (wife = marital metaphor; children = parental metaphor). As Susan Ackerman succinctly puts the matter, "the personal is political" (and vice versa).[21]

The verb 'āhab is used four times in 3:1. Hosea is commanded to love a woman who has a paramour and is thus an "adulteress" (měnā'āpet, Piel participle). The woman represents Israel, and Hosea's love for her represents God's love for the Israelites, as 3:1b makes explicit. This is the case, even though they (= Israelites) have turned to other deities and "loved raisin cakes." Even with the odd reference to raisin cakes, which are likely part of indigenous cultic celebrations, the language of love in 3:1 fits the metaphorical symbolism of religious covenant as marriage in 1:2–2:23 (MT 25). Israel should love YHWH in return for YHWH's love of them. Israel's love of other deities is harlotry and adultery, i.e., misplaced love.[22]

The nation loves Israel's harlotry and its gain (9:1). Contextually Israel's love could be for Canaanite deities or for hiring help in the international arena. The former interpretation fits best with the contextual reference to Baal-peor (9:10).

20. William L. Moran, "The Ancient Near Eastern Background of the Love of God in Deuteronomy," *CBQ* 25 (1963) 77-87.

21. S. Ackerman, "The Personal Is Political: Covenantal and Affectionate Love ('āhēb, 'ahăbâ) in the Hebrew Bible," *VT* 52 (2002) 437-58. There may be also an affective side to love in Deuteronomy as well, as proposed by Jacqueline Lapsley, "Feeling Our Way: Love for God in Deuteronomy," *CBQ* 65 (2003) 350-69.

22. The use of the verb in 4:18 is rendered less clear by textual problems. Ephraim or its leaders love illicit activities.

The term "love" is also used to express devotion to a customary activity, whether good or bad. In 10:11 Ephraim is compared to a trained cow that "loves to thresh." A merchant (lit. a "Canaanite") using false weights "loves to oppress" (12:7 [MT 8]).

God is also the subject of the verb in Hosea. Because of Israel's wicked deeds, God will "drive them from his house and love them no more" (9:15). In this context, "house" likely refers not to a temple but to the land of Israel, or more idiomatically Israel as God's household. The declaration that God no longer loves the people has close parallels with the naming of the second and third children in ch. 1. The people no longer have God's mercy and they are no longer his people. In 11:1 the great historical act of Israel's deliverance from Egypt is predicated on God's love for his "son Israel" (cf. Exod. 4:22-23). In Hos. 14:4 (MT 5) God declares that he "loves Israel freely" and will thus heal them. The adverb "free" *(nĕdābâ)* indicates that God's love for wayward Israel is not the result of coercion or merit. That the affirmation comes at the conclusion of the book apparently indicates that the anger and rage also expressed by God in Hosea's prophecies are not the last words on the relationship. The book presupposes a forceful historical judgment on Israel, but the last prophecy in it declares the way open to a more merciful future.

5. Psalm 106 and Hosea

Both Ps. 106 and Hosea are poetic renderings deeply indebted to Israel's premonarchical history as a source of continuing revelation from YHWH. Psalm 106 is a long poetic rendition of the story line of the exodus and wilderness generations (cf. Pss. 78; 105). Hosea draws from these same traditions more than any of his prophetic contemporaries. On the one hand, the psalm and the prophetic book share vocabulary that is general and widespread, and thus is not persuasive evidence of direct dependence of the one upon the other.[23] Indeed, a simple dependence of one composition on the other does not seem demonstrable. On the other hand, both share some vocabulary and angles of vision on the past in ways that suggest they are drawing on a common matrix of text and tradition.

Hosea's poetic and succinct allusiveness often make it difficult to grasp the nuance and the significance of historical detail. The commonalities with Ps. 106 listed below, however, underscore that allusion to earlier history is an important aspect of the prophet's poetry, even when nuance and detail are lost upon later readers. In particular the two also share an aversion to idolatry, its interpretation as "harlotry" (no. 10 below), the influence of Israel's experience at Baal-peor (no. 7 below), and engagement with bovine symbols (nos. 4-5 below).

1. "To forget *(šākaḥ)* God": Ps. 106:13, 21; Hos. 2:13 (MT 15); 4:6; 8:14; 13:6.
2. God as "Savior" *(môšîaʿ)* from Egypt: Ps. 106:21; Hos. 13:4.
3. "To be swallowed" *(bālaʿ)* in judgment: Ps. 106:17 (Dathan and Abiram); Hos. 8:8.

---

23. Terms such as "sin" *(ḥāṭāʾ),* "iniquity" *(ʿāwōn),* or "sacrifice" *(zābaḥ)* fall in this general category.

4. A "calf" *('ēgel)* to worship: Ps. 106:19 (calf at Horeb); Hos. 8:5-6; 13:2.

5. "Glory to exchange" *(mûr kābōd)*: Ps. 106:20 (idolatry with calf); Hos. 4:7.

6. To scatter "seed" *(zera')* and to spread *(zārâ)* it in other lands for disobedience: Ps. 106:27; Hos. 1–2.

7. Apostasy at Baal-peor: Ps. 106:28; Hos. 9:10.[24]

8. "Provoke" *(mārâ)* God: Ps. 106:33, 43; Hos. 13:16 (MT 14:1) (Samaria is subject).

9. "Idols" *('ăṣabbîm)* as "snare" *(môqēš)*: Ps. 106:36, 38; Hos. 4:17; 8:4; 13:2; 14:8 (MT 9). Hosea employs images of snare and net, but uses related terms in 5:1; 7:12; 9:8.

10. "Bloodshed" *(dām/dāmîm)*; people "unclean" *(ṭāmē')* and "playing the harlot with deeds" *(zānâ + ma'ălāl)*: Ps. 106:38-39. Hos. 4:2-3 notes the polluting aspects of "bloodshed." Harlotry is a major metaphor in Hosea; note particularly the pairing of harlotry and "uncleanness" in 5:3; 6:10. Evil "deeds" *(ma'ălālîm)* is another common term in Hosea.[25]

11. God's "abundant loving-kindness" *(rōb ḥesed)*: Ps. 106:7, 45.[26] God's loving-kindness is a gift for the restored community in Hos. 2:19 (MT 21). That which is expected from Israel in Hos. 4:1 (cf. 6:6; 10:12) is derivative from God.

---

24. Ps. 106:28 states that they "ate sacrifices of the dead *(mētîm)*" at Baal-peor. Note Hosea's relating of eating and sinning (4:6-7), and that Israel became guilty through Baal and "died" (13:1).

25. Hos. 4:9; 5:4; 7:2; 9:15; 12:2 (MT 3).

26. Reading the plural with Qere in Ps. 106:45. This matches the plural in 106:7. The phrase "abundant in loving-kindness" likely reflects the formula in Exod. 34:6, which God reveals to Moses after, and in spite of, the golden calf debacle. As proposed in the introduction, section IV.A, "Hosea's Theology: Narrative and Community Identity," Exod. 34:6-7 is a base text for Hosea.

6. Sexual Infidelity in Hosea

With the command in 1:2 that Hosea marry a woman of harlotry, the book of Hosea opens with the complicated metaphor[27] of sexual promiscuity as representing Israel's faithlessness toward YHWH and rejection of him as their sufficient and exclusive provider. The terms for harlotry employed in 1:2 are forms of Heb. *zānâ,* whose basic meaning is to perform sexual acts for payment and/or to be sexually active outside marriage.[28] This basic meaning of the word is clear from the narrative of Gen. 38, the account of Judah and his widowed daughter-in-law Tamar (cf. also Prov. 7:6-23). As he travels along his way, Judah sees a woman with a veiled face sitting alone at the entrance to a village. From these cultural cues he surmises that she is a "prostitute" (*zōnâ,* Gen. 38:15), and he proceeds to proposition her for sex. They agree on the fee of a kid from the flocks for services rendered. He does not know that the veiled woman is his daughter-in-law Tamar, or that she had set the events in motion deliberately in order to conceive an heir for the family. Eventually Judah realizes that her risky behavior is in service to the well-being of the family, and he pronounces her more righteous than he because of her familial commitment (38:26). When Tamar is first discovered to be pregnant, however, she is accused of prostituting herself (38:24). Both the verb *zānâ* and the plural noun *zĕnûnîm* ("prostitution/harlotry") are used in this verse to describe her activity. The latter term is the same one used in the phrase "woman of harlotry" in Hos. 1:2. As a plural noun *zĕnûnîm* represents an abstraction of the activity of the verb.

The root *znh* is used elsewhere in Hosea. In 2:5 (MT 7) the children's mother is accused of engaging in prostitution. In 3:3 the unnamed adulteress

---

27. Phyllis Bird, "'To Play the Harlot': An Inquiry into an Old Testament Metaphor," in *Gender and Difference in Ancient Israel,* ed. Peggy L. Day (Minneapolis: Fortress, 1989), pp. 75-94.

28. Cf. S. Erlandsson, "זנה, *zānāh,*" *TDOT* 4:99-104.

is forbidden to engage further in prostitution. In this context, prostitution and adultery are essentially synonyms for Israel's faithless activity, even if they may indicate particular activities of Gomer. In a prophetic litany of judgment upon Israel, the people are accused of engaging in faithless behavior toward the Lord, and several times the charge is "prostitution" (4:10-15, 18). The actual behaviors symbolized seem to include forms of idolatrous worship as well as sexual activity. The folly of the people collectively is attributed to a "spirit of harlotry" in 4:12. Ephraim and Israel collectively are charged with prostitution in 5:3 and 9:1.

"Adultery" is a related term in Hosea (root *n'p,* 2:2 [MT 4]; 3:1; 4:2, 13-14). Adultery presupposes sexual relations that violate the bond of marriage, whereas prostitution does not necessarily presuppose this. When used metaphorically, however, especially as a collective charge against a people, adultery is essentially a synonym for prostitution, faithless activity against YHWH. In 2:2 (MT 4) the terms "adultery" *(na'ăpûpîm)* and "harlotry/prostitution" *(zĕnûnîm)* appear to be used as synonyms.[29] There is essential overlap between the two terms also in 3:1, 3, and 4:13-14.

The feminine noun *qĕdēšâ* is used in parallel with "prostitutes" in 4:14 and in the context of the charge of adultery. The root *qdš* means "be set apart, be holy." When the noun *qĕdēšâ* is used in the context of sexual activity, it may indicate a temple prostitute and a woman dedicated to the service of a deity.[30] Interestingly, the noun is also used by Judah to describe the veiled woman in Gen. 38:21-22, where possibly it serves as nothing more than a synonym for *zōnâ,* "prostitute."

The most common root in Hosea for sexual activity is *znh,* with most references directed to Israel as represented by Gomer, the land, the people, and daughters and daughters-in-law of the people. In some cases, particularly in ch. 4, the charge of prostitution could include actual sexual practices. The charge is mostly employed, however, in metaphorical senses, using language for sexual promiscuity as a visceral charge against religious and cultural practices deemed faithless to the Lord. In metaphorical terms the tenor (or target domain) is Israel's failures vis-à-vis YHWH, the covenant Lord. The

29. A related term *ni'upîm* ("adulteries") occurs in Jer. 13:27 and Ezek. 23:43.

30. There are parallels to this in Mesopotamian culture. See Joan Goodnick Westenholz, "Tamar, *Qĕdēšā, Qadištu,* and Sacred Prostitution in Mesopotamia," *HTR* 82 (1989) 245-65. T. Hentrich has proposed that Gomer may have been a hierodule similar to those in Mesopotamia, but the connections are inconclusive. See his "Qui était Gomer, *'ēšet zĕnûnîm* (Os 1,2-3)?" *Science et esprit* 55 (2003) 5-22. In her recent study, *"Kultprostitution" im Alten Testament? Die Qedeschen der Hebräischen Bibel und das Motiv der Hurerei* (OBO 221; Fribourg: Academic Press, 2006), Christine Stark thinks that the term refers not to sacred forms of prostitution but to women who were associated with religious shrines.

vehicle (or source domain) is prostitution. Thus matters are reversed if one sees first in the terminology a depiction of sexual acts for the nation Israel. Prostitution is the source of imagery that interprets matters in the different domains of religious fidelity.

There is ample use of this sexual metaphor for faithlessness elsewhere in the OT. Indeed, it is the most common usage of the root *znh*. One finds the term so used in legal and historical sections, where a variety of cultic and social practices are described as harlotry (e.g., Exod. 34:15-16; Lev. 17:7; 20:5-6; Num. 15:39; Deut. 31:16; Judg. 2:17; 8:27, 33; 2 Kgs. 9:22 [Jezebel's "harlotries"]; 1 Chr. 5:25; 2 Chr. 21:11, 13), and in other prophetic books (e.g., Isa. 1:21; Jer. 2:20; 3:1-14; and throughout Ezek. 16 and 23). Hosea is the earliest prophet to use the language of harlotry to describe the failures of Israel, just as he is the earliest among them to employ the analogy of marriage with covenant. In these matters, however, he is less likely to be an innovator than someone who pushes the envelope on matters that he inherits from his tradition. Covenantal faithlessness is compared to harlotry in Exod. 34:15-16. Hosea employs terminology in common with Exod. 32–34, including the language of YHWH's mercy and forgiveness (cf. Hos. 1:6 with Exod. 34:6-7) and the critique of bovine symbolism (Hos. 8:5-6 and 10:5-6 with Exod. 32:1-35). It is plausible, indeed likely, that he inherited the metaphorical identity of faithlessness with harlotry from his understanding of the covenant YHWH had instituted with Israel.[31]

What, therefore, might it mean when Gomer is described in 1:2 as a "woman of harlotry"? One starts with the recognition that Gomer is a symbol for the people of God, just as her children are. In metaphorical terms she is a vehicle representing the tenor, which is faithless Israel. As a female she may more particularly represent the people as defined by land or capital city (Samaria), since both of these entities in Hebrew are feminine in gender. Her marriage to Hosea is a symbol of the covenant that God established with Israel. And the charges of prostitution and adultery (2:2 [MT 4]; 3:1) against her represent God's charge that Israel had forsaken him, served other deities, and otherwise failed to maintain the standards of covenant obedience in the realm of political relations. Does Gomer's symbolic role as harlot include actual prostitution or adultery on her part, or does the charge simply reflect that she was an Israelite engaged in the cultic and social misdeeds symbolized in the metaphor? Any answer is speculative, since the textual evidence under

---

31. Jezebel is charged with "harlotries" *(zĕnûnîm)* in 2 Kgs. 9:22. It is possible that the description is that of the Deuteronomistic Historian(s) and thus later than Hosea, but it is also possible that such language was used by the reforming circles associated with Elijah and Elisha and passed along to opposition prophets like Hosea and his circle of support.

consideration is not sufficient for drawing a firm conclusion. It seems probable that Hosea and Gomer were actually married, even though their relationship is configured literarily as a prophetic symbolic act. Stated differently, certain details of their marriage and family were adopted to illustrate a prophetic message. If this is true, then symmetry between person and portrayal would suggest that Gomer was involved in misconduct both before and during her marriage to Hosea, some of which was sexual in nature.[32]

The form of her promiscuity remains elusive because it is Israel, not Gomer, who is the primary agent being rendered as harlotrous. As readers and hearers, we must attend to the target being rendered, namely Israel. In the person of Gomer, Israel is accused of adultery and pursuing "lovers" who paid for services (2:2-13 [MT 4-15]). Possibly Gomer engaged in sex for hire, thereby rendering herself comparable to Israel's defection from YHWH, the covenant Lord. In 3:1 Hosea is commanded to love a woman who is an adulteress and involved with a paramour, a state of affairs consistent with sex for hire and marital infidelity. It is clear, however, that the "lovers" of ch. 2 symbolically represent, at least in part, other deities (2:8, 13 [MT 10, 15]). Thus some interpreters have concluded that Gomer's sexual activity may have been related more specifically to Canaanite fertility cults or sacred prostitution rather than sex for hire or literal adultery.[33] Three options have commended themselves to previous interpreters: (a) a Canaanite initiation rite for betrothed girls, whereby they lose their virginity through copulation with a stranger or a cultic representative;[34] (b) repeated participation in fertility rites, including perhaps ritual copulation, in order to ensure

32. According to Paul A. Kruger, "Israel, the Harlot," *JNSL* 11 (1987) 107-16, the vocabulary describing Gomer, while metaphorical in application to Israel, is that of a prostitute and adulteress. Hornsby, "Israel Has Become a Worthless Thing," pp. 115-28, would essentially agree that the description of Gomer is largely that of a prostitute. She questions, however, whether Gomer and Hosea were married. Perhaps she was a prostitute with whom Hosea became involved.

33. Wolff, *Hosea*, pp. 13-16, sets out the various options. For cautionary comments regarding sacred prostitution and sexual initiation rites, see K. van der Toorn, "Cultic Prostitution," *ABD* 5:510-13; A. A. Keefe, *Woman's Body and the Social Body in Hosea* (JSOTSup 338; Sheffield: Sheffield Academic Press, 2001), pp. 36-65. Keefe writes of the "scholarly fantasies concerning a Canaanite sex cult" (p. 12) that have led to fateful misinterpretations of the book of Hosea. In his treatment of Israelite religions, Richard Hess offers cautionary words on the mixed evidence that has survived for the Palestinian setting, both for scholars who have made it central to reconstructions of Canaanite theology (though lacking evidence), and for those who have completely given up on the concept of sacred prostitution because of those scholarly reconstructions. See his *Israelite Religions: An Archaeological and Biblical Survey* (Grand Rapids: Baker Academic, 2007), pp. 332-35.

34. Wolff, *Hosea*, p. 15, opts for this explanation.

the increase of family, flocks, and crops;[35] (c) engagement as a temple or cult prostitute.

The first option takes a cue from a succinct comment of Herodotus (*History* 1.199) that Babylonian women were required to present themselves once in their lives at the temple of Aphrodite and to copulate with a stranger. Whatever rite of passage (if any) is behind this strange report, there is not enough evidence elsewhere to demonstrate its widespread practice. The second option assumes rituals of sympathetic magic to support indigenous Canaanite fertility cults. Such rituals, if they can now be identified at all from allusion and innuendo, would have varied widely from place to place. Also, they may have been rooted more in popular religion than in the official rituals of the larger temples. The third option has sometimes been thought of as a public institutional setting for the rites in option two. It is true that prostitution could be associated with temples in antiquity, but the reason for it may be more for temple revenue or a means to pay the fulfillment of vows rather than sympathetic magic or sacred ritual.

In summary, Gomer's form(s) of sexual infidelity could include one or more acts of commercial prostitution, adultery, ritual copulation to enhance fertility, and possibly sex to pay a sacred vow. Her sexual practices may have been influenced by syncretistic forms of Yahwism or some of the Canaanite cults. Her harlotry, however, is primarily not about her but about Israel. This is the important matter for understanding the claims of the book. Once this issue is acknowledged, it is better also to acknowledge the difficulty of moving behind the metaphorical use of sexual terms and to remain reticent, rather than to define more specifically Gomer's sexual practices.[36] To concentrate on the person of Gomer rather than the people of Israel is to miss the forest because of attention to a symbolic tree.

The question has been raised whether the imagery of harlotry is gender specific in the OT, and if so, whether this is not inherently sexist, if not misogynist, and indeed more damaging than helpful for modern theological appropriation. The question is complicated by several factors, not the least of which is the broad gap between ancient formulations and modern sensibilities. We should start with the fact that the most common use of the term *zānâ* in the OT is the metaphorical one to describe faithless activity in the religious and social spheres, even if this meaning is derived from a term for illicit sex-

---

35. Andersen and Freedman, *Hosea,* p. 166: "Everything points to her promiscuity as participation in the ritual sex acts of the Baal cult."

36. It is possible that the metaphorical description of harlotry simply marks Gomer out as an Israelite woman, since all of Israel is under the charge of harlotry. The realism of a symbolic act, however, which is the basis of Hosea's marriage to Gomer, would suggest otherwise. It is more likely that she engaged in promiscuous sexual behavior, even if its precise form(s) cannot be further identified with certainty.

ual activity carried out by females. In the metaphorical usage, which is the primary way Hosea employs the terminology, it clearly applies without distinction to both men and women who have failed in their responsibilities before the Lord. In Hos. 4:14 *zānâ* explicitly defines inappropriate sexual activity of men, even if that is atypical for the term in the realm of sexual commerce elsewhere in the OT. Finally, the more important matter for modern appropriation is the depiction of religious faithlessness as the human violation of an intimate trust — rather than annoyance at another culture's depiction of gender.

Marriage and family constitute the most intimate bonds among the human species. Thus the power of the harlotry metaphor comes in its ability to evoke betrayal in personal terms. Hosea's claim is not just that Israel has broken certain religious requirements, mistreated inhabitants of the land, or cunningly sought deliverance through political machinations, but that at root Israel has miserably failed its Lord, rejecting outright his plea for exclusive worship and heartfelt devotion. Israel had not just rejected some things or ideas, but some One — not simply a covenant charter, but a covenant partner.

An interpreter might conclude nevertheless that the negative language about Israel is too negative, or even misanthropic, since it portrays a rotten and shameless community in toto. This conclusion at least intersects with the undeniable corporate judgment on and devastating portrait of Israelite society in the book. Whether the verdict is too harsh, or even misanthropic, is finally a judgment on the cogency of the book's premise that the political end to the house of Israel in the historical process was also the work of a just God. The real shock of the book, however, is not the negative portrayal of 8th-century Israel, but the portrayal of a God who feels justly wounded, who refused to let the failures of his people stand as the last word on human culpability.

7. Terms for Election in Hosea

Hosea employs several terms to convey the conviction that YHWH had chosen Israel as his own. They illustrate the variety of ways in which the prophet adopts and adapts historical tradition to communicate with his audience.

1. "allure/entice" *(pātâ,* Piel). In the complex presentation of his family, Gomer and the children represent Israel in various ways. In 2:14-15 (MT 16-17) Gomer represents Israel's ancestors whom YHWH chose in the wilderness (cf. no. 4 below). More particularly, Gomer is the young bride whom YHWH will again acquire to renew the marriage (cf. Jer. 2:2; Ezek. 16:8-13). The verb used in Hos. 2:14 (MT 16) is one appropriate to the man who seeks to woo or to persuade his betrothed of his intention to consummate the marriage (cf. Exod. 22:16 [MT 17]; Judg. 14:15; 16:5). In the context of Hos. 2:14-23 (MT 16-25), the "alluring" of Israel will result eventually in the transformation of the betrothed people as redeemed members of YHWH's household.

2. "take" *(lāqaḥ),* "love" *('āhab),* and "acquire/purchase" *(kārâ).* These three verbs are all used to describe Hosea's actions toward Gomer. Twice he "takes" her (1:2; 3:1), a term used for marrying a woman who is taken from her home to become a wife in another household. This is also an act of "love" (3:1). In the case of the adulterous Gomer, Hosea must pay to settle her debts or obligations, so that once again she is his (3:2). In "taking," "loving," or "purchasing" Gomer, the prophet is acting out what YHWH had done initially in making Israel his own and what YHWH would do again after a period of judgment and discipline.

3. "called/summoned" *(qārā' lĕ)* and "loved" *('āhab).* According to Exod. 4:22-23, the people of Israel were metaphorically YHWH's "firstborn son." As part of a retrospective on Israel's history, the prophet portrays them as YHWH's "son, called from Egypt" (Hos. 11:1). Such a description may presuppose the act of adoption. In any case, it is predicated on divine love.[37]

---

37. YHWH's "love" is also behind the mystery of his "choosing" *(bāḥar)* and "joining himself to" *(ḥāšaq bĕ)* Israel in Deut. 7:6-8.

This characterization of YHWH's choosing Israel is one of two others that links YHWH's choice of Israel with Egypt (12:9 [MT 10]; 13:4) and not just the desert.[38]

4. "find" *(māṣā')*. In another metaphor YHWH "found" Israel like grapes in the wilderness (9:10).[39] As with 2:16-17 (MT 18-19), there is no mention here of Egypt. The same verb is used in Deut. 32:10 to portray the circumstances of finding and protecting the people: "he found him in the wilderness land, in an empty, howling wasteland; he encompassed him, heeded him, and cared for him like the apple of his eye." There is no compelling reason to think that Hos. 9:10 is an example of an independent "finding tradition" in which YHWH's acquisition of Israel begins in the wilderness and not in Egypt. Whether such a separate wilderness tradition can be identified in the OT at all is doubtful, although several scholars have proposed it.[40] That YHWH acquired Israel in Egypt is clear in Hosea (11:1; 12:9 [MT 10]; 13:4). YHWH's finding of them in the wilderness, therefore, should not be taken as the initial point of contact, but as an indication of support for the people in a place of vulnerability. It is quite plausible that Hosea draws upon traditions of Israel in the wilderness that are not otherwise preserved in the OT.

5. "know" *(yāda')*. YHWH "knew" Israel in the wilderness (13:5). The verb can bear the nuance of "engage" or "enter into a relationship with." Such a nuance fits 13:5, since the text comes in the context of YHWH's declaration that he has been Israel's God since the land of Egypt (13:4). The use of the verb "know" with the connotation of "engage" or even "choose" is in Amos 3:2a, where YHWH addresses Israel: "you only have I known *(yāda')* of all the families of the earth." The context in Amos is one of judgment to come, with the declaration of YHWH's "knowing" as the preface to the announcement of punishment in 3:2b. There is no question about the extent of YHWH's knowledge, as if he had cognizance only of Israel among the peoples of the earth. The manner in which YHWH knew Israel made them uniquely his own.[41]

---

38. In Hos. 12:13 (MT 14) YHWH "brought up" *('ālâ)* Israel from Egypt. The redeeming act is not itself God's choosing of Israel, but the result of it.

39. The parallel phrase in 9:10 is that YHWH "saw them like early figs."

40. See the full discussion of the "finding tradition" and Hosea in Neef, *Heilstraditionen,* pp. 60-65, 116-17; Holt, *Prophesying the Past,* pp. 116-27.

41. Both NASB and NIV translate the verb *yāda'* in Amos 3:2a as "chosen." Wolff, *Hosea,* p. 197, describes Amos's use of the verb as a "less vivid word [than 'love'] for election."

8. Transjordan in Hosea

Hosea refers several times to the land east of the Jordan River. An examination of these texts is a good indication of ways in which historical geography may contribute to the book's understanding.

Perhaps the clearest reference is 9:10b, where the prophet reminds his hearers/readers of Israel's sinfulness at Baal-peor, sometimes called Beth-peor in the OT. It is located east of the Jordan Valley on the plains of Moab, near Shittim, where Israel encamped at the conclusion of the wilderness journeys to the promised land (Num. 25:1, 3; 33:48-49; Deut. 3:29). Beth-peor is assigned to the tribe of Reuben (Josh. 13:20) as part of its inheritance. Nearby is Mt. Nebo, a place associated with the burial of Moses (Deut. 34:1-6). Baal-peor cannot be located definitely, but possibilities include Ras es-Siyagah, Khirbet Ayun Musa, and Khirbet el-Muhatta, all west of Madeba overlooking the descent to the Jordan Valley and the northern edge of the Dead Sea.[42] According to a narrative account in the book of Numbers (25:1-13; cf. 31:16; Deut. 4:3-4; Ps. 106:28-31), Israel became engaged sexually (*zānâ;* Num. 25:1) with women there, apparently in conjunction with the cult of a deity known as Baal (of) Peor.[43]

---

42. Ras es-Siyagah is the location of a Byzantine period memorial to Moses, i.e., Byzantine Mt. Nebo. Iron Age Nebo (Khirbet el-Muhayyat) was just to the east of this site. The promontory of Siyagah may have had an Iron Age site or shrine, which could be identified with Pisgah (Num. 23:14), Peor (23:28), or one of the "high places of Baal" (Num. 22:41). The springs of Moses (Ayun Musa) are in the valley immediately to the north of Siyagah, and Khirbet el-Muhatta is a modest ruin on the ridge line to the northwest of Ayun Musa.

43. George R. Boudreau, "Hosea and the Pentateuchal Traditions: The Case of the Baal of Peor," in *History and Interpretation,* ed. Graham et al., pp. 121-31. Boudreau improbably thinks that Hosea alludes not to some form of the account now included in Num. 25:1-11 and Deut. 4:3-4, but to an event after the settlement in the land that was interpreted as idolatry. One may readily agree to the possibility that Hosea knew a somewhat different

Numbers 25:1 employs the verb *zānâ* ("to play the harlot") in the same metaphorical sense as Hosea uses it, with Israel as the subject (Hos. 4:15; 5:3). The prophet's charge that Israel devoted itself to "shame" *(bōšet)* is a slur elsewhere referring to Baal (Jer. 11:13)[44] and fits well with Hosea's ongoing polemic elsewhere against Baal deities. Apparently Hosea's narrative theology includes an account of transgression in the transition from the wilderness period to life in YHWH's land.[45] Although it is not stated explicitly in 9:10b, it makes sense that Hosea also knew of divine judgment associated with the transgression at Baal-peor (as do the canonical accounts in Num. 25; Deut. 4:3-4; Ps. 106:28-31); otherwise, the force of his comparison with current transgressions of Israel is considerably lessened.

Twice Hosea refers to Gilead (6:8; 12:11 [MT 12]), the hilly region east of the Jordan River. The first is a reference to a "city" with tracks of blood, and the other describes iniquity in Gilead. Neither reference is positive. The city is not otherwise named. It could refer to the place named Adam (6:7), which was associated with the western edge of Gilead and the east bank of the Jordan River, or possibly to Mizpah (5:1; see below). Both cities are named elsewhere in Hosea. It could also be a reference to a more prominent site such as Ramoth-gilead or Jabesh-gilead.

According to 2 Kgs. 15:25, Pekah led a band of Gileadites in a successful coup against Pekahiah, the king in Samaria. This report does not make Pekah himself a Gileadite, but this is probable. Minimally, Gilead was one source of opposition to Pekahiah's rule in Samaria. Pekah also allied himself with Rezin, the king of Damascus, in an attempt to replace the Davidic ruler in Jerusalem (2 Kgs. 16:5; Isa. 7:1-9). With Gilead as his base of support, the connection to Damascus makes geographical sense.[46] The

---

form of the story than the one now included in Num. 25, but Hos. 9:10b almost certainly alludes to it rather than to an otherwise unknown, postsettlement event. Hosea's charge that Israel had devoted itself to "shame" *(bōšet)* at Baal-peor is ignored by Boudreau, although its employment in Jeremiah shows rather clearly that it can be a slur for Baal (Jer. 11:13; cf. 3:24-25). It is not, therefore, just a matter of idolatry at Baal-peor, but the worship of a Baal deity. His claim that Hosea used only the tradition of an "ideal wilderness period" is also unconvincing, as is his related conclusion that the form of the indictment in 9:10-14 requires the transgression at Baal-peor known to Hosea to be postsettlement.

44. See further Dearman, "Baal in Ancient Israel," pp. 187-90.

45. Micah knows a related summary of YHWH's "righteous acts" *(ṣĕdāqôt)* that brought Israel from Egypt to the region of Moab, with local threats there (Balak and Balaam), and the names of Gilgal and Shittim as sites associated with the transition to the land of promise (6:4-5).

46. The chronological report in 2 Kgs. 15:27 that Pekah reigned twenty years is an impossibly long time. Some interpreters have suggested that the period includes a time when he claimed sovereignty in Gilead before taking the throne in Samaria from Pekahiah.

question, finally, is that of Hosea's negative references to Gilead. Pekah's connections to Gilead might be one contributor to the iniquity and political instability in Hosea's day. The Israelites settled there may have been a counterweight or opposition party to the rulers in Samaria. One may think also of these suggested connections as a tip of the iceberg, a partial reflection of regional tensions and conspiracies in Israel during the period of Hosea's prophecies.

Hosea's adaptation of traditions associated with the ancestor Jacob may also be related, at least in part, with Gilead. In Gen. 32 Jacob's encounter with a nocturnal visitor takes place at Peniel, located near a crossing of the Jabbok River, in the region of southern Gilead. Jacob's wrestling ordeal is clearly alluded to in Hos. 12:3-4 (MT 4-5), but neither Gilead nor Peniel is named.

A similar kind of obscurity applies to the reference to the cities of Admah and Zeboiim in 11:8. They are cities involved with the wickedness of Sodom and Gomorrah and were destroyed (Deut. 29:23). These cities cannot be located with certainty, but they are likely in the Jordan Rift near the Dead Sea, perhaps on the east side.

Another obscure historical allusion in Hosea is that of the destruction of Beth-arbel, carried out by a certain Shalman, cited in a threat against Bethel (10:14-15). The location of Beth-arbel, a city otherwise unattested in the OT, is unknown, and the identity of the destroyer named Shalman is uncertain. Some interpreters have identified the latter with the Moabite king Salamanu, who appears in the tribute lists of Tiglath-pileser III; and they suggest that Beth-arbel is to be identified with Irbid, the largest city in northern Jordan.[47] Given the obscurity of the city's name and the ambiguity of the destroyer's name, it is difficult to pin down the details of 10:14. The reason to consider Hosea's reference at all is the probable connection with Transjordan. It certainly illustrates the range of political tensions that Hosea identified in his prophecies. André Lemaire's proposal, in particular, shows

---

47. So Wolff, *Hosea*, pp. 187-88. André Lemaire, "Essai d'interprétation historique d'une nouvelle inscription monumentale Moabite," *CRAIBL* 1 (2005) 101-8, agrees and provides additional details. On the basis of a recently discovered Moabite inscription, which briefly indicates a defeat of Ammon by Moab, Lemaire proposes that Salamanu/ Shalman was also allied (ca. 750-740 B.C.) with Israel against the expansion of Damascus and Ammon in Transjordan. The destruction of Beth-arbel (Irbid) by Shalman was to punish the city and to bring it into line with the aims of the Israelite-Moabite alliance. As both Wolff and Lemaire acknowledge, Shalman could be a Hebrew version of Shalmaneser and refer to a destruction of a city by Shalmaneser III, IV, or V, a period of time lasting well over a century. It is less likely, as Wolff notes, that Shalman refers to Shallum, who assassinated King Zechariah (2 Kgs. 15:10-15), although others have proposed it. On Salamanu see Tadmor, *Inscriptions*, pp. 170-71.

how new material may shed light on regional tensions hitherto unknown and help explain an otherwise obscure reference in Hosea.[48] In the cases of Baal-peor, Gilead, and Beth-arbel, the brief allusive references would have evoked reaction among the prophet's contemporaries, who would have known a number of details now hidden from modern readers and thus made connections that we are unable to make without fresh evidence.

Finally, in 5:1-2 Mizpah is mentioned in conjunction with Tabor and Shittim.[49] Mizpah might refer to a site in Gilead near the territory of Ammon (Gen. 31:49; Judg. 11:29), which cannot be identified with certainty but is likely west or northwest of modern Amman. The other option is Mizpah of Benjamin, a prominent location for Samuel's work (1 Sam. 7:5-6, 16; 10:17). Mizpah of Benjamin is almost certainly Tell en-Nasbeh, ca. 5 miles north of Jerusalem. If the name Shittim is correctly restored in Hos. 5:2a, since it is located in Transjordan, perhaps 5:1 also refers to the site in Gilead called Mizpah and to some activities in Transjordan. Jacob and Laban concluded a covenant between themselves at Mizpah in Gilead (Gen. 31:43-55). Perhaps this makes Mizpah a place of assembly or even the location of an open-air shrine. Hosea may have known of this tradition, as he most certainly drew on other accounts of Jacob's life.[50]

48. One difficulty in Lemaire's stimulating proposal is the proposed political alliance between Moab and Israel, ca. 740 B.C. A century earlier, Moab freed itself from vassalage to Israel (2 Kgs. 3:4-27). A later alliance with Israel is not impossible, but there is no other evidence for it. Moreover, Israel was in league with Damascus when Pekah came to power, ca. 736, which would require that Israel make quick amends with the Arameans.

49. The name "Shittim" is reconstructed. See the comments on 5:2.

50. Neef, *Heilstraditionen,* pp. 216-20, suggests that Hosea has Gilead Mizpah in mind and more particularly is drawing on the covenant of peace concluded there between Jacob and Laban as a critique of the national leaders in 5:1.

9. Worship Centers in Hosea

Criticism of worship centers in Israel plays a prominent role in the book of Hosea. Much of that criticism comes as part of the prophet's broader institutional critique, including his opposition to the cultic practices of his day.[51]

Gilgal and Bethel (sarcastically nicknamed Beth-awen, "Wicked House" or "House of Nothing") are two places for worship paired in Hos. 4:15. They are paired also in Amos (4:4; 5:5), an 8th-century prophetic contemporary of Hosea.[52] Both have altars for sacrifice and Bethel has a temple (Amos 7:13). Gilgal is named in Hos. 9:15 and 12:11 (MT 12), where Israelite intrigue and transgressions are rooted. Hosea makes reference elsewhere to Beth-aven ("Wicked House") in 5:8 and 10:5 and to Bethel in 10:15 and 12:4 (MT 5). Amos also refers to Bethel separately in 3:14; 5:6; 7:10, 13. In both prophets, where contemporary religious practices or corporate assemblies are in view, the references are negative.

Apparently more than one site in Israel had the name Gilgal ("rolling" or "round stone"; cf. Josh. 5:9), but the references in Hosea are most likely to the best known of them, a site located on the west side of the Jordan River and east/northeast of Jericho. Its remains cannot be located with certainty, as it appears to have been more a place for assembly and cultic service rather than a permanent urban center.[53] In narrative and prophecy alike, it is the end of the wilderness wandering for Israel (Josh. 4–5; Mic. 6:5). It was likely an open-air shrine with an altar and ceremonial stones but lacking a temple. It

51. See also the full discussion in Emmerson, *Hosea,* pp. 117-55. She is of the opinion that the prophet's criticisms of activities at Bethel and Gilgal have been strengthened by the Judean editors of the book and made to seem as opposition to the sanctuaries themselves.

52. Amos 5:5 also includes Beer-sheba in the Judean Negev as a place of pilgrimage and worship that should be avoided.

53. Ely Levine, "Gilgal," *New Interpreter's Dictionary of the Bible,* ed. Katharine Doob Sakenfeld (Nashville: Abingdon, 2007), 2:572-73.

was a site of Samuel's itineration as a judge (1 Sam. 7:16) and the place where Saul was "made king" before YHWH (1 Sam. 11:15). It was also a staging ground for clans and tribes when following Saul (1 Sam. 13:4-14) or meeting David (2 Sam. 19:15 [MT 16]), and perhaps the home of a company of prophets (2 Kgs. 4:38; cf. 2:1). Possibly, Hosea's negative references to Gilgal in 9:15 and 12:11 (MT 12) play on the site's history as the location of Saul's rejection (1 Sam. 13:7-14), or because of its proximity to Gilead, a source of political intrigue in Hosea's day.[54]

Bethel is known from the ancestral period as the place of revelation to Jacob/Israel. It was earlier known as Luz (Gen. 28:10-22; 35:1-15). Its ruins are located at the village of Beitin, ca. 12 miles north of Jerusalem.[55] Jeroboam built a shrine in Bethel (1 Kgs. 12:29).[56] Nearby to the east is Beth-aven (Josh. 7:2), a name that does not seem to be polemically based like Hosea's usage; it is used straightforwardly elsewhere (Josh. 18:12). It is difficult to sort out the intertwining of geography, multiple names, and polemic involved in the various references to Beth-aven, and what follows is but one possible reconstruction. It depends on recognizing wordplay on the part of the prophet, using the roots 'wn ("strength," "wealth"), a homonym 'wn ("injustice," "deceit," "worthless"), and 'wn ("iniquity").

1. Beth-aven can mean "house of strength/substance/wealth," based on the root 'wn, with different vocalization. This explains the positive element to the name Beth-aven in Joshua (7:2; 18:12). The noun 'ôn is used in just this way in Hos. 12:3, 8 (MT 4, 9), and v. 8 also plays on the similarly pronounced term "iniquity" ('āwōn).

2. Abram built an altar and offered sacrifice on the hill east of Bethel (Gen. 12:8). This could be also the area of Beth-aven (cf. Josh. 7:2), likely a site with a smaller permanent population than the city of Bethel proper. Was this the site also of Jacob's revelation and the temple associated with the ancestral period? This is certainly a plausible conclusion, given the location of an altar east of Bethel, and given the negative evidence from the excavations at Beitin proper, which did not provide evidence for an Israelite temple. There is evidence, furthermore, in Hos. 10:8 for multiple altars and "high places" linked to the site of "Iniquity"

54. Gilgal is also the location of the treaty with the Gibeonites in Josh. 9:3-27, where they employ a ruse in order to get favorable terms in the making of a covenant (bĕrît) with Israel (9:6).

55. A. F. Rainey, "Looking for Bethel: An Exercise in Historical Geography," in *Confronting the Past: Archaeological and Historical Essays on Ancient Israel in Honor of William G. Dever,* ed. Seymour Gitin et al. (Winona Lake, IN: Eisenbrauns, 2006), pp. 269-73.

56. Klaus Koenen, *Bethel: Geschichte, Kult und Theologie* (OBO 192; Göttingen: Vandenhoeck & Ruprecht, 2003); Gomes, *Sanctuary of Bethel.*

('āwen), likely a reference to Bethel. Apparently various cultic acts were celebrated in and around Bethel. This seems a prudent conclusion from the textual evidence. The royal shrine of the Israelite period may have been located east of the settlement at Bethel or in the city itself. The negative evidence from the excavations at Beitin does not settle the matter of an Israelite temple there. Further investigations may well bring forth evidence of such a structure.

3. Hosea polemically adapted the name "House of Wealth" to "Wicked House" *(bêt 'āwen),* producing a cutting pun on the idolatrous practices at the royal shrine at Bethel.[57]

Shechem is likely another site with a shrine or altar in Hosea's day, but the one reference to the city in 6:9 mentions only priests on the "way to Shechem" and says nothing else about the city. Elsewhere, Shechem is the site of an ancestral altar (Gen. 12:6-7). The mountain to the north of the city (Ebal) is associated with an altar of sacrifice in Deut. 27:4-7 and Josh. 8:30-31. It was also a traditional place of tribal assembly (Josh. 24:1; 1 Kgs. 12:1). An old city in Israel's heartland, Shechem played a prominent role in the accounts of the judges (Judg. 9:1-2), where an abortive attempt at kingship was undertaken. For a short time it was the home (capital?) for Jeroboam I (1 Kgs. 12:25).[58]

Samaria, likewise, as the capital city would have a cultic role to play in Israel. It is difficult, however, to discern much of its cultic role from the book of Hosea. There is no reference to a Yahwistic temple in Samaria in Hosea or any other Hebrew text, but it is hard to imagine the city without some form of a Yahwistic shrine.[59] In Hos. 8:5-6 there is a polemic against Samaria's "calf." This may well presuppose a shrine in the city, whether dedicated to YHWH or another deity, but the reference in 10:5 to Samaria's inhabitants trembling for the "calf" (a plural term in Hebrew) of Beth-aven could indicate a location for the cult figure there rather than in the city of Samaria.

Finally there is brief mention of Tabor and Mizpah in 5:1. There is nothing compelling in their brief mention to conclude that either one is a cultic site, much less a worship center drawing pilgrims. In the case of Mizpah, there are two primary possibilities even for its identification, one located in Benjamin (Josh. 18:26; Judg. 20:1) and the other in Gilead (Gen.

---

57. A wordplay on Bethel also occurs in Amos 5:5, which states that Bethel will become "nothing" *('awen),* apparently contrasting its popular depiction as a house of "wealth" or "substance" *('wn).* Shalom Paul, *Amos* (Hermeneia; Minneapolis: Fortress, 1991), p. 164, suggests that this aspect of the wordplay influenced Hosea.

58. Wolff, *Hosea,* p. 122, thinks that Shechem itself is not criticized in Hos. 6:9 and that perhaps Levitical and prophetic opposition to Samaria was located there.

59. According to 2 Kgs. 10:18-27, there was a temple for Baal in Samaria.

31:49; Judg. 10:17; 11:11). There is suggestive evidence elsewhere, however, for a cultic role for both Mizpahs. Samuel offers sacrifice in Benjaminite Mizpah, where Israelite tribesmen have gathered to face the Philistines (1 Sam. 7:5-11). Jacob and Laban concluded a covenant between themselves at Gileadite Mizpah and erected a monument there (Gen. 31:43-55). The evidence for Tabor, a mountain where Israelites gathered (Josh. 19:12, 22, 34; Judg. 4:6, 12), is at best indirect.[60]

The polemics against the cities of Gilgal, Bethel, Shechem, and Samaria are to be interpreted in light of Hosea's thorough institutional critique of Israel. Hosea criticizes both the worship of YHWH (too syncretistic) and that of other deities. His cultic criticisms would have had a political component to them as well. Perhaps part of his vehemence against places like Gilgal and Bethel is the result of their historical role in handing on the traditions of Yahwism, a role that Hosea believes is being subverted in his day. Instead of being the guardians of traditions held dear by Hosea, the sites had been co-opted by leaders and infused with practices that Hosea opposed. Perhaps the prophetic circles that nurtured Hosea had been evicted or shunned by the cultic officials in charge of their shrines. We are told, for example, that Jeroboam I made significant changes in the temple service at Bethel (1 Kgs. 12:28-33). Amos was expelled from there by a priest, perhaps acting on instructions from Jeroboam II (Amos 7:10-17). In interpreting the work of prophets like Hosea, Amos, and Micah, we face the problem that they offered such severe national critiques yet they are themselves dependent upon earlier traditions, some of which were surely preserved and handed down at cult centers they excoriated in their preaching.[61] Unfortunately, if there were struggles and upheavals in the personnel associated with cult centers, perhaps resulting in the disenfranchising or expulsion of persons like Hosea, we lack crucial information about them.

---

60. See the discussion on Mizpah in Gilead and Mt. Tabor in Neef, *Heilstraditionen*, pp. 216-24. Regarding Mizpah, he suggests that the narrative of the covenant ceremony between Jacob and Laban in Gen. 31:43ff. is, in part, an etiology for a shrine *(Heiligtum)* there. For Tabor he points to the blessing of Zebulun and Issachar in Deut. 33:18-19 and particularly to the calling of people to a mountain for sacrifice. He suggests plausibly that the mountain is Tabor.

61. This was a point made forcefully some years ago by Norman Porteous, "The Prophets and the Problem of Continuity," in *Israel's Prophetic Heritage: Essays in Honor of James Muilenburg*, ed. B. W. Anderson and W. Harrelson (New York: Harper & Brothers, 1962), pp. 11-25.

10. YHWH's Self-Definition (Exod. 34:6-7) and Hosea

According to the narrative of the golden calf episode (Exod. 32–34), YHWH revealed himself to Moses in the following manner:

> YHWH, a God merciful and gracious, slow to anger and abounding in loving-kindness and faithfulness; who maintains loving-kindness for thousands, forgiving iniquity, transgression, and sin; but the unpunished he will punish, bringing the iniquity of the parents on their children and grandchildren, unto the third and fourth (generation). (Exod. 34:6-7)

This formulaic self-definition in Exod. 34, which occurs in the context of a breach of covenant, has its intertextual echoes elsewhere in the OT (e.g., Pss. 78:38; 86:15; 99:8; 103:8; 111:4; 145:8; Jer. 32:18; Joel 2:13; Jonah 4:2; Mic. 7:18-20), including the second commandment of the Decalogue (Exod. 20:5-6; Deut. 5:9-10). It is also the completion of the theophany begun in Exod. 33:19, with YHWH's expressed intent to show Moses his goodness and an assertion that he will "be gracious to whom he will be gracious, and show mercy to whom he will show mercy."

As such, YHWH's self-definition is a significant text for organizing the OT claims about divine character and activity, and it is also one of the base texts for Hosea.[62] Unlike Joel and Jonah, there is surprisingly no citation of a portion of the self-presentation formula in Hosea, and thus one cannot reconstruct the precise form in which Hosea knew this authoritative tradition

---

62. For the former see Hermann Spieckermann, "Barmherzig and gnädig ist der Herr . . . ," *ZAW* 102 (1990) 1-18; idem, "God's Steadfast Love: Towards a New Conception of Old Testament Theology" (trans. Karin Schöpflin), *Bib* 81 (2000) 305-27. For the latter see Van Leeuwen, "Scribal Wisdom and Theodicy," in *In Search of Wisdom*, ed. Perdue et al., pp. 34-39; Scoralick, *Gottes Güte*, pp. 145-60.

379

about YHWH. I have proposed elsewhere, for example, that Hosea is decisively influenced by the prologue (a self-presentation formula of YHWH)[63] and the first two commandments of the Decalogue. Since the second commandment is related to the self-definition formula, it is quite complicated to sort out the literary relationships with respect to the prophet's appropriation of the formula. That the prophet employs the formulaic vocabulary and offers congruent affirmations about YHWH's character, however, can be shown from the data in the book. The basic lexical data are as follows:

1. *rḥm* ("be merciful"). Hosea cites verbal forms of the root eight times (1:6 [twice], 7; 2:1, 4, 23 [twice] [MT 3, 6, 25]; 14:3 [MT 4]). In the rest of the Book of the Twelve, there are only three other verbal uses of *rāḥam*. Hosea also uses the plural noun once (2:19 [MT 21]).
2. *ḥānan* ("be gracious"). The verb is used once (12:4 [MT 5]).
3. *ḥesed* ("loving-kindness," "steadfast love," "loyalty"). The noun is used six times in Hosea (2:19 [MT 21]; 4:1; 6:4, 6; 10:12; 12:6 [MT 7]). Hosea has nearly half of the references in the Book of the Twelve (13 total).
4. *'ĕmet* ("faithfulness"). The term is used once (4:1).
5. *nāśā' 'āwōn* ("forgiving iniquity"). The verb and object, with God as subject, occur once in Hosea (14:2 [MT 3]). This combination occurs only one other time in the Book of the Twelve (Mic. 7:18). The verb is also used in Hos. 1:6, but without the object *'āwōn*.
6. *'āwōn* and *ḥaṭṭā't* ("iniquity" and "sin"). The two nouns are used in the same verse twice in Hosea (8:13; 9:9). The term *'āwōn* is used eight other times in Hosea (4:8; 5:5; 7:1; 9:7; 12:8 [MT 9]; 13:12; 14:1-2 [MT 2-3]).
7. *pāša'* ("transgress"). The verb is used twice in Hosea (7:13; 8:1).
8. *pāqad 'al* ("bring on"). This combination occurs five times in Hosea (1:4; 2:13 [MT 15]; 4:9, 14; 12:2 [MT 3]). The verb *pāqad* is used two other times in the context of divine punishment as part of a larger phrase common to both verses (8:13; 9:9).

Two of Hosea's common terms are the root *rḥm* (9 times) and the noun *'āwōn* (10 times), providing a basic grounding for the presentation of YHWH's judgment and forgiveness of an Israel alienated from him. It is possible, furthermore, to relate the contents of the self-presentation formula to various passages in Hosea. For example, in the naming of the children and

63. "I am YHWH your God, who brought you out of the land of Egypt, out of the house of slavery" (Exod. 20:2; Deut. 5:6). See the introduction, section IV.A, "Narrative and Community Identity," and chart 4 below on YHWH's self-presentation.

the defining of their symbolic roles (1:2–2:1, 23 [MT 3, 25]), YHWH is the one who "brings on" punishment and can no longer be "merciful" (1:4, 6), even reversing the significance of his name in 1:9. By an act of sheer grace, however, he will overcome their iniquity and embrace them with his compassion. Another is 14:1-4 (MT 2-5), where the judgment depicted in 1:2-9 is also reversed, using the same vocabulary. YHWH will be "merciful" and "forgive iniquity."

In two other passages the evidence is thematic, not lexical, and thus more subjective. The first is the divine soliloquy in 11:8-9. Perhaps the great ordeal of the divine heart is a struggle over the implications of the phrase "slow to anger" as expressed in Exod. 34:6.[64] The other matter brings together two texts, 1:2-9 and 2:4 (MT 6), which concern the role of the children in bearing the guilt and judgment of their mother. Perhaps this is the outworking of Exod. 34:7 and judgment extending from parents to children.[65]

The tension between YHWH's judgment and mercy in dealing with Israel runs throughout the book of Hosea, whether it is seen from the perspective of its repetitive vocabulary or its tripartite structure (chs. 1–3; 4–11; 12–14). It is fair to say of Hosea that "no other prophet in the Old Testament relates Israel's guilt so straightforwardly to the relationship with God, (a guilt) described directly as a breach of the first commandment."[66] It would be fair also to say of Hosea that no other prophet draws more deeply on YHWH's dynamic self-definition in rendering him as God for his hearers.

64. A suggestion made by Spieckermann, "Barmherzig," p. 13; and seconded by Scoralick, *Gottes Güte*, p. 146. Hebrew *'erek 'appayim* is always cited as a phrase, being derived apparently from the larger formula and surviving only in fixed form. Thus the phrase occurs only three times in the Book of the Twelve and in the context of other portions of the formula (Joel 2:13; Jonah 4:2; Nah. 1:3). As noted above, Hosea does not cite the self-presentation formula. Related phrases using the roots *'rk* and *'p* occur in Jer. 15:15; Prov. 19:11.

65. Scoralick, *Gottes Güte*, p. 151.

66. So Jeremias, *Hosea*, p. 20.

Chart 4: YHWH's Self-Presentation in the Decalogue and the Prophecies of Hos. 12:9 (MT 10); 13:4; and Amos 2:10

Hosea 12:9 (MT 10); 13:4	Exod. 20; Deut. 5	Amos 2
I am YHWH your God (who brought you up)[67] from the land of Egypt;	2/6 I am YHWH your God, who brought you out (*yāṣā'*) of the land of Egypt, out of the house of slavery.	10 I brought you up (*'ālâ*)[69] from the land of Egypt,
— 12:9b, I will cause you to dwell in tents as in the appointed day.		and I led you in the wilderness forty years.
— 13:5, I knew you in the wilderness, in the land of drought.		
13:4b, you know no God but me, and there is no savior except for me.[68]	3/7 You shall have no other gods before me.	

67. LXX has *anēgagon*, which presupposes *'ālā* in the self-presentation formula.

68. In 13:4 LXX has the expansion: "I am the Lord your God who establishes the heaven and creates the earth, whose hand has formed all the host of heaven; but I did not show them to you that you should go after them; and I brought you up from the land of Egypt and you shall know no God but me; and there is no savior beside me." See further Russell Fuller, "A Critical Note on Hosea 12:10 and 13:4," *RB* 98 (1991) 343-57.

69. The verb *'ālā* is the one used by Hosea elsewhere (1:11 [MT 2:2]; 2:15 [MT 17]). See further Yair Hoffman, "A North Israelite Typological Myth and a Judaean Historical Tradition: The Exodus in Hosea and Amos," *VT* 39 (1989) 169-82.

INDEX OF SUBJECTS

INDEX OF AUTHORS

INDEX OF SCRIPTURE AND OTHER ANCIENT TEXTS

5:5	143n.30
6:16	268
21:2, 9	59
22:16	143n.30

OTHER ANCIENT TEXTS

Wisdom of Sirach

49:10	7

Josephus

Ant. 9.283-87	26n.62

Dead Sea Scrolls

4Q166	8n.19
4Q167	8n.19
4QXII	8n.19

Inscriptions of Tiglath Pileser III (H. Tadmor)

Annals

13:10	23n.53, 24n.54
27:2	23n.53, 24n.54

Stele III

A5	23n.52, 24n.54

Summary

4:17-18	25n.61
9:r.10	25n.61

Hammurabi Law Code

170	57

Old Babylonian

CT 48:50	57n.139

COS

1:5-52	222n.38
2:123	213n.20
2:124	213n.20
2:126	213n.20
2:138.14-18	172n.43
2:162	45n.110
2:269-70	273n.71

Elephantine (Porten and Yardeni)

B2.6	56n.136
B3.3	56n.136
B3.8	56n.136, 57n.140
B6.1	56n.136

Herodotus

History 1.199	367

INDEX OF FOREIGN WORDS

407